LIME
5

Exploited by Choice

by

MARK CRUTCHER

LIME 5: Exploited by Choice

Published by
Life Dynamics, Incorporated
P.O. Box 2226
Denton, Texas 76202
Phone (817) 380-8800
Fax (817) 380-8700

Printed in the United States of America.

ISBN 0-9648886-0-2

Library of Congress Catalog No.: 95-82088

Current events—non-fiction; abortion.

Design and typesetting by:
Genesis Publications
Bartlesville, Oklahoma

Cover design by:
Fiegenschue Design
Irving, Texas

Printed by:
Printing Center Media, Incorporated
Fort Worth, Texas

To Jackie

Contents

Acknowledgments

I n my writing, I try desperately to avoid clichés. However, I am forced to begin this chapter with one of the most common ones in the English language: *This was a team effort.* While everyone on staff at Life Dynamics played a role, it was primarily Christina Dunigan, Mona Passignano, Dzintra Brugman Tuttle, and Lisa Dodson who helped me turn the mountain of data we accumulated into *LIME 5*. Because of their commitment, and the efforts of my wife, Tulane, the American people now have an opportunity to know what's really going on inside the abortion industry. Other staff members who worked on this project were: Tom Cyr, Marco Medina, Rita Lanning, Christine Cartin, Debbie Black, Natasha Sanford, Scott Stirling, Louann Lawson, and Robert Webb. Among non-staff people who made a significant contribution to the project were Lisa Beaulieu, Rachel MacNair, Denise Makura-Tromski, and Scott Somerville.

Whatever else these people do in their lives, they can always say with pride that they were indispensable members of a team that had the courage to tell the world a story no one else would. I am extremely proud of, and grateful to, each one of them. And though she's only five years old and too young to realize the role she played, I want to also thank my precious daughter, Sheila. Whenever things were not going well and the stress was becoming unbearable, hearing her running down the hallway toward my office was exactly what I needed to keep going.

During the research for this book, my office received information from more than 200 sources, and when the process was complete, our file of usable documents had grown from just over 2,000 to almost 6,000. If you are one of the many unselfish people who helped, I want you to realize that whether you sent a little or a lot, this book would have never happened without you. I want

to also thank those people who work undercover for us in the abortion industry. For reasons you understand better than anyone, I am not able to publicly
thank you by name, but I hope you know how appreciated you are.

If you provided information for this project but were left off the following
list, please accept my apology and my appreciation.

Advocates for Life Ministries

American Life League

American Rights Coalition

Americans United for Life

Ted Amshoff

Patricia Balaguer

Heather Brown

Nick Cicali

Cincinnati Right to Life

Brian Clowes

Mike and Vickie Conroy

Lynn Copeland

Mary Kay Culp

Mike Dare

The Denton, Texas, Public Library

Paul dePairre

Larry Donlan

Betty Essex

Kathleen Essex

Carol Everett

Feminists for Life of America

Mark Gabriel

Ted Gerk

Bill Graham

Jean Gunter

Josephine Guy

Jeannie Hill

Jim Holman

Human Life International

Human Life of Washington

Jack Humphries

Robin Jones

Mary Josius

Susan Jurecka

KS Research

Bill Lasley

Ann Leach

Legal Action for Women

Life Advocates/Houston

Life Issues Institute

Richard and Pam Mahoney

Ernest and Kathy McConnell

Vivian McNeme

Jim Miller

Elaine Morley

Lynn Murphy

Tim Murphy

Michael Noonan

Jerry Orris

Craig Parker

Michael Passignano

Fr. Frank Pavone

Priests for Life

Pro-Life Action League

Pro-Life Action Ministries

Meredith Raney

David Reardon

Right to Life of Rhode Island

Joe Scheidler

Tom Smith

Anna Sullivan

Neil Sullivan

Matt Trewella

John Walker

Ron and Mary Weaver

Lynn and Eddie Webb

Dr. Jack and Barbara Willke

Fr. Paul Witt

Charlie Wysong

Brian Young

Introduction

A good argument could be made that over the last twenty years or so, no subject has been more widely discussed or written about than abortion. Despite that, there remain fundamental issues surrounding the abortion issue about which the American people have little or no information. That's because activists on both sides have narrowly defined their turf. Abortion advocates myopically defend "the right of women to make up their own minds about abortion," while those of us who are their opponents seem equally focused on the "right to life of the unborn child."

As the president of Life Dynamics, Incorporated—an organization that provides litigation support to malpractice attorneys who sue on behalf of women who have been killed, injured, or sexually assaulted during an abortion—I get a view of this issue that not many other people see. The men and women in my office witness, firsthand, the devastation that abortion often wreaks upon the women who have them. And since we also conduct surveillance of the abortion industry, we are allowed a "behind-the-scenes" look at those who perform them.

That's what *LIME 5* is about. It is a never-before-told story about the abysmal toll often demanded of these two forgotten groups. And I want to warn you right now: *LIME 5* is not for everyone. The picture we paint is not a pretty one. The reality is, it would have been impossible for us to write this book without discussing subjects and using language that most people will find profoundly offensive. *LIME 5* is uncensored and there is no denying that parts of it are totally inappropriate for children or even adults who are sensitive or squeamish. If either of these descriptions fits you, you should strongly consider going no further.

Since virtually all the information in this book comes from public records, it would have been perfectly legal to use the actual names contained in those documents. However, I chose not to do that. Instead, out of respect for the privacy of the injured women, I chose not to identify them. As for the abortionists, they are called either John Roe (males) or Erma Roe (females), along with a number (such as John Roe 16 or Erma Roe 126). The abortion clinics are labeled as Acme Reproductive Services (ARS) with a number (such as Acme Reproductive Services 29 or ARS 51). Also be aware that the assigned names are consistent throughout the book. For example, John Roe 16 is the same person in each chapter in which he is mentioned.

The abortionists' and clinics' actual names are not used because I did not want the book to appear as a vendetta against any individual abortionist or facility. The goal was to produce an exposé on the abortion industry as a whole. Additionally, using actual names might create the illusion that these are just the abortion industry's "bad apples" and that any abortionist or facility not included is safe. Nothing could be further from the truth. Our experience has been that the quality of the practitioners and facilities in this book are representative of the entire abortion industry.

For those who might be tempted to challenge the data because it doesn't name the participants, I point out that every charge made is cited in the Endnotes and verified through information that is available to any member of the general public. Obviously, anyone who needs the names of the people and facilities involved can find them by obtaining a copy of those documents. ■

Safe and Legal

A sobering look at the price American women
have been forced to pay for "the right to choose"

The primary argument of abortion proponents has always been that abortion must be legal so it will be safe. It is an argument that clearly strikes a chord with some of the American people. Although most of them admit to being profoundly uncomfortable with the idea of abortion, many reluctantly support its legality solely on the basis of maternal safety.

But as the evidence in this chapter will show, in the real world the abortion industry's safety argument is a complete fraud. After more than twenty years of legalization, they have yet to even approach minimal safety standards, and American women are being butchered because of it.

Of course, proponents of legalized abortion will contend that the abuses detailed in this chapter are relatively few compared to the number of abortions performed. They will rightly point out that all surgery has some degree of risk and a few thousand "failures" out of more than thirty million procedures is not an unacceptable safety record.

This viewpoint erroneously assumes that the examples cited here represent all or at least most of the instances of malpractice, injury, and death. In reality, limited by our inexperience at medical research and a relatively tiny budget, our findings no more than scratched the surface.

To begin with, gaining full access to accurate data would require the cooperation of the abortion industry as well as the state and local government agencies responsible for compiling such data. Unfortunately, due to their political agendas (see Chapter 3), they have little interest in reporting abortion industry disasters, and lots of interest in covering them up. Since the mainline media, as well as some elements within the medical establishment, are participants in the cover-up, all research in this field becomes totally dependent on whether abortion-injured women seek redress in the legal system. When they don't, which is usually the case (see Chapter 4), they become invisible to researchers and eliminate the only reliable source of data about abortion injuries. During the research for this book, we stumbled across hundreds of horror stories about things that happened to women at abortion clinics, and in virtually every case we had no reason to believe that they were not true. But if the woman involved didn't file a suit, report it to the medical licensing board, or call the police, we didn't even keep a record of it much less consider it for the book.

We were also hampered because attorneys are understandably reluctant to talk about ongoing cases or cases that have not yet been filed. That is the main reason there are a disproportionate number of cases from the 1970s or 1980s compared to the 1990s. Malpractice cases take an average of two to five years to get to trial, and during that time it is extremely difficult, if not impossible, to get details about them. Therefore, there are fewer cases discussed here from the late 1980s to the present than from the preceding years. However, don't let that mislead you to believe that fewer injuries and deaths are occurring or that the abortion industry "cleaned up its act." At Life Dynamics, we are currently providing litigation support in 84 abortion-malpractice cases, 11 of which involve the death of the woman having the abortion, and only one of those cases is included in this chapter. Because it often takes years for information about abortion-malpractice cases to be "discoverable" by independent researchers, no book written on this subject is ever going to have a high number of recent cases—regardless of how many there actually are.

Another factor limiting research into this field is that the majority of these cases are settled before trial. That's a problem for two reasons. First, most abortionists demand a confidentiality agreement as part of their willingness to settle a case. Second, legal research services track only cases that actually go to trial. So, except in those rare instances in which a settled case is sensational enough to be covered by the media, there is little chance that we could even find out it exists.

In writing this chapter, we noticed a very interesting phenomenon that seems to support our contention that the data we gathered is merely a fraction of the whole story. Although there is no evidence that abortionists are any worse in one part of the country than they are in another, the abortion-malpractice activity that we were able to identify was not evenly distributed. We found that, without exception, we uncovered lots of cases in sections of the country where the media had previously investigated abortion industry abuses, or where we had researchers willing to sift through dusty courthouse documents.

Of course, abortion advocates will try to claim that in places where we didn't find significant abortion malpractice activity it's because there wasn't any. But the fact is, wherever cases were pursued—cases were found. A lack of abortion malpractice activity in a given city or state doesn't indicate that the abortionists there were better, but that the uncovering and reporting of their behavior were worse.

The point is, no one who is knowledgeable on the subject could reasonably argue that we found more than a fraction of the total number of abortion-injury cases. And even at that, we were able to print only a small portion of what we found. Under the specific injury categories later in this chapter, the case summaries represent only a sample of the typical cases we found. Had we printed everything we have, this book could easily have been a couple of thousand pages long.

You will notice in this book that there are no statistics about how often a particular injury occurs, or what percentage of women get raped while having an abortion, or how many die, etc. That was not an oversight. When the media refuses to talk about abortion injuries, the abortion industry uses raw political power to cover its tracks, an intellectually dishonest medical community is willing to look the other way, and the U.S. government is actively involved in a cover-up, publishing statistics about how often something does or does not happen during an abortion would be a joke. If you believe nothing else in this book, believe this: Anytime you see a statistical chart about abortion injury, sexual assault, or death, the person who compiled that chart either is very misinformed or is lying. Under the current system, there is absolutely no definitive way to have accurate information on this subject, and without profound systemic changes there never will be.

Another problem with abortion statistics is that, even if they were accurate, they invite unreasonable comparisons. Abortion advocates try to claim that abortion is safer than other common forms of surgery. However, they ignore that the patients are different, making the comparison irrelevant. In other surgical procedures, the patient may be old and/or deathly ill or injured, while abortion patients are always relatively young and normally in good health. In fact, it has often been observed that a woman is never more healthy in her life than when she is pregnant. Additionally, other forms of surgery can often be very complicated, while even the abortion industry touts abortion as a very quick and very simple procedure. So by any criterion, it is clearly unreasonable to draw comparisons between abortion and other surgical procedures. The circumstances under which they occur are completely different.

Before going into the case histories, I want to relate the story of one particular abortion clinic that, to me, symbolizes the entire history of legalized abortion in America.

A Shaky Beginning

In June 1970 the State of New York legalized abortion, and in less than a month freestanding abortion clinics began springing up like mushrooms. Before legalization, the National Association for the Repeal of Abortion Laws (later changed to the National Abortion Rights Action League, or NARAL) had "publicly pledged assurance that the new law would work in a safe manner" and took it upon themselves to evaluate these new facilities.

Dr. Bernard Nathanson, one of the founders of NARAL, began inspecting the new clinics and described the first one he visited as drab, dank, and unsanitary. He then visited a second clinic and described it in a similar manner. The second one was operated by John Roe 849, a *theatrical arts* graduate who had been arrested numerous times in California for performing illegal abortions, including one in which he killed a woman.

But despite knowing about the problems in these facilities, NARAL members invested in them anyway. Fortunately for women, New York health officials still had some power to regulate the safety of abortion, and these prototype clinics were soon run out of business.

Then Nathanson was approached with a challenge. The largest freestanding abortion clinic in the world, Acme Reproductive Services (ARS) 12 was in big trouble. Originally touted as a model to prove that first-trimester abortions could be performed safely in outpatient clinics, it was now in danger of being shut down. The clinic's owners asked Dr. Nathanson to take over operations of ARS 12 and save it from suffering the same demise as other New York abortion clinics.

Nathanson met with the clinic's administrator and she gave him the rundown on the precise problems ARS 12 was facing. She told him that the doctors were "atrocious...sadists, drunks, incompetents, sex maniacs, thieves, butchers, and lunatics...half of them don't even wash their hands anymore before doing an abortion, let alone scrubbing. They refuse to use masks or caps, and their mustaches are dragging into the suction machines. I swear, one of these days we're going to lose one of those guys right into the suction trap and the lab is going to tell us the tissue is pregnancy tissue and the abortion is complete."

When Nathanson inspected the facility, he found that it was chaotic, crowded, inadequately lighted, ill-equipped, poorly run, poorly staffed, dirty, and operating with no back-up emergency hospital. He also discovered that staff abortionists were paid on a commission basis and that the more experienced ones would purposely underestimate gestational ages on some patients. The idea was to trick the new abortionists into taking the messy and time-consuming late abortions, leaving the easier, quicker, and more profitable ones for themselves.

Nathanson's first task was monumental: getting ARS 12 in shape for an upcoming state health inspection. It was clear that without a complete overhaul, it had no hope of passing. Nathanson saw his goal as revamping the operation "to make it into a model clinic for all those that would arise across the nation when the laws [against abortion] fell."

First, he ordered up-to-date sterilizing equipment, scrub suits, and lights for the operating rooms. He imposed some discipline on the staff, including medical criteria for screening patients and a protocol for sending high-risk patients to a hospital for their abortions. He knew he could never get the entire clinic into shape, so he focused on the central

After the inspectors left, it was back to business as usual. The very next abortion patient ended up in the emergency room of a local hospital.

issue—the abortion itself. His theory was that the inspector might overlook irregularities in counseling, record-keeping, recovery, and other areas of the clinic if he could observe a model abortion done in a properly equipped procedure room. To that end, on the day of the inspection Nathanson selected his most qualified doctor, instructed his staff to be on their best behavior, and scheduled the calmest patient.

When the state inspection team arrived, the place was spotless and the staff behaved professionally. The "show abortion" went flawlessly with the patient calm and quiet. Nathanson said that "[the state inspector] was impressed. He was even encouraging and soothing as he offered a mild critique of our ridiculous recovery room. As he left, he winked and murmured to me, 'Don't worry.' I knew we were safe for a while."

Of course, after the inspectors left it was back to business as usual. The very next abortion patient at ARS 12 had her uterus perforated and ended up in the emergency room of a local hospital, in serious condition. Nathanson opined that, "If that operation had occurred in [the inspector's] gaze, he probably would have closed down [ARS 12] on the spot." Instead, the staff's command performance allowed the facility to keep its license, and they eventually moved to even bigger facilities.

However, Nathanson was becoming disillusioned. The clinic's administrators seemed to have a ghoulish preoccupation with doing more and later abortions. Suspicious that the lab was not doing proper pathology reports, Nathanson had a staffer extract a section of liver from a cadaver and send it to the lab. The report came back "pregnancy tissue." The wife of one of the doctors reported that her husband was having nightmares, another that her husband had developed a drinking problem. Four marriages ended in divorce and affairs between staffers were common. Nathanson resigned his position at ARS 12, and eventually renounced his "pro-choice" position. He went on to become an outspoken opponent of legalized abortion.

However, ARS 12 flourished despite its numerous problems. In 1984, 1985, and 1986, ARS 12 was cited by the state for a lack of medical supervision and administrative control. Also in 1986, it was cited for primary medical deficiencies, because it had no anesthesiologist on staff and was improperly administering anesthesia.

Unfortunately, these warnings apparently went unheeded. On August 10, 1988, 19-year-old "Christine" underwent a 14-week abortion at ARS 12. Despite her obvious signs of distress shortly after the procedure, the clinic did not instigate emergency procedures for almost an hour. After finally being transported to Cabrini Medical Center, Christine was pronounced dead from complications related to anesthesia. Incredibly, as she was receiving emergency treatment, clinic records showed that her abortionist, John Roe 44, was back on the job and performed 10 more abortions that day.

During a subsequent health department investigation, authorities found that Christine's post-operative condition was listed on clinic records as "pink, responsive, alert," even though by that time she had already gone into respiratory arrest. Investigators eventually determined that the note was written before the abortion even began. Among their other findings were that ARS 12 "did not employ proper monitoring equipment or procedures,...had no working EKG machine,...had no [cardiac defibrillator] available," and that "neither the surgeon nor the nurse were properly knowledgeable about CPR procedures and techniques." They were also critical of what they called "an inordinate delay on the part of [ARS 12] in calling for an ambulance."

In addition to issues directly related to Christine's death, health department inspections conducted in 1988 determined that ARS 12 routinely placed its patients at "continuing and serious risk" by employing "procedures and equipment that were grossly irresponsible and in contravention of accepted medical practice." Among specific allegations were that the facility:

- Had no one on staff who was qualified to administer anesthesia
- Did not employ proper procedures or equipment for administering anesthesia
- Did not administer preliminary test dosages to determine a patient's sensitivity to anesthetic drugs
- Used dosages of anesthesia that were twice as high as specified in the clinic's in-house procedure manual
- Maintained no procedures or devices to accurately gage the amount of anesthesia being given, estimating dosage "by eye"
- Conducted pre-operation medical examinations and medical histories that were cursory and inadequate
- Had no functioning emergency equipment on-site
- Had a number of emergency medications that were past their expiration date
- Had no one on staff with current CPR training
- Did not document respiration and pulse prior to anesthesia
- Had insufficient lighting in operating rooms
- Lacked proper hand-washing sinks in exam rooms, and had no soap or paper towels at either the scrub sink or recovery room bathroom
- Improperly stored oxygen and nitrous oxide canisters
- Had unsanitary conditions, including stained scrub sinks, dirty walls and floors, trash stored in operating scrub room, blood on two wheels of the operating room table, red make-up stains on the rim of oxygen and nitrous oxide masks, uncovered and dusty tubing on suction machines
- Stored medical supplies on the floor
- Stored sterile surgical supply items in dirty wash room
- Had no provisions for disposal of infectious wastes

During this time, the medical director of ARS 12 was John Roe 267. The facility, however, was unable to produce any documentation verifying his credentials or qualifications and there was virtually no evidence that he

provided any meaningful medical supervision. Despite the fact that one investigation was conducted a full two weeks after Christine's death, there was no
indication that Roe had personally reviewed the matter or directed that any
reforms be instituted. Similarly, they uncovered 18 patient medical charts that
showed complications, and not one indicated that it had been reviewed by
Roe. There was also evidence that he had never read the facility's policy
manual, and had never instituted a quality assurance program at the clinic.

In September 1988, ARS 12 was provisionally closed by the state. Although
this action was supposed to last only 60 days, the facility never reopened.
However, that did not end the mayhem of Roes 44 and 267.

Roe 44, who performed Christine's fatal abortion, finally had his license
suspended in 1991 for incompetence in performing abortions and repeatedly
testing positive for cocaine use. One of the incidents that led to this action was
a botched abortion in which the patient hemorrhaged and required a hysterectomy. An investigation revealed that contributing factors to the patient's
injuries were a lack of proper equipment and a delay in calling an ambulance.
Apparently, Roe 44 had decided not to learn from his past mistakes.

As for Roe 267, his license to practice medicine in New York was actually
revoked two months *before* Christine's death, but he had secured a judicial stay
and remained licensed at that time. However, the revocation was eventually
enforced and his license was taken. This action was originally initiated because
of his 1987 conviction for illegally selling approximately 48,000 Dilaudid
tablets to pay off gambling debts.

In 1991, his request to have his license restored was granted and he went
to work for an abortion clinic in Queens, New York. On September 16, 1994,
he performed a second-trimester abortion on a 36-year-old mother of three,
and four hours later she was dead from complications. The clinic's director
later admitted that she knew about Roe's background when she hired him, but
defended her decision, saying, "We are firmly committed to helping people
who are skilled medical professionals who have a fall from grace." It sounds to
me like what she should have said is that they decided to let their *patients* make
that commitment. After all, it wasn't this clinic director or any of her staff who
ended up dead.

As I said at the beginning of the discussion about ARS 12, for many reasons
it is symbolic of the entire American experience with legalized abortion. Since
the problems at this and other New York abortion clinics were well documented prior to the deliberations in the *Roe v. Wade* decision, they should have
been used as examples of how dangerous legal abortions are. Instead, when
the subject of safety was introduced into those proceedings, abortion facilities

in New York—of which ARS 12 was the largest—were cited as examples of how free-standing abortion clinics could provide safe and inexpensive abortions. Meanwhile, abortion proponents who knew the real story either remained silent or actively participated in the deception. The result was that on January 22, 1973, the Supreme Court struck down every state law regulating abortion, and made it possible for every American city to have its own ARS 12. (To reinforce our argument that abortion proponents knew that legalizing abortion didn't make it safe, this chapter includes several examples of *pre-Roe* injuries and deaths, *all of which resulted from legal abortions.*)

The events at ARS 12 also demonstrate an attitude toward women that is alarming, and which we continue to find among abortion providers (see Chapter 5). When ARS 12 needed to demonstrate good medical practice in order to protect themselves, they did so. They spit-shined the facility and had the staff on its best behavior, and nobody got hurt. But as soon as the inspectors went away, the very next patient ended up in the emergency room fighting for her life. And when state inspectors showed up after Christine's death, they found conditions so appalling that they wouldn't be tolerated in a veterinary clinic. Clearly, no one who truly cared about the women they treated would allow this sort of thing to go on.

But perhaps the best example of the callous disdain they had for women was that Roe 44 performed 10 additional abortions immediately after killing Christine. Despite having just seen a 19-year-old girl lose her life because of his incompetence, he immediately resumed his normal routine. Contrast that to a situation a few years back when a promising middleweight boxer killed an opponent in the ring. Although he intellectually knew that it was not his fault, this man was so unnerved by the experience that he was unable to even talk about it without being overcome with emotion. He stopped boxing for a time, and even when he returned he was never again the same. He eventually retired at an age that usually marks the height of a professional fighter's career. Unlike Roe 44, this prizefighter—a man whom many would label as violent— had enough humanity in him to be traumatized by having participated in the taking of another human being's life.[1]

Case Histories

Before you begin reading the following case histories, I want to reiterate that these are only a fraction of the total number of cases we found. In fact, these categories do not even reflect all the types of injuries we identified. Also, keep in mind that choosing the appropriate category for a case was by no means an exact science. When a woman died after an abortion and her autopsy showed that she had a perforated uterus, torn cervix, sepsis, and DIC, it was difficult to decide in which of these categories she should be placed. Our purpose was simply to include several cases in each category to show that a specific injury was not unique. Because most cases had multiple injuries, you will see quite a bit of overlap. For example, while there are only ten cases listed under "Hysterectomy," in thirty-eight of these cases the women required a hysterectomy in an attempt to stop bleeding.

Injuries to the Uterus

In February 1968, "Nancy" flew with her boyfriend from Oklahoma to Kansas City for an abortion by John Roe 416. Roe examined Nancy and told the couple that he would contact them at their hotel. He called at 11 p.m., and arrived 40 minutes later to drive them to his sinus clinic for the abortion. During the procedure, Roe created a half-inch tear in Nancy's uterus. The resulting blood loss sent her into shock and she died while still at the clinic. An autopsy revealed that parts of the fetus, which had reached four-and-a-half to five months gestation, had remained in her womb.

Roe was convicted on June 8, 1968, of performing an abortion that was not "necessary to preserve the life" of the patient. He served 14 months in prison before being released on parole, and his license was revoked on May 4, 1971. But Missouri's abortion law was found unconstitutional in the wake of *Roe v. Wade*. Roe sued to overturn his conviction and restore his medical license on the grounds that since Missouri's abortion law was unconstitutional, his conviction was likewise unconstitutional. He was eventually successful when a court ruled that Nancy's abortion "was performed by a licensed physician in a medically accepted manner under medically accepted conditions," and the state therefore could not have validly prohibited it "in terms of its interest in maternal health." Roe was released from probation and his record expunged of the manslaughter-abortion conviction.[2]

Having heard that the abortion law had been changed in New York, "Margaret" sought an abortion by John Roe 146 on June 6, 1970. A resulting uterine perforation brought her to the threshold of death and required that her reproductive organs be surgically removed. In spite of the fact that her uterus had been perforated in the abortion, she encountered difficulties in pursuing a lawsuit because, even though New York legalized abortion on April 11, hers took place before the law was enacted on July 1, and therefore was technically illegal.[3]

Nineteen-year-old "Judy" traveled to New York for an abortion on September 3, 1970. She suffered a uterine perforation, which was not noticed at the time of the abortion. She returned home to Indiana where she was later hospitalized due to nausea, vomiting, and pain. A laparotomy found the uterine perforation, a 12-week-old fetus, and 1500 ml of blood in her peritoneal (abdominal) cavity. She suffered severe hypoxia, required a tracheotomy, and suffered numerous other problems including bronchopneumonia and a cerebral artery blockage. She underwent a hysterectomy on September 10, but died September 22. An investigation of the abortion clinics and hospitals used by this particular abortionist uncovered records of five additional patients with uterine perforations who required hospitalization.[4]

"Cassandra," age 20, underwent an elective abortion at a California hospital on September 2, 1971. She was treated for heavy bleeding on September 15, and was sent home following a D&C. Two days later she returned, still complaining of heavy bleeding. She went into convulsions and was transferred to another hospital, where she died on September 19. The cause of her death was cardiopulmonary insufficience due to blood loss from a perforated uterus and lacerated uterine artery.[5]

On January 21, 1972, "Kathryn" went to a California hospital for a legal abortion by John Roe 846. During the procedure, her uterus was perforated and, according to her medical records, she suffered "retroperitoneal and intraabdominal hemorrhage and shock." The next day, at age 26, she died, leaving behind a husband and a three-year-old son. In a sad irony, on the one-year anniversary of Kathryn's death, January 22, 1973, the U.S. Supreme Court issued the *Roe v. Wade* decision legalizing abortion nationwide.[6]

In late March 1972, 14-year-old "Susan" underwent a legal abortion in New York, after which she required additional treatment to extract fetal tissue that had been left behind. During these procedures, her uterus and bowel were perforated, requiring a partial resection of the bowel and drainage of an abscess. Despite these efforts, Susan died of peritonitis and septicemia on April 16, 1972.[7]

On June 3, 1975, 35-year-old "Sandra" had an abortion at Acme Reproductive Services (ARS) 14. During the abortion, her uterus was punctured and she bled to death. Sandra left behind four children. As they had done in several other instances in which they injured women, employees of ARS 14 claimed that they were simply repairing an injury caused by the patient's botched attempt at a self-induced abortion. In fact, this is a fairly common claim made by abortionists who injure their patients. Of course, this contention defies logic. First, why would a woman self-induce when abortion is legal? Second, even if she did, why would she go to an abortion clinic for repairs instead of an emergency room? And third, since the injured woman often traveled to the clinic from out of state, the obvious question is why a woman who injured herself trying to self-induce an abortion would go out of state for help. In reality, this is simply a shabby bit of deception abortionists use to avoid responsibility for the harm they do to women.[8]

After charging her a fee, a Chicago area abortion referral service sent 16-year-old "Louise" to a local abortionist whom she was lead to believe was a physician. Actually, he was a chiropractor who had failed his licensing test at least three times, and later had his chiropractic license suspended. He used a corkscrew-like device to attempt to terminate her 21-week pregnancy. As a result, she suffered a badly perforated uterus and was hospitalized for 11 days. She eventually had to have her uterus removed. As we were investigating this story, we found information about another chiropractor and a witch doctor performing abortions in the Chicago area.[9]

On June 14, 1977, "Barbaralee" had an abortion performed by John Roe 781. After the procedure, she was noted to be pale and complaining of lower abdominal cramping, so she was kept at the clinic for an additional two hours. When she was dismissed, her sister helped her, weak and bleeding, to her car, where she lay in the back seat during the trip home. Several hours later, she was found unconscious in her bedroom and was rushed to a hospital. She was pronounced dead on arrival. An autopsy showed a badly torn uterus, a damaged ureter, and a large amount of blood in the pelvic cavity. The face and spinal column of her fetus were embedded in a hematoma inside her uterus. A subsequent investigation noted that although vital signs taken 45 minutes after the abortion showed signs of internal hemorrhage, Barbaralee was not examined again before being discharged. She was 18 years old at the time of her death, and had been referred to this National Abortion Federation member clinic by a local women's group.[10]

On July 18, 1979, "Geneva" underwent an abortion at Acme Reproductive Services 16. Later that day, the 21-year-old was in pain, which she attributed to the cramping that the clinic said to expect. At 8:30 that evening, she was admitted to a local hospital with no vital signs. Attempts to resuscitate her failed and she was pronounced dead. The autopsy found that Geneva had suffered a perforated uterus. She was the mother of two small children. ARS 16 was eventually sued by their malpractice insurer, alleging that the owner and director were negligent in allowing John Roe 26 to perform abortions after staff noted his failing manual dexterity. He was later diagnosed as having multiple sclerosis. The complaint also charged the facility with failure to meet state health standards, failure to have a sufficient number of nurses on duty, failure to have an appropriate on-call practitioner, and failure to have a professional director of medical services. ARS 16 was a member of the National Abortion Federation.[11]

"Carol" underwent a late-term abortion by John Roe 686 on May 13, 1980, at Acme Reproductive Services 17. During the two-day procedure, completed on May 14, Carol's uterus was perforated. Roe suspected that he had created a hole in her uterus and that there would be a delay in her being dismissed. He had a staff member put her on an X-ray table and roll her into a storage room. Not only was this room not private, but a security man was allowed to come in and loaf there. Carol was in severe pain, but ARS 17's staff told her to shut up because her cries were frightening patients who had not yet undergone their abortions. They left Carol cold, alone, and nauseated. Her cries were finally investigated by another patient, who said she would try to find someone to help. During the post-operative check-up, Roe blamed Carol for ruining his record of not "poking a hole through a uterus" in the last two or three years, and told her that she should have undergone the abortion in a hospital because of the fetus's age.

Meanwhile, her husband was left sitting in the waiting room and was not informed of Carol's whereabouts or condition. When the clinic closed, he was sent outside to wait. When Carol came out, she was bent over in pain and on the ride home she cried out in pain every time the car hit a bump. She had to be carried into the house, and had a pulse rate of 140–160 with a temperature of 104. They called the clinic, and Roe prescribed medication. When Carol's husband came home from the pharmacy, he found her on the hallway floor where she had collapsed after going into the bathroom to vomit. She then hyperventilated, vomited, lost feeling in her hands and feet, and turned bluish gray. On May 19, she had a follow-up visit. Roe told her that she was still pregnant and that a second procedure would be necessary. When her husband asked about the second procedure and what precautions would be taken to prevent a second perforation, Roe had the police eject him from the clinic. ARS 17 was a member of the National Abortion Federation.[12]

When "Helen," age 26, sought a tubal ligation from John Roe 822, he informed her that she was pregnant. Helen consented to an abortion on October 26, 1983. Roe failed to remove all the fetal parts and punctured her uterus, then sent her home without informing her of her injury. When she later called the clinic complaining of weakness, vomiting, and severe pain, she was instructed to take a laxative. She developed a high fever and died on November 3. Feculent fluid and feces were discovered in her abdominal cavity after her death. Helen's mother filed suit on behalf of Helen's two surviving children. When a local activist group wrote to Roe to chastise him for his poor care of Helen, he wrote back, saying, "Elective abortion refers to termination of a live viable pregnancy upon the request of the mother. I have never performed this service or even offered it." He claimed that he was only doing a D&C after Helen had a miscarriage.[13]

On March 2, 1985, 38-year-old "Ellen" sought an abortion at Acme Reproductive Services 30. Her abortion was performed by John Roe 797, who earlier that day had left portions of a fetus in another patient. (See "Patricia" under "Incomplete Abortion or Retained Tissue.") On March 4, she returned to the clinic complaining of high fever, severe cramps, and excruciating pain. The clinic's owner/director gave her tea and called Roe. He arrived four hours later, examined Ellen, performed a second D&C, and sent her home with a bottle of antibiotics. The next day, suffering from pain and high fever, she was taken by ambulance to the emergency room of a local hospital where she was rushed into surgery. She died, leaving two children behind. Her autopsy report listed the cause of death as peritonitis from uterine and bowel perforations. Roe told reporters that he did not ordinarily work at ARS 30, but was "strapped for cash" and had agreed to fill in for abortionist John Roe 338. He said that he was "not an abortionist, just an honest, easygoing guy looking for something temporary." He left the clinic after Ellen's death saying, "It was a bad month."[14]

On January 5, 1988, 18-year-old "Sarah" underwent an abortion by John Roe 73 at Acme Reproductive Services 20. She awoke in pain during the procedure, her blood pressure fell during recovery, she passed out while preparing to leave, and she was bleeding so profusely that blood had to be suctioned from her vagina. Roe told her family that her symptoms were a reaction to anesthesia and that they should take her home, but they refused to leave. After the facility closed, Sarah's family brought her soup at Roe's suggestion. About four hours after the facility closed, the family requested an ambulance, but the clinic's staff refused to call one. Sarah's aunt then called an ambulance. When paramedics arrived, they found Sarah pale, lethargic, in profound shock, and with a pulse of 132. Roe sent a note to the hospital with her which was later found to misrepresent her condition. The emergency room physician ordered IVs and eight units of blood. A surgeon found two liters of blood in her abdominal and pelvic cavities, and her uterus filled with clots, the result of a large uterine tear. She was hospitalized for six days.[15]

On December 30, 1988, "Hannah," age 19, underwent an abortion by John Roe 135 at Acme Reproductive Services 27. Roe did not administer anesthesia, and Hannah was in so much pain that she had difficulty remaining still, repeatedly begged him to stop, and eventually lost consciousness. Roe did not monitor Hannah's blood loss or assess her condition during the procedure. After pulling so hard on Hannah's internal structures that he bent his forceps, he used a pair of desk scissors. During the abortion, Roe inadvertently removed Hannah's right ovary and Fallopian tube, severed her left Fallopian tube, caused a large uterine rupture, lacerated and destroyed almost four feet of small intestine, and left the fetus floating in the abdominal cavity. She went into hypovolemic shock and was transported to an emergency hospital. After her hospitalization, Roe convinced Hannah that she should return to him for follow-up care. She attended regular appointments from January until May 1989, during which time Roe engaged in inappropriate sexual behavior with her.[16]

On June 2, 1989, "Margaret" went to Acme Reproductive Services 21 to have an abortion performed by John Roe 295. After she was dismissed, she started experiencing pain and bleeding, and called the facility about her symptoms. They did not advise her to seek medical care. Two days later, she sought medical treatment on her own and was told that she had a perforated uterus and retained fetal tissue. A D&C was performed to complete the abortion and, due to infection, a hysterectomy was also necessary. Unfortunately, despite all efforts to save her life, Margaret died of the complications of her abortion, leaving behind her husband and one-year-old son.[17]

"Christie" underwent an abortion by John Roe 339 on February 20, 1990, to terminate a 22-week pregnancy. Although the health history form completed by her indicated a history of high blood pressure, headaches, dizziness, toxemia, and a C-section during a prior pregnancy, there was no record that these conditions were ever discussed with Christie. Clinic records do not indicate that any counseling was done and there was no informed consent document signed by the patient. Additionally, no ultrasound, physical examination, or blood tests were performed, nor were vital signs taken prior to the abortion. The pre-operative, intra-operative, and post-operative charts failed to note the method of dilation of the cervix, the dosage or type of anesthesia, the personnel administering anesthesia, whether an IV was in place, or the identity of nurses or other assisting personnel. The records do indicate, however, that Roe performed a suction abortion, which is an incorrect procedure for a 22-week pregnancy. It also documents a cervical tear and repair, but fails to record the amount of blood loss, the time or duration of post-abortion observation, or by whom Christie was observed. There were also no readings of vital signs during the post-operative period, and Christie was discharged without any recorded follow-up or emergency care instructions. The next day she was taken by ambulance to the hospital, in shock due to blood loss. She had a laceration of her uterus that extended deep into her pelvis, the end of her ovarian vein had been lacerated and tied, and her ureter had been kinked by the suture Roe had used to repair her cervix.[18]

"With his patient clearly in critical condition, he sent her to the hospital in a private car during rush hour…A more egregious example of incompetence and gross negligence is difficult to imagine."

On February 27, 1990, "BJ," age 22, underwent an abortion by John Roe 73. She awoke screaming during the abortion, and begged him to stop. He then had an employee clamp a hand over her mouth. She eventually went under again but awoke this time in a chair in the recovery room, with the bottom of her shirt drenched with blood. The next thing she remembered was Roe carrying her to her car, after which a friend drove her to a hospital. The note sent by Roe to the hospital described the abortion as "uneventful," and failed to disclose all the medications he had administered. Because the ligaments around BJ's uterus had been severed and her right ovary torn loose, her uterus and ovary had to be removed. The doctor who did the emergency surgery testified: "It would take a lot of force—an extreme amount of force—to do that kind of damage." He noted that the perforation was four inches in length and had caused BJ to lose an incredible amount of blood. The medical board stated that, "having nearly eviscerated his patient and with her clearly in critical condition, he sent her to the hospital in a private car during rush hour…A more egregious example of incompetence and gross negligence is difficult to imagine."[19]

"Sandra," age 28, had an abortion performed by John Roe 67 on April 27, 1990, and was discharged soon after her procedure. Upon returning home, her babysitter stayed with her three children several hours as Sandra slipped in and out of consciousness and suffered pain and abdominal swelling. The babysitter called the abortion clinic twice and was told that Sandra's symptoms were normal. When a third call to the clinic yielded no response, the babysitter called paramedics. Sandra was pronounced dead upon her arrival at the hospital from a one-inch uterine laceration.[20]

"Anjelica" had an abortion by John Roe 468 at a Las Vegas abortion clinic on November 1, 1991. During the procedure, her uterus was perforated and she began to bleed heavily. The clinic's staff kept her under observation, but did not initiate treatment or call for emergency care for several hours. Finally, paramedics were called and they rushed her to the hospital at 7:30 in the evening. Unfortunately, she had already bled to death and was pronounced dead on arrival. She was 21 years old and left behind two daughters, ages one and three.[21]

Shortly after beginning an abortion at a Ft. Lauderdale abortion clinic, John Roe 387 stopped the procedure because the 39-year-old patient complained of pain. As it turned out, the woman was in intense pain because Roe had perforated her uterus. Roe, however, was undaunted and tried again nine days later. This time, not only did he tear a second hole in her uterus, he accidentally took out her appendix. After a subsequent medical board investigation, one member stated, "The fetus was still there, untouched, and was removed later by another doctor. That the patient is alive today is fairly miraculous."[22]

Injuries to the Cervix

On June 16, 1971, "Margaret," age 25, traveled from Michigan to a New York abortion clinic, where she underwent a legal abortion. The procedure took place at approximately 10:30 a.m. The abortionist and his staff left Margaret virtually unattended until her boyfriend returned to the facility at 2 p.m. He found her pale, and having difficulty breathing. He pleaded for the clinic employees to take action. They summoned paramedics, who were unable to revive Margaret. She was pronounced dead on arrival at a hospital directly across the street from the abortion clinic. The pathologist determined that Margaret had bled to death from a "laceration of the entire length of the cervix, lower segment of the uterus, and the broad ligament."[23]

On March 16, 1973, "Evelyn" had an abortion at ARS 13 in Chicago. She later collapsed in a driveway and was taken to the hospital. She was in shock and was hemorrhaging from a ruptured cervix and vagina. She lost her life as a result of those injuries. The abortionist later claimed that he did not perform the abortion that killed Evelyn, but was treating her for injuries received at an abortion facility in her hometown of Detroit. However, her brother pointed out that the only reason Evelyn was in Chicago was for an abortion.[24]

Twenty-five-year-old "Charlotte" underwent an abortion by John Roe 436 on April 2, 1977. Afterward, she required hospitalization and surgical treatment for shock, a lacerated cervix and uterus, and an incomplete abortion. Roe contended that the damage was done by the doctors at the hospital, and filed suit against them. He also argued that at the time of her abortion, Charlotte had signed an arbitration agreement that limited his liability to $15,000, and had agreed that she would have to pay in advance for the entire cost of the arbitration.[25]

On March 10, 1981, 19-year-old "Tina" also had an abortion by Roe 436. He lacerated her cervix, uterus, and vaginal wall, penetrating the peritoneal cavity. Tina bled, became nauseated, and vomited intermittently for approximately one hour. She finally fell asleep on a couch in the clinic waiting room. At no time following the procedure did Roe examine Tina. At home, she passed a large blood clot, began bleeding profusely, and lost consciousness. She was transported to a hospital in shock, and underwent an emergency laparotomy and hysterectomy.[26]

On January 15, 1982, 34-year-old "Shary" had an abortion performed by John Roe 368 at Acme Reproductive Services 22 in Dallas. During the procedure, she sustained a one-inch tear of her cervix and began to hemorrhage. She died the next day. The clinic where she had her abortion was a member of the National Abortion Federation.[27]

"Patricia" underwent an abortion by John Roe 13 to terminate her 24-week pregnancy on March 3, 1984. During the procedure, she suffered a deep laceration two inches long and passing through the entire cervical wall. Roe then left her alone while he performed abortions on other patients. Patricia, age 16, bled to death while at the abortion clinic.[28]

"Sylvia," age 18, underwent a second-trimester abortion on December 31, 1986, by John Roe 47. Because he used an abortion technique that is appropriate only for first-trimester procedures, Sylvia ended up with a two-and-a-half-inch laceration of her cervix, a foreign body imbedded in her uterus, and a nearly one-inch laceration of her vagina, none of which were noted by Roe. After she complained of severe abdominal cramps, he gave her Demerol and told her to go home. She then collapsed and said she was unable to walk. Roe called her "lazy," put her in a wheelchair and ejected her from his facility. Later that evening she went into shock, and was transported to an emergency room without a pulse or blood pressure. Despite an emergency hysterectomy, she bled to death, leaving one child behind.[29]

On December 6, 1988, "Katrina" had an abortion at a Jacksonville, Florida, doctor's office. As a result, she ended up with 900 cc of blood in her peritoneal cavity from a torn cervix and ruptured uterus. Emergency efforts to save her were unsuccessful. She was 16 years old at the time of her death.[30]

On July 27, 1990, 32-year-old "Mary Ann" had an abortion by John Roe 726. After being dismissed, her continued massive blood loss required that she be rushed to a local hospital. She died later that night following unsuccessful surgery to repair a badly lacerated cervix sustained during the abortion.[31]

"Theresa" underwent an abortion by National Abortion Federation member Erma Roe 137 on February 15, 1991. Theresa suffered a perforated cervix and colon, causing substantial blood loss and profound shock. In addition to a hysterectomy, she required removal of her right Fallopian tube and ovary and part of her colon.[32]

On November 10, 1993, John Roe 45 performed an abortion on 20-year-old "Jane" at Acme Reproductive Services 23 in New York. Jane had originally called Roe's New Jersey abortion clinic, but had been referred to his New York facility for what was estimated to be a second-trimester abortion. The referral was made because New Jersey law requires that second-trimester abortions be performed in hospitals, while New York allows them to be done in abortion clinics. However, a sonogram showed that the pregnancy was already in its third trimester, which even New York requires be terminated in a hospital. Although Roe's lack of qualifications prevented him from obtaining hospital privileges, he did not want to lose the sale. So he opted to defy New York State Law and scheduled the abortion for the next day.

A subsequent medical investigation determined that Jane was given a fact sheet for first-trimester abortions, and was not adequately counseled on the risky late abortion that she was about to undergo nor counseled on alternatives. It also showed that Jane's "anatomical anomalies and other risk factors" made her a poor candidate for surgery in general and for a late-term abortion in particular. During the procedure, she suffered a major laceration of the cervix, which the medical investigation said most likely occurred because of a "rupture of the lower uterine segment followed by the pulling out of a large fetus against an inadequately dilated cervix" or to grasping and pulling the original rupture. An additional laceration of the uterine wall "was probably a separate injury, done with the forceps during the dismembering of the fetus."

After Jane lost consciousness, Roe discovered the laceration but did not transfer her to a hospital and instead attempted to repair the damage himself. When Jane's blood pressure dropped, Roe administered fluids intravenously, which restored blood pressure to some extent, but did not address the injuries. Two-and-a-half hours after the injury, Jane was "woozy and pale" and exhibited signs of going into shock. When Roe helped Jane sit up thirty minutes later, she "immediately felt dizzy and expelled a gush of 200–300 cc of blood." Fifteen minutes later he finally transferred Jane to the emergency room. She was in hypovolemic shock, pale, with a pulse of 113, respiration of 86, and blood pressure of 88/52. She had a severed uterine artery, a lower uterine perforation, and a cervical laceration nearly two inches long. She required an emergency hysterectomy to save her life. When asked why he did not transfer her to a hospital after he discovered the injury, Roe said that there is nothing "magical" about a hospital. He also contended that he is an emergency room physician, and had he transferred her she would only have been seen by another emergency room physician. He also claimed that he and his staff were giving Jane more attention than she would have gotten in an intensive care unit. Among other things, the medical board found that Roe's "answer to this question and others evidences his inability to distinguish between mere attention and appropriate care."[33]

Injuries to the Intestines/Bowel

During a legal abortion on August 31, 1970, "Edith" suffered a perforated uterus with abrasions of the bowel in three places. She was hospitalized 11 days for corrective treatment, and was left sterile and with a permanent bowel problem.[34]

A 1974 suit by "Sheila" alleged that her abortionist had been negligent in performing an abortion outside a hospital setting after 12 weeks gestation. She suffered a perforated uterus and a small bowel obstruction, requiring a hysterectomy and removal of a Fallopian tube. She also suffered a periuterine abscess, multiple adhesions, external scarring, and a small bowel resection, requiring removal of some small bowel.[35]

Twenty-six-year-old "Leanne" underwent an abortion by John Roe 330 on June 25, 1975. As a result, she suffered a perforated uterus with portions of her small intestine being suctioned into her cervical cavity. After corrective surgery in a hospital, she suffered intestinal blockage that required further surgery, and a subsequent intestinal abscess required yet a third surgery. She missed nine months of work, and her weight dropped from 101 to 70 pounds.[36]

On February 23, 1979, "Sharon" had an abortion performed by John Roe 280. During the procedure, he noticed that the suction tube was clogged, and then discovered that he had punctured Sharon's uterus and severed her small intestine. She ended up losing all but about five-and-a-half inches of her small intestine, both Fallopian tubes, her appendix, and some of her large intestine. Only 28 years old, Sharon required a permanent catheter tube implanted to allow nutrients to be taken into her bloodstream, a procedure that takes up to 14 hours daily, and that she will most likely require for the rest of her life. She also suffered bloating, dizzy spells, hair loss, and her weight fell below 100 pounds. Roe's defense was that this is just "one of the complications of this procedure that happens from time to time."[37]

"Mary" underwent an abortion by John Roe 150 at Acme Reproductive Services 24 on November 11, 1980. She returned to the clinic on November 20, reporting bleeding and clots. After being kept waiting an hour and a half, she was not permitted to see a doctor. She later was admitted to the emergency room of a local hospital in shock due to hemorrhage. A one- to two-inch uterine perforation was repaired, and blood in the peritoneal cavity was evacuated. After her surgery, Mary vomited, and had a distended abdomen, tenderness, and diminished bowel sounds. Exploratory surgery performed on November 26 revealed intestinal obstruction due to loops of small bowel where the uterus was perforated. This injury was repaired and 300 cc of greenish fluid was suctioned out of her peritoneal cavity. The clinic where Mary had her abortion was a member of the National Abortion Federation.[38]

On June 25, 1982, John Roe 204 performed a third-trimester abortion on 12-year-old "Natasha" at Acme Reproductive Services 26. The girl's uterus was ruptured in three places and had to be removed. She also suffered multiple injuries to her large and small bowel. Natasha required a colostomy but her bowel was later reattached and the colostomy discontinued. The medical board referred to the abortion as "a hatchet job," and alleged "gross and repeated malpractice." Roe's attorney called him "superlative," and said he "has performed thousands and thousands of pregnancy terminations in this country and his native Cuba." One year later, "Hilda" also required a hysterectomy and colostomy after an abortion by Roe 204.[39]

On September 4, 1984, "Rebecca" had an abortion performed by John Roe 32 at a Planned Parenthood abortion clinic. She was later admitted to a local hospital to correct multiple uterine perforations. She was discharged on September 12 after having her damaged left ovary and Fallopian tube removed, but was rehospitalized on November 7 due to severe abdominal pain.

Medical tests failed to determine the cause of the pain, so Rebecca began taking her mother's prescription painkillers and became addicted. On January 30, 1985, she was admitted to a mental health center to treat her addiction. In February, Rebecca experienced extreme abdominal pain and was taken to the emergency room, with a pre-operative diagnosis of peritonitis. She had 800 cc of yellow pus drained and over two feet of gangrenous bowel removed. The gangrenous bowel was attributed to bacterial invasion through the uterine perforations created during her abortion.[40]

On May 1, 1986, "Janet" was having an abortion performed by John Roe 422 when he perforated her uterus. He then used a pair of forceps to remove what he apparently thought was fetal tissue. Instead, what he pulled out through Janet's vagina was her bowel. A general surgeon was called, a laparotomy performed, and several feet of bowel resected.[41]

On July 17, 1988, "Clara," age 24, underwent an abortion by John Roe 3. She began hemorrhaging after the procedure, but was told this was normal and dismissed. She returned in two days, reporting extreme pain. Roe performed a second abortion and Clara resumed bleeding. Roe then sent Clara and her friend home. Twelve hours later, Clara began to pass fecal matter through her vagina, so she went to her friend's doctor who admitted her to a hospital. There they found portions of fetal skull in her cervix, a uterocoloic fistula, and punctures in her vagina, uterus, and rectum. She required a colostomy. Although Roe tried to deny that he had ever treated Clara, the medical board investigated and found that he had medical records—albeit incomplete ones—for her. John Roe 3 was a member of the National Abortion Federation.[42]

In February 1989, "Phyllis," age 35, underwent a second-trimester abortion by John Roe 704. During the procedure, Roe extracted from Phyllis' vagina what he thought was the umbilical cord, but turned out to be her sigmoid colon. A general surgeon was summoned to the operating room, and found that Phyllis had also sustained injury to her right kidney and right ureter. Roe later admitted that he did not inform Phyllis of the risks of the surgery because he assumed she already understood them.[43]

On June 10, 1989, 15-year-old "Elizabeth" had an abortion by John Roe 7 at his Oklahoma City office. During the procedure, Roe pulled out some tissue, held it in his hands, and told the nurse that it was Elizabeth's small intestine and then stuffed it back into her vagina. Incredibly, not only did Roe not call for emergency care, but while Elizabeth was still under anesthesia, he left the clinic to give a friend a ride to the airport. Afterward, the clinic staff noticed a drop in her blood pressure and had her transported to a hospital. There it was determined that she had a perforated uterus, vaginal laceration, and an injury to the colon requiring a colostomy. Roe had also failed to remove the dead fetus.[44]

"Marcia," age 22, underwent an abortion on May 2, 1990, by John Roe 604. During the procedure, he perforated her uterus and intestines. Afterward, her husband wrapped her in a blanket and carried her downstairs. She was then taken by ambulance to a hospital where she was admitted, vomiting blood. The next day the abortion was completed at the hospital by another abortionist, Roe 535, who was an associate of Roe 604. Marcia continued to experience pain and vomiting and suspected that she had a perforation. When Roe 535 diagnosed her symptoms as indigestion and tried to dismiss her, Marcia refused to leave. They performed a barium enema on her which showed an intestinal blockage, but Roe 535 still discharged her. Three days later she returned to the hospital, saw a different doctor, and underwent both immediate and subsequent surgeries to remove two-and-a-half feet of intestine. She was hospitalized for 60 days and left sterile.[45]

In May 1992, "Beverly" sought an abortion from John Roe 45 to terminate her 24½-week pregnancy. After removing a fetal arm and part of the placenta, he detected a uterine perforation. He continued the procedure even though he was reaching for bony parts of the fetus and instead grasping soft tissues. In that process, he caused a three- to four-inch laceration in her uterus, perforated her sigmoid colon, cut extensive connective tissues of the colon, and damaged both of her ureters. Beverly was transferred by ambulance to the hospital, in shock. She received a blood transfusion, lost a large segment of her colon, and required a colostomy. Roe later admitted that he did not know what he was grasping with the forceps, and that the ultrasound picture was not consistent with what he felt, but that he just opened his forceps wider and grasped again, with force.[46]

"Sonia" underwent an abortion by John Roe 596 on October 12, 1993, and suffered a perforated uterus and retained fetal parts. She was evaluated by another doctor on October 21 to discover the cause of her severe abdominal pain, high fever, and vomiting. He found a bowel fistula caused by sections of her bowel being sutured to her uterine wall. She was hospitalized for corrective surgery October 23–28.[47]

After "Margaret" underwent an abortion by John Roe 223 on July 23, 1994, she had to be hospitalized. There it was discovered that her uterus had been perforated, her right Fallopian tube damaged, and her rectum perforated. As a result, part of her colon had to be removed and she required a colostomy.[48]

"Magdalena," age 23, had an abortion on December 8, 1994, by John Roe 209. During the procedure, Roe said that he knew he had "screwed up" when he had difficulty removing fetal parts, and noticed that he had perforated Magdalena's uterus and removed parts of her bowel. Because she was bleeding profusely, Roe called a hospital and asked for directions to send Magdalena there by car. He called an ambulance only when instructed to do so by the hospital staff. However, there was a half-hour delay between when the hospital was called and when an ambulance was called, during which Roe performed abortions on other patients.

Upon reaching the abortion clinic, paramedics found Magdalena lying in a pool of blood on the floor in ventricular fibrillation, with no pulse. She had no vital signs upon arrival at the hospital, was unresponsive, and had fixed and dilated pupils. A massive amount of blood was found when she was opened for surgery, and surgeons noted a "large uterine laceration with a fetal lower extremity protruding out and into the abdominal cavity,...a surgical sponge in the uterus,...cervical, vaginal, and bladder lacerations." During surgery, a female fetus, estimated by the surgeons to be of approximately 30 weeks gestation, was removed. In describing the fetus, they noted that "Both arms had been cut off; the heart, lungs, liver, and other organs had been cut out, the front of the chest and abdomen were missing, the right femur was fractured, the head was intact except for an area on the scalp which had been taken off from the back of the head." Magdalena did not survive the surgery, and her death was attributed to "complications of the acute pelvic injuries which consisted of lacerations of the lower uterus, vagina, bladder, and colon." Roe later told the medical board that he had delayed calling an ambulance because he had no admitting privileges and Magdalena had asked to be released to walk home. He also admitted that he had left Magdalena several times to perform abortions on other patients. His attorney was quoted as saying, "We don't believe this [case] was below the standard of care nor do we believe it is malpractice." Magdalena's 10-month-old daughter was left in the care of her grandmother.

This was not the first time that Roe 209 had "screwed up." He lost his license in New York in 1992, and served eight months in prison in 1990 for 17 felony counts, including forging prescriptions, grand theft, Medi-Cal fraud, aiding in furnishing of a dangerous drug without an authorized prescription, aiding and abetting unlawful prescription of a controlled substance, and assisting in unlicensed practice of medicine.[49]

Injuries to the Urinary Tract

On April 22, 1972, "Hester" underwent an abortion at a hospital in Ohio by an unidentified abortionist. During the procedure, her bladder was cut, resulting in her need to wear a Foley catheter. She also had to have a hysterectomy and required further hospitalization and treatment.[50]

In late April 1973, "Cynthia" sought pregnancy counseling at Acme Reproductive Services 36. Counselors there recommended that her pregnancy be terminated and that they be authorized to perform the procedure. She agreed, and the termination was performed by John Roe 425. Another abortionist in the facility noticed that Cynthia was jaundiced and appeared to be suffering from a severe infection. He had her transferred to a hospital where it was confirmed that she was suffering from a massive infection and acute renal failure. She had to have a complete hysterectomy and faces the possibility of future kidney and liver complications. She must also take medications for the rest of her life, and has scars on her abdomen and arms. At the time of her abortion, she was 13 years old.[51]

"Tena" underwent an abortion by John Roe 187 on October 7, 1977. As a result, she had medical bills in excess of $7,000 to treat tears in her uterus and bladder, and an infection caused by retained fetal parts. The abortionist involved is not only a member of the National Abortion Federation, but a regular presenter at their Risk Management Seminars.[52]

On July 18, 1979, "Gail" died of an infection she contracted during an abortion four days earlier at a Fort Wayne, Indiana, abortion clinic. The infection caused her red blood cells to dissolve, which in turn caused her kidneys to fail. Although she was placed on an artificial kidney machine, the combination of the kidney failure and infection caused her death. Gail was 20 years old when she died.[53]

John Roe 1 performed an abortion on "Suzanne" on November 22, 1989. He perforated her uterus and bladder, requiring surgical repair at a local hospital. Suzanne sustained permanent injuries, continuing health problems, and difficulty controlling her bladder functions. The 73-year-old Roe stated that "the placenta and a hand of the fetus had been removed, and omentum came into the cannula." A subsequent medical review of the case pointed out that omentum is fat found in the abdominal cavity, and a doctor who sees it in the cannula (suction tube) should realize that he has entered the abdominal cavity.[54]

On January 20, 1990, "Ingar" underwent an abortion at Acme Reproductive Services 28 by an unidentified abortionist. Neither the abortionist nor the facility diagnosed Ingar's kidney problems or noted the deterioration of her physical condition before, during, or after the abortion. She was hospitalized several days later for acute kidney failure, and died on January 26.[55]

"Stacey" had an abortion in April 1992 by John Roe 689 at an Alabama abortion clinic. During the procedure he perforated her uterus, suctioned her right ureter completely out of her body, and damaged one of her kidneys. She had to be transported to an emergency room where the fetus and damaged kidney were removed. The facility where Stacey had her abortion was a National Abortion Federation member.[56]

Nineteen-year-old "Crystal" had an abortion performed by John Roe 720 on March 26, 1994. Afterward, she was hospitalized in serious but stable condition with a perforated uterus, a severed uterine artery, and a lacerated bladder. She said that she had requested an ambulance three times before leaving the clinic on her own.[57]

Incomplete Abortion or Retained Tissue

"Katie," age 27, went to the University of Illinois Hospital for infertility tests. At that time, it was discovered that her uterus contained fetal bone fragments from two first-trimester abortions that she had had eight and nine years earlier.[58]

During her abortion "Cheryl," age 22, suffered a three-and-a-half-inch laceration of her uterus and a one-inch laceration of her colon. The next day she was hospitalized with symptoms of these complications and doctors discovered that the head of her fetus had been pushed through the uterine laceration into her abdominal cavity. She required a hysterectomy, a colostomy, and six units of blood.[59]

On October 10, 1970, 23-year-old "Maria" traveled from Massachusetts to New York for a legal abortion by Erma Roe 741. Roe estimated the pregnancy at two months and started the abortion, but could not extract the fetus. She concluded that Maria was not pregnant and sent her home. In fact, there was a fetus, but Roe could not find it because she had perforated Maria's uterus and pushed the fetus into her abdominal cavity. That night, Maria died from complications created by the retained fetus.[60]

"Janet," age 18, had a legal first-trimester abortion by John Roe 650 on September 11, 1971. She was released from the hospital later that day and was picked up by her brother-in-law. He reported that she was very weak and sleepy, and that she experienced intermittent stomach pains at home. When Janet called Roe on September 14 complaining of abdominal pain, he told her that he would see her in his office the next day. At around 2 a.m. that night, she experienced what appeared to be hot and cold flashes for about twenty minutes, and at about 3:30 a.m. she went into convulsions. The police and an ambulance were called, and found Janet lying in bed with a pus-like substance noted in the vaginal area. Janet was transported to a local hospital where she was pronounced dead on arrival.

Her lung and heart sacs showed serous fluid, and there was frothy tan fluid in her respiratory tract. Her uterus was boggy, with the placenta still attached. Medical records noted that her uterus contained a "macerated, lacerated and purulent male fetus of about 19 weeks gestation. This fetus measures 14.5 cm in crown–rump length, shows lacerations in the shoulder area, evisceration of the bowel through an abdominal laceration, and destruction of the skull and facial structures." Her uterus also contained "approximately 20 cc of red-brown purulent and foul-smelling liquid." Her lungs, liver, and kidneys showed vascular congestion. Janet's death was attributed to septicemia due to an incomplete abortion.[61]

Twenty-eight-year-old "Linda" was hospitalized after John Roe 477 performed a second-trimester abortion on her in June 1973. Roe had left a fetus of nearly five months gestation, missing a leg, an arm, part of the skull, and part of the torso, in Linda's uterus. Linda died from a massive infection created by the retained fetal parts. Roe was put on trial for manslaughter in the case, during which the South Dakota Attorney General is quoted as saying, "You take a three-inch leg off something, you have to know that there's more in there than just the leg." The defense argued that the state could not prove that Roe intended to harm Linda by leaving so much of the fetus inside her. The expert witness for the prosecution said that infection would result in every case when so much tissue is left behind, and the defense argued that infection is an accepted risk. Roe was acquitted. He was tried for another manslaughter following the 1985 abortion death of 18-year-old "Yvonne," and was again acquitted.[62]

On June 23, 1972, "Angela" underwent a legal abortion by John Roe 761 at a New York Planned Parenthood clinic. After the abortion, Angela "was told that the fetus had been aborted and/or the pathology specimens of the abortion did not reveal any product of conception." On December 2, 1972, Angela was admitted to the hospital and a Caesarean section was performed "for removal of a dead female child." According to her medical records, Angela "was rendered sick, sore, and disabled; sustained injuries both internal and external, sustained severe shock to her nervous system... [and] was confined to the hospital and bed for a long period of time."[63]

"Donna" underwent an abortion on June 30, 1973. The abortionist, John Roe 830, left the legs, an arm, a portion of the trunk, and other fetal parts in Donna's uterus. Her father was called by the hospital and told "she is bleeding to death." When he got to the hospital, she was in intensive care and stayed there for over five days. He said that his daughter had "tubes everywhere... a private nurse right there with her." He also stated that, after requiring a hysterectomy, Donna was upset about needing medication for the rest of her life and being unable to have children.[64]

On November 20, 1973, "Joann" had an abortion performed by John Roe 436. There was no follow-up exam prior to discharge; she was just given a follow-up information sheet and sent home. Within two days, Joann suffered excruciating pain and bleeding, and her mother-in-law rushed her to an emergency hospital. Once there, she became semi-conscious and discharged a severely mutilated female fetus. It was missing both arms and one leg, the rib cage was exposed, and lung tissue protruded from the left side of the chest. Calculated by femur length, the fetus was estimated at 19 weeks. Joann required hospitalization, followed by continued bed rest at home. She suffered severe infection, a depressive reaction, and weight loss, and was temporarily unable to return to work.[65]

On November 11, 1977, 21-year-old "Elizabeth" believed that she was two months pregnant and underwent an abortion at a local Planned Parenthood abortion clinic. She called the clinic in December to report that she was still not menstruating, but they assured her that the abortion was complete. On February 1, 1978, it was discovered that Elizabeth was five months pregnant. The Planned Parenthood facility referred her to a local hospital for a saline abortion. That evening, she packed a nightgown and told her family that she was going to spend the night at a friend's house. That was the last time they saw her alive. She died the next day from complications of the abortion. The coroner's report indicated that she had acute pulmonary edema, congestion, and hemorrhage.[66]

"Ida," age 25, underwent an abortion by John Roe 109 in January 1978. Some time later, when she started gaining weight and feeling the fetus kick, she went to another physician who informed her that she was 19 weeks pregnant. She returned to Roe on April 20 to complain. At first, he denied that this fetus was from the original pregnancy. Then he speculated that it was a twin missed in the original abortion. In either event, he refused to complete the abortion for free, as follow-up, telling Ida that he wasn't Sears and didn't have to guarantee his work. The exam he did was so painful, Ida described it as "like he just put his whole fist up there, just jammed it." After the exam, Roe told Ida and her boyfriend that he would have to charge more than before due to the complicated procedure necessary. "He showed us the diagram and how he'd have to section off the fetus," Ida said, imitating slicing movements Roe had made with his hands. She said that Roe told her, "You…whores just get in trouble all the time." Apparently, he was unable to complete the abortion even with two tries, because one week after he performed the second procedure, Ida expelled six inches of umbilical cord and a small, bloody, four-fingered hand.[67]

John Roe 609 performed an abortion on "Margie" on February 28, 1979. Roe indicated that the first abortion attempt was not complete, and had Margie return on March 2. After the second abortion, she continued to bleed and experience abnormal problems with her female organs. On July 5, 1983, after deciding that she could no longer tolerate the pain, she went to the emergency room of a local hospital. As a surgeon there performed a total hysterectomy, he discovered bones from Margie's fetus still in her uterus after more than four years. Margie had an infection, inflammatory cysts, and endometriosis spreading to her cervix and appendix.[68]

Nineteen-year-old "Gloria" underwent an abortion of her 8-week pregnancy by John Roe 523 on March 1, 1979. She called the clinic on March 3 to report vomiting and abdominal pain that radiated down both legs, and was told to increase her prescribed antibiotics. She was hospitalized later that day with blood pressure of 100/50, a pulse of 136, and a foul, brownish vaginal discharge. The doctor found a macerated fetus with one arm and one leg in Gloria's vagina, and performed a D&C to remove the remaining placental tissues. Gloria was treated for endoparametritis secondary to septic abortion and was discharged from the hospital on March 9.[69]

"Lynne" had her 16-week pregnancy terminated by John Roe 94 in his office on May 22, 1979. The abortion was incomplete, and she required a follow-up D&C. Unfortunately, Lynne allowed Roe 94 to do the second procedure as well, and that time he perforated her uterus. After an acute infection set in, Lynne ended up with a colostomy, the loss of her reproductive organs, and diminished function in her extremities.[70]

"Nancy" underwent an abortion by John Roe 308 on May 9, 1981. She called the clinic on May 26 to report severe pain and cramping, and was told that she must have appendicitis. Nancy went to a hospital, where she passed the remains of a "flattened, macerated male fetus approximately 14.5 centimeters in length, accompanied by an accumulation of mushy brown feathery tissue fragments and turbid brown fluid."[71]

John Roe 739 performed a second-trimester abortion on "Amy" in June 1983. Upon examining the extracted tissue, he noticed that the fetal skull was missing. He then "explored" Amy's uterus with forceps, but did not locate the missing head. Nonetheless, Amy was dismissed after 20 minutes in recovery and was instructed to return in three weeks for a follow-up appointment. She was not told that the abortion was incomplete, and her medical chart noted that no complications had occurred. The tissue was not sent to a pathology lab, which Roe defended by pointing out that he already knew there were parts missing. About four-and-a-half hours later, Amy called reporting heavy bleeding and was told to return to the clinic. At that time, abortionist John Roe 360 removed the fetal skull and several large blood clots.

The Medical Board found that knowingly sending a woman home with a retained fetal skull did not constitute a deviation from the standard of care, since other abortionists often leave the skull in the patient.

Two weeks later, patient "Cindy" had the identical thing happen to her while having an abortion by Roe 739. This time, however, the patient refused to allow Roe 360 to finish the procedure because she smelled alcohol on his breath. After an investigation, the Colorado Board of Medical Examiners found that knowingly sending a woman home with a retained fetal skull did not constitute a deviation from the standard of care, since other abortionists in Colorado testified that they often leave the skull in the patient. Roe 739 was later found to be performing abortions on women who weren't pregnant, but again the same Board said that was not a violation of the minimum standard of care.[72]

"Emily," age 18, underwent a second-trimester abortion by John Roe 476 on November 29, 1983. On December 1, Roe received a pathology report showing that only placental tissue had been removed, but there was no note in Emily's chart to indicate that Roe had either reviewed the report or attempted to contact her. At 5:10 a.m. on December 3, Amy was rushed to an emergency room in a coma and with shallow respirations. An hour and 10 minutes later, she was pronounced dead. The autopsy found a portion of a fetal leg protruding from her uterus and concluded that Emily had died of hemorrhage due to an incomplete abortion.[73]

Twenty-five-year-old "Patricia" underwent an abortion by John Roe 797 on March 2, 1985, at Acme Reproductive Services 30. After she returned home, she began hemorrhaging and passed the upper part of her fetus. She said, "I freaked out. I didn't know what to do. I could see the eyes, and the arms and legs." She placed the tissue in a plastic bag, and returned to the clinic where she was told by the clinic's owner/director that the tissue was just a blood clot. Not convinced, Patricia took the tissue to a hospital where she was informed that it was in fact the head and body parts of a 16-week-old fetus. She had a second procedure in the hospital to remove additional tissue. As it turns out, she fared better than another patient of Roe's on the same day. (See "Ellen" under "Injuries to the Uterus.")[74]

On February 7, 1987, "Susan," age 25, had an abortion by John Roe 16. The pregnancy was in its twenty-eighth week and the fetal head was so large that it became lodged in the cervix during the procedure, causing Susan to scream in pain. Roe requested that she not scream because she was scaring the other patients. She asked Roe to give her painkillers and to take her to a hospital. He responded that he didn't have any painkillers, and that no hospital would take her because her abortion was beyond the 24 weeks most hospitals permitted. At one point while he was trying to get the head out, Roe got his hand stuck inside Susan's vagina, and began yelling at her because his hand hurt. After removing his hand, she kicked him and requested that he stop the procedure. Three hours after beginning the abortion, with half the fetus sticking out of her body, he sent Susan to a hospital in an employee's car so he could finish the procedure with her under general anesthesia. Incredibly, during the three hours that he was treating Susan, he left her several times to perform abortions on other women. Then, after sending her to the hospital, he remained at his facility to do three more abortions before arriving at the hospital 45 minutes later.[75]

Seven months after her 1988 abortion, "Janet" discovered a fetal bone in her vagina. She called a friend who worked at a different abortion clinic, and went there for an examination. The doctor there found another fetal bone, and told her to go the hospital for a D&C. She contacted her family doctor, who performed an ultrasound that revealed "a mass of something" in her uterus. After surgical removal, the mass was found to contain additional bones. Janet bled for six weeks after the corrective surgery.[76]

On September 1, 1989, "Teresa" underwent an abortion by John Roe 556, a National Abortion Federation member. During the procedure, she was told that her pregnancy was more advanced than the 10 to 12 weeks previously estimated. The clinic staff performed an ultrasound and determined her pregnancy to be of 14 weeks gestation. Roe then requested an additional $225, which Teresa said she did not have. At that point, Roe stopped the abortion and sent her home, still bleeding. Teresa was admitted to a hospital later that day, and labor was induced to expel a fetus that was missing a leg and its intestines.[77]

In 1989, "Hattie," age 21, was told that she was 16 weeks pregnant. She underwent an abortion by John Roe 338, who sent her home after declaring that the abortion was "complete and uneventful." That night, she began to bleed heavily and lost consciousness. She was transported by ambulance to a local emergency room where surgeons removed a five-month, mutilated male fetus by Caesarean section. One doctor said, "It looked like the baby had been half-eaten by a dog." Roe later admitted that he knew the abortion had been incomplete, but that he expected Hattie to expel the fetus naturally.[78]

On April 9, 1992, "Sue," age 30, had an abortion at a California abortion clinic, Acme Reproductive Services 19. She was homeless and was living in a car owned by a friend, and on May 19 she was found dead in the car. The cause of death was sepsis that developed from fetal tissue left behind during her abortion. The clinic where she had her abortion was a member of the National Abortion Federation.[79]

Complications from Anesthesia and Other Drugs

We were able to document several anesthesia-related abortion deaths occurring in states that had legalized abortion before *Roe v. Wade*. However, details about them were sketchy at best, and we decided not to include them here.

For information about that subject, read the March and April 1994 editions of *Obstetrics and Gynecology,* the 1972 *CDC Abortion Surveillance Annual Summary,* and the *New England Journal of Medicine,* Vol. 295 No. 25. The remainder of this section relates only to abortions occurring after *Roe.*

"Janie," age 37, underwent an abortion by John Roe 501 in New Orleans on March 6, 1974. Five days later, she died from an apparent overdose of drugs administered to her during the abortion. She was the mother of three children.[80]

Seventeen-year-old "Wilma" underwent an abortion by John Roe 670 on June 19, 1974. After being overdosed with an anesthetic drug, Wilma lapsed into a coma. Roe then left her unattended at the abortion clinic for 12 hours before transferring her to a hospital. She died the next day of complications from the anesthesia. In 1980, another woman, 32-year-old "Jeannie," suffered cardiopulmonary collapse related to anesthesia during an abortion performed by Roe 670. At the time of the second woman's death, Roe's abortion clinic had been operating without a license for two years and had repeatedly violated medical standards regarding sanitation and the use of anesthetics.[81]

On July 22, 1974, "Carole" went to Hospital 31 for an abortion. Her sister-in-law had taken her there, and was instructed by the staff to return in two hours to pick Carole up. When she returned, she was informed that Carole was still sleeping and that it was against hospital policy to awaken a patient. She then called at one-hour intervals, and was told that Carole was still asleep. At 4:30, she was told that the doctor was talking to Carole in her room, and at 5:30 she was instructed to come to the hospital so the doctor could talk to her. When she arrived, they informed her that Carole was dead.

A subsequent investigation revealed that Carole died of complications from the anesthesia. It also disclosed that the hospital lacked a cardiac monitor, resuscitator, and defibrillator in the operating room. The staff was so slipshod in their handling of Carole's case that they failed to obtain a proper medical history prior to performing surgery, and in fact never even obtained her home address. The hospital had been cited for 43 violations of nursing care standards and 12 violations of physical plant standards in an October 17 inspection the year before Carole's death. They were to be allowed to remain open until their license expired in June 1974, and were open on appeal when Carole died. She was 22 years old when she died, and she had a four-year-old daughter.[82]

"Joan" underwent an abortion at Acme Reproductive Services 49. She was placed under general anesthesia. As a result of the staff's failure to monitor her, failure to provide adequate oxygen, and failure to promptly detect Joan's inability to breathe, she sustained permanent brain damage.[83]

On August 17, 1978, 32-year-old "Marina" had a first-trimester abortion by John Roe 189. Within 90 seconds after the procedure began, she stopped breathing due to a reaction to the anesthesia. Despite the fact that patients were routinely placed under general anesthesia, the abortion clinic had no resuscitation equipment. Roe was unable to take any emergency measures, aside from performing CPR. When paramedics arrived, Marina was lifeless, and was pronounced dead upon her arrival at a local hospital.[84]

On June 25, 1981, "Robin" underwent an abortion under general anesthesia by John Roe 308 at an Ohio abortion clinic. After the procedure, Robin suffered cardiac arrest in the recovery room, and went into a coma. On August 2, she died from complications of the anesthesia overdose that she was given during the abortion. She was 27 years old and the mother of three small children.[85]

"Darlene" underwent a second-trimester abortion by John Roe 645 on July 2, 1982. She was given nitrous oxide through a face mask, and started coughing as the procedure began. Afterward, she was admitted to the respiratory intensive care unit where a diagnosis of primary pulmonary hypertension was made. She suffered increasing respiratory distress over the next several days, and her blood pressure had to be maintained by medication. On July 7, Darlene went into cardiorespiratory arrest and was pronounced dead.[86]

Seventeen-year-old "Laniece" had an abortion performed by John Roe 13 on February 6, 1986. During the procedure, she suffered cardiorespiratory arrest due to the anesthesia and died.

On September 5, 1992, at another abortion clinic owned by Roe 13, "Deanna" suffered a similar fate. During an abortion, she was given a massive overdose of anesthesia and died two minutes after being sent to the recovery room. Deanna was 13 when she died. In a cynical irony, a "Thank You Note" was sent to the hospital that referred Deanna to the clinic, stating "Date of service 9/5/92, Uneventful D&C, Thank you!" It was signed by John Roe 479, the doctor who had performed her abortion. Roe 479 was a National Abortion Federation member.[87]

"Brenda," age 35, underwent an abortion at Acme Reproductive Services 14 on March 13, 1987, under general anesthesia. She later developed fever, chills, and back pain. On March 27, she had a second procedure at ARS 14 by the same abortionist. She was eventually transferred to a local hospital where, on April 20, she died. Her death certificate attributed her death to hepatic necrosis (liver tissue death) due to a toxicity reaction to the anesthesia used during the abortion.[88]

Twenty-four-year-old "Patricia" went to Acme Reproductive Services 32 for an abortion on May 4, 1987. Abortionist John Roe 333 placed her under general anesthesia, despite the fact that he was not a qualified anesthesiologist and ARS 32 was not equipped to treat anesthesia emergencies. Immediately after being given the anesthetic drug, Patricia went into cardiac arrest. When paramedics arrived, they found that no emergency care was being provided, and Patricia had not been breathing for at least 20 minutes. Roe told them that he had injected Neo-Synephrine and sodium bicarbonate into her heart in an attempt to revive her. Neither of those is recommended for such use. He later testified that he had actually injected Epinephrine, which was kept in the same drawer with Neo-Synephrine, but that he wrote down the wrong drug in the confusion. ARS 32 also advertised that it was "licensed by the state," even though abortion clinics are not state-regulated in Oklahoma. In fact, this particular facility had not been inspected since the attorney general declared state oversight unconstitutional in 1984.[89]

During her August 29, 1987, abortion, 27-year-old "Diane" was injected with Xylocaine, a local anesthetic. She began having seizures and went into cardiac arrest. Despite the fact that four physicians were present in the abortion clinic, none were able to properly perform CPR, and Diane died.[90]

On February 20, 1988, 23-year-old "Stacy" was placed under general anesthesia for an abortion by John Roe 73. After the procedure, she went into cardiac arrest. CPR was initiated and an ambulance was summoned. The paramedics found Stacy without a pulse, not breathing, and with unresponsive pupils. Resuscitation attempts by the paramedics included suctioning copious amounts of blood from the airway, inserting an endotracheal tube, administering medications and oxygen, and defibrillation of her heart. She was transported to the emergency room of a nearby hospital and found to be in sinus tachycardia with fixed and dilated pupils and no spontaneous respirations. An EEG revealed findings consistent with brain death, and after a discussion with her family, respiratory support was discontinued and the patient was pronounced dead. The cause of Stacy's death was found to be a massive overdose of the anesthetic drug Lidocaine. Contributing factors were cerebral and pulmonary edema, pulmonary hemorrhage, clotted and unclotted blood in her mouth and nose, and about 50 cc of blood-tinged fluid in her lung cavities. The coroner also noted approximately 200 cc of blood-tinged fluid present in the peritoneal cavity, and a bone marrow embolus in a pulmonary artery.[91]

In June 1988, "Joyce" had an abortion performed by John Roe 441. She died as a result of an "acute amitriptyline overdose" occurring during the abortion.[92]

In July 1989, "Debra," age 34, died as a result of anesthesia complications during an abortion. The procedure was performed by John Roe 384 at Acme Reproductive Services 33.

Later in 1989, "Suzanne" also sought an abortion at ARS 33, and again the abortionist was John Roe 384. In this instance, he continued with the abortion even after the unlicensed nurse who was attending noted that Suzanne's lips had turned blue. Emergency medical personnel were called and found that ARS 33 employees were very confused and did not seem to know what they were doing. In attempting to put an oxygen mask and bag on the patient, they were putting the mask on upside down, and the patient was not receiving any oxygen. By this time, Suzanne was not breathing, blue, limp, and had dilated pupils and no pulse, but the rescue squad was eventually able to reestablish breathing and blood pressure. After being in a coma for four months, Suzanne awakened as a quadriplegic, unable to speak, and with no memory of the abortion. She died in a nursing home in December 1993 at the age of 24.[93]

Infection

"Gloria" underwent a legal abortion by John Roe 641 in October 1970 at Hospital 7. As a result of her abortion, she suffered infection, bladder problems, and required a hysterectomy and a colostomy. In total, she was incapacitated for almost three years.[94]

On January 12, 1971, a 26-year-old underwent a legal abortion at a New York abortion clinic. She suffered an infected uterine perforation and peritonitis, which caused her death eight days later. A 33-year-old Ohio woman, who also had an abortion in New York in 1971, died from septic pulmonary emboli after drainage of a pelvic abscess created during the procedure. Her death came 19 days after the abortion, on October 13.[95]

"Julia," age 20, underwent an abortion by John Roe 427 at Acme Reproductive Services 13 on April 21, 1973. From the abortion, she developed "bronchopneumonia and generalized peritonitis complicating extensive necrotizing endometritis and myometritis with sealed perforation." She died on April 28.[96]

On March 4, 1975, 16-year-old "Rita" had a second-trimester abortion by John Roe 831. Three days later, Rita's mother called the clinic to report that Rita had a fever. Roe declined to see her, and scheduled her for a future appointment. However, later that day, Rita collapsed and was taken to a hospital emergency room where surgeons had to complete the abortion by removing a macerated fetus. Unfortunately, the decaying fetus caused an infection that led to Rita's death on March 8.[97]

On August 28, 1976, "Diane," age 23, was admitted to a Chicago hospital with an intraabdominal hemorrhage, telling the hospital staff that she had undergone an abortion in a Chicago abortion clinic. They discovered that she had a perforated uterus and septic infection, and attempted to save her life with a hysterectomy. Unfortunately, that was unsuccessful and she died on September 11.[98]

"Chris," age 20, had a second-trimester prostaglandin abortion on December 28, 1976. The next morning, intravenous antibiotics were administered because the abortionist suspected that she may have sustained a uterine perforation. However, she was later diagnosed with clostridial sepsis and required a hysterectomy. At that time, her pelvic cavity contained bloody, foul-smelling fluid and her uterus was necrotic. Cultures of the fluid and tissue removed from her abdomen revealed gas gangrene, a fermentative bacteria commonly found in soil, feces, and sewage. Eventually she began to experience kidney trouble and had to be put on dialysis.[99]

On February 25, 1980, 26-year-old "Betty" had a third-trimester abortion performed by John Roe 281. During the procedure, Roe failed to extract the entire fetus, packed Betty's vagina with gauze, gave her shots and pills, and instructed her to place any discharged fetal remnants in a bag and bring them to him later. Betty never had a chance to do that, as she died from an infection that she contracted during the procedure. A news article reported that Roe was subject to nearly two dozen lawsuits in three states. Another article reported that he filed for bankruptcy in 1979, while facing $2 million in judgments from other malpractice suits.[100]

Abortionist John Roe 268 terminated "Gwen's" second-trimester pregnancy on June 14, 1984. Four days later, she began vomiting and had abdominal pain and a high fever. The next morning, Gwen's mother found the 14-year-old dead on the bathroom floor. An autopsy estimated the pregnancy at 22 weeks and found that Gwen's abdomen was full of pus and adhesions. The cause of death was listed as "diffuse acute peritonitis; perforation of the uterus due to abortion." The medical board also noted that Roe had altered Gwen's medical records.[101]

"Terry" had an abortion by John Roe 766 on August 31, 1984. She went to an emergency room on September 3 after she started passing blood clots the size of golf balls. She told the staff about her abortion, and they called Roe but were told that he was not available. The abortion clinic staff said that Terry should drive to another hospital to be seen by one of Roe's friends. However, the emergency room staff called in their own doctor who found that Terry had tissue coming out of her uterus and was still passing large clots. After Terry continued to have problems, the doctor admitted her to the hospital, and found that she had pus up to her diaphragm, was expelling tissue from her vagina, and had a temperature of 106.[102]

In late November 1986, "Michelle" had an abortion at a Mobile, Alabama, abortion clinic after being told that her epilepsy medication would cause fetal deformity. The abortionist performed an incomplete abortion, leaving a leg bone, two pieces of skull, and some of the placenta inside her uterus. She developed sepsis caused by fetal parts that the abortionist missed during her abortion, and died after being on life support for three days. She was 18 years old.[103]

As "Marie" was undergoing an abortion by John Roe 3 on March 17, 1991, Roe stopped the procedure and told Marie's husband that the pregnancy was further advanced than he had thought, and demanded an additional $500. Marie's husband did not have the money, and pleaded with Roe to finish the procedure, promising to bring the additional $500 the following afternoon. Roe ejected Marie from his office, still under sedation and bleeding heavily. The next day, Marie's husband took her to a hospital, where she was admitted with a distended abdomen, a foul-smelling, dark, bloody vaginal discharge, and pieces of fetal tissue and laminaria protruding from her cervix. Her abortion was completed, and a septic infection treated. Afterward, Roe tried unsuccessfully to claim that he had never seen Marie and was convicted of assault and falsification of records. Roe was a member of the National Abortion Federation.[104]

In July 1991, "Ingrid," age 28, had an abortion performed by John Roe 662 during which he perforated her uterus. Because of the perforation, she subsequently developed acute peritonitis and died on August 1, 1991.[105]

On February 23, 1994, "Jamie" was admitted to the intensive care unit of a Houston area hospital after undergoing an abortion by John Roe 238. She had spiking fever, fluctuating blood pressure, respiratory distress, distended abdomen, a high white-cell count, and a very low blood-oxygen level. Doctors were unsuccessful in their treatment and Jamie died on March 2. Her autopsy found congested lungs weighing 1950 grams (expected range 685–1050) and a congested liver weighing 2600 grams (expected range 1500–1800). It also identified pelvic abscesses and hemorrhagic tissues, as well as infection in the lymphatic system. She had 800 ml of serous fluid in her abdominal cavity and her brain showed swelling and cell damage. The source of the infection was the vaginal flora, which entered the uterus during the abortion. She was 15 years old at the time of her death.[106]

Hemorrhage

On November 13, 1972, 21-year-old "Twila" traveled from her home in Colorado to California Hospital 37 for a legal abortion. Afterward, her blood pressure fell and she became cyanotic. She began bleeding profusely from her IV sites and from her vagina. Hospital staff gave her oxygen and three units of blood, and then transferred her to another hospital. Upon arrival, she was comatose and still bleeding. A D&C was performed to remove retained pregnancy tissue, and Twila was placed in the intensive care unit. However, even with aggressive treatment, the bleeding and clotting problems were not solved, and Twila died the morning of November 15. Her autopsy revealed extensive hemorrhage in her brain, internal organs, and eyes.[107]

Thirty-seven-year-old "Dorothy" underwent an abortion at Acme Reproductive Services 13 on August 16, 1974. Hours later, she died from shock related to hemorrhagic necrosis of the uterus.[108]

"Maria," age 29, had an abortion at Acme Reproductive Services 15 on May 4, 1976. Afterward, paramedics were summoned and found that she had a liter of blood in her peritoneal cavity. Maria died an hour and a half after the abortion, leaving behind four children. Her cause of death was listed as hemorrhage due to laceration of the uterus.[109]

"Mary," age 26, underwent an abortion at Hospital 38 on April 19, 1977. During the procedure, she suffered a uterine perforation and began to hemorrhage. In less than seven hours, she was dead. An autopsy found 2500 cc of blood in her abdomen.[110]

Twenty-one-year-old "Claudia" sought counseling at a Texas abortion clinic on September 17, 1977. She was concerned that the fetus she was carrying may have been harmed by medications she was taking. A counselor there told her that the baby would be deformed and advised her to abort. Claudia agreed, and the counselor—not a nurse—prepped her for surgery. The abortion was performed by John Roe 231, who perforated Claudia's uterus and tore a uterine artery. She began to hemorrhage, eventually losing approximately one-third of her blood. After being left unattended on the clinic's bathroom floor for two hours, she was transported to an emergency room where she required a total hysterectomy to save her life.

A doctor later testified that the condition of the fetus could not have been determined without tests, which the facility neither ordered nor performed. Roe also admitted that there was no emergency equipment, whole blood, or plasma available when he did the abortion, and that the private ambulance that the facility called took 40 minutes to arrive, even though the fire department's ambulance was only six blocks away. He also admitted that, typically "we went from one to another woman in a minute to a minute and a half."

Two months later, Roe was performing a first-trimester abortion on 23-year-old "Lucy" when she began to hemorrhage from a perforation he had made in her uterus. Still operating without a back-up supply of blood, Roe gave her a transfusion of his own blood, which was of an incompatible type. Lucy then went into cardiac arrest. Like before, Roe summoned a private ambulance to transport her for emergency care. In Texas, private ambulances are limited to transfers of stable patients and are prohibited from responding to emergency calls. Therefore, they do not respond with any sense of urgency. When the ambulance crew finally arrived and discovered that the case was a life-and-death emergency, they transported Lucy immediately rather than call for a fire department ambulance. Unfortunately, Lucy was not as lucky as Claudia and she bled to death on November 4, 1977. At the hospital, Roe asked that Lucy's body be released without inquiry, but a doctor at the hospital learned of the injury and requested an autopsy.[111]

"Jennifer" underwent an abortion on June 30, 1982, by John Roe 809. On her way home, she began to bleed heavily. A male friend tried to reach Roe at two different locations, but for four hours the staff at both clinics refused to put his calls through, with one nurse telling him to "be realistic" about the amount of bleeding. By that point, Jennifer had bled through two pairs of sweatpants, two blankets, and a towel. When her friend finally got through to Roe, Roe told him that the bleeding was normal. Jennifer's friend then called an ambulance, but she bled to death before paramedics arrived. She was 17 years old.

Incredibly, Roe and his attorney tried to blame Jennifer's death on this friend, asking why he wasn't booked on murder charges for "watching Jennifer bleed to death...[He] cleaned up most of six quarts of blood. Anyone who sees six quarts of blood and does not do anything about it..." A police officer testified that Jennifer's friend was "crying and verging on hysteria" when spoken to after Jennifer died. Roe's attorney suggested that the friend was crying because he feared that he might be booked for murder. Interestingly, even though Jennifer's abortion took place in a completely legal abortion clinic, by a licensed physician, it is mysteriously listed in the California vital statistics files as an *illegal* abortion death.[112]

"Melissa," age 22, underwent a first-trimester abortion by John Roe 32 on September 2, 1983. Roe failed to detect the fact that he had perforated both her cervix and uterus. On September 9, Melissa began hemorrhaging. She was taken to Planned Parenthood where she was attended by another abortionist who failed to discover the cause of bleeding. He performed a second abortion procedure and discharged Melissa to her mother. When Roe 32 reexamined Melissa on September 12 and again failed to detect the cause of her bleeding, he advised her "to increase her activity." The next day, she was rushed to the hospital suffering from massive hemorrhaging. This time, Roe performed a D&C, and noted that "blood was squirting within the cervical canal." After the D&C the bleeding continued, so Roe performed a laparotomy. He then discovered the perforation he had made during the original abortion, sutured it, and discharged Melissa from the hospital. Two days later, she was rushed back to the hospital, again with massive hemorrhaging. Roe attempted to stop the hemorrhaging by "packing" her with gauze. She continued hemorrhaging and Roe operated on her again. The hemorrhaging stopped, but started again three days later. This time she was taken to a different emergency room where a total hysterectomy was performed.[113]

"Linda" had an abortion performed by John Roe 106 on April 5, 1986. When she was examined by Roe prior to the procedure, he and several others were talking back and forth, unsure about the age of the fetus. Finally, one of them said, "We'll say 13 weeks," and the others all agreed. Roe then began performing a suction abortion and a few minutes later removed the suction cannula from the patient and left the room. Linda was led to a waiting room and then discharged. On April 9, she suffered from a bloated and sore abdomen, with pain so severe that she became alarmed and called her sister.

After she began to hemorrhage, discharging large clots of blood and tissue, her sister called an ambulance. When paramedics arrived, they found Linda bleeding profusely, in severe pain, and discharging fetal tissue. They took her to a local hospital where a D&C was performed to remove the retained tissue. When Linda called the clinic to inform them of the emergency, an employee responded, "Well, you wanted to kill the baby and it's dead now, so what's the problem?"[114]

Seventeen-year-old "Latachie" underwent a second-trimester abortion by John Roe 326 on November 2, 1991, at a Houston abortion clinic. Afterward, she started bleeding heavily and cried out to the clinic staff for help. She was told that her symptoms were normal and was sent home without any provision to monitor her. Later that evening, she stopped breathing. Her brother-in-law called 911 while her sister performed CPR. She was pronounced dead upon arrival at a local hospital. Roe reportedly called the publicity about Latachie's death "media hype and a political event." Less than two months later, another 17-year-old also underwent an abortion by Roe 326. After the procedure, the girl's mother walked into the procedure room and found her daughter with "a pan of blood between her legs." She was hospitalized in critical condition from hemorrhaging. She required multiple transfusions and a hysterectomy to survive.[115]

On June 16, 1993, "Lisa" had a second-trimester abortion performed by John Roe 96 at his New Jersey abortion clinic. She suffered a badly perforated uterus and complained of dizziness during recovery. Her medical chart showed that her injury occurred at 10 a.m., but an ambulance was not summoned until 12:06 p.m. Lisa bled to death, apparently as a result of the clinic's delay in calling an ambulance. She was 20 years old and the mother of a four-year-old boy.[116]

On July 9, 1993, "Guadalupe," age 33, underwent a second-trimester abortion at Acme Reproductive Services 39 in Queens, New York. During the procedure, abortionist John Roe 52 lacerated her cervix and punctured her uterus, causing severe bleeding. She was moved into recovery and was not monitored for over an hour. Although these injuries occurred during an abortion that began at 10:00 a.m., an ambulance was not called until 1:40 p.m. Upon their arrival at ARS 39, paramedics found a breathing tube inserted into Guadalupe's stomach instead of her trachea, causing stomach fluids to travel up the tube, into the mask, and down into her lungs. One paramedic said he found Guadalupe naked and bloody, and a nurse was screaming and trying to revive her in a small, unventilated room with an inadequate oxygen tank and no necessary equipment such as a blood pressure cuff. Guadalupe died later that day from massive blood loss. Guadalupe was a native of Honduras and had immigrated to the United States. At the time of her death, she was selling ice from a cart to raise the funds to bring her children here.[117]

On June 26, 1994, "Pamela," age 31, had a first-trimester abortion at Acme Reproductive Services 40. During the drive home, she started bleeding heavily and became unresponsive. Her friends stopped at a motel and called an ambulance, while two passers-by performed CPR. At the hospital, she underwent an emergency hysterectomy to try to save her life, but she died of massive blood loss caused by a perforated uterus. ARS 40 was a National Abortion Federation member.[118]

Masking of Ectopic Pregnancy

In 1972, a Planned Parenthood office referred "Jean" to John Roe 549 for a legal abortion. A week after the procedure, she called Planned Parenthood complaining of pain and was told to call a local medical facility. She did, and was given an appointment for one week later. Before the week was out, Jean was taken for emergency treatment because of a ruptured ectopic pregnancy. The surgeon who performed the operation found her abdomen full of blood and blood clots. Her Fallopian tube and the fetus were removed, and Jean was admitted to the intensive care unit in critical condition.[119]

"Lynette" had an abortion performed by John Roe 102 on September 13, 1975. He failed to diagnose her ectopic pregnancy and Lynette died on September 27, 1975, after her Fallopian tube ruptured. The autopsy report attributes her death to excess blood in her abdominal cavity following the abortion. She was 22 years old.[120]

"Sherry," age 26, underwent a first-trimester abortion on December 28, 1977, at Acme Reproductive Services 29. ARS 29 had a practice of discarding fetal remains without doing pathology reports, and staff abortionists did not routinely examine the products of conception, except through the transparent suction tubing as tissue was being aspirated from the patient. The tissue was not weighed or examined, and material from all the patients was collected together in a single bottle. This made it impossible for them to know whether they had failed to complete an abortion, operated on a woman who wasn't pregnant, or operated on a woman with an ectopic pregnancy. That lack of concern cost Sherry her life. On the night of January 2, friends found her cold and stiff in her bed. The coroner found 4000 ml of blood in her peritoneal cavity and a ruptured ectopic pregnancy.[121]

In 1977, an unidentified 19-year-old underwent a first-trimester abortion under general anesthesia. Clinic records noted that the procedure was "uneventful," and the girl was discharged. Later that evening, she experienced weakness, shortness of breath, nausea, and vomiting. She was examined in an emergency room, given medication, and released. Two hours later, she was dead. A review of the pathology report from the abortion clinic showed no pregnancy tissue, and the autopsy found 2000 cc of blood in her abdomen from a ruptured tubal pregnancy.[122]

"Barbara," a 22-year-old college student, had an abortion on April 18, 1981, by John Roe 559. In early May, she began to experience pain and bleeding and was treated with antibiotics. When the pain increased, her roommate called the emergency room. They were told to give the antibiotics time, but Barbara's pain did not abate and she was taken to the university health center. Upon arrival, she was unconscious, with no respiration, blood pressure, or pulse. She died from a ruptured ectopic pregnancy, which Roe did not identify at the time of her abortion, despite the fact that the pathology report identified placental tissue but no fetal parts.[123]

"Ruth" underwent an abortion by John Roe 794 on November 13, 1982. One week later, she was found unconscious in her home and was transported to a hospital. She suffered hemorrhagic shock and surgery was required to remove her ruptured Fallopian tube. The pathology report from the abortion had indicated the possibility of ectopic pregnancy, but the facility had failed to inform Ruth. Fortunately, she survived their incompetence.[124]

On May 23, 1985, "Josefina" had an abortion at Acme Reproductive Services 19, a National Abortion Federation member. The abortionist failed to notice during the procedure that she had an ectopic pregnancy, and afterward he left her unattended in the recovery room. While there, she hemorrhaged and died. She was 37 years old and the mother of two. Josefina's death certificate notes the cause of her death as "acute bronchopneumonia due to anoxic encephalopathy following cardiopulmonary arrest due to ruptured tubal gestation with hemorrhage." Mention is made elsewhere on the death certificate of "status post uterine suction curettage." Because the abortion is noted only as a suction curettage, and is mentioned in a supplementary area on the death certificate rather than as the cause of death, a search of California death certificates did not identify Josefina as an abortion death.[125]

John Roe 185 performed an abortion on "Yvette," age 26, on July 16, 1985. Afterward, he failed to examine the tissue, and did not notify Yvette that the lab report showed no fetal or placental matter. On July 27, she experienced sudden, sharp, constant, lower abdominal pains, and was taken to a hospital by her fiancé. She was admitted for emergency care and informed the doctors of her prior abortion. She was misdiagnosed as having Pelvic Inflammatory Disease, given medication, discharged, and advised to seek follow-up care in two days. She suffered continued pain throughout July 28 and was told by the hospital not to return, but to give the medication a chance to work. Early in the morning of July 29, she collapsed at home and was taken by ambulance to the hospital. She suffered cardiac arrest due to a ruptured ectopic pregnancy and was pronounced dead at 6:15 a.m.[126]

In late July 1988, 30-year-old "Laura" underwent an abortion at a California abortion clinic. Two weeks later, on August 6, she bled to death from a ruptured ectopic pregnancy that the abortionist had failed to detect. Her one-year-old daughter was in the room with her when Laura died.[127]

"Gladyss" underwent an abortion by John Roe 615 on April 25, 1989. The tissue retrieved consisted only of clots and he concluded that there had been a missed abortion. He then sent Gladyss home and prescribed medication, instructing her as though the pregnancy had been terminated. On May 12, Gladyss was found collapsed and unresponsive on the bathroom floor near her college classroom. A physician who was present initiated CPR until an ambulance arrived, but she was dead on arrival at a local emergency room. The cause of death was attributed to a ruptured ectopic pregnancy. Gladyss was 28 years old and the mother of one child.[128]

On October 15, 1990, "Angela" had an abortion by John Roe 333 during which he failed to diagnose her ectopic pregnancy. Later that day, the pregnancy ruptured and she died at her home. She was 23 years old.[129]

Misdiagnosis of Fetal Age
On January 26, 1977, 14-year-old "Cecelia" went to John Roe 674. He attempted to terminate her pregnancy, which he had estimated at 14 weeks. When Cecelia began to hemorrhage, he stopped the procedure and had her transported to a hospital in a private car. A doctor examined her and discovered that she was seven months pregnant. She was released from the hospital, but returned on February 1, and gave birth to a baby girl with a two-inch piece of scalp missing.[130]

"Robin," age 19, had an abortion by John Roe 161 on February 22, 1980. As Roe later admitted, he realized during the abortion that the fetus was closer to 16 or 17 weeks rather than the 11 or 12 weeks he had estimated, but he continued to employ an early-abortion technique on this advanced pregnancy. Robin pleaded for him to stop due to pain, but he told her that he was saving her money by not giving her an anesthetic, and "to hold on a little longer." He persisted for over an hour, perforating her uterus and bladder, and lacerating her cervix. Although Robin went into shock, there was a delay of over an hour before she was finally taken to a hospital. Even then, the clinic sent her in a taxi rather than an ambulance. In the emergency room, doctors found her abdomen full of blood. Robin required 16 units of blood, and six hours of surgery to repair her uterus and bladder. She also needed a hysterectomy. She spent four days in the intensive care unit, nearly died, and was hospitalized for about a month.

Since her release from the hospital, Robin has suffered thrombophlebitis, urinary tract infections, pain and swelling in her leg, migraines, and painful and irregular menses. Medical records show that the pregnancy was between 19 and 21 weeks. The facility where Robin had her abortion was a member of the National Abortion Federation.[131]

On August 7, 1981, "Alexandra," had an abortion performed by John Roe 299. Based on a pelvic exam and readings of her ultrasound, Roe estimated the gestational age as 24 weeks. During the procedure, he was unable to grasp the fetal head, and transferred Alexandra to a nearby hospital. There she gave birth to a four-and-a-half-pound stillborn infant, consistent with a 34-week pregnancy.[132]

"Darla" was examined by employees at a Portland, Oregon, abortion referral service and was told that she was 13 to 15 weeks pregnant. She was also given a sonogram, which indicated that she was 16 weeks along. Abortionist Erma Roe 401 then made two unsuccessful attempts to abort Darla's fetus by D&E and suction. In the process, she ruptured Darla's membranes. Darla was transferred to a hospital where physicians discovered that the fetus was of 29 to 30 weeks gestation. The next day, Darla gave birth to her infant girl, "Brandi," by Caesarean section. Brandi suffered bruises, lacerations, and abrasions from her shoulder blade to her leg. The baby was hospitalized for five-and-a-half weeks, suffering respiratory distress syndrome, infections, apnea, and jaundice.[133]

Sixteen-year-old "Jane" underwent an abortion by John Roe 821 in August 1986. Roe had estimated that her pregnancy was in the first trimester. However, when he pulled out a fetal arm, he realized that the fetus was much older. He stopped the abortion, but did not transfer the patient to a hospital for seven hours. After she was admitted, the dead fetus was removed by Caesarean section. Jane was admitted to the intensive care unit and was hospitalized for eight days. The autopsy of the seven-month fetus attributed its death to "partial dismemberment due to the suctioning during the abortion."[134]

"Eurice" underwent an abortion by John Roe 664 on January 7, 1989. Roe had told her that she was between 11 and 12 weeks pregnant. After the procedure, the clinic's receptionist became alarmed at Eurice's bleeding and asked Roe to examine her. He instructed the receptionist to put an ice bag on Eurice, and left the facility in spite of being the only medically trained person there. When Eurice's bleeding continued, the receptionist attempted to contact Roe at home but was unable to do so. She eventually called an ambulance for Eurice, who was still bleeding, unconscious, and in shock. She was performing CPR on Eurice when the paramedics arrived, and they were able to restore her breathing. Doctors at the emergency hospital performed surgery, but Eurice did not come out of her coma. She died at age 26 and left one child behind.

The heavy bleeding was found to be from a perforated uterus and severed abdominal artery, and her pregnancy was determined to have been at least 19 weeks along. The state health commissioner suspended Roe's license when an investigation showed that the receptionist had given Eurice and other abortion patients anesthesia, that Roe failed to perform medical tests prior to abortions, and that he had left Eurice in the facility with no medical supervision.[135]

Roe had estimated the fetus at six weeks gestation. Apparently, the abortion was unsuccessful because she gave birth four days later.

"Tralishia," age 17, underwent an abortion by Erma Roe 801 on December 22, 1989. Roe had estimated the fetus at six weeks gestation. Apparently, the abortion was unsuccessful because Tralishia gave birth four days later in a hospital corridor. The baby, a one-pound, critically ill girl of 24 to 26 weeks gestation, was named "D'Angela." Tralishia's attorney said of his client: "She's devastated, obviously. She would never have dreamed of having an abortion had she known it was 26 weeks old." The attorney said that Tralishia was undergoing psychiatric care.[136]

Ignoring Pre-existing Conditions

A New York woman with a history of sickle cell anemia underwent a legal first-trimester abortion on July 11, 1970. Nine days later, at age 23, she died of complications from sickle cell crisis. In March 1972, another woman traveled to New York from Michigan for an abortion to end her 20-week pregnancy. She had a history of asthma, and after the abortion went into respiratory distress. She died on March 8 at the age of 21.[137]

"Margaret," age 33, the mother of three, had a legal abortion performed by John Roe 305 on July 15, 1972. She experienced respiratory and cardiac problems during recovery, and Roe was unable to revive her. Her autopsy revealed hemorrhaging in her cervix, blood in her uterus, and congestion in her brain, windpipe, and lungs. The coroner declared that Margaret's death was caused by "acute sickle cell crisis."[138]

On March 7, 1978, abortionist John Roe 35 performed a 15-week abortion on "Gloria" at a Florida abortion facility. At the time, Gloria was obese and had asthma, chronic lung disease, and a family history of high blood pressure. During the procedure, Roe punctured her uterus badly enough to require an emergency hysterectomy. Unfortunately, that was not enough to save her life, and Gloria died at age 34. The medical examiner said that because of Gloria's health problems, Roe should not have performed the abortion in an outpatient setting, and a court-appointed panel found him negligent in her death.[139]

While living in an institution due to her mental retardation, "Diane" was raped and became pregnant. On October 22, 1981, the institution took her to abortionist John Roe 326 for him to terminate her pregnancy. The cause of Diane's mental retardation and the drugs she was taking both contraindicated the use of certain anesthetic drugs, including Valium and Sublimaze. However, the abortion clinic's staff administered those very drugs to her anyway. Diane had a reaction to the anesthesia and died. She was 19 years old.[140]

"Jane," who had a history of asthma, underwent an abortion at Acme Reproductive Services 28 on June 5, 1984. After being placed in the recovery room, she had an asthma attack and died. She was 27 years old and the mother of one child. Less than two years later, another 27-year-old woman with a history of asthma had an abortion at ARS 28. Immediately after her abortion, she too had an asthma attack and died.[141]

Nineteen-year-old "Tami" underwent an abortion by John Roe 842 on August 19, 1988. Afterward, she went into bronchial spasm, asthma-related respiratory failure, and then cardiac arrest. She was transported to the hospital, where she died shortly after arriving.[142]

"Angela" underwent an abortion on June 7, 1991, by John Roe 720. Before the procedure, the clinic director had determined that Angela was not a good candidate for an elective pregnancy termination due to her low hemoglobin and other contraindicators. The director informed Roe's wife (vice president of the corporation) that the clinic should refuse to perform this abortion. Shortly thereafter, she was called to the phone, and Roe told her that he would do Angela's abortion, because "You know we need the money. Just put her through." The clinic's staff administered general anesthesia and prepped Angela in anticipation of Roe's arrival. Once at the clinic, he aborted Angela's $21\frac{1}{2}$ week fetus, and punctured her cervix in the process. He completed the procedure and left the room. Angela started having difficulty breathing, and her blood pressure stopped registering. When Roe returned to the room, he attempted mouth-to-mouth resuscitation, and administered Epinephrine and Levophed. Angela's blood pressure became detectable, but was low, and she appeared to stabilize.

Even though she was gasping for breath, Roe ordered her to be sent to the recovery room—which lacked monitoring equipment—so that she wouldn't disturb other patients. When Angela's pulse failed, more drugs were administered. She began hemorrhaging, and Roe ordered that she be packed with gauze. At that point, the clinic director called an ambulance. Upon learning what she had done, Roe angrily screamed at her, "I'm the goddamned doctor here. If anybody's going to call the fucking ambulance, it will be me." He canceled the ambulance, apparently because another woman had been sent to the hospital for complications earlier that day. When the director was unable to stop Angela's bleeding, she informed Roe that "she's going to die." Roe replied, "Fine, call the goddamned ambulance." Then, despite being the only physician in the building, he left. While waiting for the ambulance to arrive, Angela's condition worsened. The staff contacted Roe on his car phone and were instructed to administer more medications. Angela died three days later.[143]

Hysterectomy

In July 1973, "Gladys" was referred by Planned Parenthood to Acme Reproductive Services 36, where she underwent an abortion by John Roe 226. Roe's notes indicate that the patient tolerated the procedure well and sustained minimal blood loss, and that there were no perforations. In reality, the abortion was incomplete and Gladys required a second procedure. However, that did not solve all of her problems and two days later she had to have a total hysterectomy.[144]

The television news show *60 Minutes* reported several instances of botched abortions at Acme Reproductive Services 33. One case involved "Linda," whose boyfriend described the scene to *60 Minutes*. He said that when he went to pick Linda up after her abortion, "I went back and they had a sheet wrapped around her bottom, like a baby diaper. And there was just blood everywhere...she was just lying in her own blood." Linda nearly bled to death and required a hysterectomy.[145]

On July 18, 1978, "Bonnie" had an abortion by Erma Roe 85. During the procedure, Roe called another doctor in, but due to Roe's thick accent, Bonnie could not understand what was being said. "They were awfully excited and jumping around, and I was scared to death," Bonnie said of the period just after the abortion. She remembered screaming, was evidently quite confused and frightened, and has very unclear memories of the events. She was put in the recovery room with "the second batch" of abortion patients and was given some pills. Eventually, someone told her that she was all right and could get dressed and leave. She called back several days later complaining of symptoms, which they told her were normal. They assured her that her "procedure had been a total success without any complications."

Two weeks later, Bonnie was at a concert and started to hemorrhage. At first she thought the bleeding was menstruation, and went to her van to get a pad. By the time she got to the van, "there was blood sloshing in and out of my shoes, and I was still trying to convince myself this was just a heavy period, that everything was going to be all right." She laid down in the van and covered up with a blanket. After a few minutes she decided that the bleeding was not going to stop and honked the horn to summon help. A policeman came over and saw what the situation was "and started screaming on his little walkie-talkie for them to get an ambulance there immediately." Bonnie was hospitalized for a week and required a hysterectomy to save her life.[146]

In 1978, "Carole," age 36, had an abortion by John Roe 288. She suffered a perforated uterus, and required an emergency hysterectomy, laparotomy, and removal of her left Fallopian tube and ovary. She sustained nerve damage resulting in permanent numbness and tingling in her left leg.[147]

In December 1980, "Judy" missed her period and believed that she was pregnant. On January 17, 1981, she went to Acme Reproductive Services 25 to obtain a legal abortion. By April, Judy concluded that she was still pregnant and informed the clinic. They told her to return on April 8 for a second procedure. At that visit she was told that she was too far along for ARS 25 to perform the procedure. However, she was told that they could make arrangements for the abortion to be done by John Roe 436 in North Carolina. Judy agreed, and the next evening she, her husband, and their kids drove to North Carolina for an appointment scheduled for 8:00 a.m. the next day. After Judy underwent the second procedure, she was directed to a side room, given several shots, and told that the shots would induce labor to expel the dead fetus. Some time later, when labor still had not begun, she was told to get on her feet and run back to the procedure room as fast as she could. She did so, but after making it back to the procedure room, she lost consciousness.

Her husband inquired at the front desk several times and was told that his wife was fine and recovering. After seven hours, he suspected that something was wrong and demanded to see her. At that point, an ambulance was called and Judy was taken to the hospital in deep shock and with no detectable blood pressure. A team of surgeons opened her abdomen and found it filled with blood from profuse internal bleeding. A three-and-a-half-inch hole was found in her uterus, through which a mutilated 22-week-old fetus had been pushed into the abdominal cavity, and parts of her intestines had been lacerated. In the ensuing five-hour operation, the surgical team supplied her with massive infusions of blood, performed a complete hysterectomy, and repaired her damaged organs. Fortunately, she survived and was discharged on April 16.[148]

On January 8, 1981, "Andrea" had an abortion performed by Roe 670 at his abortion clinic, Acme Reproductive Services 18. During the procedure he lacerated her uterine wall. Then, in violation of state clinic licensing statutes, he moved her to his home, designated as the "Clinic Annex." Two days later he returned her to the clinic and discharged her. The next day, she was admitted to a local hospital with complaints of severe pain. Exploratory surgery revealed an unsutured laceration creating a hole from her vagina into her abdominal cavity, with significant pelvic and intestinal inflammation. Surgeons also removed a mass of dead tissue from her abdomen, which laboratory analysis confirmed was fetal matter. Andrea required a total hysterectomy. An investigation showed that Roe 670 routinely used the company car to transport patients from the clinic to the "Annex," which was not licensed in Maryland to treat patients. Roe admitted to transporting at least three injured patients to the "Annex" for overnight stays. He also admitted that he had not had hospital privileges since 1963.[149]

In December 1984, "Mary" had a first-trimester abortion at Acme Reproductive Services 19, a National Abortion Federation member. During the procedure she sustained two cervical lacerations, and was bleeding heavily after the abortion. The abortionist was not able to bring her bleeding under control, and performed a hysterectomy on her in an effort to save her life. He was not successful, and she died on December 16, 1984. Mary was 43 years old and the mother of five.[150]

"Roxanne" aborted her 16-week pregnancy on December 29, 1984, at Acme Reproductive Services 40 in Pennsylvania. Afterward, she was transferred to a local hospital where surgeons found blood in her stomach, a large hematoma encompassing the whole pelvic sidewall, and tissue extruding through a three-inch uterine laceration. Upon further inspection, the surgeons found additional damage, and determined that it was "virtually impossible to repair the defect and also to repair the uterine artery and vein that was traumatized by the abortion. Therefore, a hysterectomy was performed." ARS 40 was a member of the National Abortion Federation.[151]

On August 19, 1988, "Tamera" had an abortion by John Roe 452 at a Fargo, North Dakota, abortion clinic. Afterward, she bled profusely, suffered low blood pressure, and drifted in and out of consciousness. The clinic staff instructed her to squeeze her legs together and attempt to clench her vagina. When they tried to move her, she had a gush of blood and her friend demanded that she be taken to a hospital. The abortionist refused, and instead performed at least one D&C in an unsuccessful attempt to stop the bleeding. Her friend demanded to see Tamera and again insisted that they "do something." Anti-abortion protesters were in front of the building during this time, and Roe waited until they left to call an ambulance. At this point, five-and-a-half hours had passed since Tamera's injury. She later recalled that emergency room personnel were shouting, "We're losing her, we're losing her." She was given transfusions of several pints of blood, and required an emergency hysterectomy to stop the bleeding.[152]

Twenty-year-old "Toby" underwent an abortion by John Roe 249 on May 10, 1991, at Acme Reproductive Services 41. She suffered a lacerated uterus and cervix, and began to hemorrhage. She was transferred by ambulance to a hospital. There she had follow-up surgery performed by another ARS 41 abortionist, John Roe 409. He observed Toby for two hours after surgery, and then, at the urging of nurses, transferred her to the intensive care unit and left the premises. Toby's condition worsened, and the hospital was unable to contact Roe 409 for eight hours. The hospital's ob/gyn consultant examined Toby and discovered that Roe 409 had sewn her cervix shut. The damage was irreparable, so an emergency hysterectomy was required. John Roe 409 was a National Abortion Federation member.[153]

Heart Failure

On July 13, 1969, "Cindy" traveled from her Iowa home to California for a legal abortion. Injuries she sustained during the procedure caused her to suffer "acute cardiac insufficiency." At 4:45 p.m. on July 16, Cindy was pronounced dead. She was 17 years old.[154]

"Sara" had a legal abortion on August 10, 1970, at Hospital 7 in California. Because the anesthesia was improperly administered, she went into ventricular fibrillation. She died the next morning at the age of 22.[155]

On December 23, 1970, a 25-year-old New York woman underwent a legal abortion to end her 18-week pregnancy. During the procedure, she suffered cardiac arrest and died. On July 1, 1971, a 44-year-old New York woman had a legal first-trimester abortion and died from heart failure. On March 8, 1972, a 31-year-old New York woman had her pregnancy terminated and died from cardiac arrest.[156]

On August 5, 1975, 31-year-old "Mitsue" underwent an abortion by California abortionist John Roe 100. She suffered cardiac arrest, became semi-comatose, and eventually died. The very next day, 29-year-old "Cheryl" had an abortion at a different California abortion facility. Afterward, she began bleeding heavily from her vagina because of a rupture that had been created in her uterus. She was transferred to a hospital where she suffered cardiac arrest twice and died.[157]

In 1976, a 35-year-old woman had a prostaglandin abortion to terminate her 15-week pregnancy. Five minutes into the procedure, she experienced nausea and vomiting. Shortly thereafter, she collapsed and was found to have no pulse. CPR was administered and she was transported to a local emergency room. Upon arrival, she was comatose with no pulse or blood pressure, and was experiencing ventricular fibrillation. She was resuscitated, then later expelled the fetus and was transferred to a university hospital. Her neurologic status never improved and she remained partially paralyzed until her death, five months after her abortion.[158]

"Lydia" had her first-trimester abortion at a doctor's office. He inserted a rubber catheter into her uterus and packed her vagina full of gauze to keep the catheter in place. She returned the next day as instructed, and the doctor removed the catheter and completed the abortion. Two days later, she was taken to an emergency room with chills, fever, severe pain, and a thick, black, bloody discharge. She was admitted to the hospital and was given IV fluids and antibiotics. Later that evening, she went into cardiorespiratory arrest and could not be resuscitated. She was 16 years old when she died.[159]

On June 14, 1980, "Linda" had an elective abortion at an unknown abortion clinic by an unknown abortionist. What is known from her death certificate is that she suffered a perforated uterus, massive blood loss, shock, and a septic infection, which led to cardiopulmonary arrest. Linda died on July 16 at age 21.[160]

On October 21, 1986, "Rena" underwent an abortion by John Roe 540. After the procedure, she was walking back to the clinic's waiting room when she collapsed, unconscious, and went into cardiac arrest. CPR was performed on her and an IV started, but no ambulance was called. In fact, an ambulance was never called, and no attempt was made by the abortion clinic's staff to determine why her heart stopped beating. After Rena was resuscitated, she was simply discharged and sent home. On November 18, she called to report heavy bleeding with clots, and was told that this was just her period. She returned 10 days later, reporting the same problem, and was again told that this was menstruation. On December 10, she returned with a clot she had passed. Roe told her that she would stop bleeding any day now, and noted "no tissue contained in the clot sample." A pathology report performed later indicated that there were fetal parts in the clot. On December 31, Rena was taken to an emergency room where a D&C was performed, yielding a portion of the placenta.[161]

After her August 3, 1991, abortion at Acme Reproductive Services 35, "Dawn" went into respiratory and cardiac arrest. She was transported by ambulance to a hospital where attempts to resuscitate her were unsuccessful. She died at the age of 21, leaving behind one child. ARS 35, a National Abortion Federation member, had four abortionists on duty the day Dawn was killed, but the one who did her procedure was not identified.[162]

Embolism

A 35-year-old New York woman underwent a legal abortion in late December 1970 to end her 14-week pregnancy. During the procedure she suffered massive pulmonary emboli, which caused her death on January 2, 1971. A Massachusetts woman who had traveled to New York for a legal, first-trimester abortion on May 17, 1972, died minutes after the procedure from arterial and venous air emboli.[163]

In 1978, a medical magazine looked at the issue of abortion-related embolism and found the following, then-recent cases: A 31-year-old woman who was eight weeks pregnant underwent an abortion and subsequently experienced nausea, chest pains, and cardiopulmonary problems. She was admitted to a hospital where she died of respiratory arrest and pulmonary embolism two hours after admission.

Another woman, nine weeks pregnant, underwent an abortion and was put on oral contraceptives. Two weeks later, she suffered swelling and pain in her left calf. She was admitted to a hospital, and a pulmonary embolism was identified. Six days later she went into cardiac arrest and died. During the autopsy, retained fetal material was found in her uterus. She was 17 years old at the time of her death.

A 20-year-old woman with a history of ventricular septal defect and pulmonary hypertension underwent an abortion. After the procedure, she suffered chest pain and abdominal bleeding and was hospitalized. Five days later, she died. Pulmonary emboli were discovered during the autopsy.

A 34-year-old woman who was 10 weeks pregnant underwent an abortion that seemed uneventful. Twelve days later, she was found unconscious at home, and pronounced dead on arrival at a hospital. Pulmonary emboli were found by the coroner.[164]

"Linda," age 34, was 15 weeks pregnant when she underwent an abortion by John Roe 436 on April 8, 1981. A week later, she contacted the clinic to report pain, chills, and bleeding. They told her to come in for an examination. When she got there, she was told that Roe was out of town and she was sent home. The next day, she went into the clinic "barely able to walk due to the pain and loss of blood." Again she was informed that Roe out of town, but this time she was taken to an examination room where she disrobed and was told to stand over a piece of paper to catch the blood. The staff reportedly called Roe, and advised Linda to travel to the other city see him. Linda was too ill to make the trip, so she stayed at the clinic until it closed and an employee drove her home. She bled heavily during the ride, and the employee told her to lie down and rest at home. The next day, Linda was taken to an emergency room and hospitalized for life-threatening complications including retained fetal parts, infection, a perforated uterus, and a pulmonary embolism. She later required a hysterectomy due to complications from her abortion.[165]

On August 7, 1983, "Mary," age 28, died at a hospital in Norwich, Connecticut. The cause of death was listed as cardiorespiratory failure due to an amniotic fluid embolus following an elective abortion.[166]

During her May 26, 1988, abortion, "Manuela" sustained a pulmonary embolus that caused her to go into cardiac arrest. She died on June 6 at age 36.[167]

"Lynn," age 24, underwent an abortion by John Roe 729, then went into violent contractions. She experienced an amniotic fluid embolism and was left in a coma. This mother of two children died one week later.[168]

John Roe 156 performed an abortion on "Erica" on March 1, 1989. After the procedure, Roe left Erica bleeding and unattended for four hours. He carried Erica to her aunt's car just before 11:00 p.m. and gave instructions that Erica be taken home and put to bed. Instead, Erica's aunt took her to a hospital where she died. The medical examiner attributed Erica's death to an air embolism caused by a uterine perforation. There was more than 100 cc of air in Erica's heart and 300 cc of blood in her abdomen. The medical examiner's report noted an irregular horizontal rupture of the uterus extending into the vagina, cervix, and endometrial cavity. An additional irregular laceration of the uterus extended into the pelvic cavity. Erica was 16 years old at the time of her death.[169]

Abscess

On July 6, 1970, just five days after New York's legal abortion laws took effect, "Lisa" underwent an abortion during which she suffered a uterine perforation. Several days later, she had to have a pelvic abscess drained, and a dead fetus was removed from the abscessed cavity. She underwent a hysterectomy to try to save her life, but died 23 days later.[170]

"Sharon," age 18, underwent an abortion by John Roe 224 on April 11, 1975. She became ill two days later and was admitted to the hospital. She was diagnosed with acute septicemia with pelvic, subphrenic, and retroperitoneal abscesses. She died on April 29.[171]

After undergoing an abortion on May 12, 1977, "Adrianne" complained of severe pain to the recovery room nurse. Her abortionist, John Roe 667, prescribed pain pills and dismissed her. Adrianne's problems persisted and she called back two days later. Roe then diagnosed a tipped uterus and prescribed pain pills and rest. Four days after that, still experiencing problems, she called the clinic again. Roe told her to meet him at the hospital. There he advised her that she was hemorrhaging and prescribed antibiotics and rest, but did not hospitalize her. This pattern continued until Adrianne had a D&C at another hospital. Her problems were found to have resulted from a perforated uterus, a pelvic abscess, peritonitis, and recurring infections caused by her abortion.[172]

"Juana" underwent an abortion by John Roe 747 on September 13, 1986. Because she suffered perforations of her uterus and bowel, she was admitted to a local hospital later that day. On September 16, she required a D&C, during which it was found that she also had an incomplete septic abortion, and possibly a tubo-ovarian abscess. Severe and continuous pain required her to be transferred to an intensive care unit on September 17, where she underwent surgery to treat intraabdominal sepsis and a pelvic abscess. She was hospitalized for five weeks.[173]

John Roe 542 performed an abortion on "Debra" on October 24, 1987. She subsequently required corrective surgery for a retrovaginal defect and intraabdominal abscesses. She also had to have a colostomy.[174]

On August 30, 1990, "Diona" went to a Planned Parenthood facility for pre-abortion counseling and a gonorrhea culture. Abortionist John Roe 143 proceeded with the abortion prior to obtaining the results of the culture. On September 2 and 3, Diona called Planned Parenthood to complain of cramps and a fever, but was unable to reach anyone. On September 4 they returned her call, and told her that since her temperature was only 99.5, she should keep taking her Tylenol. Diona's symptoms worsened, and on September 11 she was admitted to a local hospital with "bilateral tubo-ovarian abscesses." She underwent a laparoscopy, pelvic laparotomy, removal of adhesions, drainage of abscesses, and a D&C. The results of the gonorrhea culture were reported positive to Planned Parenthood staff on September 4, but they did not attempt to advise Diona of this until September 11, after she was already hospitalized.[175]

Coma

During her June 1979, abortion at an Atlanta abortion clinic, "Angela" stopped breathing. The clinic's nurse-anesthetist left another patient, "Delores," to attend to Angela. Unfortunately, she forgot to turn off Delores' anesthesia drip. Delores then went into cardiac arrest. Another staff member attempted to revive her with oxygen and intravenous fluids. However, she would not release her to an ambulance until the facility doctor arrived, resulting in a 30-minute delay. Delores, who was 15 years old at the time, went into a coma and was finally transported for emergency care. We were not able to find out if Delores recovered, but we were able to find out what happened to Angela. On June 11, 1979, at the age of 19, Angela died after spending a week in a coma.[176]

On January 24, 1985, 13-year-old "Dawn" had an abortion by abortionist John Roe 475. Her parents did not know she was having the procedure performed, and the $450 abortion fee was paid for by her 15-year-old boyfriend. Because she was given only half the dose of anesthesia necessary for the operation, she awoke five minutes into procedure. When she began to vomit and choke, Roe inserted a breathing tube. He continued with the abortion, although he failed to extract the remainder of the fetus, and left Dawn unattended in a recovery room. Dawn then suffered a heart attack and slipped into a coma. During the three weeks she was comatose, her parents tried to awaken her by playing recordings of songs they had sung together at the church where her father was pastor. Dawn died on February 11, 1985.

When a judge asked if Dawn's age had captured his attention, he responded, "Oh, no. I've done 13-year-olds before. When they're 10, maybe I'll notice."

In an interview, her mother said, "They told me I had to come in [to the hospital] right away, that Dawn is here at that hospital fighting for her life…I was going, 'How could she be fighting for her life?' She left this morning, going to school, looking healthy, never been sick…While I was in the hospital sitting there,…I had to keep my hand over my mouth to keep from screaming in horror. I could not believe this was happening. I said, 'This is a bad dream; I'm going to wake up and this would not have happened.'" She said she felt Dawn had probably sought the abortion because she feared her parents would be disappointed in her for becoming pregnant. When a judge asked Roe 475 if Dawn's age had captured his attention, he responded, "Oh, no. I've done 13-year-olds before. When they're 10, maybe I'll notice." Court testimony also showed that Roe and the abortion clinic's staff altered and fabricated medical records in an attempt to conceal their mistakes.[177]

During her August 27, 1986, abortion, "Jackie's" breathing tube was not properly inserted during the general anesthesia. She turned blue from lack of oxygen and lapsed into a coma from which she never emerged. She was declared dead on September 5. Jackie was 22 years old and had a four-year-old daughter.[178]

On January 24, 1987, "Belinda," age 37, had an abortion performed by John Roe 649. During the procedure, her uterus was badly perforated. However, she was left unattended for three hours after the abortion, and was then detained an additional two hours before she was transferred to a hospital. After being in a coma for three days, she died.

Belinda was one of 74 women who had had an abortion in the clinic's single operating room on that day, and one of 24 women who were operated on during the last two hours of the day. State inspectors contend that no post-anesthesia evaluation had been conducted. Paramedics found Belinda's bed at the clinic soaked with blood.

Her mother wrote to a Los Angeles district attorney: "I am the mother of [Belinda], victim of abortionists at [abortion clinic address]. I am also the grandmother of her three young children who are left behind and motherless. I cry every day when I think how horrible her death was. She was slashed by them and then she bled to death...She has been stone dead for two years now, and nobody cares. I know that other young black women are now dead after abortion at that address. Where is [the abortionist] now? Has he been stopped? Has anything happened to him because of what he did to my [Belinda]? Has he served jail time for any of these cruel deaths? People tell me nothing has happened, that nothing ever happens to white abortionists who leave young black women dead. I'm hurting real bad and want some justice for [Belinda] and all other women who go like sheep to slaughter."[179]

"Catherine," age 27, underwent an abortion on March 11, 1989, by John Roe 502. Afterward, she was left unattended in the abortion clinic's recovery room. When a staff person finally checked on her, she was in cardiac arrest. Although emergency personnel were able to revive her, she went into a coma from which she never emerged. She died on October 10, 1989, leaving behind an 11-year-old daughter. The abortion had been performed at Acme Reproductive Services 34, which state officials found to have serious problems. They cited the abortion clinic for administering the same doses of anesthesia to patients whose weights ranged from 107 to 167 pounds, inadequate record-keeping, and inadequate supervision of patients. Clinic staff admitted that they refused to allow state investigators to access the clinic's files because the officials had only shown their badges and did not have a subpoena. The state eventually raided the facility to seize the records. The clinic's owners complained that the raid was political harassment, despite the fact that they had failed to file the appropriate state-mandated documents after Catherine's cardiac arrest. ARS 34 was a member of the National Abortion Federation.[180]

On March 11, 1989, "Glenda" underwent an abortion at a Houston area abortion clinic. During the procedure she sustained a two-inch-long wound to her uterine artery and vein complex. After a delay, abortion clinic employees decided to transfer Glenda to the hospital. However, as is often the case, they did not call an ambulance, opting instead to transfer her in one of their cars. Glenda's husband discovered them attempting, unsuccessfully, to transfer Glenda from a wheelchair to the car, so he went over and helped them. With the IV still in her arm, Glenda was driven to a local emergency room where she was admitted in a coma, with no blood pressure and almost no pulse. She died three days later. She was 31 years old and the mother of two.[181]

Incapacitation

"Diana" underwent an incomplete abortion by John Roe 791 on July 21, 1973. She was admitted to the hospital the next day in great pain and with a high fever. She subsequently expelled the fetus into a bedpan. The high fever caused permanent damage to her brain.[182]

In January 1978, "Shelby," age 50, had an abortion by John Roe 82. Immediately after the abortion began, she had a reaction to a drug the abortionist had given her and experienced a grossly abnormal elevation in blood pressure. Roe dismissed the reaction as transient and left after completing the procedure. Half an hour later, Shelby went into cardiopulmonary arrest. The resulting lack of oxygen left her severely and permanently brain damaged. She now requires 24-hour care and lives in a nursing home.[183]

"LaVerne," a 35-year-old mother of two, underwent an abortion at a Washington, D.C. area abortion clinic in November 1987. The nurse improperly placed a tube for anesthesia in her esophagus instead of her trachea. Before the mistake was discovered, the oxygen supply to her brain was cut off, leaving LaVerne in a permanent vegetative state.[184]

"Nina" underwent an abortion by John Roe 158 on January 2, 1988. During the procedure, she went into cardiac arrest, but Roe did not have the training or equipment to deal with it. As a result, Nina was left comatose, legally incapacitated, and in need of nursing home care for the remainder of her life.[185]

On February 17, 1992, "Agusta" had an abortion by John Roe 694. During the procedure, she lost an excessive amount of blood and went into respiratory arrest. She suffered severe and permanent brain damage and remains incapacitated.[186]

On February 24, 1993, "Venus" underwent an abortion at Acme Reproductive Services 35, a National Abortion Federation member. Her abortionist was John Roe 489. Afterward, clinic staff noticed that Venus had no pulse and was ashen in color. Nine minutes later an ambulance was called and Venus was given oxygen and a cardiac massage, but the damage was already done. She was left in a permanent vegetative state with profound brain damage, and needing a respirator to breath for her. After more than five months in the hospital, she was transferred to a nursing home to live out her life. As of this writing, she is 25 years old.[187]

On July 1, 1993, "Christi" underwent an abortion by John Roe 360. After the procedure, Roe looked up to find Christi pale, with bluish lips, and no pulse or respiration. Christi's heart had stopped, and there are no records that her vital signs were monitored during the procedure. Additionally, Roe was not trained in anesthesia and the clinic had no anesthesia emergency equipment or staff trained to handle an anesthesia complication. Paramedics were able to restore Christi's pulse and respiration, but she was left blind and in a permanent vegetative state. Today, she requires 24-hour-a-day care and is fed through a tube in her abdomen. She is not expected to recover and is being cared for by her family. Christi had her abortion on her eighteenth birthday.[188]

Amputation

After her 1981 abortion by John Roe 139, "Naomi" had to have portions of three fingers amputated because the drugs that she was given were improperly administered.[189]

On April 1, 1985, 22-year-old "Laura" underwent an abortion by John Roe 320. Immediately afterward, she developed a rash and her hand swelled, but she was sent home anyway. When her arm swelled and turned purple, she went to the emergency room of a local hospital. Her arm developed gangrene and had to be amputated. Roe admitted that he may have misinjected drugs during the abortion.[190]

Aspirated Vomitus

"Gail," age 27, had an abortion at Hospital 43 in July 1978. As she was being put under general anesthesia, she began to vomit and choked to death on the vomitus.[191]

On March 30, 1988, "Erna" was having an abortion by John Roe 599. Erna's mother, who was holding her hand, said Erna jerked upright and went rigid. A medical assistant ran for smelling salts. Incredibly, Roe continued with the abortion while Erna choked to death on her vomit. Roe later admitted that he gave her a painkiller that he knew could cause vomiting and failed to ask when Erna had last eaten. She was 18 years old at the time of her death.[192]

Disease Contraction

"Pamela" underwent an abortion at Acme Reproductive Services 14 on August 7, 1976. She later became ill and was admitted to a hospital on January 27. She was diagnosed with serum hepatitis, which was caused by the unsanitary, improperly sterilized instruments at ARS 14.[193]

"Latonya" had an abortion at Hospital 7 on January 21, 1989. The next day, she began experiencing abdominal pain, vomiting, dark urine, weakness, yellowness to her eyes, and fatigue. She was taken to another hospital on January 29, and diagnosed with hepatitis B, which was eventually attributed to unsanitary equipment used during her abortion.[194]

On May 6, 1994, "Sara" had an abortion of her 17-week pregnancy after completing treatment for chlamydia infection. She was discharged without any noticeable complications. The following day, she complained of having a headache, a sore and stiff neck, and difficulty seeing. She then began exhibiting bizarre behavior and screaming, and was unwilling to get out of the car at the hospital. She was admitted to the emergency room, disoriented and in a stupor. She suffered respiratory arrest and was pronounced dead. Her death was attributed to Group B Streptocicci Meningitis, caused by infected amniotic fluid and decidual emboli created during her abortion. She was 15 years old.[195]

Abortions on Women Who Were Not Pregnant

"Sharon" was examined at Hospital 7 and was diagnosed as pregnant on January 26, 1974. Based on their representation that she was pregnant and that abortion "was necessary for her health," she was admitted for the abortion. During the procedure, she suffered injuries that required treatment. She learned afterward that she had not been pregnant.[196]

On April 16, 1983, "Patricia" had an abortion at a Kansas City, Missouri, abortion clinic. After "the painful poking had been going on probably around seven to nine minutes, ... the doctor had stopped for a second, and whispered something to the nurse, ... and the nurse raised me up and said, it had been a mistake, I had not been pregnant... I was weak and I could not respond." Patricia bled heavily, and a nurse told her that they couldn't stop the bleeding, and that she would be transferred by ambulance to the hospital. Another staff member warned her not to fall asleep. Patricia got her clothes from the nurse and dressed. When the ambulance didn't arrive, she called her sister. "I waited for…a half hour, and I was getting weaker and weaker, and nobody said anything about an ambulance. I wasn't going to wait all day…I was crying telling [my sister] what happened. And I told her to come and get me." Patricia rode to the hospital in her sister's car. She used tissues to absorb the bleeding because she hadn't been given a pad. In order to terminate a pregnancy that didn't exist, this woman suffered damage to her reproductive organs and three years of amenorrhea.[197]

On June 17, 1985, "Joann" underwent an abortion by John Roe 382, during which she suffered a perforated uterus and permanent injury that required surgical repair. It was subsequently determined that she had not been pregnant.[198]

Despite the fact that she had an IUD, "Debra" suspected that she might be pregnant and took a home pregnancy test. The test result was positive, so she went to John Roe 92 for an abortion. Without giving her another test to verify her pregnancy, Roe assumed the home test was accurate and performed an abortion on her. Then, because he obtained no tissue even after repeated procedures, he sent Debra to a hospital to look for a tubal pregnancy. There, he made an abdominal incision and noted a mass on or near Debra's ovary. Roe stated, "Because it could not be certain as to what exactly was going on, it was elected to remove the ovary and the distal segment of the tube." A lab report later found no pregnancy material in the Fallopian tube or ovary.[199]

"Synthia" underwent an abortion and tubal ligation at Acme Reproductive Services 14 on September 7, 1989. According to a subsequent medical investigation, the abortionist, John Roe 526, "performed a surgical incision at a time when the operative field was not clear and the organs at the site of the incision were not clearly visible; severed an artery; severed a vein; failed to locate the source of bleeding and hemorrhage; failed to stop the bleeding and hemorrhage; failed to summon help in a timely manner; refused to allow trained and skilled paramedics to attend to Synthia; refused to allow paramedics to transport Synthia to a hospital in a timely manner; refused to follow medical advice from medical personnel at [a local emergency hospital] who requested immediate transfer of Synthia; allowed Synthia to bleed to death." There was also evidence that Synthia's medical records were altered, and based on additional evidence that these medical records were about to be destroyed, a court order was requested to preserve them. Synthia's autopsy revealed that she was not pregnant. She was 24 years old and the mother of two children.[200]

Failed Abortion—Baby Survives

In April 1973, John Roe 602 performed an abortion on an unidentified patient. The patient later expelled a live four-and-a-half-pound infant instead of the anticipated dead fetus. The nurses called Roe, who ordered them to discontinue oxygen to the newborn. Another doctor countermanded the order and provided medical care to the infant. The infant survived and was adopted.[201]

On April 27, 1973, John Roe 724 attempted an abortion on "Linda," during which he removed only part of the placenta. During a follow-up visit, he still did not diagnose Linda's continuing pregnancy. Eventually, she gave birth to "Chad" who suffered cerebral palsy, and had serious wounds on his head, body, arms, and legs.[202]

"Joshua," age 14, filed a suit for assault and battery against abortionist John Roe 740, who had attempted an abortion on his mother on January 12, 1979. The procedure was unsuccessful and Joshua was born on September 18, 1979. He spent two weeks on a respirator and suffered brain damage and hearing loss. A lower court would not permit the suit because his mother had consented to the abortion. An appeal was made to the United States Supreme Court, but it too refused to hear Joshua's case.[203]

"Kimala" underwent an abortion by John Roe 481 in March 1979. The abortion was unsuccessful, and on November 7 Kimala gave birth to a daughter. Due to abortion injuries, the infant was born with cerebral palsy and disfigurement.[204]

"Denise" was 22 years old when Erma Roe 353, a radiologist, determined that she was nine weeks pregnant. On July 10, 1982, Roe performed two suction abortion procedures on her. Although Roe noted "scant tissue," a nurse told Denise that there was no chance that she could still be pregnant. Denise returned on July 22 with complaints of bleeding, passing clots, and pain. Roe reviewed the pathology report, which noted that no products of conception had been found, and then performed a pelvic examination. She informed Denise that she was not pregnant, but was suffering from a urinary tract infection that could be treated with antibiotics. On September 28, Denise was taken to a hospital in active labor, with a fetal foot protruding into her cervix. A 13½-ounce infant boy was delivered, but died an hour later. Denise underwent an emergency D&C, lost one liter of blood during labor and delivery, and was hospitalized for three days. She suffered depression, recurring nightmares, and two subsequent miscarriages.[205]

On July 16, 1985, "Lynette" underwent an abortion by John Roe 49 at a Planned Parenthood facility in Michigan. Prior to the abortion, no ultrasound was performed to determine the gestational age of the fetus. Roe ruptured the amniotic sac, then referred Lynette to a hospital where, five days later, she gave birth to a 2 pound, 3½ ounce premature infant boy. Because of the botched abortion attempt, the baby suffered developmental delay, intracranial bleeding, hydrocephalus, and disfigurement.[206]

On February 2, 1987, "April" had an abortion by John Roe 462. Afterward, the abortion clinic staff examined the material extracted during the procedure and found no fetal parts. However, they never informed April of this fact, and on May 7 she was diagnosed as being 22½ weeks pregnant. Because of the emotional trauma she experienced after the first abortion procedure and the numerous additional risks of a late-stage abortion, she decided not to undergo another abortion. On June 29, 1987, she went into premature labor and "Baby Girl Sandi" was delivered by Caesarean section. Unfortunately, due to the loss of amniotic fluid, the baby was born with chorioamnionitis, hypoplastic lungs, and Hyline Membrane Disease, and died the next day.[207]

"Lena" had an abortion by John Roe 57 on February 28, 1989. Roe had erroneously told her that she was two weeks pregnant. When she returned for her follow-up visit, he assured her that the abortion had been successful. On April 12, Lena experienced severe abdominal pain. She went to a hospital where it was discovered that she was five months pregnant. On July 10, she gave birth to a son who died two days later from respiratory complications caused by the abortion attempt.[208]

"Cheryl" had an abortion by John Roe 263 on January 20, 1989, at a Maryland abortion clinic. Clinic records state that her abortion was complete, even noting that there was no need to send the extracted material for a pathology report. However, on March 15 Cheryl discovered that she was still pregnant, and she delivered a baby girl on August 23.

Another young woman, "Christine," underwent an abortion by this same abortionist on December 20, 1991. After the procedure, he examined the tissue he took from Christine and determined that the abortion was successful. In a follow-up visit on January 2, 1992, he again failed to detect the fact that Christine was still pregnant. Another physician made that determination during a kidney check-up on April 6. Due to fetal distress, infant "Brandon" was delivered by Caesarean section on May 1, at approximately 29 weeks gestation. The botched abortion caused severe medical problems for the child, including brain damage, and he will require around-the-clock hospitalization for his entire life.[209]

On October 25, 1991, "Rosa" believed herself to be less than 17 weeks pregnant and came to John Roe 3 inquiring about an abortion. After telling her that he believed she was actually still in the first trimester of pregnancy, he agreed to do the procedure for $1,500. Rosa paid him $1,000 and used her passport, green card, and jewelry as collateral for the remaining $500. When she heard women screaming at the clinic, she asked Roe why someone was screaming if there was supposed to be no pain. He replied that not everyone could pay for anesthesia. After her abortion, she was sent home with instructions to call Roe's facility only if she experienced problems. She called reporting pain, and Roe's assistant told her that this was normal. Several hours later, Rosa could no longer bear the pain and a family friend called an ambulance for her. At the hospital, she gave birth to a perfectly healthy baby girl whose only problem was that her right arm had been pulled from her body during Roe's botched abortion. Doctors at the hospital estimated the pregnancy to have been in its thirty-second week. John Roe 3 was a member of the National Abortion Federation.[210]

Unauthorized Sterilizations

At the age of 13, "Barbara" had an abortion performed on her at Hospital 46. She later discovered that the abortionist had also performed a hysterectomy. He justified his actions on the grounds of Barbara's mental retardation. However, in the hospital discharge summary he also made references to her race, family size, and economic status.[211]

"Marjorie" entered a Chicago hospital on July 26, 1967, to have an abortion performed. Three doctors, John Roe 206, John Roe 480, and John Roe 4, secretly agreed to perform a tubal ligation on Marjorie, in addition to the abortion she had requested. The doctors did not inform Marjorie of their decision. After she had been sterilized without her knowledge or consent, hospital staff concealed the fact that a tubal ligation had been performed. A student nurse assisted Marjorie in obtaining a contraceptive device, knowing that the device was unnecessary in light of the tubal ligation. The chief of the hospital's Obstetrics and Gynecology Department, Roe 206, assured Marjorie in 1973 that she was fertile, even though he was aware of the tubal ligation. In 1980, Marjorie's famly physician informed her that he knew a tubal ligation had been performed on her at the Chicago hospital in 1967.[212]

On October 26, 1974, "Nancy," age 21, paid $75 for an abortion referral and was sent to John Roe 674. She thought she was being referred to a hospital, and was surprised upon arriving at Roe's clinic, which she found to be unsanitary. The pre-operative exam consisted of Roe walking into the room, putting his hand on Nancy's abdomen, and announcing "15 weeks." During the abortion, which occurred at nearly six months gestation, Roe began swearing, saying that the skull was stuck. Nancy recalled, "I felt like I had been jabbed with a knife." Because Roe tore her uterus and left the fetal skull in the tear, Nancy had to be hospitalized. The doctor who removed the skull and repaired the tear informed Nancy that Roe had also done a tubal ligation and appendectomy; Roe told him that this was what she wanted. When Nancy called Roe from the hospital to complain, he told her that she was fortunate because she got all this done and got her money back too. He said she should be happy.[213]

On July 29, 1984, "Beverly" underwent an abortion at Acme Reproductive Services 47 in New Orleans. Due to severe pain, on August 7, Beverly sought follow-up care from the abortionist who had done the original procedure. During this follow-up, he performed a tubal ligation on her without her knowledge or consent.[214]

Unsought Abortions

On January 29, 1983, "Patricia" went to abortionist John Roe 484 for routine obstetrical care. He told her that her 10-week fetus was dead, and she gave her consent for him to remove it. During the procedure, her uterus was punctured in two sites. She began to hemorrhage and went into shock. She was transported by ambulance to a hospital where her uterus, Fallopian tube, and ovary had to be removed. During her week-long hospitalization, she learned that her fetus had not been dead prior to the abortion.[215]

In November 1989, "Dianna" went to abortionist John Roe 686 for advice about health problems she was experiencing during her pregnancy. She expressed that she was opposed to abortion except as a last resort. He told her that the pregnancy was ectopic and that surgery was necessary to prevent her death, so she reluctantly submitted to an abortion. Afterward, she learned that both her pregnancy and fetus had been normal and that the surgery had been a standard elective abortion procedure. She said his behavior was "extreme and outrageous conduct, going beyond all possible bounds of decency, and was atrocious, and utterly intolerable in a civilized community." Roe was quoted in a news article as saying, "We don't do everybody that comes through the door, and we don't do people who don't want an abortion." [216]

"Alcida," age 28, went to a Planned Parenthood facility in Washington, D.C. on February 25, 1992, for birth control pills. Alcida, who speaks only Spanish, was led to a procedure room by a Spanish-speaking employee who had her disrobe, put her in stirrups, inserted a speculum, and left the room. Abortionist John Roe 180 entered the room and initiated an abortion procedure. Alcida screamed for him to stop, but Roe ignored the pleas of his patient and completed the procedure.

It turned out that Roe had gone into the wrong room and had failed to correctly identify which patient he was about to operate on. Ironically, the fact that Alcida was *not* pregnant later worked against her. Since, technically, there could not be an abortion without a pregnancy, Planned Parenthood successfully blocked her attempt to file suit anonymously, on grounds that the suit "does not involve an abortion, or a woman's right to privacy when choosing to obtain an abortion. The female plaintiff in this case was not pregnant,…did not seek, and did not obtain an abortion."[217]

Fetal Homograph

A 20-year-old patient experienced four months of vaginal discharge following her second abortion in two years. The second procedure was apparently incomplete, as recognizable fetal parts were expelled a few days later. Upon examining the patient, a doctor found that, "Projecting from the cervix was a polyp, 1 by 0.5 centimeter, which bled when touched." When he examined the polyp under a microscope, he noted that it "showed a most unusual appearance. Although it had a covering of normal endocervical epithelium, the core of the polyp was composed mainly of what appeared to be fully differentiated brain tissue." Further testing confirmed that this polyp was indeed brain tissue, and additional fragments of brain tissue were discovered embedded in the endometrium. Called a fetal homograph, this is tissue that is retained following an abortion, but instead of decomposing it embeds in the uterus and continues growing.

The articles we found on fetal homographs were from European sources, but since the United States has such a high abortion rate, and because our reporting system for complications is virtually non-existent, it can be presumed that this type of complication occurs in U.S. abortions as well, but is not as well documented. The first noted incidence was described in 1914. A researcher postulated that "the embryonic brain is implanted in the uterine lining following an abortion and grows there as a graft." The article then describes a specific case "to draw attention to a little-known condition which may not be quite as rare as the few case records would suggest."[218]

Another case of fetal homograph was noted in 1971. A patient had a 6-centimeter mass in her cervix three months after a suction abortion. A hysterectomy was performed, and the mass was found to be fetal muscle, bone, and cartilage that had been implanted into the uterus during the procedure.[219]

Psychological Injury/Suicide

The first documented case we encountered in which a suicide was officially attributed to a legal abortion involved a 19-year-old New York woman who killed herself on April 18, 1971. Three days earlier, she had submitted to an abortion and had since expressed guilt about having "killed my baby." Compounding this tragedy is the fact that it was later discovered she had never been pregnant.[220]

"Linda," age 35, was three-and-a-half-months pregnant when she underwent an abortion. She was not informed of fetal development, or of the possibility that she could later expel the fetus. The evening following the abortion, Linda suffered discomfort and discovered the upper part of the aborted fetus in her undergarments. She said, "I saw a baby that was fully formed." She suffered severe emotional trauma and now has recurring nightmares.[221]

In the fall of 1992, "Arlin" was still in high school when she learned that she was pregnant. A friend recalled that Arlin wanted to have children, but chose abortion to try to salvage the relationship with her boyfriend. As a result of the abortion, she not only suffered physical injury, but was also very depressed. In October, she was found hanging from a tree in the woods not far from her home. Under her shirt, the coroner found Arlin's favorite stuffed animal—a rabbit. Her mother said that Arlin left a suicide note saying that she wanted to be with her baby.[222]

Twenty-five-year-old "Melinda" underwent an abortion at a facility in New York City. One week later, the facility got a pathology report indicating that Melinda might still be pregnant. Despite the danger of an incomplete abortion or ectopic pregnancy, she was not notified. Prior to the scheduled follow-up appointment, she went to a local emergency room suffering severe cramps. There she delivered a four-and-a-half-inch fetus into the toilet.

Melinda screamed until she was taken to an examining room for removal of the placenta. She has since undergone psychiatric care for post-traumatic depression, nightmares, and sleeplessness. She is reluctant to enter into intimate relationships with men and remains socially withdrawn.[223]

"Stephanie," age 42, had an abortion when she was 13 weeks pregnant. The abortionist's notes accurately reflect that Stephanie did not want an abortion, but that her husband wished it. She suffered profuse vaginal bleeding after the abortion, was bedridden for two months with vaginal infection, and suffered depression and despondence resulting in psychiatric hospitalization.[224]

Disseminated Intravascular Coagulation

On January 22, 1980, the seven-year anniversary of *Roe v. Wade*, "Vanessa" underwent a second-trimester abortion at Acme Reproductive Services 42 in Dallas. During the procedure, she had a grand mal seizure, then went into cardiac arrest. Abortionist John Roe 848 and a nurse began CPR, and were able to resuscitate her. However, she went into a second arrest before the ambulance arrived. She was stabilized and transferred to a hospital where she became unresponsive. About 40 minutes into exploratory surgery, Vanessa went into cardiac arrest again. She received a total of 24 units of blood, and efforts to resuscitate her were continued for 90 minutes. Those efforts failed and she died. Vanessa was 22 years old.

An autopsy found that there were multiple vaginal punctures around the cervix and that the placenta was still attached to the uterus. The autopsy concluded that Vanessa "suffered a cardiac arrest due to the sudden entry of amniotic fluid into her blood stream during a legal abortion. The entry of this fluid into the blood stream created a condition in which the blood could not clot properly. Cardiopulmonary resuscitation was successful in restarting the heart, but also resulted in a relatively small tear of the liver. This liver injury would not normally be life threatening. However, in the presence of abnormal blood coagulation, the result was extensive hemorrhage into the abdominal cavity which could not be controlled at surgery." The cause of death was listed as amniotic fluid embolism and Disseminated Intravascular Coagulopathy (DIC).

DIC is a severe disorder in which the body, in response to initial clotting, mistakenly produces too much anti-clotting substance. It causes uncontrolled hemorrhaging and tissue death, and is a recognized potential complication of induced abortion. John Roe 848 was a co-founder and board member of the

National Abortion Federation, and ARS 42 was a member clinic in good standing.[225]

"Barbara" underwent an abortion at a New York hospital on December 11, 1981. Early in the morning five days after the abortion, she was admitted to another hospital suffering intermittent vomiting, back pain, and inability to urinate. Her admitting diagnosis was septic shock, acute renal failure, and disseminated intravascular coagulation. She had pelvic adhesions, an enlarged uterus, 1000 cc gray fluid in her peritoneal cavity, and a hardened, twisted, yellowish-brown site of obstruction of the small bowel. Her entire small bowel showed markedly dilated and inflamed loops and her lungs contained excessive pinkish watery fluid. She was pronounced dead at 11:35 a.m.[226]

"Dawn," age 28, underwent an abortion by John Roe 729 on June 29, 1988. Her brother, who accompanied her, was instructed to wait in a park across the street and come back to get her at four in the afternoon. When he did so, he was told that she was not ready to go and to return in 30 minutes. After a half hour, he was again told that she was not ready, and to return in another 30 minutes. When he returned, he found that his sister was dead. After the abortion, Dawn had started gasping for breath, and then yelled out. When her blood pressure dropped, the abortion clinic's staff attempted resuscitation, but did not call an ambulance. Her death was attributed to an amniotic fluid and chorionic villi embolism with disseminated intravascular coagulation following termination of pregnancy. Her autopsy revealed "about ½ litre of a yellowish fluid…present in the abdominal cavity" and "about 10 cc of an amber colored fluid" in her heart sac.[227]

After learning that she was pregnant, "Marla" was advised to have an abortion due to possible fetal injury caused by medications she was taking for depression. On the night after her abortion, she became ill with nausea, vomiting, and urinary incontinence, and had dried blood on her teeth. Her pulse and temperature were also elevated. Early the next morning, she became increasingly disoriented, and at 7:15 a.m. she was unresponsive, grunting loudly, and having seizures. She was pronounced dead shortly after noon. A medical article about her case indicates that Marla was diagnosed with disseminated intravascular coagulation. She was 18 years old at the time of her death.[228]

On September 18, 1990, "Sophie" underwent an abortion by John Roe 3, a National Abortion Federation member. That evening, she reported bleeding, pain, and difficulty breathing. The next day, she was taken to the hospital and was found to have a perforated uterus with sepsis. She underwent a hysterectomy, but developed disseminated intravascular coagulation. She died on September 26 at the age of 17.[229]

On August 3, 1992, "Angel" died following her abortion by John Roe 158. Her death certificate attributes her death to disseminated intravascular coagulation caused during an elective abortion. She was 22 years old and the mother of two children.[230]

"Rhonda" underwent an abortion by John Roe 470 at a Philadelphia abortion clinic on September 3, 1992. The abortionist knew that the procedure was unsuccessful. He sent Rhonda home with instructions to return on September 12, at which time he would attempt the abortion again. Rhonda experienced such severe pain, dizziness, fever, and discharge that on September 10 she sought emergency care at a hospital. She was diagnosed with "severe non-cardiogenic pulmonary edema consistent with adult respiratory distress syndrome." She underwent a laparoscopy, D&E, hysterectomy, and removal of her spleen. Despite these efforts, Rhonda died on September 14. An autopsy revealed a perforation from her vagina into the uterine cavity, sepsis, disseminated intravascular coagulation, non-bacterial thrombotic endocarditis, pulmonary infarctions, and dysplastic kidney.[231]   ■

The Canned Hunt

Rape and sexual assault in the abortion industry

There are people in America who want the experience of shooting "big game" animals without having to hunt them in the conventional manner. There are also people who will capture such animals and make them available for these "hunters" to shoot in a controlled environment. It is not uncommon for these animals to be drugged and/or staked to the ground as they are shot from a hundred yards away with a high-powered rifle. The shooter then poses majestically over the carcass for a trophy photo to hang in his office.

This noble event is called a "canned hunt," and bears some uncomfortable similarities to the situation in which women are raped or sexually assaulted by their abortionist. In both cases, the prey is often alone, drugged, powerless, and with virtually no defense against the predator.

When we originally designed the outline for this book, a chapter on rape and sexual assault was never envisioned. Although we had often heard rumors that this sort of thing happened, we had no reason to believe it was widespread enough to deserve more than a passing mention. However, as more and more data came into our office, we began to see that rape and sexual assault in abortion clinics is not uncommon at all.

What is really alarming is that we have probably uncovered no more than a tiny fraction of the total number of these instances. A recent government study estimated that at least 84 percent of all rapes go unreported.[1] However, since women who are assaulted by abortionists have additional issues to deal with that other rape victims do not, it is reasonable to believe that the percentage of unreported rapes is even higher for them. In order to speak up, these victims have to publicly admit things that may be difficult—if not impossible—for them to admit. They have to reveal that (a) they are sexually active, (b) they became pregnant, and (c) they had abortions.

Young and/or single women (an accurate description of most abortion patients) almost always need to keep this information a secret from someone. Even most married women are reluctant to come forward because there is still a powerful stigma attached to women who have abortions. Other women may remain silent because they view the assault as their "punishment" for having an abortion in the first place.

The bottom line is that the vast majority of women who are sexually assaulted by an abortionist don't perceive that they are in a position to do anything about it. For most, the only thing that matters is putting the whole miserable episode—the pregnancy, the abortion, and the sexual assault—behind them. It is not unlike the situation in which a man is robbed by a prostitute. He knows that he can't say anything because he can't afford to have his wife find out. His problem is not just that he was robbed, but *where* he was robbed and *by whom*. Women who are sexually attacked in an abortion clinic are in exactly the same predicament. Most are not going to say a word, and the people who work at abortion clinics know it.

This may explain the fact that when an abortionist is exposed as a sexual predator, it is very often one of his *non-abortion* victims who brings the allegation to light. Apparently, since these women don't have to grapple with the abortion stigmas mentioned earlier, it is easier for them to come forward. That's why we have included examples of these situations in this chapter. It is simply unreasonable to believe that a doctor who would do this sort of thing to his patients is going to discriminate among them on the basis of what kind of treatment the patient sought. If he's going to attack his non-abortion patients, he's going to attack his abortion patients. The only difference is that the non-abortion patients feel more freedom to speak up.

We have also included instances in which an abortionist sexually attacked someone who was not a patient at all. We did this because we felt that any abortionist who would, for example, kidnap and rape a 13-year-old girl, is probably not a paragon of sexual restraint when he has control of nude and anesthetized women whose feet are in the stirrups.

Keep in mind that this is by no means an exhaustive list. The following instances are simply a representative sample of the sexual misconduct of people known to be practicing abortionists.

John Roe 2

When his 11-weeks-pregnant wife refused his sexual advances, this member of the National Abortion Federation handcuffed her, dragged her to a bathroom, and performed an abortion on her against her will and without anesthesia. During the attack, he told his wife that if she didn't hold still he'd inject her with something to calm her down. Afterward, the 37-year-old victim called the police. She was taken to the hospital where a doctor confirmed that she had had an abortion. Roe was then arrested and charged with sexual battery and had his medical license suspended.[2]

John Roe 3

On October 11, 1991, "Carol" was being seen by Roe 3—a member of the National Abortion Federation—for an abortion follow-up exam. After placing her on an examining table, Roe inserted one finger into her anus while inserting another into her vagina. He had his other hand on her buttocks, then placed it on her breast. When later confronted, Roe denied that Carol was a patient of his despite the fact that his signature is on a prescription for her. Incredibly, the New York Department of Health's only criticism of Roe's actions was that he should not have been performing a simultaneous breast and pelvic examination.[3]

John Roe 7

On March 25, 1993, "Angela" was having an after-hours abortion performed by Roe 7. She awoke from anesthesia to find him putting his penis into her mouth. He called her several times afterward to find out if she remembered anything about the incident, and she taped the conversations. Police seized her medical records, which were found folded in Roe's desk rather than in her chart. As a result of this incident, Roe 7 was charged with attempted forced oral sodomy and sexual battery. He was released on $100,000 bail and left for India in May, claiming that he had to attend the wedding of a niece.

One day after Roe 7 was arrested for these crimes, "Tina" also filed a lawsuit against him. According to her suit, Roe asked Tina to meet with him to discuss her mental condition following her abortion. She claimed that at this meeting he tried to fondle and kiss her.

Two female employees also sued Roe, complaining of unwelcome sexual advances and sexual harassment.[4]

John Roe 16

On May 2, 1987, Roe 16 performed an abortion on 25-year-old "Clara" and gave her written instructions to abstain from sexual intercourse for a week. Four days later he had sexual intercourse with her in her home. Although this was clearly in violation of a state law that forbids doctors from having sexual relationships with their patients, Roe defended himself by claiming that the doctor-patient relationship ended when they had sex. His attorney contended that since Roe did not have sex with Clara during the actual abortion, he was perhaps guilty of poor judgment but not of causing any harm. The attorney also indicated that Roe had sex with Clara only because she gave positive responses to his questions about her enjoyment of sex and she was receptive to his visiting her at home.

Then, in November 1987, Roe 16 was censured by the Medical Board of Arizona for performing an after-hours abortion alone on another woman. She claimed that he had sex with her before doing the abortion. Ironically, a newspaper quoted Roe as saying, "I believe that if a woman decides to have a termination, it should be done safely, legally, and with some dignity."[5]

John Roe 28

Nineteen-year-old student nurse "Kathryn" alleged that abortionist Roe 28 wrote her an unsolicited and undesired prescription for birth control pills. Several hours later, he took her arm as she was leaving the nurses' lounge and led her down a flight of stairs. When she asked where he was taking her, he replied, "You never ask a doctor where he's going." Kathryn testified that she had no reason to fear Roe because he was a doctor and the same age as her father. However, as he brought her into a room that was still under construction, she became alarmed and asked him to let her go. At that time, Roe tried to kiss her and tightened his grip on her arms. He then began pulling down her scrub suit pants. Kathryn said she feared for her life and was afraid to scream. Because she was not physically strong enough to fend him off, she was not able to prevent her rape. Following the attack, a physical examination of the victim revealed the presence of semen.[6]

John Roe 34

Patient "Nicki" had an abortion on June 17, 1982, in Roe 34's office and returned on July 2 for a follow-up exam. She was naked from the waist down and partially covered by a paper sheet on the examining table. No nurse or assistant was present. Roe began to make sexually oriented comments and started reaching under the sheet to touch her body. Although Nicki begged him to stop and repeatedly pushed his hand away, Roe unzipped his trousers and told her to scoot down to the end of the table. She refused and again pleaded, "Please don't do this." Roe then placed his hands around her buttocks, pulled her down toward the end of the examination table, and forced his penis into her vagina.

Six years later, following a complaint for sexual misconduct, Florida placed an emergency restriction on his license. The next year, that state revoked his license altogether. Then, in 1990, Roe 34's New York license was revoked for substandard care, incompetence, and negligence.[7]

John Roe 35

Roe 35 was charged with the July 14, 1980, kidnapping and rape of a girl under the age of 13. In 1982, he was convicted of that crime and was arrested again on charges of indecent exposure, assault with intent to commit kidnapping, and assault with intent to commit sexual penetration of a female minor. Those charges resulted from a December 7, 1981, incident in which he masturbated in front of children who were exiting a high school.[8]

John Roe 38

Abortionist Roe 38 was investigated by the Oregon Board of Medical Examiners in 1994, after a 41-year-old woman and her 20-year-old daughter alleged that he tried to sexually stimulate them during examinations in 1990 and 1993. A criminal investigation was launched late in 1994 after three other women claimed that he tried to sexually stimulate them and used explicit sexual language during examinations in 1991 and 1992. After publishing an article about these allegations, *The Oregonian* reported that 21 additional women contacted them to report similar incidents. Eventually, the Oregon Board of Medical Examiners and the police received sex-related complaints about Roe from more than 100 female patients, including one who said that he photographed her genitals. Oregon medical authorities suspended his license in September 1994, and revoked it in December 1994. On May 26, 1995, he suffered a severe stroke and died three days later. He had been scheduled to go to court the following week on civil charges filed by one of his alleged victims, and to stand trial on July 10, 1995, in a criminal court for 29 counts of sexual abuse on 18 former patients. The statute of limitations had run out on all but those 29 incidents. Eighty-nine women planned to testify against him in the criminal hearing.[9]

John Roe 40

Roe 40, a nurse anesthetist at two Florida abortion clinics, was caught with photographs of clinic patients lying naked on exam tables with their feet in the stirrups. The photos focused on the victims' genital areas. It was also discovered that he would open patients' garments and fondle their breasts while they were under general anesthesia. On at least two occasions, he called other employees to look at the anesthetized patients' breasts. Additionally, he was accused of paying clinic staff members a commission for each patient they persuaded to purchase general rather than local anesthesia. It was also alleged that he routinely left the building while women were under general anesthesia, leaving the anesthetized patients under the care of unlicensed and untrained staff.[10]

John Roe 56

Several patients have accused Roe 56 of sexual misconduct, fondling, and rough treatment, including one who said that he stared between her legs and sang silly songs during an exam. Other charges against him include inappropriate behavior toward an abortion patient who had changed her mind and performing two abortion procedures on patients who were not pregnant.

At one point, Roe filed a complaint with the state bar claiming that an attorney representing these women was filing suits only to harass him. His complaint was found to be unsubstantiated when the court ruled that the attorney had reasonable grounds for filing the suits, even though the cases were unsuccessful.[11]

John Roe 70

Abortionist Roe 70, a member of the National Abortion Federation, admitted to charges of sexual misconduct with a patient after "Cheryl" accused him of placing his mouth on her breasts for several minutes on two separate occasions.[12]

John Roe 71

In 1990, the Virginia Board of Medicine noted that Roe 71 had been receiving weekly outpatient psychotherapy for "chronic and intermittent depression and anxiety resulting in increased conflictive interpersonal relations." The Board concluded that he "may be physically and/or mentally impaired to practice medicine with reasonable skill and safety to his patients." Roe was ordered to continue his psychotherapy and to be evaluated by the Board's psychiatric consultants prior to a meeting of the Board's conference committee, which was to take place in not less than a year. The conference committee hearing took place in May 1992, at which time they found that Roe "was not physically or mentally impaired to practice medicine."

Apparently, that was not a very sound decision because just two years later that same board was forced to address the following:

Patient "Gina" said that in late 1992 or early 1993, Roe kissed and hugged her, and made inappropriate comments and inquiries about her sexual activities.

Twenty-four-year-old patient "Johnna" alleged that on July 7, 1993, he made inappropriate sexual comments regarding her appearance and sexual behavior, rubbed her genitals inappropriately, advised her to chart her sexual activity, and told her, "I speak five different languages, I have practiced in five different countries. I do this for women for their own good."

Patient "Alli" reported that on November 19, 1993, Roe made inappropriate comments and inquiries about her sexual behavior and touched her genitals inappropriately. On that same day, he placed unwelcomed phone calls to the home of another woman, making sexual comments. He then went to a hotel where the woman worked and caused such a disturbance that hotel security had to intervene. Although the reasons aren't clear, Roe seems to have some sort of bizarre fetish for people who work in hotels. On December 18, 1991, a female hotel employee said that he asked her to go with him to a fitness center and help him change his clothes. Another employee complained that he also made inappropriate sexual comments to her.

On December 3, 1993, 24-year-old "Crystal" said that he kissed her neck, told her she had beautiful breasts, tugged on her navel ring, and described a sexual act he wanted to do that included suspending her from a ceiling fan by her navel ring. Then, after falsely informing her that she had genital warts, he applied a solution to her vagina that caused so much pain it left her screaming for 15 minutes. She said he also dispensed various medicines to her out of an unlabeled "ziplock" bag. Another patient told of an encounter with Roe during an appointment in May 1994 that was almost identical to Crystal's experience.

"Hillary," a 28-year-old African-American patient, complained that on April 14, 1994, Roe told her she had beautiful breasts and that if his wife saw them she would be jealous. After informing her that he liked to perform oral sex on black women, he grasped her arms, held them up and said, "I'd like to rent this for the weekend."[13]

John Roe 74

In 1995, New Jersey abortionist Roe 74 was suspended from practicing medicine for three years for having sex with patient "Katy" and prescribing unnecessary drugs for her. Katy said he made numerous sexual advances toward her
and fondled her during office visits. After inviting her to his office sometime
in 1985, he had sexual intercourse with her on a bed in the birthing room
while the staff was nearby and the door was unlocked. He was aware that Katy
suffered severe depression, had been sexually abused as a child, and had a
history of psychiatric hospitalization. Roe denied that the allegations were
true, but said he admitted to them only because he was tired of legal battles.
However, in another report he defended his having had sex with the woman
on the basis that (a) there was no emotional involvement, (b) he did not
charge for the visit, and (c) his sexual advances were not premeditated.
Subsequently, two other women also brought claims of improper sexual
behavior against him.[14]

John Roe 75

Abortionist Roe 75 was convicted of producing and mailing pornographic
videotapes. The tapes showed children as young as four years old engaged in
sexual acts such as oral sex with adults and other children. They also featured
an adult masturbating while smearing excrement on his body. Additional
charges included using a false name or making a false statement to a U.S.
agency to get a post office box for the purpose of shipping these obscene
videos across state lines. Evidence was also found showing that Roe and his
associates are affiliated with the National and International Diaper Pail Foundation. Members of this organization are infantilists who are interested in the
defecation of small children. They also enjoy wearing diapers, defecating in
the diapers, and smearing the defecation on their bodies while masturbating.
Some of the videos confiscated by federal authorities were titled *Diaper Dump*,
Baby Photos, *Shorts Dump*, and *The Nap*.

   On the day he was scheduled to appear in court to plead guilty to federal
charges related to interstate distribution of child pornography, Roe apparently ingested poison in what is thought to be a failed suicide attempt.[15]

John Roe 76

In 1983, Kentucky abortionist Roe 76 was convicted of four counts of an
unlawful sexual transaction with the 14-year-old daughter of one of his friends.
"Jana" testified that in 1982, Roe offered her a massage, then took off her
bathing suit and penetrated her vagina with his penis and his fingers. He was

also convicted of having sex with her on three other occasions and of performing oral sex on her. Jana testified that she knew what they were doing was not right but that she trusted him. When she told her aunt about the encounters, the case was turned over to county juvenile authorities.

At the trial, an 8-year-old girl testified that she had seen Roe touch other children's chests and genital areas and that he had touched her chest. Her 12-year-old sister testified that she saw Roe put his hand up a 5-year-old girl's shirt while she was sitting on his lap. Both girls also described an 'airplane game' Roe allegedly played with children whom he invited to his home for parties. This game involved picking the children up and spinning them, touching their chests or groins. Roe denied the allegations, producing in court a receipt that he said proved he was at work on the day the first encounter took place. His attorney claimed the accusations were made because the parents of the two sisters wanted to buy Roe's house.[16]

John Roe 77

"Janice," a well-known abortion-rights advocate, claimed that she was fired as co-director of a Minnesota abortion clinic because she objected to the sexual harassment of female employees by Roe 77. Another former employee said that Roe repeatedly intimidated some younger staff members with his jokes and questions about their sex lives, and told them he dreamed about how they would look without clothes. She also said that when an employee was about to undergo an abortion at the clinic, Roe asked if he could be in the room. She said he described a fantasy about having sexual intercourse with a woman on an examining table during an abortion. Roe was also reported to have put his arm around another female employee, told her she was frigid and that what she needed was a good man.

Roe admitted to doing "foolish things and telling dirty jokes," but said Janice only made the complaint because she wanted the clinic to be run entirely by women.[17]

John Roe 80

Several patients of Roe 80 claim that he fondled their breasts, injected them with medication that made them groggy, and then engaged in sexual intercourse with them against their will. One of these women testified that she was rendered physically unable to move but kept crying, "What are you doing?" Another patient testified that after Roe examined her vagina, he licked his fingers. His medical license was revoked in 1989.[18]

John Roe 88

This National Abortion Federation member was indicted with his wife on four counts of child pornography involving their 3-year-old foster daughter. One of the photographs showed the child dressed in black lace thong panties, in lewd positions with her genitals and buttocks exposed. Charges against both were dropped after Roe's wife signed a "statement of fact" admitting that some people might find the photographs to be of an inappropriate nature and that they could constitute a violation of state law. However, she maintained that she did not consider them inappropriate. She said she was an artist and the photos were meant as a keepsake for the child. Roe was arrested for possession of the photographs when he picked them up after they were developed. He said the incident was a minor family matter that became blown totally out of proportion. He also claimed that the prosecution was motivated by opposition to his abortion practice, a charge which authorities denied. The child was placed in another home by child protection services upon Roe's arrest and was later adopted by an out-of state family.

The building that houses Roe 88's abortion clinic is owned by a local used car dealer. A photo shows this man outside the building, dressed in a devil suit and exposing his genitals. Signs posted outside the building direct messages toward anti-abortion protesters. Included among them are "Jesus loves these braindead assholes," "These Bible-thumpers suffer from lack-o-nookie," "Free coat hangers to picketers' wives and mothers," "God bless these horny old sweat-hogs," and one identifying a particular female picketer as the "lard-ass in hot pink." The building owner also had a person dress as the "Condom Monster" (similar to the Muppet "Cookie Monster") and hand out condoms, some inflated with helium, to protesters' children.[19]

John Roe 99

In September 1981, 16-year-old "Ruth" was working in a cooperative nursing program when 30-year-old Roe tried to entice her into a sexual relationship. When she rejected his advances, he set up an appointment for her to come to his office for a pelvic examination and birth control pills. During the appointment, no nurse was present and he again attempted to have sexual intercourse with her.

On February 12, 1982, "Carli" went to Roe's office for treatment of a urinary tract infection and a sore throat. Roe tried to slide his hand down her chest toward her breast, but she slapped it away. He then told her he needed a urine sample. While she was in the restroom, Roe entered and asked if he could help. She told him to "Get the hell out." Roe told her he was just trying to calm her down. Later, he told her that the test showed she had a urinary tract infection and asked her if he could give her a pelvic examination. She declined.

Thirty-six-year-old "Sally" visited Roe's office for treatment of a sore throat on January 13, 1982. She told him that she was despondent because her four-year-old daughter had died about a month earlier. In response, Roe gave her his business card with his home phone number written on the back. The next day, Roe called her and asked her to meet him and she agreed. That night they engaged in sexual intercourse at his home. They continued their sexual relationship, and in February 1993 Sally became pregnant. When she told him of the pregnancy, Roe demanded that she have an abortion. She informed him that she could not kill her baby and would give birth with or without his help. She then saw another physician who later testified that Sally was three months pregnant at the time of her visit, and that she definitely wanted to keep the baby. Roe spoke with this physician and acknowledged that he was dating Sally and was the father of her baby.

On October 30, 1983, Roe went to Sally's home. She was eight months pregnant and commented that she could feel the baby moving. Roe asked her to go for a drive with him and she agreed. Roe took her to his home, examined her, and said that he could not hear a heartbeat and that the baby was dead. Sally said he was wrong and that the baby was fine. Roe did, however, convince her to take medications to calm her down, which she recalls as being two or three round blue pills. She became very drowsy, and Roe then took her to an upstairs bedroom, removed her clothes, and induced labor. Although Roe told her the baby was stillborn, Sally argued that she briefly awoke from her drug-induced sleep to hear the muffled sound of a baby's cry. Roe then threatened her with a gun, saying he would use the six bullets to kill her, her son, her minister, her father, her ex-husband, and then himself. No death certificate was ever filed for the supposedly stillborn child.

After her June 1, 1983, appointment, Roe gave "Michelle" his home phone number and asked her to call him. Later, he went to her home and told her that his beeper had gone off. She allowed him to use her telephone, and then he wandered off in her house. When she went to find him, Roe was standing naked in a bedroom. He then forcibly raped her knowing that she would not scream for help because her 10-year-old son was asleep in the next room.

On September 1, 1983, "Samantha" went to Roe's office to have her IUD removed. She requested the presence of a nurse but Roe told her that the nurse was busy. During the procedure he told her that he was going to insert an instrument into her, but instead Samantha felt him insert his penis into her vagina. She pulled away and found Roe with his erect penis exposed. Later, he telephoned her and told her to keep her mouth shut.

In early 1984, Roe made sexual advances toward patient "Maria" and engaged in sexual intercourse with her. He also performed an abortion on her without her prior knowledge or consent.

"Kelly" went to Roe's office for a gynecological exam in March 1984. She was divorced and told him that she wanted to start taking birth control pills because she had decided to date again. Roe gave her his phone number, asked her out to dinner, and invited her to his home. Subsequently, they began a sexual relationship. In December 1987, Kelly told Roe that she thought she might be pregnant with his child. He insisted that she come to his office. Once there, Roe performed a pregnancy test, assured Kelly that she was not pregnant, and suggested that he help her start her period. When she later complained of fever, chills, cramping, and excessive bleeding, Roe made arrangements for her go to a hospital, and told her that she would merely be given intravenous medications. Instead, he tricked her into signing forms for a D&C procedure. Afterward, he asked her how she was feeling about the abortion. Until that time, Kelly had no knowledge that an abortion had been performed on her.

Eventually, his license was revoked on allegations of having sex with numerous patients, including the three he was known to have impregnated and aborted without their consent.

During a December 1, 1984, pelvic examination at Roe's office, "Carrie" told him that she was addicted to the prescription drug Xanax. No nurse was present and Roe did not wear rubber gloves. As the examination continued, Roe told Carrie that he thought she was beautiful and had a nice body. He then attempted to sexually stimulate her by rubbing her breasts and rolling her nipples between his fingers. He also began rubbing her clitoris and asked if it felt good. Afterward, he wrote her a prescription for Xanax and told her that as long as she continued to have her pelvic examinations, she would have plenty of Xanax.

On June 1, 1986, "Brenda" sought medical treatment from Roe. He later called her and asked her to come to his home for dinner. She accepted, and after dinner Roe attempted to engage in sexual intercourse with her. She refused, but continued to see him for medical care until January 1989. He conducted pelvic examinations without a nurse present, and repeatedly asked Brenda to marry him during her office visits.

Thirty-three-year-old "Sandy" met Roe 99 in May 1987 after she responded to a personal dating advertisement that he had placed in the *Indianapolis Monthly* magazine. The two met at a local fast-food restaurant and then went to his home. They had sexual intercourse that night and their sexual relationship continued through July. At that time, Roe became aware that Sandy was pregnant and convinced her to allow him to examine her. He told her that she was not pregnant, and that he would help her start her period. He inserted a metal instrument into her cervix, and she jumped from the examining table and wouldn't let him proceed due to pain. She later allowed him to complete the abortion, which he had originally initiated without her knowledge or consent.

On September 1, 1988, "Trisha" went to Roe because of back pain. He told her that she was beautiful, gave her his home phone number, and asked her out for dinner. On September 15, she returned to his office for a pelvic examination. Roe did not leave the room while Trisha undressed, and he examined her without a nurse present. A month later, she was in the hospital awaiting a hysterectomy, when Roe visited her and asked, "How is my sexy lady?" He asked if the book she was reading was making her hot and told her that there were ways to pleasure a woman with his hand and that he could make her feel good.

On February 2, 1989, "Kay" sought medical treatment from Roe for stomach pain. He asked the 17-year-old if she was sexually active and whether she had a boyfriend. He also asked if her boyfriend was an older man like him and if she would be interested in an older man. During the examination, Kay said the pain was near her sternum. Roe then told her she had an ulcer, unhooked her bra, and conducted a breast exam. He also asked her to allow him to do a pelvic exam, but she refused.

Finally, on February 23, 1989, Roe 99's Indiana medical license was suspended in an emergency order. Eventually, his license was revoked on allegations of having sex with numerous patients, including the three he was known to have impregnated and aborted or attempted to abort without their consent. After he was convicted of performing and attempting to perform illegal abortions, prosecutors feared that he would flee the country, having received a tip that he had applied for hospital jobs in Canada and Africa under an assumed name.[20]

John Roe 108

John Roe 108 is a former U.S. Navy Pharmacist's Mate 3rd Class and a Licensed Vocational Nurse. A complaint was filed with the California Medical Board on

February 24, 1981, alleging that he presented himself as a physician, signed other physician's names to prescriptions, practiced "the full range of medicine including performing pelvic examinations as well as minor office surgical procedures," and performed "hypnosis on a select group of patients, who always happen to be young girls or women, and that the hypnosis is represented to the patients as being part of the medical treatment." At one medical facility a complaint of sexual advancement was filed against him with his superior, but nothing was done to modify his practice. In fact, members of the office staff who expressed any disapproval of his practice, or told the patients that he was not a physician and should not be doing vaginal examinations on them, were dismissed for one reason or another. The facility where these instances occurred is a member of the National Abortion Federation.[21]

John Roe 109

According to members of his staff, Roe 109 had a lot of mental problems, constantly took potentially addictive pain-killing drugs, and made sexual advances toward the patients. One non-physician employee claimed that she assisted in four or five abortions performed by other non-physician staff members, and performed one herself at the request of a patient who was afraid of Roe. Another employee, a nurse's aide, testified that she had several fellow employees perform an abortion on her, and that she assisted in abortions they did on others.[22]

John Roe 113

Abortionist Roe 113 engaged in sexual misconduct with several of his patients, including massaging genitals during a pelvic exam and kissing a patient on the face, neck, and breasts. He told another patient that she and her husband should engage in intercourse with him observing so he could determine why she was not climaxing. An emergency suspension of his Minnesota medical license in 1986 followed allegations of sexual abuse of seven patients. His license was revoked after similar charges by two more patients.[23]

John Roe 115

On June 19, 1987, patient "Erin" filled a complaint alleging that Roe 115 put KY jelly on his hands, reached under her blouse, massaged her breasts, pressed his body against hers, and then attempted to kiss her on the lips. As a result, Roe was eventually convicted of criminal sexual misconduct and placed on probation for two years.

Another patient, "Sharon," complained that Roe rubbed her clitoris for 10–20 seconds twice during an exam on November 6, 1992. Roe's attorney contended that Roe "didn't do it," pointing out the proximity of a nurse who was in the room during the exam. However, Sharon pointed out that because the nurse was standing at the head of the exam table she was unable to see what Roe was doing.

On two occasions in early 1994, patient "Willa" complained that Roe rubbed her clitoris with his fingers in a way she described as "constant pressure…like he was trying to turn me on." Willa said she was paralyzed with shock, and that she had never had a doctor touch her in that way.

In 1995, a Pennsylvania court sentenced Roe to prison for sexually molesting three female patients. Two additional women who had accused him of inappropriate sexual conduct were present at his trial, but did not testify because the statute of limitations had run out in one woman's case, and the other woman was pressing charges against him in another state.[24]

John Roe 116

Abortionist Roe 116 met "Maria" in 1977 when she went to him for an abortion. She later went to work for him and they became sexually involved. Maria won a lawsuit against Roe in which she alleged that his abuse of her caused her to throw their 14-month-old son to his death from the top of an apartment building. As Roe and his wife looked on, Maria also leaped from the building but survived the fall. Roe had provided her with an apartment in the building from which she jumped. Maria was charged with the murder of her baby but was acquitted on grounds of temporary insanity.[25]

John Roe 119

Roe 119 admitted that he placed his mouth on a patient's breasts in May 1988, and that between 1988 and 1993, he would occasionally ask patients inappropriate questions about their sexual practices. His license was suspended for five years, and then was reinstated with a probation agreement after only a year of suspension. The probation agreement was that Roe would attend weekly psychotherapy sessions. Nurses with whom he had worked expressed their belief that Roe should not be allowed to work with women.[26]

John Roe 123

On November 9, 1992, "Kim" underwent an abortion by Roe during which she was given an anesthetic injection to induce sleep. However, it only made her drowsy. Roe ordered the nurse to leave the room while he performed the abortion. Immediately afterward, he began to massage Kim's genitals, thighs, and buttocks as well as fondle her breasts through her blouse. While Roe was touching her breasts, she could feel him rub his groin up against her exposed vagina. He had his pants on at the time. As Kim began to cry, she asked Roe what he was doing and pushed his hand away. Roe then left the room and the nurse returned to give the patient follow-up instructions.

"Clare" underwent an abortion by Roe on June 22, 1994. During a July 7 follow-up appointment, he told Clare that she had the human papilloma virus and scheduled her for another examination. During that exam, the phone rang and Roe told his assistant to answer it, leaving Clare alone with Roe for the rest of the examination. Afterward, he told her that the infection was severe and quoted $1,500 for laser treatment. Clare began to cry when she heard the cost. At that point Roe said, "Don't worry, I like you. I'll do anything for you." On July 22, 1994, he placed Clare under anesthesia for the one-and-a-half-hour laser treatment. Before doing so, he sent the nurse out of the room and it is unknown whether she returned for the procedure.

During Clare's next visit, August 2, 1994, Roe drew blood using a latex glove instead of a tourniquet. Two fingers of the glove inflated as he tightened it around her arm. Roe tapped the inflated fingers playfully, referring to them as penises and saying, "This one's Chinese, and this one's Vietnamese." As Clare left the room, Roe grasped her firmly by the waist and pulled her close to him. She resisted his advances and was able to struggle free.

On January 28, 1995, "Abby" was having an abortion performed by Roe when she awoke from the anesthesia to find him penetrating her vagina with his penis. He then gave her a shot and she went back to sleep. When she woke up a second time, he was standing next to her with his erect penis out of his pants. She tried to push him away but he gave her another injection and she went back to sleep. When she awoke for a third time, she found her sweater had been removed and her bra partially pulled down exposing her right breast. Roe was caressing her and when she tried to scream he placed his hand over her mouth. He then told Abby that she had a beautiful body. He continued to fondle her breasts, telling her she was a very nice girl and was very sexy. He kissed her right breast and then placed his business card inside her bra and said she could call him anytime.

In February 1995, four sexual misconduct charges were filed against Roe by the state of California, his medical license was suspended, and he was released on bail pending trial. In August, detectives presented a local judge with evidence that Roe was still performing abortions. The judge revoked his bail and issued a warrant for his arrest. However, Roe had disappeared and detectives were unable to serve the warrant.[27]

John Roe 125

"Jodi" filed a suit against Roe 125, alleging that he sexually assaulted her while performing an abortion on her in June 1986. She also charged him with fraud, medical malpractice, battery, violation of her civil rights, and discrimination.[28]

John Roe 126

Documents filed with the Florida Board of Medicine state that Roe 126 sedated patient "Danielle" and then fondled and engaged in sexual activity with her.[29]

John Roe 131

In October 1979, 21-year-old "Elaine" came to abortionist Roe 131 for an annual gynecological exam, which he performed without a nurse present. During that visit, Roe manipulated her clitoris and asked her to fantasize and move her hips. He also asked her to stand, and as she did he lifted off her examination gown, leaving her nude. He then requested that she walk and move her hips, which she refused to do. Roe told her that she had a nice body and requested that she lift her leg onto the step of the examining table while she remained nude.

In July 1977, "Loren" was in the process of divorcing her husband and had consulted Roe 131 to find out if she had contracted any venereal diseases as a result of her husband's contact with other women. Without a nurse present in the examining room, Roe checked her breasts by manipulating and rubbing them instead of examining them in an appropriate manner. During the vaginal exam, Roe began manipulating the patient's clitoris and then forced his erect penis into her vagina.

On November 19, 1982, "Louise" came to Roe 131 for a diaphragm in anticipation of her upcoming marriage. After the nurse left the room, Roe said he wanted to check the fit of the diaphragm and asked Louise to resume her position on the examining table. Roe then stated that he was going to teach her how to relieve herself and began to manipulate her clitoris with his right hand while placing his left hand against her pubic area. In spite of the patient's protest, Roe forced her hand over her clitoris, placed his hand over hers and began to rub back and forth. While Louise was standing in the room after the examination, Roe put his hand inside her vagina and stated that "this is what it will feel like..." while pushing on the inside of her vagina and manipulating her clitoris.

In response to the above accusations, Roe 131 surrendered his medical license to the Board of Medical Quality Assurance of the State of California, and declared that he did not intend to seek its reinstatement.[30]

John Roe 135

On April 29, 1993, the Medical Board of California accused Roe 135 of sexual misconduct and recommended that disciplinary action be taken against him. This resulted from a December 30, 1988, second-trimester abortion that he performed on 19-year-old "Helen." Helen had been hospitalized because of life-threatening injuries she sustained during the abortion, and required follow-up visits to Roe. During those appointments, Roe kissed her face and lips, caressed her face, rubbed her shoulders, and suggested they go out together. At one point he rubbed her thigh, knee, and shoulders, hugged and kissed her, and told her he would like to see more of her. After that encounter, Helen terminated all contact.[31]

John Roe 136

A 24-year-old woman charged that Roe 136 negligently caused her to become addicted to her medication, made improper sexual advances, impregnated her, and then performed an abortion on her.[32]

John Roe 141

In a park restroom on September 10, 1982, California abortionist Roe 141 unzipped his pants and masturbated his erect penis toward one vice officer and grabbed the crotch of another. He was arrested and booked on three charges. He pleaded no contest to lewd conduct and the other two charges were dropped. He received a $60 fine and three months probation. Roe 141 worked for a National Abortion Federation member clinic.[33]

John Roe 497

Roe 497's minor half-sister "Ann" was one of his patients for several years, during which time he repeatedly raped her. He was also accused of perform-ing several abortions on her to terminate pregnancies that he may have caused.

When patient "Shannon" began dating Roe in 1988, he expressed concern about venereal disease and insisted on examining her. He then told her that she had genital warts and needed surgery. The next day he performed the surgery without obtaining adequate biopsy or Pap smear results. Eventually, Shannon became pregnant by Roe and in early 1989, he performed an after-hours abortion on her without adequate equipment or supporting personnel. Shannon went to work for Roe in February 1989, and remained in his employ until April of that year. After completing Air Force officer's training, she broke off their relationship and moved. In May, she requested her medical records, which Roe claimed he no longer had. Shannon's supervisor, an Air Force colonel, showed her a letter that Roe mailed to him May 12, 1989, suggesting that the Air Force should delay Shannon's flight training because she was an "incorrigible liar." The letter also disclosed details about her medical history.

More than 160 women accused this California abortionist of sexually assaulting them.

In 1992, more than 160 women accused this California abortionist of sexually assaulting them. Most of the allegations made against him related to one or more of the following activities:

- Forcibly raping patients
- Sexually abusing minor patients
- Attempting to sexually stimulate patients by manipulating the clitoris and fondling the breasts of patients against their will
- Using sexually abusive language with patients and asking unnecessary and inappropriate questions about their sex lives
- Manual or instrumental intercourse with patients without their permission
- Inserting his tongue into the vagina of a patient who was in labor
- Inducing patients to perform oral sex on him
- "French-kissing" his patients
- Sticking his hand inside the underwear of a patient and telling her she had a nice "pussy"
- Rubbing his penis against the legs or bodies of patients on exam tables
- Performing abortions without anesthesia
- Twirling a patient's pubic hairs around his fingers, pulling out the loose ones and blowing them across the room while saying how he loved blondes

- Initiating sexual contact with a nurse who was attending an obstetrics patient

- Sexually harassing and assaulting a hospital employee and then having her fired because she reported him

- Boasting about his fertility and offering to "help" a patient get pregnant

- Offering to "break the cherry" of a virgin patient

- Offering to surgically cut a patient's clitoris so she could have stronger orgasms

- Performing surgery to "tighten" the vaginal openings on patients without their knowledge or permission

Deputy Attorney General for the State of California, Randy Christison, called Roe 497 a predator in a white coat who used his position for his own perverse sexual gratification. Unfortunately, the state was not able to pursue criminal charges against him because the statute of limitations had expired on many of the instances and corroborating evidence was not available in the others. However, the California Medical Board charged him with sexual abuse, sexual misconduct, gross negligence, incompetence, and immorality. On May 15, 1992, Roe surrendered his California medical license.[34]

Erma Roe 813 / Acme Reproductive Services 1

This Chicago abortion clinic was featured in a 1974 *Playboy* article entitled "Take Two Aspirins and Masturbate," which described ARS 1's "Sexual Attitude Restructuring Workshops." The magazine said that the weekend was a bargain at $75 for two, including a pizza-and-wine supper and a cold-chicken box lunch. It went on to describe a film shown on the first day that featured a woman masturbating with a big square green vibrator. Then, in what they labeled the highlight of the evening, a nude "Reverend Shaw" anointed and nibbled someone's toes, while a few attendees engaged in a bit of extracurricular massage dressed only in their underwear. As an aside, the article mentioned that on this first day of the workshop eighty abortions were performed in an adjacent room.

The second day started with what the abortion clinic called a "Fuckarama." *Playboy* described this as a heavy porn collection projected onto several screens at one time. It called them "desensitizing films" consisting of "lots of good-looking people engaging in intercourse and oral sex in groups of two, three, or four; girls with eye shadow fondling rubber dildos." In one scene, a young woman had sex with a dog to the tune of songs with lyrics such as "She's a hooker, she fucks and sucks any schmuck with twenty bucks." Meanwhile, Roe 813 danced to "Jimmy fucks Sue and Sue fucks Sam / Mary balls Dave and then eats Dan." Other participants reclined or sat on big pillows on the floor. One young man had come in with his wife, and by Sunday had abandoned her for the wife of another attendee, although he had to share her with a second man as well. His wife was okay, as she had teamed up with yet another man.

The *Playboy* article said that the "Sexual Attitude Restructuring Workshops" were just one of a variety of similar "services." (One workshop targeted professional and church groups, staffs of social agencies, etc.) It also revealed that sex therapists who were in attendance created the term "psycho-physiological genitourinary disorder," in the hope they could get insurance companies to pay for future workshops.

After this article was published, Illinois health officials closed ARS 1 until it agreed to stop offering the workshops on the premises. They also required ARS 1 to satisfy health inspectors that its counseling of abortion applicants was adequate, and to address other reported problems such as physicians washing their hands in a soiled utility room and women undergoing abortions in street clothes.

Roe 813 was quoted in the *Playboy* article as saying, "Any and all sexual expression is legitimate, provided it does not infringe on the rights of others... to me, good and evil have nothing to do with how you express yourself sexually. That's overemphasizing harmless physical acts and giving them ethical powers." The article elaborates, "she does mean all—whether it's casual, group, adulterous, prepubertal, adolescent, oral or anal, with devices, animals, or partners of the same or opposite sex."

Roe attributed the health department's closing of her abortion clinic to "hysterical, arbitrary arrogance" on the part of city officials. She was a founder and board member of the National Abortion Rights Action League. ARS 1 was a member of the National Abortion Federation.[35]

Conclusion

In reality, the instances contained in this chapter can be nothing more than the tip of an enormous iceberg. If more than 84 percent of all sexual assault victims remain silent, and if those attacked during an abortion are even more silent, then the actual number of women assaulted at abortion clinics must be staggering. And while we will never know what the real numbers are, it would be hard to argue that there is any business establishment in America in which a woman is more likely to be raped than in an abortion clinic. ■

CHAPTER 3

Speak No Evil

Abortion industry self-policing, and other selected fairy tales

In most areas of medicine, state legislatures operating through medical licensing and/or medical examiner boards will, to some degree, police bad medical practitioners. However, in the case of abortion they have shown a remarkable unwillingness to pursue bad doctors or clinics. And even when they do, it is not at all uncommon for the abortion industry to search for a court to rule that governmental oversight of abortion is an unconstitutional infringement on a woman's right to abortion.

Today, abortion industry efforts to resist regulation are easy to find in practically every state. That is somewhat understandable, since any industry would rather be allowed to self-police than have the government do it. However, history has proven that virtually no industry will, in practice, actually police itself. Relying on an industry to do something simply because it is the right thing to do is naive. One example of that is pollution. Does anyone really believe that American industry would have enforced upon itself the strict anti-pollution regulations that are now law? The fact is, most regulation of industry comes about to solve a problem that the industry itself refused to solve.

Although they may not always like it, most industries recognize that reasonable regulation is ultimately in the best interest of all concerned. A notable exception is the American abortion industry, led primarily by either the National Abortion Federation or Planned Parenthood, or both. These groups desperately want the public to embrace, with childlike naiveté, the view that they are selfless champions for women whose every motive and action is pure, making any sort of external oversight unnecessary meddling. And because they are so adept at projecting this image, and because they have a virtual stranglehold on the American media, they have successfully beaten back almost every attempt to impose even minimal oversight. But as this chapter will show, there is an enormous gap between their claim to self-police, and what actually happens. Of course, the best proof of that is seen in Chapters 1 and 2.

The National Abortion Federation

The National Abortion Federation (NAF) claims that they "ensure continued high standards for safe, quality abortion care. We meet this charge in three ways: offering continuing medical education to reproductive health care providers; chronicling abortion-related complications; and establishing new standards of care."[1] Generally, their argument is that regulation would drive the cost up and deny some women access to abortion services. That has prompted some critics to argue that what NAF wants is not "*safe* and legal" abortions, but "*cheap* and legal" ones.

While it is true that NAF publishes standards for the operation of abortion clinics, they openly admit that they have no way of enforcing them, even within their own membership. Suzanne Poppema, head of NAF's Clinical Guidelines Committee, recently pointed out that NAF "has no credentialing power ... [it] isn't a board," and therefore has no enforcement power. Warren Hern—who is a NAF board member, former head of its Clinical Guidelines Committee, and author of the book *Abortion Practice*—helped write NAF's abortion standards, but now calls them "ornamental," "cosmetic," and "meaningless." He admits that NAF "has never pursued a serious program of standards implementation and program evaluation," adding that, "Following good standards costs money. And people don't want to do that." He also pointed out that NAF has never implemented a system to monitor whether its facilities are following its standards.[2]

Not only does NAF lack the power to enforce its standards, it clearly doesn't want anyone else enforcing them either. When the CBS news show *60 Minutes* did a story about a Maryland abortion clinic that had killed at least two women during botched abortions in 1989, they asked Barbara Radford, executive director of NAF, if they knew about these problems. She responded that NAF was aware of them, but had decided to remain silent because, "This is the last thing we need. We had hoped that it wouldn't get national publicity because of the political nature of all this." *60 Minutes* reported that they discovered other pro-choice activists who also knew about the problems at this clinic, but who remained silent out of fear that the bad publicity would prompt state legislators to start regulating clinics. The *60 Minutes* reporter, Marilyn Viero, pointed out that even though these laws could make clinics safer, abortion advocates usually fight them. That was reaffirmed when she interviewed pro-choice State Senator Mary Boergers about regulating abortion clinics. Boergers said, "There's only so much of a willingness to try to push a group like the pro-choice movement to do what I think is the responsible thing to do because they then treat you as if you're the enemy." Radford tried to justify NAF's position: "We want to make sure that women have choices when it comes to abortion services, and if you regulate it too strictly, you then deny women the access to service."[3]

Apparently, Radford believes that the goal of legalizing abortion was to make it cheap and widespread, rather than safe. Furthermore, by admitting that they knew of these instances and yet remained silent in the hope that the media wouldn't find out, these pro-choice activists were really saying that they are willing to sacrifice women to protect their political agenda. It is exactly like a police department remaining silent about the fact that a serial rapist is loose in their city, to avoid embarrassment over not having caught him.

One service NAF offers is an 800 number that abortion-minded women can call for information about NAF member clinics and doctors. In October 1995, we decided to see what they would tell a woman who called and asked about a particular NAF abortionist. In Chapter 1 is a story about "Deanna," a 13-year-old who died from a massive overdose of anesthesia during an abortion at a NAF facility. It turns out that the abortionist involved is very active in NAF. When a Life Dynamics (LDI) employee called, she was told by the counselor, "Stacey," that this abortionist is "a very, very excellent doctor; very well respected."

When the LDI employee indicated that she had heard something about an abortion being botched at this facility, Stacey interrupted, "All of the complications are reported here, and if there is an excessive amount of complications, or unnecessary complications, they would not be members of the National Abortion Federation." When pressed, she said that this story about a botched abortion was "just a rumor."

At that point, the LDI staffer got even more specific, saying that her brother-in-law had told her to ask about someone named Deanna who had died at this clinic. Stacey then asked the LDI employee to hold for a moment. When she returned, she suggested that the brother-in-law was confused, and had Deanna mixed-up with another girl who died from "an illegal abortion.

She hadn't called the National Abortion Federation; she obviously did not go to a NAF member." Stacey went on to suggest that the brother-in-law "might be an anti-choice person." When the LDI employee again brought up Deanna, Stacey was even more emphatic that there was a mistaken identity, saying "it was not a NAF doctor. Basically she wasn't aware that there was an organization that could refer her to a clinic…There are still poor abortions performed in the United States, not by NAF doctors. All of our physicians are licensed by the state…the risks are very, very, very minimum…All our physicians are licensed by the state; they're all trained, skilled providers, and they're all very, very excellent clinics."

We had contacted NAF the day before this conversation, asking them to fax us their protocol for dealing with complaints and complications, as well as their quarterly complication reports. The person we talked to, Susan Shapiro, agreed to send us the material. Following the conversation with Stacey, we called Susan back to inquire about the fax, as we had not yet received it. At this point, she reversed her previous position, saying, "Since you're not a member, I can't send them to you." As the conversation continued, we asked what their policy would be if a consumer called the 800 number with a question about a facility:

> SS: "Um, well, we just only refer people to NAF members, so as long as they're checked out and they were fine, we could refer them to them."
>
> LDI: "Okay, and if they asked if there was malpractice or deaths at that facility or by that practitioner, would you inform them?"
>
> SS: "We don't have that—no, we would not inform them of anything specific, unless there was a problem. Then they wouldn't be NAF members if there was something—if there was a serious problem, and if the complications were—were serious, you know. Our NAF members are the best abortion providers in the country."

The next day, we called Ms. Shapiro back and became more specific:

> LDI: "Since you said that you would not inform a consumer of anything specific unless there was a major problem, in which case the person would no longer be a NAF member, what do you do in the case of something like [John Roe 479] in Chicago, where he had that 13-year-old girl die? Would you tell a

consumer about that if she asked if anyone had died at that clinic?"

SS: "Well, I don't have that information, and our—the people that work on the hotline don't have that information readily available, and they tell the person on the phone, 'We just don't have that information readily available right now.' Their basic goal is to refer them to a NAF member clinic, and that's what they do. They don't get into specifics on the phone."

LDI: "Okay, so if..."

SS: "We don't say yes, we don't say no. They don't know on the phone."

LDI: "Even in a case like the situation with [Roe 479] where there was a death, and the consumer specifically asked 'Was there a death?', your hotline counselors would not even have access to that information to share it?"

SS: "Right. And they would say—they would not say, 'No, there was not a death.' They would say, 'I don't have that information.' And we can give them the number of the medical board and they could research that themselves. But if it was something that a doctor lost his license, he wouldn't be a NAF member, or lost his privileges at a hospital."[4]

Obviously, when NAF thought they were talking to a potential customer, their story was considerably different than when they knew they were talking to Life Dynamics. We chose the "Deanna" case because the abortion occurred in one of NAF's flagship clinics and was performed by one of its premier abortionists, John Roe 479. In fact, he is a regular presenter at NAF conventions.

To prove that their willingness to cover for bad practitioners was not a fluke, we made another call to NAF on November 10, 1995. This time we had an employee (Lisa) pose as a pregnant 15-year-old from Aurora, Colorado. We selected this city because two weeks earlier a NAF abortion provider from that area, Acme Reproductive Services 50, settled a major abortion malpractice lawsuit. We wanted to hear what NAF would tell a client about that incident. The first part of the conversation was pretty routine. Then, after the counselor ("Linda") referred Lisa to ARS 50, Lisa started asking more pointed questions:

Lisa: "And it's a real doctor that's going to do [the abortion], right?"

Linda: "Yeah, it's a very good clinic."

Lisa: "Do you know who?"

Linda: "I don't; I can't give you the name of the doctor..."

Lisa: "Okay."

Linda: "...but we check out all of our clinics to make sure they're very good places."

Lisa: "And also, I've been so nervous because there's been on the news that this girl was—I guess she's in a coma or something because she had an abortion a couple years ago, and I'm so scared that something like that would ever happen to me because then my parents would know, and..."

Linda: "Yeah. This is actually—it's a very safe procedure. It's the safest surgical procedure in the United States. So it's safer than having your tonsils out. There are fewer complications. There's a very, very low likelihood that anything is going to go wrong."

Lisa: "Okay. So that was just like a fluke or something?"

Linda: "Yeah, yeah. And, you know, we know these are very good clinics, so probably the likelihood that something's going to go wrong at this clinic is even less than normal. 'Cause it is a good place."[5]

At this point, the conversation returned to the routine issues: "How much does it cost?" "Will it hurt?" "How long will it take?" and so on. Since Linda was obviously trying to avoid talking about the situation at ARS 50, we decided to have Lisa call back the next day with questions that were more focused on that subject:

Linda: "National Abortion Federation Hotline. How can I help you?"

Lisa: "Hi, is this Linda?"

Linda: "Yes, it is."

Lisa: "Hi. I called you earlier. I'm the one who was so nervous about going for an abortion in Aurora. And, um, I've been trying to get the money together and everything."

Linda: "Okay."

Lisa: "And I talked to one of my friend's mom, 'cause my friend thought her mom would lend me the money, and it turns out that, um, this lady, um—well, her daughter didn't think she'd be like this, but she's not really all that keen on abortion and everything, I guess, and, um, she was telling me that she thinks [ARS 50] is the place that that girl that I told you about ended up in a coma."

Linda: "Uh-huh."

Lisa: "And I was wondering if you know anything about that or…"

Linda: "Um, I think what, I'm not sure, but this may be the case, um, where there was a—she had some sort of condition, and I don't know and I can't say any of this officially, but she had some sort of condition that was not related to any of the procedure itself. It was a problem she had, she had a bad reaction—it was a strange thing, but it wasn't anything—there was nothing, nothing medically wrong with the procedure. Um, it's just kind of a—it was really a fluke kind of thing. Um…"

Lisa: "So the abortionist didn't do anything wrong or anything. It was just…"

Linda: "No, the doctor—there's no, like no problem on their part. It was that her body had a strange reaction. Um…"

Lisa: "To the abortion or the medication or…"

Linda: "To, to the procedure. And it wasn't—this was a totally—this is a very rare, very rare thing. Um, and it's not a normal thing. It could have been—it could have been anything for her that would have set off this, um, this problem."

Lisa: "I don't know if I have something like that that could make something go wrong, though, you know?"

Linda: "Yeah, you know, you probably don't. Like, you know, and I can't say you definitely don't, but it's probably, you know, one in every million people that have it or something. The chances are very rare. I mean, it's like saying, you know, you shouldn't drive because there are car accidents and people die. You know, it's, yeah, but you go in the car anyway because you know that the chances are very rare that that's going to happen. It's the same kind of thing with this. Like, there are risks involved. They are very low risks. Um, there are things that you can do to reduce those risks."

As the conversation continued, Linda kept telling Lisa how safe abortions are, especially those performed at NAF facilities. Lisa was told for a second time that abortion is "a safer procedure than even having your tonsils out," and on four occasions she was told that an abortion is safer than giving birth, regardless of the stage of the pregnancy at which the abortion is performed. We found that to be an especially odious assertion, since Lisa never once asked what the relative risks were between abortion and child birth. Clearly, this "counselor" was determined to convince Lisa that she was in more danger from not having an abortion than from having one. She even went so far as to suggest that whatever happened to the girl who is in a coma following her abortion could have happened if she had continued the pregnancy. That seems a strange position considering the fact that she claims she didn't know what actually happened. When Lisa again expressed her concern that ARS 50 is the place where this girl was injured, Linda countered with:

Linda: "That's possible. Um, you know, that doesn't—we've followed up on that here. There was nothing that they could do to prevent that. It was, like, out of their hands. It was—I can't really explain it, but, um..."

Lisa: "Well, do you know what happened to the girl now, or anything? Do you know if she's okay?"

Linda: "No, I don't know. I don't know, you know, what happened. I, I haven't followed that."

Lisa: "Yeah."

Linda: "But you're always—there's always going to be stories, you know, for everything. And they're scary, and, you're saying, gosh, you know, 'What if that happens to me?' There's always that, and you need to, like, think about it as it's an incredibly unlikely chance that that's going to happen. And you kind of have to go from there. It's like, I don't know, it's like everything you do in your life. There are risks involved. It's like when you go to the bathroom and the floor is wet. There's a risk. You know, there is someone in this country, maybe someone even around you that has fallen in the bathroom and died, but you still go to the bathroom. You know, it's not—and this is a different thing, because this involves a decision, but what I'm saying is that the risks are very rare. You know, it's very low, and you need to consider them, but also realize that carrying to term, there are more risks involved. So if that's your only decision for not having an abortion, then, you know, you need to rethink that."

In the blink of an eye, Linda went from having followed the situation well enough to know that what happened wasn't their clinic's fault and that there was nothing they could have done to prevent it, to not having followed it well enough to know what happened to the woman involved.

The facts are that on her eighteenth birthday, July 1, 1993, a perfectly healthy "Christi" went to ARS 50 for an abortion. Less than three hours later, after complications related to the anesthesia, she was blind and in a permanent vegetative state. Furthermore, what happened to her had absolutely nothing to do with a problem she already had, it was not a fluke, and NAF's contention that Christi's injuries were beyond the control of the clinic's staff is simply a lie. Even though they were administering powerful anesthetic drugs, the abortionist involved was not trained in anesthesia and no one on the staff was trained to handle an anesthesia complication. Additionally, the clinic had no respiratory or heart-monitoring equipment, nor any of the equipment necessary to handle an anesthesia emergency.[6] Because of this reprehensible behavior, Christi now wastes her life away, requires 24-hour-a-day care, and is fed through a tube in her abdomen. And her doctors say that she will never get any better.

Of course, abortion apologists dismiss events like this as rare and unavoidable accidents. But this kind of callous irresponsibility is not an accident. When someone who is drunk makes a conscious decision to get behind the wheel of a car, the destruction he causes is not an accident. In the same light, when an abortion clinic puts an 18-year-old girl under general anesthesia knowing that they are not qualified to do so, and are not equipped to handle an emergency, the harm done to her is no accident. And unfortunately, as Chapter 1 shows, incidents such as this are not at all rare.

Another interesting issue is that prior to Christi being injured, a Colorado dentist was involved in an almost identical situation with one of his patients. He too was untrained in anesthesia, and lacked monitoring and emergency equipment. After his patient died, the Colorado Dental Board implemented much tougher regulations on dentists to prevent this sort of thing from recurring in the future.[7] That's called self-policing. In the wake of Christi's tragedy, the abortion industry has done nothing similar. That's called self-serving.

Although the National Abortion Federation publishes standards of conduct for abortion clinics, it lacks both the power and the will to enforce them. Instead, it is what one of its own former members called it: "a group of abortion providers that bind together for the purpose of their own benefit."[8] We found incident after incident proving that women entering NAF clinics find pretty much the same conditions that they would find at any independent, free-standing abortion facility. The decor may be more tasteful, the paperwork more professional, and the sales pitch more polished, but none of this makes it any less likely that she will end up butchered, sexually assaulted, or dead. Even with our limited resources, we found over 330 lawsuits or other substantiated cases of malpractice, including 21 deaths, by NAF members or at NAF member clinics. And this does not include cases against people we could not confirm as NAF members.

After a patient died, the Colorado Dental Board implemented much tougher regulations on dentists. That's called self-policing. In the wake of Christi's tragedy, the abortion industry has done nothing similar. That's called self-serving.

The apparent problem with NAF is its focus. In looking at how it operates, it is clear that NAF sees its mission as protecting the abortionist, not his patients. No better proof of that exists than two meetings NAF sponsored in 1994. At the first, NAF's 18th Annual Meeting on April 24–26, Colorado abortionist Dr. Warren Hern—identified earlier as a NAF board member, former head of its Clinical Guidelines Committee, and author of the book *Abortion Practice*—addressed the group. He was attacked by some in attendance for his willingness to review potential abortion-malpractice cases to see if a violation in the standard of care had occurred. He also provides expert witness testimony in cases where he feels that such a violation caused a patient harm. Defending his practice of working with pro-life groups and individuals, he said, "I do not conceal my views from these people, but I have to say this—there's a lot of crummy medicine being practiced out there in providing abortion services, and I think that some of the stuff I see coming across my desk is very upsetting. And I think that I have said for 20 years in this movement, we have to do this right or we shouldn't do it…If we're not practicing good medicine, we're gonna get nailed."

At that point, he was cut off and the topic changed. After a bit more discussion by others on the evils of malpractice suits, Hern spoke up again, but stammering and clearly disturbed. "I think that our best defense is to practice good medicine. I think if you follow the NAF standards and you really try to do that, you're gonna be in good shape," Hern said. "I think that your colleagues who are being called to do this [reviewing cases and testifying] are not going to nail people who are practicing good medicine. But, I think if you're not practicing good medicine, it is gonna be very difficult to defend a bad case, okay—that's all."

Again, Dr. Hern was cut off and the topic changed. For the remainder of the time, the discussion centered around legal strategies for avoiding suits, rather than medical strategies for preventing injuries and deaths. Additional discussion focused on how to attack the women who sue, including ideas about how to discredit, frighten, and/or intimidate them into dropping their suits. Hern spoke up yet again, trying to get the discussion onto providing quality care. He stressed that there was a lot of bad practice that he wanted to see eliminated. Again, his opinion was summarily dismissed, and the discussion returned to attacking the injured woman, her attorney, and any individuals or organizations helping with her case.[9]

By September of that year, NAF was getting even more frantic about malpractice suits. For their Fall Risk Management Seminar, they brought in a malpractice consultant. She told the group, "There are a lot of really bad abortion places out there…" and then discussed some tactics they could use to manage lawsuits that arise from an abortion injury. However, to her credit, the basic thrust of her presentation was that the most effective way not to get sued for malpractice is to not commit malpractice. And once again, Dr. Hern offered his opinion that, "The way to keep from being sued by these idiots is to practice good medicine. It's really very, very simple."

However, as it was in the April meeting, this view was completely discounted, and the theme of the seminar reverted to how to manage malpractice suits, not how to avoid causing injuries in the first place. Discussions were held about the need to do the following things: keep clinic records as vague as possible; keep written records to a bare minimum; keep employees from knowing too much so that if they quit they can't testify in a malpractice action; get crisis pregnancy centers out of the phone book so women won't know who to call if they get injured; and harass attorneys who represent women injured by abortion. One presenter even offered to supply a list of the attorneys who attended the Life Dynamics Abortion Malpractice Conference to anyone who would target them.

The list of "action plans" went on and on, but the underlying theme was the same and typified by an attendee who lamented that, "We do have bad practitioners. And it's affecting all of us. And we have been reluctant to do anything or say anything or whatever because of the physician shortage. We don't want bad press, but when something happens, under our breaths we all say, 'Well, it was just a matter of time.' You know, that stuff is going to come to the surface more and more... I want to know how we can control this."[10]

The seminar discussion centered around legal strategies for avoiding suits, rather than medical strategies for preventing injuries and deaths.

Apparently, Hern is finding that his position continues to be out of favor with NAF and the rest of the abortion industry. Five months after this seminar, he commented about the abortion malpractice campaign being implemented by Life Dynamics, saying, "In my view, there are many legitimate cases that would not happen if people were following good standards of medical practice... There are people out there providing abortion services that do not recognize fundamental principles of surgery."[11]

Planned Parenthood

In 1992, Life Dynamics created a new "abortion-rights" group called Project Choice. Our goal was to go undercover, infiltrate the abortion industry, and gain information that we had no other way of getting. (More about that in Chapter 5.) One of the things we discovered is that among certain quarters of that industry there exists a sort of mental caste system. In simple terms, one of the factions in the abortion-rights community thinks it is better than all the others. That group is Planned Parenthood. To hear them tell the story, all the disgusting things that appear in the press about bad abortionists, filthy clinics, or criminal behavior by abortion clinic personnel is never about a Planned Parenthood affiliate. While undercover, when we would ask someone from Planned Parenthood about an example of shoddy behavior, we would consistently hear things like, "Oh, that must have been a NAF clinic or an independent. You'd never hear of such a thing from Planned Parenthood," or "We'd never do something like that; Planned Parenthood is better than that." To put it mildly, Planned Parenthood people were seldom bashful about the fact that they viewed everyone else in the abortion industry as the scum of the movement. We found this view especially hypocritical since many Planned Parenthood facilities that don't do abortions actually refer women to NAF and independent abortion clinics.

The question is whether this arrogance has any basis in fact. Is Planned Parenthood really better than the rest of the abortion industry? The answer is yes and no. During the research for this book, our observation was that a woman probably is less likely to be injured, raped, or killed at a Planned Parenthood facility than at a non-Planned Parenthood facility. On the other hand, the difference is insignificant and in no way justifies their "holier-than-thou" attitude. About the best they could claim to be is the cream of a rotten crop. In our research, we were able to identify approximately 100 lawsuits and/or disciplinary board actions against Planned Parenthood facilities, with complaints covering virtually the entire range of problems seen at other abortion clinics. We also found many examples of Planned Parenthood clinics operating in the same filthy conditions, and with the same outrageous practices, as NAF or independent abortion clinics. And again, the dynamics I've mentioned elsewhere apply here: The cases we found can be no more than a fraction of what really exists.

Generally speaking, with few functional differences, the typical NAF, independent, and Planned Parenthood abortion clinics are indistinguishable. The most obvious thing separating Planned Parenthood from the rest of the pack is the arrogance I mentioned earlier. When a NAF clinic gets caught doing something, they will usually try to lie their way out of it. Even when the evidence is stacked against them, they'll claim it never happened and is instead part of a vendetta by some pro-life group or over-zealous bureaucrat. And while Planned Parenthood clinics are certainly not above trying that same stunt, more often than not they'll own up to the charge but say there was no impropriety. Then they'll stick their nose in the air and suggest that the real problem is that the rest of us—the great unwashed masses—are simply not smart enough to understand why they did whatever it is they're accused of doing. Just name the social issue, and Planned Parenthood will not hesitate to tell you that they are the experts.

A good example of this arrogance is seen in a situation that happened in Tennessee. In October 1990, "Charity's" stepfather murdered her mother, then killed himself after his sexual abuse of Charity's older sister was revealed. Charity, then 14 years old, moved in with her grandmother. Six months later, her biological father called her, threatening to commit suicide unless she came to live with him. After she refused, he hanged himself.

Quite understandably, these events caused Charity to end up in a psychiatric hospital. For about a month and a half, she was treated for post-traumatic stress disorder, dysthymic disorder, and oppositional defiant disorder, and released. Then, on January 19, 1993, Charity told her 17-year-old boyfriend that she believed she was pregnant. Two days later, he took her to a Planned Parenthood facility where she was counseled by an employee who also happened to be the mother of her boyfriend. After being told that she was 11 to 12 weeks pregnant, Charity insisted that she would never consider an abortion, despite pressure to do so from both her boyfriend and his mother. Her boyfriend then started calling her nightly, threatening to commit suicide if she did not have an abortion. His mother also played a role, telling Charity that in refusing to get an abortion she was not thinking of the best interests of the boy who got her pregnant. The boyfriend took Charity to Planned Parenthood again on January 25 for counseling by another woman, at which time Charity reiterated that she did not want an abortion.

On January 27, the boyfriend and his mother took Charity back to Planned Parenthood, where she repeated that she would not consider having an abortion. After her boyfriend again threatened suicide, the second counselor asked Charity to sign a written consent form, telling her that there was no need to read it. At this point, Charity gave in. Immediately afterward, the medical director of this facility performed an abortion on her, knowing that she had repeatedly stated she did not want one. Two weeks later, she was taken to an emergency room and admitted to the psychiatric unit. She remained hospitalized until March 9, and was diagnosed with major recurrent depression and thoughts of suicide as a result of being pressured to get an abortion. She also began demonstrating a pattern of increasing alcohol and drug abuse. Charity was discharged to her grandmother's care, but the psychological damage she exhibited was so severe that she was eventually placed in the custody of the Tennessee Department of Human Services at a temporary residence for adolescents in crisis.[12]

Incredibly, the Planned Parenthood facility involved continues to deny any wrongdoing, even though it allowed Charity to be counseled by a particular employee, knowing Charity was pregnant by that employee's son, and performed an abortion on this troubled young girl, completely aware that she consistently said she didn't want one. Today, Planned Parenthood contends that Charity alone must bear responsibility for the damages she sustained because she signed a consent form for the abortion.

This disgraceful type of arrogance goes beyond just their attitude toward their abortion industry colleagues and their clients. For some unexplained reason, they sometimes seem to believe that laws passed regulating abortion don't apply to them. They have also demonstrated an unhealthy enthusiasm for taking over the parental role in the lives of American children. One example of both these phenomena involves "Kathy," a pregnant 16-year-old. When her mother sought prenatal care for her, she learned that her daughter had an abnormality of the cervix and womb, and that an abortion could present a threat to her health, leave her unable to carry future children to term, or even result in her death. In spite of that, Kathy made clandestine plans to have an abortion. However, her mother learned of her intentions and got a court injunction against the area abortion facilities, preventing them from performing surgery on her daughter.

Despite inserting themselves between a child and her parent, disregarding the stated wishes of the mother, ignoring the advice of a physician, and violating two court orders— Planned Parenthood claims they did nothing wrong.

The order was issued on May 14, 1986. Among those served was John Roe 851, executive director of a local Planned Parenthood facility, who ordered his staff to notify him if Kathy appeared at the offices. When she did so, Roe and a staff counselor told her that in spite of the injunction she could obtain an abortion in a bordering state. Roe also told Kathy that the restraining order would not prevent him from assisting her in obtaining an abortion, and that "Planned Parenthood was not bound by local laws and courts." Kathy later said they never asked her about the medical condition upon which the injunction was based. Instead, they contacted an out-of-state abortion clinic and made an appointment for her. Additionally, in callous disregard for Kathy's well-being, they never informed the personnel at this abortion clinic about the medical complications that led to the injunction.

Kathy's mother learned of these arrangements and had an additional restraining order served, preventing Planned Parenthood from counseling Kathy for an abortion. She also contacted the Planned Parenthood staff, asking for the name of the abortion clinic at which they had scheduled Kathy for an abortion. She wanted to make the people there aware of her daughter's medical complications and risks, but Planned Parenthood refused to provide her with that information.

The next day Kathy had her abortion. She ended up in an emergency room with sepsis, a potentially life-threatening infection. Eventually, both Kathy and her mother filed suits against Planned Parenthood, but its attorneys were able to get the cases transferred to a jurisdiction where a judge would dismiss them.[13] (If there is one thing in which Planned Parenthood is undeniably an expert, it is the hiring of good lawyers.)

Again, Planned Parenthood claims that they did nothing wrong here. Despite the fact that they inserted themselves between a child and her parent, totally disregarded the stated wishes of the mother, ignored the advice of a physician who had examined the daughter, and violated two court orders— *they did nothing wrong*. Like the case of "Charity" mentioned earlier, this is classic Planned Parenthood.

Another interesting tactic of theirs involves the standards manual that they produce for the operation of their affiliates. We've tried several times to obtain one from them, only to be denied. We've been repeatedly told that they are confidential, not for public release, etc. It seems odd that an organization that brags about its high standards would want to hide them. Most organizations would behave in the opposite fashion. If they demand high standards of their affiliates, only good can come from as many people knowing about it as possible. Of course, if the organization created these standards as nothing more than a legal tool to insulate themselves against lawsuits, and doesn't actually demand that its affiliates abide by them, then a wide distribution is risky.

And that appears to be the case here. Planned Parenthood knows that if one of their facilities is found violating their own published guidelines, it is not just a public relations nightmare but practically an admission of guilt in a malpractice action. And not only would the individual facility be exposed, but Planned Parenthood's failure to enforce its standards would probably make them liable as well. Therefore, it is in their best interests to see that the injured woman's attorney doesn't have access to the standards. That would explain why they don't want their standards made public.

On November 9, 1995, we decided to talk directly to Planned Parenthood about their standards, especially as they relate to John Roe 326, the medical director of one of their facilities in Missouri. This particular abortionist has a very unenviable track record, with at least 12 abortion malpractice actions against him, including two in which women died. After avoiding us for two days, we finally cornered Ann Glazier, a spokesperson at Planned Parenthood's national office. We asked her if Planned Parenthood furnished its affiliates with a protocol for hiring doctors. She said they did, but that they were proprietary. When we asked how someone with Roe 326's background could pass any sort of reasonable hiring protocol, she told us that we would have to talk to Roe himself. She was actually suggesting that we call Roe and ask him why someone with his abysmal history would pass Planned Parenthood's protocol for hiring. The whole conversation was, I believe, a textbook example of the circular logic used by someone who knows that her position is indefensible:

LDI: "How are we going to [get] a copy of the protocol for hiring physicians?"

AG: "That's proprietary information. We don't release that."

LDI: "Okay, um, so it would only be available to members?"

AG: "Yeah. If you're an official Planned Parenthood certified affiliate."

LDI: "Uh-huh. Okay. What about situations such as Dr. [Roe] that would really raise some questions? He does have, um, quite a bit of malpractice in his background. We have quite a number of some very alarming-looking suits here. But he's a medical director of Planned Parenthood in, I believe it's Missouri. Let's see. Yes, Missouri. And, um, I just have, uh, some trouble understanding how somebody with this kind of background would be able to pass a protocol."

AG: "You'll have to talk to Dr. [Roe]."

LDI: "I would have to speak with Dr. [Roe] directly?"

AG: "Yes."

LDI: "Okay, so, um, Planned Parenthood does have protocol for dealing with situations like this, but you do not reveal it to anybody but, um, your member facilities?"

AG: "I didn't say that."

LDI: "Okay. Can you clarify for me then, since I'm obviously not understanding you?"

AG: "I said I don't release the information. We don't release the information you've asked for. It's proprietary."

LDI: "Okay. Which means it's only for affiliates."

AG: "Yes."

LDI: "Uh-huh. So if a patient were to call with a question about Dr. [Roe's] background, if she was concerned, she had heard about these cases—would she be able to get an answer about his background?"

AG: "I'm not going to discuss that with you."

LDI: "Uh-huh. Okay. So there is no way—is there any way that somebody who is not a Planned Parenthood affiliate would be able to find out how somebody with this kind of background is working at a Planned Parenthood facility?"

AG: "They could call me."

LDI: "I am calling you."

AG: "And I'm telling you the information you've asked for is proprietary and I'm not going to release it."

LDI: "To whom would you release it?"

AG: "I'm not going to discuss that with you."[14]

By this time, it was clear that we were just chasing our tail by talking to this woman. She had no plausible explanation for why Planned Parenthood hides their standards, because there simply isn't one. The fact is, they can't afford to make them public for the reason I stated earlier. They know these guidelines would come back to haunt them in some future malpractice trial, but since she obviously can't say that, she is relegated to the nonsense above. (The day after this conversation, Ms. Glazier sent a fax to all of their U.S. affiliates warning that LDI was trying to get these standards, and reminding them that they are proprietary.)

What Ms. Glazier didn't know was that we had already called the Missouri abortion clinic that hired Roe, and at which he still works. We talked to the director of that facility, who admitted that she knew of Roe's history when she hired him. As we found with the national Planned Parenthood office, she would not provide us with a copy of the phantom hiring protocol, but when asked whether employing somebody with his questionable background was in violation of it, she was emphatic that it was not. Then, we asked what she would tell a patient who inquired about his malpractice history. Her reply was that she "was not in the business" of giving out that sort of information. She repeated that answer when we asked what she would tell a woman who specifically asked whether he had ever killed a patient during an abortion. When we pressed her for what she thought women should do to find out if Roe was competent, she suggested they contact the AMA, or the state board of medical examiners, or the courthouses in the states where he practices. (Some of Roe's problems were in Texas.)

At this point, it was clear that she was trying to hop-scotch around the issue. No one can seriously believe that a fifteen-year-old girl in a crisis pregnancy situation is going to call the American Medical Association in Chicago, the Texas Board of Medical Examiners in Austin, the Missouri Board of Medical Examiners in Jefferson City, and then start sifting through courthouse records in two states. Of course, the real question is why she should have to when the person she's talking to at Planned Parenthood already has that information. When we asked Ms. Glazier whether she thought it was reasonable to expect this kind of effort out of a woman in this situation, her answer was, "Well, uh, I have to tell you that, uh, I have all the confidence in Dr. [Roe's] skills and judgment."[15]

Again, a Planned Parenthood associate was proving to us that they are unequaled in question-avoidance techniques, and we abandoned the chase. But before doing so, we found out that Planned Parenthood also provides a referral protocol to their facilities that don't do abortions. This is apparently to ensure that any abortion clinic to which they send patients meets Planned Parenthood's standards. Naturally, we were told that we couldn't have a copy of these referral standards either, because they are—you guessed it—proprietary. By now, I'm convinced that I would have a better chance of getting the formula for Coca-Cola than I would of getting a copy of Planned Parenthood's standards for running an abortion clinic. I visualize them lying majestically on a white marble altar in some distant cave, perpetually bathed in a golden light of unknown origin, while a host of angels sing in the background.

Back in the real world, we were somewhat suspicious of Planned Parenthood's claim to have such high standards for the clinics they refer to, since it was they who referred Christi to ARS 50. So we decided to contact other Planned Parenthood facilities and see where they would send us. While we found several examples of Planned Parenthood referring women to people who were, at best, questionable, one referral really caught our attention. On November 10, 1995, we had an employee call a Planned Parenthood hotline in California asking where she could go to terminate her 20-week pregnancy. The number they gave her was for an organization that runs a chain of abortion clinics. We were already very aware of this group, having identified eight women who died as a result of abortions performed by them, plus over 70 other documented allegations relating to botched abortions. Among many other things, patients and health department officials have alleged that this organization performs abortions on women who are not pregnant, falsifies medical records, pays kickbacks for abortion referrals, maintains unsanitary and unsterile conditions, improperly maintains its medical equipment, and allows non-physicians to practice medicine. The California Department of Health Services once said that this chain's primary abortion clinic "lacks the ability to conform to licensing requirements and is not of reputable and responsible character."[16] Apparently, however, their character and ability is good enough for Planned Parenthood.

In the section on NAF, I asserted that abortion advocates have shown a willingness to sacrifice women to protect their political agenda. To illustrate that point, I used the example of them admitting to *60 Minutes* that they remained silent even though they knew about an abortion clinic where women were being killed and injured.

Be assured that while Planned Parenthood can posture all they want about being both morally and intellectually superior to the rest of the abortion industry, the fact is that they are neither. They too have shown that they will martyr women for political reasons. For example, in a segment on NBC's *Dateline* about a study indicating that an abortion might increase a woman's risk of breast cancer, the following dialog took place between *Dateline*'s reporter and Pamela Maraldo, then-president of Planned Parenthood:

> Reporter: "If indeed your panel of medical experts studies this study by Dr. Daling and you find it to be solid good science, what are the chances you will begin warning women about this possible link?"
>
> Maraldo: "Even if it's solid good science, then to begin to warn women, and upset women, on the basis of one study is clearly irresponsible. One study is not an adequate, uh, uh—evidence for us to change a policy, or—or to upset or frighten women."
>
> Reporter: "Five studies—say you have five studies?"
>
> Maraldo: "Well I think we're a long ways away from that."[17]

Not only are Maraldo's remarks undeniably patronizing and insulting to women, but they are dishonest. The Daling study is not the only one suggesting this link, but simply the latest. There are actually over two dozen, and Maraldo is aware of them (see Chapter 6). Therefore, when she asserts that "we're a long ways away from" five studies showing a link between abortion and breast cancer, she is lying. And again, Planned Parenthood is displaying their unmatched arrogance. She readily admits that even if her own experts found the information credible, that would not be enough to "change a policy"—regardless of the implications for women. Since she's simply talking about a *Planned Parenthood* policy, she apparently believes that their policies came down the mountain with Moses. I also point out that—for all their bleating about how much they care for women—since this program aired they have yet to demand further investigation into whether abortion causes breast cancer. They aren't studying it themselves, and neither are they demanding that the government do so. Call me cynical, but I suspect they're silent on the issue, not because they're convinced that abortion does not cause breast cancer, but because they're afraid that it does.

The Dark Legacy

Those in the abortion-rights movement say that they want abortion to be safe and legal. However, the *safe* and *legal* aspects are often at odds with each other. And when that happens, the abortion industry has always been willing to sacrifice women for their political objective. Please note that I did not say they are enthusiastic about sacrificing women, but that they are *willing* to do so. I don't believe that these people enter this arena with either the intent or the desire to harm women; it's just that when they have to choose between safe and legal, they always choose legal.

A good example of that was seen when a Florida newspaper ran a story about a Miami area abortion clinic that no one could describe as anything other than a cesspool. The place was filthy, and being run by a woman with a police record with convictions ranging from hit-and-run to cocaine possession. At one point, she actually received her paycheck from the clinic while in jail. Her brother, a clinic "go-fer," also ended up in prison as an ax murderer. One of the clinic's abortionists had even lost his license in another state for having sexual intercourse with a 14-year-old. After another abortionist quit, he described the place as "a scum hole," and commented, "I wouldn't send a dog in there…they should be put in jail."

After the death of one woman and the butchering of a few more, the story became public. And as always happens when the light finally shines on one of these places, local abortion advocates crawled out of the woodwork to reluctantly admit that they knew what was going on, but kept silent for political reasons. The newspaper quoted a local full-time pro-choice activist, Janis Compton-Carr, as saying, "In my gut, I am completely aghast at what goes on at that place. But I staunchly oppose anything that would correct this situation in law."[18]

Ms. Carr was simply articulating what is a long and honored tradition within the American abortion-rights movement. The operative attitude is: safe if possible, but legal regardless. Of course, for abortion advocates that attitude is made somewhat more palatable by the fact that it's always someone else who pays the cost when safety is traded for legality.

A classic example of this phenomenon is the issue of instillation abortions. The first instillation abortion technique was developed in Rumania in 1939. It used a strong saline solution that was injected directly into the amniotic fluid. After World War II, the saline abortion technique was adopted and used extensively in Japan with many serious effects being reported. In only five years, at least 60 women were known to have died of saline abortion complications, and over 70 papers were published documenting the hazards of this technique. After the Japanese Obstetrical and Gynecological Society declared the risks too great, Japan quickly abandoned saline and adopted other abortion methods that were less likely to injure or kill the mother.[19]

Little was known of this experience outside Japan until other countries began popularizing the saline technique. Two Japanese doctors, Takashi Wagatsuma and Yukio Manabe, were appalled by the Western nation's enthusiasm for saline. They each published a number of articles and letters in Western medical journals, revealing to the world the disastrous results of the Japanese experience with saline. In 1965, Wagatsuma wrote that, due to the increasing popularity of saline, "It is, I think, worthwhile to report its rather disastrous consequences which we experienced in Japan."[20] Manabe virtually begged the United States and Great Britain to use safer methods. "It is now known," he wrote, "that any solution placed within the uterus can be absorbed rather rapidly into the general circulation through the vascular system of the uterus and placenta. Thus, any solution used in the uterus for abortion must be absolutely safe even if given by direct intravenous injection." He stressed, "A solution deadly to the fetus may be equally toxic and dangerous to the mother." He acknowledged that many Western abortionists dismissed the Japanese tragedy with an assertion that the Japanese were untrained and worked in dirty facilities, but he pointed out that if the facilities rather than the technique had been at fault, the Japanese would not have been able to improve their maternal mortality rate immediately upon abandoning saline instillation. He pointed out that other countries had experiences similar to those in Japan. "In spite of the accumulating undesirable reports, the use of hypertonic saline for abortion is still advocated and used...in the United

States and Great Britain. I would like to call attention to the danger of the method and would predict the further occurrence of deaths until this method is entirely forgotten in these countries."[21]

Some Westerners did express misgivings about saline. In 1966, British researchers noted that instillation abortions could cause damage to the brain and spinal cord. They found that once hypertonic saline enters the blood stream, the salt-rich blood of the patient draws fluid out of the brain cells. Just as the woman's kidneys were flushing out the excess saline, the body would pump extra fluid into the brain to offset the dehydration. As a result, her brain would swell. The authors noted that "the amniotic-fluid-replacement technique for inducing abortions should be used with caution until further information is available of any potential danger to the mother."[22]

By the mid-1960s, the data against saline was simply overwhelming. But that didn't dissuade the American pro-choice community. In the same year that Manabe published his warning, a 27-year-old California woman became what may be the first verified death from a saline abortion in the United States. After the legal procedure was performed at a Sacramento hospital, she died from cerebral edema and an electrolyte imbalance, common complications of instillation abortions.[23]

Unfortunately, while this woman may have been the first known death from a saline abortion in the U.S., she was far from the last. Despite the dire warnings, when large-scale abortion began in New York and California, American abortionists enthusiastically embraced saline. Before long, the corpses started piling up, and articles about saline deaths and injuries began showing up in mainstream medical literature.[24] One, published by the American Medical Association, stated that, "Saline amniocentesis abortion has the highest fatality rate of any elective surgical technique, second only to cardiac transplantation. The ethical, sensible answer to this problem would be to place a moratorium on saline abortions..."[25]

Of course, the American abortion industry was deaf to suggestions like that, and the carnage continued. But that was not the case everywhere. Since the early 1960s, saline had been the abortifacient of choice among the Swedes. However, by 1966 an unacceptable body count was forcing them to reconsider. One study even cited Manabe's review expressing "astonishment that the far-from-risk-free method of [saline] is still extensively used in the Western countries." It also noted that Japan and the Soviet Union had abandoned this practice, implying that Sweden should follow suit, which they shortly did.[26]

Just a few weeks later, the United States Supreme Court issued the *Roe v. Wade* decision, making unregulated abortion-on-demand legal in all 50 states.

Ironically, at about the same time, another medical journal article came out showing a 50 percent complication rate with saline abortions.[27] The question was, now that the abortion industry was free to push saline beyond the boundaries of New York and California, would they do so in the face of overwhelming evidence that it was brutally dangerous for women? Of course, we now know the answer to that question. Regardless of the human cost, they were not backing down.

Over the next few years, the evidence mounted that the very things Wagatsuma and Manabe predicted were coming true. By 1981, even the clandestinely pro-abortion Centers for Disease Control (CDC) had to grudgingly admit that saline abortions were maiming and killing women.[28] Meanwhile, the abortion industry was beginning to have problems with them as well.

However, their concerns had nothing whatsoever to do with the harm that abortion was doing to women, but the harm it was doing to abortionists. From the abortion industry's standpoint, the problem wasn't that saline sometimes killed the woman, but that it sometimes *didn't* kill the fetus. This created real headaches for the abortionist. Now he had a badly injured baby to deal with, and a woman who was probably going to sue him. Of course, some dealt with the problem by killing the baby even after it was born. But that's a risky gambit. After all, if someone were to tell the authorities, he would be looking at the possibility of a murder indictment. Interestingly, abortionists who wrote about the possibility of a live birth often referred to it as "The Dreaded Complication." [29] It seems odd that this term would be saved for a situation where a fetus survived, but not used when the woman dies. Clearly, for the typical abortionist, the latter is of less concern.

It seems odd that the term "The Dreaded Complication" is used when a fetus survives, but not when the woman dies. Clearly, for the typical abortionist, the latter is of less concern.

So in the early 1980s, the abortion industry began slowly moving away from saline abortions in favor of the Dilatation and Evacuation (D&E) method. Since, with this procedure, the fetus is dismembered while still in the womb, there is virtually no chance of a live birth, plus it has the advantage of being faster and cheaper.

Old habits die hard in the abortion industry, and while saline abortions are rare today, they are not completely gone from the scene. In a 1987 *Technical Bulletin*, the openly pro-abortion American College of Obstetricians and Gynecologists (ACOG) describes how to perform instillation abortions, with virtually no mention of the extraordinary dangers of the procedure.[30] A 1994 patient information brochure published by this same organization lumps instillation abortions in with other abortion techniques and dismisses them as "a low-risk procedure."[31]

In 1991, Warren Hern was still describing how to perform instillation abortions in his book *Abortion Practice*. He compared the perceived benefits and drawbacks of various refinements of instillation, but never mentioned the abandonment of the technique in Japan, the USSR, and Sweden. Nowhere in his book, considered the definitive work on abortion, does he suggest that this deadly technique should be rejected. In 1992, abortionist Don Sloan wrote a book, *Abortion: A Doctor's Perspective/A Woman's Dilemma*. In it, he blandly describes the saline technique as "biochemically simple, sound and effective—the fetus and placenta are destroyed and nature then takes over with an expulsion by labor." He notes that this method carries "a distinct advantage for the abortionist, who doesn't have to be around when the fetus, macerated and lifeless, is expelled." He does admit that the saline experience is emotionally hard on the woman, but makes no mention whatsoever of the terrible risks to her life, health, and bodily integrity.

The point is, to this day—42 years after saline abortions were abandoned in Japan, 30 years after Wagatsuma and Manabe warned us of their terrible dangers, 22 years after an American Medical Association article called for a moratorium on saline abortions, and 14 years after the Centers for Disease Control finally recognized that the technique was dangerous and should be abandoned—many U.S. abortionists have yet to acknowledge the dangers of instillation abortions. The real tragedy is that it is this sort of abject dishonesty that killed and injured so many American women. Any way you look at it, the only abortionists concerned about these women were the Japanese, who cared enough to warn the U.S. physicians.

Current Betrayals

On several fronts, the abortion industry now seems poised to again sacrifice women for political gain. Currently, two of their biggest efforts are trying to pass legislation allowing non-physicians to perform abortions, and trying to find an effective chemical abortion. Regarding the first issue, we found a rather interesting phenomenon. On November 4, 1995, Planned Parenthood held its 79th Annual Conference, at which it bestowed its highest honor, The Margaret Sanger Award, on Minnesota abortionist Jane Hodgson. Interestingly, at a NAF meeting in 1990, Hodgson said that, "When I first started doing abortions, I took my boards in obstetrics and gynecology, and therefore I knew

I was competent to do it. After I had done my first few hundred, I realized how silly I had been. At this point, having done somewhere around 12,000 procedures, I'm beginning to think I'm reasonably competent."[32] The obvious dichotomy is how a board-certified obstetrician/gynecologist has to perform 12,000 abortions before she feels "reasonably competent" while NAF and Planned Parenthood claim that nurses and physician's assistants can pick it up in no time. There has also been at least one study showing that complication rates are significantly higher when abortions are performed by residents rather than licensed physicians.[33] In one study, cervical injury was found to be twice as likely to occur in abortions carried out by residents than in those carried out by physicians.[34] If these studies are accurate, it seems highly unlikely that the safety of abortion would improve by allowing them to be performed by nurses and physician's assistants who have even less medical training.

For the abortion industry to seriously propose that the standards for providing abortion be lowered demonstrates the utter disdain they have for American women. As Etienne-Emile Baulieu, the inventor of the French "abortion pill," RU-486, said, "To demedicalize abortion by removing doctors from the process—it's insane!"[35]

That, of course, brings us to their quest for a chemical abortion. The most public manifestation of this effort has been their love affair with Baulieu's pill, and they are feverishly working to see it made available in the United States. In the meantime, they're experimenting with chemical abortions by combining two drugs, methotrexate and misoprostol, which have not been approved as abortifacients. Methotrexate is intended for the treatment of cancer, severe rheumatoid arthritis, and severe psoriasis. The *Physician's Desk Reference (PDR)* contains the following warning:

> "Methotrexate should be used only by physicians whose knowledge and experience includes the use of antimetabolite therapy...Because of the possibility of serious toxic reactions, the patient should be informed by the physician of the risks involved and should be under a physician's constant supervision. Deaths have been reported with the use of methotrexate in the treatment of [certain diseases]...Methotrexate use should be restricted to patients with severe, recalcitrant, disabling disease, which is not adequately responsive to other forms of therapy, and only when the diagnosis has been established and after appropriate consultation."

Among other warnings in the *PDR* are that methotrexate can cause hemorrhagic enteritis and death from intestinal perforation, unexpectedly severe (sometimes fatal) marrow suppression, and gastrointestinal toxicity. There is also evidence that methotrexate can cause chromosomal damage to human bone marrow cells.

According to the *PDR*, the other drug, misoprostol, can cause incomplete miscarriages, leading to potentially dangerous bleeding, hospitalization, surgery, infertility, or maternal death. In studies of women undergoing elective termination of pregnancy during the first trimester, it caused either partial or complete expulsion of the products of conception in only 11 percent of the subjects and increased uterine bleeding in 41 percent.[36]

Clearly, this methotrexate/misoprostol abortion is just the latest example of the abortion industry's willingness to play Russian roulette with the lives of American women. When the abortion industry insists that this new procedure is the latest "silver bullet," perhaps we should all remember that they said the same thing about saline. After all, the stakes are pretty high.

They Knew All Along

To sell America on the idea of legal abortion, its proponents had to convince the public that an illegal abortion meant some greasy old man with a coat hanger, hovered over a frightened 15-year-old shivering on a filthy mattress in a dark and abandoned warehouse. And while there is no denying that situations like this occurred, to contend that they were the norm is simply a lie.

It has been shown time and again that the overwhelming majority of illegal abortions were performed by physicians who were simply breaking the law. In one study, 89 percent of women who obtained an illegal abortion found a physician to do the procedure, and an additional five percent found a nurse or other medically trained person. In short, 94 percent found a medical or paramedical abortionist.[37] And while one can logically assume they weren't the most wholesome of people, take another look at Chapters 1 and 2 before you decide that they were worse than what we have today.

In order to appreciate the kind of deception that was employed to market legalization, consider the way the abortion industry just completely lied about maternal mortality related to illegal abortions. They used to claim that, before legalization, 5,000 to 10,000 women died each year from botched illegal abortions. In fact, some still throw these figures around. However, the American Medical Association (AMA) says that the figure for 1950 was 263 and that it had dropped to 119 by 1970.[38] Even Planned Parenthood's research arm, the Alan Guttmacher Institute,[39] published a graph showing that the number of induced abortion-related deaths fell from about 200 in 1965 to about 110 in 1967.[40] Finally, the Centers for Disease Control (CDC) pointed out that beginning in 1940, the death rate from abortion was falling faster than the overall maternal mortality rate.[41]

This clearly had nothing to do with abortion's legal status, an argument the AMA made in 1992 when they pointed out that abortion deaths were declining "long before abortion laws became less restrictive." They attributed this to improved antibiotics management and a contraception-driven drop in the number of unintended pregnancies, resulting in a corresponding reduction in the number of illegal abortions being performed.[42]

Several other factors were also causing this drop in complications. First, medical technology was making abortions easier to perform and complications easier to treat. Additionally, because women viewed criminal abortion as seedy and dangerous, there was a more powerful incentive to avoid unwanted pregnancies in the first place. Today, with more than 40 percent of all abortions being repeat abortions,[43] the abortion industry no longer even bothers to deny that abortion is being used as just another method of birth control.

A major factor in reducing complications was that illegal abortionists had far more incentive to do clean, careful work. When one of them injured or killed a woman, the police sought to shut down his operations and had a legal mechanism with which to do so. During the research for this book, we found several examples of states that had vigorously investigated illegal abortion deaths, but stopped doing so when the procedure became legal. Dr. Alan Guttmacher, former president of Planned Parenthood, wrote that before decriminalization, "The technique of the well-accredited criminal abortionist is usually good. They have to be good to stay in business, since otherwise they would be extremely vulnerable to police action." He also said that a "Dr. B" of Baltimore "made the statement at a public meeting, in which the danger of abortion was being overemphasized by some well-meaning do-gooder, that in 12,000 illegal abortions with which he had been personally associated there had been only 4 deaths. It is to be remembered that this remarkable record predated antibiotics."[44] Even abortion-guru Dr. Christopher Tietze observed that during the 1960s the illegal abortion community was largely an enclave of experienced and skilled practitioners.[45]

Obviously, abortion advocates knew all this information. Contrary to their public statements, among themselves they had to know that maternal deaths from illegal abortions were rapidly declining, and that nothing was on the horizon to reverse that trend. They also had to recognize that removing the threat of prison terms for botching abortions would simply open the floodgates to marginal practitioners who otherwise would not risk performing abortions for fear of going to jail. Legalization would also make abortion *seem* safer, which would discourage the use of contraceptives as women would come to rely more on abortion. Actually, just the simple fact that abortion was legal would cause a certain percentage of women to be less responsible about sexual activity and contraception. That view has been confirmed many times, including in a 1977 article published by The Population Council. In it, the author summarized one woman's rationalization for not using contraception: "It's embarrassing to ask him to get out of bed and get a condom...I probably won't get pregnant because the doctor says I have a tipped uterus, but if I get pregnant he will probably marry me. Or worst coming to worst (sic), I can always get an abortion."[46]

This woman's attitude has obviously caught on pretty well as evidenced by the 40 percent repeat abortion rate. It also illustrates one of the primary reasons the abortion industry's "safe and legal" argument is a fraud. In order for legalizing abortion to reduce injuries and deaths, the abortion rate would have to remain relatively stable both pre- and post-legalization. If illegal abortions were replaced one for one by legal abortions, then it would be reasonable to speculate that the complication rate might be less. As a practical matter, however, that's not what happens. It's laughable to argue that the rate at which people will participate in an act is not affected by whether the act is legal or not. If that were so, it would make no sense whatsoever to waste our time making anything illegal.

Even hardcore abortion proponents saw that legalization would not mean replacing every 1,000 illegal abortions with 1,000 legal ones. Christopher Tietze was making that very point when he said, "Because a higher incidence of abortion enables more women to return to the fecundable state, sooner than if they had chosen to carry their pregnancies to term, more than one abortion is required to replace one birth. Thus, the *total* number of *pregnancies* tends to increase, even if no changes occur in the proportion of fecund women who are sexually active; in coital frequency; in contraceptive practice; and/or in contraceptive effectiveness."[47]

A real-world example of this phenomenon was found in Maryland. In 1968, the first year after abortion was decriminalized there, 2,134 legal abortions were performed in that state. The second and third years saw 5,530 and 7,757, respectively. Clearly, a trend was developing, and by 1988 the number had reached 23,707. In other words, within 20 years of legalization, the abortion rate skyrocketed by more than a factor of 10.[48] While it *may* be true that a smaller *percentage* of women were being injured and/or killed after legalization, the actual *number* has to be higher simply because the total number of abortions had increased so dramatically. It is simply not rational to believe that with a tenfold increase in the abortion rate, fewer women are going to be killed and/or injured.

In the final analysis, legalized abortion means more abortions, by less-skilled practitioners, on less wary women. And this is not just theory—it was the experience of every country that had preceded America in legalizing abortion.[49] In 1971, three British doctors warned that "the public is misled into believing that legal abortion is a trivial incident, even a lunch-hour procedure, which can be used as a mere extension of contraceptive practice. There has been almost a conspiracy of silence in declaring its risks. Unfortunately, because of emotional reactions to legal abortion, well-documented evidence from countries with a vast experience of it receives little attention in either the medical or lay press. This is medically indefensible when patients suffer as a result." After describing types of problems they were seeing as severe and "disquieting," they pointed out that their high incidence of complications was observed despite the excellent credentials and experience of their practitioners. "It is perhaps significant that some of the more serious complications occurred with the most senior and experienced operators. This emphasizes that termination of pregnancy is neither as simple nor as safe as some advocates of abortion-on-demand would have the public believe. Moreover, the incidence of such delayed complications as infertility, recurrent abortion, premature labor, ruptured uterus, or emotional manifestations cannot be assessed at this stage."[50]

> *British doctors warned that "the public is misled into believing that legal abortion is a trivial incident. There has been almost a conspiracy of silence in declaring its risks."*

One of the more cautious American voices was that of Dr. Albert Altchek, a surgeon who had performed about 5,000 abortions. In a 1973 editorial, he reflected on *Roe v. Wade* and its likely consequences: "As one who was active in promoting [legal abortion], I was elated. However, in a short while an inner deep concern developed. The Court indicated that first-trimester abortion may be performed by any physician without any government restriction. This opinion was based on...the Court's finding that such abortion is safer than regular childbirth. The latter observation, based on a carefully controlled series of abortions performed in New York State, may not necessarily hold true if the floodgates of completely unsupervised abortion are suddenly opened nationwide. I predict that within one year our profession will sadly record a far greater morbidity and mortality rate than has been reported so far."[51] ■

Cooking the Books

When it comes to abortion-industry disasters,
cover-up is spelled "CDC"

This chapter is somewhat similar to Chapter 2, in that when I started writing the book I had no idea it would be necessary. Like most Americans, I had no reason to question that the Centers for Disease Control (CDC) was anything other than what it appeared. At Life Dynamics, we knew abortion complications were grotesquely underreported, but just attributed it to garden-variety bureaucratic incompetence. As our research continued, however, we were getting suspicious that the flawed abortion data being released by the CDC was not the product of ineptitude, but of dishonesty and manipulation. By the time we discovered that a large percentage of CDC employees have direct ties to the abortion industry, we were no longer suspicious, we were convinced.

As you will see in this chapter, when it comes to abortion, CDC stands for Center for Damage Control. The CDC doesn't oversee abortion, it justifies it. Just as Planned Parenthood and the National Abortion Federation work to eliminate political opposition to abortion, and just as the American Civil Liberties Union (ACLU) aims to eliminate judicial opposition, the CDC's role is to eliminate medical opposition.

The CDC, ASB, and ICD

Based in Atlanta, Georgia, the CDC is part of the U.S. Department of Health and Human Services. After being chartered in 1946, it began by conducting studies on certain diseases such as smallpox, diphtheria, malaria, and leprosy.[1] In the late 1960s, as the first few states started legalizing abortion, the CDC created the Abortion Surveillance Branch (ASB) to examine the impact legal abortion would have on public health. The ASB also took over a project that was begun in 1970 by the Population Council. Overseen by Dr. Christopher Tietze, this project focused on abortion morbidity (the assessment of complications) and was called the Joint Program for the Study of Abortion (JPSA).[2] All morbidity data is collected by case reporting and investigation.

The ASB is also supposed to conduct "surveillance of abortion-related deaths to assess their preventability."[3] It gets this mortality data by compiling vital statistics from death certificates obtained from the health departments in each state, the U.S. territories, the City of New York, and the District of Columbia. The causes of death are classified by a numerical coding system called the International Classification of Diseases (ICD). When the ASB issued its first report, these codes were called ICD-7. The medical community, state health departments, and the CDC currently use a revised version called ICD-9. All complications related to pregnancy and childbirth are coded from 630 to 677, with the following specific codes for abortion:

632 missed abortion
634 spontaneous abortion
635 legally induced abortion
636 illegally induced abortion
637 unspecified abortion
638 failed attempted abortion
639 complications following abortion and ectopic or molar
     pregnancies

Code 633, which is excluded from the list, designates an ectopic pregnancy.[4] Although the CDC does not include ICD-9 code 633 as an abortion-related citation, we will prove later that it is actually quite relevant in identifying instances of abortion morbidity and mortality.

Although abortion surveillance began in 1969, the CDC did not issue a report on abortion injuries and deaths until 1974, and that report covered only 1972. The last year for which a "full" report was released was five years ago, in 1990, and it did not include figures for deaths.[5]

Deaths that come to the attention of the CDC can be added to the statistics at any time. In 1988, the National Pregnancy Mortality Surveillance Program was initiated to study maternal mortality.[6] A joint project of various federal, state, and local health programs, as well as the American College of Obstetricians and Gynecologists (ACOG), this retrospective study uncovered eleven abortion deaths that had not been previously reported to the CDC. These deaths occurred from 1978 to 1985, yet they were not added to the total number of deaths for these years until September 1992.[7]

All the coded vital statistics gathered by health departments throughout the nation are submitted to the National Center for Health Statistics (NCHS). This department of the Federal Government was part of the Public Health Service, but in June 1987 it was incorporated into the CDC.[8] The NCHS reviews death certificates to determine the number of fatalities caused by a particular injury or disease. The CDC then gathers statistics from the NCHS on women whose deaths were coded as having been caused by an abortion-related complication.

Issues Hindering Mortality Data

Deaths related to abortion are often missed by the coding system used by the NCHS. However, these deaths are sometimes brought to the attention of the CDC through state medical associations, reports from other federal agencies, private sources, and published case histories. The CDC is then supposed to investigate them by obtaining information from state health agencies, the attending physician at the time of death,[9] the abortion provider if the provider was not the attending physician, medical examiner's reports, police reports, trial transcripts, medical records, and the family of the deceased.[10] Many times, case investigations are impeded because there is not enough information available to draw conclusions about a death. Either investigators have trouble contacting the involved parties or the involved parties are unable to remember information. In other cases, the information needed is simply not in the medical records.[11]

An example of how this works is seen with the death of a 16-year-old in Maryland. This girl underwent an abortion of a 19-week pregnancy at a local doctor's office. Once she was released by the doctor to return home, the aunt who had taken her in for the abortion instead took her to a hospital because she was so ill. The girl died that night. An autopsy showed a perforation of her uterus that caused an air embolism (bubble) to travel to her heart.[12] The State of Maryland does not have this girl's death counted in their abortion tabulation, therefore neither does the NCHS.[13] Since this death was reported to the CDC by a private source, an investigation should have been performed. However, because the CDC is so secretive, there was no way for us to find out whether they actually investigated her death. Moreover, once a death is counted, almost all identifying information is removed, including the woman's name, date of birth, and even the state in which her death occurred.[14] When another death is later found, it is virtually impossible for the CDC to determine whether it's the same woman.

Another way mortality can be tracked is by looking for specific ICD codes from National Hospital Discharge Survey databases available from the states. However, these records are not always accurate, and they can only report complications that are actually treated in a hospital. A look at North Carolina Medical Database Commission's search for abortion complications shows how far off these databases can be. According to a 16-year-old girl's hospital discharge information, she was hospitalized for one day after her abortion and then died. Her ICD-9 code shows that she had a legally induced abortion, and does not mention complications.[15] The obvious question is how a 16-year-old girl dies from an abortion with no complications. In any event, this death was not counted in North Carolina's vital statistics records as an abortion death.[16]

There are also abortion deaths reported to the CDC that it places in a non-abortion category. The CDC defines a legal abortion as one performed by a licensed physician. An illegal abortion is one that the woman performs on herself or that is performed by someone other than a licensed physician. A spontaneous abortion (miscarriage) is one that occurs with no intervention before the twentieth week of pregnancy.[17] Another problem is that, occasionally, a death certificate does not specify whether the abortion was legal, illegal, or spontaneous. In those cases, the CDC classifies it as unknown.[18]

It is interesting that the last report issued by the CDC that included any numbers on deaths from abortion was in 1987. Currently, they claim that suspected deaths from 1988 and 1989 are still under investigation and have yet to be placed in the appropriate categories.[19] Remember, the CDC is charged with investigating abortion morbidity and mortality in order to identify problems and recommend solutions. Statistician Jack Smith and Dr. Willard Cates, both with the CDC, have stated that, "In the absence of accurate, complete, and timely health statistics, there is little basis for rational decision-making regarding the effectiveness and efficiency of health care, be it preventative or therapeutic."[20] In the same article they conclude that "health questions related to abortion should be answered by sound epidemiological reasoning based on adequate abortion statistics."[21]

Clearly, what Cates and Smith say should happen is far from what is actually happening. Despite the fact that abortion surveillance reports are printed in a government document entitled *Morbidity and Mortality Weekly Report*, morbidity has not been tracked since the JPSA studies in the 1970s, and mortality data is released at a snail's pace. In fact, abortion deaths have even been added to the tally a full 14 years after the death occurred.[22] It seems incredible that in the age of computers, fax machines, and the information superhighway, the United States Government takes years to figure out how many women have died from abortion. Consider that if a professional football player is hurt at the start of a game, by halftime the whole world knows the full extent of his injuries and how they were caused. There's also a chance they've seen X-rays, and you can be assured they have been told how many games he will miss. Why does it take 14 years to find out that a woman died from an abortion? This absurd system caused one critic at the *New York Post* to call abortion statistics gathered by the CDC "a joke."[23]

Issues Hindering Morbidity Data

Abortion morbidity has been shown to be even harder to track than mortality. Cates and Smith go so far as to say that "because definitions of abortion complications are not uniform, it is often difficult to obtain comparable morbidity data. Moreover, because follow-up of postabortion patients is variable, only the immediate effects of the procedure are usually known."[24] Complications can be tracked by looking for specific ICD codes from the National Hospital Discharge Survey databases. However, as mentioned, this is not always an accurate source of mortality data, and is certainly suspect with morbidity, which is more difficult to track.

Even in a controlled study like the JPSA of the late 1970s, information on complications was not readily available. In that project, more than 40 percent of the women involved never went back to the abortion provider, making accurate data virtually impossible to obtain. Although the CDC has not officially conducted any studies on morbidity since the JPSA, individual employees often collaborate on articles about morbidity, such as those published by the *Journal of the American Medical Association*.[25]

Demographic Data

The abortion-related demographic information collected by the CDC includes, among many other things, age, race, marital status, number of live births, weeks of gestation of the pregnancy at the time of abortion, type of procedure used, and whether the woman had the abortion in the state in which she resides.[26] There is also a count given on the total number of abortions performed that year, although the CDC admits that this number is probably underestimated. For comparison, in 1988 the number of abortions reported by abortion providers to the Alan Guttmacher Institute (a research division of Planned Parenthood) was 16 percent higher than the CDC's figures. This means that more abortions are being performed than are reported to central health agencies. This doesn't speak well for the accuracy of the CDC's information on abortion morbidity and mortality, since most of it comes from the same source as the demographic data, which even they admit is inaccurate.[27]

Much of the demographic information collected by the CDC seems clearly unrelated to any health issue, and more related to marketing and politics. It's interesting that while the CDC's health data often takes many years to be compiled (in November 1995 we're still waiting for a mortality count for 1988), their demographic (marketing?) data is out in three years or less.[28]

Creative Coding at Work

One of the main sources of the CDC's information are the vital records provided by health departments. They are gathered from death certificates completed by the attending physician at the time of death, or by the medical examiner or coroner's office. This person must record their determination of what caused the death. Most states have death certificates with three blanks that can be filled in for this and another blank where other significant medical information can be included. The physician or coroner fills in these blanks with an account of events leading to the death, and then sends the completed certificate to the state. The state writes the appropriate ICD code in the margins, if the doctor has not done so already. If the death certificate has not been completely filled out, it is returned to the doctor for completion.

Since only about seven percent of all abortions are performed in a hospital,[29] the attending physician at the time of death is usually not the doctor who performed the abortion. This physician must be told important information by the abortion doctor, the woman's family, or the woman herself. If none of these parties specify the cause of her illness, the physician must try to determine events based on clinical or physical evidence. For a physician to accurately classify an abortion death, he must know that an abortion took place, must think it important enough to mention, and then must report it on the certificate.[30] There are times when the physician does not know the cause of death until an autopsy has been performed. Unfortunately, more than one-third of all maternal deaths do not result in an autopsy.[31] Even when an autopsy is performed, the true cause of death is still sometimes unknown. The death of a woman in California shows how this happens.

A 39-year-old, who had just returned from a trip with her truck driver husband, was admitted in shock to a hospital near her home. The woman was not able to talk, so they got her medical history from her husband. The woman subsequently died and an autopsy was performed. Neither the woman's mother nor the husband would tell the police what had caused her death. At first, the husband told investigators that he had not known that his wife was pregnant. He subsequently confessed that his wife had presented him with a fetus in a plastic bag and told him to get rid of it. Later, while still on the road, she handed him another bag with the placenta and requested that he do the same thing. He denied an induced abortion ever took place and insisted that his wife had a miscarriage. Despite the autopsy's findings that her death was caused by an induced septic abortion, it was counted as a spontaneous abortion death because there was no way to prove otherwise when the family insisted that the woman had a miscarriage.[32]

If the physician suspects or knows that an abortion has taken place but is unable to classify it as legal, illegal, or spontaneous, he can choose not to record it as abortion-related, or he can code the death as 637 (an unspecified abortion). For example, the death of a 39-year-old woman in Kentucky was coded as 637.6—an unspecified abortion, with the ".6" denoting "complicated by embolism." No autopsy was performed and the case was not referred to the medical examiner's office.[33] This woman may very well have been killed during an elective abortion, but there is no way of knowing from the death certificate.

The death certificate of a 36-year-old woman in North Carolina does not mention an abortion taking place; in fact, it does not even mention that she had been pregnant.[34] In this case, however, an autopsy was performed and the findings were available before the death certificate was completed. The autopsy shows that this woman had an abortion the day before her death. The physician filling out the death certificate either did not find the abortion worth mentioning, or he just failed to note it on the certificate.[35] Despite an autopsy showing that this woman died from complications of an elective abortion, her death certificate does not mention the word "abortion." This may explain why some abortionists always send their injured patients—even those needing emergency care—to a particular hospital when another one may be closer. Is it possible that a buddy at this distant hospital covers his tracks with a little "creative coding"?

Even if a physician knows and correctly states the cause of death on a death certificate, errors and manipulation are still possible. A case in point is the death of a 40-year-old woman from Alabama. Although the coroner recorded the cause of death as "Coagulation complications following abortion of a second-trimester fetus," whoever coded the death certificate assigned the code as 666—the ICD code for postpartum hemorrhage.[36] Not only is this code unrelated to abortion, but it falls under the category of complications occurring mainly during labor and delivery.[37] Obviously, the code totally misidentified the cause of death for this woman, and this "error" was never corrected on the death certificate. If the CDC accepts the ICD code on the death certificate (likely), and does not look at the autopsy (even more likely), then a death gets counted against childbirth that should have been counted against abortion. Ironically, the CDC then uses these flawed statistics to show how much safer childbirth is than abortion. And be assured, mislabeling an abortion death is *not* an uncommon occurrence. Furthermore, this does not "come out in the wash" with an offsetting childbirth death counted as an abortion death. That *never* happens.

More Roadblocks

There are often hurdles at the state level that affect how abortion injury data is collected. For example, in late 1978 the *Chicago Sun-Times* ran a series of articles about the Chicago-area abortion industry. After five months of investigation, the authors concluded that while the Illinois Department of Public Health "can quote statistics on the age, race, and marital status of every woman who has received an abortion since 1973, it does not even know how many have died from their abortions."[38] Since the CDC gathers its information from the states, it is safe to say that the information is not only suspect in its accuracy, but it is undeniably incomplete as not all states report this information to the CDC.

Since the data collection process is not governed by a uniform national standard,[39] we wanted to find out how each state gathers its abortion data, what is gathered, and how it is distributed. To determine that, we called the health departments of every state, plus the District of Columbia, New York City, Guam, Puerto Rico, and the Virgin Islands.

We quickly learned that each state has its own rules on what data is gathered and who has access to these records. For example, two of the largest states have vastly different methods of reporting abortion deaths to the public. In California, one merely requests the desired information and pays the fee for copying and research. In our case, we requested, and received, a print-out of all abortion and ectopic deaths that occurred in the state from 1960 to 1993, including the appropriate ICD codes.

On the other hand, when we asked the State of Texas for information concerning abortion deaths, we were told that only the number of deaths could be released. Therefore, all one gets out of Texas is that there was one abortion death in each of the years 1986, 1990, 1991, 1992, and 1994. We found this interesting because, without even conducting a search, we came across two deaths occurring in 1988, one in 1989, and two in 1994 *in addition* to the ones the state is aware of. When we informed them of this, the health department requested that we provide them with information on these other deaths so that they could be investigated. They refused, however, to verify if they had a record of any of the deaths that we had provided to them, or if our deaths for each year matched up with theirs. We asked for no personal information on any woman involved, and in fact provided that information to them, yet they refused to answer even "yes or no" questions.

Sometimes, as is the case with Texas, it is simply policy not to release information to the public. Usually this policy is a result of legislation passed in the state,[40] and even applies to death certificates filed with each state. Twenty-seven states and the District of Columbia will not release information about a death unless you are a member of the immediate family. Eight states conceal the cause of death from public requests for death certificates. Presumably, immediate family members would have access to the cause of death if that specific information was requested. The remaining fifteen states, including California, allow public access to death certificates.[41]

In Delaware, the health department is prohibited by state law from officially tracking abortions. This state does not even code its own death certificates; that is done by the NCHS, which is part of the CDC. Allegedly due to budget cuts and the loss of senior staff, our request for information from the New York City Department of Health has been indefinitely delayed. Although we have had all the required paperwork into the department since mid-July 1995, our request has not even been brought up for consideration. In Iowa, although the legislature's Joint Appropriations Committee has allotted $500,000 for teen pregnancy monitoring, a bill that would allow this information to be collected was killed in the House of Representatives. House Bill 522 is currently in the Human Resource Committee; only if this bill is passed in both houses will the state have the authority to collect information on teenage pregnancy.[42] This is especially important considering teenagers have the highest abortion rate of all age groups.[43]

In Missouri, all sorts of maternal health data is collected, but the form in which it is released renders it practically useless for analysis. The data is not broken down into usable categories for determining the cause of death. All one can discern for any given year is the total number of maternal deaths.

Illinois illustrates the problems states have collecting usable abortion data. It collected abortion data until the early 1980s, when a restraining order was issued prohibiting its collection. This remained in effect until mid-1993, when the state was once again permitted to collect this data.[44] The restraining order was issued six years after the *Chicago Sun-Times* abortion exposé blasting the state's health department for not doing a thorough job of regulating the industry. An official at the state health department remarked that the American Civil Liberties Union (ACLU) was heavily involved in getting the restraining order issued.[45] This is a pattern we've seen repeated elsewhere, as abortion-rights groups like the ACLU try to censor information related to abortion problems.

That sort of "abortion-protection" mentality may also have been a factor in a situation in Santa Monica, California. In 1972, a local newspaper tried to obtain abortion-injury data from the county. When the newspaper petitioned the county for the records, it was denied access and the county health department stated that they did not have the information. When the state health department was asked for the information, they refused to release it, claiming that doing so would not be in the public interest. The president of the California Public Health Association tried to help the newspaper gain access to the information, but he was also refused. Finally, the State Attorney General's Office was informed of the situation, and told the state health department to release the information.[46]

Because criminal charges were filed against the doctor, the state counted this death from a legal abortion as a death due to an illegal abortion.

In Oregon, not only are death certificates unavailable to the public, but so are autopsy reports, even though both are officially classified as public records.[47] When we requested two autopsy reports on suspected abortion deaths, we supplied the woman's name, date of death, and the case file number for the autopsy. The request was made because neither death certificate was filled out adequately to determine the real cause of death. One death certificate lists the cause of death as "septic abortion with complications."[48] There is no determination about whether the abortion death was spontaneous, illegal, or legal. The other death certificate attributes the woman's death to "pulmonary embolus originating in uterine veins."[49] This was all the state would provide as explanations for these deaths, and no autopsies were made available to us. Evidently, Oregon's definition of "public records" is different than ours.

Abortion deaths are also missed because states make their own rules on how data is collected and how deaths are classified. The death of a California woman in 1982 illustrates how this can affect mortality accuracy. Her abortion was performed by a licensed physician in a licensed facility, but because criminal charges were filed against the doctor, the state counted this death from a legal abortion as a death due to an illegal abortion.[50] According to the CDC's definition of legal and illegal, this was clearly a death due to legal abortion, and we can only assume that when the CDC investigated the death they came to the same conclusion. However, we cannot verify this because the CDC will not inform the public how deaths are classified.

Sometimes a physician intentionally does not complete a death certificate in the correct manner. For example, embolism has been documented as being overreported on death certificates, and several CDC employees stated that this may be done because a doctor is less likely to be sued after a death from an embolism. The doctor's legal concerns may cause him to list the death as such to avoid any action being taken against him.[51] A federal health official told *The Washington Times*, "There have always been problems identifying deaths secondary to abortions." The official explained that it is likely that many abortion-related deaths go unreported if the true cause of death is concealed.[52] The chairman of the Los Angeles County Medical Association's committee on maternal mortality stated in an interview about the underreporting of legal abortion deaths, "We need to know what risk there is to therapeutic abortion, and we don't know."[53]

Finally, the collection of abortion injury data is impeded because some states simply don't report certain information to the CDC. For example, in a 1989 abortion surveillance report, several states did not supply data requested by the CDC, and some of the missing states (Alabama, California, Florida, Illinois) have fairly influential numbers.[54] In fact, since approximately 20 percent of all abortions performed in the U.S. occur in California alone,[55] these results would be profoundly affected.[56]

Stacking the Deck

According to the "Standards of Ethical Conduct for Employees of the Executive Branch," government officers and employees are to follow certain rules to ensure public trust. These standards were written "to ensure that every citizen can have complete confidence in the integrity of the Federal Government." These Standards of Ethical Conduct state, "Employees shall act impartially and not give preferential treatment to any private organization or individual." Government employees are also instructed not to engage in outside activities that would conflict with official governmental duties or responsibilities. This rule is further expounded upon when employees are told not to even "create the appearance" that they are violating ethical standards.[57]

The question is whether that standard has been met by the CDC. Starting at the top, since at least 1975, Dr. Willard Cates and Dr. David Grimes have both held various positions at the CDC and both have served terms as head of the Abortion Surveillance Branch. Each is also a practicing abortionist. In February 1976, they were presenters at an abortion conference sponsored by the Abortion Referral and Counseling Service of Colorado, Catholics for a Free Choice, Colorado National Organization for Women, Colorado Women's Political Caucus, Denver National Organization for Women, the National Abortion Rights Action League, Rocky Mountain Planned Parenthood, and Zero Population Growth.[58] In 1990, Grimes chaired a symposium held by the National Abortion Federation and ACOG,[59] and 1991 the National Abortion Federation listed him as a member.[60]

We found a lengthy list of ties between these two men and the American abortion industry. The point is, their pro-abortion pedigree cannot be challenged. They are true believers. Although Grimes is no longer employed by the CDC, he and Cates remain the CDC's most prolific writers on abortion. And though it's logical to assume that they make an effort to hide their political bias, it inevitably seeps through. (There are several examples below.) However, even if their writings were not so transparently pro-abortion, there is still an indefensible conflict of interest in having two people with such close ties to the abortion industry in the CDC.

After identifying Cates and Grimes, we decided to see if there were any other abortion industry operatives at the CDC. We first created a list of CDC employees by finding their names and job titles listed in the surveillance summary reports and in the Federal Staff Directory.[61] Then we analyzed that list for names of people we knew to have links with the abortion industry. Not surprisingly, we discovered that a significant number of CDC employees, especially its leadership, are indeed involved in the abortion industry. Out of 68 upper-level employees of the CDC, we were able to identify 48 as medical doctors. Of these, 17 are actually practicing abortionists and nine others have an obvious connection with the abortion industry.

Of the remaining 20 non-physician employees, eight had identifiable links with the abortion industry. These links range from participation in a symposium on ensuring that there are doctors who will do abortions,[62] to serving on an Editorial Advisory Committee of a Planned Parenthood publication.[63] This gives a total of 34 employees, or one-half, who are somehow involved with the abortion industry. These figures are not the result of extensive research into the professional or private lives of these employees, but are from public

information. One would reasonably expect these numbers to increase significantly if a more intensive search were conducted.

This situation is clearly in violation of the government's code of employee
ethics. While the public would never tolerate people with ties to the tobacco
industry being in charge of an agency that monitors the impact of cigarette
smoking on public health, that is precisely what is happening at the CDC. And
one would have to be incredibly naive to believe that this does not affect the
information released by this agency. Any way you look at it, people with an
outspoken abortion agenda have been placed in an influential position that
allows them a government-funded forum to spread their message.

The Agenda Promoted

How does the link between the CDC and the abortion industry manifest itself?
First, remember that the CDC has not officially conducted any studies on
morbidity since the JPSA study in the late 1970s. This is not to suggest that
CDC employees have been ignoring the subject. In fact, they have been quite
busy. As long ago as November 1985, the CDC published a document containing a seven-page listing of abortion-related articles written by CDC employees
in only a four-year period.[64]

These articles cover a wide variety of topics, ranging from complications
and deaths, to restrictions of publicly funded abortions, to regulations on the
abortion industry, to abortions in Bangladesh. Despite the fact that these
people had to know what was happening to women inside America's abortion
clinics, their political agenda is clearly evident in their writings on the subject.[65] In fact, we identified many situations in which the CDC used data they
obtained directly from openly pro-abortion organizations such as Planned
Parenthood, the National Abortion Federation, and the Alan Guttmacher
Institute.[66] They are also not shy about citing individual pro-abortion researchers and writers.[67] However, we did not find a single example where they
used materials from pro-life groups or researchers with known pro-life view-
points.

We even found several examples where the CDC published materials
directly lifted from the abortion industry. In their 1976 annual summary, the
CDC used Planned Parenthood's standards to determine how well a community was doing in providing abortion services. In one incident, the CDC used
these same guidelines to affix blame on the community in which a woman died
from a legal abortion, rather than on the abortionist who killed her.[68] Another
example of how the CDC used Planned Parenthood guidelines to color the
writings they published is seen in one of their 1981 reports. In it, one death

from each of the legal, illegal, and spontaneous categories was examined in detail. For the section on the illegal abortion death, little information was given except that the woman had not tried to get a legal abortion nor had she seen a doctor about her pregnancy.[69]

The section on the legal abortion death had much more information available, though most of it was obtained from the doctor who had done the abortion. They concluded that the woman was partially at fault for her own death because she was not using contraceptives and got pregnant. (That's like excusing a drunk driver by arguing that the person he killed should not have been on the highway in the first place.) In any event, this standard was not applied to the woman who died from the illegal abortion, although apparently she did not use contraception either. The woman who had the legal abortion and her family also refused her hospitalization on the day of the procedure, even though the doctor was almost certain that he had perforated the uterus. In addition, she did not keep a follow-up appointment. No mention is made of the possibility that the woman might not have been cooperative with the doctor because he is the one who had just poked a hole in her uterus. Nor is the doctor ever accused of so much as contributing to the death, much less causing it.[70]

In the spontaneous abortion category, the woman was not blamed for her death. While she too failed to keep a follow-up appointment, her behavior was not cited as a contributing factor in her death. All blame was placed on her physicians for failing to abort the pregnancy even though they knew she had an infection. They did this because *the patient* said she wanted to continue the pregnancy. In other words, the CDC was critical of these doctors because they would not go against their patient's stated wishes. The CDC stated that if the doctors had just aborted the pregnancy immediately after admitting her to the hospital, the complication that led to her death "could possibly have been avoided."[71]

To recap, this official CDC publication used Planned Parenthood standards to determine that (a) a legal abortion death was the fault of the woman; (b) an illegal abortion was simply tragic, but no one's fault; and (c) a spontaneous abortion death was caused by doctors who *irresponsibly* failed to perform an abortion on a woman who didn't want one. The overriding theme here is that legal abortion is good and everything possible must be done to prove it so.

This habit of blaming everyone but the abortionist is endemic to writings of people associated with the CDC, even when Planned Parenthood is not involved. A classic example is a 1981 article by Cates and Grimes. In it, they discuss seven deaths during D&E abortions in abortion clinics. These deaths occurred in states that require second-trimester abortions to be performed in hospitals rather than outpatient abortion clinics. The authors point out that, in every case, the abortionist may have deliberately underestimated gestational age to justify doing a prohibited second-trimester abortion in his clinic. Cates and Grimes also point out that in at least five of the seven deaths, there was an unnecessary delay in sending the injured women for emergency care. They claimed that, "Some physicians delayed referral because they feared criticism from their colleagues for performing unconventional D&E procedures. Others were afraid of prosecution. In those states that require that all abortions later than 12 weeks gestation be performed in hospitals, clinicians were reluctant to admit that they had inadvertently initiated an abortion in a non-hospital facility on a woman beyond the legal gestational age. Fearing both rejection by their colleagues and prosecution by law enforcement officials, these physicians were hesitant to send their patients for further treatment. In these situations, the abortion regulations requiring hospitalization in the second trimester hindered rapid and appropriate care."[72]

This is equivalent to a rapist killing his victim so she couldn't identify him, then claiming that he wouldn't have had to kill her if the state hadn't made rape illegal.

Now let me see if I've got this right. In each of these cases, an abortionist lies about gestational age to justify performing an illegal abortion. Then, in the process of performing this illegal procedure, he gravely injures the patient. However, to protect himself, he lets her languish without emergency care, and she dies. Later, two guys from the CDC come along and blame the state for making these abortions illegal, while subtly suggesting that the abortionists were the victims! This is equivalent to a rapist killing his victim so she couldn't identify him, then claiming that he wouldn't have had to kill her if the state hadn't made rape illegal. In reality, these abortionists proved the wisdom of the state's decision not to allow second-trimester abortions to be performed in clinics. The bottom line is that a state law intended to protect women was ignored, and seven women died.

Despite that, Cates and Grimes used this article to justify their view that these regulations are unreasonable (a very shop-worn theme for them), by suggesting that second-trimester abortions may be performed just as safely in a clinic as in a hospital. Clearly, that's untrue. Anyone associated with emergency medicine knows that when someone is injured, one of the most important factors in determining the outcome is how fast emergency care is rendered. Obviously, a woman who is injured at an abortion clinic is not going to receive hospital care as quickly as she would if she were already at the hospital. In addition, the whole premise that an abortion clinic is as capable as a hospital is patently ridiculous. Just ask a thousand physicians the following question: "If your daughter was going to have an abortion, would you rather she have it at an abortion clinic or a hospital?"

The bizarre logic exhibited by Cates and Grimes in this article is typical of their writings on abortion. Just as in this example, the majority of their rhetoric is indistinguishable from anything published by the National Abortion Federation or Planned Parenthood.

Same Song, Second Verse

This section includes comparisons with abortion-reporting policies in other countries. Studies from countries in which the legal status of elective abortion is substantially different were excluded.

There are a multitude of ways in which CDC employees deceive the public with their writings. One is to ignore knowledge that has been gained in foreign countries. A case in point involves saline abortions, which were discussed in Chapter 3. In 1965, Japanese abortionist Takashi Wagatsuma, M.D., published an article in an American medical journal about his country's experiences with saline abortions. In this article, he explained the types of complications that arose from this abortion method and reported that the procedure had been abandoned by Japanese physicians because they were seeing too many deaths from saline. The author concludes with this warning: "In order not to repeat Japan's tragedy, one would think this method should be applied very cautiously."[73]

By 1969, another Japanese doctor, Yukio Manabe, was warning Americans of the dangers of saline abortions. U.S. doctors were advised that there were complications from these procedures that could not be predicted or avoided, mainly because the solution that can kill the fetus can also kill the mother. Manabe stated, "In spite of the accumulating undesirable reports, the use of hypertonic saline for abortion is still advocated and used by some physicians in the United States and Great Britain. I would like to call attention to the danger of the method and would predict the further occurrence of deaths until this method is entirely forgotten in these countries."[74] As early as 1966, British doctors began writing about cases in their country where saline was used with tragic results.[75]

Meanwhile, some American doctors were beginning to express profound misgivings about saline,[76] and others were insisting it was so safe that it could be done on an outpatient basis.[77] The CDC did not warn against this practice, despite the evidence that it was potentially fatal. It was not until 1977 that the CDC began to heed these warnings and started looking for a different method of second-trimester abortion.[78] Why did it take the so-called experts twelve years to come around? One answer might be that they had nothing with which to replace it. In light of a political agenda that says even a dangerous abortion is better than no abortion, the obvious thing to do is to continue with saline. And when the bodies start piling up, just manipulate the already complex ICD codes to hide them.

Another issue is whether abortion complications affect subsequent pregnancies. Again, foreign studies differ greatly from their American counterparts. A British study found that abortions done vaginally seem to create cervical incompetence in succeeding pregnancies. As Chapter 1 demonstrates, cervical lacerations, uterine perforations, infection, hemorrhage, and bowel complications occur frequently. Because of these complications, this British study found that women who have had induced abortions are at greater risk for miscarriage in their next pregnancy.[79] An Israeli study comes to the same conclusions and states that the connection between induced abortion and cervical problems has been well documented.[80] Almost all abortions performed in the United States are done vaginally, yet Grimes and Cates want to extend the gestational age at which these abortions can be done. Although they discuss how much cheaper and less stressful it will be for the woman, they never even mention the possibility of these other problems.[81] Since most abortions are performed on young women, it would stand to reason that this information would be particularly important if they wanted children later.

There is also the issue of uterine perforation. A study from India found that one in every 250 abortions performed in a hospital ended with a perforation of the uterus. While vacuum aspiration with suction is touted worldwide as the safest abortion procedure, more than half of the injuries in this study were caused by the suction machine.[82] The authors warned that any time a perforation is caused by the suction machine, the bowels must be checked for damage. A Swedish study on the same subject had approximately the same results, with one in every 230 abortions causing a perforation. This author agreed with those from India that perforations were going to occur with this type of abortion, and the damage should be evaluated.[83] Meanwhile, an American study reported that the third most frequent cause of abortion-related death was hemorrhage, primarily from uterine perforation.[84] However, American researchers stated in 1991 that there were no extensive articles (presumably American) that dealt with managing postabortive hemorrhage.[85] The foreign researchers stated that perforations should be checked out, yet in a study of 24 American deaths caused by hemorrhage, a lack of treatment after the perforation led to the fatal outcomes.[86]

So, while foreign doctors were stressing the importance of identifying and treating perforations, these American women did not receive adequate post-abortion treatment for the doctor to even notice that a problem existed. The authors of the 1991 study—all of whom have been affiliated with the CDC—stated, "No woman in the United States should die from hemorrhage caused by legal abortion, yet these deaths continue to occur."[87] They maintain that everything necessary to keep these women from dying of hemorrhage is available to physicians, and they have no idea why these deaths happen. Incredibly, the answer is in their article—these women did not receive proper care. The authors will just not be honest enough to admit it.

Foreign authors also mention that very little has been written about conditions that arise later as a consequence of abortion. These conditions are especially important because most women having abortions are young, and it is their first pregnancy.[88] While Norwegian physicians were concluding that induced abortion in young women is "far from an innocuous procedure,"[89] a CDC author, Dr. Carol Hogue, wrote that there seems to be little evidence that abortion causes these subsequent problems unless some very rare other conditions are present also.[90] Throughout the article, she cites five of her *own studies* as proof that her position is correct. In some instances, she does not even tell the reader what studies she is attacking, only that they are flawed and she will not be addressing them.

Don't Question the Party Line

Obviously, not all American physicians have the same attitude as those at the CDC. But dissenters are often either ignored or lambasted. In 1974, two physicians wrote about the psychological problems with unwanted pregnancies and the decision to abort. They had discovered that several claims made by those who advocated abortion on demand were unproven. In fact, studies that had been conducted showed different results. For instance, the "fact" that legal abortion provides a beneficial alternative to those who would otherwise have illegal abortions was belied by nine studies. These studies showed that 80 to 90 percent of the women who have legally induced abortions would not opt for the abortion if it were illegal.[91]

Several physicians, including Dr. John Jewett of Massachusetts, have written articles citing errors committed by abortionists. Dr. Jewett looked at the case of a woman who began having problems with her pregnancy and was told by her doctors that the best course of action would be to abort. He dared to suggest that there were other ways to have handled the crisis that would have been much more beneficial to the patient.[92] A reasonable argument can be made that Dr. Jewett was right, since the woman died from complications of the abortion. But the CDC completely ignored his view.

In 1979, a Fort Lauderdale Ob/Gyn wrote about the increased number of teenage patients he was seeing as a result of abortion complications. He stated that, "of the 54 teenage patients seen with significant complications after legal abortions, one factor common to all of them stands out. None of them felt they had been afforded any meaningful information about the potential dangers of the abortion operation."[93] Some of these girls had stopped taking their birth control after reading of its dangers. They were unconcerned about going without contraceptives because they felt they could always have an abortion. Their attitude was that since abortion was legal, it had to be safe. Two physicians in Minnesota stated, "All members of the medical profession must be cognizant of the methods and possible complications of therapeutic abortion so that counseling and care may be delivered to every woman who considers having an abortion."[94] Again, these dissenters to the "abortion-is-always-good" philosophy were ignored by the CDC.

If a person dares to question data released by CDC people, or state that there might be a better way to tabulate the data, this person is quickly informed that he or she is misguided and mistaken. Dr. Denis Cavanagh has butted heads with Cates, Grimes, and others at the CDC on several occasions. In one instance, CDC employees became so engrossed in trying to prove Cavanagh wrong that they totally changed his words to fit their argument.

At the end of a medical journal article, Cavanagh had written some remarks concerning a hypothesis of another physician (Dr. Thomas Hilgers of Australia). The CDC employees took offense at his words, although they had misquoted him in the article. Cavanagh had been quoted by the CDC employees as saying "liberalized abortion laws have caused more deaths of women of childbearing age than they have prevented." What he had actually said was, "I believe it is possible that had liberalized abortion not been introduced in 1967 there might have been fewer deaths than were in the last year recorded." As you can see, the meaning is quite different. The guys in Atlanta had also taken exception to the data Dr. Hilgers had used. Cavanagh explained that the reason Hilgers used that data was because he thought it was more accurate.

Ironically, the data that caused the CDC employees so much grief had originally come from the CDC.[95]

Finally, several people from a medical college in Wisconsin took exception to the CDC's comparison of mortality between women with live births and women with abortions, in order to show that abortion is safer. These people felt that it would be better to compare women with abortions to women with vaginal deliveries, and exclude women who give birth by C-section. Since most abortions are vaginal, not abdominal, this seemed only fair. It is known that abdominal delivery has a much higher complication rate than vaginal delivery. When vaginal childbirth was compared to abortion, abortion had almost twice as high a mortality rate as childbirth. The CDC employees felt that these comparisons could not be done because precise national data was not available for vaginal and abdominal deliveries. Precise national data is not available on abortion either, yet they make comparisons with these numbers whenever it suits their purpose. The CDC concludes that childbirth is more dangerous than abortion, and refuses to acknowledge that in comparing vaginal childbirth to vaginal abortion, the numbers favor childbirth.[96]

Massaging the Data

Occasionally, the CDC takes a direct route to distort results. In 1978, CDC employees published an article on the use of vital statistics and the surveillance program in monitoring abortion deaths. Their intent was to assess how well they were doing. They used a certain mathematical method, called Chandrasekaran-Deming, to tabulate the number of deaths that are not reported by the CDC. They compared abortion data gathered by the NCHS with abortion data collected by the CDC. By using the above mathematical method, they determined that the CDC could account for 94 percent of all abortion deaths in the country during the years of the study.[97]

There is only one small problem with this. The Chandrasekaran-Deming method is supposed to be used to compare "the results of two independent systems of ascertaining the same event and provides an estimate of the completeness of ascertainment in both systems."[98] But according to one researcher, the CDC failed to use the Chandrasekaran-Deming method properly because the surveillance information provided to the CDC came primarily from the same sources that should have reported the death to NCHS in the first place.[99] Therefore, the CDC's results cannot be valid using this method of tabulation. The CDC attempts to prove its competency by comparing its data with that from the NCHS, knowing that its data has to be better because it uses NCHS data as its starting point. The only conceivable reason for the CDC to make these comparisons would be to boost how the public perceives its performance.

Another deceitful practice used by the CDC is "incestuous citing." Remember how one CDC employee, Dr. Carol Hogue, used her own studies to prove her point about late-term effects of abortion? This is similar, except that instead of citing themselves, the CDC employees cite each other to prove their points. When we researched articles by CDC employees, we found them literally teeming with examples of this.

In one instance, in an attempt to discredit Dr. Thomas Hilgers' criticism of American abortion policies, Cates writes a response to Hilgers' testimony before the Australian Royal Commission on Human Relationships. Cates just happens to reference his co-workers' articles to defend his position. He, like Dr. Hogue, also cites himself.[100] In another article, written by CDC employees as well as several abortionists, the authors use 37 references to back up their findings. Of those, 35 were by known abortion advocates or practicing abortionists. The other two may also have been, but we were not able to identify them. Another interesting thing about this particular article is that, with only one exception, every CDC employee writing this article was an abortionist.[101]

One final example of CDC employees using their own cohorts for their sources comes from the *1981 CDC Abortion Surveillance Annual Summary*. This report states that the CDC makes a "critical review of scientific literature on the effects of induced abortion on subsequent childbearing." It then lists one hundred such articles. However, they fail to mention that every single article cited was written by CDC employees.[102]

When we were examining the data on deaths reported by the CDC, we noticed a very strange phenomenon. There were some women who were counted as abortion deaths one year, but were not counted the next year.[103] We later learned that in the mid-1970s, the CDC assembled a panel of experts on abortion to create definitions for each category of abortion deaths. Their job was to determine what constituted an induced or spontaneous abortion. For induced abortion, they also defined terms for legal, illegal, and unknown abortions. By 1977, the new definitions for classifying abortion deaths were in place. One change was that if an abortion was induced to expel a fetus who was already dead, and a maternal death also occurred, the woman's death would be counted as a *spontaneous* abortion death. Previously, this death would have been counted as a legal abortion death because it was the abortion procedure that caused the woman's death. Based on the new definitions, abortion deaths that the CDC had previously labeled as legal were reclassifed as spontaneous.

Hidden Killer—Ectopic Pregnancy

Another decision the CDC made was that ectopic deaths occurring after an abortion would no longer be counted as abortion deaths.[104] This enabled them to avoid counting women who died because their abortionist failed to diagnose their ectopic pregnancies. According to Dr. James Breen of New Jersey, "The diagnosis of ectopic pregnancy is not usually difficult if the physician keeps in mind the fact that this is a potential hazard in any woman in her reproductive years."[105] However, when the CDC published an article covering ten deaths from ectopic pregnancy following a legal abortion, it found that no diagnostic action was taken by the physicians at the time of the abortion, because an ectopic pregnancy was never suspected. The CDC authors also state that most deaths from ectopic pregnancy after legal abortion can probably be prevented. The key is early diagnosis, which is the responsibility of the doctor providing the abortion. He has a prime opportunity to do this by simply examining the contents of the uterus. If no signs of fetal tissue are found, ectopic pregnancy has to be suspected.[106]

The problem is that many abortion clinics simply discard the fetal tissue with no examination. In one of many examples, a woman died from an ectopic pregnancy after an abortion in Chicago. The clinic, in an attempt to save up to $50,000 a year, would throw away tissue from the abortion procedure instead of sending it in for a pathology report. They did not even keep the tissue samples from different woman in separate containers. Instead they allowed the bottle in which the tissue was collected to fill up before dumping the tissue. A newspaper reported that they found three other abortion clinics and one lab not following proper procedures in collecting, examining, and reporting results from tissue samples.[107]

Sometimes, tissue that is to be sent to a lab for inspection is improperly collected. In Florida, state inspectors found that a "clinic's procedure for collecting products of conception included the use of a kitchen strainer, which was contaminated with dried blood. This would compromise any pathological testing of the tissue." They went on to say, "The clinic does not notify patients whose pathology tests indicate their abortion was incomplete—or that no products of conception were removed, which would mean their pregnancy was tubal or that they were never pregnant at all."[108] The clinic also had an old suction machine that was not used anymore that still had tissue in it. Whoever had this tissue removed was placed at risk because their tissue was never tested. Several CDC employees found that although women seeking abortions had fewer ectopic pregnancies than those not having an abortion, the risk of death from ectopic pregnancy is greater for the woman having the abortion.[109]

Three pathologists wrote a letter to the editor of a pathology lab journal in 1993. In it, they urged pathologists to use their influence on the national and state levels to see that abortion clinics are adequately regulated, especially in regard to pathology reports. They concluded that if the abortion doctors followed regulations, fewer women would be dead.[110]

So what do researchers say about the causes of ectopic pregnancy? They all agree that it is a very pressing problem, since ectopic pregnancy is the leading cause of maternal deaths in the U.S. during the first trimester.[111] Interestingly, several studies suggest that ectopic pregnancies can be caused by legal abortions. So, not only does an abortion increase a woman's chances of dying from an ectopic pregnancy, but it may actually cause the ectopic pregnancy. One such study showed a clear association between having infection or retained tissue following an abortion and ectopic pregnancy.[112] Another study shows a parallel increase in induced abortions and ectopic pregnancies, suggesting that ectopic pregnancies may be caused by induced abortion.[113] An article in a leading medical journal found that,

Since abortion was legalized, ectopic pregnancies have sky- rocketed. Ironically, in these instances, abortion doesn't terminate just the current pregnancy, but future preg- nancies as well—and may also terminate the mother.

"Ectopic pregnancy, estimated to be responsible for 5% to 10% of maternal deaths in the United States, was listed as a sequela of suction curettage [abortion] in New York City after one year's experience with liberalized abortion and also has been reported increasingly common in Japanese women after abortion."[114] Since abortion was legalized, ectopic pregnancies have skyrocketed. In 1970 there were 17,800, and by 1987 the number had swelled to 88,000.[115] Ironically, in these instances, abortion doesn't terminate just the current pregnancy, but future pregnancies as well—and may also terminate the mother.

Ectopic pregnancies are also related to other factors that may initially seem unconnected. For example, throughout the world, the rate of Pelvic Inflammatory Disease (PID) found in any nation correlates with the incidence of ectopic pregnancy in that nation.[116] A study from the CDC states that the most generally accepted cause of ectopic pregnancy is PID.[117] This does not bode well for induced abortion either, since one of the side effects of abortion is PID.[118] One major factor in the occurrence of pelvic inflammatory disease is the presence of chlamydia. As a triple whammy to induced abortion, the chlamydia that causes the PID, which causes the ectopic pregnancy, is some-times introduced into the uterus and Fallopian tubes by an induced abortion procedure.[119] All these studies recommend that women, especially the young, be screened for chlamydia and other Sexually Transmitted Diseases (STDs) before the abortion procedure.[120]

This is not being done on even a modest scale in the United States. The reason is that the woman would need to be tested at least a day before her abortion so that the results would be at the clinic by the time the abortion is performed. If the results are not known at that time, the woman would need to be treated just in case. Antibiotics have proven very effective in treating this particular STD as long as the dose is taken in full and started no later than the day of the abortion.[121] But because the American abortion industry is based on high-volume, quick-turnaround clinics, few women receive antibiotics appro-priate for treating STDs, puting them at greater risk for the complications mentioned above. This is another way the abortion industry shows that its concern is not for the woman's health but for their bottom line.

Despite the fact that an ectopic pregnancy with induced abortion has a higher risk of death than an ectopic without an abortion attempt, the CDC did not separate them and instead lumped all ectopic deaths into one category. So now, instead of a death from an ectopic pregnancy after an abortion being counted as an abortion death, it is purely ectopic—therefore, nobody knows how many ectopic deaths can be linked to abortion. To test the effect of this statistical maneuver, we obtained a list of California's ectopic pregnancy deaths for 1960 to 1993. We chose California because their health department was unusually cooperative, and because California legalized abortion quite some time prior to *Roe v. Wade*, and therefore has a longer experience with it than the nation as a whole. In addition, with 20 percent of all the abortions in America, their numbers would be large enough to be statistically significant.

We then obtained 25 randomly selected death certificates for women who were counted as having died from ectopic pregnancies. From those, we randomly chose four cases and requested their autopsy reports. We did not get a larger number because copies of autopsy reports in California are very expensive. Of the four, we confirmed that two had undergone abortions immediately prior to their deaths,[122] and another one was questionable. If our admittedly small sample was extrapolated over the entire country, the num-bers could be significant. By the way, the CDC does not count either of the cases we found as deaths due to abortion.

Since abortion is implicated in the increase in ectopic pregnancies and deaths, the CDC's 1977 change in ectopic reporting removed from the picture a potential major player in legal abortion deaths. If you're trying to conceal deaths due to abortion, this is a very nice move if you can get away with it. And they did.

AIDS and Breast Cancer

There are two other possible complications from abortion that may have long-range effects on women's health: AIDS and breast cancer. As discussed in other chapters, equipment that must be kept sterile is sometimes used on multiple patients before being sterilized. Indeed, some equipment is never sterilized properly. Incredibly, the CDC has been virtually silent on this issue. In fact, we could not find one reference to it in CDC literature, despite the tragic potential for cross-contamination.

As for breast cancer, to date there have been more than twenty studies showing a possible link with abortion. (See Chapter 6.) However, only one CDC employee, Dr. Willard Cates, has chosen to write on the subject. Of course, he gave the party line and was predictably hostile to the theory.[123] Some cancer researchers feel the evidence is inconclusive at this time while others feel that women, especially those under 18, should be told that breast cancer is a risk factor after induced abortion.[124] Every researcher we've found who does not have a political loyalty to the abortion industry, and even some who do, feels there should be more research. It seems to be only a few hardcore abortion advocates who are so sure there is no link. I'll let you draw your own conclusion as to why.

Illegal Abortions

In 1977, the CDC advised the American people that if publicly funded abortions were available to low-income women, they might not get illegal abortions.[125] But the evidence does not seem to back them up. Three years after this report, CDC employees published an article stating that in 1978 three women in one area tried to self-induce abortions, and one died as a result. The CDC ignored that this occurred in a state that pays for abortions for low-income women.[126]

Two years later, the same employees published an article saying that, "In areas where public funding was unavailable, most low-income women apparently paid for legal abortions from private funds rather than resort to illegal procedures." But at the conclusion of this article, they again stated that public funding for abortions could reduce the number of illegal abortion deaths. Flopping once more, they go on to say, "However, because many women seek illegal abortion for idiosyncratic reasons unrelated to cost or availability, a small number of illegal-abortion deaths will probably continue to occur."[127]

Proof that they had inadvertently stumbled across the truth is the illegal abortion death of a 32-year-old California resident. She had an appointment at a local abortion clinic on April 30, 1990, to terminate her second-trimester pregnancy. But two days before this appointment, she allowed her boyfriend to insert a plastic tube into her uterus in an attempt to abort the fetus. It is not clear why she did not wait for her scheduled appointment. An additional problem for the CDC is that this woman didn't fit too well into any of their stereotypes. She had been a systems analyst at a defense contractor for five years, she was college educated, and it is doubtful that she was ignorant of the dangers of illegal abortion. Also, she was fully aware that legal abortion services were available because she had an appointment at an abortion clinic. Finally, at 32 years old, she was not too young to know any better.[128]

The CDC writers constantly call for federal funding of abortion to protect the health and safety of American women, but conveniently ignore research conducted over twenty years ago. This research shows that complication rates for women whose abortion was paid for by the government were significantly higher than for abortions that were paid for by the woman herself.[129]

The Federal Courts

Not only does the public get duped by the CDC, but so does the judicial system. One example occurred in June 1983, as the Supreme Court again heard arguments on the safety and regulations of abortion. This time, second-trimester abortions were the point in question and the Court used the testimony of Cates and Grimes to rule in favor of easing some regulations on these abortions. The Court also used public health recommendations based on the premise that outpatient Dilatation and Evacuation (D&E) procedures were safer than those performed in the hospital.[130] However, this recommendation failed to take into account that, by this time, the overwhelming majority of abortions were being performed in clinics. Normally, the only patients who have the procedure performed in a hospital are those who were too ill to have it done in a clinic. Therefore, the comparison was being made between healthy women having abortions in outpatient clinics, and unhealthy women having abortions in a hospital. Also, it is likely that the procedures performed in clinics were done at earlier gestational ages than those in the hospital. It stretches the imagination to believe that Cates and Grimes were not aware of the problems with the study being used to decide the Supreme Court case, and yet they remained silent.[131]

Field Testing New Products

Many times, women having abortions are unknowingly used in the research and development of new products for the market. One example is saline abortions, a technique that had been abandoned in almost every other developed nation in the world. U.S. abortionists were somewhat stuck with saline and prostaglandin abortions for late-stage pregnancies because no other available method was any safer and yet still killed the fetus. In fact, two other late-term procedures, hysterectomy and hysterotomy, had even worse complication and death rates. It was not until the late 1970s that doctors realized they could use the D&E method at higher gestational ages. After that was learned, literature written by CDC employees finally started appearing in medical journals that encouraged its use in place of the more dangerous instillation procedures.[132] Prostaglandin procedures were even being done in physician's offices despite the drug manufacturer's recommendation that it be used only in a hospital setting.[133] Just like the reusing of instruments that are meant to be discarded, this was a violation of the law.

Another glaring example of allowing women to be experimented upon is the super-coil method. These coils were forty centimeters (almost 16 inches) long and were wound into a spiral. The abortionist would straighten out the coil, put it in an inserter, and place the coil in the uterus.[134] As many coils were inserted as would fit into the uterus, and they were removed by an attached string within 12 to 24 hours. At that time, the fetus should be expelled. The coil's inventor stated that they were safe for use by paramedical personnel.[135] When this method was tested on 15 women in Philadelphia, two were lost to follow-up so their outcome is not known. Nine of the 13 who were available for follow-up had some complication. Of these nine, three had major complications. One had lacerations severe enough to require a total hysterectomy, one had an infection that caused her to be hospitalized for twenty days, and one had heavy vaginal bleeding that caused anemia.[136]

After investigating the usage of the coils, the CDC stated, "Until the super-coil abortion technique is demonstrated to be safe in the hands of competent medical personnel and in a controlled research setting, the CDC findings suggest that it is not appropriate for use by paramedical personnel."[137] None of the women in the test knew that the procedure they were undergoing was experimental, or that they were being taped by a television crew of an educational station in New York.[138]

Two months before the Philadelphia incident, the super coil's inventor asked the United Nations to help get abortion providers and supplies to villages in Bangladesh. This abortion aid was sought because of approximately

20,000 pregnancies that resulted from Pakistani soldiers raping Bengali women during a war between the two countries. The inventor was in Bangladesh as a member of a team of abortion experts assembled by the International Planned Parenthood Federation and a New York women's health group.[139] One of the techniques used in these Bengali abortions was the super coil.[140]

The inventor of the super coil called himself Dr. Harvey Karman. Unbeknownst to the abortion industry, the CDC, and all the women who had his procedure done on them, Karman was not a doctor at all. He was actually an ex-convict with a master's degree in theater arts. The man's police record included nine felonies in Los Angeles County alone. He had been convicted of grand theft, had caused the death of a woman in an illegal abortion by using a nutcracker on her in a hotel room, and was involved with multiple other illegal abortions that resulted in injuries to the women. The most cursory of background investigations by the CDC would have revealed this information, but apparently one was never done.[141] Amazingly, all the CDC ever did was issue a tepid recommendation that paramedical personnel not be allowed to use his super-coil method.

The CDC Today

As we tried to determine what the CDC is currently doing regarding abortion, we discovered that the people involved were extraordinarily reluctant to talk to us. Time and again, when we attempted to get even the most rudimentary information, we were "handed off" from one person to the next, asked what we wanted the information for, or told we would have to file a request under the Freedom of Information Act. It became crystal clear that asking questions about abortion made some people at the CDC extremely nervous.

What we wanted to discover was: Is the Abortion Surveillance Branch still being run by people with a political agenda, or has it been cleaned up? The first thing we learned is that the Abortion Surveillance Branch no longer even exists. When we asked to speak to the people overseeing statistics on abortion, we were directed to the Division of Reproductive Health. A woman there told us that abortion mortality is handled by Dr. Clarice Green in the Pregnancy and Infant Health Branch. As it turns out, Green is not a permanent employee of the CDC, but is instead a two-year research fellow. She explained that she researches the death reports she receives to gather enough information so that a panel of CDC doctors can determine their correct classification (legal, illegal, spontaneous, or unclassified).

We could find no evidence that Dr. Green has any ties to the abortion industry. However, she did tell us that all death certificates must first go through a department run by a woman named Lisa Koonin. In fact, Green told us that even if she learns of a possible abortion death from an outside source, she cannot investigate it until Koonin's office confirms the death as being abortion-related. If her office does not confirm it, the investigation ends there. Interestingly, Lisa Koonin is currently listed on the Editorial Advisory Committee of a magazine published by the Alan Guttmacher Institute—the research arm of Planned Parenthood.[142] She was also a presenter at a 1995 National Abortion Federation conference.[143]

Also interesting is the insignificance that the CDC places on the study of abortion morbidity and mortality. When asked why the collection and dissemination of this data is so poor, Dr. Green said, "…resources are very scarce now. I mean, there really was a large cohort of staff involved in abortion epidemiology surveillance and mortality [but] there were cuts everywhere. It's just basically gone from a four- to six-man team, to one to two. And resources are just not there anymore."[144] However, during one of our conversations with Koonin, she pointed out that the Division of Reproductive Health had grown from 25 or 30 to almost 140. It seems strange that this department would experience an explosion in personnel, while there was a simultaneous reduction in the staff assigned to investigate complications from the most common surgical procedure performed in America.

The CDC is actually going to publish a study on the safety of abortion based on information supplied by the abortion industry!

When we asked Dr. Green when the CDC was going to release updated abortion morbidity information, she responded that they are in the process of "editing" data gathered from a research project that began in 1973 and concluded in 1988. She volunteered that their current goal was to have this "new" data ready for release in the summer of 1996, adding, "We're really looking forward to getting our hands on that data, but until that point all we have is the more, what I would consider, obsolete data on abortion morbidity."[145]

Now, if you think it's outrageous that the CDC takes eight years to publish information—which is as much as 23 years old—wait until you hear where they got the data. After more than a week's investigation, we were able to confirm that the data the CDC intends to release in 1996 is from a joint project between the CDC and a St. Louis area abortion clinic. In short, the CDC is actually going to publish a study on the safety of abortion based on information supplied by the abortion industry!

When we contacted the clinic involved, its director denied that it had ever received money for participating in this study. However, we tracked down the doctor who was the facility's medical director while the study was underway, and he confirmed that the CDC did indeed fund the project. It will probably not surprise you to learn that when we tried to find out how much money was paid to this abortion clinic, the people at the Division of Reproductive Health were quite uncooperative. (In an unrelated, but important, statement, this former medical director volunteered that when Grimes and Cates were at the CDC, they "always came to all the National Abortion Federation meetings, and all the Planned Parenthood meetings" at taxpayer expense.[146])

As we have discussed before, the CDC may not be able to produce much in the way of morbidity and mortality statistics, but they can crank out demographic (marketing) data almost overnight. Currently, they have a "hotline" that the public can call 24 hours a day to find out such "vital" information as the following:

- Reported legal abortions by marital status and state of occurrence

- Reported legal abortions by number of previous legal abortions and state of occurrence

- Percentage of abortions obtained by out-of-state residents and state of occurrence

- Reported legal abortions by Hispanic origin and state of occurrence

- Reported legal abortions by number of previous live births and state of occurrence

- Number and percentage of reported legal abortions by race, age, and marital status

This hotline even offers to fax you the marketing data listed above. When we accepted the offer, within 10 minutes we had 12 pages of text, graphs, and charts that would be invaluable to an abortion clinic owner who's trying to decide where and how to advertise, and who the advertising should target. However, it had absolutely no value to someone wanting to know the safety record of abortion, or the rate of complications. For that, the hotline gives the phone number of the Pregnancy and Infant Health Branch. Of course, this is not a 24-hour-a-day service, but if you know how to jump through the right hoops and have the patience to do so, you can get some morbidity/mortality information that Dr. Green admits is "obsolete."

When we questioned Lisa Koonin about the public health value of this demographic information, she readily admitted that it "doesn't relate to morbidity" and gave some vague justifications about "trends" and "utilization of services." Again, as someone with an extensive marketing background, I can tell you that all this sounds strangely familiar. When we pressed Koonin about why so much emphasis was placed on demographic data, and so little on the morbidity and mortality that the CDC is supposed to be tracking, she remained completely silent and spoke only to change the subject.

We later had information about the CDC that needed verification, as well as some statements Koonin had made that conflicted with what we had been told by other CDC employees. When we called her with questions, she insisted that we fax them to her. We agreed, and sent her a fax asking her to address nine very simple issues, all of which could have been answered "yes" or "no." She stalled for three days, claiming that she had to consult with various other people, and repeatedly promised to call us back. Not surprisingly, she never returned a single call during that time.

Eventually, Koonin told us that (a) they were not going to respond to the nine issues raised in our fax, (b) her supervisor had ordered her to no longer answer our questions over the phone, and (c) we would have to submit the text of our book for review before they would answer questions. She tried to justify her position by claiming that her answers might be used "out of context," when the answers to these questions could not possibly change based on their context. It seemed to us that the CDC wanted editorial control over what were going to publish before they would answer our questions. Eventually, Koonin told us that the CDC would no longer answer our questions—even if they were submitted in writing. She said that, from this point on, we could get information only by filing a claim under the Freedom of Information Act.

To learn whether the entire CDC worked this way, or just those involved in abortion, we changed gears and called to request information about tobacco. Contrary to our earlier experience, the people at the Office on Smoking and Health were quite willing to answer any question we asked, and in fact supplied us with far more data than we wanted. They not only seemed eager to help, but their attitudes were the complete opposite of those whom we contacted about abortion information. When we asked whether they would ever collaborate with the tobacco industry in a study on the health effects of smoking, a spokeswoman said, "I can't imagine us ever doing this...we never would."[147] Among the people we talked to at the Office on Smoking and Health, the consensus was that it would be unthinkable to let the tobacco industry control the health-related data that the CDC releases on smoking. We also noticed that the data they supplied was current (they faxed us five studies, with the oldest relating to data compiled in 1990) and was directly related to the health issues surrounding tobacco. And they do not disseminate health-related statistics compiled by the tobacco industry.

At the Office on Smoking and Health, the consensus was that it would be un-thinkable to let the tobacco industry control the health-related data that the CDC releases on smoking.

They too have a hotline but this one actually contains current morbidity and mortality data, including 12 articles on quitting smoking, 10 on the effects of second-hand smoke, and 14 on teenage smoking. And even the articles that appear to concentrate on demographic data have some readily apparent health component. Lastly, the abortion hotline refers callers to the Alan Guttmacher Institute for additional information, and even repeats their phone number twice. By contrast, the tobacco hotline never suggests that the caller contact R. J. Reynolds Tobacco Company, nor does it give their phone number.

In the Final Analysis

Clearly, when it comes to information about abortion, the CDC is a complete fraud. It is my opinion that if a private sector company or organization were found to be engaging in a similar coverup, those responsible would stand a good chance of ending up in prison. Since the day it was created, the Abortion Surveillance Branch was run by people who functioned as abortion-industry operatives. Today, though this department no longer exists, the goal of those who took over its role remains the same: (a) to keep to a minimum the reporting of abortion morbidity and mortality, (b) to neutralize any outside sources that claim there may be problems with abortion, and (c) to perpetuate the view that abortion is safer than childbirth—even when there is evidence to the contrary. As stated at the beginning of this chapter, when the subject is abortion, the CDC has decided that its mission is not surveillance but damage control.

Interestingly, I am apparently not the first to come to that conclusion. During a conversation with Dr. Jack Willke, president of Life Issues Institute in Cincinatti, Ohio, he mentioned that he had made a similar observation almost 10 years ago. In a follow-up letter to me, he stated:

> As president of the National Right to Life during Reagan's second term, I grew increasingly concerned about the lack of definitive data regarding abortion morbidity and mortality. I

shared this with Dr. James Mason, Assistant Secretary of Health, and with the Surgeon General, Dr. C. Everett Koop.

They both agreed that the time had come for a major study. We all agreed that with almost no exception, the published studies on abortion's psychological aftermath were invalid, and those on the physical dangers were inadequate. Accordingly, a meeting was arranged at the Centers for Disease Control in Atlanta on July 25, 1986, to consider such a study.

Dr. Mason welcomed us but then had to leave. Attending were Dennis Tolsma, James Marks, and other senior staff. Pro-life attendees included Matthew Bulfin, Gene Diamond, Richard Glasow, Thomas Hilgers, Dennis Horan, Jacqueline Kasun, and myself. It lasted all afternoon.

After a lengthy explanation of the CDC's surveillance system, the staff spent most of the rest of the day on every possible detail of the dangers of pregnancy and birth. We were given exhaustive details on why, in their opinion, it was more dangerous than induced abortion.

The extreme difficulty of setting up a valid study on abortion was repeated ad nauseum. Every imaginable objection was presented at great length.

By 5:00 p.m. an unsophisticated observer would have been convinced that such a study was all but impossible and, since it was so obvious that pregnancy was more dangerous, why even try.

My initial skepticism slowly changed to conviction and finally to anger. It was painfully obvious that these staff members were confirmed pro-abortion advocates, and that they didn't have the slightest intention of doing our study.

At the end I spoke in professional language, but rather directly. I all but condemned their thinly veiled bias. I repeated what was needed—a five-year, prospective, double-blind study of perhaps 20,000 women in different locations. I accused them of deliberately trying to so confuse the issue, and to make it so difficult that such a study would not be done.

Sadly, I was correct. Faced with a stonewall at CDC, and the study's high cost, nothing was done. My report to the Department of Health and Human Services was probably duly filed away.

I remain convinced that there is a conspiracy of silence by the administration at the CDC. Nothing less than their replacement will change this unfortunate situation.[148]

Noted economist Milton Friedman once observed that government agencies inevitably become the servants of those they are created to oversee, stating that, "it's in the clear and immediate interest of the regulated industry or industries to either neutralize the effect of that agency or use it to their advantage."[149]

Friedman was not talking specifically about the CDC, but he obviously could have been. Of course, some readers of this book may be tempted to overlook the fact that the CDC is run by people with an undeniable pro-abortion agenda. Perhaps they want to give these people the benefit of the doubt, and just blindly accept that they are too noble to allow their political beliefs to compromise the safety of American women. If someone is naive enough to believe that, fine. The only problem is that they then have to answer some rather provocative questions. For example:

- Why does the CDC always have its demographic (marketing) data out in no more than three years, but take at least twice that long to publish data about morbidity or mortality? (As of November 1995, we're still waiting for an official death count for 1988.)

- Why do CDC writers ignore or denigrate foreign studies that state anything negative about abortion while citing and praising those that say positive things—regardless of the health implications for women? And why do they either attack or ignore American researchers who say negative things about abortion? (The only acceptable attitude about abortion seems to be: "If you can't say something nice, don't say anything at all.")

- How is an agency that takes years to release abortion data to the public able to respond overnight to any medical journal article that raises questions about the safety of abortion?

- Why is it that even when the CDC grudgingly admits to a particular problem with abortion, they make no legitimate proposals for solutions?

- Why does the CDC allow American women to be used as guinea pigs for dangerous abortion techniques and unproven abortion products?

- Why does the CDC publish almost no information about the management of abortion complications, or about managing a problem pregnancy through any means other than abortion?

- Why do CDC authors publish articles in which they cite other articles they wrote, or articles written by their colleagues at the CDC, as proof of their position? (How much credibility would this book have if all the articles cited in the endnotes were written by employees of Life Dynamics, National Right to Life, and the American Life League?)

- Why are CDC employees willing to give deceptive testimony to the United States Supreme Court?

- Why are obvious conflicts of interest that violate the government's ethics guidelines openly tolerated at the CDC?

- Why do articles written by CDC employees inevitably blame complications of legal abortion on the mother, abortion restrictions, or the lack of federal funding for abortion, but never on the abortionists or on the possibility that the procedure itself is dangerous?

- Since the CDC admits that abortion can spread chlamydia thereby causing PID, which leads to sterility, why do they rail at the suggestion that abortion can cause sterility? It's like admitting that driving too fast on a rain-slick road can cause a skid leading to a fatal accident, while claiming that driving too fast in the rain is not related to traffic deaths.

- Why do CDC writers consistently allege that the lack of public funding for abortion poses a threat to the health and safety of women, when studies have shown that complication rates are significantly higher for publicly funded abortions than those paid for by the patient?

The list of questions is endless, but the point is that the time has come for Congress to exercise its authority, and either turn the CDC into what it was originally intended to be or defund it. With over 6,000 employees and a budget of approximately $250,000 *an hour*—24 hours a day, 365 days a year[150]—the performance of this organization should outrage taxpayers, regardless of their political position on abortion. It is utterly indefensible that after more than 20 years of legalized abortion, we have absolutely no statistics that the public can feel confident are unbiased, reliable, and accurate on the most commonly performed invasive surgery in America. And it is even more indefensible that we allow people to work for an agency of the U.S. Government who, in order to protect their political agenda, are willing to see young women put in nursing homes and early graves.

While what we have included in this chapter is far from all we found, it is simply all we could prove. With a larger budget, experienced researchers, and access to information that is currently off-limits to us, we are confident that we could prove conclusively that the CDC is not a watchdog over abortion, but a guard dog for the abortion industry. Ironically, as conspirators often do, the folks at the CDC are actually proving by their actions what they set out to cover up. Don't forget, they know the real story about abortion's safety. And with their clearly defined political positions, if the story was good, statistics would be released instantly and with complete accuracy. The fact is, people don't cover up good news.

■

Vacant Souls

Powerful evidence that the punishment for doing abortions
is life as an abortionist

In every legal abortion there are three main participants: the unborn, the woman, and the abortionist. Throughout the history of the abortion struggle, much has been written about the politics of abortion and about what the procedure itself does to the unborn and the women involved. But virtually nothing has been written about what the procedure does to the abortionist. That's what this chapter is about. It begins by looking at the bizarre environment in which abortionists live and the incredible amount of stress it creates in their lives. It also examines the toll that stress takes on them, and then documents the many ways women are impacted by the stress their abortionists are under. In the end, it is clear that abortion doesn't play favorites. It devastates everyone it touches.

Environment

The Misery of Inner Conflict

Political advocates of legal abortion fiercely claim that abortion is just an ordinary medical procedure and that those who participate in it are merely practicing regular medicine. Yet many actual abortion providers say that life in the abortion industry is not like life in the rest of the medical community. And the distinctions are seldom, if ever, positive. In 1976, Magda Denes released *In Necessity and Sorrow*, a book about day-to-day life in an abortion facility. In it, one of the counselors who had worked there for over two years disclosed some of her feelings: "I don't know, I feel emotionally beaten up. And when I leave here every day, I have a hard time turning it off, and turning on the next thing...And I think it wouldn't be so bad if my work were not this kind of painful and draining as it is to me, here...The drain is from what the system is like, in addition to whatever the procedure is like. And the emotional built-in thing, because it's abortion. A lot of the drain is from the way people don't work or tell lies to each other all the time. It's a horrible environment to work in."[1]

Her opinion is not unique. Charlotte Taft, the former administrator of a Dallas abortion clinic, says, "Abortion providers are isolated. We haven't really done a very good job of making the physicians who work with us really feel connected...They're isolated in terms of the medical field, because, as you well know, it's been marginalized as a sub-specialty of gynecology...And then there's the social isolation that happens when someone is scared to tell what they do...These guys are pitiful."[2]

Our research for this book showed no shortage of evidence that the first problem abortionists must grapple with is their own internal conflict regarding the procedure itself. Here are just a few examples of this:

> Abortionist David Zbaraz told the *Washington Post*, "It's a nasty, dirty, yucky thing and I always come home angry." The article went on to say that, "on those days when he performs an abortion, his wife can tell as soon as he walks in the door."[3]

> Sallie Tisdale, a nurse in an abortion clinic, writes, "There are weary, grim moments when I think I cannot bear another basin of bloody remains, utter another kind phrase of reassurance...'How can you stand it?' even the clients ask. They see the machine, the strange instruments, the blood, the final stroke that wipes away the promise of pregnancy. Sometimes I see that too: I watch a woman's swollen abdomen sink to softness in a few stuttering moments and my own belly flip-flops with sorrow."[4]

> In a *New York Times* editorial, Dr. Susan Conde said, "I observed during my medical training as an Australian physician many abortions by experienced practitioners. They experienced, without exception, physical revulsion and moral bewilderment."[5]

A nurse in the Midwest remembers how the nurses and physicians all began to have internal problems over the abortions performed at a hospital. In a demonstration of uneasiness with the abortions she was doing, a woman physician "walked out of the operating room after doing six abortions. She smeared her hand [which was covered with blood] on mine and said, 'Go wash it off. That's the hand that did it.'"[6]

One abortionist confessed, "As a physician I'm trained to conserve life and here I am destroying life...I guess I feel guilty because according to the Hippocratic oath you're not supposed to do abortions, and according to the Maimonides oath you're not supposed to do abortions. So how could you be trained and raised one way, and suddenly be told it's okay to do it?" He went on to talk about his experience with saline abortions and the fact that the fetus moves around before the injection, thrashes around immediately after it, but then the movement ceases: "You know that there is something alive in there that you're killing."[7]

During a workshop sponsored by the National Abortion Federation, one nurse described her horror as an abortionist she worked for pulled out a cannula (the suction tube used in a D&C) and a tiny foot was sticking out of it.[8]

Judith Fetrow, a former clinic worker from San Francisco, revealed that in her experience, "clinic workers have very mixed emotions about abortion...Clinic workers may say they support a woman's right to choose, but they will also say that they do not want to see tiny hands and tiny feet. They do not want to be faced with the consequences of their actions...There is a great difference between the intellectual support of a woman's right to choose and the actual participation in the carnage of abortion. Because seeing body parts bothers the workers."[9]

Beyond these sorts of anecdotal statements, there has also been some research done in this area. Researchers Constance Nathanson and Marshall Becker observed, "Some studies have suggested that some physicians experience considerable personal disturbances over the abortion procedure itself." Nathanson and Becker's own study found that 41.8 percent of Maryland

Ob/Gyns who support the *Roe v. Wade* ruling are often or sometimes disturbed by abortion. Of those who are disturbed, 37.1 percent admit that the disturbance is severe or moderate.[10] A study of 130 San Francisco abortion clinic workers conducted between January 1984 and March 1985 found that 77 percent of them see abortion as a destructive act against a living thing, and 18 percent actually talked about it as murder. The study's author stated, "Particularly striking was the fact that discomfort with abortion clients or procedures was reported by practitioners who strongly supported abortion rights and expressed strong commitment to their work. This preliminary finding suggested that even those who support a woman's right to terminate a pregnancy may be struggling with an important tension between their formal beliefs and the situated experience of their abortion work."[11]

This type of internal conflict includes the issue of women who have repeat abortions. When a woman comes in after having had several abortions, the counselors start to question whether they should continue to see her. They differ on what their cutoff is for an acceptable number of abortions. Some say two, some four, some ten. Some realize that if abortion is truly a woman's choice, they have to treat every abortion as if it is just as acceptable as the last one. But most are not comfortable with that position. Of course, the problem that abortion advocates have with nonchalant repeat patients is largely their own doing. They have spent so much time downplaying any ethical considerations surrounding abortion that patients naturally don't think it should be a problem if they come back for another abortion in a few months. The clinic workers tell them that an abortion is nothing more than the removal of a small bit of tissue. Therefore, the patients don't expect those same nurses and doctors to have a problem with seeing more of that "tissue."

Then there is the problem of mid- and late-term abortions. As the fetus begins to physically resemble a newborn, it becomes harder to watch the abortion procedure. Employees have stronger emotional reactions to second-trimester abortions because "it's just that it's very easy not to need to face some of these issues...in first trimester."[12] One counselor admitted, "I am having difficulty with my feelings about late abortions also. More and more, I don't even know anymore if I believe in it. There is just so much pain."[13] A director of nursing points out that some of the later term fetuses are "getting pretty big...It is very traumatic for the staff to pick this up and put it in a container and say, 'Okay that's going to the incinerator.'"[14]

The procedure most commonly used in the second trimester is Dilatation and Evacuation (D&E), in which the abortionist uses forceps to dismember the fetus and pull it out of the woman's uterus one piece at a time. From an emotional standpoint, this method is particularly difficult because the abortionist and all those nearby have to view the torn pieces of the fetus. Then they "reassemble" the fetus to verify that none of it was left in the uterus. By contrast, in the first trimester, the fetus is pulled down a suction tube, so that only the person who cleans the machine has to view it. This D&E procedure meets a lot of resistance by abortionists, with the head of obstetrics at a Philadelphia teaching hospital admitting that they are "far more 'psychologically traumatizing' for doctors...I can't do them anymore."[15] In a paper presented to a Planned Parenthood conference, Dr. Warren Hern reported a intense emotional reaction from his staff after D&E operations. These included "physiological symptoms, sleep disturbances, effects on personal relationships, and moral anguish." He observed that the staff's reactions to the fetus ranged from refusal to look, dismay, and amazement, to disgust, fear, and sadness. The abortionist admitted that the procedure also caused him problems, saying, "The sensations of dismemberment flow through the forceps like an electric current."[16]

In addition to their own aversion to the procedure, the abortion providers also have to deal with the emotions of the women involved. Charlotte Taft, the former abortion clinic director mentioned earlier, once observed that, "For many women nowadays, they're angry that they had a choice. It's too bizarre, but it's like, 'If you weren't here, I wouldn't have had to make this choice.' And so, instead of feeling gratitude toward the physician and a sense of, you know, 'You've helped me so much,' a lot of times that woman [is] in her own pain or anger, or whatever, and the doctor may not get a lot of that [gratitude] these days. The woman herself may be anti-abortion."[17] When a woman doesn't want an abortion, but simply accepts it as her fate, she is unlikely to feel any gratitude toward the one who provided it. As one doctor said, "No one ever says 'Thank you' to an abortionist."[18]

The woman may also be ungrateful because she felt forced into the abortion by a boyfriend, husband, parent, school teacher, or even the society that says abortion is bad, but offers her no options. She may even feel that society is telling her she has no right to have her baby because she is poor or because the baby is handicapped. Even hardcore abortion activists sometimes suggest that women have not only a right—but a responsibility—to abort. For example, abortion advocate Ann Taylor-Flemming once urged the pro-chioce community to encourage more men to participate in the fight for legalized abortion by stating, "I dare say that many of them have impregnated women along the way, and been let off the hook in a big, big way; emotionally, economically, and every other way when the women went ahead and had abortions...The sense of relief for themselves was mixed with sympathy for, and gratitude towards those women, whose ultimate responsibility it was to relieve them of responsibility by having abortions...and it would sure be nice to hear from all those men out there whose lives have been changed, bettered and substantially eased because they were not forced into unwanted father-hood."[19]

Another problem for abortionists is that there is seldom a conventional doctor-patient rapport. To move as many women through the clinic as possible, the nurses and counselors completely prep the woman for abortion and oversee her recovery; the doctor is involved only during the actual procedure. According to abortionist David Grimes, the "communication may be limited to a brief discussion with the patient on the operating table before the surgery."[20] So there is little time to get to know the patient, or to allow the patient to see the doctor as anything more than someone who walks in a room, performs her abortion, and moves on to the next woman. Additionally, since the only service many abortionists provide is abortion, patients have no reason to come to him on a regular basis. They may return for a repeat abortion, but it's not like there will be any regular contact established. Therefore, no loyal customer base, which is often important to maintain a healthy practice, can be maintained. In fact, a woman's feelings about the abortion may cause her to purposely avoid him should she encounter him in a social environment.

Changing gears between being a protector of pregnancy and a terminator of pregnancy can be troubling. One such doctor admitted, "You have to become a bit schizophrenic."

Then there is the situation in which a woman immediately regrets her choice. These cases can profoundly rattle the abortion clinic staff. During a workshop designed to allow abortion providers to talk about these problems, a nurse said she saw women "who had just had an abortion...lie in the recovery room and cry, 'I've just killed my baby. I've just killed my baby.' I don't know what to say to these women. Part of me thinks, 'Maybe they're right.'"[21] One abortionist, apparently tiring of the despair behind abortion, said, "I don't think there's anyone doing abortions who hasn't wished at some point that the situations creating the demand for them wouldn't just go away. That includes me. There have been plenty of times when I've wanted to say 'Enough! This is more human tragedy than I want to deal with.'"[22]

Another internal conflict relates to abortionists who also practice obstetrics. Changing gears between being a protector of pregnancy and a terminator of pregnancy can be troubling. One such doctor admitted, "You have to become a bit schizophrenic. In one room you encourage the patient that the slight irregularity of the fetal heart is not important, everything is going well, she is going to have a nice baby, and then you shut the door and go into the next room and assure another patient on whom you just did a saline abortion, that it's fine if the heart is already irregular, she has nothing to worry about, she is *not* going to have a live baby. I mean you definitely have to make a 180 degree turn, but somehow it evolved in my own mind gradually..."[23] A New York abortionist expresses a similar sentiment, "On some mornings I leave my office, and if I turn right I go down the hallway to the [abortion facility] and terminate. I am a destroyer of pregnancies. If I turn left down the same hallway, I go toward the nursery and the labor and delivery unit and take care of the myriad of complications in women who are in the throes of problem pregnancies—and I do things to help them hold on. It's all so schizophrenic. I have a kind of split personality."[24]

One doctor who was dedicated to performing abortions eventually had to quit his obstetrics practice to alleviate his conflicts: "I felt that you can't do both. You do a delivery and then you do a late abortion," he says. "I couldn't take the emotional roller-coaster ride."[25]

Medical Community Stigma

In 1973, over half of all abortions in America were performed in hospitals. Today, well over 90 percent are done in free-standing clinics. This has resulted in the abortion industry not only being physically isolated from mainstream medicine, but philosophically isolated as well. Abortionists are the first to admit that this is true. Life Dynamics, posing as a pro-choice organization called Project Choice, sent a survey to 961 doctors who do abortions as their primary business. Having received a large response, it can be considered reliable. Among others, questions were asked regarding the way abortionists perceive their place within the broader medical community:

- 69 percent felt they were not respected by the rest of the medical community
- 65 percent felt ostracized for doing abortions
- 61 percent have been verbally confronted by a pro-life physican
- 60 percent feel their prestige has been damaged because they do abortions

- 51 percent feel isolated from the medical community for doing abortions

- 19 percent have been denied hospital privileges because they perform abortions

Not only is the abortion industry isolated from the legitimate medical community, occasionally abortionists are even isolated from others within the abortion industry. Abortionist Warren Hern once observed, "Increasingly, doctors have been made to feel irrelevant. Feminist abortion clinics treat doctors like technicians and are especially contemptuous of male physicians. Entrepreneurs who treat abortion strictly as a retail business also tend to treat doctors as technicians. Doctors who perform abortions have usually acquiesced in these roles, and their status has plummeted lower than that of physicians who do insurance company examinations."[26]

Additionally, separating abortion clinics from mainstream medicine has increased the natural stigma surrounding abortion. Alexander Sanger, president of Planned Parenthood of New York City, pointed out that, "Back in the early '70s, Planned Parenthood led the fight to get abortions to be done in outpatient clinics, and it seemed like a good idea at the time, a way of providing easy access to good, cheap care...But it turns out that it has led to a stigmatization of abortion, as something most doctors opt out of."[27] Abortionist David Grimes, formerly with the Abortion Surveillance Branch of the Centers for Disease Control, writes, "Clinicians whose practice is limited to abortion services may become estranged from the medical community."[28] One abortionist who responded to the Project Choice survey lamented that he knew of another physician who would not refer patients to him because he performed abortions, and went on to say, "I am sure I have lost other patients from this sort of abuse." Another respondent said, "Many feel you are less than a good physician because 'their doctor' doesn't perform abortions. I did stop performing abortions—the stress and harassment wasn't worth it."

The view that abortionists are the black sheep of the medical community appears to be pretty universal, even among abortion supporters. An Ohio medical student observed, "There's a real stigma on physicians who provide abortion. It's almost like: 'They do abortions. They don't do real medicine.'"[29] A Birmingham, Alabama, physician told an Atlanta newspaper that "the majority of abortionists are seen by their peers as not able to do well in other areas of medical practice, so they gravitate toward abortions for the money."[30] In a *Glamour* magazine article, an Ob/Gyn resident said she sees the abortion stigma in school administrators, faculty, and their peers who give the impression that "abortion is a sleazy and offensive procedure...A doctor who does abortions—even if they are only a small part of her practice—is known as an abortionist. This label is supposed to be the kiss of death for any professional hopes she might have."[31]

Even practicing abortionists admit to this reality. As soon as abortion became legal in 1973, Bruce Stier came under attack because it was known that he would be performing abortions. He recalls that one day shortly after the *Roe v. Wade* decision, as he was scrubbing up, a colleague standing next to him asked, "So, Bruce, how many babies are you going to kill today?"[32] Abortionist Morris Wortman says, "Abortion has failed to escape its back-alley associations." In his mind it is still treated as the "dark side of medicine...Even when abortion became legal, it was still considered dirty."[33] Finally, a Florida newspaper quotes abortionist Robert Crist, lamenting that some physicians who don't do abortions treat him "like a second-class citizen. Some of the ones who do—especially the younger, inexperienced ones—have added to an increasing level of discomfort." Later in the article, Crist says he knows of others who have quit because "the stigma had become overwhelming."[34]

In many cases, the low regard with which abortionists are held within the medical community is apparently shared by the abortionists themselves. One of many examples we found of this situation involves John Roe 840. During hearings to determine whether he would lose his medical license, he spoke with pride about the fact that in more than 17 years of doing abortions, he had never killed any of his patients. He went on to brag that most of the malpractice charges ever brought against him were dismissed for lack of proof, and that authorities were content to suspend his license for six months and put him on probation for a year and a half. While most physicians would be devastated by having this sort of disciplinary action taken against them, this abortionist saw it as the high point of his medical career.[35] In reviewing actions taken against abortionists accused of malpractice, we discovered that this sort of defense is fairly common. Abortionists who haven't killed a patient, or turned someone into a vegetable, see themselves as the abortion industry's elite. And while they may be right, that seems like a pretty low standard to set for oneself.

It is often observed that "Many a truth is spoken in jest." In light of that, consider the following dialog from the television show M*A*S*H. It seems to sum up the medical community's view of abortionists.

> Henry: "May I remind you both that not everybody you'll meet down there is going to be lovable Colonel Henry Blake."

Hawkeye: "What are you trying to tell us, lovable Colonel Henry Blake?"

Henry: "Just take my advice—don't show up looking like a couple of freelance abortionists. Shape up."[36]

Societal Stigma

If you consider the large number of abortions performed every year, you would suspect that it reflects large societal support for abortion. However, just as we saw with the medical community, even the part of society that seems to approve of the existence of abortion does not seem eager to support either the practice itself or those who perform them. The general viewpoint seems to be that abortionists are unsavory characters. Take as an example a newspaper article that reported the murder of a clinic owner/abortionist. The article itself was titled, "Creepy Kenny Died in the Gutter Where He Belonged." In reviewing his life, it read, "When Ken Yellin moved to Chicago, he put his business acumen and money into concerns that were characterized by their increasing sordidness and which have known links to organized crime. He ran a marriage counseling service which a former prosecuting attorney said was a front for prostitution, and was then believed to have operated or invested in X-rated movie theaters. The abortion business seemed a natural progression."[37]

A *Newsweek* article about teenage sexual habits in the 1990s points out that high standards are not exactly expected of abortionists. "Access [to abortion] was rarely a problem: every big city and most college towns had a clinic or at least an abortion doctor, and if he wasn't Marcus Welby, well, at least he had an office."[38] Even *Newsweek* doesn't expect very much from an abortionist, apparently believing that having an office is about the best that can be reasonably hoped for.

The stigma that society places on abortion was never more evident than when Dr. Henry Foster was nominated to be U.S. Surgeon General. When it was revealed that he had performed abortions, he and his supporters became obsessed with covering up the number of abortions he had performed. At first, he reported only a handful, then around 60, and someone else came forward with a report of 700. The exact number was never established and doesn't really matter here. What is important is the fact that there was a question at all over how many abortions he had done. If it is a basic right, and there is nothing wrong with it, why should it matter if he had done one, a dozen, or a million? Evidently, while pro-choice activists claim that America is firmly behind the legality of abortion, they know that the reality is quite different. Repeatedly during his nomination process, we heard even hardcore abortion advocates loudly proclaiming that Foster was not "an abortionist." The two obvious questions are: (a) How many abortions does someone have to do before he is an abortionist? and (b) Why were Foster's supporters so defensive about people calling him an abortionist?

Because of the lack of respect that society has for individuals who work in abortion clinics, it is often difficult for the clinic employees to even talk about where they work. One clinic employee explained that when you "have a hard time answering the question that other people ask you about what you do...you come to not feel so good about what you're doing even when you thought you were doing something wonderful."[39]

One indication that abortion providers really do sense that they have no respect in society is their reaction to critical comments, or even jokes, about themselves. At Life Dynamics, we created a joke book called *Bottom Feeder* by converting jokes that lampoon and insult lawyers into jokes that lampoon and insult abortionists. We then mailed copies to over 33,000 medical students across America. Instantly, the pro-choice and medical communities went nuts. We got literally hundreds of phone calls and letters, including several death and bomb threats. The response was nothing less than astonishing, and very revealing. While attorneys may feel perfectly comfortable sitting around swapping lawyer jokes, abortion advocates threaten to kill when people say exactly the same things about abortionists. Why is that? The answer is that lawyers can afford to laugh because in their hearts they know that what's being said isn't true. But for abortionists, jokes that insult and ridicule hit too close to home. The *Bottom Feeder* campaign was extraordinarily successful in several areas, such as revealing that even the abortion industry realizes the depth of the stigma associated with being an abortionist.

Emotional Abandonment

When we were conducting the Project Choice survey, we encountered a very interesting phenomenon. Within the abortion industry, there is often bitter animosity between what we call the "doers" and the "talkers." While there is some overlap generally speaking, talkers are the people who work in the public and political arena to keep abortion legal; doers are the ones who work in the abortion clinics. We found that talkers tend to view doers as the ghouls of the movement who perform the disgusting, but necessary, dirty-work. Meanwhile, the doers think the talkers are a bunch of prima donnas who live to go on national television and talk about what a terrific thing abortion is, but couldn't stomach watching one if their lives depended on it.

Over 78 percent of the abortionists who responded to the Project Choice survey said they don't get enough support from pro-choice activists, and some were downright hostile about it. One doctor complained, "I have heard women state they go to Dr. 'X' because he's pro-choice. These various Dr. X's frequently talk a good game and have busy practices, but I have yet to see them provide abortions. Privately they tell me they are afraid to lose patients and physician referrals. I wish I had the luxury of reaping the rewards of being pro-choice without the above problems." Another wrote, "The pro-choice majority has done nothing to support physicians who provide abortion service. It seems that even pro-choice women are reluctant to go to an office that provides abortion care, for fear that they may be thought to be obtaining an abortion."

While the activists sit in their ivory towers and coldly discuss the statistics of abortion, the abortionists pull those statistics out of women's bodies one tragedy at a time.

In yet another example of frustration voiced by abortionists, abortionist Warren Hern wrote an editorial for the *New York Times* in which he complained, "Pro-choice organizations often ignore, patronize and disparage the contributions of physicians who specialize in abortions, in contrast with their support for well-known physicians in conventional specialties."[40] Similarly, Diane Derzis, an administrator for an abortion clinic in Birmingham, confided to an Atlanta newspaper, "There's still the shame thing, even among people who are pro-choice...We are still seen as dirty, even among our own people."[41]

We found the hostility between the abortion industry's "talkers" and "doers" to be similar to that which often exists during wartime. To the frontline soldier, who lives in constant terror while killing other mother's sons whom he doesn't know or hate, the war is not some abstract political philosophy—it's real and horrible. And while he might crawl through hell on his knees for his buddies in the trench, he is profoundly resentful of the bloated politician who talks about how noble the war is over a $50 lunch in Washington, D.C.

Someone once said, "One death is a tragedy, a million is a statistic." In a way, that defines the conflict between abortionists and political activists. While the activists sit in their ivory towers and coldly discuss the statistics of abortion, the abortionists pull those statistics out of women's bodies one tragedy at a time. The talkers comfort themselves with rhetoric about how legal abortions empower and liberate women, while the doers know the real-world desperation and despair of the women who actually have them. They know what pro-life feminist Frederica Mathewes-Green recognized when she wrote: "For the question remains, do women want abortion? Not like she wants a Porsche or an ice cream cone. Like an animal caught in a trap, trying to gnaw off its own leg, a woman who seeks abortion is trying to escape a desperate situation by an act of violence and self-loss. Abortion is not a sign that women are free, but a sign that they are desperate."[42]

There are some talkers who acknowledge this problem. One abortion advocate recently wrote, "We who are pro-abortion-rights leave the doctors in the front lines, with blood on their hands...This is blood that the doctors and clinic workers often see clearly...And we who are pro-choice compound their isolation by declaring that that blood is not there."[43] However, this person is almost alone in her warnings to fellow talkers, with most seeming completely disinterested in the real problems faced by frontline abortionists. When asked about the issues facing the abortion-rights movement, activists inevitably talk about how all of their problems are brought on by the pro-life community. They suggest that if those religious fanatics would mind their own business, everything would be all right. But when a writer for the American Medical Association interviewed abortion clinic personnel about the problems they face, not one word was printed about anti-abortion activity. Instead, the entire discussion centered around the psychological problems they have, all of which are caused by the abortion procedure itself.[44]

Actually, this is simply one of several examples of a lack of camaraderie within the abortion industry. While both talkers and doers agree that they are under siege, during Project Choice we noticed that there is not the "drawing together" normally experienced by people who perceive that they are under attack from a common enemy. At best, there is sometimes a false unity within the clinics, based on fear of dissent. Judith Fetrow, a former Planned Parenthood worker, summed up this problem at a pro-life conference: "It is extremely difficult to watch doctors lie, clinic workers cover up, and hear terrifying stories of women dragged out of clinics to die in cars on the way to the hospital without beginning to question the party line. I began to wonder if we were really caring for these women, or if we were just working for another corporation whose only interest was the bottom line. But these are questions that one does not voice at Planned Parenthood."[45]

Not only do they not draw together, but the large abortion organizations viciously fight against each other. The National Abortion Federation, the

National Abortion Rights Action League, and Planned Parenthood all want to be recognized as *the* voice of legal abortion, and none seem willing to share the credit with the others. This is especially true between Planned Parenthood and the remainder of the field. One respondent to Project Choice wrote, "Planned Parenthood is a problem. Elitist snobs who think they are the only providers. The rest of us are scum to them."

Politics Are No Help

Ironically, another source of low morale within the abortion industry is President Bill Clinton. Since 1973, the abortion industry has been able to blame most of its problems on the fact that anti-abortion presidents, mainly Reagan and Bush, have prevented them from creating their "pro-choice" utopia. And it really didn't matter whether Reagan and Bush were really the cause of their problems or not. As long as the abortion industry *believed* they were, they could avoid dealing with their real problems and keep the dream alive that one day a "fellow traveler" would be in the Oval office and make their problems just magically disappear.

Then, in 1992, they got what they always wanted—and it is destroying them. After three years of a hardcore, no apologies, abortion-on-demand president, the *real* problems faced by the abortion industry are worse than they've ever been. And that fact is taking a heavy toll on them. Today, they are like the man who thought that being rich would make him happy. If he wins the lottery and is still unhappy, he is in worse shape than before. As long as he didn't have any money, he could continue to believe that there was hope for being happy. But now that he's rich and unhappy, he has nothing left to dream about.

That's exactly what Bill Clinton has done to the abortion industry. He has given them everything they asked for, and yet their problems are worse today than they were at the height of Ronald Reagan's power. The election of Bill Clinton destroyed the abortion industry's dream. They had been concentrating on imagined problems and ignoring the fact that the most threatening problems they have relate to the abortion procedure itself and the environment surrounding it.

Boredom

Most physicians see themselves as problem-solvers and enjoy the practice of medicine for the challenges it presents. But as one journalist discovered, "[Doctors] regard abortions as boring and repetitive procedures that use up time they would prefer to devote to more interesting and challenging cases."[46]

The sense of boredom is magnified since abortionists generally have little or no personal contact with their patients. Because they are only present to do the abortions, unlike other physicians they don't get any of the challenges associated with diagnosis, or the satisfaction of being personally involved with a patient's progress. Charlotte Taft describes the problem this way: "In most clinics, the doctor is pretty much the technician. We do the counseling, we do the blood testing, we do the sonogram, and then the doctor sees the patient for the abortion. And for many reasons that's cost effective, and you need to do that in order to keep the cost low. It does mean that the doctor's interaction with the patient is very limited. So they don't get a lot of the goodies that you get when you're in a relationship. They get to go inflict pain on someone for five minutes. That's a tricky piece."[47]

In his book *Abortion: A Doctor's Perspective/A Woman's Dilemma*, abortionist Don Sloan agrees. "I've [aborted] tens and tens of thousands of women, and I know so little about so many of them—most of them...How could I? In a sense, the doctor is only a tradesperson, a technician performing a task, like any other."[48]

This situation also affects other abortion clinic staff. A director of nursing at one abortion facility made the following incredible statement: "In some ways it is very boring, these abortions—the same thing day after day. In fact, the nurses are excited about complications because it's something different."[49]

High Turnover

Another source of discouragement in the abortion industry is an unusually high employee turnover rate. For example, we identified one abortion clinic that had a 200 percent turnover in staff in less than six months.[50] This not only adds to the lack of camaraderie mentioned earlier, but heightens the sense of isolation felt by the long-time workers who are left behind.

Many factors contribute to this problem, one of which is the exploitation of junior employees. Though administrators and abortionists received good salaries, support staff salaries are very low. This is a "chicken-or-egg" situation in that they pay poorly because they expect a high turnover, and they get a high turnover because they pay poorly. Clinic management also keeps salaries low for the same reasons many companies do: to keep prices low and profits high. Another reason they do this is simply because they can. For all their rhetoric about women's rights, the reality is that they hire mostly women and one would have to be pretty naive not to believe they take advantage of the fact that they can hire women cheaper than men. In fact, not only do they hire mostly women, but they appear to prefer women who are in vulnerable situations.

Joy Davis, who managed abortion clinics in Alabama and Mississippi stated, "If the doctor had somebody come and apply for a job whose husband was a big hot shot that made a lot of money, then he didn't want her working for him. But if they were single, and had children, that's the one he wanted. He could control them. And he controlled me probably most of all. I had two children, I had a son that had severe problems...And he preyed on that. Because when I started getting into such financial problems with my son's medical care, that's when he started making all the demands on me. That's when he really started pushing on me hard, to change records and to treat patients, and to be a doctor and not get paid a doctor's wage. And it wasn't just me, he did that to a lot of people...I can refer to [the abortionist] like I can an abused woman, and I've seen this with a lot of abused women, where their husbands abuse them and they make them think it's their fault, and they won't leave their husband, even though he beats them... I find that to be true with [the abortionist]. He will abuse his employees, mentally, just put them through the wringer, then he'll turn around and do something very wonderful for them, to make them think he really cares about them...He was always doing things for me that made me feel obligated to him."[51]

A woman who used to work for a Louisiana abortionist reports, "At the time, I needed a job. I'm a single mom with three children...I was hired as a receptionist. And they so-called 'promoted' me to doing the urine tests and the recovery room...What [the abortionist] does is he seeks out people that really need to make the money...Most of the women that do work there are single women with children.[52] (This woman asked not to be named, because she fears the abortionist she worked for will retaliate against her.)

Sexual harassment is also a problem for abortion clinic employees. In one case, a prominent abortion-rights advocate filed a complaint with the Minnesota Department of Human Rights, saying she was fired from the abortion clinic where she worked "because she objected to the sexual harassment of female employees by her co-director." Confirming her story, another former employee said this man "repeatedly intimidated some younger staff members with his jokes and questions about their sex lives, and telling them he dreamed or fantasized how they would look without clothes." She also reported that he asked a female staff member, who was to undergo an abortion at the clinic, if he could be in the room during the procedure, because "he said he had a fantasy about having sexual intercourse with a woman on an examining table during an abortion."[53]

Former employees in another clinic also alleged discrimination and sexual harassment. In depositions they claim that the abortionist they worked for always talked about the female employees' legs and that he started hiring only young girls with short skirts. One staff member testified, "he was calling other women dogs...If you're young and your skirt is short, you're fine. If you're older, we're gonna get rid of you...And we're gonna make you quit so that we don't have to pay the unemployment. We're gonna make your life so miserable that you're gonna walk out...You could check with the [unemployment office]. There's at least 10 older other women who have gone there."[54]

Another cause of employee dissatisfaction and high turnover is that they feel powerless to affect conditions within the clinics for which they work. Inside the clinics, important issues seem to be ignored, possibly because no one wants to mention problems for which they fear there may be no solution. When Joy Davis was asked about that, she said, "We don't have conversations. Sometimes the employees faint. Sometimes they throw up. Sometimes they have to leave the room. It's just problems that we deal with, but it's not talked about...If you really dwell on it, and talk about it all the time, then it gets more personal. It gets more real to you. You just don't talk about it, try not to think about it...if [the abortionist] ever caught you discussing something like that, he'd fire you."[55]

Another abortion clinic worker reinforced the view that there was no room for questioning the party line: "Privately, even grudgingly, my colleagues might admit the power of abortion to provoke emotion. But they seem to prefer the broad view and disdain the telescope. Abortion is a matter of choice, privacy, control. Its uncertainty lies in specific cases: retarded women and girls too young to give consent for surgery, women who are ill or hostile or psychotic. Such common dilemmas are met with both compassion and impatience: they slow things down...One person might discuss certain concerns, behind closed doors, or describe a particularly disturbing dream. But generally there is to be no ambivalence."[56]

Not only do abortion clinic staff not have a mechanism within the clinic to address issues that bother them, but they dare not take their problems to an outside source. The abortion industry is definitely one that does not want its dirty laundry aired in public. The woman who worked for the Louisiana abortionist mentioned above pointed out that employees couldn't report dangerous medical practices to the authorities because to do so they would have to give their name, and the employees knew that they would be fired if they got caught.[57] And apparently, her concern about being fired for reporting problems is not unfounded. Two employees of a Florida abortion clinic claimed they were fired because they reported unsanitary and dangerous conditions. A clinic counselor and the clinic's manager say they were fired immediately after another employee overheard them calling the National Abortion Federation in Washington, D.C., to file a complaint. To add insult to injury, one of them had her last paycheck docked $3 for the long-distance bill.[58]

In another incident, a woman reported grievances against an abortionist but then the abortionist tried to discredit her by having her arrested for libel. The abortionist had discovered that his former clinic administrator stated that "abortions were being done on women who had negative pregnancy tests; that narcotics and drugs were not locked up around the clinic; that the fetuses obtained from the abortions were not identified and were not pathologically examined at the clinic; that women who had complications who could have needed hospital treatment were sometimes not taken to the hospital." These allegations were reported in the newspapers, and the abortionist wanted retaliation. Since she had already resigned, he couldn't fire her, so he had her prosecuted for malicious libel. When the case was found in her favor, she counter-sued for false charges with malicious intent and won.[59]

No Way Out

Few people are ever as frustrated as when they find themselves in a miserable situation from which they can see no escape. This would be especially true for doctors who must generally be intelligent and self-confident people in order to become doctors in the first place. It is logical to assume that, by their nature, most physicians feel they are in control of their lives.

So imagine the frustration of suddenly finding yourself trapped in an environment such as described here, with little hope of returning to a more acceptable practice. During the Project Choice campaign, many abortion providers openly admitted that they would like to stop performing abortions. Joy Davis even said, "I've seen [the abortionist] cry because he couldn't get hospital privileges, or couldn't get out [of the business]." She went on to say that during all the years she spent in the abortion industry, she never met one abortionist who didn't want out.[60]

The question is, if they want out of the abortion business, why don't they just get out? The answer is simple. First, when a physician enters the field of abortion, his medical career is effectively over. Because of the shortage of physicians willing to perform abortions, the patient load will overwhelm the other parts of his practice. Second, many abortionists readily admit that other patients leave when they discover that a doctor performs abortions. Third, if an abortionist attempts to quit his abortion practice and find other work with someone else, the odor of having been an abortionist is one he will never lose. It will make him very unattractive to any future employer. Finally, most physicians who have been in practice for any length of time can sell their practice and purchase another one. But an abortion practice has no intrinsic value and cannot be sold. In fact, there are brokers in America who help physicians sell their practices and clinics, and every one we talked to said they would not accept a client who was trying to sell an abortion clinic; they simply don't have any value on the open market.

Naturally, one of the biggest traps is the money involved. Most of these men and women can make significantly more money performing abortions than they can doing anything else. The abortion industry often denies this by pointing out that top-flight Ob/Gyns can easily earn more than an abortionist at even a high-volume abortion clinic. They will also contend that an abortionist makes only $200 to $300 on a woman he aborts, while an Ob/Gyn charges several thousand to take a woman to term and deliver her baby. What they leave out of the equation is that the abortion takes five minutes while a full-term delivery takes nine months.

Actually, from a financial standpoint, the motivations and entrapments of abortion have not changed much since the days of its illegality. In one account from the late '50s, Alan Guttmacher stated, "Doctors do not start out as illegal abortionists. They are ordinarily driven to it as a means of supplementing their income during a time of dire financial crisis. In order to pick up some quick cash they do a few abortions, then have difficulty in calling a halt to so easy a source of revenue."[61]

Of course, the reason people who work at abortion clinics don't quit and become top-flight Ob/Gyns is that they simply don't have that option. In fact, for the overwhelming majority, the unavailability of that choice influenced them to become abortionists in the first place. Work at an abortion clinic is not something that the cream of the medical community seeks; it is what the washouts of the medical community are relegated to before they're out the door altogether. So for someone who works at an abortion clinic, his option isn't to quit and start a successful practice in legitimate medicine; he has already proven that is not a reality. His choice is whether to remain an abortionist or to get out of medicine altogether. Period.

Even non-physician staff discover that it is hard to find work elsewhere if they've been in the abortion industry for a substantial length of time. Joy Davis realized that when she tried to leave and had a prospective employer ask, "Were you so cold that you could do that for 11 years?"[62]

Finally, there is also a strong psychological factor keeping providers tied to the abortion industry. Understand that this is a business where you can have absolutely no doubts that what you are doing is right. The consequences of being wrong are simply too horrific to contemplate. Combine that with a view that quitting is the same as admitting guilt, and quitting becomes next to impossible. In a sense, the only way an abortionist can justify the abortions he's already done is to do some more.

Abortion Provider Stress

The *American Heritage Dictionary* defines cognitive dissonance as: "A condition of conflict resulting from inconsistency between one's beliefs and one's actions." As you read this section, I think you will become convinced that the overarching problems of abortionists are directly related to this internal conflict. Abortionists are trapped between a belief in the legality of abortion and the undeniable reality that it is the taking of human life. In public, they have to argue that abortion does not kill a child, while in private, they have to dispose of the dismembered bodies. To their dismay, abortionists find that although political rhetoric might persuade our society to allow the killing to continue, it does not insulate them from the effects of being the killers.

There is also a strong psychological factor keeping providers tied to the abortion industry. In a sense, the only way an abortionist can justify the abortions he's already done is to do some more.

To date, little research has been done regarding the toll abortion takes on the people who perform them, but that which has been done suggests they suffer from incredible stress. One research report shows they have "obsessional thinking about abortion, depression, fatigue, anger, lowered self-esteem, and identity conflicts...The symptom complex was considered a transient reactive disorder similar to combat fatigue."[63] Another journal article states, "Ambivalent periods were characterized by a variety of otherwise uncharacteristic feelings and behavior including withdrawal from colleagues, resistance to going to work, lack of energy, impatience with clients and an overall sense of uneasiness. Nightmares, images that could not be shaken and preoccupation were commonly reported. Also common was the deep and lonely privacy within which practitioners had grappled with their ambivalence."[64]

According to a report that appeared in a psychiatric journal, the personnel react with anxiety, depression, and periods of obsession. This was true even for those who intellectually supported abortion. There were reports of withdrawal from the procedure. The stress would overflow into resentment and hostility toward the patients for getting pregnant in the first place. The physicians involved demonstrated their hostility to the situation by treating these patients in a "perfunctory manner" that was a deviation from their standard manner.[65] In discussing people who counsel at abortion facilities, one author stated, "The effect is staggering and uniform. They become devoted, guilty, erratically pious, and explosively grateful to the blind fates that have chosen to spare them...as in the case with many who survive catastrophes, nearly all the counselors change while working here."[66] In another observation, Dr. Julius Butler, a professor of obstetrics and gynecology at the University of Minnesota Medical School, expressed his concern about the mental health of abortionists, saying, "We've had guys drinking too much, taking drugs, even a suicide or two...There have been no studies I know of of the problem, but the unwritten kind of statistics we see are alarming."[67]

It seems clear that abortion workers often exhibit behavior consistent with that of people who suffer Post-Traumatic Stress Disorder (PTSD). In laymen's terms, PTSD is a strong emotional reaction to intense trauma. According to literature on the subject, a person who suffers PTSD experienced, witnessed, or was confronted with an event (or events) that involved actual or threatened death or serious injury, or a threat to the physical integrity of self or others, and the person's response involved intense fear, helplessness, or horror. Symptoms include recurrent recollections of the event, distressing dreams of the event, and/or intense psychological distress. In reaction to this, the individual may avoid conversations, feelings, and thoughts associated with the trauma, may be unable to remember part of the event, or feel detached or estranged from others. Also, they may have difficulty falling asleep, outbursts of anger, difficulty concentrating, hyper-vigilance, exaggerated startle response, and experience significant distress or impairment in social, occupational, or other areas of functioning.[68]

It is important to note that while PTSD can be brought on by fearing for one's own life, it can also be caused by the pain of injuring and killing others. One study about battlefield killing concluded that after 60 days of combat, 98 percent of all soldiers will be psychological casualties. According to Lieutenant Colonel Dave Grossman, who recently released his book *On Killing*, "The resistance to the close-range killing of one's own species is so great that it is often sufficient to overcome the cumulative influences of the instinct for self-protection, the coercive forces of leadership, the expectancy of peers, and the obligation to preserve the lives of comrades."[69]

It stands to reason that whatever stress a soldier is under may actually be greater for an abortionist. First, his victim is completely different. The one comfort a soldier might take is that at least the person he killed was also trying to kill him. But the abortionist doesn't have that emotional sanctuary because the fetus poses no personal threat. Another stress reliever that the soldier has and the abortionist doesn't is camaraderie. As was illustrated earlier in this chapter, the abortionist basically exists without a support network, either within or outside the abortion industry. This could have a profound effect, as studies have shown that the magnitude of PTSD is inversely proportional to how strong the individual's social support is.[70]

It is also important to note that if abortion providers experience PTSD, its effect would not spare those who work as support staff in the clinic. Truck drivers who delivered ammunition to the soldiers in Vietnam suffered PTSD in degrees comparable to those who actually took part in combat. They had to drive the dead bodies back. "There was no definitive distinction between the guy pulling the trigger, and the guy who supported him in Vietnam...They may not have killed, but they were there in the midst of the killing, and they were confronted daily with the results of their contribution to the war."[71] The role of these drivers seems distinctly parallel to that of the support staff at an abortion clinic. Even though they may not actually take part in the procedures, they too have to dispose of the bodies.

PTSD has very well-established symptoms. The following is a look at how these issues impact the lives of those who work in the abortion industry.

Visions and Nightmares

Recurring visions, obsessive thoughts, and graphic nightmares about abortion appear to be common problems for abortion providers. The fact that we found no shortage of such experiences shows how remarkably widespread this problem is, and provides insight into just how psychologically distressing abortion must be on the people who do them. Following are a few of the cases we found:

- One nurse reported dreaming of shoving babies with pleading faces into a vase, with a feeling of condemnation coming from a white ring that she believes represents other nurses.[72]

■ Another clinic worker describes dreams in which she sees "aborted fetuses stare at [her] with ancient eyes asking, 'Why? Why did you do this to me?'"[73]

■ One former abortionist said he dreamed about delivering a healthy baby and then holding that baby up in front of a jury panel who give a thumbs up or down. If it's thumbs down, he drops the baby into a bucket of water.[74]

■ A former abortionist relayed a story about one of his doctors having nightmares involving blood and children. He became very disturbed because he was afraid that justice would be inflicted on his own children.[75]

■ An abortion clinic nurse reports in detail, "I have fetus dreams, we all do here: dreams of abortions one after the other; of buckets of blood splashed on the walls; trees full of crawling fetuses. I dreamed that two men grabbed me and began to drag me away, 'Let's do an abortion,' they said with a sickening leer, and I began to scream, plunged into a vision of sucking, scraping pain, of being spread and torn by impartial instruments that do only what they are bidden…"[76]

■ Sometimes the dreams are enough to keep health-care workers from participating in abortions. A nurse from a maternity unit of a New Jersey hospital relates, "I've met some nurses who had thought that they could work on an abortion patient…But after the first one they changed their minds. They had nightmares."[77]

The problems of nightmares and obsessive thoughts seems to especially affect those who are involved with D&E abortions. One-fourth of abortion providers reported an increase in nightmares after viewing one of these procedures.[78] Dr. Warren Hern interviewed the 24 members of his staff who took part in the D&E procedures. Of those, 18 admitted that they had a preoccupation with the procedure outside the clinic. He also observed, "Several others felt that the emotional strain affected interpersonal relationships significantly or resulted in other behavior such as an obsessive need to talk about the experience." He added, "Two respondents described dreams which they had related to the procedure. Both described dreams of vomiting fetuses along with a sense of horror. Other dreams revolved around a need to protect others from viewing fetal parts, dreaming that she herself was pregnant and needed an abortion or was having a baby…In general, it appears that the more direct the physical and visual involvement the more stress experienced. This is evident both in conscious stress and in unconscious manifestations such as dreams...Both individuals who reported several significant dreams were in these roles."[79]

Numbing and Desensitization

Another sign of stress is that abortion providers appear to lose interest in activities that they previously found important in their lives. One clinic worker refers to a numbing sameness that settles into their days: the same questions, the same trembling tones in their voices. But more than monotony, there is a psychological numbing. She went on to say that in order to endure, "I've cultivated a certain disregard. It isn't negligence, but I don't always pay attention. I couldn't be here if I tried to judge each case on its merits; after all, we do over a hundred abortions a week."[80] Joy Davis reflected, "When I was active in the abortion clinics, I don't know that any of us had any feelings about anything."[81] Another former abortion clinic worker stated, "When I started at Planned Parenthood, I saw two types of women working at the clinic. One group were women who had found some way to deal with the emotional and spiritual toll of working with abortion. The second group were women who had closed themselves off emotionally. They were the walking wounded. You could look in their eyes, and see that they were emotionally dead. Unavailable for themselves, or for anyone else."[82]

One-fourth of abortion providers reported an increase in nightmares after viewing D&E abortions.

Another former abortionist described how he became accustomed to performing abortions. He says that during his medical training, he first had to observe abortions. At one point he was asked to identify the fetal parts to ensure all the pieces had been removed. He identified an arm, some ribs, a piece of a leg, and the other parts as well. When it came time for him to perform one, he said, "It was like somebody put a hot poker into me. I believe that God gives us all a conscience. And I wasn't a Christian, but I had a conscience, and that hurt...That was a really hard experience to go through emotionally." He admitted that the next one he did also bothered him, but that, "After a while it got to where it didn't hurt. My heart got calloused."[83]

What this abortionist discovered was that the initial horror one experiences in these situations soon fades. This can be seen in many instances throughout history. In training soldiers for combat during the Vietnam war, the U.S. military undertook large-scale efforts to desensitize them to the killing they would have to do.[84] Those who ran the Nazi death machine experienced the same phenomenon without any training. The simple process of participating automatically desensitized them, and mass executions that were initially carried out with revulsion and horror were soon no problem at all. One writer who studied this process wrote, "Their direct participation in the killing was not only less personal but more finite. Habituation played a role as well. Having killed once already, the men did not experience such a traumatic shock the second time. Like much else, killing was something one could get used to."[85]

This numbing of basic human emotion can lead to ghoulish behavior. In wartime, traumatic stress reactions are known as the Ganzer Syndrome. An example of this is a soldier in Vietnam who walked into his quarters with a dead man's arm and introduced it to everyone as his friend Herbert. He even proceded to try to pick his nose with it.[86] Compare that with a story told by a former employee of a Louisiana abortion clinic about the abortionist: "He had a fetus wrapped inside of blue paper. He stuck it inside of a surgical glove and put another glove over it. He was standing in the hall, speaking with myself and two of his assistants. He was tossing the fetus up in the air and catching it. Like it was a rubber ball. I just looked at him..." She also said this abortionist seemed obsessed with leaving dead fetuses lying around the office. She related the following: "One Saturday, another employee and I were working, we were closing up, and we went down the back hallway to get the garbage. Well, we smelled this awful smell—it wasn't coming from the garbage. So we opened the door to a storage room. Inside that storage room was a bunch of fetuses, wrapped up in the blue paper in the gloves that had been sitting in there for, I would say, at least a week. There were maggots. It stunk like—I couldn't even describe it. We gagged and closed the door. There were at least six or seven of these fetuses just sitting in there, just rotting away."[87]

Another example of this kind of numbing and desensitization is gallows humor. We found several examples of this including the following story about a Texas abortionist. Several days after he struggled through a particularly difficult abortion, the patient's mother returned to the abortion clinic upset and angry. She brought in a milk carton containing a three-inch fetal head that her daughter had passed after she had massaged the girl's abdomen to alleviate her pain. One employee stated, "I remember the eyes were bugging. That's when I decided to quit." Another employee opened the refrigerator a couple of weeks later and found the milk carton, still containing the head, with a sign taped to it saying, "Hi, do you remember me?" It had been left as a homecoming surprise for an employee who had been away on vacation.[88]

Such numbing to the point of indifference can be seen in the jokes tossed around at one National Abortion Federation conference. During a discussion about how to respond in a social atmosphere to direct questions about their work, they came up with some pretty harsh responses. One question explored was, "How do you respond when somebody says 'you kill babies,' or 'doesn't it bother you?'" Some of the responses offered were, "No, it doesn't bother me, bub!" and "Try it, you'll like it!" Another question was, "What do you do with the babies that you take out of there?" The answers were, "We buy a lot of Drano" and "Don't come for breakfast." These jokes illustrate how abortionists have to use humor to try to remain sane in their daily conflicts. But some of their answers really demonstrated a depraved view of their work. A participant asked what the response should be when someone inquires if there is a minimum age for an abortion. The suggested answer was, "Yes, for the girls under 10." The group responded with wild laughter. They were so proud of this clever response that they couldn't see what a sad scenario they were painting. During this session, one comment apparently hit too close to home. In response to questions about the issue of killing, a staff worker said that a colleague of hers simply replied, "Many women would rather kill than wound." The audience remained largely silent.[89]

An employee opened the refrigerator and found a milk carton, containing a three-inch fetal head, with a sign taped to it saying, "Hi, do you remember me?"

This numbing causes not only a calloused insensitivity toward the work, but toward patients as well. In one example we found, it almost cost a woman her life. A former employee of a San Francisco Planned Parenthood facility stated, "The most horrifying complication that I witnessed was a woman who stopped breathing during the abortion. [The abortionist] just walked out of the room when he was finished. Despite my telling him that the client was not breathing, he left me alone with her. When [he] was forced to return, we didn't even follow emergency protocol for that situation. It was a miracle that this woman didn't die."[90] A similar incident occurred at another Planned Parenthood facility, this one in Washington, D.C. A non-pregnant Spanish-speaking woman came there for birth control pills and was led to a procedure room by a Spanish-speaking employee. The worker had the patient disrobe, put her in the stirrups, inserted a speculum, and left the room. Subsequently, the abortionist entered the room and initiated an abortion procedure, oblivious to the patient's screams for him to stop. It turns out that the abortionist had gone into the wrong room and had failed to correctly identify the patient upon whom he was about to operate. Obviously, mistakes can happen. But what cannot be so easily dismissed is that the abortionist was so completely indifferent to the screams of this terror-filled woman.[91]

Distancing

Doctors learn early in their medical training not to be bothered by blood and guts. However, many abortionists and their staff seem to remain bothered by the sight of an abortion, even after many years in the business. To overcome this problem, abortion clinic employees often develop a method of distancing themselves from their work and the actual procedures. Former clinic director Joy Davis describes it this way: "Each person who worked there had a different way of dealing with it. [One] would look at the ultrasound the entire time she was in the room, but she would never look down in the pan. She would never look at the tissue being removed. She never wanted to see that. She would just never take her eyes off the screen. And then I had one who would never look at the screen...she would never look at the tissue and never look at the screen, she just didn't want to see anything."[92]

In his book, *Abortion: A Doctor's Perspective/A Woman's Dilemma*, abortionist Don Sloan shows how this tactic is used deliberately: "As the pregnancy advances, the idea of abortion becomes more and more repugnant to a lot of people, medical personnel included. Clinicians try to divorce themselves from the method. In a saline or prostaglandin abortion, the doctor administers the agent to the patient and the wait-and-watch period is a labor process, which is not predictable. It may take several hours or even longer; up to twenty-four hours is fairly common. The care of the patient is usually left to specially trained nurses and abortion technicians. There is a distinct advantage for the abortionists, who don't have to be around when the fetus, macerated and lifeless, is expelled."[93]

Another way of distancing is to refuse to address the psychological issues of patients who come into the clinic. Many clinic workers cannot cope with the heaviness of their own problems, much less those of the dispair-filled women they see. In one clinic, a nurse said she would be willing to do all the technical work needed, but, "For me, the limit is allowing my clients to carry their own burden, to shoulder the responsibility themselves. I shoulder the burden of trying not to judge them."[94] One abortion advocate described emotional distancing in the following way: "At the present time, the fetus is sent down the sewer, without any form of farewell, and the operation obeys the rituals of medicine. In many cases, abortions are serial operations, and it may happen that not one word is addressed to the woman, except to verify that she has fasted and filled out four copies of the bureaucratic forms. Perhaps she does not even see the doctor's face, for she has already been given sedatives. She is stretched out on her back with her legs apart when the doctor, passing from one table to another, proceeds with the next abortion. He opens the neck of the uterus, often provoking a flood of emotion to which no one pays any attention...What happens to all the fear, the guilt, the pain, the solitude, and the suffering? The guilt, and sometimes revolt, may be crushing and unjust, insofar as the woman bears alone a burden that belongs to all of us."[95]

Abortionists are no longer able to distance themselves from what they are doing when an abortion is unsuccessful and results in a live birth. Many in the medical profession point out that abortion is risky because it is a blind procedure. Unlike a heart surgeon, for example, who sees the procedure he is performing, the abortionist operates by feel and cannot see what he is doing. While this makes the procedure riskier for the woman, ironically, it makes it psychologically safer for the abortionist. He does not have to watch the baby die. However, sometimes a baby will evade the abortionist and emerge from its mother alive. At that moment, the abortionist no longer enjoys his emotional protection. That is why many abortionists refer to this as the "dreaded complication."

Most states require that, in those instances, the baby be given the same life-saving medical care afforded anyone else. However, that is often not what happens. In July 1979, John Roe 279 attempted to abort a 23-week pregnancy after which the one-pound, two-ounce infant boy gasped and attempted to breathe. No efforts were made to revive the infant due to his parents' wishes and the infant's size. He was placed in a utility closet used as an infant morgue. Roe instructed a nurse, "Leave the baby there—it will die." The nurse testified that the infant was still gasping in the closet when she returned to work 12 hours later. Roe then agreed to transfer the baby to a hospital, where he died four days later. The child's death was ruled accidental.[96]

According to five abortion clinic employees, Texas abortionist John Roe 109 was performing an abortion when a one-foot-long infant girl with light brown hair was born. They testified that the baby curled up in Roe's hand and attempted to breathe as Roe held the placenta over her face. He then dropped her into a bucket of water, and several employees testified that bubbles rose to the surface. They went on to say that Roe then "dropped the fetus into a plastic bag...The bag was tied and placed at the end of the operating room...[The] sides of the bag pulsated as though someone were breathing into it. Then the bag stopped moving." One witness said he was holding the bag in which Roe placed the infant, and that he later put the bag in the freezer where aborted fetuses were stored.

Roe was later convicted of murder in connection with this incident and sentenced to 15 years in prison. He was also convicted of altering his hospital records, hindering the state's attempts to locate the woman. Former employees alleged that Roe falsified records on all patients over 20 weeks pregnant, saying they were all exactly 20 weeks pregnant, and that such abortions were routine. One former employee said she assisted in abortions in which Roe would sedate the patient, dilate the cervix, and pull the fetus out with forceps. "He wanted them in pieces, but a lot of times they would come out whole." She also said she saw signs of life in at least two fetuses aborted this way. Another former employee said she watched as Roe placed one fetus in a plastic bag in a bucket "and just waited until it stopped moving." She said the fetus squirmed and wiggled for about 10 seconds.

Yet another former employee said that during late abortions, Roe would walk in, close and lock the door, tell staff to look away when the fetus was extracted, and warn that, "If you see any movement or anything, you don't see anything, you don't know anything." While Roe 109 was free on appeal for the above murder conviction, he botched an abortion on a 28-year-old woman, causing her death.[97] (Although most live births involve saline abortions, which are generally no longer performed, we did identify some instances occurring in the last few years.)

It is revealing that abortionists apply the term "dreaded complication" to this event. What has happened in a doctor's mind when he starts to view killing the mother, or putting her in a nursing home for the remainder of her life, as simply unfortunate, but the survival of the fetus as "dreaded"? The answer is simple: the moment an abortionist sees a baby he attempted to abort move or gasp for breath, he is no longer insulated from his actions. This is precisely why distancing is so vitally important to abortionists. I think it also explains why they desperately want things like the "abortion pill," RU-486, available in the United States. In fact, even some abortion advocates have openly admitted that one of the benefits of RU-486 would be to psychologically protect abortionists. They accurately point out that while the woman may have to see the dead fetus floating in her commode, at least the abortionist won't have to.

There is an interesting, and macabre, issue surrounding RU-486 of which many people are not aware. One reason the Nazis went from mechanically executing (shooting) their victims to chemically executing (gassing) them was to allow the killers some distance between themselves and their victims. In short, they would still be doing the killing, but at least they wouldn't have to see it. The gas the Nazis used, Zyklon B, was developed and manufactured by an old-line German pharmaceutical company named I.G. Farben. After the war, the name I.G. Farben was naturally linked to the holocaust, with stories even circulating that the company was actually involved in helping design the gas chambers in which millions perished. In order to break all ties with their past, company leaders changed the name of the company. So I. G. Farben became known as Hoechst AG. Today, this company is a pharmaceutical giant with subsidiaries all over the world, including the United States. One of those subsidiaries is a French company named Roussel Uclaf, the developer and manufacturer of RU-486. ("RU" stands for Roussel Uclaf, and 486 refers to April 1986—the date the company first introduced the drug.)

Distancing was the issue that gave this book its title. In February 1992, a young woman went to a Tennessee abortion clinic to terminate her eight-week pregnancy. At the clinic, her name was taken from her and she was told to answer to the name "Lime 5" while at the facility. This allowed the staff to distance themselves from the woman, much like the Nazis distanced themselves from the Jews by giving them numbers in place of their names. It is also interesting to note that when this woman sued the clinic for botching her abortion, she asked the court to allow her to sue anonymously to protect her privacy. The abortion clinic opposed this effort and demanded that she use her real name. She could have her abortion as Lime 5, but she couldn't sue under that same name. This case was also an example of several other types of outrageous, yet typical, abortion clinic behavior. The patient testified that:

- She was "counseled" in a room with 20 other patients

- She was not given copies of anything she signed

- No staff was available to answer any of her questions

- The state law requiring a 48-hour waiting period was ignored

- The abortionist performed the procedure with his shirt unbuttoned

- During the procedure, the abortionist repeatedly used profanity, including the word "fuck"

- While apparently fondling the nurse, the abortionist told the patient that he believed "Nothing is better in life than sex and money."[98]

Compartmentalizing

Another way to avoid having to deal with too many burdens in the abortion clinic is to assign specific duties in isolated compartments. By compartmentalizing, the person doesn't have to recognize all the factors involved in the event, just his own. He knows they are there, but can ignore them. This way, only one person has to worry about taking the patient's information, another one counsels, yet another one holds the woman's hand in the procedure room, but she does not have to hear the woman's story in the counseling room to complicate her own emotions. One Alabama abortionist even went to the point of not allowing nurses to ask him about medical matters, requiring that they go through one specific contact person.[99]

A non-medical employee in a New York abortion facility was asked whether she had ever seen an abortion. She responded, "No. I am a chicken. I stay as far away as possible from that area…I went up to the lab one day and on the pathologist's table saw what I thought was a little rubber doll until I realized it was a fetus. I got sick, I got really shook up and upset and I couldn't believe it. It had all its fingers and toes, you know, hands and feet, and I really didn't know what a fetus was going to look like. I never thought it would look—so real. I didn't like it…"[100]

A former employee states that the Planned Parenthood facility she worked for completely understood those dynamics and intentionally divided the work. She explains, "Planned Parenthood is set up so clinic workers never have to see the babies. It's set up that way because having to look at the babies bothers the workers. Planned Parenthood workers talk about how seeing parts is emotionally painful for them…The smell of blood penetrates the clinic on the killing days. Generally there is one clinic worker in charge of the babies…I was that clinic worker. I had to look at the babies. I had to store them, I had to sent them to pathology. And I was the person who had to dispose of them…In order to maintain my sanity, I established a personal mourning ritual. I said Shiva for the babies. I said prayers for the dead. I also named the babies as I put it in a waste container. There were days when I would go home and think, 'You know, maybe this isn't right.' "[101]

In Nazi battalions, responsibilities were divided up to foster the killing process. One set of men would round the Jews together and another would eventually shoot them in the forest. Of course, the execution squads came into direct contact with the Jews, but they were usually "specialists" brought in to do the killing.[102] This division is similar to the division of labor needed to keep an abortion clinic calm: someone does appointments, another counseling, another basic nursing, and a specialist is called in to do the actual procedure.

Manipulated Language

People involved in mass killing have always found it necessary to control language in order to sugar-coat what they do. U.S. soldiers in Vietnam called the enemy "gooks" because dehumanizing them made it easier to kill them. When innocent people are killed in a military bombing, they are called "collateral damage." The list is endless and always has the same purpose: to soften the sting of one's involvement in killing.

The fact that abortionists feel they have to play this same game is generally seen as a public relations issue. It is true that manipulating language does have marketing advantages. However, it is revealing that abortion clinic workers who are completely out of the public spotlight still use some very convoluted euphanisms. For them, an abortion becomes a "pregnancy termination," the fetus becomes a "product of conception," the head of a fetus is called "number one," and some of them become enraged if you call someone who does an abortion an abortionist. For example, when the pro-life community labeled Henry Foster as an abortionist, he claimed that he wasn't really an abortionist because he delivered most babies alive and in one piece. That's like someone on trial for robbing a 7-Eleven Store saying that he isn't really a thief because there are a lot of 7-Eleven Stores that he didn't rob!

Language manipulation was common in Nazi-controlled Germany. Jews became known as "useless eaters," while Auschwitz wasn't a death camp but a "relocation center." And Nazis always referred to "removing the Jewish element" in the same impersonal way that abortionists call induced abortion the "removal of the products of conception." Consider the following analogy: Nazi doctor Fritz Klein stated that he could justify killing the Jews based on the belief that "when you find a gangrenous appendix, you must remove it."[103] In a similar way, Alan Guttmacher, former president of Planned Parenthood, compared performing an abortion to operating on an appendix or removing a gangrenous bowel.[104] Another example of deceptive language is found in abortionist Warren Hern's book *Abortion Practice*, in which he repeatedly describes pregnancy as an illness or disease for which abortion is a cure.[105]

This sort of language can lead to serious miscommunication between abortionists and their patients, often with disastrous results. We found a case in which a woman in her 23rd or 24th week of pregnancy went into labor. Her physician, an abortionist, told her that she had an infection "and that for her safety the pregnancy would have to be terminated." She interpreted this to mean that her *pregnancy* would be terminated by way of early labor, not that the life of the fetus would be terminated by deliberate killing. She entered the hospital, where labor was induced, with the fetus in breach position. The infant survived only six minutes. The woman requested that the nurse take all possible measures to save her baby, but no action was taken because the nurse had been informed to treat this as an abortion. The abortionist later stated that since the patient had undergone a prior abortion, he assumed that she understood that "terminating a pregnancy" meant an abortion.[106]

Abortion proponents are not opposed to changing their rhetoric when the need arises. For example, a 1962 Planned Parenthood pamphlet stated that, "An abortion kills the life of a baby after it has begun. It is dangerous to your life and health. It may make you sterile so that when you want a child you cannot have it. Birth control merely postpones the beginning of life."[107] Clearly, nothing has come along since 1962 to refute the fact that the fetus is a living baby. In fact, technology such as ultrasonography supports Planned Parenthood's original statement. However, being the nation's number-one abortion proponent is somewhat inconsistent with that statement. So what they used to call a "baby" they now call a "product of conception."

> *A 1962 Planned Parenthood pamphlet stated that, "An abortion kills the life of a baby after it has begun. Birth control merely postpones the beginning of life."*

Rationalization

Some individuals take a different approach to rectifying their feelings about abortion. They determine that they can accept identifying the fetus as a baby, while at the same time promoting abortion. Their thinking goes something like this: "Yes, abortion is a terrible, sad thing. Realistically, the thing growing in the woman's uterus is a baby. But we have to think of the woman, and how hard this pregnancy experience is going to be for her, and let her abort the baby if that is what she decides." They are actually saying that it *is* a baby, but have no problem with it being killed. Interestingly, this concept is embraced primarily by pro-choice activists, rather than by the actual providers, and is just another issue that separates the two. Since the advocates are not the ones who have to dirty their hands with the procedures, they can afford to accept it as the death of a baby and not care. It could not be so simple if they were in the operating rooms every day. What's more, these advocates are not the ones who are scorned by society for knowingly taking human lives.

Of course, in deciding *Roe v. Wade*, which brought legality to abortion, the U.S. Supreme Court left the field wide open for accepting the killing of human beings. Incredibly, Justice Blackmun's position was that the issue of abortion could be decided without addressing the question of when life begins. In other words, abortion could be legal even if it was murder. So by example of the law, it became perfectly logical that someone could promote abortion while agreeing that it is the killing of an unborn child. A classic illustration of that muddled thinking was expressed in a recent magazine article. The author asserted that, "Abortion should be legal; it is sometimes even necessary. Sometimes the mother must be able to decide that the fetus, in its full humanity, must die. But it is never right or necessary to minimize the value of the lives involved or the sacrifice incurred in letting them go."[108]

Although this viewpoint is primarily advanced by the advocates rather than the abortionists themselves, there are exceptions. One New York abortionist has acknowledged that the procedure is "inherently negative. I don't think that anyone can say that abortion is right…It's a form of life…This has to be killing…The question then becomes, 'Is this kind of killing justifiable?' In my own mind, it is justifiable, but only with the informed consent of the mother…Why kid ourselves? It's better to say, 'This is a life, albeit an early life. Give it that kind of respect and then make the decision.'"[109] In another example, Charlotte Taft, a former clinic administrator, admitted, "We have learned a great deal from the movement that calls itself pro-life. We were hiding from women some of the pieces of truth about abortion that were threatening…It is a kind of killing, and most women seeking abortion know that."[110]

One abortion worker admitted that she rationalizes by basically ignoring the whole issue of the fetus. She stated, "This may sound like repression: however, it does work for me…When I find myself identifying with the fetus—and I think the larger it gets, that's normal…then I think it's okay to consciously decide and remind ourselves to identify with the woman. The external criteria of viability really isn't what it's about. It's an unwanted pregnancy and that's the bottom line."[111] The need to subvert feelings about the fetus seems to be a common theme in the issues with which abortion providers struggle. Another illustration of this comes from *ObGyn News*: "Sonography in connection with induced abortion may have psychological hazards. Seeing a blown-up, moving image of the embryo she is carrying can be distressing to a woman who is about to undergo an abortion…Staff members also may be affected by sonographic images and may need opportunities for venting their feelings and reconfirming their priorities."[112]

Another common method of removing discomfort about abortion is to give blind and unbending loyalty to pro-choice ideology. It can be very handy to be able to ignore moral misgivings by rationalizing that they are less important than "the cause." The Nazis found that "ideological justification is vital in obtaining willing obedience, for it permits the person to see his behavior as serving a desirable end."[113] Leaders of sociopolitical movements realize that there will inevitably be times when a movement's ideology will conflict with the experiences and moralities of their followers. At those moments, followers must reject their own consciences and blindly fall back on the accepted dogma. One abortion advocate who saw this in her own experiences said, "A struggle evolves between reason and conscience, between pragmatic morality and one's own commitment to all human seed. With the struggle there also evolves a shamefaced solution." In interviews with clinic employees, she heard them try to convince themselves that they had no responsibility, with statements such as, "I do not decide for these women, I just do my job," and, "I give them what they want," and, "I only help out."[114] This sounds eerily similar to Nazi war criminals who defended their actions by claiming that they had only followed orders.

Rationalization is sometimes an evolutionary process. An abortionist may initially do only first-trimester procedures, but then slowly evolve into performing later procedures. We identified one hospital that started doing D&E procedures only up to 15 weeks, then very slowly moved the cutoff date up to 24 weeks. With this progression, the employees couldn't argue, since the earlier procedures had seemed fine to them. It's reasonable to believe that if they had started at 24 weeks, they would have been appalled. One abortionist admitted that if he had started with late abortions, he would have had "conflicts of murder," but having started with D&Cs made it easier for him to move up to later term procedures.[115]

Abortion advocates often try to rationalize their position by not bothering to deny that abortion is wrong, but saying that it is better than whatever fate might await the child after its birth. They might contend, for example, that a baby is better off being killed in the womb than living a miserable life. This sounds reminiscent of how some Nazis defended their actions. They later used excuses like, "Even without me, the Jews were not going to escape their fate anyway." One executioner shot children, rationalizing that they could not live without their mothers who had already been shot. Someone else tried to make himself feel better by claiming that they "shot only the poorest of the poor."[116] They were clearly struggling to convince themselves that they were serving a worthwhile end, or hastening a destiny that was unavoidable.

There are times when abortion workers' efforts to rationalize what they do appears to get the better of them. In one example, an abortion counselor said,

"At first I was very upset by the [abortions]. I'm not one to see blood and mess and things like that. But I have since gotten so excited about it that I've thought about going back to nursing school. When you think about it on a certain level, it's a really interesting thing that is happening. It's fascinating, when you can think about it clinically and not get involved in the people, or the babies. What happened when I was first working here was that I just thought about the baby and that was very upsetting. I'm very pro-abortion...I think I must have overcompensated, you know, overreacted and tried to look, and like really get into it, and not shy away from it. And several times I saw really beautiful things happen, I mean it's physically beautiful...Sometimes you can see the vagina opening up and the entire thing coming out at once. Most of the times the water will break, and then the fetus will come out and then the afterbirth. You know, in sequence. But sometimes this all comes out at once, like a balloon with the fetus inside and the afterbirth just sitting on top. It's a really interesting thing, and it got me very excited."[117]

To have this much excitement over an abortion after previously being revolted by it indicates that this woman has, as she herself admits, overcompensated and forced herself to see it this way. She has rationalized away her concern and replaced it with a bizarre obsession. We have observed that when abortion workers defend what they do, it often sounds more like they are trying to convince themselves than someone else. That may be the case with the woman above. If not, her efforts to rationalize her behavior have clearly taken a dreadful toll on her emotional stability.

Manifestations

After observing the actions of abortionists, a pro-abortion researcher once warned that, "Reknown is no guarantee of skill. Skill is no safeguard against cruelty. Patients are utterly vulnerable to the mental health of their helpers. The helpers should, therefore, be watched like potential enemies."[118] While conducting research for this book, we discovered what sound advise that is. When people are living with high levels of stress and inner conflict, it is inevitably going to impact the way they deal with others. In the case of abortionists, their most likely targets are their patients and we found literally hundreds of instances in which abortionists treated them with everything from callous indifference to dangerous hostility. The remainder of this chapter looks at a few instances showing how the stress abortionists are under affects their patients.

Blame and Punish

We noticed that when abortionists treat their patients badly, it is not simply a matter of poor "bedside manners." More often than not, their abusive or cruel behavior is deliberate. When someone is living in the hell that these people are living in, it is human nature to blame someone, and our experience has been that they blame the women. In the Project Choice responses, we had several abortionists make that very point. Their attitude seems to be that, "If these women wouldn't jump into bed with every guy that comes along, I wouldn't be in this mess." When women who have had abortions call our office, at least half will tell us that someone at the clinic made inappropriate or insulting comments to them. The most frequent is something like, "Well, take off your pants and spread your legs. You obviously know how to do that."

When women who have had abortions call our office, at least half will tell us that someone at the abortion clinic made inappropriate or insulting comments to them.

This is a phenomenon that has been recognized by the abortion industry itself. Abortionist David Zbaraz was quoted earlier in this chapter about how he always comes home angry, and how his wife knows the moment he walks through the door if he's done abortions that day. In one paper about the effects that abortion has on providers, the author wrote about nurses who had to work with abortion patients in the early 1970s: "Unfortunately, before their anger became conscious and was verbalized in the group, there had developed a tendency to act it out toward each other and the patients."[119] Another study about this issue concludes, "They also reported some anxiety and depression, as well as a good deal of anger towards the patients for their sexual acting out."[120] One doctor confessed during a National Abortion Federation workshop that he is "angry at the woman." He added, "I have angry feelings at myself for feeling good about grasping the [head of the fetus], for feeling good about doing a technically good procedure which destroys a fetus, kills a baby."[121]

Former clinic director Joy Davis reported that one abortionist she worked for routinely slapped his patients. "[I]f they talked during the procedure, or moved or flinched in any way, he would hit them...I've seen him hit so many patients." She also talked about another abortionist she worked for: "I was very uncomfortable around [the abortionist], so I decided not to work for him any longer. He invited me to go out to dinner with him to discuss it. I went to dinner with him to discuss how I felt about the way he treated his patients, and how he acted. He stated to me that he loved inflicting pain on women, which was the reason he did not use any medications for pain."[122] Another abortion advocate/researcher described an abortionist she studied as someone who "gets along poorly with people and makes a cult of this impediment. He especially dislikes women and among women most especially those who work and those who get pregnant. He is married and has a child. One time I asked him what would happen if his wife got pregnant again. His response was succinct: 'Scrape it out, throw it away.'"[123]

Another abortionist's poor opinion and treatment of women became known in a lawsuit brought against him during divorce proceedings. The court found that he had "deserted/abandoned his wife and had subjected her to physical cruelty (choking her, body-slamming her, kicking her, throwing her down the stairs, beating her face, pulling her hair, and screaming at her)." It was also alleged that he referred to women as "cunts." A close relative suggested that this man "hates women." His "attitudes and behavior toward women evidences a psychological need and desire to control and use vulnerable women or women in vulnerable positions for his own purposes, resulting in an indifference to, and reckless disregard for, the welfare of female patients."[124] In one example, a woman alleged that after her abortion, this abortionist "stood drinking coffee and watching [her] suffering from severe sustained pain…without even examining or treating her for excessive bleeding, large blood clots and severe pain."[125] Here are a few of the many other examples we found of physical and psychological trauma inflicted by abortionists:

- In response to a woman's screams of pain during her abortion, a clinic worker stuffed a tampon in her mouth. During the procedure, she was so badly injured that she lost all of her reproductive organs and spleen and ended up with a colostomy, as well as permanent damage to her heart, lungs, and kidneys. She spent eight months in the hospital—three of those in intensive care—and then had to learn to walk and talk again. After other patients complained of this abortionist's sadistic behavior, an undercover investigator found that, "You could hear the patients screaming…nearly all [his] patients vomit from the pain."[126]

- An abortionist showed a 12-week-old fetus that he had just aborted to the patient, threw his glove on the floor and asked her if she was "satisfied."[127]

- An abortionist was suspected of intentionally performing incomplete abortions so that patients would have to come back a second time for an additional fee. One such woman was five months pregnant when she returned to him. She told him that she planned to sue him and keep the baby. He convinced her to have another abortion because he claimed the baby would be deformed from the first attempted abortion. After she finally agreed, he kept her a virtual prisoner in his clinic and in his secretary's house for three nights. For the actual procedure, "she was tied to a table while the fetus was 'pulled out' of her."[128]

- A woman claimed that her abortionist "ordered [her] on the table and threw her legs apart." She said she felt like she was some animal at which the doctor was irritated. After the abortion he told her to stand up, at which time everything the doctor was supposed to have "cleaned out" via suction passed onto the floor—fluids, tissue, and what she believed to be segments of the fetus. She said that he then became irritated with her and without any apology or reassurance ordered her back onto the table to finish the procedure.[129]

- An Arizona woman claimed that her abortionist "stared between [her] legs and sang silly songs during the exam."[130]

- A Kansas abortionist lost the support of a local women's group after one of its members "went with him while he did some abortions, accompanied him, and didn't like the way he treated the women—real rough, and arrogant, and not respecting their privacy."[131]

- An undercover investigator found an abortionist who would perform abortions after consuming two to four glasses of champagne with his lunch. She also claimed that "as one patient stumbled out of a procedure room and fainted, [the abortionist] began to laugh. 'He stood a few feet away, leaning against a pillar, laughing and acting giddy as the aide struggled to get the woman up.'"[132]

- A female abortionist (a member of the National Abortion Federation and director of a Planned Parenthood facility) seems to enjoy seeing abortion patients suffer. According to a suit filed against her, after telling a patient to "Drop your pants and get up on the table," she performed an abortion without anesthesia. When the patient screamed in pain, the abortionist told her to shut up or they would gag her and have her "put in a psycho ward." She then had a nurse hold her hand over the patient's mouth. After the ordeal, the abortionist said, "Here are your pants, put them on and get out of here. This will make you think twice before having sex without a contraceptive." The patient said she saw at least one other woman who was hysterical in the recovery room, crawling on her hands and knees and screaming uncontrollably.[133]

Although not as bad as beating or verbally humiliating a patient, some doctors show their disdain for the women they treat by not talking to them at all. Frequently an abortionist will come into the procedure room, perform the abortion, and leave without speaking a word to the woman.[134] This is something we routinely hear from women who come to us for legal advice about their abortion injury.

There is also the issue of sexual abuse. As Chapter 2 demonstrates, this is not an uncommon occurrence at all. What is revealing is that many of the instances seem to have been perpetrated not for the sexual gratification of the abortionist, but for the degradation of the woman. Researchers often point out that rape is not about sex, but about power. If a study were ever done about sexual assault in the abortion industry, I suspect it would conclude that the attacks are not about sex or power, but about punishment. These abortionists are punishing women for destroying their medical careers and, in some cases, their lives. That may seem odd, but this is an odd environment and it has bizarre sexual overtones. For example, consider what one abortionist said when asked about the relationship between abortionists and patients: "The patients are subservient to us, and when they rebel it's very simple: Go to somebody else." He went on to say, "What better relationship can a man have with a woman? Besides if you fuck thirty women a day with your fingers, and in a way you do, this is a form of sexual violation."[135]

These abortionists are punishing women for destroying their medical careers and, in some cases, their lives.

In our research for this book, we also discovered that abortionists' disrespect for the standards of the medical profession and the well-being of their patients affects how they deal with their non-abortion patients. However, the nature of the injuries they inflict upon their non-abortion patients is different than those they inflict upon their abortion patients. As mentioned elsewhere in this book, abortionists are generally considered the losers and washouts of the medical community, and the injuries they cause their non-abortion patients usually reflect the kind of incompetence one would expect from that quality of person. However, while there were some exceptions, we didn't find many examples of the kind of disrespect, outrageous remarks, and "punitive" injuries that they inflict upon their abortion patients. This seems to lend credence to our observation that they punish these women.

Money Changes Everything

Virtually all abortion clinics require that their customers pay cash before going into the procedure room; many won't accept credit cards; they almost never accept checks; and, not suprisingly, we have never found one that would bill for the procedure. While this system may be tacky, it is not unscrupulous. However, what is indefensible are the inappropriate sales and marketing techniques they employ to make extra money off their patients. Two former employees of an abortion clinic summed up the situation when they stated, "The real philosophy is, each woman is worth X amount of money and the more women we can see, the more money we can make." One said that the day the clinic "hit peak patient load, the doctor took everyone out to celebrate." Both women said they were trained to "maximize the marketing potential" of the women calling the facility and to sell procedures that were more profitable even though they were also more dangerous. As business began to pick up, they were pressured to move women rapidly through the clinic so [the abortionist] could attend to other commitments. They also alleged that the clinic originally would not do abortions prior to eight weeks because the smaller size of the fetus makes it difficult to abort successfully, but that when "patients were few" they would do them as early as five weeks to increase profits.[136]

One former employee of a Kansas abortion clinic said that after she had worked at the clinic for a few weeks answering phones, the supervisor gave her a handbook. She expected it to cover how to counsel a woman, or something similar. Instead, it explained how to be a high-pressure salesperson over the phone.[137] At another clinic, the abortionist was paying counselors commissions based on the type of anesthesia they sold. The dangerous—but profitable—general anesthesia brought a $2 bonus, Demerol and Valium were 75 cents, and a local was only worth 25 cents.[138]

Sometimes this greed can cost patients their lives. In a malpractice trial, John Roe 831 was accused of deliberately performing incomplete abortions in order to charge more for the follow-up visit. Unfortunately, one of these patients died, resulting in a second-degree murder charge against Roe. The state charged that Roe had a "malicious interest in making more money, cutting his costs and saving his time in disregard for the life and health of his patients."[139] Similarly, "Angela" came to the abortion clinic of John Roe 720 on June 7, 1991. A female employee later testified that Angela was not a proper candidate for an elective termination in the office due to her low hemoglobin levels and other problems. The employee wanted to send her to a hospital, but Roe insisted that Angela be aborted at his clinic, saying, "You know we need the money." The staff administered general anesthesia and prepped Angela in the normal way. As Roe began the abortion, he punctured her cervix and her blood pressure stopped registering. Angela started having difficulty breathing. The staff tried to stabilize her and eventually called an ambulance. Angela died three days later from complications of the abortion.[140]

We also found several instances in which an abortionist was caught over-stating the fetal age to justify charging more for abortions. We also found instances in which sedated patients were sometimes asked "to get up off the table and pay more money when the doctor found the pregnancy was further along than originally thought."[141] One example was a New York woman who underwent an abortion by John Roe 3 on March 17, 1991. Roe stopped the procedure and told the woman's husband that the pregnancy was further advanced than he had thought, and demanded an extra $500. The husband said he did not have the money and pleaded with Roe to finish the procedure, promising to bring the additional money the following afternoon. Roe refused the offer and ejected the woman from his office, still under sedation and bleeding heavily. The next day, her husband took her to a hospital where she was admitted with a distended abdomen, a foul-smelling, dark, bloody vaginal discharge, and pieces of fetal tissue and laminaria protruding from her cervix.[142]

Another abortionist had a "Bargain Day," during which he charged a 17-year-old girl $110 for an abortion. Afterward, the girl returned with her mother and "sat doubled over in a chair, sobbing." Her mother did not have the additional $25 cash the abortionist demanded in order to assist the daughter, so she "stood by the door to the operating room for five hours, pleading with anyone who came out" and asking to talk to the abortionist. She offered to pay by check or to be billed, but was refused. Eventually, the abortionist called the police to remove the mother and daughter from the clinic.[143]

One of the most deplorable marketing tactics used by abortionists is the well-documented practice of performing abortions on women who are not pregnant (see Chapter 1). These women are especially easy victims because they come into the clinic suspecting they are pregnant, and are often already prepared to have an abortion if that is the case. After a New York abortionist had his license revoked because he "repeatedly offered to and did perform abortions and abortional acts which were not medically indicated, without ascertaining or attempting to ascertain whether patients were pregnant," the local district attorney said it was likely that 25 percent of the patients who underwent abortions in this clinic were not pregnant. A newspaper investigating the allegations said this abortionist and his wife "tricked women who were not pregnant into having phony abortions."[144]

A Texas newspaper investigated charges that an El Paso abortionist was engaged in this practice and found former staff members who stated that it was routine for them to tell non-pregnant women they were pregnant in order to sell them abortions. These staff people also reported being told not to run pregnancy tests at all during "slow weeks," but to make them all positive. Patients who needed time to get the money were told to ignore any vaginal bleeding, because "the onset of a seemingly normal five-day menstrual period means nothing." Allegedly, even the ultrasound was fudged to convince patients they were pregnant. Non-pregnant reporters were sent in posing as patients, and were told they were pregnant and advised to have abortions immediately. One was actually menstruating at the time of her visit and was told that it was likely she was pregnant and to return in two weeks.[145] Likewise, a Florida newspaper sent 10 non-pregnant reporters into a Miami abortion clinic. Two tested positive, and eight tested negative but were told their tests were probably "false negatives." One was advised to rush home and get cash, and told she should not wait until next week because then she would need $450 instead of $250. She was encouraged to go ahead with the abortion because she was "probably pregnant, but either too far along or not far enough for the test to show positive."[146] (By the way, it is impossible for a woman to be "too far along" for a doctor to tell if she is pregnant.)

We found numerous other incidents of shady financial dealings by abortionists, including the following:

- Paying kickbacks to agencies that refer women for abortions
- Paying for abortion referrals from taxpayer-funded agencies that are legally prohibited from referring for abortion
- Charging indigent clients for abortions that were also charged to the government
- Collecting money from taxpayer-funded programs for services never rendered
- Charging twice as much for government-paid abortions as those paid for by the patient

■ Charging insurance companies as much as $4,000 for the same proce-
  dure that they charged cash customers $400

■ Illegally billing Medicaid for abortions that don't qualify for payment by
  Medicaid[147]

Since these matters don't have a direct bearing on the care given to women
who seek abortions, we've listed only a few examples here. Obviously, they
don't compare to someone subjecting a non-pregnant woman to the risks of
abortion (Chapter 1 includes an incident in which a non-pregnant woman
died during an abortion), or selling a woman extremely dangerous general
anesthetic for a $2 commission. However, they reinforce the view that abor-
tionists are willing to sacrifice their medical ethics for money.

Filthy Conditions

Hardly a week goes by that we don't learn of another abortion clinic being
cited by authorities for non-compliance with health and safety standards.
These are not just failures to meet some bureaucratic requirement for ceiling
height or size of doorways, but items that could pose a serious threat to the
health of the women who go there.

At a Tennessee abortion clinic, authorities discovered the following: intravenous needles and packages of curette tips in a box on the floor containing
dead bugs; alcohol-soaked sponges stored in a plastic ice cream container;
brownish-red residue or dirt on the floors of the waiting room and the
treatment rooms; an instrument cleaning room floor that was "blackened;"
cobwebs and dead insects on the floor of the recovery room; dirty lavatories
with no soap or towels; toilet facilities needing repair; soiled linens on the beds
in the recovery room; a microwave containing a "fast-food bag which emitted
a foul odor and contained a gray and green fur-covered object;" red-stained
rubber gloves; two blackened sponges; a vaginal speculum that shed pieces of
brownish-red tissue when handled; and 18 individually bagged abortion tissue
specimens from the previous week in a garbage bag sitting on boxes of
formaldehyde.[148]

In another facility, the suction machine container and tubing were
clogged with tissue; unsterile instruments, expired supplies, and soiled gauze
were found in the procedure room; the refrigerator contained expired medications, three syringes, a bottle of Yoo Hoo, a half-full bottle of Riuniti peach
wine, a quarter-full bottle of Asti Spumanti with a paper towel stuffed in the
top, a carving knife, a specimen envelope containing a tube of blood collected

22 days earlier, one mostly-eaten salad, and partially-empty bottles of Coca-Cola and Sunkist soda.[149]

Following are just a fraction of other things we've uncovered:

- A suction device with "green mold" growing on it
- Restrooms that were filthy, with toilets that wouldn't flush and no toilet paper
- Blood splattered on floors, walls, and curtains of clinic operating rooms
- Clinics smelling of rotted tissue and rancid blood
- Instruments encrusted with tissue
- Cockroaches and rat droppings in clinic operating rooms
- Garbage cans uncovered and overflowing onto the clinic's floor
- Autoclaves overloaded with stained cloth wrappings
- Stirrups covered with blood
- Chairs in client dressing rooms with brown stains, consistent with blood or Betadine
- Blankets and recliners in the recovery room that were not cleaned between patients
- Reusing disposable syringes and leaving used syringes out on tables in the procedure rooms
- Abortionists using unsterilized instruments and reusing instruments from one patient to the next without having them sterilized
- Abortionists not wearing gloves or not changing gloves between patients
- Employees cleaning hoses used in abortions by running cold water through them while flexing them back and forth to flush out blood and tissue
- Employees dumping tissue jars into the sink and running the solid contents through the garbage disposal
- Abortion clinics operating with no scrub sink
- Patients being made to wear robes and lie on sheets that are covered with blood from previous patients
- Patients being made to use gas masks covered with lipstick from previous patients
- A dog being allowed in the operating room, which sniffed at a patient as she lay bleeding and then lapped blood off the floor[150]

Another public health problem with abortionists is their common practice of inappropriate disposal of fetuses and abortion waste. While it would be farfetched to imagine a hospital throwing hearts, livers, amputated limbs, or dead bodies out with the ordinary trash or burning them in a field, this is exactly what many abortionists have done.

John Roe 436 was investigated for dumping fetuses and medical waste in a hotel dumpster during the summer of 1992. He claimed his abortion clinic sent such material out through a disposal firm, but the firm's records showed no materials received from that facility for two months. On August 12 and August 22, 1992, a local newspaper reporter identified a considerable amount of fetal tissue in a dumpster adjacent to the clinic. The remains—deposited in 10 to 15 large plastic trash bags—included many readily identifiable body parts, such as a forearm and hand, a leg and foot, and a spinal column and rib cage. In several cases the remains had been dumped in trash bags along with ordinary garbage: coffee grounds, cigarette butts, and remnants of chicken dinners.[151]

Among other similar incidents we discovered are:

- A restaurant owner called the police in October 1992, after he caught John Roe 459 putting 10 fetuses and some bags of medical waste in the restaurant dumpster. The restaurant owner said that he had seen Roe put trash in the dumpster several times before. Some of the small plastic jars containing the fetuses were leaking when the restaraunt owner found them.[152]

- An abortion practitioner filed an affidavit against John Roe 473 in opposition to his highly disgusting method of disposing of fetuses. The affidavit stated that the doctor vomited after observing Roe grinding up aborted fetuses of 15 to 22 weeks gestation in a standard kitchen meat grinder and flushing the tissue down the sink. In another instance, a different practitioner stated that Roe told him he had developed this method because the fetuses would "stop up" the toilet and he didn't want to put them in the trash.[153]

- John Roe 7 admitted in news articles that he dumped and attempted to burn at least 60 fetuses in a vacant lot. The fetuses were described by a medical examiner as being "in various states of dismemberment...and preservation."[154]

■ At least one clinic installed an "industrial gauge" garbage disposal. Employees of the clinic told investigators that they routinely placed 8- to 20-week-old fetuses down the disposal.[155]

Bizarre Behavior

Frederick Douglass' experience as a slave, and his understanding of how slavery affected his master, serves as a good comparison for the problems abortionists have. He saw how his master's behavior grew strange and heartless, which he attributed to the fact that he owned slaves. Douglass writes that though this man at times showed attention that "was of remarkably mild and gentle description, a few months only were sufficient to convince me that mildness and gentleness were not the prevailing or governing traits of his character...He could not only be deaf to the appeals of the helpless against the aggressor, but he could himself commit outrages deep, dark, and nameless." Douglass observed that "the slave holder, as well as the slave, was the victim of the slave system," and that his owner gave the impression of an unhappy man who "wore a troubled and at times a haggard aspect." Douglass said the man would "walk alone...muttering to himself, and he occasionally stormed about as if defying an army of invisible foes. Most of his leisure was spent in walking around, cursing and gesticulating as if possessed by a demon. He was evidently a wretched man, at war with his own soul and all the world around him."[156]

The Nazi execution squads are another example of the amplified cruelty that comes with taking part in brutality. A lieutenant named Gnade was described as "affable and approachable at times, brutal and vicious at others. His worst traits became more pronounced under the influence of alcohol." His sadism became apparent during a roundup and execution of the Jews in Lomazy, Poland. He had not been particularly brutal before, but this changed as he decided to entertain himself while waiting for the Jews to finish digging their own graves. Even before the shooting began, Gnade picked out 20 to 25 elderly Jews and made them undress and start crawling toward the grave. At this point, Gnade began screaming at those around, "Where are my non-commissioned officers?...Don't you have any clubs yet?" The non-commissioned officers went to the edge of the forest, fetched clubs, and vigorously beat the Jews. Gnade then began to chase Jews from the undressing areas into the grave.[157]

Gnade's strange behavior is often mirrored by abortionists, and John Roe 652 is a prime example. His neighbors described him as "either mentally disturbed or on some sort of drug," and the "strangest man I've ever met in my life." He would pace outdoors at night, flailing his arms and talking to himself. He'd sit in the parking lot alone at night, talking to himself and ranting, "I trusted you! I trusted you!" This man was shot dead in an apparent robbery attempt as he was exiting an adult movie theater. The owner of the establishment said Roe was a regular at the theater, arriving on Saturdays at about 3:00 p.m. and staying for three or four hours.[158]

John Roe 831 was known to be exceptionally inattentive during procedures, with witnesses testifying that he would "operate with one hand and eat a tuna fish sandwich with the other, and talk to his stock broker on the phone."[159]

In a similar fashion, a former clinic administrator for abortionist John Roe 194 said he routinely engaged in telephone conversations while performing abortions. Even more odd was her claim that on October 23, 1990, he left a patient on the table, went outside, and threw rocks at the procedure room window. He never offered an explanation for this, though he signed a letter of compliance from the medical board vowing not to do such things in the future. Not only could Roe not treat his patients properly, but his animals also suffered under his care. In June 1992, an officer from the humane society confiscated four of his eleven horses and two of his dogs because they had been so terribly neglected. The horses were near starvation, despite stacks of hay—although of inferior quality—just outside their reach. Also, his barn had a foot-deep layer of mud and excrement.[160]

Since many abortionists feel that they have sunk to the bottom of the barrel, their pride won't stop them from making declarations that most people would consider ridiculous. Abortionist Erma Roe 190 was found guilty of 65 counts of "practicing with gross negligence; 29 counts of permitting, aiding, or abetting an unlicensed person to perform activities requiring a license; 90 counts of practicing fraudulently; 65 counts of practicing with gross incompetence; and 139 counts of unprofessional conduct." She later appealed to have her license reinstated, insisting that she had "committed the crimes because of a domineering husband who manipulated her through voodoo."[161]

Some abortion providers seem to be disreputable even before they come into the business. It sounds like Robin Dragin was one of this kind. He was known to be a professional burglar with mob connections. Police wanted to question him about the murder of Kenneth Yellin (the administrator of a Chicago abortion clinic). According to a top investigator, Dragin organized a Chicago abortion clinic that had been in competition with Yellin's operation.

Before abortion was legalized, Dragin was a principal in the operation of an illegal abortion ring. That racket, which was based in various motels, was tied to the crime syndicate.[162]

After abortion became legal, Erma Roe 230 opened an abortion clinic in Florida. Previously, she ran an abortion referral company in Michigan where, for a fee, she would arrange for women to go to New York for their abortions. At that time, she was using Planned Parenthood as a name, even though her facility had no association with the national organization. Two of Roe's children worked with her in the family abortion business. However, her daughter was eventually jailed for drug convictions, and her son incarcerated for life for karate chopping and axing his roommates to death. He claimed that it was justifiable homicide because they were picking on him about his sloppiness. He had also stabbed his mother in the neck with a steak knife, claiming she deserved it for having poisoned his father (who actually died of a heart attack in 1969). After both of her children were put in jail, Roe ran the clinic with her two granddaughters.[163]

John Roe 109, mentioned often throughout this book, was also an oddball at best, even before entering the abortion business. After graduating from high school, he worked at a Dallas ice cream company before being offered a football scholarship by the Texas College of Mines and Metallurgy. There he studied—as he put it—"the birds and the bees." Eventually he entered medical school after securing a recommendation from a prominent El Paso physician. However, Roe was not able to finish his residency, having been "dismissed from the hospital for demonstrating a disregard for the nursing staff." We were never able to determine what that means, but with his medical career on hold he turned to professional wrestling, becoming known as "The Chinese Bandit." When that also failed, he tried his hand at being a wrestling promoter, but this venture—as well as a karate school he had opened—soon fizzled. By this point, abortion had been legalized, so Roe reactivated his medical career and became an abortionist. During this time, Roe seemed to cultivate an interest in art, with a particular passion for the huge, sexually explicit, surrealistic works of Raymond Douillet. Roe described one of Douillet's paintings as capturing women "as they essentially are." It depicts several nude women leaning forward with paintbrushes protruding from their bottoms. He also became a fan of Adolph Hitler whom he suggests was "one of the most misunderstood men in history. He was really a great man." Eventually, Roe was convicted of murder for killing a baby that was born alive during one of his abortions. As mentioned earlier in this chapter, while out of jail on appeal he botched another abortion, which resulted in the death of his 28-year-old patient.[164]

Self-Destructive Behavior

Given the emotionally damaging nature of their lifestyles, it is not surprising that many abortionists engage in various forms of self-destructive behavior. In fact, a significant percentage of the abortionists discussed in this book abuse drugs and/or alcohol.

Joy Davis discussed the problems exhibited by one abortionist she worked for: "I'm using [John Roe 720] as a basis here because I worked more with him than any other doctor. I can't say alcohol and drugs started once he got into the abortion industry, but I can say it got really bad once he got into the abortion industry. It would be so bad that I would come into the office some time in the morning and open up this office, and find him lying on the floor, totally nude, lying in a pool of vomit, where he had been on drugs all night...which is actually what got me started in practicing medicine without a license in the state of Alabama—because he was incapable of doing it." When asked if this was a prevalent problem among abortionists as a whole, compared to other medical people, she replied, "I used to work at a hospital. I can't tell you ever once seeing a doctor come in there just bombed out of his mind, or smelling alcohol on his breath. I can't remember ever seeing that happen, and I worked with hundreds of doctors there. And it was a daily thing in the abortion industry."[165]

Given the emotionally damaging nature of their lifestyles, it is not surprising that many abortionists engage in various forms of self-destructive behavior.

Ms. Davis also points out that sometimes a drug or alcohol problem can work to the benefit of an abortion clinic. Remember, most doctors who work in one of these places do so because they were not able to make it in mainstream medicine. With the shortage of abortionists being the abortion industry's biggest problem, its chances for obtaining a new recruit increase every time a physician is drummed out of legitimate medicine because of a drug or alcohol problem. With his career in a downward spiral, his next stop may very well be the local abortion clinic. Ms. Davis told of a nurse anesthetist who became available to work at her clinic because she lost a teaching position due to her alcohol problem.[166]

A former employee of Louisiana abortionist John Roe 328 described another doctor who came to work at the abortion clinic: "The word I got was that this particular doctor had a drug problem...The man definitely had some type of problem, because he would come to work and you could tell that he was either drunk or high on drugs or something. One day I recall telling him, 'Look, you don't have any shoes on your feet. Why don't you put your shoes on before you see patients?' "[167]

In a petition to revoke John Roe 409's license, the Medical Board presented its concern that the "licensee has the inability to practice the branch of Healing Arts for which he is licensed with reasonable skill and safety to patients by reason of illness, alcoholism, excessive use of drugs, controlled substances, chemical or any other type of material or as a result of any mental or physical condition." In addition, he had been convicted in Oklahoma for the sale of marijuana and LSD and for possession of hashish on September 2, 1970. He failed to disclose these convictions on a federal application, an application for hospital privileges, and an application for a Kansas license. He was therefore given a four-year suspended prison sentence and a $5,000 fine in 1984.[168]

Another common problem is abortionists and abortion clinic employees who illegally distribute drugs. In 1984, John Roe 652 had to close his Mississippi abortion facility after two of his employees were arrested for illegally distributing drugs. After this incident, he surrendered his Mississippi medical license and his federal license to dispense drugs.[169] Michigan abortionist John Roe 420 lost his license for giving out 384 prescriptions for Dilaudid within four months. Medical experts testified that this drug is typically prescribed for terminal cancer patients, but Roe prescribed it for pain no more severe than headaches. Police said that drug dealers were paying Roe $50 for each 24-capsule prescription, which they then sold on the street for $10 to $15 per capsule.[170]

In two other examples, John Roe 517 was the subject of a drug diversion and Medicaid fraud investigation being conducted by the Federal Drug Enforcement Administration and the Oklahoma Attorney General's Medicaid Fraud Control Unit. At the same time, he was also being investigated for performing second-trimester abortions in his home and throwing the fetuses away in his regular trash.[171] And John Roe 18 had his license suspended for 180 days and received five years probation for insurance fraud. While he was still on probation, he prescribed controlled substances "other than for legitimate medical purpose[s] and not in the usual course of medical practice...to persons not under [his] treatment for a pathology or condition other than addiction." On December 15, 1986, he pleaded guilty to 10 counts of unlawful distribution of controlled substances. He was given a suspended five-year prison sentence, five years probation, and was fined $20,000. He was also required to undergo psychiatric care for anxiety, stress, agitation, and suicidal thoughts, and was diagnosed as having dependent personality disorder.[172]

Another self-destructive behavior to which abortionists seem especially prone is excessive gambling. One study of the billing practices of abortionists found that those with the most ambivalence about the procedure itself are the ones who charge the least for it. Apparently, they don't feel entitled to profit from something they are so uncomfortable doing.[173] If that's so, it may explain the seemingly high percentage of abortionists with gambling problems. Perhaps they don't feel entitled to the money they've made from abortions and subconsciously look for a way to get rid of it.

Whatever the motivation, we identified several abortionists who either have well-acknowledged habits or have undergone therapy for their gambling problems. One example is John Roe 267 (discussed in Chapter 1), who was convicted of illegally selling 48,000 Dilaudid tablets to pay off gambling debts. John Roe 652's gambling habit may have even led to his death. By 1990, he had filed for personal bankruptcy with assets of less than $50,000 and debts of more than $500,000. He was reputed by police to be a "heavy gambler" and there was even speculation that his murder during an apparent robbery may have actually been a "hit" by people to whom he owed gambling debts.[174] ∎

The Hidden Killer

*A complication that the abortion industry doesn't
want anyone talking about*

n recent years, American women have suffered a dramatic increase in the
rate of breast cancer. The popular press has been filled with articles such as,
"In Pursuit of a Terrible Killer"[1] and "A Puzzling Plague: What Is It About
the American Way of Life that Causes Breast Cancer?"[2] Although some of
the increase is commonly attributed to known risk factors, the reasons for
approximately 60 percent of the increase remain a mystery, and the medical
community is seemingly unable to provide a conclusive explanation.

Statistics indicate that the increase in breast cancer, although general in
nature, is more prevalent among certain subgroups. Logic suggests that whatever factor accounts for the disparity in the rate of increase between women
as a whole and women in these subgroups could be a large piece of the puzzle.
Some medical research indicates that one answer may be abortion. There is a
powerful and well-documented body of evidence to suggest that having an
abortion, especially of a first pregnancy, may place a woman at a higher risk
for this devastating disease. If true, then the rapid growth in the abortion rate
over the last twenty years could at least partially account for the tragic growth
in the breast cancer rate during that same period.

The Theory

Before a woman's first pregnancy, her breasts consist mostly of connective tissue surrounding a branching network of ducts, with relatively few milk-producing cells. When a woman conceives for the first time, progestational hormones flood her system. Under the influence of these hormones, her breast cells undergo massive growth. The network of milk ducts begins to bud and branch, developing more ducts and new structures called "terminal end buds." These end buds begin to form "alveolar buds," which will later develop into the actual milk-producing glands called "acini." This period of rapid growth toward maturity is when breast cells are most likely to be affected by carcinogens. Research shows that when a woman completes her first full pregnancy, hormonal changes occur which permanently alter the structure of her breasts in a way that greatly reduces her risk of breast cancer.[3] Conversely, a premature termination of a first pregnancy interrupts this process, circumventing the protective effects of a full-term pregnancy and possibly leaving millions of breast cells in transitional states.[4]

To date, the most comprehensive discussion of the potential abortion/breast cancer link has been published by Dr. Nancy Krieger in the journal *Breast Cancer Research and Treatment.* She writes: "According to this hypothesis, an early FFTP [first full-term pregnancy] would provide the greatest protection against breast cancer by drastically reducing, early on, the presence of undifferentiated and hence vulnerable breast cells, thereby decreasing the risk of subsequent transformation...Other types of pregnancies, however, might increase risk of breast cancer. If a woman's first pregnancy resulted in a first-trimester abortion, the dramatic rise in undifferentiated cells that takes place during the first trimester would not be followed by the marked differentiation occurring during the second and third trimesters. The consequent sharp increase in the number of vulnerable cells would thus elevate breast cancer risk..."[5]

Krieger's hypothesis predicts that studies which carefully control for age and timing of the abortion (before or after the first live birth) should find a moderate increase in the risk of breast cancer. Two dozen published, peer-reviewed studies tend to support that position, and include the following major findings:

> *Study 1.*   There was a higher rate of both spontaneous and induced abortions among breast cancer patients; increased risk ranged from 100 percent to 400 percent among the different subgroups.[6]

Study 2. More Israeli women who terminated pregnancies in the first trimester developed breast cancer than did the control group.[7]

Study 3. "There was a significant excess of [cancer] cases reporting one or more abortions."[8]

Study 4. Women with one or more abortions had a cancer risk 50 percent higher than that of women who have not had an abortion; with two or more abortions, the risk rose to 100 percent.[9]

Study 5. In Brazil, more breast cancer patients reported having had abortions than did the control group.[10]

Study 6. Thirty-seven percent of patients who developed breast cancer after menopause have had at least one abortion, while only 27 percent of women with other cancers reported having had an abortion.[11]

Study 7. The rate of breast cancer among women in Finland increased with the number of abortions.[12]

Study 8. Women whose pregnancies lasted four months or less showed a statistically significant increase in breast cancer.[13]

Study 9. A case-controlled study in the North Caucasus, Soviet Union, found an increased risk of 240 percent in women with three or more induced abortions. With one or two induced abortions, the increase in risk was 100 percent.[14]

Study 10. "Pregnancies of less than four to five months duration may be associated with an increased risk."[15]

Study 11. First-trimester abortion of first pregnancies led to increased risk of 140 percent among women under 32 years of age.[16]

Study 12. Raw numbers in this study nearly duplicate findings of Study 11, completed two years earlier.[17]

Study 13. Women with one abortion had twice as many recurrences of cancer as those with none; women with two or more abortions had three times as many recurrences of cancer.[18]

Study 14.   The risk of developing breast cancer was 52 percent higher among women with an induced abortion than for women who had no abortions.[19]

Study 15.   Abortion before a first live birth, after adjusting for other known risk factors, increased the risk of developing breast cancer by 250 percent.[20]

Study 16.   The risk among Italian women with one or more legal abortions before a first live birth was increased by 42 percent.[21]

Study 17.   The termination of a first pregnancy before 28 weeks increased the risk of cancer by 43 percent; two or more abortions before the first full pregnancy increased the risk by 73 percent; one induced abortion with no live births increased the risk by 285 percent.[22]

Study 18.   Among Chinese women who developed breast cancer before the age of 40, abortion before first full-term pregnancy led to an increased risk of 140 percent.[23]

Study 19.   Among women who developed breast cancer while pregnant: those who carried pregnancy to term had a 20 percent survival rate; women who miscarried received more aggressive treatment and had a 42 percent survival rate; but every woman who chose abortion died.[24]

Study 20.   The abortion of a first pregnancy led to an increased risk of 90 percent, and repeated abortions heightened the risk by 300 percent.[25]

Study 21.   Women who had an abortion before a live birth had an 88 percent greater risk of breast cancer than did women who had a live birth before an abortion.[26]

Study 22.   Aborting a first pregnancy led to more aggressive cancer tumors.[27]

Study 23.   Breast cancers of women who aborted their first pregnancy showed many times the normal rate of INT2—a specific gene associated with breast cancer.[28]

Study 24.   Legal abortions in Italy before a first birth led to an increased risk of 30 percent.[29]

Krieger's theory seems to maintain its credibility even *after* adjustments for other known risk factors. In Study 21 cited above, researchers examined 3,315 Connecticut mothers and found that those who had experienced the early loss of a first pregnancy were 350 percent more likely to develop breast cancer. Some of this difference may be attributable to the later age at first birth among women who miscarried. However, after adjusting for this and other known risk factors, there was still a 250 percent increase.

A related issue concerns women who develop breast cancer during pregnancy. Known as "coincidental breast cancer," it has been called "the ultimate challenge" for physicians, since it pits the mother's needs for aggressive radiation and/or chemotherapy against the needs of the developing fetus. Although this phenomenon is often cited as a justification for induced abortion to save the life of the mother, if abortion may actually contribute to breast cancer, then it is clearly contraindicated.

One study that examined the relationship between coincidental breast cancer and abortion found that induced abortion seemed to yield disastrous results. Of the women who carried their pregnancies to term, 20 percent were alive more than 20 years after developing cancer. On the other hand, women who had spontaneous abortions were able to take advantage of more aggressive treatments and enjoyed a survival rate more than twice that of the women carrying to full-term. But all the women who chose to have an elective abortion died of their cancer within 11 years.[30]

Further studies address the immigration issue. People who come to the United States have a low breast cancer risk if they enter the country as adults, but young immigrants and second-generation Americans take on the same breast cancer risk as indigenous Americans.[31] Non-Western societies that have traditionally had very low breast cancer rates are now experiencing rapidly rising breast cancer rates and a more Western pattern of tumor types.[32] It could be that expanded access to abortion is a contributing factor.

Another interesting factor involves male breast cancer. Although rare (one-percent of the rate of female breast cancer), it does occur. However, while breast cancer is on the rise among women worldwide, it is not increasing among men.[33] Obviously, if breast cancer were on the rise in men as well as women, attention could be focused on non-reproductive factors like diet and pollution. But because only women seem to be at increased risk, the prime suspects for the escalation in breast cancer must logically have some link to female hormones or reproduction. Contributing factors could include changing patterns of childbearing, lactation, oral contraceptive use, or abortion.

There is also the "cross-over effect," the well-documented and highly troubling fact that young African-American women have a higher breast cancer rate than do young white women.[34] In the Krieger study, it was suggested that the popularity of the birth control pill and/or abortion might account for this. Krieger theorized that if this were true, one would expect to find higher breast cancer rates among young, upwardly mobile black women, because they use the pill and have abortions more often than do women on welfare. Krieger followed up her theory with a careful study of racial and economic patterns in the breast cancer rates of women in the San Francisco Bay area. She found a significant increased risk of breast cancer for young African-American women living in higher status neighborhoods, thus supporting her hypothesis regarding the cross-over effect.

Soviets have had one of the world's highest abortion rates, and the incidence of breast cancer among Russian women has tripled.

Of course, the question then becomes whether the culprit is the pill, abortion, both, or neither. Obviously, the pill could be at least partially responsible for breast cancer, but its use alone cannot account for the sudden worldwide jump. Women in the former Soviet Union have had little access to Western-style drugs, including the pill or any other contraceptives. Yet the Soviets have had one of the world's highest abortion rates. If the pill alone were the sole cause of the sudden jump in breast cancer, one would expect no rise in breast cancer rates among women in Soviet countries. If, on the other hand, abortion contributes to the onset of breast cancer, one would expect a very sharp rise in the incidence of breast cancer among Soviet women. And the latter is precisely what has happened. The incidence of breast cancer among Russian, Estonian, and Soviet Georgian women tripled between 1960 and 1987. According to one researcher's analysis, more than three-quarters of breast cancer cases in the former Soviet Union can be attributed to reproductive factors such as abortion, woman's age at first birth, cumulative fertility rate, age at marriage, and breastfeeding.[35]

The rise in breast cancer cases has also been blamed on changes in diet, but a recent report states that the popular theory that eating fatty foods in adulthood might cause breast cancer seems to have "bombed out."[36] It is hard to provide much concrete evidence that dietary changes are responsible for the dramatic rise in breast cancer around the world. In Japan, the rising rate of breast cancer has been blamed on the introduction of red meat into the Japanese diet. Women in the former Soviet Union, however, have not been eating more red meat; yet their breast cancer rate, as noted earlier, has tripled. Recently, women in the U.S. have become very health-conscious, and have reduced their consumption of red meat. However, they too have seen a huge rise in the rate of breast cancer. It is clearly problematic to blame diet, unless one is willing to believe that the rate of breast cancer is rising in Japan because women are eating richer foods, in the former Soviet Union because women are eating poorer foods, and in the United States because women are eating more healthful foods.

Other demographic factors impacting the sudden rise in breast cancer might be explained only by legalized abortion. For example, early studies on breast cancer that included socioeconomic status usually found that wealthy women have a higher rate of the disease than poor women.[37] Before 1969, a legal abortion in a hospital was likely to cost more than $500, which meant that women of higher economic status were much more likely than other women to obtain abortions.[38] If there is indeed a link between abortion and breast cancer, that may account for the link between breast cancer and socioeconomic status. In a study that seems to confirm this, researchers found that women in Taiwan (which until recently had little to no experience with Western-style abortion) experience no significant difference in breast cancer rate based on socioeconomic status.[39]

Inexpensive and/or free abortions would change this pattern, and studies in states that provide free abortions indicate the pattern *has* changed. Washington legalized abortion in 1970, three years before the U.S. Supreme Court decided *Roe v. Wade*. As a result, rich women in Washington have had little trouble getting abortions. In the early 1970s, Washington began to publicly fund abortions for the poor. The results are striking. After the state started funding abortions, the breast cancer rate among poor women rose by 53 percent in the period from 1974 to 1984, while it actually dropped by one-percent among wealthy women.[40] The latter, who supposedly have always had access to abortions, experienced no increase in the rate of breast cancer, while the rate among poor women rose substantially.

A similar study in California (which also funds abortions for the poor) found that by 1990, among young white women, there was no difference in the rate of breast cancer between rich and poor.[41] Washington and California have, to some extent, equalized access to abortion among poor and rich women, and appear to have simultaneously equalized their risk of breast cancer.

Finally, one factor often cited as a risk factor for breast cancer is occupation. White females in professional, managerial, clerical, and teaching environments suffer statistically higher instances of breast cancer death than women in lower socioeconomic positions.[42] Some, but not all, of this increased risk can be attributed to well-established risk factors like the woman's age when she first gives birth. As the U.S. Supreme Court has noted, however, abortion has become a way of life for women who hold these kinds of jobs.[43] Recognizing that, it would seem at least plausible that a higher rate of breast cancer among these women could be attributed to their higher rate of abortion.

In summary, while it is hard to conclusively prove a 50 percent increase in risk through studies alone, the demographic effects of such an increase would be impossible to miss. If abortion causes even a slight increase in the risk of cancer, the staggering abortion rate in our society must eventually make that risk evident, and tragically, population-based studies seem to suggest just that. And although some cite many other possible causes (diet, genetics, radiation, miscarriage, environmental pollution, and so on), most of these factors have always existed to some degree. They may be responsible for the relatively stable *base level* of breast cancer, but are certainly unlikely to be fueling its recent global surge.

Theory Opposition by Researchers

Scientists who disagree with the theory that there is a connection between abortion and an increased risk of breast cancer often claim that there are studies showing no link. That is true. However, Russian researcher Larissa Remennick observes, "An initial attitude of researchers towards abortion usually determines the way they interpret results, since outcome risk measures are often of moderate value and/or borderline statistical significance."[44] Remennick's observation may be compounded by the political battle over abortion. Like all human beings, breast cancer researchers are not immune to the possibility that a deeply held personal view might impact their professional conduct.

Additionally, some studies showing such a link have been questioned because of what is often described as "recall bias." According to this theory, women with breast cancer are more likely to remember or admit previous abortions than are other women,[45] and therefore, studies which detect an increased risk of cancer find a risk that isn't really there.

However, even if one accepts the contention that women who have breast cancer remember their abortions better than women who don't, the "recall bias" theory can only explain away an abortion link if the study in question depends on the memory of women who now have cancer. Yet many studies that cannot be affected by "recall bias" still show an increased risk of breast cancer[46] or more aggressive tumor types.[47]

A study conducted by researcher Holly Howe, in conjunction with other researchers at the New York State Department of Health, seems to discredit the "recall bias" theory. In this study, Howe found a 90 percent increased risk of breast cancer among women who had first-pregnancy abortions, and did so in a way that could not have been influenced by "recall bias." The data for this research was derived solely from official records made at the time of the abortion, and therefore did not depend on the woman's memory or honesty.

Another problem with the "recall bias" theory is that it cannot explain why women who have had abortions seem to have deadlier cancers than women who have not had abortions. According to the "recall bias" theory, every woman with breast cancer should be equally likely to tell the truth about her abortion history. Thus, abortion should have no influence on the patient's case. Instead, we find that in every study that checks for abortion among women with breast cancer, abortion is linked to a deadlier form of cancer.

Abortion advocates realize that this connection, if confirmed, could be politically devastating, and are therefore openly hostile to it.

An additional measure of the deadliness of cancer is its recurrence. In one study, women who developed breast cancer had a 10.5 percent rate of recurrence within three years if they had only live births. Those women who had one abortion were twice as likely (20.5 percent) to have a recurrence of cancer within that amount of time. Women with two or more abortions were three times as likely (32.3 percent) to have such a recurrence.[48]

Theory Opposition by Abortion Advocates

Many advocates of legal abortion have been aware of evidence suggesting the possible link between breast cancer and abortion since at least 1982. In March of that year, Willard Cates, Jr. wrote an article in *Science* that discussed evidence of the link.[49] His manuscript was reviewed by D. A. Grimes, C. Tietze, R. W. Rochat, and C. W. Tyler, authors who have contributed many articles to publications like *Family Planning Perspectives*, *Studies in Family Planning*, and *American Journal of Obstetrics and Gynecology*.

Understandably, they realize that this connection, if confirmed, could be politically devastating, and are therefore openly hostile to it. In November

1993, Planned Parenthood, which is involved in approximately 40 percent of all abortions performed in the U.S., issued the following statement:

> There is not one study in mainstream medical literature that proves a cause and effect relationship between abortion and breast cancer. In fact, there are many studies that show no relationship. The largest—and most comprehensive—study to date of a possible link between abortion and breast cancer was done in Sweden and reported in the *British Medical Journal* on December 9, 1989. It followed, for as long as 20 years, 49,000 women who had received abortions before the age of 30. Not only did the study show no indication of an overall risk of breast cancer after an induced abortion, it suggested there could well be a slightly reduced risk. Many other studies have shown no relationship.
>
> The two studies cited by those promoting the alleged link are of limited value because they don't account for the rest of the woman's pregnancy history. These studies are not considered conclusive from a medical point of view. Those who allege the breast cancer/abortion link rely on a self-published booklet by an author with no known expertise in the field. This document, and a shorter brochure, are distributed by an organization in Virginia ("AIM") which is unrecognized in the medical field and fails to describe its mission or source of support. Studies establishing this alleged link have not appeared in accepted medical journals or undergone mainstream peer review.
>
> Researchers don't know what causes breast cancer. In looking at possible risk factors, it is known that having a full-term pregnancy before age 35 is protective against breast cancer. Studies have shown that nuns, for example, have a much higher rate of breast cancer than the general population. If a woman were to have an abortion and no full-term pregnancy before 35 years of age, she would not have the protection offered by a full-term pregnancy. But neither would a woman who gets pregnant after age 35, or a woman who never has a child. In any event, the relationship between pregnancy and breast cancer is a meaningful element of a woman's medical

history, but hardly a reason in and of itself to make decisions about childbearing...or becoming a nun.

Since no reliable, accepted study shows a link between abortion and breast cancer, this is not information that should be conveyed to clients. In fact, to do so would be irresponsible. Bogus medical arguments and flawed conclusions serve only to create unwarranted fear in women; in no way do they contribute to informed consent.

Recognizing that breast cancer takes the life of five women every hour, that one woman in nine will get breast cancer during her lifetime, and that there has been no real progress in curing breast cancer in the last 40 years, we support greatly increased efforts to determine the causes of breast cancer, expand education and screening, and improve treatment.

Obviously, Planned Parenthood's response is patently dishonest. First, they argue that "no study has proven a cause and effect relationship between abortion and breast cancer." However, as every medical professional realizes, scientific proof of causation would require ethically prohibited direct experimentation on living women. (This is precisely how the tobacco industry perpetuates the myth that it's questionable whether smoking causes lung cancer.)

Second, Planned Parenthood cites a Swedish study that they claim shows abortion to cause no increase in the "overall risk" of breast cancer. But "overall risk" was not the issue. Connection theorists have never claimed that *every* woman who loses a pregnancy has a greater risk of breast cancer, but that women who have their *first* pregnancy terminated are at greater risk. The Swedish researchers made no effort to identify a control group, nor did they focus on women who aborted their first pregnancy. (In Sweden, unlike America, most women who get legal abortions have already had one or more children, and thus most women in this study have the lower risk of breast cancer associated with the protective effect of the first full pregnancy.) The Swedish study included women who already had a child with women who aborted their first pregnancy. They then compared the combined results to the total population (which included a high number of women who had had abortions) rather than to women who had not had abortions. Because of these methodological errors, the Swedish researchers effectively masked any possible link between first-pregnancy abortions and breast cancer and then concluded: "Contrary to most earlier reports, this study did not indicate any overall increased risk of breast cancer after an induced abortion in the first trimester in young women."[50]

Interestingly, when first-pregnancy abortions are distinguished from the whole, the statistics show that women who had an abortion *after* a live birth had a breast cancer risk of only 58 percent of the "average" risk in the study, while women who had an abortion *before* a live birth had a risk of 109 percent of the "average." (Comparing these two numbers yields an increased risk factor of nearly 88 percent, which is consistent with the 90 percent figure found in the Howe study mentioned earlier.)

Every study of induced abortions performed before the first live birth is consistent with an initial increase in risk of at least 50 percent.

Additionally, the "average" risk in the Swedish study is based on the population at large. According to the authors, the "average" risk of breast cancer is 40 percent higher than it had been prior to the legalization of abortion. If one converts the risk factors to reflect this 40 percent rise, one sees that women who have an abortion *after* a live birth have an adjusted risk factor of 81 percent, while women who have the abortion *first* have an adjusted risk of 153 percent. In short, even though this study is cited by Planned Parenthood to *refute* the connection theory, if one simply counts the women who aborted before their first live birth, the figures actually *confirm* the theory.

In another part of their statement, Planned Parenthood suggests that only two studies support the hypothesis. However, as this report demonstrates, there are over twenty studies in support of the theory. They also imply that connection proponents are without credentials. In reality, the abortion/breast cancer link has primarily been advanced by Dr. Joel Brind, professor of endocrinology at Baruch College, City University of New York, who is also a breast cancer researcher on staff at Beth Israel Hospital and Mount Sinai Hospital in New York City. Moreover, he has submitted his research on this subject to the *Journal of the American Medical Association (JAMA)* for peer review. Dr. Brind and a team of researchers are currently performing a "meta-analysis," which compiles every research result to date. (As of November 1993, based on work in progress, Brind reported that every study of induced abortions performed before the first live birth is consistent with an initial increase in risk of at least 50 percent.)

Don't Be Misled

Information continues to be released suggesting that there may be a connection between abortion and the onset of breast cancer. In November 1994, Dr. Janet Daling released a study indicating a minimum 50 percent increased risk, with a 250 percent increase for girls who have an abortion before their eighteenth birthday. Although the author stated that the results were not definitive and more study was needed, she did say that, "Our data support the hypothesis that an induced abortion can adversely influence a woman's subsequent risk of breast cancer." This study also showed, as have others before it, that women experiencing a naturally occurring abortion (miscarriage) were not at a higher risk for breast cancer.[51] That would seem to support the theory that it is *induced* abortion that causes problems.

As these studies emerge, pro-abortion organizations—probably led by the Centers for Disease Control—will undoubtedly attempt to discredit them. The bitter political struggle over abortion always has the potential to cloud the process of scientific inquiry, and those wishing to make an honest appraisal must take steps to avoid falling victim to that phenomenon. Accurate analysis of data about a possible abortion/breast cancer link must begin by applying the following standards:

1. Does the information distinguish between abortions before and after the first live birth? Studies that lump all abortions together often fail to find an increase in breast cancer.[52] The important point is that those studies are not inconsistent with the possibility of a connection between an increased risk of breast cancer following the termination of a first pregnancy.

2. How many induced abortions are counted in the study group? Prior to the relatively recent legalization of abortion, first-pregnancy abortions were less frequent. Because of this, some studies depend on very small numbers of first-pregnancy abortions in their sample.[53] Sound statistical research requires having enough cases to be able to rule out chance as the explanation.

3. Does the study exclude women who have never given birth? Several studies exclude from the analysis all women who have had abortions but no live births,[54] or segregate them from the rest of the abortion cases.[55] Obviously, if one is researching the question of whether abortion is related to the onset of breast cancer, these are the very women who should not be excluded from the analysis because they are the ones at the highest risk of developing breast cancer.

4. How carefully are the ages matched? In two studies funded by drug companies, researchers compared women with cancer to women without cancer, and made little or no effort to match the ages of the two groups.[56] This is a major flaw since it's commonly accepted that the single biggest risk factor for cancer is *age*. One study compared a group of women with cancer and a median age of 52 to another group without cancer and a median age of 40. It makes no sense to compare women who discover they have cancer at age 52 to women without cancer at age 40, since some of the younger women can expect to detect cancer sometime in the next 12 years.

Another potential "age-related" distortion of data is caused by the tendency of drug company researchers to employ five-year age-grouping. This ignores the fact that the risk of breast cancer increases so steeply for women from 30 to 35 years of age that each additional year adds 30 percent more risk. It is virtually impossible to identify even a 50 percent increase in risk when the subjects within the five-year block differ in risk by 150 percent.

A final "age-related" problem is more subtle. The median age of cases in a five-year block will tend to be older than the median age of controls, thereby distorting the statistical findings. According to the authors of the definitive paper on analyzing statistical data from retrospective studies, it is inappropriate to gather data in five-year age blocks when studying diseases with a steep age curve.[57]

5. Does the reporting match the data? Occasionally, a study claiming not to find a link contains data that supports just the opposite.

6. Does the study depend on retrospective recall of abortions? Such studies could be easily skewed as women are not always candid about their abortion history.[58]

7. Does the study distinguish between women who use oral contraceptives and those who don't? If the theory of a connection between abortion and breast cancer is legitimate, one disturbing implication is that many oral contraceptive studies may need to be reconsidered. When researchers compare women who take the birth control pill with women who don't, they could actually be comparing women who get breast cancer from oral contraceptives to women who get breast cancer from elective abortions. This could partially explain why studies of oral contraceptives produce inconsistent results.

Conclusion

Obviously, at this point no one can definitively state that abortion does, or does not, cause breast cancer. However, anyone who honestly cares about the health and safety of women should be demanding a large-scale, politically unbiased study. Such a demand, however, has yet to be heard from America's self-appointed "women's rights" groups. They have clearly made the decision that if informing women of this risk creates a risk for the abortion industry, then it is the women who will be sacrificed. Recall from Chapter 3 the story of how then-president of Planned Parenthood, Pamela Maraldo, responded to the Daling study. When a reporter for the NBC program *Dateline* asked her, "If indeed your panel of medical experts studies this study by Dr. Daling and you find it to be solid good science, what are the chances you will begin warning women about this possible link?" She replied, "Even if it's solid good science, then to begin to warn women, and upset women, on the basis of one study is clearly irresponsible. One study is not an adequate, uh, uh—evidence for us to change a policy, or—or to upset or frighten women." Then the reporter asked, "Five studies—say you have five studies?" Maraldo's reply was, "Well I think we're a long ways away from that."[59]

Planned Parenthood would martyr American women, rather than risk the possibility that some of them might forego abortions if told about the potential breast cancer link.

Obviously, Maraldo knew that Daling's study was just the latest of many to suggest a link between abortion and breast cancer. So not only were her statements condescending to women, they were also a public confession. She was openly admitting that Planned Parenthood would martyr American women, rather than risk the possibility that some of them might forego abortions if told about the potential breast cancer link. While Planned Parenthood routinely says that the central issue of abortion is not its morality, but who decides, in this case their attitude seems to be that *Planned Parenthood* will decide. ∎

Just Sit Down and Shut Up!

What abortion-injured women are told when they
seek justice in the court system

ven in many modern countries, it is not uncommon for the judicial system to be accessible only to the wealthy or politically powerful. But since its founding, the American legal system was intended to be available to every citizen. In the *Roe v. Wade* decision that legalized abortion, Justice Blackmun alluded to that concept when he wrote, "If an individual practitioner abuses the privilege of exercising proper medical judgment, the usual remedies, judicial and intra-professional, are available."[1]

Unfortunately, abortion malpractice (ABMAL) victims often find that Blackmun's words are meaningless. While an increasing number of Americans have come to believe that the criminal justice system is one in which only the criminal receives justice, few realize that the same can be said about the civil court system. In both, our country's zeal to protect the accused often stacks the deck against the victim.

Regardless of how seriously she was hurt, and regardless of how legitimate her claim may be, before an abortion-injured woman can receive compensation there are basically three hoops she has to jump through. First, she must be willing to seek legal action. Second, she must be able to get her case filed. And finally, through either settlement or trial, she has to win her case.

Without being successful in each of these areas, she will get nothing. This chapter will examine the powerful forces working against these women as they weave their way through this grueling process.

Barriers to Seeking Compensation

Stigma and the Desire for Secrecy

One recent study found that "Most of the women kept their pregnancies and abortions a secret from their parents. Some feared physical retaliation, but most wanted to spare their parents stress, worry, or shame. These women kept the silence (some to this day) so that their parents' dreams would not be dashed..."[2]

The fact that the largest group of women who have abortions are young and/or unmarried and have their abortions without telling family or friends creates a very real dilemma for the ones who are injured. A woman seeking help has to admit that she (a) was sexually active, (b) became pregnant, and (c) had an abortion.

The problem is, most of these women realize that, even today, these are not generally viewed by society as wholesome behaviors. So when injured, it is not unusual for them to insist that if they can't get help while maintaining the same secrecy with which they had their abortion, they will "just have to live with it." For them, their reluctance may not be just about their abortion, but in having to admit that they were sexually active. This is particularly true when they come from a social structure that does not approve of pre-marital sex or abortion. Women in these situations may believe that revealing the abortion to their family and friends will destroy all the relationships they depend upon. Whether that is true or not is irrelevant if they believe it to be true. In addition, if they were coerced into having the abortion (which is often the case), they may find it even more difficult to disclose their injuries through a lawsuit.

This desire for secrecy may go beyond the legal arena and include a refusal to seek medical help. We have had underage clients who would not see a doctor for treatment of their abortion injuries because doing so would require getting parental permission. One of the bitter ironies is that most of these girls live in a state where they can legally get an abortion without parental knowledge, yet when they are mutilated during that abortion they find that they cannot get medical treatment or seek legal redress without the consent of their parents. The fact that so many of these girls then choose to remain silent about their injuries may explain why the abortion industry fights so viciously against legislation requiring that parents be notified before abortions can be performed on their minor children. At some point it must have dawned on them that the lack of parental involvement in the initial abortion decision reduces the reporting of injuries that occur. And even if that was not the intent, it is certainly a result.

Unfortunately, it is not only young and/or unmarried women who desire to keep their abortions secret. While concealing the fact that they are sexually active or pregnant is probably not a concern for most married women, concealing the fact that they had an abortion might be. Even after more than two decades of legality, abortion still carries a powerful social stigma. Most women, even those who are married, probably have someone in their circle of family and friends to whom they do not wish to reveal their abortion. Whether married or not, most women are not interested in having their abortion known by a society that says women have a right to an abortion while looking down their noses at the women who exercise that right.

> *Some abortion-injured women, like many rape victims, will not seek legal help because doing so would remind them of an event they would prefer to forget.*

Also, it is not uncommon for women to keep silent because they feel profound guilt about having had an abortion. For some, this sense of remorse or guilt can be so powerful that it causes them to accept their injury as punishment. We often hear such women say things like, "Maybe I just got what I deserved for killing my baby," or "Maybe God's punishing me for what I did." These women do not seek compensation because they don't feel entitled to it. Sadly, some do not even seek medical treatment for the same reason.

One thing we have observed is that married women often experience these feelings to a greater degree than unmarried women. This seems especially true if they have already given birth to other children.

Desire for Closure

For some abortion-injured women, their primary concern is getting the whole episode behind them. Like many rape victims, they will not seek legal help because doing so would remind them of an event they would prefer to forget. We have even seen this with the parents of young girls who've been killed during abortions. They sometimes choose not to pursue legal action against the person who killed their child because the legal action itself would revisit the tragedy and reopen old wounds. They may even question what difference it makes, arguing that winning a lawsuit won't bring their daughter back.

Ignorance and Deception

Some abortion-malpractice victims are not even aware that they can seek compensation. While there are many reasons for this, the bottom line seems to be that many Americans, especially those from lower socio-economic backgrounds, do not perceive that the judicial system is available to them.[3]

In our experience, most abortion-malpractice victims come from this group. And though they may feel that the criminal courts, traffic courts, and family courts relate to their lives, the thought of instigating a civil lawsuit against a physician seems far-fetched. While being a member of a society's "upper class" often creates completely unjustified attitudes of superiority, being a part of the other extreme can create equally unjustified attitudes of inferiority. For a person from the latter group, it may seem inconceivable that they would have a chance of winning a lawsuit against someone they perceive as more intelligent, more powerful, more successful, and in general a better and more valuable member of society. That feeling is strongly reinforced if they suspect that the legal system is rigged to protect just those people.

In other instances, abortion-malpractice victims don't file suit because they've been convinced that they can't. Abortion providers typically require their customers to sign a statement agreeing not to sue if something goes wrong during the procedure. From a legal standpoint, this document is not worth the paper it's written on and the abortionist knows it. But if an abortion-injured woman doesn't know it, and doesn't seek legal advice because she believes she signed away her right to seek compensation, the document served its sinister purpose.

From the abortionist's standpoint, this dirty little trick has another advantage. Every state has legal limits on how long after an injury the injured party can bring suit. Called a "statute of limitations," this time restriction varies from state to state but typically the injured party must bring a claim within seven years from the date of the injury, or two years from the date they discover the injury—whichever comes first. In this example, if an abortion customer immediately realizes that she has been injured but doesn't even talk to an attorney because she thinks she has signed away her legal rights, in two years she permanently loses her ability to seek compensation. So for the abortionist to profit, his victim's belief that she can't sue doesn't have to last forever, just until the statute of limitations runs out.

Unfortunately, the scenarios described here are all too common. We have been contacted by many women facing permanent, debilitating injuries who had not previously sought legal assistance because they didn't know (or had been lied to) about their legal rights. This may at least partially explain a situation involving New York abortionist John Roe 3. After area newspapers ran articles about him botching an abortion on 20-year-old "Rosa," more than 30 additional complaints were immediately filed against him charging botched abortions and sexual abuse.[4] Clearly, those women had made a conscious decision to keep quiet, and it is likely that if Rosa had not come forward that would still be the case today. The question is, how many of them had been suffering in silence only because they didn't know, or had been deceived about, their legal options?

Client Reluctance to Endure the Process

The typical abortion-malpractice case is a grueling process in which the client must continually relive the physical and emotional agony of the abortion. In fact, defense attorneys often make the process as horrible as possible for the plaintiff in the hope that she will withdraw.

For example, defense attorneys sometimes put the client on trial for her behavior in order to take the focus off the wrongdoing of the abortionist. Historically employed as a method of defending accused rapists, this "Slut Defense" introduces the victim's medical, gynecological, criminal, and sexual history into the trial in a cowardly attempt to disqualify her as a person deserving compensation. If the client does nothing worse than work in a less than socially acceptable job, that will be used to discredit her. An abortion or sexual indiscretion at age 15 may be used against a woman who was killed during an abortion that she had at age 25. In our research, we even found a case in which a defense attorney tried to use the sexual history of a relative to discredit a woman who was seeking compensation for an abortion injury.

Obviously, none of these issues are relevant to the botched abortion, but the judge may allow them into the trial—especially if he is an abortion rights supporter. And although it is clearly a reprehensible tactic, the "Slut Defense" has proven amazingly effective and is attempted by ABMAL defense attorneys in virtually every case. One well-known abortion advocate has even admitted that they do this, and that it is very effective. Barbara Radford, former executive director of the National Abortion Federation, once said that, "No one wants to get on the witness stand and tell the world that they had an abortion. They don't want to be cross-examined about how many men they had in how many days."[5]

Another defense tactic is to stall. Even under the best of circumstances, an ABMAL case can take several years to resolve. Procedural stalling by the defense can greatly prolong the process. This is almost always an advantage to the abortionist and a barrier to his injured victim. The passage of an excessive amount of time can (a) discourage the client or her attorney so that they give up on the case, (b) motivate them to settle for a fraction of the compensation she deserves, (c) result in witnesses dying or disappearing, or (d) cause juries to be less sympathetic to the woman since her injuries occurred many years before the trial.

There are many other unsavory tactics used by defense attorneys against abortion-injured women. Once advised of them by her attorney, the client must be strongly motivated, have a reliable support system among friends and family members, and firmly believe that the lawsuit is in her best interest. Without all of those, the chances are slim that she will begin—much less survive—the litigation process.

Client Reluctance/Unavailability Due to Geography

A client who lives in a rural area may find it difficult to obtain legal services. Even if she is able to recruit an attorney who is interested in her case, it may be impossible for her to attend all the proceedings necessary to properly pursue it. That can cause delays and even dismissals. In addition, geography may be a major barrier to her obtaining the follow-up medical care she needs in order to prove her injuries. Some defense attorneys even use the client's geographical difficulties against her by opposing continuances (court-permitted delays) and arranging depositions at times when he knows she will be unavailable. These tactics can be so discouraging to the client and her attorney that they abandon the case.

Client Reluctance Due to Perceived Financial Requirement

Most people believe that hiring an attorney costs a lot of money and have heard horror stories about huge fees being paid to attorneys with minimal results. However, they probably do not know that medical malpractice attorneys normally take cases on a contingency basis. Under this arrangement, the attorney or law firm finances the case with an agreement that their fees come out of any damages awarded to the client. If the suit fails, the attorney loses all the time, effort, and money that he put into the case. In any event, the client does not have to risk any of her own money. The problem is that if an abortion-injured woman is not aware of this, she may erroneously believe that she has no access to the court system and simply remain silent.

Inability to Find Representation

Although it is often lamented that there are too many lawyers in America, Life Dynamics is routinely contacted by abortion-injured women who are not able to find attorneys willing to take their cases.

There are many personal, political, and pragmatic reasons why an attorney might turn away abortion-injured clients (sometimes in good cases and always in marginal ones) and this rejection can be a powerful roadblock for these women to overcome. It has even caused some women to believe that they did not have a legitimate claim for compensation when, in fact, they did.

Some attorneys will not represent abortion-injured clients because they do not want to be associated with such a controversial issue or risk the notoriety they fear will result from a potentially high-profile case. Others just do not want to confront their own feelings on the subject.

Attorneys who are political supporters of legalized abortion will sometimes refuse to represent an abortion-injured woman because of the harm such a case could do to the abortion industry. In some instances, attorneys have wanted to represent abortion-injured women, only to find pro-abortion partners or staff members threatening to quit before assisting in a suit against an abortionist.

Cost of Litigation

Often, the most overwhelming barrier to filing an ABMAL lawsuit is the astronomical cost of the litigation. These expenses start piling up even before the case is filed, as medical records and other information must be gathered and sent to a medical expert (normally a physician) who can review them to determine if the abortionist violated the standard of care. This will usually cost a minimum of about $1,500 with a realistic potential of between $5,000 and $10,000.[6] If it is a more complicated case, or if more than one medical expert is needed, the cost can be significantly higher.

If the case is deemed worthwhile, there will be costs related to filing fees, service fees, discovery, depositions, document preparation, investigations, research, client preparation, telephone calls, travel, and whatever out-of-pocket expenses the attorney has for his support staff. Once these expenses are factored in, a typical and relatively uncomplicated ABMAL case can easily cost between $25,000 and $50,000 before the first day of trial—not counting attorney fees. If it is a complex case, the costs go up dramatically.

As mentioned earlier, almost all ABMAL cases are funded by the attorney on a contingency basis. The problem is that even when an attorney is willing to accept these risks, unless his practice is financially sound it is unlikely that he can fund a high-dollar contingency case. Additionally, since only about 29 percent of all medical malpractice cases that go to trial are concluded in favor of the plaintiff,[7] even those attorneys and law firms who are capable of financing such cases may choose to avoid this kind of high-risk venture.

Insufficient Recovery Amount

Some women are unable to secure legal representation only because the potential recovery amount in their cases might not be enough to pay the bill amassed during the litigation. This is a particularly acute problem for women with less severe injuries like infection, excessive bleeding, or Rh sensitization. While these injuries can present profound and life-altering problems to the women who suffer them, they do not have a lot of "courtroom appeal" and are less likely to result in an award that is large enough to justify the time and expense required. If a woman has a $10,000 emergency room bill for complications caused by retained fetal parts (the most common abortion complication), and her attorney does not think he could recover more than just her "out-of-pocket" expenses, the chances that her case will be heard are poor. This problem has been identified in a government study that found, "The present system works to the serious disadvantage of the patient whose injury due to negligence is of small monetary value."[8]

Inability to Collect

Another issue that the attorney must consider when deciding whether to accept a case is the likelihood of collecting if the case is successful. As any experienced attorney will verify, it is one thing to be awarded damages but quite another to collect them.

One potential source for collecting damages is through malpractice insurance. However, our experience is that a relatively high percentage of abortionists choose not to buy malpractice insurance. Then, if sued, they shield their personal income by declaring bankruptcy, hiding their assets in another country, or putting them in a family member's name. At that point, the malpractice claim is worthless, regardless of how severely the woman is injured, because there is no money to collect even if she wins. We have also observed that those abortionists who decide not to purchase insurance seem to be the ones who need it the most. Apparently, the disregard they show for their patients when they consciously decide not to buy insurance is mirrored in the way they treat them in the procedure room, and makes them more likely to injure or kill someone.

Malpractice Coverage Limits—Risks Beyond Policy Guidelines

Even when an abortionist has malpractice insurance, there is no guarantee that it will be available to an abortion-injured patient. Generally, malpractice insurance is tailored to the medical practice of the individual doctor, with the cost of the policy dependent upon how many and which risks are covered. If an abortionist claims to perform only first-trimester abortions, only that type of procedure will be covered. If he then misdiagnoses the stage of the pregnancy (as often happens) and botches what is actually a second- or third-trimester abortion, the insurance company can legally refuse to pay the injured woman. This situation often arises when the doctor intentionally underinsures himself in order to lower policy costs, and then intentionally underestimates fetal age in order not to lose a sale.

Malpractice Coverage Limits—Exclusions

Malpractice policies can also have numerous exclusions to coverage. Medical negligence is sometimes not covered if it involves a lack of informed consent. Abortion providers have a legal duty to make certain that every patient seeking abortion receives *and understands* all relevant information about the abortion procedure and its "material risks" before consenting to have one. If an abortion clinic doctor or counselor fails to meet this responsibility, or remains silent despite an obvious lack of understanding by the patient, informed consent for the procedure does not exist.

The term "material risk" can be defined on the basis of what the abortionist thinks is relevant or on the basis of what the woman thinks is relevant. But regardless of how it is defined, abortion clinics rarely provide their clients with enough information to meet either standard. If the woman would not have had the abortion had she known all the risks, then the abortionist should, at the very least, be held legally responsible for whatever injury she suffers. As one attorney observed on national television, the way in which abortionists counsel their patients means that the vast majority of abortions performed in the United States today are legally actionable for malpractice.[9] But that is a moot point if the abortionist is judgment-proof because he has hidden his assets and his malpractice insurance policy does not cover injuries from a procedure for which there was no informed consent.

Malpractice Coverage Limits—Intentional Acts

Malpractice policies are designed to cover injuries that occur when an abortionist fails to meet the accepted minimum standards of medical care and *unintentionally* injures a patient. These policies do not normally cover *inten-*

tional acts. An example of how this can work against the abortion-injured woman relates to informed consent. If an abortionist's insurance company can show in court that the injured woman did not give informed consent to the abortion, then it follows that she did not give her consent to be touched by the abortionist. In most states, that is considered a battery or *intentional* tort and may release the insurance company from liability. At that point, the abortionist has no applicable malpractice coverage, and if he has hidden his assets the injured woman will receive nothing. It is sadly ironic that, in this case, the fact that the woman's injuries were *intentionally* inflicted protects the doctor who injured her and the company who insured him, but does not protect her.

Malpractice Coverage Limits—General Limits

When abortionists are covered by malpractice insurance, there are almost always general limits to the policy. The injured woman will only be able to recover damages to the extent that the abortionist has purchased insurance. If his policy limit is less than the amount awarded by the court, she will simply have to settle for that amount. To address that problem, a few states have established catastrophic injury funds to which all health care providers are required to contribute. It is intended to cover damage awards in excess of these private insurance limits. Unfortunately, women who do not live in one of those states do not have access to such funds.

Malpractice Coverage Limits—Punitive Damages

Another way in which malpractice insurance companies limit an abortion-injured woman's ability to be compensated for her injury is by excluding coverage for punitive damages. Since punitive damages are supposed to punish the wrongdoer, there is some justification for the company's unwillingness to cover punitive damages. After all, if an abortionist does not feel some economic pain because the insurance company has paid the bill, then the punitive damage award cannot achieve its objective. Some courts have upheld insurers' rights to refuse coverage for punitive damages on the premise that they are not good public policy.[10] But regardless of that, not covering punitive damages clearly produces unfair results for the woman who is injured by abortion.

Malpractice Coverage Limits—Cumulative Provisions

Some malpractice policies stipulate that the coverage amount does not apply to each incident of negligence but to all negligence incidents combined during a particular time period. For example, if an abortionist has a policy containing a $200,000 cumulative limit, and an injured woman receives a damage award for $175,000, the most the next injured woman can receive is $25,000 regardless of the nature of her injuries. Any woman injured after that is completely without recourse. This system guarantees that the most negligent abortionists will be the least likely to compensate their victims, since the limits of their insurance coverage will be quickly exhausted. So even if an injured woman knew on the day of her abortion that her abortionist had insurance, by the time her case is resolved, there may not be any insurance funds left.

Malpractice Coverage Limits—Claims-Made Policies

In this type of policy, only claims made or reported during the policy year are recoverable, regardless of when they occurred. Therefore, if the abortion took place while the policy was in effect, but was not reported until later, after the policy ended, the insurance company would not have to pay any damages that a court awarded. This is particularly egregious if an insurer canceled the policy of an abortionist because of the excessive number of negligence lawsuits filed against him, thereby ending the ability of his victims to recover damages.

State Limitations on Damages

There are two types of damages available to victims of ABMAL. Economic damages compensate the victim for the financial cost of past and future medical care. Non-economic damages compensate the victim for pain and suffering. Non-economic damages include punitive damages, which are intended to punish a negligent abortionist and provide a deterrent to future wrongdoing. Punitive damages are usually awarded only in cases of intentional harm or gross negligence.

In recent years, many states have enacted ceilings on the damages that can be awarded in personal injury cases. In those states, attorneys must take these caps into account when determining whether the case is worth filing. Consequently, these caps can present a significant barrier to women injured by abortionists. If a state has a $100,000 limit on wrongful death claims (such as in Kansas), why would an attorney risk $50,000 of his own money funding a case that statistics show he has only a 29 percent chance of winning?

Statutes of Limitations

Every state has time limits for filing lawsuits, and about a third of the states have special statutes for medical malpractice cases. Commonly referred to as "statutes of limitations," they require that litigation be instituted within a certain timeframe.

In some states, the time limit starts to run when the wrongful act occurs, regardless of whether or not the victim of the negligence realizes that the doctor caused the injury. If a state has a two-year statute of limitations but the effects of the abortionist's negligence do not become apparent until more than two years after the abortion took place, even though the client may have been legitimately injured by her abortion, she no longer has the right to seek recovery. Unfortunately, this situation is not unusual when it comes to abortion injuries. For example, a woman might not discover that an injury caused by the abortionist's negligence has left her infertile until she attempts to become pregnant again.[11] Another example would be psychological injuries that do not become apparent until many years after the abortion takes place.[12] If it takes years of psychoanalysis to discover the repressed feelings associated with the abortion,[13] and the statute of limitations has run out, the woman has no recourse against the abortionist who caused the problem. Incredibly, many states actually apply a shorter statute of limitations for medical malpractice than for other types of personal injury actions.

The statute of limitations may also be abbreviated if the injury caused by the abortionist is construed to be intentional rather than negligent. For example, the lack of informed consent is often considered an assault and battery, which is an intentional tort, and the statute of limitations for intentional torts may be shorter than that for personal injury or medical malpractice. In Florida, for example, the statute of limitations applying to medical malpractice is three years, but the statute applying to assault and battery is two years. This cuts a full year off the time that the abortion-injured woman has to file her lawsuit. In other words, if the abortionist injures someone on purpose rather than accidentally, his liability is actually less.

Sometimes an abortion injury suit is based on a contention that the injury occurred because the clinic or doctor violated the agreement they had with the patient to deliver a safe abortion. One advantage of using this "contract law" approach is that the statute of limitations may be longer than it is for personal injury or medical malpractice. While this may give the injured woman a longer time to file, the downside is that recovering damages for pain and suffering is normally prohibited in this kind of litigation. Given the large expenses involved in medical malpractice cases, that could make the suit not worth filing,

Statutes of limitations may be "tolled" (suspended) if the injured patient is suffering from some type of disability, such as being underage, imprisoned, insane, or mentally incapacitated. However, in states that have a separate statute of limitations for medical malpractice, some courts have applied a strict interpretation. Unless the statute specifically incorporates the disability exceptions, these courts have held that the normal disability exceptions do not apply in the case of medical malpractice.[14] In such instances, the extra time these women would normally be given to file lawsuits is eliminated. Clearly, this is not justice but a way of cheating them out of their right to compensation.

Statutes of Limitations—Discovery Rule

Some state courts have adopted the "discovery rule" under which the time limit does not start until the patient discovers, or reasonably could have been expected to discover, the injury. While this does give an abortion-injured woman more time to file her case, it does not completely solve the problem. Even with the discovery rule, the time may begin running when the initial manifestation is felt although the client may not feel that the pain is severe enough to cause much disability. By the time the full impact of the injury is revealed, the statute may have run out and the client will be forever barred from recovering damages. Again, because of the unique nature of abortion injury—particularly psychological injury—it may take many years before a woman discovers she was injured and recognizes that the injury was caused by the abortion. If there is no legal basis to claim that the statute of limitations should be tolled because of a disability, the woman—no matter how severely injured—will not be able to recover any damages. There have been a few cases in which courts have ruled that the statutory period began when the woman discovered that her injury was caused by malpractice, and not just when she discovered the injury. However, this is the exception, not the rule.[15]

Statutes of Limitations—Unavailability of "Blocking" Defense

As mentioned, one of the disabilities that prevents the statute of limitations from beginning to run is mental incapacity, or some condition of mental derangement that prevents the injured party from comprehending rights that she would otherwise, as a reasonable person, have known about. Recently, this rule has been expanded in a few jurisdictions to include cases where the injured person has repressed or blocked the memory of the injury, mainly in sexual abuse cases.[16] In addition, some states have been motivated by the child abuse phenomenon to enact legislation that provides for an extended discovery period. The question in these cases is whether it is credible that the victim's repression actually prevented or delayed an awareness of the injury and whether there is objective, verifiable evidence of the psychological injury and the repression. This type of Post-Traumatic Stress Disorder (PTSD) is used to nullify a statute of limitations deadline in child abuse cases.

There is a large body of evidence that postabortion trauma is also a type of PTSD and that the psychological injury which some women experience from an abortion can cause them to block or repress a true understanding of their psychological injuries. However, at this point courts are generally unwilling to accept that. Until postabortion trauma is widely recognized by the courts as a variant of post-traumatic stress disorder, or until the legislatures act to extend the discovery period in such cases, abortionists who psychologically injure their patients will be able to escape liability. Currently, the brief statute of limitations period simply does not allow sufficient time for these women to discover the true nature of their injuries.

Statutes of Repose

In recent years, lobbyists for large malpractice insurance companies have successfully obtained the repeal of the discovery rule in four states.[17] In addition, forty states have enacted statutes of repose, which cut off all claims after a certain number of years, without regard to the discovery rule, disabilities, or repressed memories.[18] These states have sided with insurance companies that seek this legislation in order to avoid having to maintain large cash reserves for claims arising many years after the injuries occurred. Clearly, while this is great for abortionists and their insurance carriers, it is particularly restrictive for those women who are psychologically injured by abortion and seek to recover for their injuries years later.

Existing Barriers to Winning an ABMAL Case

Attorney Incompetence and/or Naiveté

The catalog of differences between ABMAL cases and other personal injury and medical malpractice litigation is far too extensive to detail here. However, any attorney who wants to be an effective advocate for abortion-injured women must know what they are. If he simply applies the same standards to an ABMAL case that he would to litigation involving other surgical procedures performed by legitimate physicians in conventional medical environments, he is guaranteeing that his client will never get the compensation she is due.

Unfortunately, in researching ABMAL cases, we find that this is exactly what often happens. In some instances, because attorneys are not completely familiar with the abortion procedure, they will tell deserving clients that they do not have actionable injuries. In those cases, either someone with knowledge of the procedure must step in as an advisor, or the case will never be filed.

When a case does get filed, the attorney must be prepared for the fact that it will be fought more viciously than any other kind of personal injury case, have issues routinely introduced that would never be allowed in other areas of litigation, may feature overt political bias from the bench, and is likely to generate a level of publicity that he is not fully prepared to handle. Additionally, he had better anticipate and know how to handle the fact that the defense is going to make the trial a referendum on abortion rights.

Keeping the Client

The typical abortion-injured client is so traumatized by the injury and frightened by the litigation process that she is particularly susceptible to giving up on the case. She may require therapy to develop sufficient strength to sustain herself through the rigors of the litigation process, and even when she agrees to go, there may be many difficulties in keeping her in a therapy program. Abortionists, their attorneys, and their insurance carriers know this and capitalize upon it. Combined with the fact that they have far more resources than the injured woman, this can be devastating to her.

Getting Records

Normally, the first step in litigation involving a medical procedure is to review the injured party's medical records. Legitimate physicians usually take the view that patients are entitled to these documents and have little reluctance when asked to make them available.

Abortion clinics, on the other hand, are notoriously uncooperative about releasing medical records. We have encountered situations in which the clinic claimed they had no record of the woman having been there, in spite of the fact that she had several witnesses to back her up. In other situations, abortion clinics set up a bureaucratic maze of corporate personnel and independent contractors. Their unmistakable goal is to make it difficult to assess who is responsible for which function, whether it is securing the signature on an informed consent form, doing the actual procedure, or providing post-operative care. In other instances, they have told us that medical records can only be released by a particular clinic employee who mysteriously never seems to be around. Sometimes, abortion clinics put up so much resistance that the only recourse is to seek a court order.

And even when abortion clinic records are provided, it is not at all unusual to discover that they are incomplete, unreadable, or significantly altered. This is particularly common if the clinic stalls before releasing the records. Although they realize they will have to eventually furnish them, stalling for a couple of days gives them time to "correct" any damaging information.

Juror Confusion

It is often joked that a jury consists of twelve people who were not smart enough to get out of jury duty. Although insulting, like most humor it contains at least an element of truth that can profoundly impact the chances of an abortion-injured woman being successful in court.

In an ABMAL trial, if the jury is unsure or confused about what happened, they invariably side with the doctor. Being aware of this, defense attorneys often try to confuse the jury. Since the case revolves around a medical procedure, confusion is seldom difficult to accomplish. If the injured woman's attorney is not able to clear up that confusion and make the jury completely comprehend what happened, she will lose her case. This is also true of the doctor who is testifying as an expert witness on her behalf; her case could literally depend upon his ability to accurately draw what happened on a chalkboard.

Abortion-Injured Clients as Witnesses

In all personal-injury litigation—and especially abortion-injury litigation—if the jury does not like the client they will not award her compensation regardless of the facts of the case. Defense attorneys know this and will use every trick in the book to make the woman as unattractive as possible. Unfortunately, for a variety of reasons, abortion-injured women do not always make effective witnesses for themselves.

In some cases, feelings of remorse, regret, and/or guilt are communicated to the jury or judge, making it more difficult to convince them of the worthiness of the client's claim. Also, if an abortion-injured woman has led a less than exemplary lifestyle, she will be particularly vulnerable to the loathsome "Slut Defense" described earlier in this chapter.

Another defense tactic is to suggest to the jury that the client "got what she asked for—a dead baby—so why is she complaining?" The "Dead Baby" argument makes the jury less sympathetic toward the client and is particularly difficult to overcome if she was injured during a repeat abortion.

Difficulties in Locating Expert Witnesses

In any medical malpractice action, quality expert witnesses are absolutely critical to a successful outcome. Before an attorney recommends that a case be filed, he will almost always have an expert evaluate it to determine if the abortionist did not meet the standard of care owed to the patient. An expert can also establish which material risks were inherent to the abortion procedure and therefore not actionable. If a case is eventually filed, the expert must then be available to refute the abortionist's ubiquitous claim that he met the highest standards of medical care, no matter what he did to the patient.

Historically, it has been difficult to find physicians who are willing to testify against other physicians. Even when doctors know that a particular colleague is performing below the standard of care, there is a "circle the wagons" mentality that discourages them from testifying against him. While the goal of any true medical professional should be to ensure that the public receives the best care possible, in some corners of the medical establishment there is no concern greater than that of protecting physicians—regardless of what they do. One of the more egregious examples of this kind of intellectual dishonesty is that some medical institutions will allow their staff to testify for the defense in a malpractice action, but specifically prohibit them from testifying for the plaintiff.

In abortion-injury cases, there are often additional dynamics at work. For example, many doctors view abortion as so distasteful that they refuse to be associated with it in any way. For them, the fact that abortion is also politically volatile reaffirms that staying out of ABMAL litigation is best.

Standard of Care Requirements

In order to win an ABMAL case, the attorney must do more than simply prove that the woman was injured during an abortion. He must prove that her injuries were caused by the abortionist's failure to provide the appropriate standard of care.

Of course, in order to do that, he must also identify the standards by which the abortionist's actions should be measured. The problem is that there are many different standards and they vary according to the area of the country in which the case is tried. If the area applies a national standard, the court may use standards published by the National Abortion Federation,[19] the American College of Obstetricians and Gynecologists,[20] or Planned Parenthood.[21] In addition, there are textbooks[22] that outline the standard of care for abortion procedures, as well as the provision of informed consent.

Measuring the performance of an abortionist against one of these national standards will typically allow the woman to recover for substandard care. However, some jurisdictions still use a "neighborhood," "state," or "same or similar community" approach.[23] Unfortunately, when it comes to abortion these standards are often so low that it is virtually impossible for even the most incompetent abortionist to violate them. When that happens, the abortionist is not going to be held accountable for his actions regardless of the type or degree of injuries he inflicts upon his patient.

Proximate Cause Requirement

Once the attorney has demonstrated that an abortion injury occurred because the abortionist violated the standard of care, he must then prove that this standard of care violation was the proximate cause of the woman's injuries.

On the surface, this seems very reasonable. After all, people should not be held responsible for injuries they did not cause. However, in practice this legal doctrine often works against the abortion-injured woman. For example, if an abortion-injured woman does not seek medical care but eventually seeks legal compensation, the abortionist may be able to escape liability by claiming that her failure to seek medical treatment was the proximate cause of the injury. Although the abortionist might actually admit in trial that he contributed to the problem, and the court agrees that there was medical negligence, the doctrine of proximate cause may mean that the injured woman will not be compensated for her injuries. This is obviously a bigger problem in abortion-injury situations than in any other kind of medical malpractice case. Most women who have abortions do not want their abortions or pregnancies made public, guaranteeing that they are far more likely to keep silent about any injuries that occur. This makes them far more vulnerable to a claim that they were the proximate cause of their own injuries.

Limitations on the Res Ipsa Loquitur Doctrine

There are two ways in which an attorney can prove an ABMAL case. Direct evidence of the actions that caused the injury (such as an eyewitness or medical records) can be produced. Or the attorney can use circumstantial evidence to prove that the abortionist was negligent. The latter method is often referred to as the doctrine of *res ipsa loquitur*, which is a Latin phrase meaning "the thing speaks for itself."

In order to use this strategy, the woman's attorney must introduce evidence that the three elements of the doctrine are present. First, the abortion injury must have resulted from an occurrence that does not ordinarily happen in the absence of negligence. For example, a sponge does not usually remain in a patient's body after an abortion unless there was negligence. Second, the injury must have been the result of an action under the exclusive management or control of the abortionist. Third, the injury must not have resulted from any voluntary act or negligence on the part of the patient.

The most difficult element to prove is the first one, since most medical procedures pose an inherent risk of injury. The attorney must prove that there could not have been any other cause for the injury except for the negligence of the abortionist. The burden would then shift to the abortionist to show that he was not negligent. However, in recent years some courts have held that applying *res ipsa loquitur* only creates a permissible inference of negligence, and that the burden is still on the plaintiff to establish that negligence took place. This means that the injured woman's attorney would still have to use expert witnesses to establish that the standard of care was breached. In addition, over twelve states have limited the doctrine to particular injuries. This is an additional barrier to successfully holding abortionists liable for the injuries they inflict.[24]

The Definition of Material Risk

There are some risks that are inherent to certain medical procedures. Even if the abortionist does everything right, there is a chance that certain injuries will occur. If a woman gives her informed consent to the procedure, and then suffers an injury due to one of these inherent risks, her claim will not be actionable in a court of law.

But what constitutes informed consent? Generally, it has two parts. First, the patient must have enough information concerning the material risks, benefits, and alternatives to the abortion so that she is able to decide whether or not to consent to the procedure. Some states define "material risks" as those that a reasonable person in the patient's position would want to know in deciding whether to undergo the procedure. This definition generally requires that the abortionist give more information than he would have under his own view of what material risks are. If the abortionist did not provide this information, he may liable for inherent injuries. Using this definition also makes it easier to prove to a jury that, by withholding information, the abortionist did not meet the standard of care, since expert testimony is not needed to establish a professional standard of care.

However, many states define "material risks" as those that the *doctor* deems important, according to professional practice standards. In these "doctor-oriented" states, it is far less likely that the woman will be informed of all the risks that she might deem important to her decision. If she gives her consent, it will not be with the knowledge that she might have her uterus perforated unless the *abortionist* believes that a perforated uterus is a material risk.

Allowing an abortionist to dodge liability for injuries in this situation is like allowing a person accused of armed robbery to avoid prosecution on the basis that he did not believe armed robbery was wrong.

Other Informed Consent Limitations

A new legal theory is that an abortionist should not be held responsible for ensuring that the woman has given her informed consent prior to the abortion. The contention is that the staff of the abortion clinic, not the actual abortionist, is responsible for making certain that the forms are appropriately signed. If this idea becomes widely accepted, it will effectively be impossible to hold an abortionist liable for either an intentional or negligent tort. This would remove an entire cause of action from abortion-injured women and leave them with absolutely no legal recourse.

Signed Informed Consent Form

Many new state laws have been passed that require a woman to sign a consent form before undergoing an abortion.

Ironically, these consent forms can help abortionists escape liability under both common and statutory law. Since few consent forms contain all the information the woman has a right to receive, it will be difficult to prove, other than by her testimony, that she was not actually given the required information before signing the form. She will not know whether the abortionist has fully disclosed all the information on every material risk, since she is depending on him to know what those risks are. Yet by simply introducing the form as evidence, the abortionist can show in court that she gave her informed consent.

Some of these statutes specifically exempt the doctor from liability if the form is signed, and it is not always clear whether the statute preempts the common law requirements. In states with this type of statute, if a woman suffers an abortion-injury that she was not told was a possibility because the doctor did not consider it to be material, her signature on the informed consent form may make it impossible for her to obtain compensation.

Contributory Negligence

Once the plaintiff in an ABMAL suit presents her case, the defendant abortionist may argue that the injured woman was negligent in some way and contributed to her own injuries. For example, if the woman did not follow postabortion procedures to the letter, the doctor may escape liability even if the injury was not related to a lack of follow-up care.

In other jurisdictions, courts use the principle of comparative negligence and assess fault on a percentage basis. If the court decides that the woman was 20 percent responsible for her injuries, then she will receive only 80 percent of the damage award. Under either system, the woman is prohibited from being fully compensated for her injuries.

Illegality of the Abortion

Many states still have laws on the books that prohibit abortion after a certain gestational period. While most of these laws are unconstitutional, if they have not been challenged they will remain as valid laws.

Generally, a person who is injured while committing an illegal act cannot sue for damages. So if a woman obtains a late-term abortion in a state that prohibits them, and therefore participates in an illegal act, most likely she will not be permitted to sue the abortionist even though she may have been seriously and permanently injured. Additionally, since the abortionist is far more likely than the woman to be aware of the laws regarding abortion, and since she is the only one with the possibility of being injured, this law protects only him.

Frivolous Defenses

The complaint that there are many frivolous claims filed against doctors is frequently raised as a rallying cry for tort reform. While there is powerful evidence that too few malpractice claims are filed rather than too many (as discussed later in the chapter), people often believe this "frivolous lawsuit" claim. However, there is seldom any discussion of frivolous defenses. "Even in the most obvious cases—where no honest person would doubt that malpractice occurred—the physicians and their insurance companies almost always deny liability, refuse responsibility, and defend against the lawsuit vigorously."[25] Since the abortionist usually has an insurance company with far greater resources than the injured woman, she is often at an overwhelming disadvantage even when she has profound injuries resulting from a clear case of malpractice.

Limits on Liability

Under the existing law in most states, if an abortion-injured woman wins compensation, everyone involved (the clinic, the abortionist, etc.) is potentially liable for paying 100 percent of the damages. If only one of the defendants has insurance or attachable assets, that person is responsible for paying the entire amount even though the fault was shared by all the defendants. The defendant who pays may seek contributions from the other defendants, but in any event the victim will be paid.

While this system is clearly in the best interest of the injured party, some states choose to limit payments in proportion to the percentage of fault ascribed to each defendant. For example, a court could rule that an abortionist was 20 percent responsible for a woman's injury and the clinic 80 percent, and order them to compensate her in those percentages. If the total award is $100,000, the abortionist owes her $20,000 and the clinic owes her $80,000.

While, on the surface, it seems fair to hold a defendant responsible for only the portion of an injury that he causes, this approach has severe flaws. To begin with, the proportioning of responsibility is subjective and can easily be manipulated, resulting in the victim not receiving all the compensation she is owed. In the example above, if the abortion clinic has no insurance and no assets, the maximum this woman could recover is 20 percent of her award, even if the abortionist has full coverage and the awarded amount falls within the limits of his policy. The victim cannot possibly gain from proportional compensation, so the best she can hope for is to break even.

In other instances, the proportional compensation doctrine may actually prevent a woman from receiving even the percentage of compensation that the court awards. For example, let's say a woman was left sterile because of complications due to an incomplete abortion, but admits that she did not keep a follow-up appointment set for her by the abortion clinic. The jury might decide that her failure to properly follow the clinic's instructions made her 51 percent responsible for her injuries and that she should receive only 49 percent of whatever the award is. However, in some jurisdictions if a plaintiff is found to have been more than 50 percent responsible for her own injuries, by law she receives nothing.

Additionally, twenty states have legislation stating that if an abortion-injured woman wins her case but her own insurance has already covered her medical expenses, then the award will be reduced by that amount. If the primary purpose of damage awards is to compensate the victim, then the fairness of this rule is debatable. In addition, another generally accepted goal of the tort liability system is to deter future negligence. However, if an abortionist is able to escape liability simply because the woman he injured has her own insurance, this second purpose is also obviously circumvented.

Barriers to Psychological Recovery

A well established principle of medicine is that, while counseling a patient prior to surgery, the physician has a duty to screen the patient for contraindicators. For example, if he is going to anesthetize a woman with a drug that the manufacturer says should never be given to people who suffer asthma, he has a responsibility to screen her for asthma. If he does not, he has clearly breached the minimum standard of care and is liable for whatever damage occurs to the patient.

That applies to abortion as well. However, unlike most other medical procedures, there are not only physical contraindicators for abortion but emotional ones as well. To date, there have been literally hundreds of studies on the negative psychological aftereffects of abortion. In 1992, one researcher observed that, "There is now virtually no disagreement among researchers that some women experience negative psychological reactions postabortion."[26]

Even many abortionists openly acknowledge that women can be psychologically injured by abortion. In a *Dallas Morning News* article, abortionist William West called a local Planned Parenthood representative's assertion that women never suffer negative postabortion reactions "outrageously dishonest." He went on to cite a study showing that about 10 percent of postabortive women experience psychiatric disturbances that are "marked, severe, or persistent." He also pointed out that such a figure translates into about 160,000 American women being psychologically injured by their abortions each year.[27]

"There is now virtually no disagreement among researchers that some women experience negative psychological reactions postabortion."

In another newspaper article about malpractice suits brought against abortionists, Sylvia Stengle, executive director of the National Abortion Federation, admitted that about one in five abortion patients should be refused the procedure due to their philosophical opposition to abortion.[28] Even the Supreme Court has acknowledged that, "In attempting to ensure that a woman apprehend the full consequences of her decision, the State furthers the legitimate purpose of reducing the risk that a woman may elect an abortion, only to discover later, with devastating psychological consequences, that her decision was not fully informed."[29]

The problem is that the law does not usually acknowledge these realities. In most jurisdictions, it is virtually impossible to win a case where an abortion client suffered psychological injury unless she had an accompanying physical injury.

Potential Future Barriers for ABMAL Victims

Tort Reform

In America today, certain groups are demanding legislation that would do away with what they claim is an avalanche of frivolous lawsuits. Among the most vocal proponents are physician trade organizations, which argue that the doctors they represent are being buried in malpractice claims. They also contend that the public is being harmed because these lawsuits create higher medical bills, although most independent research shows that malpractice insurance coverage is actually a tiny fraction of overall health care costs.[30]

Obviously, the near hysteria over tort reform is justified only if there is no basis for the lawsuits being filed. If the suits are *not* frivolous, then the reform that is needed is not *legal* but *medical*. And while few would disagree that some attorneys and clients abuse the judicial system, it is absolutely laughable to argue that the filing of frivolous medical malpractice lawsuits is common. Some of the research that has been done on this subject has found that "the real tort crisis may consist in too few claims,"[31] and that "eight times as many patients suffer an injury from medical negligence as there are malpractice claims."[32]

In spite of that, many states are now considering legislation which, if enacted, would present overwhelming new obstacles to women seeking justice for their abortion-related injuries. Currently, most states' rules of civil procedure do not require a unanimous decision by the jury in order for the plaintiff to prevail. However, several states have introduced measures that would do so in all personal injury and malpractice cases. Some would also like to increase the standard of proof required for the plaintiff to win. In most civil suits, the standard is now a "preponderance of the evidence" with some proposals calling for that to be increased to "clear and convincing evidence" or even the criminal standard of "beyond a reasonable doubt."

Another proposal is the creation of review (or screening) panels. Under this system, an abortion-injured woman would be required to submit her claim to one of these panels before it could be filed in court. The panel would then evaluate it and issue a ruling regarding its merit. And while the panel may not legally be able to prohibit her from pursuing her case, if their findings are admissible in court, the primary effect of this system may be to discourage legitimate claims from proceeding. After all, if a jury hears that a panel of "experts" has determined that there is not sufficient evidence of negligence, they cannot help but be prejudiced against her.

Other states want to implement various legislation that would lock poor and middle-income women out of the system. One example would be a "loser pays all" rule requiring the loser of a civil case to pay all court costs including the winner's expenses, *even if the suit was not deemed frivolous.* Another requirement would be that any abortion-injured woman who sues her abortionist must post a "good-faith" bond of several thousand dollars, whether her case has merit or not. Clearly, both of these measures would ensure that only the wealthiest women would have access to the civil court system.

Some state legislatures have imposed limits on the contingent fees that an attorney may charge, and others are beginning to permit judges to review the reasonableness of lawyers' fees. Given that the enormous expense of a medical malpractice case must be borne by the attorney, and given that the success rate of these cases is relatively low, limits on contingent fees will make abortion-injury cases less attractive to attorneys and deny even more women access to the court system.

Conclusion

After the state of Indiana implemented legislation providing a $750,000 cap on all tort awards, *The Indianapolis Star* conducted an investigation into its effects. Their conclusion was that "the act turned out to benefit the two groups who lobbied hardest for its passage—doctors and their insurance companies...far more than it benefits malpractice victims and their families."[33]

That quote sums up what I believe is the motivation for so much effort and money being funneled into tort reform by the American medical community and their insurance companies. Their interest cannot be in preventing frivolous medical malpractice suits because they know such litigation rarely exists. Better than anyone else, they realize that there is simply no incentive for attorneys to spend tens of thousands of their own dollars financing frivolous contingency cases and exposing themselves to countersuits for frivolous prosecution.

What these people are really looking for is a way to shift the burden of caring for malpractice victims away from themselves and onto the backs of the taxpayer. They know that when an abortionist puts a woman in a nursing home for the rest of her life, and tort reform has either eliminated his liability or limited it to an amount that is insufficient to pay for her care, Medicare or Medicaid will be forced to pick up the tab.

The great irony here is that the tort reform movement gained most of its current momentum from Republican victories in the elections of November 1994. As candidates for office, these individuals claimed to favor smaller government and more personal responsibility. But once elected, they started openly pushing legislation that would allow doctors to escape responsibility for their actions and force government to grow larger through increases in Medicare and Medicaid.

In the final analysis, it is indeed true that the whole system is in need of an overhaul. However, contrary to what the abortion industry, the medical establishment, and the insurance lobby want the public to believe, the kind of tort reform that is needed is that which will make it *easier* for abortion-injured women to recover, not harder. In the case of abortionists, a legitimate argument can be made for holding them to a *higher* standard of medical conduct than other physicians, not lower as is currently the case. After all, unlike other physicians, the overwhelming majority of an abortionist's patients come to him young, strong, and in perfect health. It is utterly indefensible that a physician who makes an honest mistake while trying to save the life of an injured or desperately ill patient should be held more accountable than one who injures or kills a perfectly healthy young woman while performing non-medically-indicated surgery that the abortion industry claims is simple and virtually without risk.

America's political leaders lack the courage to stand up for these women against the powerful and vicious abortion lobby.

The time has come for elected officials to decide whether they want to continue defending a system that provides sanctuary to the perpetrators of malpractice at the expense of its victims. It is also time for the American public to recognize that personal injury attorneys play the same role in civil law that prosecuting attorneys play in criminal law. Each exists to make sure that people who prey upon others are brought to justice.

In the case of abortion, the last twenty years have proven at least two things. While the pro-choice community urges women to make their voices heard loud and clear in support of the right to an abortion, it turns right around and tells women who are injured during one to just sit down and keep their mouths shut. We also have irrefutable proof that America's political leaders lack the courage to stand up for these women against the powerful and vicious abortion lobby. With those harsh realities in mind, it is crystal clear that if the nation's personal injury attorneys are not allowed to protect these women, they are nothing more than sitting ducks for the abortion industry. ∎

A Contract With American Women

As long as abortion remains legal, it's the least we should do

As the rest of this book attests, abortions are often far more legal than they are safe. Of course, some of these problems occur as a result of the natural risks associated with any type of surgery. However, most are an indirect result of the political power of the pro-choice movement. For over 20 years, abortion proponents have been extremely effective in insulating abortionists from the usual checks and balances applied to other forms of medicine. Practices that are so far beneath the minimum standard of care that they would never be tolerated in any other health care environment are "business as usual" in abortion clinics.

Primarily, these are the issues that the nine initiatives in this chapter are intended to address. As long as abortion is legal, our nation has a moral obligation to see that women who have abortions are protected against the criminal acts, anti-social behavior, and inferior medical practices of abortion providers. Of course, the most radical advocates of unrestricted abortion will argue that these proposals are too harsh and go beyond what is required of other physicians. This is not true. But even if it were, a legitimate argument can be made that abortionists should be held to a higher standard of care than other physicians, not a lower one as is currently the case. After all, the overwhelming majority of their patients come to them young and in perfect health. In fact, women are often healthiest when they are pregnant. It is indefensible that a physician who makes an honest mistake while performing a delicate, complicated procedure intended to save the life of an injured or desperately ill patient should be held more accountable than one who injures or kills a strong, young, and perfectly healthy woman while performing non-medically indicated surgery that the abortion industry claims is simple and virtually risk-free. The following are Life Dynamics' proposals for addressing that issue.

1
Revise the Standards for Informed Consent

Any woman who seeks an abortion has a right to be completely and accurately informed about the risks she faces. If an abortion is likely to aggravate her physical, psychological, or social problems, the abortionist should either refuse to perform the procedure, or at least fully inform her of these risks and allow her to decide whether to accept them. (Where is the freedom to choose if one is not allowed to make an informed choice?) One widely published abortionist has even concurred that an abortion should not be performed until the patient's preexisting medical or psychological conditions have been treated.[1]

Unfortunately, that is not what is happening. Today, there are abortionists who openly admit—even flaunt—the fact that they provide no decision-based counseling whatsoever. Wisconsin abortionist Elizabeth Karlin recently confessed that, "I—we—are not doing pregnancy options counseling because people have made their choice when they come in…Women know exactly what they want."[2] In another example, New Jersey abortion clinic counselor Marilyn Bennett said, "If a woman comes in and clearly states that she wants to have this termination, I don't ask her, as though I think she is a moron, 'Have you thought about this?'"[3]

Obviously, with irreversible elective surgery, counseling a patient does not mean you think she is a moron. For example, if this same woman went to a legitimate physician for a tubal ligation, any reasonable person would expect the physician to counsel with the woman, even though he could probably assume she had thought about it.

The result of such irresponsible behavior is that every year thousands of women suffer devastating emotional injury from abortions they wished they had never had. As stated in Chapter 7, even Sylvia Stengle, executive director of the National Abortion Federation, admitted that about one in five abortion patients should be refused the procedure due to their philosophical opposition to abortion. Without legislative intervention, this situation will not improve. We should establish in law that it is the abortionist's responsibility to screen women for emotional and physical factors that might contraindicate abortion.

Regarding physical injury, there must be new guidelines requiring that a woman be informed about all the risks relative to the actual circumstances under which her abortion will be performed. For example, studies show that abortion injuries are far more likely to occur when the procedure is performed by a resident rather than a practicing physician.[4] If a woman is told that a particular injury occurs only once in every 100 abortions, but there is evidence that residents inflict this injury once in every 50 abortions, she has been lied to if the clinic is having a resident perform her abortion. (This problem is especially relevant today, since the abortion industry is working overtime to pass legislation that would allow non-physicians to perform abortions.)

Often, the informed consent information given to a woman does not match the circumstances of her abortion because counselors quote risk factors for all abortions combined, rather than for the type of abortion she will undergo. Since virtually every risk factor increases dramatically with gestational age, statistics that relate to all abortions are deceptive when given to a woman who is having a second- or third-trimester procedure.

To lower the risk of coercion, there should also be legislation prohibiting abortion clinics from either taking payment from a client or giving her relaxant drugs before she signs the consent form. Likewise, the abortionist should be required to meet with the woman privately before performing the procedure, and abortion clinics should be prohibited from counseling women in a group setting. It is astounding that the abortion industry's political rhetoric centers on the issue of privacy, yet a woman who is considering abortion is counseled in a room with five to ten other people. Women have even told us that they were counseled in a setting that included husbands or boyfriends of other patients.

Finally, each state should mandate that all informed consent documents inform the woman that she has the right to seek compensation if injured. This legislation should also prohibit abortionists from asking their patients to sign statements saying that they will not sue if injured.

2

Reduce the Incidence of Abortion Malpractice

Obviously, the most desirable way to deal with abortion injuries is to prevent them. The problem is that, like any surgical procedure, abortion has inherent risks so there will always be a certain number of women who are injured regardless of the quality of care. However, it can be made considerably safer than it is today.

First, our experience at Life Dynamics indicates that as many as one-third of all abortion complications and deaths are related to anesthesia. The main problem is that general anesthesia is often administered by unqualified people in an environment that is unequipped to manage complications. There is a pressing need for legislation mandating that general anesthesia be administered only by licensed anesthesiologists, and that appropriate monitoring and emergency equipment—and people trained in its use—be on-site.

Another common cause of injury and death is ectopic (tubal) pregnancies, which have increased dramatically since the legalization of abortion. Our experience indicates that many of these women are actually the victims of botched abortions. When a woman has an abortion, the abortionist is supposed to perform an examination of the material removed to make certain that the abortion was complete. If fetal remains are left in her uterus, the woman is exposed to a potentially deadly infection. Often, when no "products of conception" are found, there is the possibility of an ectopic pregnancy that could rupture and cause her death.

The problem is, many abortion clinics routinely dispose of abortion waste without a pathology report, and even when one is done the results are often ignored. Moreover, many clinics are so careless in their record-keeping that they are unable to contact a woman whose pathology report indicates a potential problem. These factors could at least partially explain the alarming rise in ectopic pregnancy deaths over the last twenty years. Legislation should require a pathology report after every abortion. It should also require that abortion clinics obtain the necessary information to contact their patients should the need arise. Since negligence in this area could result in a woman's death, there should be criminal penalties for any clinic employee who fails to comply.

We also need legislation establishing minimum uniform standards for anyone who performs abortions or counsels women about them. This should be accompanied by a licensing procedure to ensure that abortion providers and clinic employees understand and are capable of meeting these standards. Part of this legislation would include a provision for revocation of this license as well as a requirement that all such licensing information be public record. Another requirement should be that all abortion clinic employees and agents be routinely tested for drug abuse and prevented from working in an abortion clinic if they fail. States must also be required to share licensing information with other states. Currently, an abortionist who has a licensed revoked in one state simply moves to another state, and people have no way of knowing his history. Abortionists especially have a very mobile nature.

Next, there should be a requirement that abortion facilities meet the same medical standards as other ambulatory surgical clinics. Additionally, there should be demands that the government enforce the existing OSHA guidelines regarding blood-borne pathogens, which were implemented to help avoid the spread of hepetitis B and AIDS.

Finally, as documented in Chapter 2, there is indisputable evidence that some women are raped or sexually assaulted while having abortions. How frequently this occurs, or why it occurs, is debatable. However, there can be little argument that a significant decrease could be expected if legislation was passed requiring that a female clinic employee be present anytime an abortionist is counseling a woman or performing an abortion.

3

Reduce the Time Between Abortion Injury and Medical Treatment

In any injury, a critical factor for recovery of the patient is the speed at which emergency care is obtained. Regrettably, an abortionist who has injured a woman will sometimes send her to a hospital many miles away, thus increasing her chances for a poor outcome. The usual motivation for this is that the abortionist is affiliated with a closer facility and does not want it to be aware of the incident, especially if he has previously sent several other abortion-injured women there. In other cases, he has an associate at the distant hospital (usually another abortionist) who will cover his tracks in case of a lawsuit. Additionally, abortionists will often transfer an injured woman to the hospital in a private car to avoid the publicity associated with an ambulance arriving at their clinics. This is especially true when protesters are present as witnesses. Obviously, the emergency care the woman needs is delayed since a private car cannot transport her as fast as an ambulance can, and she will not receive any emergency treatment in a car whereas she would in an ambulance.

Legislation should be passed preventing abortion clinics from transporting injured women by any means other than an ambulance. They should also be required to maintain an advance transfer agreement with the nearest emergency hospital and to send all injured women to that facility.

Additionally, states should require that "circuit riders" (abortionists who come in from out of the area) maintain an on-call agreement with a physician who is a permanent resident of the area. All patients should be given this name as they are dismissed from the clinic. Otherwise, a woman may have no one to call if six hours after her abortion she experiences complications. No other physician would even dream of leaving his patients in such a situation, and abortionists should not be allowed to either.

4

Make It Easier for Abortion-Injured Women to Recover Damages

As Chapter 7 illustrates, abortion-injured women find the deck stacked against them when they seek compensation from the civil court system. A few reasonable reforms could alleviate this.

First, as mentioned, abortion providers commonly require their patients to sign a statement saying that they will not hold the facility liable for injuries that occur during an abortion. Of course, these statements are not worth the paper they are written on, but the women signing them may not know that and erroneously believe they have surrendered their right to redress. If this misconception causes abortion-injured women to not seek compensation, it could be reasonably argued that they have not only been victims of malpractice, but also of fraud. This calls for legislation preventing abortionists from asking their patients to sign such an agreement.

Second, there should be a uniform standard of care with which abortionists must comply and which will be used in all malpractice proceedings as the guideline for determining when malpractice has occurred. There should also be a minimum civil penalty in all cases where there is a finding of abortion malpractice.

Third, abortion-injured women should be allowed to sue their abortionist anonymously or with the use of a pseudonym. Some women who are seriously injured during an abortion will not seek justice, simply because there is someone whom they do not want to find out about the pregnancy or the abortion. Currently, a request for plaintiff anonymity is granted or denied at the discretion of the judge hearing the case. If he is politically pro-choice, he may decide that the best way to get rid of the case is to make the complainant publicly admit that she has had an abortion. If for no other reason, the anonymity decision must be the woman's and not the judge's.

Fourth, there should be legislation lowering the burden of proof that women must meet in order to recover damages from an abortionist. Under the current system, she must normally show that she was injured because the abortionist violated the standard of medical care typical in elective abortions. This seems reasonable except that the abortion industry has been so successful at fighting regulations on abortion that violating the minimum standard of care has become virtually impossible. For example, recall from Chapter 1 that the Colorado Board of Medical Examiners ruled that knowingly sending a woman home with a retained fetal skull did not constitute a deviation from the standard of care, since other abortionists in Colorado often leave the skull in the patient. The same Board said that performing abortions on women who were not pregnant also did not violate the minimum standard of care.[5]

Fifth, there needs to be an extended amount of time for women to sue after an abortion injury. Most states have "statute of limitations" provisions that prevent plaintiffs from seeking compensation after a certain amount of time has passed. Normally, the limit is one or two years and is a reasonable check against frivolous litigation. But in the case of abortion, injuries often do not manifest themselves for many years. For example, a 15-year-old girl might be left sterile from a botched abortion, but not find out about it until she tries to get pregnant at age 25. If her state's statute of limitations stipulates that she cannot sue more than seven years after the injury occurred or two years after the injury is discovered, she is powerless to receive compensation.

Sixth, there should be legislation mandating minimal requirements for medical record-keeping, and legislation making it easier for women to obtain their medical records from abortion clinics. There should also be mandatory criminal penalties for the alteration, destruction, or forgery of these documents.

Seventh, hospitals and other medical institutions should be prevented from barring or punishing doctors who testify on behalf of plaintiffs in medical malpractice litigation. Some medical institutions actually have official policies allowing their doctors to be expert witnesses for the defense side of a medical malpractice trial, but not the plaintiff side. If the goal of the medical establishment is to provide the best medical care possible, it should welcome the opportunity to deal with bad practitioners rather than shielding them.

Eighth, there should be legislation preventing defense attorneys in malpractice cases from introducing the injured woman's personal history into trial. Often called the "Slut Defense," this is the shabby but effective practice of putting the abortion-malpractice victim on trial for her past behavior. Once common in rape trials, the victim's medical, gynecological, criminal, and sexual history—no matter how irrelevant—is introduced into the trial in a shameless attempt to disqualify her as a person deserving compensation. Most states now prohibit this practice in criminal trials, but not in civil litigation. Defense attorneys currently use this tactic in virtually every case in which a woman seeks compensation from an abortionist who has injured her.

Finally, American women deserve legislation that would make it easier for them to bring a civil action for psychological injury. Currently, it is virtually impossible for a woman to recover damages for an emotional injury unless she has an accompanying physical injury. In addition, since emotional injuries from abortion often are not apparent for several years, there should be extensions in the statute of limitations for women who are diagnosed with abortion-induced post-traumatic stress disorder.

5
Increase Malpractice Insurance Requirements

When an abortion-injured woman seeks compensation in court, it is not uncommon for her to discover that she will receive nothing even if a jury rules in her favor. Abortionists often hide their personal assets and either carry no malpractice insurance or carry so little that it is insufficient to cover her injuries. Thus she cannot recover damages even if a jury determines that she is entitled to them.

This can be corrected by legislation requiring abortionists to have either adequate medical malpractice insurance or proof of financial responsibility. Most states will not let someone drive a car without demonstrating financial responsibility—why would they let someone perform a potentially life-threatening surgery without it? States should be concerned not only about people injuring women with cars, but with medical instruments as well.

In the absence of such legislation, there should be a requirement that all abortionists who do not have malpractice insurance, or proof of financial responsibility, inform their patients of this fact—both verbally and in writing—

prior to performing their abortions. Furthermore, abortionists who refuse to purchase insurance should be required to make available a "single-event" insurance policy that the client could purchase at her option and expense. This would be similar to airports offering single-trip insurance to passengers about to board a plane. At least with this arrangement, the woman could choose for herself whether she wanted to take her chances. Under the present system, the abortionist makes the choice for her.

6
Expand Third-Party Liability

Most reliable information suggests that at least one other person or organization probably played some role in a woman's decision to seek an abortion. It seems only fair that since she did not get into this situation alone, she should not have to face all the risks alone.

In the case of minors, there should be legislation requiring that the person who performs an abortion on an underage girl—without her parent's knowledge—be liable for the cost of any subsequent medical treatment she might require because of the abortion. It should include not only the person who performs the abortion but also the person who causes the abortion to be done. For example, if a public school employee, family planning counselor, or another physician refers a minor to an abortionist who injures her, that person should be held liable.

If these individuals are comfortable usurping the parents' role during the decision-making process, they must also assume the parents' financial responsibility when something goes wrong. It is outrageous that we hold parents financially responsible for something that is done to their minor daughters, while telling them that they do not have a right to know about it beforehand. Additionally, if the parents do not have the financial means to pay for this medical care, it becomes a burden on the taxpayer.

Furthermore, regardless of a woman's age, if a third party (individual, insurance company, or government entity) pays for her abortion, that party should be liable for complications. Among other things, this would force irresponsible males who use abortion as an easy way out to share in at least one of the risks faced by the women they impregnate.

Finally, we should seek legislation which addresses the fact that every unmarried minor girl considering an abortion may have been the victim of criminal sexual abuse. She could have become pregnant only as the result of

(a) a relationship with another minor, (b) a consenting relationship with an adult, (c) forcible rape, or (d) incest.

With three of the four being illegal, it would seem that every medical professional encountering an unmarried, pregnant minor has a moral and legal obligation to inquire how she became pregnant. Most states already have legislation requiring that any person who knows—or in some cases just suspects—that a minor is being sexually abused must report it to law enforcement authorities. If our society is serious about protecting children from sexual abuse, we must strengthen these laws and enforce them among abortionists and abortion counselors. Obviously, no one in our society is in a better position to know about such activity.

7
Reform the System of Identifying and Reporting Injuries and Deaths

At Life Dynamics, our experience has been that it is impossible to accurately gage the safety of abortion, despite widely used statistics. The information gathered is spotty, and even accurate data tends to get "cleaned up" by an overtly pro-abortion agency within the federal government. (See Chapter 4.)

Of course, the first priority is a complete overhaul of the abortion surveillance system at the Centers for Disease Control (CDC). Legislation should prohibit CDC employees with responsiblities in this area from having ties to the abortion industry, or known political prejudices on legalized abortion. It must also feature strict enforcement guidelines with criminal penalties for failure to comply. Then, federal legislation should be passed that creates a universal standard for reporting of injuries and deaths due to abortion, including a requirement that every state report its figures to the newly revamped CDC. Currently, reporting of deaths and injuries is voluntary. Additionally, all ectopic pregnancy deaths and injuries should be investigated to determine if the woman has had a recent abortion.

In order to obtain complete and accurate information, legislation is also needed to prevent abortionists and insurance companies from seeking confidentiality as part of an agreement to settle a case. (This legislation should be written in a way that does not prevent the woman from initiating a confidentiality agreement.)

Finally, there should be federal funding for a politically neutral scientific study to determine the degree to which abortion can, or cannot, trigger post-traumatic stress disorder. Far too many women report severe emotional problems following abortion for this to be ignored.

ß
Restructure State Medical Licensing Boards

In many, if not most, states, the medical licensing board is uninterested in disciplining bad doctors. More often than not, these boards are run by physicians. Unfortunately, history has shown that they are extremely reluctant to take disciplinary action against other physicians. A few relatively simple procedural changes could transform these boards into the unbiased oversight committees they were originally intended to be.

State medical licensing boards should be required to do the following:

- Include a majority of non-physician members
- Publicize their proceedings, including the results of all investigations
- Prohibit the purging of physician records as long as the physician is alive
- Report any disciplinary actions they take against a doctor to the National Physician Databank
- Establish a universal standard for completing medical records
- Automatically revoke the license of any physician or nurse who attempts to prevent a patient from getting her medical records
- Automatically revoke the license of any physician or nurse who is involved in the alteration of medical records to conceal mistakes made in the treatment of a patient

This legislation should be accompanied by a bill making all the information contained in the National Physician Databank public record.

There should also be legislation passed requiring insurance companies to inform the state medical board when they pay a claim for abortion malpractice or restrict/terminate the policy of an abortionist. This legislation should include a requirement that abortionists report all out-of-court settlements they make with injured women. Another feature of this legislation should require civil courts to report all awards for abortion malpractice to the state medical licensing board, which would then be required to investigate for possible disciplinary action.

9
Strengthen Basic Consumer Protection Legislation

Women seeking an abortion should be afforded the same consumer protection that is common in other areas of commerce. One step toward ensuring that they receive the necessary counseling is to prohibit organizations that refer women for abortions from taking commissions or kick-backs from the abortionists to whom they refer. Another would be to require that all abortion-related counseling be done by people who are not directly connected to any abortionist or abortion clinic. There is an obvious conflict of interest when a woman is counseled about an abortion decision by someone who is employed by an organization that profits from abortion. This legislation could be patterned after laws that prohibit people who conduct vision exams from being employed by companies that sell eyeglasses.

In the absence of this legislation, we should pass a bill that prohibits abortion facility counselors from being paid on commission. Counseling women in crisis pregnancy situations should never be done by someone with a financial interest in her decision.

Other protective legislation could include a requirement that pregnancies be proven viable before an abortion is performed. Why should a woman pay three or four hundred dollars for an abortion to end a pregnancy that is going to naturally miscarry the next day? This would also reduce the number of abortions performed on women who are not pregnant.

Additionally, women should be given data that compares their abortionist's malpractice and criminal history against that of other abortionists in her state. If a woman is going to place her life in the hands of an abortionist who has the worst record in the state, she has a right to know it beforehand. She also has the right to know the abortionist's real name and whether he is a "circuit rider" or a permanent resident of the area.

Finally, legislation is needed that requires state agencies to enforce all regulatory legislation once it is passed. Passing protective legislation will be a hollow victory if the agency charged with enforcing it is run by someone with an abortion-on-demand political agenda. ■

Epilogue

The story you have read in this book is clearly one of tragedy and pain, and it should be obvious by now that American women have been betrayed and exploited—not only by the abortion industry, but by several institutions that they should have been able to count on. There was a time when organizations like the American Medical Association (AMA) and the American College of Obstreticians and Gynecologists (ACOG) would have involved themselves in remedying a situation such as this. But they, and other members of the "medical establishment," have sold their souls to the abortion industry. The AMA has evolved from an organization that once admonished its members to shun abortionists as people who brought dishonor upon the medical profession, to one that joined with the National Organization for Women (NOW) in arguing before the Supreme Court that federal anti-racketeering legislation should be used against individuals who protest abortion. As for ACOG, on at least one occasion it has co-sponsored with the National Abortion Federation a symposium on solving the abortion industry's shortage of abortionists.

In another arena, state medical review and licensing board—which were created specifically to police bad medical practitioners—routinely turn their backs on women who are killed, mutilated, or raped in abortion clinics. Sometimes the lack of action is due to hardcore abortion advocates running the board. But more often than not, board members are fearful of confronting a bad abortionist because they know that doing so will inevitably result in a vicious political assault by state, and even national, abortion-rights groups.

The other institution to abandon these women is the media. Today, the decision-makers in the American press are almost completely under the thumb of the abortion industry, and they simply refuse to tell this story. In fact, many don't want anyone else telling it either. Several national publications refused to run ads for this book. For example, *USA Today*, returned our check for over $75,000 after pre-approving our ad copy. We were told by the advertising department that it got kicked back by someone "higher up" the corporate ladder. When we called this person, we were summarily dismissed after being told there was basically nothing we could do about it. Furthermore, they refused to reimburse us for the production costs we incurred after they pre-approved our ad copy. And this scenario was repeated with several other publications.

When I see how the media covers the abortion issue, I am reminded of a joke I heard while in high school:

The fastest runner in America was going to race the fastest runner in the USSR to determine which political system produced better athletes. When the race was over, the American had won. The next day, Soviet newspaper headlines read, "Soviets Come In Second In Big Race, Americans Finish Next To Last!"

In the 1960s, that was just good-natured satire about how the Soviet Union used their government-controlled press to manipulate public opinion. In the 1990s, however, it hits a little too close to home to be humorous. Notice that the above headline is factually accurate, but its implied message is the complete opposite of what actually happened. Unfortunately, the current operating principle of the American media is that a reporter with a predetermined agenda can remain technically accurate, but functionally deceptive. Today, it has evolved into a snake pit of hidden, and often not so hidden, political agendas—one of which is the protection of the abortion industry.

In our research, we noticed that even during those rare times when the media reluctantly covers a story about a woman who was victimized by an abortionist, they do so in a clearly apologetic manner. For example, when a 25-year-old New York woman was killed by her abortionist, the local newspaper was practically forced into writing an article about it. However, they reserved the last three paragraphs for a thinly disguised effort at mending fences with local abortion advocates. After a minimal account of what happened to the victim, they concluded: "Maternal deaths during legal abortions are quite rare, occurring fewer than once every 200,000 operations in this country, according to the Centers for Disease Control and Prevention in Atlanta. The death rate has been heading down steadily, from 0.9 deaths for every 100,000 in 1984, to 0.8 deaths for every 100,000 in 1985 and 1986, and 0.4 for every 100,000 deaths in 1987, said Dr. Cynthia Berg, a medical epidemiologist with the CDC. In contrast, an average of seven to eight women die during every 100,000 child-births, Berg said."[1]

How's that for subtle? It sounds like something the National Abortion Federation would have written. Who knows, perhaps it was. In any event, it proves even further that the contemporary American media has about the same relationship to legitimate journalism as professional wrestling has to legitimate sports.

Obviously, if you have read this book, you now know at least a small portion of what *USA Today* and their ilk have withheld from you all these years. Hopefully, that allows you to have a sense for the abysmal toll abortion takes on the women who submit to them, and the devastation it wreaks upon the people who perform them. Of course, it is natural to wonder what changes can be made to prevent these problems in the future. Clearly, the things we propose in Chapter 8 could do a great deal, but ultimately they do nothing more than treat symptoms. The question is whether anything can be done to cure the disease.

To answer that requires an understanding of two fundamental and unchangeable truths about the abortion procedure itself. First, because the women involved are vulnerable and often unconscious, abortion demands practitioners of the highest moral character. And second, even though abortion is a relatively simple procedure, the fact that it is carried out in a part of the body that is very unforgiving of sloppy work demands that it be done by practitioners with the highest degree of technical skill.

If you have read this book, you have a sense for the abysmal toll abortion takes on the women who submit to them, and the devastation it wreaks upon the people who perform them.

The problem is that the overwhelming majority of the people who enter the field are spectacularly unqualified in both of these crucial areas. In the case of character, a quick reexamination of Chapter 2 should put to rest any suggestion that this standard is met. What's frightening is that, from a pragmatic standpoint, it may not even be possible to meet this standard. For whatever reason, the practice of abortion seems especially attractive to the kinds of degenerates who sexually assault their patients. And even when it attracts someone who is not a sexual predator, the abortion clinic environment often transforms him into one.

As for technical expertise, during the research for this book we found only one or two abortionists—out of a couple thousand we looked at—who were even remotely qualified to operate in a situation where there is almost no room for error. In fact, we found just the opposite. With virtually no exceptions, abortionists are the losers, rejects, and washouts of the medical community who couldn't compete in, or were drummed out of, legitimate medicine. Over and over, we saw irrefutable proof that good physicians don't ascend into the practice of abortion, but instead bad ones descend into it.

The reality is, whether you're talking about moral character or technical proficiency, elective abortion is just not done by the "best and brightest" of the medical community, and it never will be. The impact of this phenomenon has been so powerful that the abortion industry has been reduced to lobbying medical schools to require that their students and residents participate in elective abortions. This sort of desperation also controls their political agenda. Twenty-five years ago they were saying that abortion should be legalized so it could be performed by doctors in a controlled and regulated environment. But having discovered that cleaning up their industry would destroy it, those same people now viciously oppose even the most benign attempts to control or regulate abortion, and are even calling for legislation that would allow non-physicians to perform them.

However, abortion proponents are beginning to find that coercion and the lowering of standards does not work. They may have the money and political muscle to pass the legislation they want, and they may be able to intimidate or trick a few ivory-tower academicians into doing their will. But when the dust settles, they inevitably find that abortion clinics are still the medical community's "red-light district" and that legitimate, competent physicians are still not interested. Borrowing the punch line from an old joke...the operation was a success, but the patient died.

The abortion industry needs to acknowledge that they are not being destroyed by any pro-life success but by one of their own failures. Despite their virtual strangle hold on the media, they have been unable to make abortion socially acceptable. Instead, abortion remains a bone that's stuck in the throat of the American people. They may not know what to do about it, but they know for certain that they can't swallow it. And because that dynamic also permeates the medical community, it traps the abortion industry in what might be called a "circular dilemma." They realize that they can't keep doing the things outlined in this book and survive, but they also know that they will never attract practitioners who are capable of anything else. They clearly see their defeat on the horizon—and they know what's going to cause it—yet they are powerless to do anything to prevent it. The energy of people who once truly believed in their cause has been replaced with the anger, frustration, and bitterness of people who are not quite so sure anymore, but just can't find a graceful way out.

Like many others before them, abortion advocates are finding that conflicts are much easier to start than they are to stop. That's what happened at the end of the American Civil War, as poor communication with distant troops resulted in some battles being fought well after the South had surrendered. And while every death in that war was a tragedy, the idea of men dying for a cause that was already lost seems especially heartbreaking.

Today, the abortion industry's stubborn refusal to accept its fate is placing a lot of women in that same situation. Every time one of them submits to an abortion, and is then raped or mutilated or killed by her abortionist, she becomes a martyr for a failed social experiment with no long-term future. In the final analysis, it appears that the only thing left to decide is how many women will be sacrificed because the abortion industry wants something it can never have. ■

Endnotes

Chapter 1

1 New York Health Department Order No. 83383136, Case No. 11097; Associated Press 9/30/88; *Questionable Doctors*, Ingrid Van Tuinen, ed., Public Citizens Health Research Group, 1993; New York Medical Board Statement of Charges, Calendar No. 12022 as well as correspondence and documents relating to Calendar No. 11018; *New York Daily News* 9/17/94; *New York Newsday* 9/17/94; *Abortion & Sterilization*, Jane E. Hodgson, ed., Grune & Stratton Inc., New York: 1981.

2 United States District Court, Western District of Missouri, Western Division Civ. No. 73CV497-W-3

3 New York Court of Appeals 369 N.E.2d 766, 42 N.Y.2d 1038

4 *Obstetrics and Gynecology* October 1972

5 California Coroner's Report No. 71-10001

6 California Death Certificate No. 72-014193; Alameda County (CA) Superior Court Case No. 447479-5

7 *Obstetrics and Gynecology* March 1974

8 *Chicago Sun-Times*, "Abortion Profiteers" Series 11/12/78–12/3/78; Illinois Death Certificate No. 614138

9 *Chicago Tribune* 5/24/77; *Chicago Sun-Times*, "Abortion Profiteers" Series 11/12/78–12/3/78

10 Perry County (IL) Coroner's Report 6/20/77; *Chicago Tribune* 8/31/77; *CDC Abortion Surveillance Annual Summary* 1977; *St. Louis Post-Dispatch* 6/15/79

11 *The Altanta Daily Report* 7/20/94; *Atlanta Journal and Constitution* 7/21/79

12 Sedgwick County (KS) District Court Case No. 82C1309

13 Kern County (CA) Death Certificate No. 2665, Local Registration District 1500; Kern County Superior Court Case No. 85936

14 *Miami Herald* 3/7/85, 3/20/85, 9/17/89; Dade County (FL) Circuit Court Case No. 85-14112; Florida Death Certificate No. 85-026164

15 *Southeast Missourian* March 1990; *St. Louis Post-Dispatch* 3/5/90, 8/2/92; *Springfield Post-Dispatch* 8/19/92; Missouri Administrative Hearing Commission Case No. 90-00255HA

16 Medical Board of California Case No. D-5193

17 Richmond City (VA) Circuit Court Case No. LU441; Virginia Death Certificate No. 89-020384

18 Colorado Board of Medical Examiners AG File No. CRL 9104545.1CL "Notice and Citation" 11/5/91 and AG File No. CRL 9104545.2CL "Formal Complaint of the Attorney General"

19 *St. Louis Post-Dispatch* 8/2/92; *Springfield Post-Dispatch* 8/19/92; Missouri Administrative Hearing Commission Case No. 90-000255HA

20 Ohio Death Certificate Registrar's No. 158; *Fremont News-Messenger* 4/29/90; *Columbia Dispatch* 5/23/90; Ohio Post-Mortem Examination, Autopsy No. OA-90-8

21 *Las Vegas Review-Journal* 11/1/91, 11/2/91, 12/10/91; *San Francisco Examiner* 11/4/91; *The Washington Times* 11/21/91

22 *St. Petersburg Times* 10/1/94

23 *Obstetrics and Gynecology* March 1974; W.D. New York, United States District Court Case No. Civ-75-79

24 *Chicago Sun-Times* 3/24/73, "Abortion Profiteers" Series 11/12/78–12/3/78; Death Certificate No. 608195

25 U.S. District Court, Western District of North Carolina, Charlotte Division Case No. C-C-78-083

26 Mecklenburg County (NC) Superior Court File No. 82CVS406

27 Texas Autopsy Report No. 0120-82-0057; Texas Death Certificate No.01316

28 *Daily Breeze* 3/2/85; *Los Angeles Herald Examiner* 3/3/85; Los Angeles County (CA) Coroner's Report and Amended Coroner's Report No. 84-2948

29 Illinois Appellate Court, 1st District, 3rd Division, 216 Ill.App.3d 453, 160 Ill., Dec. 21; Associated Press 11/1/88; *Chicago Tribune* 2/18/87, 3/2/87, 7/23/87, 2/10/88, 2/11/88, 6/15/88, 8/6/88, 9/9/89, 9/14/89, 10/4/89, 1/3/92; *Chicago Sun-Times* 2/18/87, 3/3/87, 2/8/88, 2/10/88, 8/5/88, 8/27/88, 11/1/88, 9/15/89, 10/12/89, 1/3/92; Cook County (IL) Circuit Court Case No. 87L 15971; Cook County (IL) Postmortem Case No. 720, December 1986; *Modern Healthcare* 3/2/87; *Southtown Economist* 11/5/91

30 Florida Death Certificate No. 88-123938; Jacksonville, Florida Medical Examiner's Report No. 88-1392

31 *Raleigh News & Observer* 7/29/92; *Medical Malpractice Reporter* Vol. 10 No. 9, September 1994

32 Jefferson (KY) Circuit Court Case No. 92CI00493

33 New York Administrative Review Board "Decision and Order" Nos. 94-98 and 94-146; New York State Board for Professional Medical Conduct "Statement of Charges"; *New York Post* 1/7/94; *Newark Star-Ledger* 1/7/94, 6/1/94; *Rockland Journal-News* 8/3/94, 12/10/94; Associated Press 10/25/94, 12/15/94, 12/22/94; Middlesex County (NJ) Superior Court Civil Action Docket No. L-5004-94

34 Maryland Court of Special Appeals Case No. 832

35 Wayne County (MI) Circuit Court Case No. 74-040309-NM

36 *Nashville Tennessean* 3/19/77, 3/23/77

37 *Durham Herald Sun* 5/18/82

38 Queens County (NY) Supreme Court Index No. 17619/81

39 *Houston Chronicle* 7/4/82; *Chicago Sun-Times* 8/4/82; *Miami Herald* 2/13/83, 2/5/84, 3/29/88

40 Lake County (IL) Superior Court Docket No. 586 709

41 Bergen County (NJ) Superior Court Docket No. L-38313-86MM

42 *New York Post* 11/20/91, 11/21/91, 11/26/91; *New York Newsday* 11/22/91, 11/26/91; *New York Daily News* 11/24/91, 11/26/91; New York Department of Health Case No. BPMC-92-13-A "Determination and Order"

43 Orange County (CA) Circuit Court Case No. 601087

44 Oklahoma State Board of Medical Licensure and Supervision Case No. 87-7-514; *Daily Oklahoman* 12/17/92

45 San Diego (CA) Superior Court Case No. 640957

46 New Jersey Board of Medical Examiner "Interim Decision and Order" Docket No. BDS-01303-945; New York Administrative Review Board "Decision and Order" Nos. 94-98 and 94-146; New York State Board for Professional Medical Conduct "Statement of Charges"; *Newark Star-Ledger* 1/7/94; *Rockland Journal-News* 12/10/94; *Philadelphia Inquirer* 12/15/94; *Atlantic City Press* 12/15/94; *Courier-Post* 12/22/94

47 Orleans Parish (LA) Civil District Court Division C Docket No. 94-15394

48 Jefferson Circuit (KY) Court Case No. 95CI03741; *Louisville Courier-Journal* 7/8/95

49 *San Diego Reader* 12/13/94; *San Diego Union-Tribune* 12/13/94, 12/17/94; *Orange County Register* 12/15/94; *Santa Monica Outlook* December 1994; *Los Angeles Times* 3/21/95; San Diego County,

    South Bay Judicial District, California Superior Court Case No. S6003494; San Diego County Superior Court Case No. 661720; San Diego County Court Case No. 643695; Los Angeles County Superior Court Case No. SEC 76210; *Questionable Doctors*

50 Cuyahoga (OH) County Court of Common Pleas Case No. 916389

51 Los Angeles County (CA) Superior Court Case No. SWC30375

52 Hamilton County (OH) Court of Common Pleas Case No. A7802715

53 *Huntington Herald-Press* 7/19/79; *Ft. Wayne Journal-Gazette* 7/20/79, 8/4/79, 8/12/79; *Ft. Wayne News Sentinel* 7/20/79, 7/23/79, 8/3/79, 8/4/79, 8/8/79, 8/9/79; *The Harmonizer* 8/12/79

54 Rutland County (VT) Superior Court Docket No. S0806-91RC; *Portsmouth Herald* 8/3/94; *Rutland Herald* 9/24/94, 9/26/94, 9/27/94, 10/14/94

55 East Baton Rouge Parish (LA) District Court Case No. 365423

56 *The Birmingham News* 10/15/92

57 *Hattiesburg (MS) American* 4/30/94

58 *Obstetrics and Gynecology* March 1990

59 New Orleans (LA) Civil District Court Case No. 83-3049-A

60 *New York Times* 10/17/70; *Obstetrics and Gynecology* March 1974

61 Los Angeles County (CA) Coroner Case No. 71-9846; Los Angeles County (CA) Superior Court Case Nos. A 310874 and C34424

62 *American Medical News* 8/29/77; *Minneapolis Tribune* 10/21/77; *American Medical Association News* 12/12/77, 1/23/78; South Dakota Death Certificate No. 140 85-003853; personal communication between Life Dynamics and South Dakota Deputy Attorney General

63 New York County (NY) Supreme Court Index Nos. 655/75 and 10838/75

64 Hamilton County (OH) Court of Common Pleas Case No. A73109

65 Lincoln County (NC) Superior Court Case No. 74CVS247

66 California Death Certificate No. 78-063811; Los Angeles County (CA) Autopsy Report No. 78-1763

67 *El Paso Times* 4/5/81

68 *The Memphis Commercial Appeal* 2/13/85; Memphis (TN) Circuit Court Case No. 08238TD

69 Cook County (IL) Circuit Court Case No. 79L24949

70 Cook County (IL) Circuit Court Case No. 79L16622

71 Summit County (OH) Court of Common Pleas Case No. CV 81 12 3466

72 Colorado Board of Medical Examiners Case No. ME 86-07

73 New York Department of Health: State Board for Professional Conduct "Statement of Charges" 2/19/91

74 *Miami Herald* 3/20/85, 9/17/89

75 *Arizona Daily Star* 6/21/87, 8/12/87, 8/14/87; *Phoenix Gazette* 8/13/87, 8/14/87, 8/15/87, 9/12/87; *Tucson Citizen* 8/13/87

76 *The Banner* 6/30/93, 7/2/93

77 Montgomery County (OH) Court of Common Pleas Case No. 89-4426; *Dayton Daily News* 8/18/90

78 *Miami Herald* 9/17/89

79 California Death Certificate No. 92-121785; Los Angeles County (CA) Autopsy Report No. 92-04539

80 Jefferson Parish (LA), 4th Judicial District Court, Case No. 168162; Orleans Parish (LA) Autopsy Report No. 974-3-89

81 Washington, D.C. Superior Court Civil Action No. 75-1156; *The Washington Times* 4/19/84; Washington, D.C. Death Certificate No. 80-0000237

82 Michigan Death Certificate No. 9655; *Detroit News* 8/31/74

83 DuPage County (IL) Circuit Court Case No. 85L 0833/88-483

84 *Miami Herald* 8/18/78

85 Summit County (OH) Court of Common Pleas Case No. CV 82 4 1036

86 Philadelphia (PA) Court of Common Pleas Case No. 83-01/77

87 *Chicago Sun-Times* 9/6/92, 9/7/92; *Daily Herald* 9/6/92, 9/7/92; *Chicago Tribune* 9/6/92, 5/5/94; *Southtown Economist* 9/8/92; *Washington Times* 6/4/94; Cook County (IL) Circuit Court Civil Action No. 94L 05372; Orange County (CA) Autopsy Report No. 86-0682-AK; Orange County (CA) Superior Court Case No. 51-04-15

88 Cook County (IL) Circuit Court Case No. 89L 2906; Illionis Death Certificate No. 607697

89 *The Tulsa Tribune* 7/13/87; Tulsa County (OK) District Court Case No. CJ 87 04861

90 Cook County (IL) Circuit Court Case No. 87 L 24404; Cook County (IL) Death Certificate No. 617011; Cook County (IL) Postmortem Report Case No. 575, August 1987

91 *Southeast Missourian* March 1990; *St. Louis Post-Dispatch* 3/5/90, 1/30/91, 8/2/92; Associated Press 3/7/90; *Columbia Daily Tribune* 1/29/91; *Springfield News-Leader* 1/29/91, 2/9/91, 3/18/92; *Kansas City Star* 8/7/92; *Springfield Post-Dispatch* 8/9/92; Missouri Administrative Hearing Commission Case No. 90-000255 HA; Greene County (MO) Circuit Court Case No. CV 188-675 CC 2; Missouri Autopsy Report N-88-A-1

92 Los Angeles County (CA) Superior Court Case No. WEC139590; California Death Certificate No. 88-127625

93 Maryland Autopsy Report No. 89-1873; CBS News, *60 Minutes* 4/21/91; *The Washington Post* 12/11/91; Associated Press 12/20/91

94 Los Angeles County (CA) Superior Court Case No. C13671

95 *Obstetrics and Gynecology* March 1974

96 *Chicago Tribune* 4/30/73, 5/3/73, 7/17/73; *Chicago Sun-Times*, "Abortion Profiteers" Series 11/12/78–12/3/78; Illinois Death Certificate No. C612195

97 *Times Review* 7/19/79; *People* 7/26/82; *Boston Globe* 8/31/82, 9/10/82, 9/15/82, 10/1/82; *New York Times* 10/6/82; *St. Louis University Public Law Review* Vol. 13:1, p. 347

98 Illinois Death Certificate No. C621450; *Chicago Sun-Times*, "Abortion Profiteers" Series 11/12/78–12/3/78

99 *International Journal of Gynecology and Obstetrics* 1978

100 *Denver Post* 5/22/81; *Rocky Mountain News* 12/4/81; Medical Board of Colorado Case No. 81-JEF

101 New Jersey Board of Medical Examiners "Consent Order" 5/20/88

102 Fulton County (GA) Superior Court Civil File No. D-21147

103 Mobile (AL) Supreme Court Case No. 1911048/1911049

104 *New York Post* 11/20/91, 11/21/91, 11/26/91; *New York Daily News* 11/24/91, 11/26/91; *New York Newsday* 11/26/91; *Milwaukee Journal* 6/15/93; *New York Times* July 1993; New York Medical Board Case No. BPMC-92-13-A "Determination and Order"

105 Michigan Death Certificate No. 0548962; Oakland County (MI) Autopsy Report No. 91-1967

106 Harris County (TX) Autopsy Report No. A-94000025

107 Los Angeles County (CA) Coroner Report Case No. 72-12165

108 *Chicago Sun-Times*, "Abortion Profiteers" Series 11/12/78–12/3/78; Illinois Death Certificate No. 621691

109 California Coroner's Report No. 76-5654

110 California Death Certificate No. 77-051142; Santa Clara County (CA) Autopsy Report No. CA77-364

111 *Dallas Times Herald* 6/20/78; *Dallas Morning News* 6/20/78, 6/23/78, 7/28/78; Texas Autopsy Report No. 2262-77-1103

112 *Press-Telegram* 6/28/83

113 Lake County (IN) Superior Court Case No. 584-198

114 Allegheny County (PA) Court of Common Pleas Case No. G.D. 88-05725

115 *Houston Chronicle* 11/3/91, 11/6/91, 11/11/91, 9/2/92; *Kansas City Star* 11/6/91; *Houston Post* 11/7/91, 11/12/91; *The Washington Times* 11/21/91; *Springfield News-Leader* 11/24/91

116 *North Jersey Record* 7/16/93

117 *New York Times* 7/11/93, 7/16/93, 8/4/95, 8/5/95, 8/9/95, 8/13/95, 8/21/95; *New York Daily News* 7/13/92, 7/3/93, 7/11/93, 7/14/93, 8/22/95; *Staten Island Advance* 7/16/93; *New York Post* 8/4/93, 8/11/93, 8/10/95; Associated Press 3/15/95, 7/13/95; *New York Times Metro*

7/13/95, 7/18/95, 7/20/95, 8/8/95; *Lima News* 7/13/95, 8/9/95; *New York Newsday* 8/5/95, 9/26/95; *Dallas Morning News* 8/9/95; *San Diego Daily Transcript* 8/9/95; *Sarasota Herald-Tribune* 8/9/95; *Minneapolis Star-Tribune* 8/9/95; *USA Today* 8/9/95; *Lansdale Reported* 8/10/95

118 *Panama City News Herald* 6/29/94; *Pensacola News-Journal* 6/29/94; *USA Today* 6/30/94; *St. Petersburg Times* 6/30/94; *Miami Herald* 6/30/94, 7/30/94; Florida, District 1, Autopsy Report No. MLA94-266

119 Los Angeles County (CA) Superior Court Case No. C64485

120 Los Angeles County (CA) Superior Court Case No. SWC34625; Los Angeles (CA) Coroner's Report No. 75-11665

121 *Chicago Sun-Times*, 12/18/79, 11/20/80, "Abortion Profiteers" Series 11/12/78–12/3/78; *Chicago Tribune* 11/17/78, 11/18/78, 1/27/79, 1/22/82; *CDC Abortion Surveillance Annual Summary* 1978

122 *Morbidity & Mortality Weekly Report* 3/4/77; *Journal of the American Medical Association* 10/10/80

123 520 N.Y.S.2d 751(A.D. 1 Dept. 1987); New York Appellate Court 134 A.D.2nd 159

124 Illinois Appellate Court Case No. 1-91-2485; *Medical Malpractice Verdicts, Settlements, and Experts* 12/94; Cook County (IL) Circuit Court Case No. 84L 23584

125 *Press-Telegram* 4/25/88; California Death Certificate No. 85-106566

126 Charleston County (SC) Court of Common Pleas Case Nos. 86-CP-10-3283 and 86-CP-10-3284

127 California Death Certificate 88-146505; Los Angeles County (CA) Autopsy Report No. 88-07800

128 Maryland Health Claims Arbitration Office Claim No. 91-240; *Archive of Pathology and Laboratory Medicine* July 1993

129 Oklahoma Autopsy Report No. T-332-90; Oklahoma Death Certificate No. 23934

130 *Detroit Free Press* 11/14/82; *Chicago Sun-Times*, "Abortion Profiteers" Series 11/12/78–12/3/78

131 Suffolk (MA) Superior Court Civil Action No. 47117

132 California Board of Medical Quality Assurance "Accusation" Case No. D-3132 L-31034

133 Multnomah County (OR) Circuit Court Case No. A8605 03177

134 *St. Petersburg Times* 5/12/88; *Tampa Tribune* 8/6/88; Associated Press 8/8/88; *Tampa Bay and State* 2/9/92

135 *New York Post* 1/10/89; *New York Daily News* 1/12/89, 1/16/89; Associated Press 1/16/89, 2/3/89

136 Associated Press 1/11/90, 1/26/90, 1/29/90; *Today's Tennessean* 2/2/90; *Nashville Banner* 3/15/90; *The Tennessean* 3/15/90

137 *Obstetrics and Gynecology* March 1974

138 Coroner's Report Case No. 72-7646; Los Angeles County (CA) Superior Court Case No. C 53501

139 *Orlando Sentinel Star* 4/20/78; *Miami Herald* 7/20/79

140 St. Louis (MO) City Circuit Court Cause No. 812-11077; *Kansas City Star* 11/6/91; *Houston Chronicle* 11/6/91, 11/11/91

141 East Baton Rouge (LA) Parish 19th Judicial District Court Case No. 289518; *Baton Rouge Morning Advocate* 7/11/84; Louisiana Death Certificate File No. 119-8419478

142 Riverside County (CA) Death Certificate No. 38833005990; Riverside County (CA) Autopsy File No. 64442

143 Jefferson County (AL) Circuit Court Case No. CV-93-632; *New York Times* 4/23/94; *Jackson Clarion-Ledger* 4/1/95

144 Los Angeles County (CA) Superior Court Case No. C64484

145 CBS News, *60 Minutes* 4/21/91

146 St. Louis (MO) Circuit Court Cause No. 802 02960

147 Nassau County (NY) Supreme Court Case No. 1151/80

148 Chattanooga (TN) Circuit Court Case No. N-26762; *Charlotte Observer* 6/3/82

149 Washington, D.C., Court of Appeals, Case No. 82-1077

150 *Press-Telegram* July 14–22, 1985; Los Angeles County (CA) Coroner's Report No. 84-16016

151 Allegheny County (PA) Court of Common Pleas Case No. GD86-21097

152 Cass County (ND) District Court Civil Case No. 901491; *Bismark Tribune* 10/13/91

153 *Topeka Capital-Journal* 3/22/92, 6/19/93; Wyandotte County (KS) District Court Case No. 93C2142

154 California Death Certificate No. 21728; Fresno County (CA) Superior Court Case No. 146000

155 Los Angeles County (CA) Coroner's Report No. 70-8468; Los Angeles County (CA) Superior Court Case No. C857

156 *Obstetrics and Gynecology* March 1974

157 Los Angeles County (CA) Coroner's Report Nos. 75-10935 and 75-9493; California Death Certificate No. 118660

158 *CDC Abortion Surveillance Annual Summary* 1976

159 *American Journal of Obstetrics and Gynecology* 9/1/77

160 Tennessee Death Certificate No. 80 021135

161 Lubbock County (TX) District Court Case No. 88-523649

162 *New York Post* 8/7/91; New York County (NY) Supreme Court Index No. 104592/93

163 *Obstetrics and Gynecology* March 1974

164 *American Journal of Obstetrics and Gynecology* 9/15/78

165 Cumberland County (NC) Superior Court File No. 84CVS1381

166 Connecticut Death Certificate No. 106-83-017389

167 California Death Certificate No. 88-087890

168 New York County (NY) Supreme Court Docket No. 4492-81

169 *Prince George's Journal Weekly* May 30–31, 1990

170 *Obstetrics and Gynecology* March 1974

171 *Chicago Tribune* 1976; Illinois Death Certificate No. 611030; *Chicago Sun-Times* 11/19/78

172 Cook County (IL) Circuit Court Case No. 79L 10033

173 Los Angeles County (CA) Superior Court Case No. SEC61659

174 Cook County (IL) Circuit Court Case No. 89L 15261

175 Philadelphia County (PA) Court of Common Pleas Case No. 92-04-683

176 *Atlanta Journal* 6/27/79; *Atlanta Constitution* 6/28/79

177 New York County (NY) Supreme Court Docket No. 22504/85; *New York Daily News* 12/11/90; *New York Post* 12/11/90, 8/7/91, 8/15/94

178 Cobb County (GA) Superior Court Case No. 88A16621-2; Cobb County (GA) State Court Case No. 89A 004263-3

179 California Department of Health Services Case No. 8-0001 "Accusation"; Amici Brief by Christine Smith Torre filed in support of Appellants in *Webster v. Reproductive Health Services* No. 88-605, reprinted in toto in *Studies in Prolife Feminism*, Vol. 1, No. 1; *Los Angeles Times* 12/3/87, 8/12/89; Associated Press 7/15/89

180 Associated Press 5/12/89, 7/28/89, 8/7/89; *The Atlanta Journal and Constitution* 5/12/89, 7/28/89, 1/5/90; *Chattanooga News-Free Press* 5/13/89, 1/4/90

181 Harris County (TX) District Court Case No. 89-028771

182 Hamilton County (OH) Court of Common Pleas Case No. A745102

183 Cook County (IL) Circuit Court Case No. 80L 1539; Illinois Appellate Court, First District, Case Nos. 1-89-2165, 1-89-2244, 1-89-2357; Associated Press 4/15/89, 4/16/89, 4/17/89; *York Daily Record* 4/17/89

184 Washington, D.C. Superior Court Civil Action No. 10616-87

185 Wayne County (MI) Circuit Court Case No. 90-016792 NH

186 Tulsa County (OK) District Court Case No. CJ-92-1308

187 New York County (NY) Supreme Court Index No. 112763/93

188 Colorado Board of Medical Examiners Case No. MB0294044 "Letter of Admonition"; *Channel 9 Evening News,* Denver, 2/3/94

189 Los Angeles County (CA) Superior Court Case No. WEC073497

190 *Houston Chronicle* 7/18/85; *Suburbia Reporter* 7/24/85, 8/21/85

191 New York County (NY) Supreme Court Case No. 8517-80

192 Associated Press 5/10/88, 3/5/95; *Kansas City Star* 6/3/90; *Topeka Capital-Journal* 6/4/90

193 Cook County (IL) Circuit Court Case No. 78L 9382

194 Los Angeles County (CA) Superior Court Case No. C 749 762

195 Georgia Autopsy Report No. A1994-13

196 Los Angeles County (CA) Superior Court Case No. 109113

197 St. Louis (MO) Circuit Court Cause No. 852-01457

198 Oakland County (MI) Circuit Court Civil Action No. 86 320211

199 Denver (CO) District Court Case No. 86 CV 7389

200 Cook County (IL) Circuit Court Case No. 89L 13692; Illinois Department of Professional Regulation Case No. 89-2096 "Complaint"; Cook County (IL) Autopsy Report, Case No. 125 of September 1989; Illinois Death Certificate No. 617111; Associated Press 10/26/89; *Chicago Tribune* 10/26/89, 12/7/89, 5/3/90, 6/13/90

201 *Philadelphia Inquirer* 8/2/81

202 Lake County (IL) Circuit Court Case No. 78L 445

203 *Milwaukee Journal* 11/1/93

204 Cook County (IL) Circuit Court Case No. 81L 26210

205 *Medical Malpractice Verdicts, Settlements, and Experts* August 1993 and November 1993; Illinois Appellate Court, 1st District, 6th Division, Case No. 1-91-738; Cook County (IL) Circuit Court Case No. 84L 13308; *Chicago Daily Law Bulletin* 6/15/90, 6/16/90; *Peoria Journal Star* 8/9/90

206 Washtenaw County (MI) Circuit Court Case No. 85-30344 NM

207 Hamilton County (OH) Court of Common Pleas Case No. A-8905595

208 Ector County (TX) District Court Case No. C-88-212

209 Maryland Health Claims Arbitration Board Claim No. HCA-90-242 and No. HCA-93-154

210 New York Department of Health Case No. BPMC-92-13-A "Determination and Order"; *New York Post* 11/20/91, 11/21/91, 11/22/91, 11/26/91; *Washington Times* 11/21/91; *New York Times* 11/21/91, 11/22/91, 11/23/91, 11/24/91; *New York Daily News* 11/21/91, 11/24/91, 11/26/91; *USA Today* 11/22/91; *New York Newsday* 11/26/91

211 New Haven (CT) Judicial District Court Case No. 270206

212 Illinois Appellate Court, 1st District, 4th Division, Case No. 86-1162

213 *Detroit Free Press* 11/14/82

214 Orleans Parish (LA) Civil District Court Division C Docket No. 85-12171

215 Cook County (IL) Circuit Court Case No. 83L 1941

216 Sedgwick County (KS) District Court Case No. 92C1280; *Wichita Eagle-Beacon* 9/8/91

217 *Washington, D.C. Legal Times* 5/24/93

218 *American Journal of Obstetrics and Gynecology* 2/15/73

219 *Southern Medical Journal* May 1974

220 *Obstetrics and Gynecology* March 1974

221 Caddo Parish (LA) District Court Case No. 329, 969; *Shreveport Times* 2/27/91

222 Christian Broadcasting Network, "Pennsylvania Abortion/Suicide," 11/6/92

223 New York County (NY) Supreme Court Docket No. 14033/84; 582 N.Y.S.2d 673 (A.D. 1 Dept. 1992); 597 N.Y.S.2d 636 (Ct.App. 1993); *Malpractice Reporter* January/February 1994; *Medical Malpractice Verdicts, Settlements, and Experts* Vol. 9 No. 11, November 1993; *American Medical News* 3/25/93

224 *Medical Malpractice Verdicts, Settlements, and Experts* Vol. 9 No. 10, October 1993; New York County (NY) Supreme Court, Index No. 24454/86

225 *The Dallas Morning News* 1/24/80, 1/25/80; *American Journal of Obstetrics and Gynecology* 10/1/81; Texas Autopsy Report No. 0190-80-0095; Texas Death Certificate 07018

226 New Jersey Death Certificate, Coroner Report Case No. 11-81-0996

227 New York Autopsy Report No. 88-1488; *New York Post* 7/4/89

228 Allegheny County (PA) Court of Common Pleas Civil Action No. G.D. 91-14565; *American Journal of Forensic Medicine and Pathology* Vol. 14 No. 2, 1993

229 New York Department of Health Case No. BPMC-92-13-A "Determination and Order"; *New York Daily News* 11/21/91; *Washington Times* 11/21/91; *New York Post* 11/21/91, 11/22/91; *USA Today* 11/22/91; *New York Times* 11/22/91, 11/23/91, 11/24/91

230 Michigan Death Certificate No. 443133; Wayne County (MI) Circuit Court Case No. 84-423794 NM

231 Philadelphia County (PA) Court of Common Pleas Civil Action No. 291, September term, 1994

Chapter 2

1 "The Response to Rape: Detours on the Road to Justice," prepared by the Majority Staff of the United States Senate Judiciary Committee, May 1993

2 *Miami Herald* 5/4/88, Associated Press 4/29/88, *Spokane Chronicle* 4/29/88

3 New York Department of Health "Determination and Order" for Case No. BPMC-92-13-A

4 *USA Today* 4/17/92; *The Daily Oklahoman* 5/28/93; *Dallas Morning News* 6/11/93; *Questionable Doctors*, Ingrid Van Tuinen, ed., Public Citizens Health Research Group, 1993

5 *Phoenix Gazette* 8/13/87, 8/14/87, 8/15/87, 9/12/87 et al.; *Arizona Republic* 1/21/90; *Tucson Citizen* 8/13/87; *Arizona Daily Star* 6/21/87 et al.; *Questionable Doctors*

6 Richland County Court of General Sessions Case No. 30159; "Prosecutive Summary" for Case No. 73-5456

7 Orange County Circuit Court Case No. 84-1969; *Questionable Doctors*

8 Michigan Board of Osteopathic Medicine and Surgery Department of Licensing and Regulation Complaints

9 *The Oregonian* 9/22/94, 5/27/95, 5/31/95, 6/1/95

10 Florida Board of Nursing Department of Professional Regulation Case No. 89-010853

11 Arizona Superior Court Case No. CV 89-18758; Arizona Board of Osteopathic Examiners "Prior Area of Concern"; Arizona Board of Osteopathic Examiners Case No. 1208 "Letter of Concern" 3/9/92; Osteopathic Licensure Verification; *New Times* Dec. 8–14, 1994

12 Physician Registration Renewal Application Registration No. 46563; Boston Globe 9/2/89, 9/6/89; *Cape Cod Times* 5/18/89, 5/31/90

13 Virginia Board of Medicine documents: letters 4/14/88, 5/27/88, 4/17/90, 3/11/92, 5/4/92; "Order of Summary Suspension" 5/13/94; "Amended Notice and Statement of Particulars" 6/9/94; *Fairfax Journal* 8/5/94; *Washington Post* 8/5/94

14 *Bucks County Intelligencer* 10/28/93; *Philadelphia Inquirer* 10/29/93; *Levittown-Bristol Courier Times* 3/22/95

15 *Clarion-Ledger* 9/30/89, 10/3/89, 10/19/89, 8/30/90; Associated Press 9/30/89, 10/19/89, 10/27/89; *Questionable Doctors*

16 *Kentucky Post* 10/21/82, 11/9/82, 11/11/82; *Cincinnati Inquirer* 11/2/82; *Kentucky Inquirer* 11/9/82, 11/11/82, 1/13/83; *Miami Herald* 5/7/88; *The Cleveland Free Times* Jan. 20–26, 1993; Department of Professional Regulation Case No. 0057913

17 *Minneapolis Star and Tribune* 5/28/82

18 The University of the State of New York Board of Regents "Disciplinary Proceeding" and Order No. 10761; New York Department of Health "Administrative Law Judge's Report" 11/2/89

19 *Chicago Tribune* 9/24/94, 11/17/94; *Courier-News* 11/17/94; *New York Times* 9/24/94; *Chicago Sun-Times* 9/24/94, 10/16/94; *Rockford Register-Star* 3/14/92, 9/23/94, 9/24/94, 10/13/94, 11/16/94, 11/18/94, 11/19/94; *The Oregonian* 11/17/94; Life Dynamics' photographs of site

20 Indiana Medical Board Disciplinary Action Cause No. 89 MLB 0003; Associated Press 2/9/89; *Tyler Morning Telegraph* 6/12/91, 6/13/91; *Questionable Doctors*

21 California Board of Medical Quality Assurance "Investigation Report" for Case Nos. 5-01161 and 5-01810; Los Angeles Municipal Court Case No. 31206712; Los Angeles County Superior Court Case No. C396206

22 *El Paso Times* 9/24/83

23 Minnesota Board of Medical Examiners Case No. SBME-87-003-AK

24 Affidavit of Probable Cause for Police Complaint 0694600543; *Delaware County Daily Times* 2/24/95, 3/1/95; *Scranton Times* 4/9/95; Letter from the Delaware Department of Professional Regulation 4/11/95; New York Office of Professional Discipline Calendar No. 11869; New York Department of Health "Amended Statement of Charges" 3/22/91; *The News of Delaware County* 5/11/94; *Questionable Doctors*
25 *North Jersey Herald & News* 12/22/89
26 *Springfield (MA) Advocate* 8/3/95
27 Medical Board of California Accusation No. 17-95-46707; *The Culver City Independent* 8/24/95
28 San Francisco County Superior Court Case No. 943763
29 Florida Board of Medicine Case Nos. 0070744 and 0073882
30 California Board of Medical Quality Assurance Case No. D-3191
31 Medical Board of California Case No. D-5193
32 King County, WA Court Case No. 82-2-11592-4
33 Los Angeles Municipal Court Case No. P006285
34 *Los Angeles Times* 1/1/93; *Orange County Register* 3/28/95; Medical Board of California Department of Consumer Affairs Case No. D-4660
35 *Playboy* 7/74; *Daily News* 8/13/74; *Chicago Tribune* 8/15/74, 8/27/74, 9/6/74; *Chicago Sun-Times* Nov. and Dec. 1978; "Sexual Health Services," Midwest Population Center (Chicago, IL)

Chapter 3

1 *1991 Annual Report*, National Abortion Federation
2 All the quotes in this paragraph are from *The American Medical News*, "Claiming Abortion Malpractice," by Diane Gianelli, 2/6/95
3 CBS News, *60 Minutes*, 4/21/91
4 Conversations between the National Abortion Federation and Life Dynamics, recorded 10/18/95 and 10/19/95
5 Conversation between the National Abortion Federation and Life Dynamics, recorded 11/10/95
6 Channel 9, *The I-Team News*, Denver, Colorado, 2/4/94
7 Ibid
8 Jefferson (KY) Circuit Court Case No. 94-CI-01970, Deposition of Ronachai Banchongmanie
9 National Abortion Federation, 18th Annual Meeting, 4/24/94–4/26/94
10 National Abortion Federation, Fall Risk Management Seminar, 9/18/94–9/20/94
11 Diane Gianelli, "Claiming Abortion Malpractice," *The American Medical News*, 2/6/95
12 Davidson County (TN) Circuit Court Case No. 94C-259
13 Boone County (IN) Circuit Court Cause No. C86-293; Marion County (IN) Superior Court Cause No. S287 0782; *Indianapolis News*, 6/11/86
14 Conversation between Planned Parenthood and Life Dynamics, recorded 11/9/95
15 Conversation between Planned Parenthood and Life Dynamics, recorded 11/9/95
16 Letter from California Department of Health Services, 8/12/85
17 NBC *Dateline*, 11/1/94
18 *The Miami Herald*, 9/17/89
19 Yukio Manabe, M.D., "Artificial Abortion at Midpregnancy by Mechanical Stimulation of the Uterus," *American Journal of Obstetrics & Gynecology*, 9/1/69
20 Takashi Wagatsuma, M.D., "Intraamniotic Injection of Saline for Therapeutic Abortion," *American Journal of Obstetrics & Gynecology*, 11/1/65
21 Yukio Manabe, M.D., "Danger of Hypertonic-Saline-Induced Abortion," *Journal of the American Medical Association*, 12/15/69
22 J. M. Cameron, M.D., Ph.D., M.C.PATH.; A. D. Dayan, M.D., B.Sc., M.R.C.P., M.C.PATH., "Association of Brain Damage with Therapeutic Abortion Induced by Amniotic Fluid Replacement: Report of Two Cases," *British Medical Journal*, 4/23/66
23 California Death Certificate No. 65-077063

24 Christopher Tietze, Sarah Lewit, "Early Medical Complications of Abortion by Saline: Joint Program for the Study of Abortion (JPSA)," *Studies in Family Planning*, June 1973; Morton A. Schiffer, M.D., F.A.C.O.G.; Jean Pakter, M.D.; Jacob Clahr, M.D., F.A.C.O.G., "Mortality Associated with Hypertonic Saline Abortion," *Obstetrics and Gynecology*, November 1973 and March 1974

25 Norman R. Kaplan, M.D., "Hazard of Saline Abortion: letter," *Journal of the American Medical Association*, 7/3/72

26 Carl-Axel Ingemanson, M.D., "Legal Abortion by Extra-Amniotic Instillation of Rivanol in Combination with Rubber Catheter Insertion Into the Uterus After the Twelfth Week of Pregnancy," *American Journal of Obstetrics and Gynecology*, 1/15/73

27 Niels H. Lauersen, M.D.; Joseph D. Schulman, M.D., "Oxytocin Administration in Mid-Trimester Saline Abortions," *American Journal of Obstetrics and Gynecology*, 2/1/73

28 Richard M. Selik, M.D.; Willard Cates, Jr., M.D., M.P.H.; Carl W. Tyler, Jr., M.D., "Behavioral Factors Contributing to Abortion Deaths: A New Approach to Mortality Studies," *Obstetrics and Gynecology*, November 1981

29 *The Philadelphia Inquirer*, 8/2/81

30 *Technical Bulletin*, American College of Obstetricians and Gynecologists, October 1987

31 *Patient Education Pamphlet*, American College of Obstetricians and Gynecologists, May 1994

32 *Who Will Provide Abortions?*, National Abortion Federation, 1991

33 Ibid

34 *The Lancet*, 5/28/83

35 "Interview," *Omni*, September 1991

36 *Chicago Tribune*, 9/12/94; *Abortion Reporter*, 3/15/95, *Physician's Desk Reference*, 1995

37 Nancy Howell Lee, *The Search for an Abortionist*, University of Chicago Press, 1972

38 Council on Scientific Affairs, American Medical Association, "Induced Termination of Pregnancy Before and After *Roe v. Wade*: Trends in the Mortality and Morbidity of Women," *Journal of the American Medical Association*, 12/9/92

39 "Abortion Providers Share Inner Conflicts," *The American Medical News*, 7/12/93

40 Rachel Benson Gold, *Abortion and Women's Health*, Alan Guttmacher Institute, 1990

41 David A. Grimes, M.D.; Willard Cates, Jr., M.D., M.P.H., "Gestational Age Limit of Twelve Weeks for Abortion by Curettage," *American Journal of Obstetrics & Gynecology*, 9/15/78

42 Council on Scientific Affairs, American Medical Association, "Induced Termination of Pregnancy Before and After *Roe v. Wade*: Trends in the Mortality and Morbidity of Women," *Journal of the American Medical Association*, 12/9/92

43 *Morbidity and Mortality Weekly Report: CDC Surveillance Summaries*, United States 1989, Issued 1992

44 Alan F. Guttmacher, M.D., *Babies by Choice or by Chance*, Doubleday and Co., Inc., 1959

45 Christopher Tietze, "The Effect of Legalization of Abortion on Population Growth and Public Health," *Family Planning Perspectives*, May/June 1975

46 Kristin Luker, "Contraception Risk Taking and Abortion," *Studies in Family Planning*, August 1977

47 Christopher Tietze, "The Effect of Legalization of Abortion on Population Growth and Public Health," *Family Planning Perspectives*, May/June 1975

48 Robert J. Melton, M.D.; J. King B. E. Segar, Jr., M.D., F.A.C.O.G.; John I. Pitts, M.D., "Therapeutic Abortion in Maryland, 1968–1970," *Obstetrics and Gynecology*, June 1972; *Centers for Disease Control, Abortion Surveillance Summary*, July 1991

49 "Abortion and Maternal Death," *British Medical Journal*, 7/10/76; Thomas W. McDonald, M.D.; Leonard A. Aaro, M.D., "Medical Complications of Induced Abortions," *Southern Medical Journal*, May 1974

50 J. A. Stallworthy; A. S. Moolgaoker; J. J. Walsh, "Legal Abortion: A Critical Assessment of Its Risks," *The Lancet*, 12/4/71

51 Albert Altchek, M.D., F.A.C.O.G., "Editorial: Abortion Alert," *Obstetrics and Gynecology*, September 1973

Chapter 4

1 *Morbidity and Mortality Weekly Report: CDC Surveillance Summaries*, 1982–1983, Issued 1987

2 Christopher Tietze, M.D.; Sarah Lewit, "Joint Program for the Study of Abortion (JPSA): Early Medical Complications of Legal Abortion," *Studies in Family Planning*, Vol. 3, No. 6, June 1972

3 J. C. Smith, W. Cates, "The Public Health Need for Abortion Statistics," *Public Health Reports*, Vol. 93, 1978

4 *Medicode's Physician ICD-9-CM*, Fourth Edition, 1995, Vol. 1&2.

5 *Morbidity and Mortality Weekly Report: CDC Surveillance Summaries*, 1990, Issued 1993,Vol. 42, No. SS-6

6 *CDC Maternal Mortality Surveillance*, United States, 1979–1986

7 *Morbidity and Mortality Weekly Report: CDC Surveillance Summaries*, "Maternal Mortality Surveillance, United States, 1979–1986," Issued 1992

8 *Morbidity and Mortality Weekly Report: CDC Surveillance Summaries*, June 26, 1987

9 J. C. Smith and W. Cates, "The Public Health Need for Abortion Statistics," *Public Health Reports*, 1978

10 James D. Shelton, Albert K. Schoenbucher, "Deaths After Legally Induced Abortion," *Public Health Reports*, Vol. 93, 1978

11 Richard M. Selik, M.D.; Willard Cates, Jr., M.D., M.P.H.; Carl W. Tyler, Jr., M.D., "Behavioral Factors Contributing to Abortion Deaths: A New Approach to Mortality Studies," *Obstetrics and Gynecology*, Vol. 58, No. 5, November 1981

12 Larry Perl, "Teen's Death After Abortion Brings Suit," *The Prince George's Journal Weekly*, May 30–31, 1990

13 James A. Miller, "In Indiana and Maryland, a Tale of Two Abortions," Other Voices, *The Evening Sun*, February 15, 1991

14 Letter to the Surgeon General, Dr. Antonia Novello, p. 1; Letter to Assistant Secretary for Public Affairs, Department of Health and Human Services, Dr. Kay James, p. 1, K.S. Research

15 North Carolina Medical Database Commission Special Run, July 14, 1995

16 Detailed Mortality Statistics Report, North Carolina, 1991

17 Richard M. Selik, M.D.; Willard Cates, Jr., M.D., M.P.H.; Carl W. Tyler, Jr., M.D., "Behavioral Factors Contributing to Abortion Deaths: A New Approach to Mortality Studies," *Obstetrics and Gynecology*, Vol. 58, No. 5, November 1981

18 *Morbidity and Mortality Weekly Report: CDC Surveillance Summaries*, Vol. 41, No. SS-5, September 4, 1992

19 *Morbidity and Mortality Weekly Report: CDC Surveillance Summaries*, 1989, Issued 1992

20 J. C. Smith and W. Cates, "The Public Health Need for Abortion Statistics," *Public Health Reports*, Vol. 93, 1978

21 Ibid

22 *Morbidity and Mortality Weekly Report: CDC Surveillance Summaries*, 1989, Issued 1992

23 *New York Post*, June 10, 1992

24 J. C. Smith and W. Cates, "The Public Health Need for Abortion Statistics," *Public Health Reports*, Vol. 93, 1978

25 M. E. Kafrissen, K. F. Schultz, D. A. Grimes, W. E. Cates, "Midtrimester Abortion: Intra-amniotic Instillation of Hyperosmolar Urea and Prostaglandin F2α v Dilatation and Evacuation" *Journal of the American Medical Association*, Vol. 251, No. 7, February 17, 1984

26 *Morbidity and Mortality Weekly Report: CDC Surveillance Summaries*, 1989, Issued 1992

27 *Morbidity and Mortality Weekly Report: CDC Surveillance Summaries*, 1990, Issued 1993

28 Ibid

29 Stanley K. Henshaw, Jeniffer VanVort, "Abortion Services in the United States, 1991 and 1992," *Family Planning Perspectives*, The Alan Guttmacher Institute, Vol. 26, No. 3, May/June 1994

30 James D. Shelton, Albert K. Schoenbucher, "Deaths After Legally Induced Abortion," *Public Health Reports*, Vol. 93, 1978

31 Andrew M. Kaunitz, M.D., et al., "Causes of Maternal Mortality in the United States," *Obstetrics and Gynecology*, Vol. 65, No. 5, May 1985

32 County of San Bernardino (CA) Coroner's Investigation, Case No. 71314

33 Commonwealth of Kentucky Certificate of Death, File No. 81-25243

34 North Carolina Medical Examiner's Certificate of Death, Vital Records No. 044550, issued October 13, 1993

35 Report of Investigation by Medical Examiner, Case No. 93-1948

36 Alabama Certificate of Death, File No. 85-10613

37 *ICD-9-CM*, 1995, Vol. 1

38 *Chicago Sun-Times*, "Abortion Profiteers" Series, 11/12/78–12/3/78

39 Andrew M. Kaunitz, M.D., et al., "Causes of Maternal Mortality in the United States," *Obstetrics and Gynecology*, Vol. 65, No. 5, May 1985

40 Arizona Revised Statutes, Title 36, Chap. 3, Art. 2; Texas Statutes and Codes, Title 4, Subtitle B, Chapter 245, Wisconsin Statutes, Chapter 69, Subchapter 1, et al.

41 Taped telephone conversations with individuals in the state health departments, June and July 1995

42 State information on abortion data collection and requests gathered from Iowa Department of Health, June 20, 1995

43 *Morbidity and Mortality Weekly Report: CDC Surveillance Summaries*, 1989, Issued 1992

44 State information on abortion data collections and requests gathered from Illinois Department of Public Health, June 1995

45 Taped telephone conversations with Illinois Department of Public Health, June 1995

46 "State Releases Data on County Abortions," *Evening Outlook*, 9/27/72

47 Multnomah County (OR) Medical Examiner's Office, Letter 11/1/95

48 Oregon Certificate of Death, File No. 87-019149

49 Oregon Certificate of Death, File No. 84-000045

50 California Resident Deaths by ICD Code, 1960-1993, Department of Health Services, issued July 1995; *Long Beach Press Telegram*, June 28, 1983

51 Andrew M. Kaunitz, M.D., et al., "Causes of Maternal Mortality in the United States," *Obstetrics and Gynecology*, Vol. 65, No. 5, May 1985

52 *The Washington Times*, June 4, 1994

53 *Los Angeles Times*, November 10, 1972

54 *Morbidity and Mortality Weekly Report: CDC Surveillance Summaries*, Vol. 41, No. SS-5, September 4, 1992

55 Stanley K. Henshaw, Jeniffer VanVort, "Abortion Services in the United States, 1991 and 1992," *Family Planning Perspectives*, The Alan Guttmacher Institute, Vol. 26, No. 3, May/June 1994

56 Hani K. Atrash, M.D.; H. Trent MacKay, M.D.; Nancy J. Binkin, M.D.; Carol J. R. Hogue, Ph.D., "Legal Abortion Mortality in the United States: 1972–1982," *Journal of Obstetrics and Gynecology*, 1987

57 "Standards of Ethical Conduct for Employees of the Executive Branch," United States Office of Government Ethics, August 1992

58 *Abortion in the Seventies*, National Abortion Federation, 1977

59 "Who Will Provide Abortions? Recommendations From a National Symposium," National Abortion Federation, American College of Obstetricians and Gynecologists, 1991

60 "Annual Report," The National Abortion Federation, 1991

61 *Federal Staff Directories*, 1988–1995, Centers for Disease Control and National Center for Health Statistics

62 "Who Will Provide Abortions? Ensuring the Availability of Qualified Practitioners," National Abortion Federation, American College of Obstetrics and Gynecology, 1990

63 *Family Planning Perspectives*, The Alan Guttmacher Institute, Vol. 26, No. 1, January/February 1994, Editorial Advisory Committee–Lisa M. Koonin.

64 *Centers for Disease Control Surveillance*, 1981, Issued November 1985

65 The following are just a very few of the instances we found: M. E. Kafrissen, K. F. Schultz, D. A. Grimes, W. E. Cates, "Midtrimester Abortion: Intra-amniotic Instillation of Hyperosmolar Urea and Prostaglandin F2α v Dilatation and Evacuation" *Journal of the American Medical Association*, Vol. 251, No. 7, February 17, 1984; H. K. Atrash, T. MacKay, C. J. R. Hogue, "Ectopic Pregnancy Concurrent with Induced Abortion: Incidence and Mortality," *American Journal of Obstetrics and Gynecology*, Vol. 162, No. 3, March 1990; Hani K. Atrash, M.D., et al., "Legal Abortion Mortality in the United States: 1972 to 1982," *American Journal of Obstetrics and Gynecology*, Vol. 156, No. 3, March 1987; Frederick P. Zuspan, M.D. Ed., "Second Trimester Abortion a Symposium by Correspondence," *The Journal of Reproductive Medicine*, Vol. 16, No. 2, February 1976; Harold Schulman, M.D., F.A.C.O.G.; Irwin H. Kaiser, M.D., F.A.C.O.G.; Georgia Randolph, BS; "Outpatient Saline Abortion," *Obstetrics and Gynecology*, Vol. 37, No. 4, April 1971; Gary S. Berger, M.D., et al., "One Death and a Cluster of Febrile Complications Related to Saline Abortions," *Obstetrics and Gynecology*, Vol. 42, No. 1, July 1973; David A. Grimes, M.D.; Kenneth F. Schulz, MBA, "Morbidity and Mortality from Second-Trimester Abortions," *The Journal of Reproductive Medicine*; Stephen, L. Corson, M.D., Assoc. Ed., Vol. 30, No. 7, July 1985; Nancy Binkin, M.D., M.P.H., et al., "Women Refused Second-Trimester Abortion: Correlates of Pregnancy Outcome," *American Journal of Obstetrics and Gynecology*, Vol. 145, No. 3, February 1, 1983; Tai-Kuen Park, M.D., M.P.H., Ph.D., et al., "Preventing Febrile Complications of Suction Curettage Abortion," *American Journal of Obstetrics and Gynecology*, Vol. 152, No. 3, June 1, 1985; David A. Grimes, M.D.; Kenneth F. Schulz, MBA; Willard J. Cates, Jr., M.D., M.P.H., "Prevention of Uterine Perforation During Curettage Abortion," *Journal of the American Medical Association*, Vol. 251, No. 16, April 27, 1984; Kenneth F. Schulz; David A. Grimes; Willard Cates, Jr., "Measures to Prevent Cervical Injury During Suction Curettage Abortion," *The Lancet*, May 28, 1983

66 *Centers for Disease Control Abortion Surveillance*, 1976, Issued 1978; *Center for Disease Control*, 1977, Issued 1979

67 *Morbidity and Mortality Weekly Report*, "Abortion Surveillance 1986–1987," Issued 1990; *Center for Disease Control*, 1972, Issued 1974

68 *Center for Disease Control, Abortion Surveillance*, 1976, Issued 1978

69 *Centers for Disease Control Abortion Surveillance*, 1981, Issued 1985

70 Ibid

71 Ibid

72 Willard Cates, Jr., M.D., M.P.H.; David A. Grimes, M.D., "Deaths from Second-Trimester Abortion by Dilatation and Evacuation: Causes, Prevention, Facilities," *Obstetrics and Gynecology*, October 1981

73 Takashi Wagatsuma, M.D., "Intra-Amniotic Injection of Saline for Therapeutic Abortion," *American Journal of Obstetrics and Gynecology*, Vol. 93, No. 5, November 1, 1965

74 Yukio Manabe, M.D., "Danger of Hypertonic-Saline-Induced Abortion," *Journal of the American Medical Association*, Vol. 210, No. 11, December 15, 1969

75 J. M. Cameron, M.D., Ph.D., M.C. PATH., D.M.J; A. D. Dayan, M.B., B.SC., M.R.C.P., M.C. PATH., "Association of Brain Damage with Therapeutic Abortion Induced by Amniotic-Fluid Replacement: Report of Two Cases," *British Medical Journal*, April 23, 1966

76 Gary K. Stewart, M.D.; Phillip Goldstein, M.D., F.A.C.O.G., "Medical and Surgical Complications of Therapeutic Abortions," *Obstetrics and Gynecology*, Vol. 40, No. 4, October 1972

77 Harold Schulman, M.D., F.A.C.O.G.; Irwin H. Kaiser, M.D., F.A.C.O.G.; Georgia Randolph, B.S., "Outpatient Saline Abortion," *Obstetrics and Gynecology*, Vol. 37, No. 4, April 1971

78 David A. Grimes, M.D., et al., "Mid-Trimester Abortion by Dilatation and Evacuation," The *New England Journal of Medicine*, Vol. 296, No. 20, May 19, 1977

79 Charles S. Wright, Stuart Campbell, John Beazley, "Second-Trimester Abortion After Vaginal Termination of Pregnancy," *The Lancet*, June 10, 1972

80 Dov Dicker, M.D., et al., "Etiology of Cervical Pregnancy Association with Abortion, Pelvic Pathology, IUDs and Asherman's Syndrome," *The Journal of Reproductive Medicine*, Vol. 30, No. 1, January 1985

81 David A. Grimes, M.D.; Willard Cates, Jr., M.D., M.P.H., "Gestational Age Limit of Twelve Weeks for Abortion by Curettage," *American Journal of Obstetrics and Gynecology*, Vol. 132, No. 2, September 15, 1978

82 Suneeta Mittal; Sneh Lata Misra, "Uterine Perforation Following Medical Termination of Pregnancy by Vacuum Aspiration," *International Journal of Gynaecology and Obstetrics*, Vol. 23, 1985

83 Peter J. Moberg, "Uterine Perforation in Connection with Vacuum Aspiration for Legal Abortion," *International Journal of Gynaecology and Obstetrics*, 1976, Vol. 14

84 David A. Grimes, M.D., et al., "Fatal Hemorrhage from Legal Abortion in the United States," *Surgery, Gynecology and Obstetrics*, Vol. 157, November 1983

85 Duane E. Townsend, M.D., et al., "Vasopressin and Operative Hysteroscopy in the Management of Delayed Postabortion and Postpartum Bleeding," *American Journal of Obstetrics and Gynecology*, Vol. 165, No. 3, September 1991

86 *Surgery, Gynecology and Obstetrics*, 1983

87 David A. Grimes, M.D., et al., "Fatal Hemorrhage from Legal Abortion in the United States," *Surgery, Gynecology and Obstetrics*, Vol. 157, November 1983

88 Oddmund Koller; Siri Nome Eikhom, "Late Sequelae of Induced Abortion in Primigravidae," *Acta Obstetrics and Gynecology Scandanavia*, Vol. 56, 1977

89 Ibid

90 Carol J. Rowland Hogue, Ph.D., M.P.H., "Impact of Abortion on Subsequent Fecundity," Chapter 8 in Termination of Pregnancy, *Clinics in Obstetrics and Gynaecology*, Vol. 13, No. 1, March 1986, W.B. Saunders Company

91 Richard R. Parlour, M.D.; James H. Ford, M.D., "The Unwanted Pregnancy: Psychiatry on the Rocks," *Medical Counterpoint*, October 1974

92 John Figgis Jewett, M.D., "Massachusetts Medical Society Committee on Maternal Welfare, Saline Abortion and Lupus Erythematosus," *The New England Journal of Medicine*, Vol. 294, No. 14, April 1, 1976

93 Matthew J. Bulfin, M.D., "A New Problem in Adolescent Gynecology," *Southern Medical Journal*, Vol. 72, No. 8, August 1979

94 Thomas W. McDonald, M.D.; Leonard A. Aaro, M.D., "Medical Complications of Induced Abortions," *Southern Medical Journal*, Vol. 67, No. 5, May 1974

95 Denis Cavanagh, "To the Editors: Reply to Drs. Cates, Schulz, and Grimes," *American Journal of Obstetrics and Gynecology*, Vol. 130, No. 3, February 1, 1978

96 Mary Jo Lanska, Douglas Lanska, Alfred A. Rimm, Ph.D., Letter to the Editor: "Mortality From Abortion and Childbirth," *Journal of the American Medical Association*, Vol. 250, No. 3, July 15, 1983; David A. Grimes, M.D.; Scot A. LeBolt; Willard Cates, Jr., M.D., M.P.H., "In Reply," *Journal of the American Medical Association*, Vol. 250, No. 3, July 15, 1983

97 Willard Cates, Jr.; Jack C. Smith; Roger W. Rochat; John E. Patterson; Alice Dolman, "Assessment of Surveillance and Vital Statistics Data for Monitoring Abortion Mortality, United States, 1972–1975," *American Journal of Epidemiology*, 1978

98 Ibid

99 David Reardon, The Elliot Institute, Springfield, IL, non-published, 1984

100 Willard Cates, Jr., M.D., M.P.H., "'Abortion Myths and Realities': Who is Misleading Whom?" *American Journal of Obstetrics and Gynecology*, Vol. 142, No. 8, April 15, 1982

101 Willard Cates, Jr., M.D., M.P.H., et al., "Dilatation and Evacuation Procedures and Second-Trimester Abortions: The Role of Physician Skill and Hospital Setting," *Journal of the American Medical Association*, Vol. 248, No. 5, August 6, 1982

102 *Centers for Disease Control: Abortion Surveillance*, 1981, Issued 1985

103 Tabulated from CDC Summaries 1972–1992

104 *Centers for Disease Control: Abortion Surveillance*, 1977, Issued 1979

105 James L. Breen, M.D., "A 21 Year Survey of 654 Ectopic Pregnancies," *American Journal of Obstetrics and Gynecology*, Vol. 106, No. 7, April 1, 1970

106 George L. Rubin, M.D., et al., "Fatal Ectopic Pregnancy after Attempted Legally Induced Abortion," *Journal of the American Medical Association*, Vol. 244, No. 15, October 10, 1980

107 *Chicago Sun-Times*, "Abortion Profiteers Series," 11/12/78–12/3/78

108 *Miami Herald*, 9/26/89

109 H. K. Atrash, T. MacKay, C. J. R. Hogue, "Ectopic Pregnancy Concurrent with Induced Abortion: Incidence and Mortality," *American Journal of Obstetrics and Gynecology*, Vol. 162, No. 3, March 1990

110 Jane M. Hardman, M.D., et al., "Ectopic Pregnancy in Association With Induced Abortion: Message for the Pathologist," *Archives of Pathology and Laboratory Medicine*, Vol. 117, July 1993

111 *Morbidity and Mortality Weekly Report: Centers for Disease Control*, "Ectopic Pregnancy-United States, 1990–1992," Vol. 44, No. 3

112 Chin S. Chung, et al., "Induced Abortion and Ectopic Pregnancy in Subsequent Pregnancies," *American Journal of Epidemiology*, Vol. 115, No. 6, 1982

113 Victoria L. Holt, M.P.H., et al., "Induced Abortion and the Risk of Subsequent Ectopic Pregnancy," *American Journal of Public Health*, Vol. 79, No. 9, September 1989

114 Thomas W. McDonald, M.D.; Leonard A. Aaro, M.D., "Medical Complications of Induced Abortions," *Southern Medical Journal*, Vol. 67, No. 5, May 1974

115 *Morbidity and Mortality Weekly Report*, "Ectopic Pregnancy–United States, 1987," Vol. 39, No. 24, June 22, 1990

116 Jack G. Hallatt, M.D., F.A.C.O.G., "Repeat Ectopic Pregnancy: A Study of 123 Consecutive Cases," *American Journal of Obstetrics and Gynecology*, Vol. 122, No. 4, June 15, 1975

117 Hani K. Atrash, M.D., M.P.H., et al., "Ectopic Pregnancy Mortality in the United States, 1970–1983," *Obstetrics and Gynecology*, Vol. 70, No. 6, December 1987

118 Lars Heisterberg, "Pelvic Inflammatory Disease Following Induced First-Trimester Abortion," *Danish Medical Bulletin*, 1987; Per-Göran Larsson, M.D., et al., "Incidence of Pelvic Inflammatory Disease after First-Trimester Legal Abortion in Women with Bacterial Vaginosis after Treatment with Metronidazole: A Double-Blind, Randomized Study," *American Journal of Obstetrics and Gynecology*, Vol. 166, No. 1, Part 1, January 1992; Erik Qvigstad, et al., "Therapeutic Abortion and Chlamydia Trachomatis Infection," *British Journal of Venereal Diseases*, Vol. 58, 1982

119 Erik Qvigstad, et al., "Therapeutic Abortion and Chlamydia Trachomatis Infection," *British Journal of Venereal Diseases*, Vol. 58, 1982; Marguerite B. Barbacci, BSN, M.P.H., et al., "Postabortal Endometritis and Isolation of Chlamydia Trachomatis," *Obstetrics and Gynecology*, Vol. 68, No. 5, November 1986; Lars Westergaard, M.D., et al., "Significance of Cervical Chlamydia Trachomatis Infection in Postabortal Pelvic Inflammatory Disease," *Obstetrics and Gynecology*, Vol. 60, No. 3, September 1982; Stellan Osser, M.D.; Kenneth Persson, M.D., "Postabortal Pelvic Infection Associated with Chlamydia Trachomatis and the Influence of Humoral Immunity," *American Journal of Obstetrics and Gynecology*, Vol. 150, No. 6, November 15, 1984

120 Ibid

121 David A. Grimes, M.D., et al., "Prophylactic Antibiotics for Curettage Abortion," *American Journal of Obstetrics and Gynecology*, Vol. 150, No. 6, November 15, 1984

122 California Certificate of Death, File No. 88-146505; Los Angeles County (CA) Autopsy Report, File No. 88-07800; California Certificate of Death, File No. 86-087497; Los Angeles County (CA) Autopsy Report, File No. 86-6084

123 Willard Cates, Jr., M.D., M.P.H., "Legal Abortion: The Public Health Record," *Science*, Vol. 215, 1982

124 "Does Abortion Increase Breast Cancer Risk?," *Journal of the National Cancer Institute*, Vol. 85, No. 24, December 15, 1993

125 *Centers for Disease Control Abortion Surveillance*, 1975, Issued 1977

126 Julian Gold, M.D.; Willard Cates, Jr., M.D., M.P.H., "Herbal Abortifacients, Editorials," *Journal of the American Medical Association*, Vol. 243, No. 13, April 4, 1980

127 Nancy Binkin; Julian Gold; Willard Cates, Jr., "Illegal-Abortion Deaths in the United States: Why Are They Still Occurring?" *Family Planning Perspectives*, The Alan Guttmacher Institute, Vol. 14, No. 3, May/June 1982

128 California Certificate of Death, File No. 90-079380; San Bernardino County (CA) Coroner's Investigation, Case No. 90-2384

129 Christopher Tietze, M.D.; Sarah Lewit, "Joint Program for the Study of Abortion (JPSA): Early Medical Complications of Legal Abortion," *Studies in Family Planning*, Vol. 3, No. 6, June 1972

130 *City of Akron v. Akron Center for Reproductive Health, Inc., et al.,* 103 Supreme Court Reporter, 1983

131 Willard Cates, Jr., M.D., M.P.H.; David A. Grimes, M.D., "Deaths from Second-Trimester Abortion by Dilatation and Evacuation: Causes, Prevention, Facilities," *Obstetrics and Gynecology*, October 1981

132 Ibid; Richard J. Guidotti, M.D., et al., "Fatal Amniotic Fluid Embolism During Legally Induced Abortion, United States, 1972 to 1978," *American Journal of Obstetrics and Gynecology*, Vol. 141, No. 3, October 1, 1981

133 Willard Cates, Jr., M.D., M.P.H., et al., "Sudden Collapse and Death of Women Obtaining Abortions Induced with Prostaglandin F2α," *American Journal of Obstetrics and Gynecology*, Vol. 133, No. 4, February 15, 1979

134 Judith P. Bourne, R.N., et al., "Medical Complications from Induced Abortion by the Super Coil Method," *Health Services Report*, Vol. 89, No. 1, January–February 1974

135 *Centers for Disease Control Abortion Surveillance*, 1972, Issued 1974

136 Gary S. Berger, M.D., et al., "Termination of Pregnancy by 'Super Coils': Morbidity Associated with a New Method of Second-Trimester Abortion," *American Journal of Obstetrics and Gynecology*, Vol. 116, No. 3, June 1, 1973

137 *Centers for Disease Control Abortion Surveillance*, 1972, Issued 1974

138 *New York Times*, 12/13/72

139 Bernard N. Nathanson, M.D., with Richard N. Ostling, *Aborting America: A Doctor's Personal Report on the Agonizing Issue of Abortion*, Life Cycle Books, 1979

140 *The Washington Post*, 3/22/72

141 Bernard N. Nathanson, M.D., with Richard N. Ostling, *Aborting America: A Doctor's Personal Report on the Agonizing Issue of Abortion*, Life Cycle Books, 1979

142 *Family Planning Perspectives*, The Alan Guttmacher Institute, September/October 1995

143 Program Schedule, National Abortion Federation, 19th Annual Meeting, New Orleans, LA, 4/3/95

144 Taped conversation on file at Life Dynamics, Inc., 11/9/95

145 Taped conversation on file at Life Dynamics, Inc., 11/9/95

146 Taped conversation on file at Life Dynamics, Inc., 11/29/95

147 Taped conversation on file at Life Dynamics, Inc., 11/27/95

148 Personal correspondence from John C. Willke, M.D., 12/4/95, on file at Life Dynamics, Inc.

149 "Playboy Interview: Milton Friedman," *Playboy*, February 1973

150 *Budget of the United States Government, Fiscal Year 1996*, Office of Management and Budget, Washington, D.C.

Chapter 5

1 Magda Denes, *In Necessity and Sorrow*, New York: Basic Books, Inc., 1976

2 Interview with Charlotte Taft by Jane Reynolds of Project Choice (Jane Reynolds was a pseudonym for an LDI employee)

3 *Washington Post*, 3/3/80

4 Sallie Tisdale, "We Do Abortions Here," *Harper's Magazine*, October 1987

5 *New York Times*, 10/19/94

6 *The Philadelphia Inquirer*, 8/2/81

7 Magda Denes, *In Necessity and Sorrow*, New York: Basic Books, Inc., 1976

8 Diane Gianelli, "Abortion Providers Share Inner Conflicts," *American Medical News*, 7/12/93

9 "Meet the Abortion Providers III: The Promoters," audiotape, Pro-Life Action League Conference, Chicago, IL, 4/3/93

10 Constance A. Nathanson and Marshall H. Becker, "The Influence of Physicians' Attitudes on Abortion Performance, Patient Management, and Professional Fees," *Family Planning Perspectives*, July/August 1977

11 Kathleen M. Roe, "Private Troubles and Public Issues," *Social Science and Medicine*, Vol. 29, No. 10

12 Diane Gianelli, "Abortion Providers Share Inner Conflicts," *American Medical News*, 7/12/93

13 Magda Denes, *In Necessity and Sorrow*, New York: Basic Books, Inc., 1976

14 Ibid

15 *Philadelphia Inquirer*, 7/18/93

16 Warren Hern and Billie Corrigan, "What About Us? Staff Reactions to the D&E Procedure," presented at a meeting of the Associations of Planned Parenthood Physicians, San Diego, 10/26/78

17 Interview with Charlotte Taft by Jane Reynolds of Project Choice

18 *Philadelphia Inquirer*, 7/18/93

19 *Spectrum*, National Public Radio, 5/11/90

20 *Philadelphia Inquirer*, 7/18/93

21 Diane Gianelli, "Abortion Providers Share Inner Conflicts," *American Medical News*, 7/12/93

22 Don Sloan with Paula Hartz, *Abortion: Doctor's Perspective/A Woman's Dilemma*, New York: Donald Fine, Inc., 1992

23 Magda Denes, *In Necessity and Sorrow*, New York: Basic Books, Inc., 1976

24 Don Sloan with Paula Hartz, *Abortion: Doctor's Perspective/A Woman's Dilemma*, New York: Donald Fine, Inc., 1992

25 Karen Tumulty, "The Abortions of Last Resort," *Los Angeles Times Magazine*, 1/7/90

26 *New York Times*, 3/13/93

27 *New York Times*, 3/22/92

28 *The Philadelphia Inquirer*, 7/18/93

29 S. G. White, "Under the Gunn," *Hartford Advocate*, 4/15/93

30 *Atlanta Journal and Constitution*, 5/16/93

31 Anonymous, "Why I Am an Abortionist," *Glamour*, October 1993

32 *San Francisco Chronicle*, 3/22/93

33 *Democrat and Chronicle*, 7/5/92

34 *St. Petersburg Times*, 6/3/90

35 *Reporter Dispatch*, 9/18/95

36 M*A*S*H, original air date 10/19/73

37 *Chicago Tribune*, 11/18/79

38 Michele Ingrassia, "Virgin Cool," *Newsweek*, 10/17/94

39 Diane Gianelli, "Abortion Providers Share Inner Conflicts," *American Medical News*, 7/12/93

40 *New York Times*, 3/13/93

41 *Atlanta Journal Constitution*, 5/16/93

42 Frederica Mathewes-Green, "Abortion: Womens' Rights...and Wrongs," *Sisterlife*, Winter 1994

43 Naomi Wolf, "Our Bodies, Our Souls," *The New Republic*, 10/16/95

44 Diane Gianelli, "Abortion Providers Share Inner Conflicts," *American Medical News*, 7/12/93

45 "Meet the Abortion Providers III: The Promoters," audiotape, conference held by the Pro Life Action League, Chicago, 4/3/93

46 *Philadelphia Inquirer*, 7/18/93

47 Interview with Charlotte Taft by Jane Reynolds of Project Choice

48 Don Sloan with Paula Hartz, *Abortion: A Doctor's Perspective/A Woman's Dilemma*, New York: Donald Fine, Inc., 1992

49 Magda Denes, *In Necessity and Sorrow*, New York: Basic Books, Inc., 1976

50 Letter from Martha Jo Billy to the Personnel Board of Planned Parenthood of Central and Northern Arizona, 12/18/84

51 Interview with Joy Davis by Life Dynamics, 1993

52 Interview with former employee of abortionist John Roe 328 by Rachel McNair, 3/10/92

53 *The Minneapolis Star and Tribune*, 5/28/92

54 Cook County (IL) Circuit Court Case No. 91-L-50928

55 Interview with Joy Davis by Life Dynamics, 1993

56 Sallie Tisdale, "We Do Abortions Here," *Harper's Magazine*, October 1987

57 Interview with former employee of abortionist John Roe 328 by Rachel McNair, 3/10/92

58 *Miami Herald*, 10/7/89

59 Mecklenburg County (NC) General Court of Justice, Case No. 75 CVD 311

60 Interview with Joy Davis by Life Dynamics, 1993

61 Alan F. Guttmacher, *Babies By Choice or By Chance*, Doubleday & Company, Inc., 1959

62 Interview with Joy Davis by Life Dynamics, 1993

63 Marianne Such-Baer, "Professional Staff Reaction to Abortion Work," *Social Casework*, July 1974

64 Kathleen M. Roe, "Private Troubles and Public Issues," *Social Science and Medicine*, Vol. 29, No. 10

65 F. J. Kane, M. Feldman, S. Jain, and M. A. Lipton, "Emotional Reactions in Abortion Services Personnel," *Archives of General Psychiatry*, Vol. 28, 1973

66 Magda Denes, *In Necessity and Sorrow*, New York: Basic Books, Inc., 1976

67 *The Philadelphia Inquirer*, 8/2/81

68 *Diagnostic and Statistical Manual of Mental Disorder*, Fourth Edition, American Psychiatric Association, 1994

69 Lt. Col. Dave Grossman, *On Killing*, Boston: Little, Brown, and Company, 1995

70 Ibid

71 Ibid

72 Howard D. Kibel, "Staff Reactions to Abortion," *Obstetrics and Gynecology*, Jan. 1972

73 Diane Gianelli, "Abortion Providers Share Inner Conflicts," *American Medical News*, 7/12/93

74 "Meet the Abortion Providers," videotape, Pro Life Action League, Chicago, 1989

75 Bernard Nathanson, M.D., *Aborting America*, Toronto: Life Cycle Books, 1979

76 Sallie Tisdale, "We Do Abortions Here," *Harper's Magazine*, October 1987

77 Richard K. Rein, "The War of the Roses," *New Jersey Monthly*, July 1979

78 Bruce Jancin, "Emotional Turmoil of Physicians, Staff Held Biggest D&E Problems," *ObGyn News*, 12/15/81–12/31/81

79 Warren Hern and Billie Corrigan, "What About Us? Staff Reactions to the D&E Procedure," presented at a meeting of the Associations of Planned Parenthood Physicians, San Diego, 10/26/78

80 Sallie Tisdale, "We Do Abortions Here," *Harper's Magazine*, October 1987

81 Interview with Joy Davis by Life Dynamics, 1993

82 "Meet the Abortion Providers III: The Promoters," audiotape, conference held by the Pro Life Action League, Chicago, 4/3/93

83 "Meet the Abortion Providers," videotape, Pro Life Action League, Chicago, 1989

84 Lt. Col. Dave Grossman, *On Killing*, Boston: Little, Brown, and Company, 1995

85 Christopher Browning, *Ordinary Men*, Harper Collins Publishers, Inc., 1992

86 Lt. Col. Dave Grossman, *On Killing*, Boston: Little, Brown, and Company, 1995

87 Interview with former employee of abortionist John Roe 328 by Rachel McNair, 3/10/92

88 *El Paso Times*, 4/5/81

89 National Abortion Federation conference, Cincinnati, Ohio, April 1994

90 "Meet the Abortion Providers III: The Promoters," audiotape, conference held by the Pro Life Action League, Chicago, 4/3/93

91 *Legal Times*, 5/24/93

92 Interview with Joy Davis by Life Dynamics, 1993

93 Don Sloan with Paula Hartz, *Abortion: A Doctor's Perspective/A Woman's Dilemma*, New York: Donald Fine, Inc., 1992

94 Sallie Tisdale, "We Do Abortions Here," *Harper's Magazine*, October 1987

95 Ginette Paris, *Pagan Meditations*, Dallas: Spring Publications, 1986

96 *Philadelphia Inquirer*, 8/2/81

97 *New York Times*, 4/29/84; *Des Moines Register*, 5/5/84; El Paso County (TX) Offense Report No. 00-380101; *El Paso Times*, 9/22/83, 4/5/81–4/8/81; *Dallas Morning News*, 4/20/84; *Dallas Times-Herald*, 9/29/83

98 Hamilton County (TN) Circuit Court Docket No. 92CV-1999

99 Interview with Joy Davis by Life Dynamics, 1993

100 Magda Denes, *In Necessity and Sorrow*, New York: Basic Books, Inc., 1976

101 "Meet the Abortion Providers III: The Promoters," audiotape, conference held by the Pro Life Action League, Chicago, 4/3/93

102 Christopher Browning, *Ordinary Men*, Harper Collins Publishers, Inc., 1992

103 *Los Angeles Times*, 2/11/82

104 Robert E. Hall, ed., *Abortion in a Changing World*, Columbia University Press, 1972

105 Warren M. Hern, *Abortion Practice*, Philadelphia: J. B. Lippincott Company, 1990

106 483 A.2d 718 (Me. 1984)

107 "Plan Your Children," Planned Parenthood, 1962

108 Naomi Wolf, "Our Bodies, Our Souls," *New Republic*, 10/16/95

109 *Democrat and Chronicle*, 7/5/92

110 *Dallas Observer*, 5/18/95–5/24/95

111 Diane Gianelli, "Abortion Providers Share Inner Conflicts," *American Medical News*, 7/12/93

112 "Warns of Negative Psychological Impact of Sonography in Abortion," *ObGyn News*, 2/15/86–2/28/86

113 Christopher Browning, *Ordinary Men*, Harper Collins Publishers, Inc., 1992

114 Magda Denes, *In Necessity and Sorrow*, New York: Basic Books, Inc., 1976

115 Ibid

116 Christopher Browning, *Ordinary Men*, Harper Collins Publishers, Inc., 1992

117 Magda Denes, *In Necessity and Sorrow*, New York: Basic Books, Inc., 1976

118 Ibid

119 Howard D. Kibel, "Staff Reactions to Abortion," *Obstetrics and Gynecology*, 1/72

120 F. J. Kane, M. Feldman, S. Jain, and M. A. Lipton, "Emotional Reactions in Abortion Services Personnel," *Archives of General Psychiatry*, Vol. 28, 1973

121 Diane Gianelli, "Abortion Providers Share Inner Conflicts," *American Medical News*, 7/12/93

122 Interview with Joy Davis by Life Dynamics, 1993

123 Magda Denes, *In Necessity and Sorrow*, Basic Books, Inc., New York: 1976

124 Fairfax County (VA) Circuit Court Case No. 133092; Washington, D.C. Superior Court, Action No. 91-CA-13039, "Deposition"; Fairfax County (VA) In Chancery No. 121765, 8/13/92

125 Fairfax County (VA) Circuit Court Case No. 133092; Northern Virginia Daily, 11/20/93

126 *Chicago Sun-Times*, "Abortion Profiteers Series," 11/12/78–12/3/78

127 *Sarasota Herald-Tribune*, 1/17/86

128 *Boston Globe*, 8/31/82

129 "Readers Respond," *Feminist Voices*, December 1988/January 1989

130 Arizona Board of Osteopathic Examiners, "Osteopathic Licensure Verification," 1/24/92

131 Interview with Luhra Tivis by Rachel McNair, audiotape, 1/19/94

132 *Chicago Sun-Times*, "Abortion Profiteers Series," 11/12/78–12/3/78

133 Hennepin County (MN) District Court File No. 89-15330

134 St. Louis (MO) Circuit Court Cause No. 792-2376

135 Magda Denes, *In Necessity and Sorrow*, New York: Basic Books, Inc., 1976

136 Tami J. Friedman, "Abortion Clinic Masks For-Profit Practice in Feminist Garb," *Feminist Voices*, September 1988

137 "Meet the Abortion Providers III: The Promoters," audiotape, conference held by the Pro Life Action League, Chicago, 4/3/93

138 *Miami Herald*, 10/7/89

139 *New York Times*, 10/6/82

140 Jefferson County (AL) Circuit Court Case No. CV-93-632; *New York Times*, 4/23/94; *Jackson Clarion-Ledger*, 4/1/95

141 *The Raleigh News and Observer*, 8/29/92

142 *New York Times*, 6/15/93; *New York Post*, 11/26/91; State of New York Administrative Review Board for Professional Medical Conduct, Case No. BPMC-92-13-A

143 *Chicago Sun-Times*, "Abortion Profiteers Series," 11/12/78–12/3/78

144 *New York Post*, 3/8/85; State of New York Board for Professional Medical Conduct, Case No. 4407, 9/6/85

145 *El Paso Times*, 4/7/81

146 *Miami Herald*, 9/17/89

147 *San Diego Union*, 10/12/80, 7/18/81; *Chicago Sun-Times*, "Abortion Profiteers Series," 11/12/78–12/3/78; *San Diego Union*, 10/13/80; *The North Jersey*, 12/22/89; *American Medical News*, 10/10/86; Transcript of *CBS This Morning*, 4/7/94

148 *Knoxville News-Sentinel*, 5/27/87

149 New Jersey Administrative Complaint, filed 10/3/89

150 *Los Angeles Times*, 1/31/93; California Consumer Complaint Form, 3/21/95; Medical Board of California Case No. D-5286; Jefferson County (KY) Circuit and District Court, ABO#22113, "Memorandum in Support of Findings"; Jefferson County (KY) Circuit and District Court, ARO-1 Reference Nos. 21451 & 22113, "Investigative Reports"; Richland County (SC) Fifth Judicial Court of Common Pleas, Case No. 95-CP; *Detroit Free Press*, 11/14/82; *Chicago Sun-Times* "Abortion Profiteers Series," 11/12/78–12/3/78; *Miami Herald*, 9/26/89; *Panama City News Herald*, 9/28/89

151 *Charlotte Observer*, 9/2/92

152 *Boca Raton News*, 10/23/92

153 Letter from John Roe 785 to the Colorado Medical Board, 6/15/92; David Iler, "Politics Suggested in Fetal-Disposal Issue," *Up the Creek*, 9/11/92; Arapahoe County (CO) District Court Case No. 90CV432, John Roe 473's deposition, 2/4/91

154 Oklahoma Medical Board Case No. 87-7-514; *USA Today*, 4/16/92

155 *Willmington News Journal*, 8/22/93, 12/15/93, 12/3/94, 12/4/94

156 Frederick Douglass, *The Life and Times of Frederick Douglass*; New Jersey: Citadel Press, 1983

157 Christopher Browning, *Ordinary Men*, Harper Collins Publishers, Inc, 1992

158 *Pensacola News Journal*, 8/24/93; *Fort Walton Beach Daily News*, 8/29/93

159 Suzanne Adelson, et al., "License to Kill?" *People*, 7/21/82

160 *Omaha World-Herald*, 8/11/92; Letter to the Nebraska Health Department, 6/21/94; *The Bellvue Leader*, 7/25/92

161 The University of the State of New York Case No. 4407, 2/4/86; Associated Press 12/14/89

162 *Chicago Sun-Times*, 11/6/79

163 *Miami Herald*, 9/17/89

164 *El Paso Times*, 4/7/81

165 Interview with Joy Davis by Life Dynamics, 1993

166 Ibid

167 Interview with former employee of abortionist John Roe 328 by Rachel McNair, 3/10/92

168 Kansas Medical Board Case Nos. 92-0073 and 92-00205; *Topeka Capital-Journal*, 6/13/93; United States District Court, District of Kansas, Case No. 84-20019-01, 5/15/84

169 *Fort Walton Beach Daily News*, 8/29/93

170 *Chicago Sun-Times*, "Abortion Profiteers Series," 11/12/78–12/3/78

171 *The Sunday Oklahoman*, 7/5/92

172 California Medical Board Case No. D-3825

173 Constance A. Nathanson and Marshall H. Becker, "The Influence of Physicians' Attitudes on Abortion Performance, Patient Management, and Professional Fees," *Family Planning Perspectives*, July/August, 1977

174 *Fort Walton Beach Daily News*, 8/29/93

Chapter 6

1 *Newsweek*, December 10, 1990

2 *Time*, January 14, 1991

3 M. Ewertz and S. W. Duffy, "Risk of Breast Cancer in Relation to Reproductive Factors in Denmark," *British Journal of Cancer*, Vol. 58 (1988); J. L. Kelsey; D. B. Fischer; R. K. Holford; V. A. LiVoisi; E. D. Mostow; I. S. Goldenberg; C. White, "Exogenous Estrogens and Other Factors in the Epidemiology of Breast Cancer," *Journal of the National Cancer Institute*, Vol. 67 (1981); J. L. Kelsey, "A Review of the Epidemiology of Human Breast Cancer," *Epidemiology Review*, Vol. 1 (1979)

4 J. Russo and I. Russo, "Susceptibility of the Mammary Gland to Carcinogenesis, II. Pregnancy Interruption as a Factor in Tumor Incidence," *American Journal of Pathology*, Vol. 100 (1980)

5 N. Krieger, "Social Class and the Black/White Crossover in the Age-Specific Incidence of Breast Cancer: A Study Linking Census-Derived Data to Population-Based Registry Records," *American Journal of Epidemiology*, Vol. 131 (1990)

6 M. Segi; I. Fukushima; M. Kurihara, "An Epidemiological Study of Cancer in Japan," *GANN*, Vol. 48 (1957)

7 H. L. Stewart and L. J. Dunham, "Epidemiology of Cancer of the Uterine Cervix and Corpus, Breast and Ovary in Israel and New York City," *Journal of the National Cancer Institute*, Vol. 37 (1966)

8 S. Yuasa and B. MacMahon, "Lactation and Reproductive Histories of Breast-Cancer Patients in Tokyo, Japan," *Bulletin of the World Health Organization*, Vol. 42 (1970)

9 T. M. Lin; K. P. Chen; B. MacMahon, "Epidemiologic Characteristics of Cancer of the Breast in Taiwan," *Cancer*, Vol. 27 (1970)

10 P. Mirra; P. Cole; B. MacMahon, "Breast Cancer in an Area of High Parity," *Cancer Resources*, Vol. 31 (1971); *Cancer Incidence in Sweden 1971–1984*, Stockholm: National Board of Health and Welfare (1987)

11 K. Stavarky and S. Emmons, "Breast Cancer in Pre-Menopausal and Post-Menopausal Women," *Journal of the National Cancer Institute*, Vol. 53 (1974)

12 I. Soini, "Risk Factors of Breast Cancer in Finland," *International Journal of Epidemiology*, Vol. 6 (1977)

13 N. W. Choi; G. R. Howe; A. B. Miller; V. Matthews; R. W. Morgan; L. Munan; J. D. Burch; J. Feather; M. Jain; A. Kelly, "An Epidemiologic Study of Breast Cancer," *American Journal of Epidemiology*, Vol. 107 (1978)

14 V. V. Dvoirin and A. B. Medvedev, "The Role of Reproductive History in Breast Cancer Causation," *Methods and Results of Studies of Breast Cancer Epidemiology*, Tallinn, Estonia (in Russian) (1978)

15 J. L. Kelsey, "A Review of the Epidemiology of Human Breast Cancer," *Epidemiology Review*, Vol. 1 (1979)

16 M. C. Pike; B. E. Henderson; J. T. Casagrande; I. Rosario; G. E. Gray, "Oral Contraceptive Use and Early Abortion as Risk Factors for Breast Cancer in Young Women," *British Journal of Cancer*, Vol. 43 (1981)

17 L. A. Brinton; R. Hoover; J. F. Fraumeni, Jr., "Reproductive Factors in the Aetiology of Breast Cancer," *British Journal of Cancer*, Vol. 47 (1983)

18 H. E. Ownby; S. Martino; L. D. Roi; L. Howard; J. Russo; S. Brooks; M. J. Brennan, "Interrupted Pregnancy as One Indicator of Poor Prognosis in T1, T2, No, Mo Primary Breast Cancer," *Breast Cancer Resources and Treatment*, Vol. 3 (1983)

19 T. Hirohata, T. Shigematsu, A. M. Y. Nomura, "Occurrence of Breast Cancer in Relation to Diet and Reproductive History: A Case-Control Study in Fukuoka, Japan," *National Cancer Institute*, Vol. 69 (1985)

20 O. C. Hadjimichael; C. A. Boyle J. W. Meigs, "Abortion Before First Live Birth and Risk of Breast Cancer," *British Journal of Cancer*, Vol. 53 (1986)

21 C. LaVecchia; A. Decarli, F. Parazzini, A. Gentile, E. Negri, G. Cecchetti; S. Franceschi, "General Epidemiology of Breast Cancer in Northern Italy," *International Journal of Epidemiology*, Vol. 16 (1987)

22 M. Ewertz; S. W. Duffy, "Risk of Breast Cancer in Relation to Reproductive Factors in Denmark," *British Journal of Cancer*, Vol. 58 (1988)

23 J. M. Yuan; M. C. Yu; R. K. Ross; "Risk Factors for Breast Cancer in Chinese Women in Shanghai," *Cancer Resources*, Vol. 48 (1988)

24 R. M. Clark and T. Chua, "Breast Cancer and Pregnancy: The Ultimate Challenge," *Clinical Oncology of the Royal College of Radiology*, Vol. 1 (1989)

25 H. L. Howe; R. T. Senie; H. Bzduch; P. Herzfeld, "Early Abortion and Breast-Cancer Risk Among Women Under 40," *International Journal of Epidemiology*, Vol. 18 (1989)

26 B. M. Lindefors-Harris; G. Edlund; O. Meirik; L. E. Rutqvist; K. Wiklund, "Risk of Cancer of the Breast After Legal Abortion During First Trimester: A Swedish Register Study," *British Medical Journal*, Vol. 299 (1989)

27 H. Olsson; J. Ranstam; B. Baldetorp; S. B. Ewers; M. Ferno; D. Killander; H. Sigurdsson, "Proliferation and DNA Ploidy in Malignant Breast Tumors in Relation to Early Oral Contraceptive Use and Early Abortions," *Cancer*, Vol. 67 (1991)

28 H. Olsson; A. Borg; M. Ferno; J. Ranstam; H. Sigurdsson, "Her-2/neu and INT2 Proto-Oncogene Amplification in Malignant Breast Tumors in Relation to Reproductive Factors and Exposure to Exogenous Hormones," *Journal of the National Cancer Institute*, Vol. 83 (1991)

29 F. Parazzini; C. La Vecchia; E. Negri, "Spontaneous and Induced Abortions and Risk of Breast Cancer," *International Journal of Cancer*, Vol. 48 (1991)

30 R. M. Clark and T. Chua, "Breast Cancer and Pregnancy: The Ultimate Challenge," *Clinical Oncology, The Royal College of Radiology*, Vol. 1 (1989)

31 H. Shimizu; R. K. Ross; L. Bernstein; R. Yatani; B. E. Henderson; T. M. Mack, "Cancers of the Prostate and Breast Among Japanese and White Immigrants in Los Angeles County," *British Journal of Cancer*, Vol. 63 (1991)

32 M. Makita and J. Sakamoto, "Natural History of Breast Cancer Among Japanese and Caucasian Females," *Gan To Kagaku Ryoho, Japanese Journal of Cancer and Chemotherapy*, Vol. 17 (In Japanese) (1990)

33 M. S. Simon; E. McKnight; A. Schwartz; S. Martino; G. M. Swanson, "Racial Differences in Cancer of the Male Breast—15 Year Experience in the Detroit Metropolitan Area," *Breast Cancer Research and Treatment*, Vol. 21 (1992)

34 C. P. Hunter; C. K. Redmond; V. W. Chen; et al., "Breast Cancer: Factors Associated With Stage at Diagnosis in Black and White Women. Black/White Cancer Survival Study Group," *Journal of the National Cancer Institute*, Vol. 85 (1993); J. M. Liff; J. F. Sung; W. H. Chow; R. S. Greenberg; W. D. Flanders, "Does Increased Detection Account for the Rising Incidence of Breast Cancer?" *American Journal of Public Health*, Vol. 81 (1991)

35 L. I. Remennick, "Reproductive Patterns and Cancer Incidence in Women: A Population-Based Correlation Study in the USSR," *International Journal of Epidemiology*, Vol. 18 (1989)

36 E. Marshall, "Search for a Killer: Focus Shifts from Fat to Hormones," *Science*, Vol. 259 (1993)

37 N. W. Choi; G. R. Howe; A. B. Miller; V. Matthews; R. W. Morgan; L. Munan; J. D. Burch; J. Feather; M. Jain; A. Kelly, "An Epidemiologic Study of Breast Cancer," *American Journal of Epidemiology*, Vol. 107 (1978); S. S. Devesa and E. L. Diamond, "Association of Breast Cancer and Cervical Cancer Incidence with Income and Education Among Whites and Blacks," *Journal of the National Cancer Institute*, Vol. 65 (1980); J. L. Kelsey; D. B. Fischer; R. K. Holford; V. A. LiVoisi; E. D. Mostow; I. S. Goldenberg; C. White, "Exogenous Estrogens and Other Factors in the Epidemiology of Breast Cancer," *Journal of the National Cancer Institute*, Vol. 67 (1981); J. L. Kelsey and N. G. Hildreth, *Breast and Gynecological Cancer Epidemiology*, Boca Raton, FL: CRC Press (1985); C. Lowe and B. MacMahon, "Breast Cancer and Reproductive History of Women in South Wales," *The Lancet*, Vol. 1 (1970)

38 W. Cates, Jr., "Legal Abortion: The Public Health Record," *Science*, Vol. 215 (1982)

39 T. M. Lin; K. P. Chen; B. MacMahon, "Epidemiologic Characteristics of Cancer of the Breast in Taiwan," *Cancer*, Vol. 27 (1970)

40 E. White; J. Daling; T. L. Norsted; J. Chu, "Rising Incidence of Breast Cancer Among Young Women in Washington State," *Journal of the National Cancer Institute*, Vol. 79 (1987)

41 N. Krieger, "Social Class and the Black/White Crossover in the Age-Specific Incidence of Breast Cancer: A Study Linking Census-Derived Data to Population-Based Registry Records," *American Journal of Epidemiology*, Vol. 131 (1990)

42 C. H. Rubin; C. A. Burnett; W. E. Halperin; P. J. Seligman, "Occupation as a Risk Identifier for Breast Cancer," *American Journal of Public Health*, Vol. 83 (1993)

43 *Planned Parenthood v. Casey*, 1992

44 L. I. Remennick, "Induced Abortion as Cancer Risk Factor: A Review of the Epidemiological Evidence," *Journal of Epidemiology and Community Health*, Vol. 44 (1990)

45 W. Cates, Jr., "Legal Abortion: The Public Health Record," *Science*, Vol. 215 (1982)

46 K. Stavraky and S. Emmons, "Breast Cancer in Pre-Menopausal and Post-Menopausal Women," *Journal of the National Cancer Institute*, (1974); O. C. Hadjimichael; C. A. Boyle; J. W. Meigs, "Abortion Before First Live Birth and Risk of Breast Cancer," *British Journal of Cancer*, Vol. 53 (1986); B. M. Lindefors-Harris; G. Edlund; O. Mierik; L. E. Rutqvist; K. Wiklund, "Risk of Cancer of the Breast During First Trimester: A Swedish Register Study," *British Medical Journal*, Vol. 299 (1989); C. La Vecchia; A. Decarli; F. Parazzini; A. Gentile; E. Negri; G. Cecchetti; S. Franceschi, "General Epidemiology of Breast Cancer in Northern Italy," *International Journal of Epidemiology*, Vol. 16 (1987); F. Parazzini; C. La Vecchia; E. Negri, "Spontaneous and Induced Abortions and Risk of Breast Cancer," *International Journal of Cancer*, Vol. 48 (1991)

47 H. Olsson; J. Ranstam; B. Baldetorp; S. B. Ewers; M. Ferno; D. Killander; H. Sigurdsson, "Proliferation and DNA Ploidy in Malignant Breast Tumors in Relation to Oral Contraceptive Use and Early Abortions," *Cancer*, Vol. 67 (1991); H. Olsson; A. Borg; M. Ferno; J. Ranstam; H. Sigurdsson, "Her-2/neu and INT2 Proto-Oncogene Amplification in Malignant Breast Tumors in Relation to Reproductive Factors and Exposure to Exogenous Hormones," *Journal of the National Cancer Institute*, Vol. 83 (1991); R. M. Clark and T. Chua, "Breast Cancer and Pregnancy: the Ultimate Challenge," *Clinical Oncology, The Royal College of Radiology*, Vol. 1 (1989); H. E. Ownby; S. Martino; L. D. Roi; L. Howard; J. Russo; S. Brooks; M. J. Brennan, "Interrupted Pregnancy as One Indicator of Poor Prognosis in T1, T2, No, Mo, Primary Breast Cancer," *Breast Cancer Research and Treatment*, Vol. 3 (1983)

48 H. E. Ownby; S. Martino; L. D. Roi; L. Howard; J. Russo; S. Brooks; M. J. Brennan, "Interrupted Pregnancy as One Indicator of Poor Prognosis in T1, T2, No, Mo Primary Breast Cancer," *Breast Cancer Research and Treatment*, Vol. 3 (1983)

49 W. Cates, Jr., "Legal Abortion: The Public Health Record," *Science*, Vol. 214 (1982)

50 B. M. Lindefors-Harris; G. Edlund; O. Meirik; L. E. Rutqvist; K. Wiklund, "Risk of Cancer of the Breast After Legal Abortion During the First Trimester: A Swedish Register Study," *British Medical Journal*, Vol. 299 (1989)

51 J. R. Daling; K. E. Malone; L. F. Voigt; E. White; N. S. Weiss, "Risk of Breast Cancer Among Young Women: Relationship to Induced Abortion," *Journal of the National Cancer Institute*, Vol. 86 (1994)

52 S. P. Helmrich; S. Shapiro; L. Rosenberg; D. W. Kaufman; D. Slone; C. Bain; O. S. Miettinen; P. D. Stolley; N. B. Rosenshein; R. C. Knapp; T. Leavitt, Jr.; D. Schottenfeld; R. L. Engle, Jr.; M. Levy, "Risk Factors for Breast Cancer" *American Journal of Epidemiology*, Vol. 117 (1983); R. S. Paffenbarger, Jr.; J. B. Kampert; H. G. Chang, "Characteristics that Predict Breast Cancer Before and After the Menopause," *American Journal of Epidemiology*, Vol. 112 (1980); G. Kvale; J. Heuch; G. F. Eide, "A Prospective Study of Reproductive Factors and Breast Cancer: I. Parity," *American Journal of Epidemiology*, Vol. 126 (1987); B. M. Lindefors-Harris; G. Edlund; O. Meirik; L. E. Rutqvist; K. Wiklund, "Risk of Cancer of the Breast After Legal Abortion During First Trimester: A Swedish Register Study," *British Medical Journal*, Vol. 299 (1989)

53 H. O. Adami; R. Bergstrom; E. Lund; O. Meirik, "Absence of Association Between Reproductive Variables and the Risk of Breast Cancer in Young Women in Sweden and Norway," *British*

Journal of Cancer, Vol. 62 (1990); L. A. Brinton; R. Hoover; J. F. Fraumeni, Jr., "Reproductive Factors in the Aetiology of Breast Cancer," *British Journal of Cancer*, Vol. 47 (1983)

54 H. O. Adami; R. Bergstrom; E. Lund; O. Meirik, "Absence of Association Between Reproductive Variables and the Risk of Breast Cancer in Young Women in Sweden and Norway," *British Journal of Cancer*, Vol. 62 (1990)

55 L. A. Brinton; R. Hoover; J. F. Fraumeni, Jr., "Reproductive Factors in the Aetiology of Breast Cancer," *British Journal of Cancer*, Vol. 47 (1983)

56 S. P. Helmrich; S. Shapiro; L. Rosenberg; D. W. Kaufman; D. Slone; C. Bain; O. S. Miettinen; P. D. Stolley; N. B. Rosenshein; R. C. Knapp; T. Leavitt, Jr.; D. Schottenfeld; R. L. Engle, Jr.; M. Levy, "Risk Factors for Breast Cancer," *American Journal of Epidemiology*, Vol. 117 (1983)

57 N. Mantel and W. Haenszel, "Statistical Aspects of the Analysis of Data from Retrospective Studies of Disease," *Journal of the National Cancer Institute*, Vol. 22 (1959)

58 H. L. Howe; R. T. Senie; H. Bzduch; P. Herzfeld, "Early Abortion and Breast-Cancer Risk Among Women Under 40," *International Journal of Epidemiology*, Vol. 18 (1989)

59 NBC *Dateline*, November 1, 1994

Chapter 7

1 *Roe v. Wade*, 410 US. at 166

2 A. Bonavoglia, *The Choices We Made*, Random House, 1991

3 *Findings of the Comprehensive Legal Needs Study*, American Bar Association, 1994

4 *The New York Times*, July 1993

5 *The Miami Herald*, 9/17/89

6 Frank M. McClellan, *Medical Malpractice Law, Tactics, and Ethics*

7 National Center for State Courts, 1992

8 "Report of the Secretary's Commission on Medical Malpractice," Department of Health, Education and Welfare, 1/16/73

9 CBS News, *Eye on America*, 12/1/93

10 *Greenbrook v. Heckler*, 592 F. Supp. 1311, 1312 (D.D.C. 1984)

11 Radberg and Hamberger, *Chlamydia Trachomatis in Relation to Infections Following First Trimester Abortions*, Acta Obstricia Gynecological (Supp 1993)154:478 (1980)

12 D. Reardon, *Aborted Women: Silent No More*, Chicago: Loyola University Press, 1987 (One of the negative outcomes in postabortive women included the delayed onset of stress with 62 percent reporting experience of their worst reactions one year or more postabortion.)

13 Vincent M. Rue, Ph.D, "Postabortion Trauma—Controversy, Diagnosis and Defense," Life Dynamics Inc.

14 51 Am Jur 2d 146

15 4 Am Jur Trials 35

16 *Mary D. v. John D.*, (1989, 6th Dist.) 216 CAL App 3d 285, 264 Cal Pptr 633, review gr 268 Cal Rptr 283, 788 P2d 1155, & rev. dism, cause remanded, 275 Cal Rptr 380, 800 P2d 858, *Hoult v. Hoult*, 792 F Supp 143

17 Delaware, Indiana, New Mexico, South Dakota

18 Paul C. Weiler, *Medical Malpractice on Trial*, 1991

19 *Standards for Abortion Care*, National Abortion Federation, 1986

20 *Standards for Obstetric-Gynecologic Services*, American College of Obstetricians and Gynecologists (ACOG), 1985

21 "Abortion Services in Planned Parenthood Affiliates," *Abortion Standards and Guidelines*, Planned Parenthood Federation of America (PPFA), 1977

22 Warren M. Hern, *Abortion Practice*, Boulder, CO: Apenglo, 1990

23 Paul C. Weiler, *Medical Malpractice on Trial*, 1991

24 Ibid

25 Harvey F. Wachsman, M.D., J.D. and Steven Alschuler, *Lethal Medicine: The Epidemic of Medical Malpractice In America*

26 G. Wilmoth, "Abortion, Public Health Policy, and Informed Consent Legislation," *Journal of Social Issues*, Vol. 48 (1992)

27 *The Dallas Morning News*, 2/12/95

28 *The Wall Street Journal*, 10/28/94

29 *Planned Parenthood v. Casey*, 112 S. CT. at 2823

30 Harvey F. Wachsman, MD., J.D. and Steven Alschuler, *Lethal Medicine: The Epidemic of Medical Malpractice in America*

31 Paul C. Weiler, Howard H. Hiatt, Joseph P. Newhouse, William G. Johnson, Troyen A. Brennan, Lucian L. Leape, *A Measure of Malpractice (Medical Injury, Malpractice Litigation and Patient Compensation)*, 1993

32 Harvey F. Wachsman, MD., J.D. and Steven Alschuler, *Lethal Medicine: The Epidemic of Medical Malpractice in America*

33 *The Indianapolis Star*, 6/26/90; *Roe v. Wade*, 410 U.S. at 166

Chapter 8

1 Warren M. Hern, *Abortion Practice*, Boulder, CO: Apenglo, 1990

2 ABC News, *Nightline*, 2/20/95

3 CBS News, *Eye on America*, 12/1/93

4 Kenneth F. Schulz, David A. Grimes, Willard Cates, Jr., "Measures to Prevent Cervical Injury During Suction Curettage Abortion," *The Lancet*, 5/28/83

5 Colorado Board of Medical Examiners Case No. ME 86-07

Index

THE SONGS OF FRANK E. TOURS

1251-1

THE SONGS OF FRANK E. TOURS

Edited by Eric Davis and Brian Thorsett

Studio for the Early American Musical
San Francisco, California

Published by Studio for the Early American Musical
1849 Geary Blvd.
P.O. Box 15643
San Francisco, CA 94115-9991

Produced by A-R Editions, Inc., Middleton, Wisconsin
Printed in the United States of America

ISBN 978-0-578-34285-6

Cover: Frank E. Tours, ca. 1920.
Frontispiece: Frank E. Tours, ca. 1934.

Photograph of *The Great Waltz* reproduced by permission of
The New York Public Library. All other photographs reproduced
by permission of the family of Frank E. Tours. The sheet music for
"West of the Sun" is reproduced by permission of Peter Simek.

Publisher's Cataloging-In-Publication Data
(Prepared by The Donohue Group, Inc.)

Names: Tours, Frank E., 1877-1963, composer. | Davis, Eric, 1966-
     editor. | Thorsett, Brian, editor.
Title: The songs of Frank E. Tours / edited by Eric Davis and Brian
     Thorsett.
Description: San Francisco, California : Studio for the Early American
     Music, [2022] | Includes bibliographical references.
Identifiers: ISBN 9780578342856
Subjects: LCSH: Tours, Frank E., 1877-1963. | Composers--England--
     Biography. | Conductors (Music)--England--Biography. | Musicals--
     Excerpts--Vocal scores with piano. | Ballads. | LCGFT: Biographies.
     | Excerpts. | Songs.
Classification: LCC ML410.T6848 T68 2022 | DDC
     782.42164092--dc23

This book is dedicated to the family of Frank E. Tours

CONTENTS

ACKNOWLEDGMENTS

This book was made possible by the invaluable support and assistance of many people to whom we would like to express our thanks. More than any single person, we are indebted to Jack Bethards, who has been our guiding light on this project throughout its many stages. Jack grew up visiting his uncle Frank and hearing him play the piano and talk about his career in the entertainment industry. It was his vision and generosity that brought this work into being, and his steadfast and patient belief in us has been both a reassurance and an inspiration. We also owe our deep and abiding appreciation to other members of the Tours family, whose stewardship of Frank's musical legacy has made this book possible. During the course of this project, we have been fortunate to get to know two of Frank's children, Joan and Elliott, who have carried the torch for their father's legacy the longest, and who deserve much of our gratitude for their steadfast faith in the value of his work. Among the next generation, Joey and Jill Townsend were wholeheartedly enthusiastic about this project from the beginning, and their warmth and friendship over the years has been a rare delight. The trust that they and Peter and Jan Simek have given to us in loaning their heirloom Tours sheet music volumes and photographs has been a treasured gift of which we are all the beneficiaries. In addition, Peter's generosity and support in granting us copyright permission to use the sheet music for this volume has been an essential component in making all of Frank Tours' music available to the public. Our research was aided enormously by Christina Tours Royston, who gave us access to Frank's scrapbooks, which are a magnificent tapestry of unique photographs and rare newspaper articles documenting his life and career. We are equally grateful to John Emerson, who has been gracious and painstaking in sharing his knowledge of Tours family history, information, and lore. Without his kind and unstinting assistance, the biography would have lacked many important details that animate the early and late passages of Frank's story. He also provided us with many rare photographs that have enriched the book immensely.

We were assisted in our research by many people that made this book much better than it would have been otherwise. In gathering information on Tours' music and training, we wish to thank Jeffrey Smith, Isabelle Demers, Peter Mintun, Vince Giordano, and staff members at the music libraries of UCLA, Baylor University, The Royal College of Music, and The British Library. In the preparation of this book for publication, we were very fortunate to have the collaborative guidance and editorial acumen of A-R Editions, who have believed in the value of this book from the beginning and have brought their expertise, stewardship, and caring to this project. The creation of the facsimile involved image capture and consultation from several people whose technical advice and craftsmanship is greatly appreciated, including George Helfand (Luna Imaging), Michael Adamo (Virginia Tech), Nathan Hall (Virginia Tech), Lindsay Brown, Andrew Justice, and Louise Smith. We are particularly grateful for the editorial assistance we received from Thomas Riis, Miles Kreuger, Corey Jamason, and Jack Bethards, whose close readings of our text were invaluable for their insights and careful attention to detail. Our effort to revive interest in the performance of Frank Tours' songs have benefitted enormously from musical collaborations with John Churchwell, Eric Choate, and Richard Masters. The editors are grateful beyond measure to their spouses, Rachel Lopez and Amy Cowan, and to their families for their unfailing support, patience, and enthusiasm throughout this project, without which we would not have come this far.

FRANK E. TOURS: A LIFE IN MUSIC

by Eric Davis

Frank E. Tours was a musician whose career embraced the distinct, but related worlds of classical and popular music in the early twentieth century. As a music director in London, he brought his training at the Royal College of Music to George Edwardes' musical comedies with scores by Lionel Monckton, Paul Rubens, and Ivan Caryll. And when he migrated permanently to the United States in 1910, he brought his skill and experience to musicals by Irving Berlin, Jerome Kern, and Cole Porter on Broadway, shows that helped to define an emerging American musical identity in popular music. As a composer, though, he took a different path, one where he remained faithful to his upbringing in a multi-generational musical family and to his education as the student of the finest composition teacher of his generation in England. Though he occasionally wrote the scores for musical comedies early in his career and later for films, Tours was a dedicated and accomplished composer of songs for voice and piano. Throughout his career as a music director, he constantly returned to the genre as an outlet for his creative energies, setting more than seventy poems over a thirty-year period, while most of his evenings were spent in the orchestral pits of London's West End and Broadway.

In retrospect, it might seem inevitable that at least one of the children of Berthold Tours would have made a career in music. As the chief editor at Novello, Ewer & Company, one of London's finest music publishing houses, Frank's father became a well-known and respected figure in British musical circles of the Victorian Era.[1] In fact, the Tours family saw professional musicians rise to prominence among them for several generations before Frank developed his own distinguished career in the theatre. The family name was acquired when Antoine, whom family lore maintains was probably a farmer from Tours, France, resettled first in Geneva and took the surname La Tour.[2]

He later moved to Rotterdam in the mid-eighteenth century where he simply went by the name Antoine Tours, thus distinguishing himself from many other Latours in the region. His son, Jacob, who was Dutch by birth, became the first in the Tours lineage to become a distinguished musician, when he became both the principal organist of Rotterdam's *Groot Kerk* ("Great Church") and a composer of liturgical music, as was the custom of the day. Before assuming this esteemed position, he was an organist in Maassluis, a city in the southwest province of the Netherlands, and later at the church of the Remonstrants in Rotterdam. Jacob's son, Bartholomeus, who was born in 1797 in Rotterdam, was a violinist of high regard within his region, as demonstrated by the fact that he received a gift of jewels from the Queen of Württemberg in the 1840s when he played for her at Bad Kissingen. In addition to being a fine organist, who followed his father into his post at the *Groot Kerk*, a position he kept with distinction until his death 34 years later, Bartholomeus helped to establish the musical society Eruditis Musica in Rotterdam. During this time, he also oversaw the building of a new organ, which was Holland's largest instrument of its kind until it was destroyed in a German air attack in 1940. The Tours name subsequently became associated through marriage to one of Germany's leading musical families when Bartholomeus' daughter, Jeanne Hermine, wedded the composer Woldemar Bargiel, who was the half-brother of Clara Wieck-Schumann. Indeed, Frank Tours recalled family members during his youth in the 1880s speaking of Robert Schumann as "Uncle Bobby."[3]

Bartholomeus' son Berthold (also named Bartholomeus, who then took a new name when he immigrated to England) was similarly surrounded by music at a young age and received his first training from his father. After continuing his studies in organ, violin, and musical composition in Leipzig, and then taking a brief position with Prince Yuri Golitsyn in Russia, Berthold settled in London, where he would establish his career and spend the rest of his life. His quiet industriousness made him a

---

[1] *The Musical Times and Singing Class Circular*, Vol. 38, No. 650, April 1, 1897, 238–39; *The Etude*, Vol. XV, No. 12, December, 1897, 318.

[2] J. T. Anema and O. Schutte, *Nederlandse Genealogieën, Deel 10* (Koninklijk Nederlandsch Genootschap Voor Geslacht- en Wapenkunde 'S-Gravenhage, 1993), 331–63, December, 1897, 318; The International Magazine, No. 1, March, 1885, 66; The Strand Magazine: An Illustrated Monthly, edited by George Newnes, Vol. IV, July to December, 1892, 87-89.

---

[3] Many details of the Tours family lore were conveyed to me by John Francis Emerson, one of Frank Tours' grandchildren.

prolific composer, whose catalogue includes 125 songs for voice and piano, 50 sacred vocal works, and over 90 instrumental works for piano solo, piano four-hands, and various chamber ensembles. An appreciation in *The Etude* referred to Berthold Tours' compositions as being "characterized by refinement of melody, originality of harmonization, and admirable workmanship generally."[4] His instrumental tutor *The Violin*, published by Novello, was widely in use, having sold more than seventy-five thousand copies during his lifetime. During the 1870s and 1880s, he welcomed visits by many esteemed musicians and was highly regarded for his editorial acumen by England's leading composers, whom he encountered through his work.[5] His leading position at Novello enabled him to purchase a house of eleven rooms in the Hammersmith district of London and to employ two servants that gave Frank's mother time to attend to his and his four brothers' education and upbringing (their only sister had died in her youth). Some of the brothers studied organ with their father, but it was Frank who showed early signs of having a prodigious musical talent, as he became the organist at St. John's Church in Hammersmith when he was fourteen.

Frank's dedication to music along with his natural ability at the piano and organ led him to pursue professional training at the Royal College of Music. The RCM was a relatively new institution when Frank applied in 1893, having been established by Sir George Grove a little more than ten years earlier, when the Royal Academy of Music was already sixty years old.[6] The school was founded with the mission to offer educational opportunities of the highest order, with support from the Royal family, to qualified music students irrespective of their social circumstances. Since he did not need a scholarship, Frank's reasons for choosing the Royal College lay in its outstanding faculty and location in nearby South Kensington. When he began his studies, the RCM employed several of the best musicians in England, including Charles Villiers Stanford (composition), Hubert Parry (composition), Franklin Taylor (piano), Walter Parratt (organ), Jenny Lind (voice),

and J. Frederick Bridge (organ). This distinguished roster of teachers attracted the likes of Gustav Holst, Ralph Vaughan Williams, Samuel Coleridge-Taylor, John Ireland, Frank Bridge and many other talented and ambitious young musicians who would surpass their professors in acclaim and compel the musical world to recognize a distinguished English school of composition in the twentieth century. Frank declared the piano as his principal area of study during his first term, but then changed it to organ two years later.[7] This was most likely a practical decision, given the high demand for church musicians in England and the fact that his technical ability at the piano was not that of a virtuoso. He declared at this time that his secondary area would include composition, perhaps encouraged by Charles Stanford with whom he was studying.[8] Since both Stanford and his organ teacher Frederick Bridge were also accomplished conductors, they must have both played a central role in Frank's eventual decision to become a music director, although his records do not indicate that he studied conducting formally at school.

Having entered the RCM at an early age, Frank took his examinations, which occurred in the spring of 1896, when he was still eighteen. Although he could have settled into a comfortable profession as a church musician at that time, he hoped to pursue further training in composition at the Leipzig Conservatory, as both Stanford and his father had done. His fortunes would change over the course of the next year, though, in a way that determined his future career. During the first Christmas holiday after leaving music school, he accepted a brief stint as the music director for the pantomime *Robinson Crusoe* in Ireland. A few months later, Stanford asked him to conduct his comic opera *Shamus O'Brien* on its second national tour.[9] At first, he hoped it would merely be a summer position to keep him occupied before heading to Germany. However, his father's death on March 11, 1897, occurred within days of his taking the job, forcing him to accept Stanford's offer to lead the production through October.[10] As a result, Frank turned to conducting in the theatre as a reliable occupation in which he was regularly employed over the next fifty years.

Just as vaudeville and burlesque circuits were a training ground for aspiring performers in America during the early twentieth century, pantomime offered British performers similar opportunities to hone their theatrical

[4] *The Etude*, December 1897, 318.

[5] Novello, Ewer & Co. published music by many of the finest living musicians in England, including John Stainer, Arthur Sullivan, Charles Stanford, Hubert Parry, and many others. For more information, see *The Complete Catalogue of Novello, Ewer & Co.* (London: Novello, Ewer & Co., 1890). Elgar submitted his cantata *The Black Knight* to Novello in 1892 and was encouraged by their response, even though Berthold Tours had told him that the piano part was too difficult for the average choral accompanist. His response was to make the necessary changes: "Since my interview with Mr. Tours on Wednesday last I have most carefully gone through the P. F. accompaniment of the above-named Cantata & have removed all the difficulties which he was so kind as to point out." Jerrold Northrop Moore, *Edward Elgar: A Creative Life* (Oxford: Oxford University Press, 1984), 166.

[6] Jeremy Dibble, *Charles Villiers Stanford* (New York: Oxford University Press, 2002), 133.

[7] Frank's matriculation sheet is housed at the RCM Archive: *RCM Student Register*, Vol. 3, 1889-1894, 1035.

[8] *Baker's Biographical Dictionary of Musicians*, revised and enlarged by Alfred Remy (New York: G. Schirmer, 1919), 959.

[9] Frank Tours compiled a list of his jobs as a musical director that he called "Fifty Years with my Back to the Audience" from which much of the basic information about his career for this essay was drawn.

[10] "Berthold Tours," *Grove's Dictionary of Music and Musicians*, Vol. V (New York: Macmillan, 1945), 366.

craft. After getting his first taste of professional life as a music director during the year after his graduation, Tours continued to accept jobs with itinerant and seasonal companies. At Christmas time during the next several years, he conducted *Robinson Crusoe* and *Cinderella* in Aberdeen, Dundee, Brighton, Manchester, and Liverpool. He was also increasingly hired at this time to conduct the tours of British musical theatre productions that had already made a hit in London. In 1898, he was the music director for the *The A.B.C.; or, Flossie the Frivolous*, featuring Music Hall star Marie Lloyd playing the role of a waitress in her only musical play. The music for the show was by "Graban" as was the music for *Sweet Brier*, a musical play in three acts by Herbert Shelley that Tours took up the baton for later that year.[11] Eventually Frank came to the attention of musical-comedy impresario George Edwardes through one of his scouts. Ever since the concurrent successes of *A Gaiety Girl* and *The Shop Girl* in 1894, Edwardes had dominated British musical theatre with his up-to-date shows that combined attractive singing actors, charming light music, and scenarios with a keen eye for modern style and sensibility.[12] When Edwardes met the nineteen-year-old Tours in London, he was prepared to give him an assignment as a music director based upon his stellar reputation, but was concerned that his youthful features would not inspire confidence in his orchestral musicians, especially on a long and exhausting tour. Instead he told the young conductor to return when he had grown a large walrus mustache that would hide his boyish appearance behind an imposing display of facial hair.[13]

Once he had acquired the necessary lip accessory, Frank was sent on the English tours of a succession of Edwardes' Gaiety Theatre hits—*A Greek Slave* (1900), *San Toy* (1901), *A Country Girl* (1902), and *Three Little Maids* (1903). In 1901, having established himself as a music director for touring shows in the United Kingdom, he turned once again to composition; but instead of working with the classical forms he had learned at home and in school, Tours began to compose for the theatre, a natural development that demonstrated his growing commitment to the field. The property he selected for his first effort was *The Lady of Lyons*, a venerable, but, according to *The Sketch*, "old and somewhat time-worn Love-*versus*-Pride drama" by Edward Bulwer-Lytton.[14] Presented to the public as *Melnotte: or The Gardiner's Bride*, the musical version of the play was designed as a comic opera with choruses amidst the individual solo and duet numbers. Frank had known librettist Herbert Shelley from his recent tour of *Sweet Brier*, which had originally opened at the Lyric Theatre in Hammersmith near the Tours family home. The production of *Melnotte* did not succeed, never having made it out of the Coronet Theatre in nearby Notting Hill, where it was given a tryout. Local critics seemed to think that Tours' music was not primarily at fault for the opera's lack of success, writing that the music was "tuneful and pleasing, and gives evidence of artistic earnestness of purpose."[15] Despite the lack of enthusiasm for the project displayed by *The Musical Times*, the journal made a point of singling Tours out as a promising young composer. He could thus take both the experience and encouragement with him into later theatrical ventures while continuing to earn his bread and butter from conducting.

Tours' clout within the Edwardes organization had risen by 1903 to the extent that he was asked to conduct Paul Rubens' *Three Little Maids* at Daly's Theatre in London, in addition to his usual work touring the provinces. And when the impresario forged a plan to expand his empire abroad and send a company around the world, he entrusted Tours with the job of musical director for the ambitious enterprise, which traveled to North America and Australia and lasted sixty-five weeks.[16] Following two weeks of rehearsal in New York, the show opened at Daly's Theatre on Broadway near 30th Street on September 1 to excellent reviews. *The New York Times* critic effused later that night in his appraisal: "It is just possible that there have been better musical comedies… but, if there have, nobody in the audience could think of them at the end of the evening."[17] The show played on Broadway through Christmas at Daly's, later moving to the Garden Theatre. When the production left for Washington D. C., Tours would not perform again in New York for another seven years.

By the turn of the twentieth century, the first flowering of musical comedy in England, precipitated by George Edwardes' smart productions in the West End, took place alongside a concurrent ripening of British art song that would be a key development in a broader renaissance of

Complete Dramatic Works of Lord Lytton, (Sir Edward Lytton Bulwer, Bart.), edited by John M. Kingdom (New York: Robert M. De Witt, 1875).

[11] Kurt Gänzl, *British Musical Theatre* (New York: Oxford University Press, 1986), 682; *The Era Almanack*, 1899, 85.

[12] Len Platt, *Musical Comedy on the West End Stage, 1890–1939* (New York: Palgrave Macmillan, 2004), 30–33.

[13] Unidentified newspaper clipping, Frank Tours personal scrapbooks.

[14] *The Sketch*, September 25, 1901, 245. The present standard hyphenated version of the playwright's name is different from how it was given originally. For more information, see *Bulwer's Plays: Being the*

[15] *The Musical Times*, November 1, 1901, 731.

[16] The company set forth out of Southampton on August 8, 1903 and did not return home until October 25, 1904. The tour took the company through New York, Washington D. C., Buffalo, Cleveland, Pittsburgh, Boston, Philadelphia, Toronto, Chicago, San Francisco, Melbourne, Adelaide, Sydney, Perth, and Paris. Frank Tours personal scrapbooks.

[17] "'Three Little Maids': A Masterpiece of Musical Comedy at Daly's," *The New York Times*, September 2, 1903.

English classical music. The revival of a distinguished school of English composition, which for centuries had been lurking in the shadows of a European musical culture dominated by artistic forces from the continent, had, according to Stephen Banfield, "reached maturity by 1900," forged largely through the choral and orchestral music of Edward Elgar.[18] The groundswell of sophisticated new music by young British composers was also animated by a heightened attention among them to the capacity for English poetry to provide a vehicle for innovative musical settings for voice and piano. As they sought to elevate an aesthetic discourse that had for so long been unresponsive to progressive musical ideas throughout the nineteenth century, English composers turned less often to sentimental verse employed in the typical British ballads of the Victorian Era, and instead sought the more disciplined and ironic language of Heinrich Heine, William Butler Yeats, and A. E. Houseman for musical interpretation.

While there are no surviving scores from his studies at the RCM to support the assumption, it is difficult to imagine that Tours didn't compose any art songs while studying with Stanford.[19] His teacher's dedication to the genre was not only evident in his own work (comprising more than sixty songs by the time Tours entered the RCM), but more significantly in the outpouring of songs from his students, which included every English composer that made noteworthy contributions to the genre during the first two decades of the twentieth century.[20] Stanford's notorious short temper with students who lacked sufficient discipline and respect for tradition would leave an indelible imprint on a generation of composers, whether they flourished or suffered under his tutelage. Though Tours' sentimental aesthetic interests, which revealed an obedience to convention and tradition, compelled him to resist the modern sensibility that was forming in the choices of text and musical settings of Ralph Vaughan Williams, Frank Bridge, John Ireland, and Ivor Gurney (to name but a few), the striving for idiomatic vocal lines, solid modern harmonic architecture, and elegant rhythmic clarity that he consistently displayed (and probably acquired from his exposure to Stanford), enabled him to bring a dignified pathos to the romantic and spiritual verses he regularly chose to set.

The first two songs by Tours that were accepted for publication were settings of verse by Arthur Anderson, who would go on to write the books and lyrics for many musicals in New York over the next twenty years.[21] Many of Tours' collaborators over the next two decades would likewise be theatrical colleagues who enjoyed creating for and speculating in the field of the commercial ballad, both in England and the United States. Anderson's words for "Lover Mine" and "'Tis Passing Strange" reflect the social and romantic anxieties particular to courtship among the Edwardian middle class: in the first case, a woman questioning whether her fiancé has represented his financial wherewithal honestly, and, in the second, a man questioning whether a woman will remain in love with him through the years. The musical settings for these bourgeois sentiments together are an impressive first effort that bear the hallmarks of Tours' craftsmanship and lyricism. In his choice of text and in their elegant and sophisticated gentility, they also reveal his commitment to elevating the artistic expression of the Victorian ballad (as his father had done before him), rather than to composing art songs in the way so many other Royal College of Music students of his generation would over the next thirty years.

Tours found his next lyric in Rudyard Kipling's early novel *The Light That Failed*. Presented as a prologue to the book, the poem that became "Mother o' Mine" is the paean of a son who imagines enduring an improbable series of tribulations—hanging, drowning, damnation—only to find that his mother's love and devotion remains unshaken through it all.[22] Having been buried for more than ten years in Kipling's book, which was considered a failure among literary critics, the verse became widely known through Tours' musical setting and remained popular over the next two decades. "Mother o' Mine" continued to occupy the public imagination well into the 1920s, and the music remained in print nearly three decades after it was

[18] Stephen Banfield, *Sensibility and English Song* (Cambridge: Cambridge University Press, 1985), 1–3.

[19] The only composition that exists from Frank's youth is the "The Skelsmergian Song" (words by Donald T. Glassford). The Skelsmergh School for Young Gentlemen in Kent was attended by all the Tours boys from the ages of 7 to 12. The song was composed in 1889 by Frank as a precocious student and was good enough for them to keep. He had it printed many years later for an "Old Boys Dinner" that the brothers attended and where it was surely performed.

[20] Banfield, *Sensibility and English Song*, 26–41, 513–14.

[21] Arthur Anderson contributed to the productions of *The Girl Behind the Counter*, *Two Little Brides*, *The Merry Countess*, *The Marriage Market*, and *Chu Chin Chow* during his career. Richard C. Norton, *A Chronology of American Musical Theatre*, Vols. I–III (New York: Oxford University Press, 2002), I: 870 990; II: 6, 37, 128, 184.

[22] While the poem's message is clear, its origin and purpose remain murky. Forced to speculate, Kipling biographer Phillip Mallett suggests that the author wrote the verse to ameliorate his concerns that the autobiographical elements of the book's tortured protagonist might implicate his mother unfairly. But an alternative scenario seems more probable. Since the poem did not appear when *The Light That Failed* originally appeared in Lippincott's journal, it is perhaps more likely that Kipling wrote the poem when he published it as a book the following year with a tragic ending that he had written first and that had met with his mother's disapproval. Phillip Mallett, *Rudyard Kipling: A Literary Life* (New York: Palgrave Macmillan, 2003), 58; Geoffrey Annis, "*The Light That Failed:* An Introduction," The Kipling Society, http://www.kiplingsociety.co.uk/rg_light_intro.htm (accessed February 26, 2020).

first published.[23] With the rise of the recording industry, the song was issued by at least five labels between 1907 and 1933: twice by Columbia, OKeh, and Brunswick, and no less than seven times by The Victor Talking Machine Co.[24] The pathos and fervent poignancy of the song that was endearing to people on both sides of the Atlantic for so many years was all but lost on audiences by mid-century however, rejected by a post-Freudian society that had become cynical toward such overt and sincere Oedipal impulses.[25] But what may seem like an embarrassing out-pouring of maternal affection by a young man to someone with a modern social sensibility was in its time considered to be a natural emotional expression of a commonplace familial bond.

Though he would never match the success of "Mother o' Mine" with any of the more than five dozen songs that he published over the next twenty years, Tours likewise never composed another song setting that did not rise to the same level of craftsmanship. His lack of creative ambition and iconoclasm, which made him content to be a composer of middlebrow salon songs rather than to join the ranks of the artistic elite that emerged out of Stanford's studio at the RCM, would all too often lead him to expend his considerable talent for musical interpretation on inferior English lyrics. If his discrimination in the choice of texts was, generally speaking, uneven, his sense of artistic integrity was, nonetheless, reliable and sure, enabling him regularly to transform a mediocre lyric into a work of genuine value and interest. Sometimes, when the words he set were irredeemably sentimental and earnest, the eloquence and appeal of his musical voice remains fresh and devoid of nostalgia. However, when he did find a sophisticated or meaningful poem to set, the results are uniformly satisfying and worthy of the company of songs by his better-known British contemporaries. Tours established himself with several publishing houses over the course of a few years: G. Ricordi & Co. published the Anderson songs as well as "My Darling" with words by J. Edward Fraser; Novello & Co., his father's old firm, published the enchanting lullaby "Hush-a-By, Sweetie"; Boosey & Co. took two early Tour songs "Oh! Cupid" and "Love's Quiet"; after the success of "Mother o' Mine," Chappell & Co. published several more art songs, including "Il pleure dans mon coeur," a setting of the familar text by symbolist poet Paul Verlaine, along with the scores from his British musical comedies;

and M. Witmark & Sons published nine songs between 1903 and 1909, a prescient decision by an American firm before Tours had relocated to New York and developed a name for himself as both a composer and a music director on Broadway.

Throughout his career, songwriting coincided with Tours' regular work as a conductor for musical comedies. The twelve songs that he published in 1903 and 1904 were largely composed while he was the music director for *Three Little Maids*, which was touring England in late 1902 and continued through the 14-month world tour that began in the fall of 1903. Given that he had been exercising his compositional inclination with increasing regularity, and since he had been immersed in performing the scores of Paul Rubens, Ivan Caryll, Percy Greenbank, Lionel Monckton, Howard Talbot, and Adrian Ross all year round, it did not take long for him to begin to collaborate on new musical comedies himself. After working as musical director for Rubens' *Lady Madcap* and Caryll's *The Little Cherub* during 1905 and the spring of 1906 at the Prince of Wales Theatre, Tours was asked to contribute songs to Sidney Jones' *See-See*, which appeared at the same venue as the others in the fall.[26] Meanwhile his clout as a composer had risen to the point where he shared the composing responsibilities as well as the lead billing for *The Dairymaids*, which opened at the Apollo Theatre in April 1906.[27] He was asked to contribute additional numbers to *The New Aladdin* and *The Gay Gordons*, the latter being a "Play with Music" by Seymour Hicks, who also played the lead. By the time he was asked by Hicks in 1909 to be the lead composer for *The Dashing Little Duke*, Tours had been contributing numbers to music comedies for nearly three years and conducting them in London and on the road for over ten, so he was well prepared for this substantial assignment when it came. Hicks had played the role of the young Duc du Richelieu in an 1899 version of the original French play (*Les Premières Armes de Richelieu*, Palais Royal, 1839), but he handed it over to his wife Ellaline Terriss to turn it into a pants role for the musical version that he wrote and produced.[28] For his part, Tours was acknowledged to have composed a light opera instead of another "Play with Music" as advertised. But this was apparently not an unwelcome preponderance of music, even for a play that, according to one critic, "might be very successfully

[23] Chappell & Co. even promoted a version for tenor and baritone duet on their cover in the 1920s.

[24] For more information, see Appendix 3: Discography of this volume.

[25] As a reflection of how such unabashed expressions of maternal affection had shifted away from social acceptability by mid-century, see Preston Sturges' parody of the "mother song" ("Home to the Arms of Mother") in his 1944 film *Hail, the Conquering Hero*.

[26] Gänzl, *British Musical Theatre*, 888, 949, 955.

[27] Ibid., 952, 956, 989, 1040.

[28] Producing the play was more akin to directing in the age where the theatre manager had the primary creative responsibility for the production. Charles Frohman, in fact, had controlling interest in the property, which, in today's parlance, would have made him the producer and Hicks the writer-director. Frank E. Tours, *The Dashing Little Duke*, lyrics by Adrian Ross, vocal score (London: Ascherberg, Hopwood & Crew, 1909).

given without musical numbers at all."[29] The composer was the show's music director for the duration of the run from February 8 through May 28, first at the Theatre Royal, Nottingham, and later at the Hicks Theatre in London.

Not surprisingly, Hicks was already planning his next musical while *The Dashing Little Duke* was still on the boards. The production he mounted, based upon a successful farce by the American playwright Richard Harding, was called *Captain Kidd* after the show's aristocratic, globetrotting protagonist.[30] Despite the auspicious array of talent Hicks had assembled, which included himself and Terriss in the lead roles and Leslie Stuart (composer of the outstanding hit *Florodora*) to write the score, the show would not only fail at the box office, it would bring to an end Hick's dominance on the London stage. Tours was asked to lead the orchestra and the swift demise of *Captain Kidd* left him unexpectedly without work for the duration of the season, although he seems to have taken over the baton at some point during the run of *The Balkan Princess*, which opened at the same time but lasted through the summer and well into the fall of 1910. For, in July, the American producer William Brady and his wife, Grace George, herself a noted actress, came to London, partly as as emissaries of Sam and J. J. Shubert, to scout properties and talent for the forthcoming Broadway season, and he offered to hire Tours to lead the orchestra in the Broadway production of *The Balkan Princess*, the American rights of which he had just acquired (in addition to two original cast members).[31] Though Tours had already finished the score for a new show with Hicks and Terriss based on the story of Joan of Arc, he took the assignment and sailed for New York in October only to find that the local musicians union would not allow him to work as a conductor for six months.[32] The Shuberts, knowing Tours' value and experience as a composer of light music, hired him instead to collaborate with Jerome Kern on the score for *La Belle Paree*, the brothers' first production at the Winter Garden Theatre. Only the year before, both composers had contributed songs to Leo Fall's operetta *The Dollar Princess*, which was being adapted for London audiences. Having landed on his feet, Tours submitted an application for naturalization within a month of his arrival, and thus commenced his stay in the United States with the conviction that he intended to immigrate permanently and seek his fortunes in New York without looking back.[33]

Tours continued to work for the Shuberts throughout 1911, taking over the conducting duties for *La Belle Paree* and *The Balkan Princess* at different times once he was free to work in the city. The first Broadway show that he was in the pit opening night for was the American adaptation of *Liebeswalzer* ("*The Kiss Waltz*").[34] The Shuberts once again asked Tours and Jerome Kern to work together, this time providing interpolations for an imported score by Carl Michael Ziehrer in an attempt to facilitate the assimilation of a Viennese operetta that the producers had bought to satisfy New York audiences' appetite for middle-European theatrical fare in the wake of *The Merry Widow*. As he was quickly establishing himself among the elite music directors on Broadway, Tours was also busy composing ballads. Being a staff musician at the Shubert organization with limited conducting and composing duties at first must have felt like a paid vacation for Tours, who prided himself on never being without work since he started conducting professionally fifteen years earlier. As a result, he had his most prolific year to date, publishing twelve songs along with one of his numbers from *La Belle Paree*. M. Witmark & Sons, which had been issuing Tours songs since 1903, became his principle publisher over the next decade, along with a couple of other leading American firms.

His immigration to the United States was marked by the setting of one of the most idiomatically American lyrics to be found among his songs. Frank Lebby Stanton was a journalist and poet from Charleston who was working in Atlanta when he wrote "Wearyin' for You" for an 1894 collection of verse called *Songs of the Soil*.[35] Tours must have learned about the text from the well-known song setting by Carrie Jacobs-Bond, the success of which continues to overshadow his version. But despite never getting any traction with the public, the Tours setting may justifiably be said to have outdone its more famous counterpart in many respects, not least of which being its uncannily natural musical rendering of Stanton's vernacular, which Jacobs-Bond had sought to suppress (the most obvious examples of which being her changing the words "jest" to "just" and "fer" to "for"). Among his finest achievements, "Jest a-Wearyin' fer You" revealed Tours' uncommon

[29] For good measure, the critic noted that "[t]he book by Seymour Hicks is good; so, too, are the lyrics by Mr. Adrian Ross, while the music by Mr. Frank Tours is a shade better than merely that." Unidentified newspaper clipping, Frank Tours personal scrapbooks.

[30] Andrew Lamb, *Leslie Stuart: The Man Who Composed* Florodora (New York: Routledge, 2002), 206.

[31] "Brady Back with Many New Plays," *The New York Times*, August 1, 1910, 7.

[32] Unidentified newspaper clipping, Frank Tours personal scrapbooks; "Theatrical Notes," *The New York Times*, April 4, 1911, 11.

[33] Tours would become a citizen six years later. Petition for Naturalization, U. S. District Court, S. District of New York by Frank E. Tours, July 2, 1917.

[34] Norton, *A Chronology of American Musical Theatre*, I: 971.

[35] Frank Lebby Stanton worked for the *Atlanta Constitution* and wrote and published several volumes of poetry, including *Songs of a Day* (1893), *Songs of the Soil* (1894), *Comes One with a Song* (1899), *Songs from Dixie Land* (1900), and *Little Folks Down South* (1904). John W. Leonard, ed., *Who's Who in America: A Biographical Dictionary of Living Men and Women of the United States: 1899–1900* (Chicago: A. N. Marquis & Co.), 687.

sensitivity to American linguistic and musical dialect and laid the groundwork for his songs over the next decade in collaboration with American lyric writers. None of his later work would be nearly as entrenched in dialect as "Jest a Wearyin' fer You," but still Tours was often able to cultivate in his personal style an American musical sensibility in the process. Elsie Janis' lyric "From the Valley," for example, bears no hint of the romantic angst that was so common in Tours' English songs, but rather describes a spiritual journey from darkness into light and back to darkness that was unrelated to love and loss. The candor and maturity of Janis' poetic voice was matched by a restrained elegance in Tours' music, which itself had matured from the ambitious and sometimes overwrought sentimentalism of songs like "The Alternative" from his British period. Janis would be the first of many performers among his Broadway milieu who would collaborate with him on ballads.

Tours became one of the leading composers of the "Black and White Series" at M. Witmark & Sons during the 1910s, which was an economy division of their catalogue that focused on music with classical leanings (the series name referring to their no-frills, monochromatic sheet music covers).[36] Julius Witmark began expanding the company's catalogue beyond popular music, which had been their mainstay since the 1880s, for about ten years before the time when the company first began to publish Tours' songs during the New York run of *Three Little Maids* in 1903. Isidore Witmark described how his brother, who was a fine singer in addition to being one of the company's founding managers, travelled to England and acquired the publishing rights to "a catalogue of better-grade songs," which later grew into the Black and White Series comprised of "semi-classical" ballads and sacred music. The Witmarks would first publish music by Tours more than a decade later, around the same time as they began to issue many successful songs by American ballad composers Ernest R. Ball, Caro Roma, and many others.[37] Isador would later write of Tours that "as a composer of better-grade songs he has no peer.[38] Among his numerous love ballads and songs of spiritual yearning, Tours also contributed several songs with religious texts to the Witmark catalogue. Given his early training on organ and the fact that his father was a prolific composer of sacred music, it was natural that Frank should want to write music for use in the Christian liturgy. Novello, Ewer & Co. had published a *Short Service of the*

Office of Holy Communion by Frank around the turn of the century (dedicated "To the Memory of My Dear Father, Berthold Tours"). Although contemporary accounts and unpublished scores from the earliest years of his career indicate that he was equally preoccupied with composing sacred music as he was with opera (the latter, again, likely the result of Stanford's influence and his immersion in the score of *Shamus O'Brien*), he only began to compose liturgical songs for solo voice once he arrived in America. Over the next two years he gave the Witmarks several songs for their sacred music catalogue, including settings for Christmas ("Thou Blessed Man of God") and Easter service ("Breaks the Morning"). While Tours had dedicated himself for more than a decade to conducting musical comedies and had already logged thousands of performances in British and American theatres, his ability to create inspirational religious music of great dignity and solemnity was undiminished by his constant immersion in light music.

Tours was next assigned by the Shuberts to conduct *The Wedding Trip*, which opened on Christmas Day of 1911 with music and lyrics by Reginald DeKoven and Harry B. Smith.[39] The show was another disappointment for the team that created *Robin Hood* (which opened in 1890) and was still searching for its successor nearly twenty years later. After the show closed in February, DeKoven returned to the tried-and-true by reviving *Robin Hood* once again and he hired Tours to be his musical director for a brief run at the New Amsterdam Theatre followed by a lengthy tour and then a production of *Rob Roy* at the Liberty Theatre the following year.[40] Tours then returned to London in 1914 to replace Cuthbert Clarke at the Empire Theatre, but was lured back to New York again by the Shuberts to be the musical director for *Tonight's the Night* with a score by Paul Rubens and interpolations by Kern.[41] He worked temporarily on *The Lady in Red* before it closed out of town in Chicago, but fortunately Irving Berlin's *Watch Your Step*, which had a successful run on Broadway in the spring, was scheduled to play for two months at the Illinois Theatre before continuing on the road, and Tours was hired by producer Charles Dillingham to lead the orchestra.[42] And when composer and conductor Robert Hood Bowers left the production of Berlin's *Stop! Look! Listen!* at the Globe Theatre the following year, Dillingham hired Tours again, a decision that cemented a musical relationship that would

---

[36] Isidore Witmark described the catalogue in this way: "The series contained not only ballads for all voices but sacred songs, arranged for solos, duets, and quartettes, and each song was offered in at least three keys, so that it could come within the range of any voice." Isidore Witmark and Isaac Goldberg, *The Story of the House of Witmark: From Ragtime to Swingtime* (New York: Lee Furman, 1939), 271.

[37] For more information about the composers of The Witmark Black-and-White Series, see their catalogue *Songland*.

[38] Witmark and Goldberg, *From Ragtime to Swingtime*, 413.

[39] Norton, *A Chronology of American Musical Theatre*, I: 980.

[40] Norton, *A Chronology of American Musical Theatre*, I: 991; II: 36–37.

[41] John Franceschina, *Incidental and Dance Music in the American Theatre from 1786 to 1923*, Vol. 3 (Albany, GA: Bear Manor, 2018), 486.

[42] Information on out-of-town and touring Broadway productions was drawn from Herbert Goldman's musical theatre research for Packard Humanities Institute.

continue for two decades with Frank becoming the music director for nearly a dozen of Berlin's shows.

Jerome Kern's career in the theatre began in London's West End, where he contributed songs to over ten productions and occasionally worked with Frank Tours before both men moved to New York within a year of each other. And though the trajectory of their careers was ultimately quite different, the parallel paths that these men took in their early professional lives gave them a bond of artistic and personal familiarity that would continue for thirty years. Tours was leading the orchestra when Kern's *Love o' Mike* opened at the Shubert Theatre in 1917, and the composer had three hit shows on Broadway at the same time. Dubbed his "Annus mirabilis" by biographer Gerald Bordman, 1917 was the year when Kern finally unseated Victor Herbert as the dean of American theatre composers, an occasion which similarly marked the conductor's rise in prominence as a musical director on Broadway to the top of his field, a position he would not relinquish for twenty years.[43] Just as he established himself professionally, Frank began to court one of the production's attractive and talented female cast members, Helen Clarke.[44] Born and raised in Manhattan by parents with connections to New York's elite cultural and intellectual life, Helen worked as a stage performer from her early youth and was discovered by Elisabeth Marbury, who cast her at the age of twenty-one as a dancer named Dolly Dip in *Nobody Home*, the first Kern show in the famed Princess Theatre series that transformed the American musical theatre. She then appeared in several other musical comedies, including *Very Good Eddie*, *Oh, My Dear!*, and *La-La-Lucille!*[45] Her career was pre-empted by her blossoming love affair with Tours and ended permanently when the two married on July 3, 1920.[46] By the end of the decade, Frank and Helen had five children and were living comfortably in Great Neck on Long Island.[47]

As he worked to establish himself as a first-call musical director on Broadway, Tours' composition for voice and piano slowed down from its heightened pace during the year after his arrival in the United States. The relatively few songs he set between 1913, when he returned to England briefly to conduct at the Empire Theatre, and 1917, when the United States joined the Allied Powers in World War I, were, nonetheless, indicative of a continued maturation of his compositional sensibility. Perhaps through a rekindling of his British associations during his year back home, Tours began working with the lyricist Edward Teschemacher, whose poems had been favored by British ballad composers since he rose to prominence with "Because" in 1902 (music by Guy d'Hardelot). Although the content of Teschemacher's lyrics in a song such as "Apple Time" represented a retreat to the sentimental Edwardian romanticism of his earlier work, Tours found a charming textural economy in his accompaniment to match the naive sentiment imploring young maidens to go apple picking in the orchards. In "Son of My Heart" Tours found an inspired melodic strain reminiscent of the music of Ernest Ball, while at the same time exploring new avenues of expressivity for its sentimental lyric through an elegant modern harmonic language that would have been inconceivable for the composer of "When Irish Eyes Are Smiling" and "Mother Machree." The romantic pathos behind the lyrics for "No Voice But Yours," "Hidden in Your Heart," and "Give Me Your Hands" strikes a more universal tone of desire and longing rather than the concerns of young men and women looking to negotiate their future happiness, which was the subject of many early texts he chose to set. Tours met this plaintive tone of yearning with unsettling progressions and sonorities that defy expectation on key turns in the lover's narrative that can disarm even the listener that is ordinarily inclined to resist the emotional language of romantic poetry. Knowing the composer's own personal story only helps us to understand how the intensification of his musical language for these particular texts at this time was attributable to some extent to his own courtship of Helen, and that the passionate musical language of these songs was born more of personal authenticity than of mere craft and creative aspiration.

During America's involvement in the war, Tours worked consistently at the conductor's desk in the theatres of Broadway, beginning with four shows for the Shuberts: *The Highwayman* (5-2-17, 44th St.) with music by Reginald DeKoven; *Maytime* (8-16-17, Sam S. Shubert) with music by Sigmund Romberg; *Over the Top* (11-28-17, 44th St.) also with music by Romberg; and *Girl o' Mine* with a score that he composed. In 1918, he was the music director for Jerome Kern's *Rock-a-Bye, Baby*, Irving Berlin's military musical *Yip Yip Yaphank*, and *Sinbad* starring Al Jolson, musicals that centered around three of the biggest names on Broadway. During the war, Tours was also moved to compose some of his most serious and sophisticated songs, even as he was immersed in the theatrical levity that characterized the shows for which he was working. The verse he set at this time was occasionally of a higher order of

[43] *Love o' Mike* (1-15-17, Shubert) opened four day after *Have a Heart* (1-11-17, Liberty) and one month before *Oh, Boy!* (2-20-17, Princess), at which point he had an unprecedented three simultaneous hits on Broadway open nearly within a month of each other. Norton, *A Chronology of American Musical Theatre*, II: 110–14.

[44] Helen Clarke was the spelling that Helen Veronica Gaylord Clark used on the stage.

[45] Selma Jeanne Cohen and Dance Perspectives Foundation, *International Encyclopedia of Dance* (New York: Oxford University Press, 1998).

[46] Anema and Schutte, *Nederlandse Genealogieën*, 349.

[47] *U. S. Census Bureau, 1930* (Washington, D. C.: Government Printing Office). Viewed at https://www.ancestry.com (accessed on June 28, 2020).

poetic expression, which in turn was the catalyst for powerful musical interpretations that exceeded even his own usual standards of excellence. John McCrae's poem *In Flanders Fields* epitomized the desolation of the European battlefield and the war's cruel futility, and in so doing it inspired no less than fifty-five composers to set its melancholy imagery of death and destruction.[48] In his interpretation, Tours paints the grim scene in suitably macabre chords and swiftly shifting modalities that evoke the unstable ground that these soldiers fought and died upon. The voice that emerges from beyond the world that the listener inhabits expresses musically the entire range of emotion contained in McCrae's message: he begins in solemn, unhurried phrases to describe the masses of graves; reaches up to describe the flight of birds; arcs down at the memory of the roar of gunfire; meanders in halting phrases above spectral harmonies to remember life on earth; forcefully calls to arms the brothers who would take up their cause in their absence; and chants repeatedly the name of their final resting place where they will not sleep if they are betrayed. By interpreting the text closely and illustrating carefully its series of moods, Tours finds a satisfying middle ground between the disturbing nightmare evoked in Charles Ives' setting and by the trivializing combination of religious anthem and military tribute in the one by John Philip Sousa. There is a Tours family anecdote that Sousa said he would give all of his marches to be able to write a single ballad like Frank Tours. Hearing their respective settings of "In Flanders Fields" side-by-side, one can imagine him saying such a thing.

The hardships of the Great War inspired the creation of a set of lyrics from Irene Castle, who revolutionized modern dancing with her husband, Vernon, and then endured months of separation when he trained and fought for the British Royal Flying Corps.[49] When he returned from the European conflict, he trained other young pilots in Canada and later in Texas, where he died in a tragic airplane accident. As her books amply demonstrate, Irene was a woman of great intelligence, style, determination, and grit. Frank Tours and Irene had become close on the road with *Watch Your Step* when Vernon was overseas, and their song set *Four Little Love Songs* was the product of their intimate friendship at a difficult time in her life.[50] *Musical America* delivered an uncompromising verdict upon her work, stating that "her texts are of that intensely subjective variety

that leave nothing to persons possessing imagination" and then concluding rather callously that "one cannot write a great poem immediately upon the death of one's loved ones."[51] By contrast, their appraisal of Tours' music was generous, concluding that "we can say of him that he resembles our highly esteemed Victor Herbert, in that he writes just as good music to poor texts as to real poetry." Her lyrics, obviously, were the work of someone who was not an experienced poet, but rather a public figure who was using the medium of verse to contain her profound sadness and devotion, which she continued to do with her two books about her husband and their relationship. As a tribute to Vernon Castle, a genuine war hero and one of the most charismatic and influential cultural figures of the early twentieth century, the songs are not merely fascinating documents; they have the power to conjure a deep emotional response, especially if one is familiar with Irene Castle, her marriage to Vernon, and his extraordinary talent, bravery, integrity, humanity, and *joie de vivre*.

After the war, Tours continued to be in high demand as a music director on Broadway. Following a three-month stint at the helm of *Morris Gest's Midnight Whirl*, staged on the roof of the Century Theatre with George Gershwin receiving the lead billing as composer, he returned to London with Edith Day when she took the city by storm as the star in *Irene*. *The London Times* referred to her introduction to British audiences in historical terms, stating that she achieved "one of the most striking successes of any American actress on her first appearance on the London stage since the evening Miss Edna May burst upon the horizon" twenty years earlier in *The Belle of New York*.[52] The original London cast recorded nearly the entire score of *Irene* for the British Columbia label with Tours conducting. Despite being the result of a commercial enterprise, the recordings also serve as a document of the musical performances and interpretive style, a form of historical preservation of the music that was rare and would not become standard until the 1940s with the regular appearance of original cast albums.[53] He returned to New York to conduct Morris Gest's extravaganza *Mecca* with sets and staging by *Ballets Russes* veterans Leon Bakst and Michel Fokine, which Alexander Woollcott said was a show "as rich and sumptuous in pageantry as the American theatre has known."[54] From one lavish spectacle to another, Tours joined the production of the *Ziegfeld Follies of*

[48] Jennifer A. Ward, "American Musical Settings of 'In Flanders Fields' and the Great War," *Journal of Musicological Research* 33 (2014), 96–129.

[49] Irene Castle, *Castles in the Air* (New York: Doubleday and Co., 1958), 138–74.

[50] It should not be inferred that her poetry was about anyone other than her husband, despite the fact that Castle wrote that "Frankie Tours and I were inseparable" while on the road together and even suggested they had a brief affair. Ibid., 136–37.

[51] *Musical America*, August 3, 1918, 28.

[52] "Irene" at the Empire: A Welcome American Invasion, *The London Times*, April 8, 1920, 8.

[53] *"Irene" with Edith Day*, Monmouth Evergreen, MES 7057, LP. The first American production to be documented on record with this degree of completeness was Marc Blitzstein's *The Cradle Will Rock* in 1938.

[54] *The New York Times*, October 10, 1920, 81. Norton, *A Chronology of American Musical Theatre*, II: 228–29.

1921 the following summer, dominated by the talents of Fannie Brice, Van and Schenck, Raymond Hitchcock, and W. C. Fields and featuring new music by operetta composers Victor Herbert and Rudolf Friml, along with Follies regular Dave Stamper. By far the smartest, most sophisticated revue to play on Broadway, at a time when the genre was flourishing like no other, was the *Music Box Revue*.[55] Designed to feature the unique talents of Irving Berlin, it was a star vehicle unlike any in the history of the American musical, not only because it cast the spotlight on a songwriter instead of a performer, but because it demonstrated that a Broadway show could be built around words and music as its primary attraction. Tours was the natural choice for music director, both because he had conducted most of Berlin's musicals since 1914 and because the two were great friends, Berlin having served as best man at Tours' wedding during the previous year.

After a two-to-three-year hiatus following World War I, Tours composed a handful of songs that represent the culmination of his work in the genre. With more than twenty years of experience composing for voice and piano, he was in full command of his craft and thus able to demonstrate the continued currency and viability of the ballad in the 1920s through his settings of several romantic lyrics. Throughout his career, Tours dedicated his music to some of the finest singers in the theatre, such as Maurice Farkoa, Orville Harrold, John Charles Thomas, and John McCormack. Although there was no remunerative benefit for the performer and the gesture was primarily made out of collegial friendship, these dedications may also be seen as a twentieth-century manifestation of the royalty ballad, since they served a reciprocal function of honoring the singer with the distinction of association with the published song while at the same time giving them a reason to program it in their concerts.[56] In the case of John Steel, concert tenor for the 1919, 1920, and 1921 editions of the *Ziegfeld Follies* as well as the 1922 and 1923 editions of the *Music Box Revue*, he collaborated as a lyricist with Tours on ballads while the two of them were working together on the Berlin shows. In his lyric for "Hope Dreams," Steel indulged in arcane language and imagery to craft a portrait of a man yearning for the fulfillment of his dreams by wishing on a "Star of Hope." Despite the challenge presented by this less-than-promising idea, it inspired Tours to create one of his finest melodies, a long, arcing line in octaves amidst throbbing sonorities that evokes a celestial communion

with greater sincerity than anyone may reasonably have expected. The esoteric narrative of Steel's lyric was grounded by Tours' setting, which balances harmonic richness and melodic elegance with natural vocal scansion. In this late period of creativity, Tours also revealed his capacity, in at least one instance, to make a credible contribution to the classical tradition of art song that his training with Charles Stanford had once suggested he might participate in more fully. "Fury of the Sea," a setting of a poem by Edmund Goulding, offers a glimpse of the artistic heights that Frank Tours might have ascended to had he regularly chose superior texts and sought to convey their meaning in forceful, uncompromising musical language. The unrelenting torrent of arpeggios that course beneath its stentorian vocal line are drawn freely from German and French art song traditions of the nineteenth century in their ability to clearly illustrate the text. While Tours would continue to compose songs through the end of the decade for projects upon which he was working as a conductor, he essentially stopped composing ballads for publication (with one notable exception) in the middle of the 1920s at the height of his creative and technical powers.

Advances in the motion picture industry after World War I precipitated the construction of massive theatres in every major city that would put films in direct competition with live theatre for the entertainment dollars of local audiences. These movie palaces needed large orchestras to supply music for a variety of needs, since even the most extravagant film productions at the time could not stand alone as an evening of entertainment, especially when vaudeville and Broadway were offering spectacular productions and talent all over the city. Paramount Pictures, which was making great strides to monopolize the distribution of its films, took over the Rialto Theatre in Times Square in 1919 after S. L. "Roxy" Rothapfel had made it the "Temple of the Motion Picture" a few years earlier.[57] As music was central to Roxy's vision of elevating moviegoing into the realm of high-class entertainment at the Rialto, he installed Hugo Riesenfeld as music director. A violinist, conductor, and composer who had worked with Gustav Mahler and Arnold Schoenberg in Vienna during the early years of his career, Riesenfeld would revolutionize the cinema orchestra and create over a hundred scores for silent films. In 1925, Tours was hired to take over as the music director of the Rialto Orchestra as theatre managers sought to maintain the high quality of their musical programming, which included several light instrumental numbers in addition to the underscoring for shorts and a feature film. He also worked in the same capacity at the Criterion Theatre, another Times Square movie palace

[55] Jeffrey Magee, *Irving Berlin's American Musical Theater* (New York: Oxford University Press, 2012), 202–86.

[56] An example of this relationship at work can be found in the press notice of a concert by John McCormack where he was reported to have sung Tours' "The Littlest of All," "which pleased greatly in the McCormack reading." *The Music News*, Chicago, IL, January 25, 1918, 3.

[57] Ben M. Hall, *The Best Remaining Seats: The Golden Age of the Movie Palace* (New York: Clarkson N. Potter, 1961), 42–51.

leased by Paramount to screen their films. After quickly establishing himself as an elite music director for high-end movie theatres in New York, he was asked to open the Plaza Theatre in London, which was located in Piccadilly Circus and built to be Paramount's flagship theatre in England. According to the opening night program: "The Plaza has been designed in the confident hope that it will prove a real home of entertainment in the heart of London for all who seek relaxation and amusement."[58] The opening was attended by dozens of members of British Royalty and other distinguished guests, a list of whom was given in the program to add to the evening's pomp and glamour. In addition to conducting the Plaza Orchestra in three selections and background music for the feature film *Nell Gwyn* with Dorothy Gish, Tours composed a waltz song for the occasion as an introductory number. "Sweet Nell" is both nostalgic and modern, evoking in words and music the historical figure of Nell Gwyn—the orange seller and actress who became the mistress of Charles II—as presented in the 1926 novel by Marjorie Bowen and in the film. The Plaza Orchestra was one of the finest ensembles in the city and their sound and repertoire were captured in several recordings for British Columbia. The venue gave Tours the opportunity to exercise his gift for composing and performing light music for orchestra, which recordings such as "Minuet," "A La Gavotte," "The Busy Bee," and "Lovers' Lane" have preserved for posterity.[59]

Tours' association with Paramount Pictures would grow over the next few years, when he began working at their film studio in Astoria, Queens, scoring and conducting films over the next eight years. Joining the film industry in 1925, as Tours did, presented several substantial challenges for a music director. The role of music in the cinematic arts was in flux at the time, and with the technological advancement of the soundtrack still on the horizon, movie managers in the big cities needed live orchestras to provide underscoring for increasingly complex and lengthy cinematic dramas. The solution that many music directors arrived at was to use pre-existing musical scores and parts from libraries created by publishers (Carl Fisher being one of the biggest in New York) or from in-house collections. But techniques for using new music created specifically to support the action were slow to evolve. When Tours arrived in London to begin his tenure at the Plaza, he wrote an essay for the British trade magazine *Kinematograph Weekly*, in which he describes the current situation in which some musical directors ("M. D.'s") prefer to play indiscriminately chosen classical and popular works complete while others cut and edit pieces to suit the action. At the end, he makes "A Plea for Special Music," apparently a novel idea in January 1926 that involved "synchronising [*sic*] the picture with appropriate music and as nearly as musically possible with music of the period of the story."[60] One may assume that he implemented these ideas in *Nell Gwyn*, a prescient view in light of Warner Bros.' release of *Don Juan* later that year, which was the first feature-length motion picture with a recorded soundtrack. One of his early contributions to a film score was the song "Desert Stars," the theme of which he composed and arranged in his score for the 1926 film *Beau Geste* starring Ronald Colman. By the time he began to work full time on the Paramount Astoria lot in 1928, the studio had fully transitioned to sound pictures and synchronized soundtracks had already become standard practice. Over the next seven years he worked on many films for Paramount (along with a few for Samuel Goldwyn and United Artists) as musical director and composer. His credits include *The Cocoanuts* (1929) featuring the Marx Brothers, *Glorifying the American Girl* (1929) featuring performers in the Ziegfeld Follies, *Laughter* (1930) starring Nancy Carroll, *One Heavenly Night* (1930) with John Boles and Evelyn Laye, *The Emperor Jones* (1933) starring Paul Robeson, *Crime Without Passion* (1934) starring Claude Rains, *Gambling* (1934) written by George M. Cohan, who also played the lead, and *The Scoundrel* (1935) starring Noel Coward.[61]

Tours remained in high demand as a music director on Broadway throughout the time he worked for Paramount. On a typical day, he would leave Great Neck in the morning, travel to Astoria by train, put in a day of work at the studio, and then take another train to Times Square to conduct a show in the evening. After he returned from a second run at the Plaza Theatre in London, Tours conducted Noel Coward's *This Year of Grace* at the Selwyn Theatre starring the author and Beatrice Lillie, followed the next season by Coward's colossal operetta *Bitter Sweet*, which opened at the Ziegfeld Theatre in November 1929. Tours sailed to London in September to "go over the score" and to oversee the making of a silent film of the production to aid in mounting the show. He returned to New York three weeks later with the film, 123 singers and dancers, producer Charles B. Cochran, and Coward.[62] Having worked on the *Ziegfeld Follies of 1927*, Tours was asked by the famed producer in the fall of 1930 to be the music director for the ill-fated musical *Smiles*, starring Marilyn Miller and Fred and Adele Astaire and with a score by Vincent Youmans. Then, after several years in creative doldrums, Irving Berlin emerged in 1932 with an outstanding contemporary score

---

[58] A reproduction of the opening night program can be found at the website "ArthurLloyd.co.uk" (accessed on July 14, 2020).

[59] Of these works, only "Lovers' Lane" is an original Tours composition. For more information, see Discography of this volume.

[60] "The Plaza's Music: Piccadilly House and New Orchestral Ideas," *Kinematograph Weekly*, January 28, 1926.

[61] For more information, see the Internet Movie Database.

[62] "Frank Tours Sails," *The New York Times*, September 21, 1929, 24.

for *Face the Music*. Tours once again conducted, and he returned two seasons later with the same team of Moss Hart (sketches) and Hassard Short (staging) to mount *As Thousands Cheer*, which surpassed their earlier success with a revue that some consider to be the pinnacle of the genre. During the run, Tours was honored in the press for having conducted his 2,000th performance of an Irving Berlin musical, an unprecedented collaboration in musical theatre history.[63] He concluded his Broadway career with two operettas—Kern's *Music in the Air* and *The Great Waltz* with music by the Strausses (Johann Sr. and Johann Jr.)—and two hit musical comedies by Cole Porter in the prime of his career—*Jubilee* and *Red, Hot and Blue!* Over the course of twenty-five years, Frank Tours was at the conductor's podium as the Broadway musical evolved from a medium dominated by European light opera to one that fully integrated vernacular American musical styles and in the process became one of the world's most distinctive theatrical art forms.

As commercial radio became a ubiquitous part of American life, Tours was hired to be a music director on several high-profile programs. Will Rogers was asked to ply his theatrical trade on radio in 1930 and was convinced only reluctantly at first. By the time he appeared on the *Gulf Headliners* in 1933, he was the country's most beloved radio personality. Tours joined the program in January of 1935, and when Rogers died tragically in a plane accident in August, Frank continued to lead the orchestra even as the country mourned and the show limped along for another month.[64] The Vince Program was created for the Blue Network in 1933 to showcase the singing of John McCormack, and when John Charles Thomas took over for the 1935–1936 season, Tours conducted the in-house orchestra.[65] Later, he led the orchestra for the *Gulf Screen Guild Show*, featuring a panoply of Hollywood stars, who donated their time and talent for the Motion Picture Relief Fund and other entertainment charities.

RKO Studios contracted Tours in 1937 to work in their music department as a conductor, composer, and arranger, which prompted him to relocate to Los Angeles. The decision to accept a long-term contract at that time (he worked on RKO films exclusively until 1945) was likely precipitated not only by the anticipation that the studio would continue to work on musicals with top composers such as Irving Berlin, Jerome Kern, and George Gershwin, but also by the attraction of not having to renegotiate a new contract every season, as he had done for the past thirty-five years. But in 1937 Irving Berlin moved over to Twentieth-Century Fox, George Gershwin unexpectedly died, and Fred Astaire had become increasingly uncomfortable working at the studio, prompting him to leave within a couple of years.[66] In addition, new studio boss Sam Briskin began to implement a plan to increase revenue by reducing the number of A-pictures produced on the lot in favor of low-budget films. Being contractually obligated to a music department at a studio that valued cost-effectiveness over production quality, Tours was now forced to do yeoman's work for at least twenty-three films in various capacities over the next eight years, mostly B-pictures for which the studio needed a competent music director and stock underscoring by a stable of uncredited composers. After spending his entire career at the apex of every facet of musical theatre in London and New York, he was only involved in two musicals during these years: *Joy of Living*, with a score by Jerome Kern, starring Irene Dunne and Douglas Fairbanks, Jr.; and a loosely adapted version of Rodgers and Hart's *Too Many Girls* featuring Lucille Ball and Desi Arnaz. With his long experience in musical comedy and operetta, Tours would have been better suited to work at Metro-Goldwyn-Mayer or Twentieth Century-Fox, which were committed to producing musicals with glamorous stars, often based on nostalgic themes where he could have had more opportunities to make a valuable contribution to the field.

His years in Los Angeles, however, were not entirely spent in the service of mediocrity. His long association with John Charles Thomas brought him to the attention of Edwin Lester, who was in the process of establishing a first-class musical theatre production company in Los Angeles. Tours brought his unparalleled experience and skill to the Los Angeles Civic Light Opera for five years, conducting revivals of *Blossom Time*, *Roberta*, *A Waltz Dream*, *The Gypsy Baron*, *Tonight at 8:30*, *Charlot's Revue*, *Music in the Air*, and *Bitter Sweet*, with Thomas frequently in the lead. And then, when Gene Mann, an ex-vaudeville performer turned theatrical producer, envisioned operetta seasons at the outdoor 4,000-seat Greek Theatre, he knew Frank Tours was just the person to entrust with being the music director for his enormous (and risky) undertaking.[67] The productions attracted some of the finest singers on the West Coast, many of whom had appeared on Broadway, and it succeeded in prospering for three seasons, during which time the company produced two-week runs of *Rose-Marie*, *Blossom Time*, *The Firefly*, *The New Moon*, *Rosalie*, *Bitter Sweet*, *The Merry Widow*, *The Vagabond King*, and

---

[63] "Mr. Tours Chalks Up a Conductor's Record: Directs an Irving Berlin Score for the 2,000th Time Today," unidentified newspaper article, Frank Tours personal scrapbooks.

[64] John Dunning: *On the Air: The Encyclopedia of Old-Time Radio* (New York: Oxford University Press, 1998), 722–24.

[65] The Vince Program was named after its sponsor Vince Toothpaste. Ibid., 180.

[66] Richard Jewell, *RKO Pictures: A Titan Is Born* (Berkeley, CA: University of California Press, 2012), 141–46.

[67] Gladwin Hill, "Hollywood's Musical Missionary," *The New York Times*, August 8, 1948, X1.

Music in the Air. Three years after being mercifully released from his obligations to RKO, Tours was back in his element, once again leading glamourous productions of live musical theatre for appreciative audiences, a fitting end to an illustrious career as a conductor of light music.

Tours published one final song during this period after nearly two decades of inactivity as a composer. A memory painting of a western traveler in the South Pacific, "West of the Sun" conjures an image of a tryst remembered and longed for again through the sensory experience of a warm and fragrant land. Unlike many Tin Pan Alley songs that essentialized Polynesian culture and women in the wake of the United States' establishment of the territory of Hawaii as a National Park in 1916, the lyric of "West of the Sun" by Dorothy K. Thomas carefully avoids colonialist allusions while indulging in romantic imagery of westerners falling in love in a tropical paradise. Tours' music uses the habañera rhythm to evoke the gentle swaying of palm trees in perfumed trade winds, and his colorful harmonic language—fluctuating easily between major and minor—depicts the rich sensory experience of the poet's dreamscape. The eloquence and sophistication of this swan song shows that he had not lost any of his creative powers during his years of musical menial labor in the music department of RKO.

By the early 1950s, musical culture in the United States, which was dominated by big band jazz and rock-and-roll, had evolved to a point where it had become largely independent from its European heritage. Even Broadway musicals, with the rare exception of a show like *My Fair Lady*, were thoroughly infused with American musical idioms that bore little resemblance to the grand musical romanticism of light opera. As a result, Tours found that his services were no longer being requested by producers in any medium and so he settled into a somewhat uneasy retirement. He returned to New York one more time in 1954 to look for work, and though he was not hired as a conductor, he was employed as a musical secretary by Irving Berlin, who saw that his old friend needed a job when retirement had left him without the dignity of a pension after a lifetime of work. Berlin ultimately rewarded Tours' decades of service to his stage career with a generous monthly stipend that kept him free of financial insecurity for the rest of his life.

During these years of professional inactivity, Tours found himself surrounded by a large family that both revered him and was endeared to him as a constant source of fun, warmth, and affability. His love of puns and telling amusing stories was as much a part of their cherished memory of him as their knowledge of his distinguished musical heritage. Several of his fifteen grandchildren recall him happily performing familial duties when he came to live with them intermittently or they with him. Just as he had been an avid maker of photographic scrapbooks during the 1900s and 1910s and of silent home movies in the 1920s and 1930s that documented his life and work, he also loved making personal sound recordings with his children and extended family where he would talk and play the piano for them. Once he was no longer working for the music industry in any capacity, he dedicated more and more of his time to playing the piano, where he would improvise for hours at a time in long, sustained streams of invention. No longer composing songs or music of any kind, he crystalized his musical ideas into impromptu instrumental rhapsodies that those who witnessed them remember with a mixture of awe and delight. Tours also spent time preserving his legacy, creating bound copies of his personal sheet music collection and compiling detailed lists of the musical productions he directed and of his published musical works. Frank and Helen had spent their years in Los Angeles living in several different parts of the city, from Santa Monica to Beverly Hills to Hollywood. They lived in a modest house in Westwood when he died of natural causes at the age of eighty-five on February 1, 1963.[68] At the end of his life, Frank Tours' music was out of print, no longer performed, and largely forgotten by a public for whom "Mother o' Mine" would have been thought of as the old fashioned music of one's parents' or grandparents' generation, if it was remembered at all. But the legacy that his family has kindled for five decades is not just the memory of an ancestor's former glory; it is a living legacy in music that contains a wealth of artistic beauty in addition to being a window to a different age. If given due consideration, the songs of Frank Tours, will once again be valued as an elegant and meaningful reflection of their time and place.

---

[68] "Frank Tours, Orchestra Conductor, Dies at 85," *Los Angeles Times*, February 3, 1963, H9.

PLATES

Plate 1. Berthold Tours Family Portrait (circa 1893). From left to right: Frank, Herman (seated on the floor), Berthold George (Frank's eldest brother), Henry, Susan (née Taylor, Frank's mother), Berthold, and Louis.

MR. FRANK E. TOURS
Musical Director

Plate 2. Frank Tours, circa 1912, from a souvenir program of the DeKoven Opera Company revival of *Robin Hood*.

Plate 3. Frank Tours, circa 1914, still sporting his walrus mustache, *en route* to London to conduct at the Empire Theatre.

Plate 4. Frank Tours and the Plaza Theatre Orchestra on stage in 1926.

Plate 5. Frank Tours conducting on a pit with a hydraulic lift in *The Great Waltz*, circa 1934.

Plate 6. Frank Tours with Irving Berlin around the time of his 2,000th performance of Berlin's music for the theatre in 1934.

Plate 7. Frank Tours and his family, circa 1933. Standing, from left to right are Joan, Susan, and Frank; seated, from left to right, are Helen, Phoebe, Elliott, and Frank Jr.

Plate 8. Frank Tours at the piano, circa late-1950s.

INDIVIDUAL SONGS

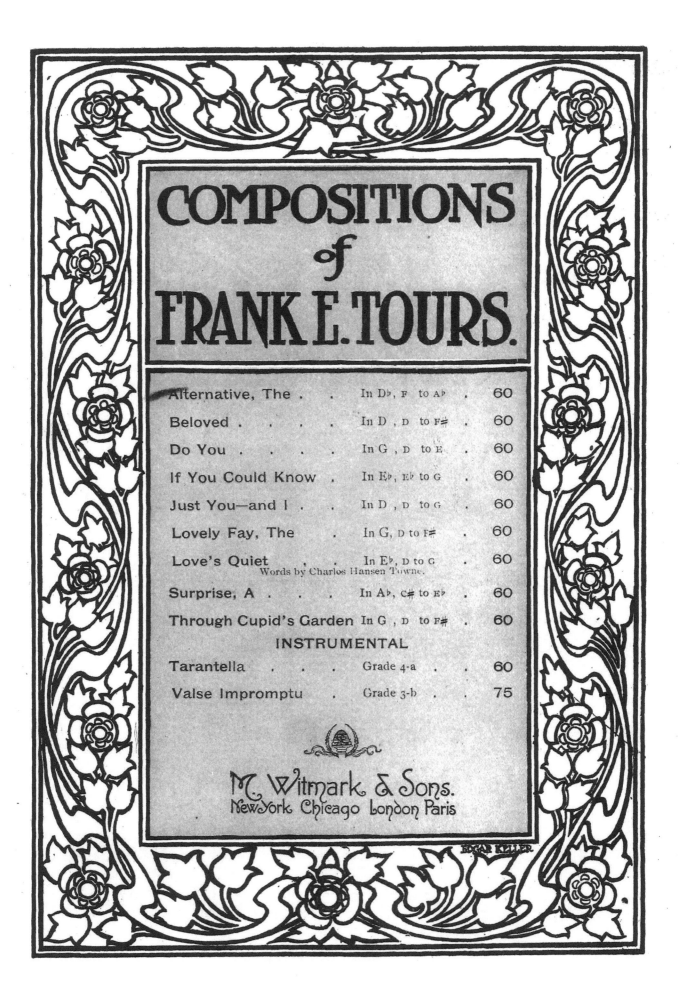

COMPOSITIONS
of
FRANK E. TOURS.

M. Witmark & Sons.
New York Chicago London Paris

The Alternative.

Words by
ARTHUR ANDERSON.

Music by
FRANK E. TOURS.

If I have dared my love to tell, Know- ing 'twere best un-said — Will you not say 'tis just as well,

6115-6

4

DAVIS AND THORSETT

poco accel.

And be my friend in - stead? Since I de - cide to play the

poco accel.

man, And dare to drink the cup,———

Will you not help me all you can, And strive to— lift me

up?

The Alternative. 6115-6

4

If you will still be-lieve in me, Prom-ise to be my

Allegretto.

friend, Trust - ing in my sin - cer - i - ty, Re -

main so to the end: I am con-tent that

you should know All that my heart doth fill, The

The Alternative. 6115-6

The Alternative. 6115–6

Tempo I.

You will not light - ly cast a - way   All that I have to

give;   Spurn with the love of yes - ter - day To-

day's___ al - ter - na - tive.   For you must know, the way is

rough,   When we are far a - part,___

The Alternative. 6115-6

Sure - ly there must be room e - nough, For friend - ship, for

friend - - ship in your heart. Sure - ly there must be

colla voce.

room e - nough, for friend - ship, For friend - - ship

in your heart.

Beloved.

Words by
J. EDWARD FRASER.

Music by
FRANK E. TOURS.

6077-4

Davis and Thorsett

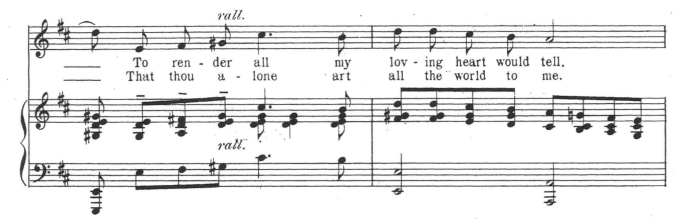

rall.

To ren - der all my lov - ing heart would tell.
That thou a - lone art all the world to me.

a tempo

The gift of love is sure - ly high and ho - ly,
Ah!___ take me up! thy lips in an - swer giv - ing,___

stringendo

___ Nor sound nor song it's full in - tent di - vine;
___ Thine arms en - fold, in pas - sion - ate em - brace,

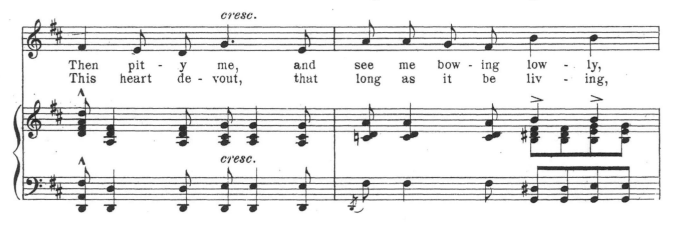

cresc.

Then pit - y me, and see me bow - ing low - ly,
This heart de - vout, and that long as it be liv - ing,

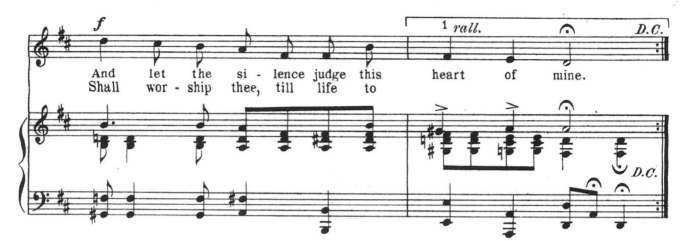

And let the si - lence judge this heart of mine.
Shall wor - ship thee, till life to

death give place, This heart de - vout, that

long as it be liv - ing, Shall wor - ship thee, till life to

death give place.

Sung by
HERBERT WITHERSPOON

Beyond The Sunset.
(And God Is Overhead.)

Lyric by
HOLMAN QUINN.

Music by
FRANK E. TOURS.

Slowly with expression.

O do not mourn, be-lov-ed, Or weep when I am
O kla-ge nicht, Ge-lieb-te, Wenn ich im To-de

dead; For the life of man Is but a span, And God is o-ver-
bleich; Denn der Er-den-lauf Führt ja hin auf Zu Got-tes sel-'gem

5315

M.W.& SONS 11743-4

14

Davis and Thorsett

wing through the sun - set bars.
e - wi - ge Son - ne scheint

Then
D'rum

Tempo I.

do. not mourn, be - lov - ed, Or weep when I am
wei ne nicht, Ge - lieb - te, Wenn ich im To de

Little slower:

dead: For the life of man Is but a span, And
bleich Denn der Er - den - lauf Führt ja hin auf Zu

God is o - ver - head.
Got - tes sel - 'gem Reich.

DAVIS AND THORSETT

M.W.&SONS 11743-4

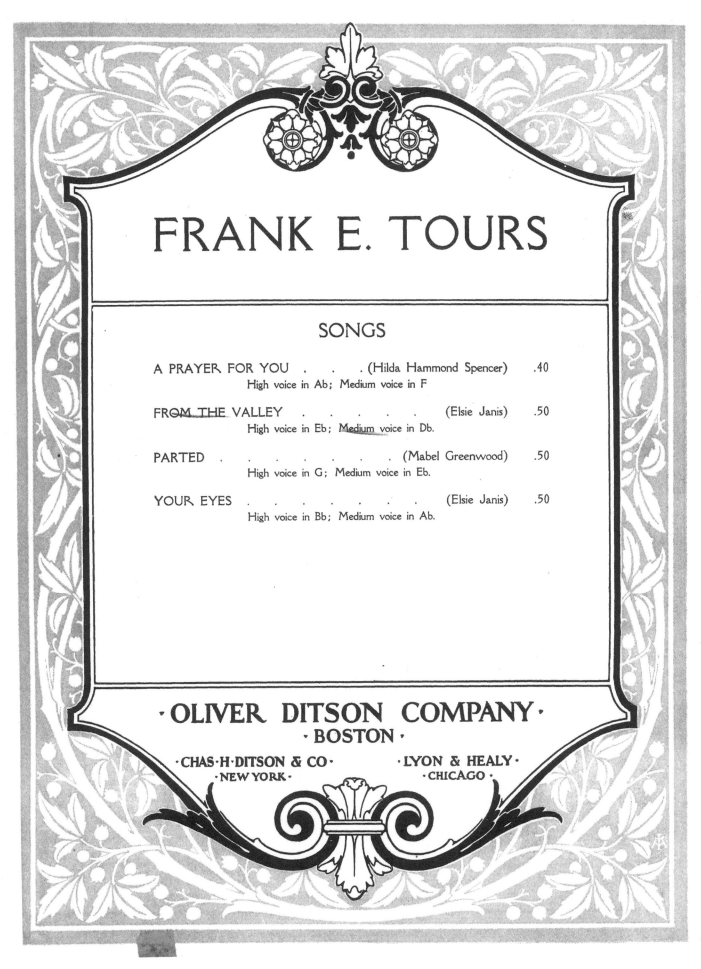

FRANK E. TOURS

SONGS

A PRAYER FOR YOU . . . . (Hilda Hammond Spencer) .40
High voice in Ab; Medium voice in F

FROM THE VALLEY . . . . . (Elsie Janis) .50
High voice in Eb; Medium voice in Db.

PARTED . . . . (Mabel Greenwood) .50
High voice in G; Medium voice in Eb.

YOUR EYES . . . . (Elsie Janis) .50
High voice in Bb; Medium voice in Ab.

OLIVER DITSON COMPANY
· BOSTON ·

CHAS·H·DITSON & CO· LYON & HEALY·
·NEW YORK·   ·CHICAGO·

FROM THE VALLEY

(Original Key, E♭)

ELSIE JANIS

FRANK E. TOURS

Out of the val-ley of dis-con-tent, In - to the fields of joy I went, One sum - mer day. I gath - er'd a few of the flow'rs of life, And left be - hind me

5-79-68711-3

DAVIS AND THORSETT

4

The years have pass'd, my dream is o'er, And here am I in the

val-ley once more: Life is sweet and to all I say: Gath- er the flow-ers

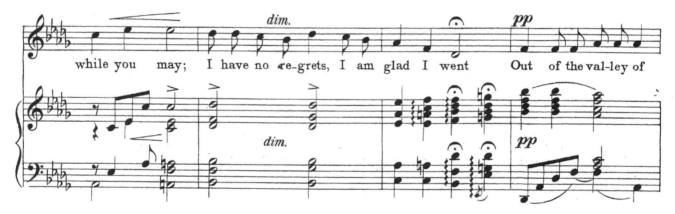

while you may; I have no re-grets, I am glad I went Out of the val-ley of

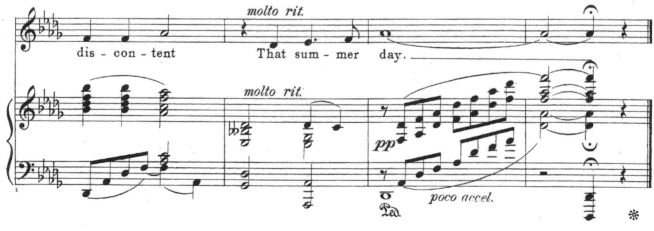

dis - con - tent That sum - mer day.

5-79-68711-3

Fury of the Sea

Poem by Edmund Goulding

Music by FRANK E. TOURS

High Voice E♭

Low Voice D♭

Price, 50 cents
(In U. S. A.)

THE BOSTON MUSIC CO.
BOSTON, MASS.

Fury of the Sea

Poem by
Edmund Goulding

Music by
Frank E. Tours

B.M.Co.7190

DAVIS AND THORSETT

Wake me with her red gold

hope at dawn,

Shroud me in my even - ing ____ in her

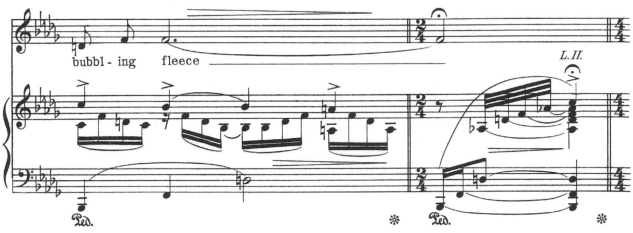

bubbl - ing fleece _____

4

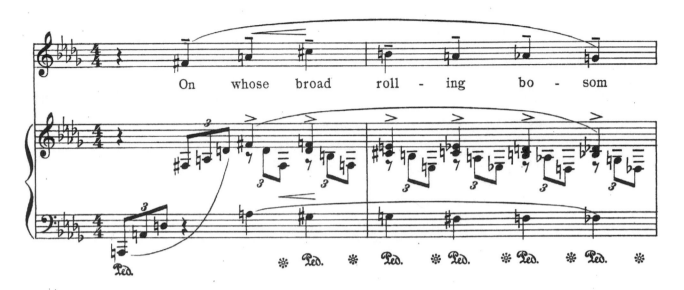

On whose broad roll - ing bo - som

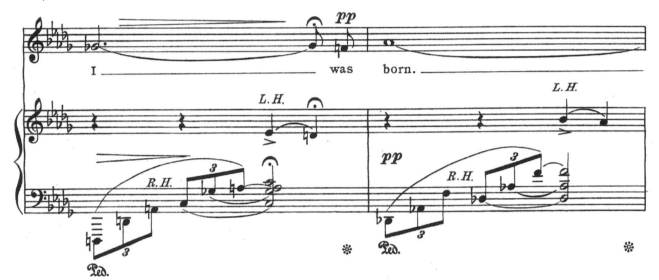

I _____ was born. _____

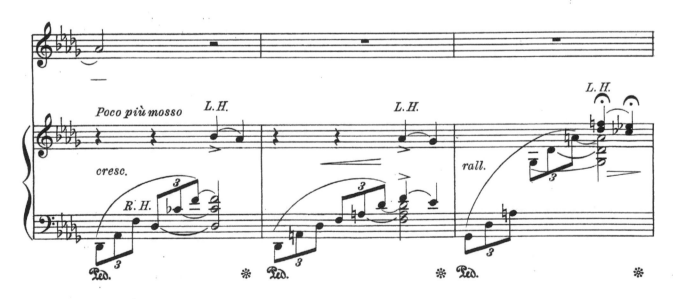

B.M.Co. 7190

DAVIS AND THORSETT

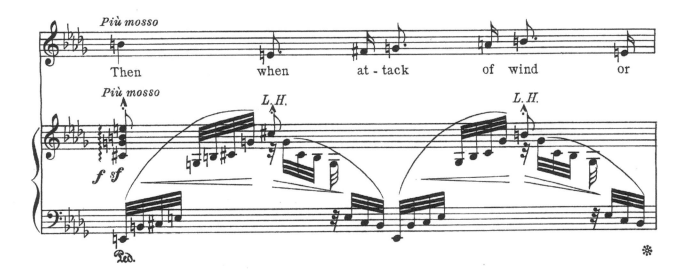

Then when at-tack of wind or

will Shall

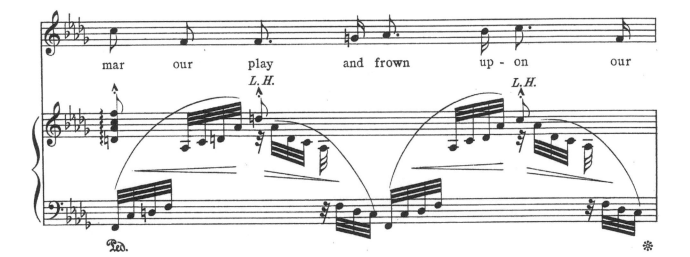

mar our play and frown up-on our

B.M.Co.7190

glee,

cresc.

Scream - - ing, we'll

rise and

crush and

B.M.Co.7190

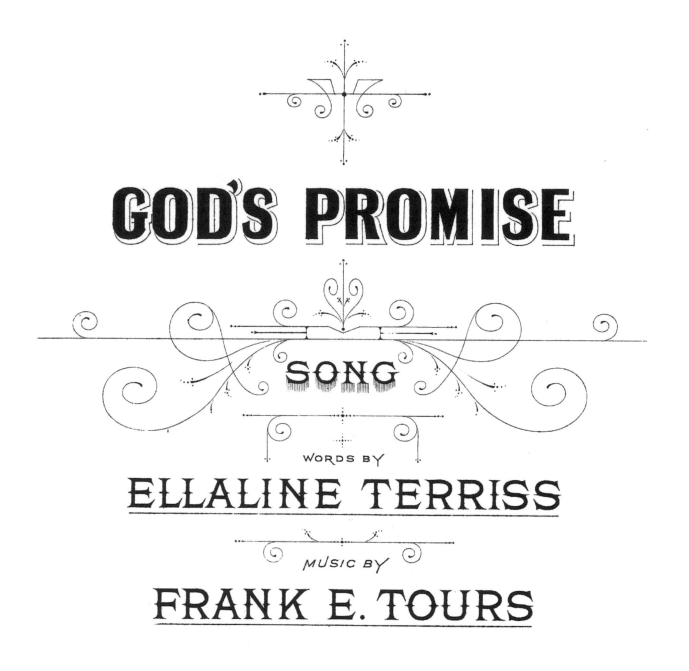

GOD'S PROMISE

SONG

WORDS BY

ELLALINE TERRISS

MUSIC BY

FRANK E. TOURS

CHAPPELL & Co LTD.
50, NEW BOND STREET, LONDON, W.

NEW YORK:
37, WEST SEVENTEENTH STREET.

MELBOURNE:
11 & 12, THE RIALTO, COLLINS STREET.

5767.

TO BETTY.

GOD'S PROMISE.

Song.

Words by
ELLALINE TERRISS.

Music by
FRANK E. TOURS.

Fai - ry pink and — bloom of a - zure, Gen - tle — pan - sies, Mig - non - ette, Bor - d'ring paths of my Life's Gar - den, Ways I'd — trod - den

23686

THE SONGS OF FRANK E. TOURS

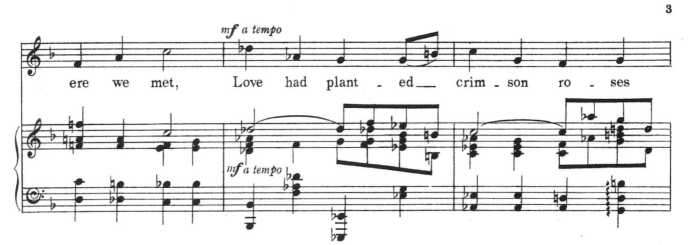

ere we met, Love had plant _ ed__ crim _ son ro _ ses

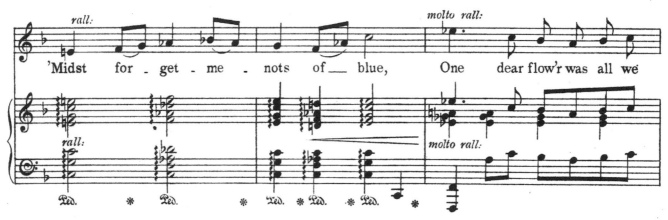

'Midst for _ get _ me _ nots of __ blue, One dear flow'r was all we

prayed for,_____ God gave a pro_mise, love, to

me____ and you.

23686

4

Ev - en-song and an - gels' voi - ces Whis - p'ring from a world of rest, Bid us seek our won - d'rous blos - som, Flow'r of Pro - mise He had blest, Stand - ing 'midst love's crim - son ro - ses, Snow - white pet - als, Kissed by ev - 'ning dew, We

23686

found a li - ly pure and ten - der,_____

This was God's Pro - mise, love, to me___ and you.

tenuto

colla voce

Tempo I.

con Ped.

Gold - en curls and dear brown eyes,___ Pat - ter - ing feet and

voice of bells, Ev - 'ry thought to you is giv - en,

23686

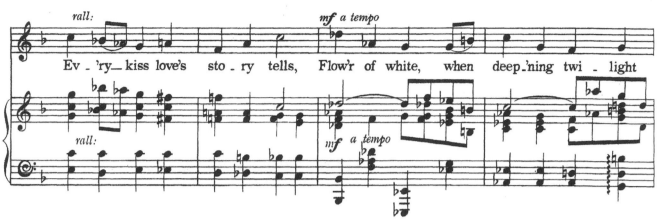

Ev - 'ry_ kiss love's sto - ry tells, Flow'r of white, when deep'ning twi - light

Fades the_ col - our of rose and_ blue, Pure and sweet we see our

Li - ly_____ God sent an an-gel, Ba-by mine, 'Twas you,

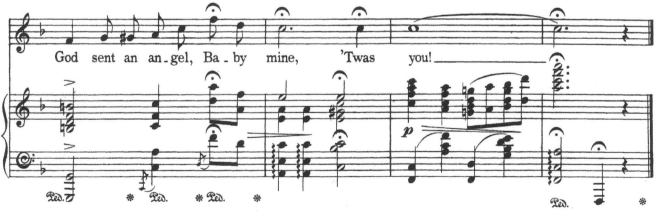

God sent an an-gel, Ba-by mine, 'Twas you!_____

LOW   MEDIUM   HIGH

HOPE DREAMS

SONG

WORDS BY

JOHN STEEL

MUSIC BY

FRANK E. TOURS

PRICE **40** CENTS
NET – NO DISCOUNT

UNITY MUSIC PUBLISHERS
· INCORPORATED ·
GRAND CENTRAL PALACE BUILDING
NEW YORK CITY

DAVIS AND THORSETT

Hope Dreams

Words by
JOHN STEEL

Music by
FRANK E. TOURS

found a book of mem-o-ries That Time had cast up from its seas, ___ I

gazed with-in its sa-cred seal, And found a Hope I now re - veal. ___ The

Hope was mine to keep or slay, With - in my heart 'twill live for aye.

Moderato

O Star of Hope shin-ing bright-ly, Where is your cheer-ing

ray? For in your Heav'n to me night-ly You ev-er seem to

say, You'll bring back the Spring-time of ro - ses,

Hope Dreams 5

Turn skies of gray to blue; Give me all your mes-sage dis-clos-es, And my hope dreams will come true._____

Andantino e con moto

A

hope is found in ev-ry heart, There's one in mine, 'twill ne'er de-part;_____ Not

Hope Dreams 5

like the rose, that blooms and dies, My hope will live, though Death de - fies, _____ And

ev - er flam-ing in my breast, It fills my soul with per-fect rest.

Moderato

O Star of Hope shin-ing bright-ly, Where is your cheer-ing

ray? For in your Heav'n to me night-ly, You ev-er seem to

Hope Dreams 5

say,　　You'll　bring back the Spring-time of　ro - ses,

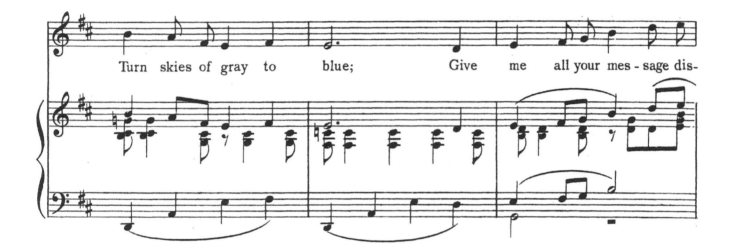

Turn skies of gray to　blue;　Give　me　all your mes - sage dis-

clos - es,　And my　hope dreams will come true.

pp

ppp

Hope Dreams 5

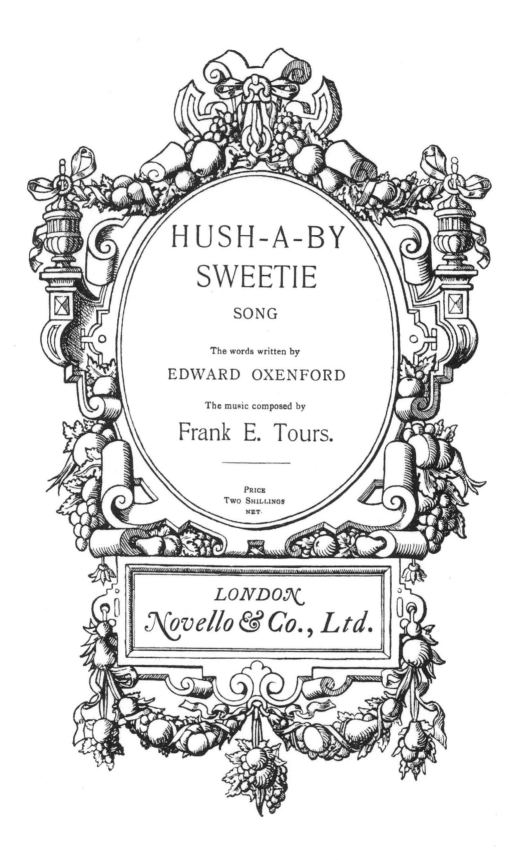

HUSH-A-BY SWEETIE

SONG

The words written by

EDWARD OXENFORD

The music composed by

Frank E. Tours.

Price
Two Shillings
Net.

LONDON
Novello & Co., Ltd.

Davis and Thorsett

HUSH-A-BY, SWEETIE.

Edward Oxenford.

Frank E. Tours.

11715

West. The flow'rs that you love now their pet - als all close, And

hide pret - ty col-ours a - way: Like good lit - tle peo - ple, they

calm - ly re-pose Till a - rous'd by the dawn of the day.

Hush - a - by, Sweet-ie; Hush, Hush-a -by! Gone has the day - light, and

DAVIS AND THORSETT

mu - sic is o'er, And so sleep, as the right thing to do. The

dear lit-tle lambs are no long - er at play, But rest in the fold where they

dwell; So now, pret-ty mite, till the dawn of the day Shut your

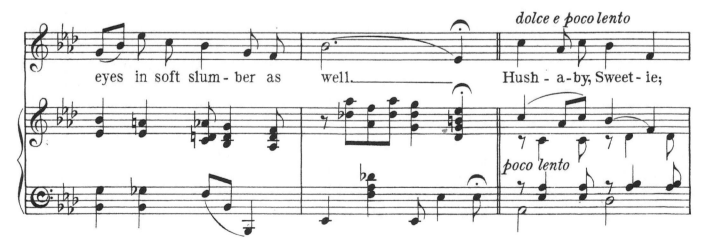

eyes in soft slum - ber as well._____ Hush - a-by, Sweet - ie;

Davis and Thorsett

FRANK E. TOURS

VOCAL

ALTERNATIVE, THE In C, c to G	*Lyric by Arthur Anderson*	60
BELOVED In D, d to F♯	*Lyric by J. Edward Fraser*	60
BEYOND THE SUNSET (And God Is Overhead)		60
Four keys, C Minor, B to D; D Minor, c to E; E Minor, d to F♯; G Minor, F to A		
	Lyric by Holman Quinn	
DO YOU? In G, d to E	*Lyric by Fred. E. Weatherly*	60
HE GIVETH HIS BELOVED SLEEP In A♭, E♭ to E♭	*Lyric by Wm. H. Gardner*	60
I DREAMED In G, c♯ to G	*Lyric by Holman Quinn*	60
IF THE WEALTH OF THE WORLD WERE MINE (The Price)		60
In A♭, E♭ to F	*Lyric by Wm. H. Gardner*	
IF YOU COULD KNOW In E♭, E♭ to G	*Lyric by Wilton Heriot*	60
JUST TO FORGET In G, d to F♯	*Lyric by Edward Teschemacher*	60
JUST YOU AND I In D, d to G	*Lyric by Wilton Heriot*	60
LOVELY FAY, THE In G, d to F♯	*Lyric by Arthur Anderson*	60
LOVE NOT IN VAIN In A♭, D♭ to F	*Lyric by Harold Simpson*	60
LOVE'S QUIET In E♭, D to G	*Lyric by Charles Hanson Towne*	60
OH BRING ME LOVE In F, c to F	*Lyric by Harold Simpson*	60
SUPPOSE (If You Loved Me) In A, E to F♯	*Lyric by Hilda Hammond Spencer*	60
SURPRISE, A In A♭, c♯ to E♭	*Lyric by D. Eardley Wilmot*	60
THROUGH CUPID'S GARDEN In G, d to F♯	*Lyric by Wilton Heriot*	60
THOU BLESSED MAN OF GOD	*Lyric by Wm. H. Gardner*	60
Two keys, C, c to E; E♭., E♭ to G		
WAITING FOR GOD AND THEE (Longing)	*Lyric by Katherine Stagg*	60
In F, c to F		
WHEN SUMMER DAYS DEPART In D, d to E	*Lyric by Harold Simpson*	60
WHEN I AM ALL YOUR OWN	*Lyric by Louis Weslyn*	60
Two keys, A♭, B to G♭ B♭, c♯ to A♭		
WHEN YOU ARE NEAR In G, d to F♯	*Lyric by Harold Simpson*	60
YEAR AGO, A In D Minor, d to D	*Lyric by Edward Teschemacher*	60

INSTRUMENTAL

Title	Grade	Price
BALARIA (Russian Dance)	4-a	.50
CUPID (Valse Brillante)	3-b	.75
LOVE'S PROMISE (Valse)	3-b	.75
TARANTELLA	4-a	.60
TRUANT LOVE (Valse)	3-b	.75
VALSE IMPROMPTU	3-b	.75

M. WITMARK & SONS

NEW YORK   CHICAGO   SAN FRANCISCO   LONDON   PARIS

I Dreamed.

Lyric by
HOLMAN QUINN.

Music by
FRANK E. TOURS.

I dreamed last night of days long dead, Van - ished was my pain;___ The bit - ter bar - ren years rolled back And Youth was mine_ a -

gain.__ For she Death stole, was at__ my side, And hand was fond - ly

clasped in hand; We watched the sea - birds in their flight, The waves break on the

strand.__ A south wind blew from the sap - phire sea; The air was sweet with

flow - ers; And heart, re-spons-ive, beat to heart,_____ For

Love and Hope were ours.____

Then changed the spir - it of__ my dream, It

seemed but yes - ter - night;____ Up - on__ a shadow-y heath we stood, Where

no star shed its light.__ But ra - diant as the dawn she shone, Such

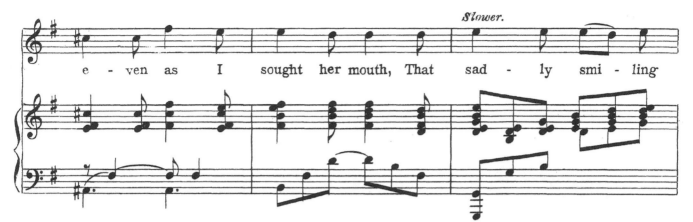

e - ven as I sought her mouth, That sad - ly smi - ling

seemed,___ E'en then, e'en then I knew, a-las, I knew, a-las, I

dreamed!___ E'en then, e'en then, I knew, a-las, I knew, a-las, I

dreamed!___

IF YOU LOVED ME

SONG

LYRIC BY

Hilda Hammond Spencer

MUSIC BY

FRANK E. TOURS

Composer of "MOTHER O' MINE", "BEYOND THE SUNSET" *etc.*

Price 60 cents.

M. WITMARK & SONS,

NEW YORK   CHICAGO   SAN FRANCISCO
LONDON   PARIS   MELBOURNE.

623

If You Loved Me

Lyric by
HILDA HAMMOND SPENCER.

Music by
FRANK E. TOURS.

6164

Copyright MCMXIV by M. Witmark & Sons.
International Copyright Secured.

THE SONGS OF FRANK E. TOURS

Sum-mer here a - gain.__ The hours would glide a - way too soon, For

life would be_ a per - fect tune.___

When woods were dark and

blos - soms dead, O, hand in hand_ we'd stray,___ Though grey the heav - ens

o - ver - head, And sad the path where leaves are shed, We'd
dance a - long the way. Our glor - ious world would
bud a - new, If you loved me as I love you! The
flow'rs would wake on mead - ow lea, When mer - ry Spring-time came, Glad

accel. *rit.* *broadly*

slowly *lunga pausa.*

With animation

Tempo I.

birds would mate in ev - 'ry tree, Their lit - tle hearts make mel - o - dy, And

gradual retard to finish

we__ should do the same!_____ O, Love, how sweet__ the

world would be. (Since I love you,)__ If you loved

me!_____

M.W.&SONS 12105-4

IN FLANDERS' FIELDS

Lyric by
Lieut-Col. JOHN MᶜCRAE

Music by
FRANK E. TOURS

·7112

M.W.&SONS 15783-5

Copyright MCMXVIII by M. Witmark & Sons

Davis and Thorsett

Scarce___ heard a-mid the guns___ be - low.___

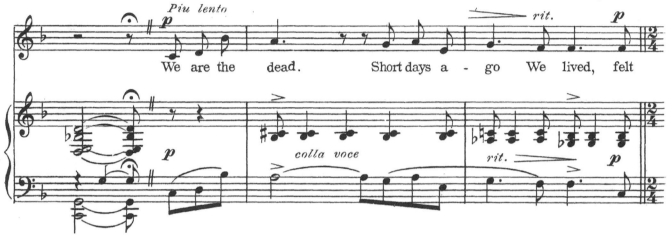

We are the dead. Short days a - go We lived, felt

dawn, saw sun - set glow;

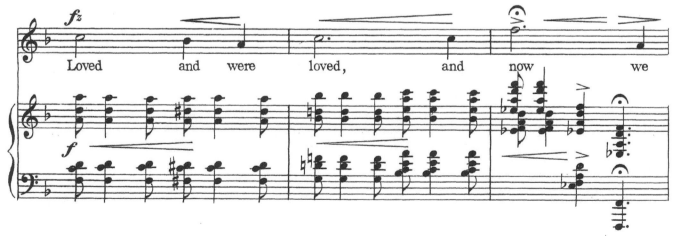

Loved and were loved, and now we

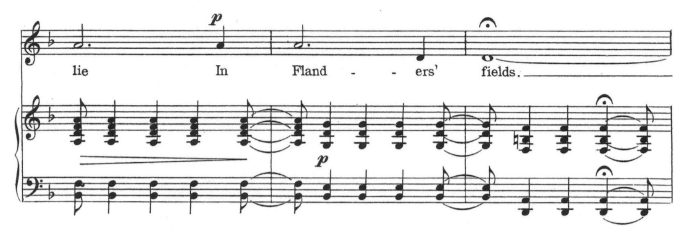

M.W.& SONS 15783 — 5

hold it high! If ye break faith with us who die, We _____ shall not sleep, though pop - pies grow _____ In Fland - ers' fields, _____ In Fland - ers' fields.

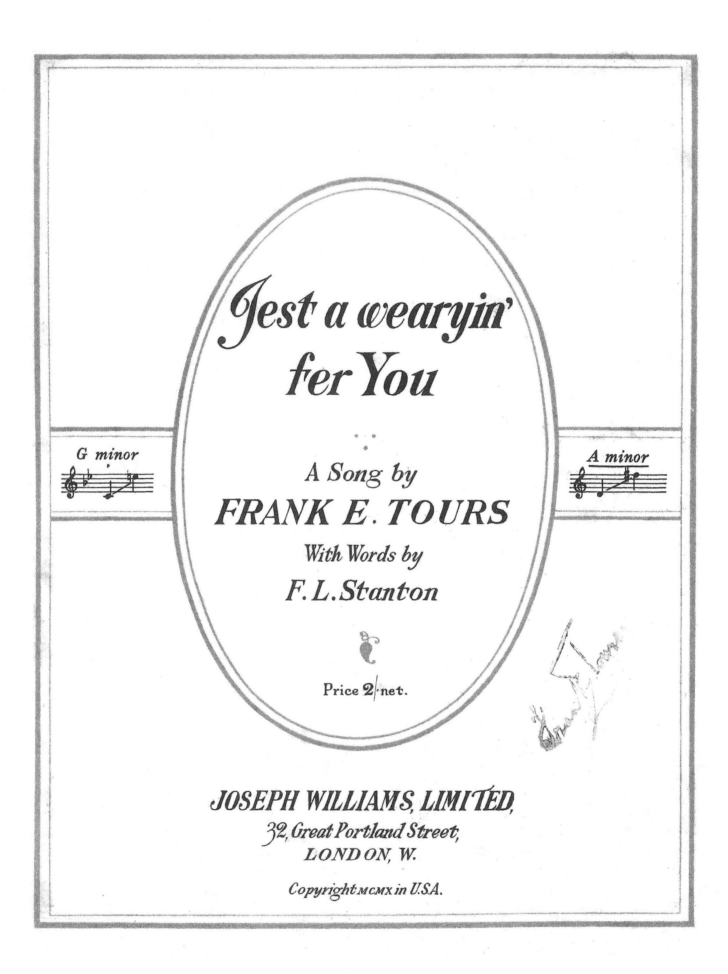

Jest a wearyin'
fer You

A Song by
FRANK E. TOURS

With Words by

F. L. Stanton

Price **2**/net.

JOSEPH WILLIAMS, LIMITED,
32, Great Portland Street,
LONDON, W.

Copyright MCMX in U.S.A.

G minor

A minor

Jest a wearyin' fer you.

Words by
F. L. STANTON.

Music by
FRANK E. TOURS.

J. W. 15101.

Rooms so lone-some with your chair Emp-ty by the fire-place there

Jest can't stand the sight o' it go out doors and roam a bit

But the woods is lone-some, too,............ Jest a wea-ry - in'............

.... fer you Eve - nin' comes I miss you more............

Davis and Thorsett

When the dark is in the door........ 'Pears as like you

or - ter be there to op - en it fer me................. Latch goes

Quasi recit.

tink - lin'........ Thrills me through sets............ me

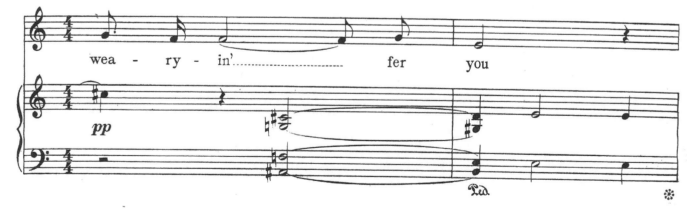

wea - ry - in'........................ fer you

pp

Crome. Printer. 12. Ham Yard, G! Windmill Street. W.

Sung by
Mr. JOHN CHARLES THOMAS

THE LONG DAY

(But I Am Over Here And He Is Over There)

SONG

LYRIC BY

GEORGE V. HOBART

MUSIC BY

FRANK E. TOURS

Composer of "IN FLANDER'S FIELDS" "LITTLEST OF ALL" "NO VOICE BUT YOURS" *Etc.*

Price 60¢ net

M. WITMARK & SONS

NEW YORK   -   CHICAGO   -   PHILADELPHIA
SAN FRANCISCO   -   BOSTON
LONDON

The Long Day

(BUT I AM OVER HERE, AND HE IS OVER THERE!)

George V. Hobart

Frank E. Tours

7179

M.W.& SONS 15862-4

Davis and Thorsett

Noon - day_____ on the

hill!_____ Breez - es_____ soft - ly blow;_____

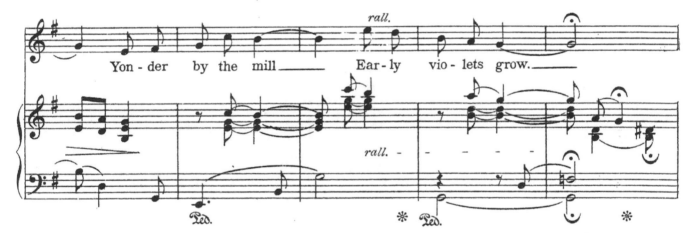

Yon - der by the mill_____ Ear - ly vio - lets grow._____

Chil - dren play - ing near, Na - ture's face is fair,— *But I am o - ver*

M.W.& SONS 15682 - 4

THE SONGS OF FRANK E. TOURS   69

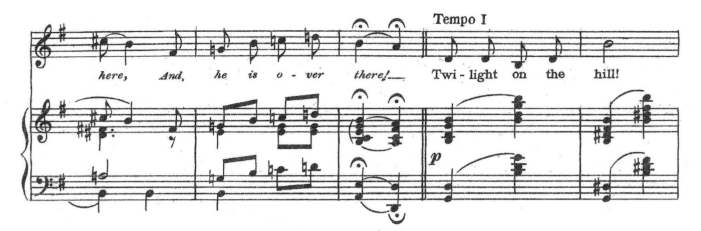

here, And he is o-ver there!___ Twi-light on the hill!

A-zure sky and red; La-zy clouds are still Loi-t'ring home to

bed. Gen-tle stars ap-pear, Night winds croon a pray'r,— But

I am o-ver here, And he is o-ver there!___

M.W.&SONS 15862-4

Davis and Thorsett

MOTHER O'MINE

SONG

WORDS BY

RUDYARD KIPLING

MUSIC BY

FRANK E. TOURS

PRICE R 60 CENTS

EXCEPT CANADA AND FOREIGN COUNTRIES

CHAPPELL & Co., Inc.
RKO BUILDING - ROCKEFELLER CENTER
NEW YORK, N.Y.

CHAPPELL & Co., Ltd.
LONDON — PARIS
SYDNEY

THE WORDS OF THIS SONG ARE REPRINTED FROM MR RUDYARD KIPLING'S "THE LIGHT THAT FAILED"
BY PERMISSION OF THE AUTHOR

PRINTED IN U.S.A.

Mother o' Mine!

Song

Victor Record No. 64332
Pathe   „   „   020690
Vocalion   „   „   30127
Gennett   „   „   10073

Words by
RUDYARD KIPLING

Music by
FRANK E. TOURS

If I ____ were hang'd on the high - est hill, ____ Moth-er o' Mine, I know whose love ____ would fol - low me still, ____ Moth - er o' Mine. ____

By permission of Miss Louise Sington, to whom Mr. Kipling assigned the exclusive rights of the original setting.

C. 6809

If I were drown'd in the deep-est sea,_____

colla voce

_____ Moth-er o' Mine, I know whose tears would come

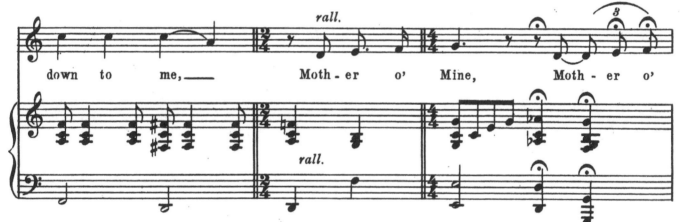

down to me,_____ *rall.* Moth-er o' Mine, Moth-er o'

rall.

Mine.

cantabile

If I were

C. 6309

THE SONGS OF FRANK E. TOURS

damn'd of bod - y and soul, I know whose pray'rs would

make · me whole, I know whose pray'rs ___ would

crescendo

make me whole, ___ Moth - er ___ o' Mine, O, ___

lunga pausa

Ped. ✻

___ Moth - er ___ o' Mine. ___

p

Ped.

ppp ✻

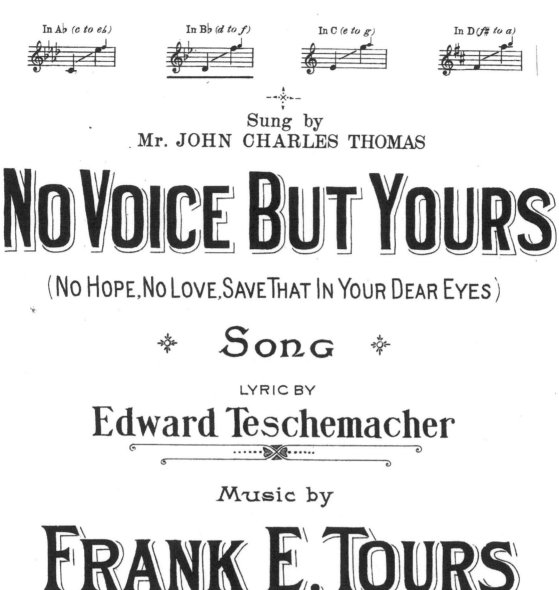

In A♭ (c to e♭)   In B♭ (d to f)   In C (e to g)   In D (f♯ to a)

Sung by
Mr. JOHN CHARLES THOMAS

No Voice But Yours

(NO HOPE, NO LOVE, SAVE THAT IN YOUR DEAR EYES)

Song

LYRIC BY

Edward Teschemacher

Music by

FRANK E. TOURS

Composer of "BEYOND THE SUNSET," "MOTHER O'MINE" etc.

Price 60 cents Net

M.WITMARK & SONS,
NEW YORK • CHICAGO • PHILADELPHIA
SAN FRANCISCO • BOSTON
LONDON.

No Voice But Yours
(No Hope, No Love, Save That In Your Dear Eyes)

No voice but yours I need to gently cheer me,
No other eyes but yours to gleam and shine;
No other hands I need to fondly bless me,
No other joy, if you are ever mine.

No other dreams I need save those you bring me,
No pray'rs but yours for which my spirit sighs,
No other heart I need till life shall fail me,
No heav'n of love, save that in your dear eyes.
No other heart I need till life shall fail me,
No hope, no love, save that in your dear eyes.

Edward Teschmacher

No Voice But Yours

(No Hope, No Love, Save That In Your Dear Eyes)

Lyric by
EDWARD TESCHMACHER

Music by
FRANK E. TOURS

Andante
No voice but yours I
need to gent - ly cheer me,
No oth - er eyes but
yours to gleam and shine;
No oth - er hands I
mp
l.h.
p

6666
M.W.&SONS 15329 4

Copyright MCMXVI by M. Witmark & Sons
International Copyright Secured

need to fond - ly bless me, No oth - er joy, if you are

ev - er mine! No oth - er dreams I

need save those you bring me, No pray'rs but yours for which my spir - it sighs,

No oth-er heart I need till life shall fail me,

No heav'n of love, save that in your dear eyes. No oth-er heart I

need till life shall fail me, No hope, no love, save that in your dear eyes.

molto rall.

M.W. & SONS 15329-4

FRANK E. TOURS

Bring Me Love

VOCAL

ALTERNATIVE, THE	.60
In C, C to G *Lyric by Arthur Anderson*	
BELOVED	.60
In D, D to F# *Lyric by J. Edward Fraser*	
BEYOND THE SUNSET (And God Is Overhead)	.60
Four keys, C Minor, Bb to D; D Minor, C to E; E Minor, D to F#; G Minor, F to A	
Lyric by Holman Quinn	
DO YOU?	.60
In G, D to E *Lyric by Fred. E. Weatherly*	
I DREAMED	.60
In G, C# to G *Lyric by Holman Quinn*	
IF YOU COULD KNOW	.60
In Eb, Eb to G *Lyric by Wilton Heriot*	
JUST TO FORGET	.60
In G, D to F# *Lyric by Edward Teschemacher*	
JUST YOU AND I	.60
In D, D to G *Lyric by Wilton Heriot*	
LOVELY FAY, THE	.60
In G, D to F# *Lyric by Arthur Anderson*	
LOVE NOT IN VAIN	.60
In Ab, Db to F *Lyric by Harold Simpson*	
LOVE'S QUIET	.60
In Eb, D to G *Lyric by Charles Hanson Towne*	
SURPRISE, A	.60
In Ab, C# to Eb *Lyric by D. Eardley Wilmot*	
WHEN SUMMER DAYS DEPART	.60
In D, D to E *Lyric by Harold Simpson*	
THROUGH CUPID'S GARDEN	.60
In G, D to F# *Lyric by Wilton Heriot*	
WHEN I AM ALL YOUR OWN	.60
Two keys Ab, B to Gb – Bb, C# to Ab *Lyric by Louis Weslyn*	
WHEN YOU ARE NEAR	.60
In G, D to F# *Lyric by Harold Simpson*	
YEAR AGO, A	.60
In D Minor, D to D *Lyric by Edward Teschemacher*	

INSTRUMENTAL

	Grade	Price
BALARIA (Russian Dance)	4a	.50
CUPID (Valse Brillante)	3b	.75
LOVE'S PROMISE (Valse)	3b	.75
TARANTELLA	4a	.60
TRUANT LOVE (Valse)	3b	.75
VALSE IMPROMPTU	3b	.75

M. WITMARK & SONS

NEW YORK   CHICAGO   SAN FRANCISCO   LONDON   PARIS

Dedicated to Orville Harrold.

Oh, Bring Me Love!

Lyric by
HAROLD SIMPSON.

Music by
FRANK E. TOURS.

With much expression.

bring   me tears,   to ease me of my pain,   And

let   me weep   with - in thine arms a - gain.   Oh,

M.W.& SONS. 12135 - 4

bring me love, that love may not be vain, Oh,

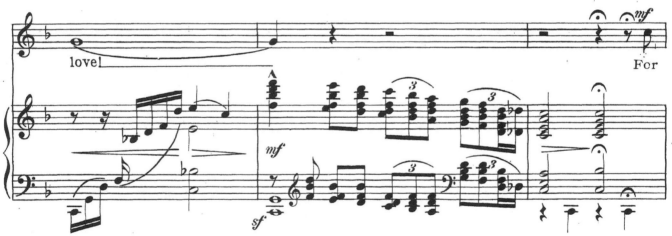

bring me love,_____ Oh, bring me

love!_____ For

what, but tears, can heal the a-ching smart? And

DAVIS AND THORSETT

what, but love, can calm my rest-less heart? Then

bring me love, though soon we have to part,

Oh, bring me love, Oh, bring me love!

M.W. & SONS. 12135 - 4

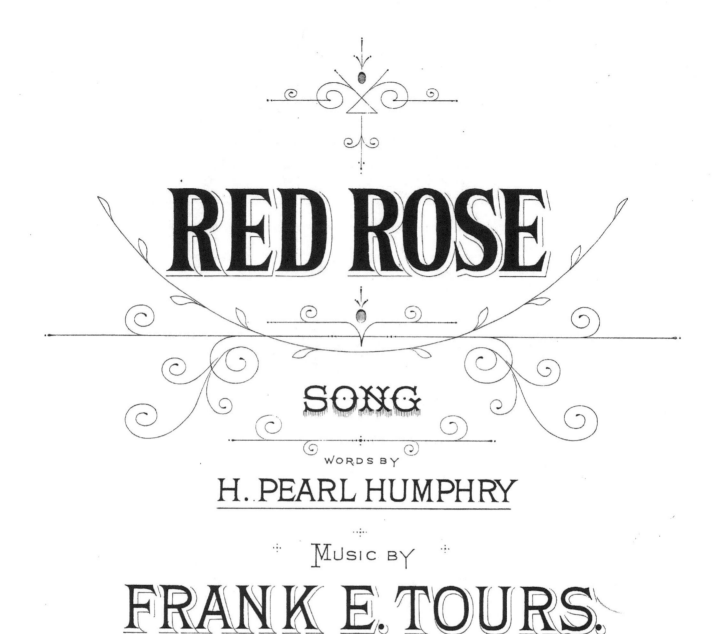

RED ROSE

SONG

WORDS BY

H. PEARL HUMPHRY

MUSIC BY

FRANK E. TOURS.

CHAPPELL & Co LTD.
50, NEW BOND STREET, LONDON, W.

NEW YORK:
37, WEST SEVENTEENTH STREET.

MELBOURNE:
11 & 12, THE RIALTO, COLLINS STREET.

DAVIS AND THORSETT

RED ROSE.

Song.

Words by
H. PEARL HUMPHRY.

Music by
FRANK E. TOURS.

23280

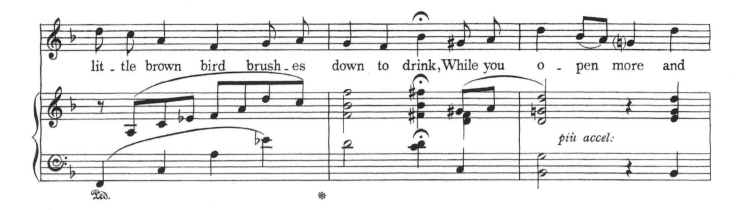

lit _ tle brown bird brush _ es down to drink, While you o _ pen more and

più accel:

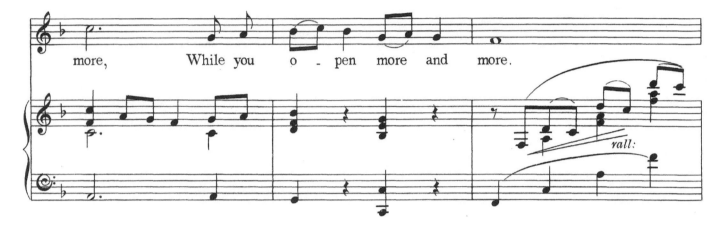

more, While you o _ pen more and more.

rall:

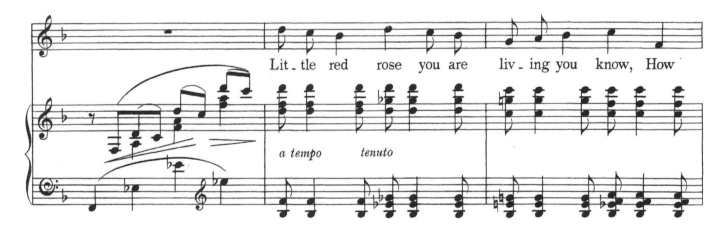

Lit _ tle red rose you are liv _ ing you know, How

a tempo *tenuto*

long, lit _ tle rose, how long? Live as hard as you can for your

time will go And lit_tle pluck'd ro_ses may on_ly blow For the

length of a lit_tle birds' song. Lit_tle brown rose are you

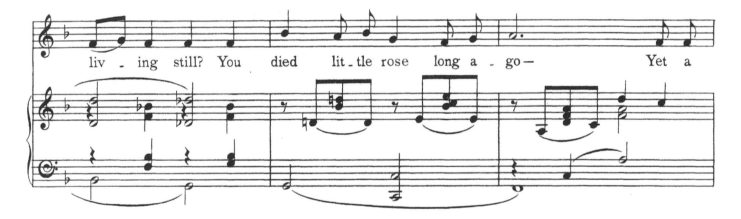

liv_ing still? You died lit_tle rose long a_go— Yet a

ro_se's thought that no time__ can kill With

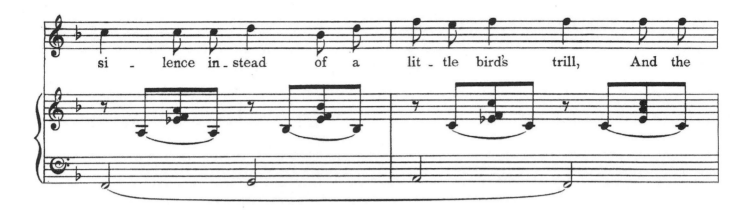

si _ lence in _ stead of a lit _ tle bird's trill, And the

beat of a heart for the rush of a rill, Keep the lit _ tle brown rose a _

meno mosso

_glow And the beat of a heart for the rush of a rill Keep the

rall:

lit _ tle brown rose a _ glow. _____

dim:

23280

Davis and Thorsett

Son Of My Heart

SONG

LYRIC BY

EDWARD TESCHEMACHER

MUSIC BY

FRANK E. TOURS

Composer of "MOTHER O' MINE", "BEYOND THE SUNSET" *etc.*

Price 60 cents.

M. WITMARK & SONS,

NEW YORK · CHICAGO · LONDON.

Son Of My Heart

Oh! you're a bonny lad and true,
    Son of my heart,
And oh! I'm fond and right proud of you,
    Son of my heart,
With your brow all curls and your rosy lips
That are set with smiles apart;
And you're mine, all mine, that's the best of it,
    Son of my heart.

I've no sermon to preach you, never fear,
    Son of my heart,
For the goal for you shines bright and clear,
    Son of my heart,
You must take your song from the wind and waves
'Ere the troubles rise and start,
And make what is best in life your own,
    Son of my heart.

Oh! you'll be a great big man one day,
    Son of my heart,
And you'll have to fight as you take your way,
    Son of my heart,
Oh! be brave and strong through the roughest storm
And be true and just bear your part,
And you'll take God's blessing and mine with you,
    Son of my heart.

Edward Teschemacher

M.W. & SONS 15013 - 4

Son Of My Heart

Lyric by
EDWARD TESCHEMACHER

Music by
FRANK E. TOURS

Son of my heart. _____

I've no ser-mon to preach you, nev - er fear, Son _____ of my heart. For the

goal for you shines bright and clear, Son _____ of my heart;— You must take your song from the

wind and waves 'Ere the troub-les rise and start,— And make what is best in life your own,—

M.W.& SONS 15012 - 4

DAVIS AND THORSETT

A WAYSIDE PRAYER

SONG

The Words by

ELSIE JANIS

The Music by

FRANK E. TOURS

PRICE 2/- NET

BOOSEY & CO., LTD.
295, REGENT STREET, LONDON, W.
AND
STEINWAY HALL, III-II3, WEST 57TH STREET, NEW YORK.

CLASS (B)

PRINTED IN ENGLAND

DAVIS AND THORSETT

A Wayside Prayer

God, let me live each lovely day
So I may know that come what may
I've done my best to live the way
    You want me to.

Forgive me, if I do not pray
The ordered and the formal way
In church on ev'ry sabbath day
    As some folks do.

Just let me know if I should stray,
That I may stop along the way
At any time of night or day,
    And talk to You.

ELSIE JANIS.

A WAYSIDE PRAYER.

Words by
ELSIE JANIS.

Music by
FRANK E. TOURS.

God, let me live each love-ly day............ So

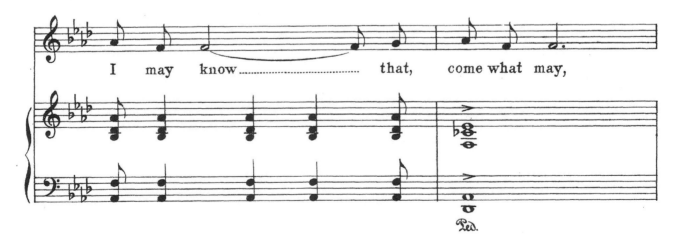

I may know.................... that, come what may,

H. 12130.

Davis and Thorsett

I've done my best to live the way You want me to.

For-give me, if I do not pray The

ordered and the for-mal way In church on ev-'ry

rit. - - -

rit. - - - legato

sab-bath day As some folks do........

A wayside Prayer.

H. 12130.

West of the Sun

Dorothy K. Thomas

Frank E. Tours

My heart is dream - ing____ Of a love - ly trop - ic
Trade winds are blow - ing____ In a land where I would

land____ Where days are long, the air is
be,____ All night and day they seem to

41574 c

Davis and Thorsett

41574

West of the sun,_____ And be-yond the moon, my dear,

Un-der the palms_____ By a blue la - goon, my dear, I

found you,_____ and you whis-pered, Dear, I'll ev - er be near you, I

DAVIS AND THORSETT

hear you,_____ in my dreams your voice I hear.

Back of the moon,____ More than half a

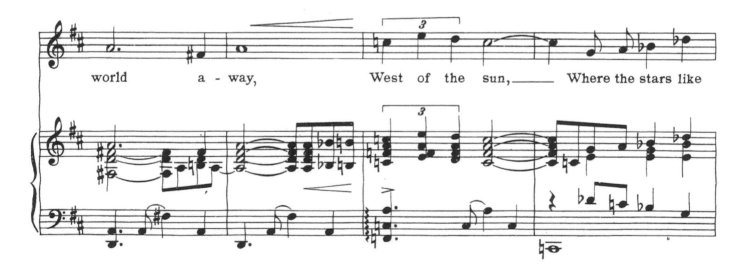

world a - way, West of the sun,_____ Where the stars like

lan - terns sway. And soft winds breathe per-fume On the

sum - mer air, Star - white flow'rs you wore in your

dark brown hair. West toward the sun,_____ When the low hung

DAVIS AND THORSETT

41574

moon is new, Wait-ing is done, I am on my way

to you.

you.

riten.

The Songs of Frank E. Tours

SONG SETS

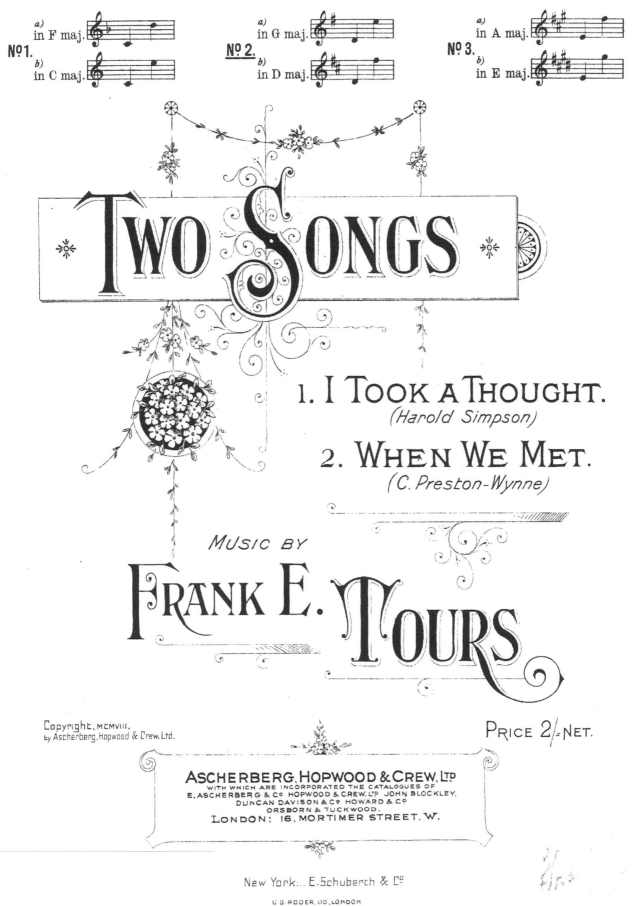

Two Songs

1. I Took a Thought.
(Harold Simpson)

2. When We Met.
(C. Preston-Wynne)

Music by

Frank E. Tours

Copyright, MCMVIII,
by Ascherberg, Hopwood & Crew, Ltd.

Price 2/= Net.

Ascherberg, Hopwood & Crew, Ltd
WITH WHICH ARE INCORPORATED THE CATALOGUES OF
E. Ascherberg & Co Hopwood & Crew, Ltd John Blockley,
Duncan Davison & Co Howard & Co
Orsborn & Tuckwood.
London: 16, Mortimer Street. W.

New York:.. E. Schuberth & Co

C. G. Röder, Ltd., London

I TOOK A THOUGHT.

Words by
HAROLD SIMPSON.

Music by
FRANK E. TOURS.

-way in-to the dis - tant blue.　　　　　　　　I took a

thought and wove it in-to song,_____ A glad sweet thought, and in the af-ter

years　　　　One who in grief and pain had sor-row'd long___ Bless'd my sweet

song, And dried his weary tears.

A. H. & C. Ltd. 48134

WHEN WE MET.

Words by
C. PRESTON-WYNNE.

Music by
FRANK E. TOURS.

The leaves lay deep, The wood-land bare, The earth a-sleep In win-ter's care, Thro' branches grey The March wind boomed! You trod the path:— A primrose bloomed.

A. H. & C. Ltd. 4813ᵃ

I look'd on high—A drea - ry waste! A-cross the sky The dull clouds raced;

poco accel.

They fled a - part And showed heav'ns blue, You smiled, sweet-heart, The

poco accel.

sun shone through!

cresc. ed accel.

You smiled, sweet -

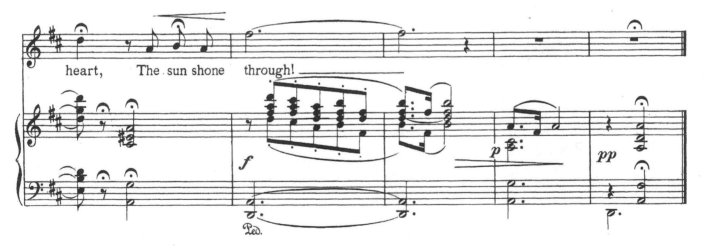

heart, The sun shone through!

f   *p*   *pp*

Ped.

A. H. & C. Ltd. 48134

Three Songs of Love

by Frank E. Tours

To Jack with all my best wishes always! Frank Tours

I.

"HIDDEN IN YOUR HEART"

II.

"GIVE ME YOUR HANDS"

III.

"COME BACK TO ME"

P₁ Price, 50 cents T ts net

NEW YORK

G. SCHIRMER

BOSTON

"HIDDEN IN YOUR HEART"

Give me the flow'r you are holding in your hands,
    And from your lips let fall one tender smile,
Give me the hope that is running through your life,
    Then say "farewell," or stay with me a while.

Give me the love that is hidden in your heart,
    Give me your prayers, all faithful and divine,
And I'll love you, and bless you, and keep you, beloved,
    While life lasts, till Death comes, mine, only mine.

FRANK E. TOURS

27320

"Hidden in your heart"

Edward Teschemacher

Frank E. Tours

Give me the flow'r you are holding in your hands, And from your lips let fall one ten-der smile, Give me the hope that is running through your life, Then say "fare-well," or

27320 c

DAVIS AND THORSETT

stay with me a while.

Give me the love that is hid-den in your heart,

Give me your prayers, all faith-ful and di-vine, And I'll

27320

love   you, and bless 'you, and   keep   you, be-lov - ed,   While life   lasts,   till

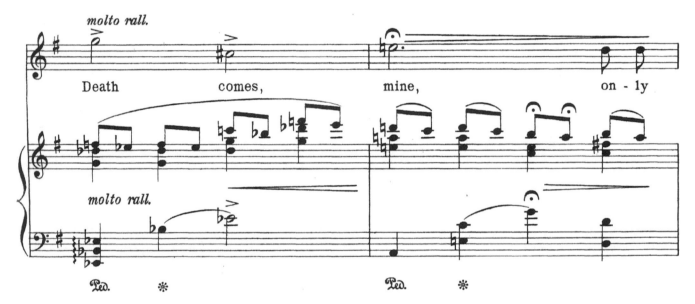

Death   comes,   mine,   on - ly

mine.

27320

"Give me your hands"

Edward Teschemacher

Frank E. Tours

THE SONGS OF FRANK E. TOURS

hold!

Give me your heart to hold, that it may be

A ho-ly trea-sure through the years to me, _____ And I will set it

from all grief a-part: Give me your heart! Give me your heart to hold!

27322

DAVIS AND THORSETT

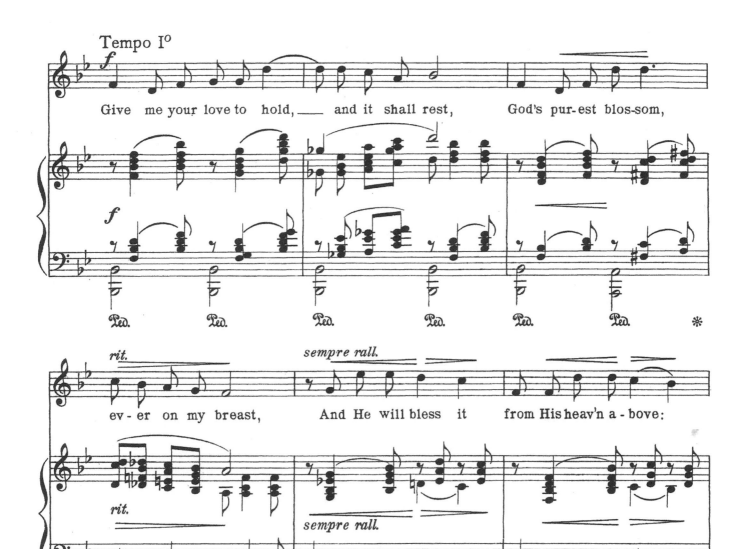

Give me your love to hold,___ and it shall rest, God's pur-est blos-som,

ev - er on my breast, And He will bless it from His heav'n a - bove:

Give me your love!___ Give me your love to hold!___

The Songs of Frank E. Tours

Come Back To Me!

Milton Goldsmith

Frank E. Tours

27321 c

122

Un - til I hold you safe a - gain In my _____ pro-tect - ing

arm?

A - wake-a - sleep,— My time in long-ing spent,

27321

I strive to keep My ach-ing bo-som in con-tent,

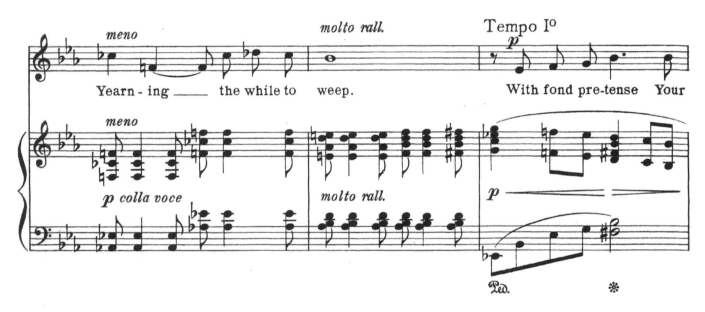

meno *molto rall.* Tempo I°

Yearn-ing ____ the while to weep. With fond pre-tense Your

pic-ture I embrace; And if sad tears be-dew my face, I'll strive to drive them hence.

DAVIS AND THORSETT

'Tis mis - er - y! The world is dark and drear;

My heart is cry-ing for you, dear. Come back,_____ come back to

me!

27321

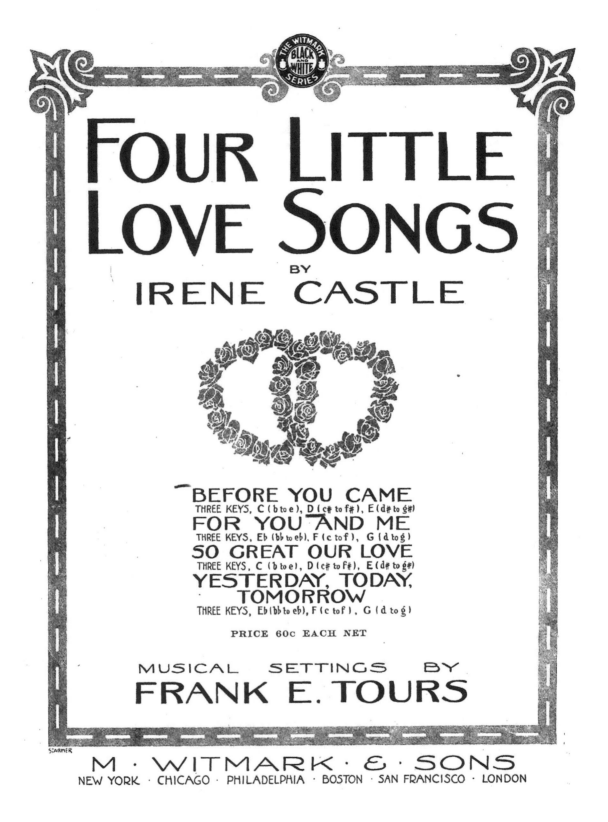

FOUR LITTLE LOVE SONGS

BY
IRENE CASTLE

BEFORE YOU CAME
THREE KEYS, C (b to e), D (c# to f#), E (d# to g#)
FOR YOU AND ME
THREE KEYS, Eb (bb to eb), F (c to f), G (d to g)
SO GREAT OUR LOVE
THREE KEYS, C (b to e), D (c# to f#), E (d# to g#)
YESTERDAY, TODAY, TOMORROW
THREE KEYS, Eb (bb to eb), F (c to f), G (d to g)

PRICE 60c EACH NET

MUSICAL SETTINGS BY
FRANK E. TOURS

STARMER

M · WITMARK · & · SONS
NEW YORK · CHICAGO · PHILADELPHIA · BOSTON · SAN FRANCISCO · LONDON

Davis and Thorsett

Before You Came

Irene Castle

Frank E. Tours

7067

M.W.& SONS 15731-4

THE SONGS OF FRANK E. TOURS

The Songs of Frank E. Tours

me at last, I shall for-get the years that passed.

Since you have come to me at last,_____ I shall for-get_____ the years that

passed _____ Be - fore_____ you came, Be -

- fore you came._____

Davis and Thorsett

For You And Me

Irene Castle

Frank E. Tours

7070

M.W.&SONS 15732 - 4

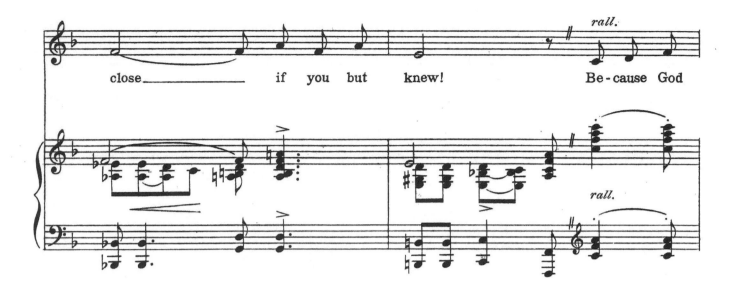

close_____ if you but knew! Be - cause God

made me, dear, for you!

Tempo I

Since I have known your love so deep and true_____ And I have

Davis and Thorsett

So Great Our Love

Irene Castle

Frank E. Tours

There is no sun - shine, __ dear, for me, __ How- ev- er fair the day may be, __ With you a - way. __ But I know, too, __ Each day will seem a year to you, __ So great our love.

7068

M.W.&SONS 15733 - 4

Davis and Thorsett

When we have climbed life's

wind-ing way, I know that both of us will say:

"There has not been a day go by Where-in___ to find___ a

tear or sigh, So great our love, our love!"

When sleep shall come _____ to you and me, _____

O peace - ful sleep, _____ E - tern - i - ty, _____ Our souls shall

wan - - der hand in hand _____ Through all the end - less sha - dow - land, _____

So great our love, So great our love! _____

M.W.&SONS 15733-4

Yesterday, To-day, To-morrow!

Irene Castle

Frank E. Tours

7120

M.W.&SONS 15780 - 4

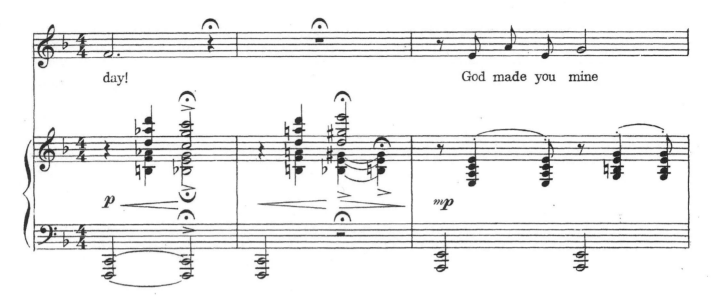

day!

God made you mine

in one long kiss,   The world seems mad   with   joy   for this.

piu accel.

My   heart be-fore____ your   feet   I   lay,   And this, dear one,   this

molto rall.

is To - day!

I dare not look _____ a - head to see _____ What God has planned for you and

me. _____ It may be joy un - told, or sor - row, But aft - er

all, that is To - mor - row!

SACRED SONGS

Easter Music

✕✕✕✕

	NET RETAIL PRICE

• **Breaks the Morning** 40
In A♭, D to F
Lyric by Jessie Villars.
Music by Frank E. Tours.

Christ is Risen 40
In A♭, E♭ to F.
Lyric by Wm. H. Gardner.
Music by Sadie Harrison.

Easter Dawn, An 40
Two keys, C, c to A.   G, G to E.
Lyric by Glen MacDonough.
Music by Victor Herbert.

Give Praise in Gladsome Song 40
In D♭, F to A♭
Lyric by Geo. Graff, Jr.
Music by Jessie Mae Jewitt.

Hail, Thou Blessed Saviour! . 40
In D, c♯ to D.
Lyric by Wm. H. Gardner.
Music by Henry L. Gideon.

Song of Triumph, The . . . 40
In B♭, F to F.
Lyric by Wm. H. Gardner.
Music by Sadie Harrison.

M. WITMARK & SONS
NEW YORK

2

Breaks The Morning.

(Christ Is Born Again.)

EASTER SONG.

Lyric by
JESSIE VILLARS.

Music by
FRANK E. TOURS.

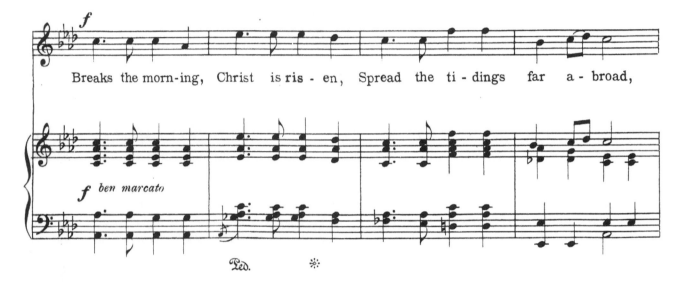

Breaks the morn-ing, Christ is ris - en, Spread the ti - dings far a - broad,

Come all ye who seek sal - va - tion, Come and mag - ni - fy the Lord;

Davis and Thorsett

Sa - viour like a shep - herd lead us Through the ho - ly light of dawn,

Sing - ing prais - es, loud Ho - san - nas, Gra - cious Lord this Eas - ter morn.

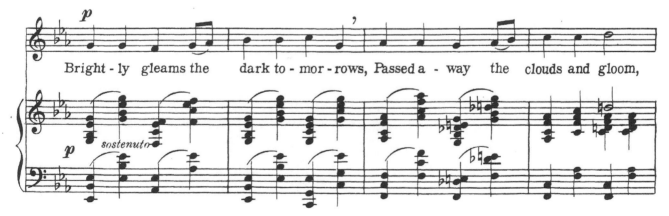

Bright - ly gleams the dark to - mor - rows, Passed a - way the clouds and gloom,

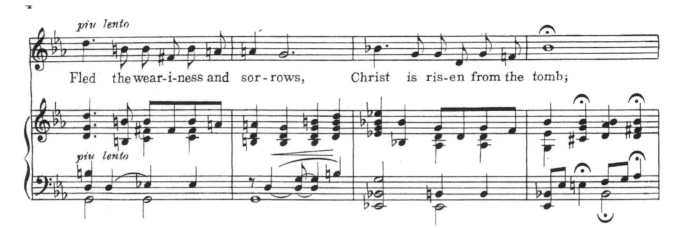

Fled the wear-i-ness and sor-rows, Christ is ris-en from the tomb;

Bend we low in praise and pray'r, Ho - ly Je - sus at thy feet,

We have found for - giv-ness there, We have found a rest com-plete.

Tempo Primo.

Christ is ris - en! Our Re-deem-er— Praise, O praise His Ho - ly___ name,

Hal - le-lu - jah, Hal - le-lu - jah! Christ is born, is born a - gain.

Christ is ris - en! Our Re-deem-er, Praise, O praise His Ho - ly name,

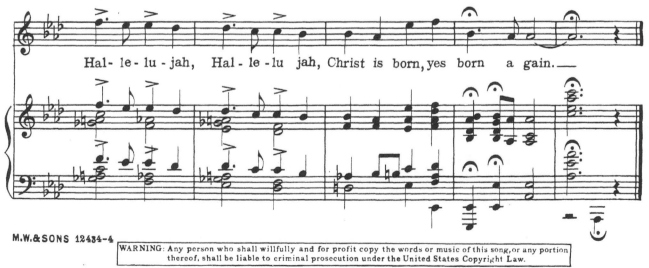

Hal - le-lu - jah, Hal - le-lu jah, Christ is born, yes born a gain.___

THE SONGS OF FRANK E. TOURS

HE GIVETH HIS BELOVED SLEEP

Sacred Song

LYRIC BY

WILLIAM H. GARDNER

MUSIC BY

FRANK E. TOURS

Composer of "MOTHER O'MINE," "BEYOND THE SUNSET" *etc.*

Price 60 cents

M. WITMARK & SONS,

NEW YORK · CHICAGO · SAN FRANCISCO · LONDON · PARIS.

Davis and Thorsett

Dedicated by the Author to the beloved memory of his Mother.

He Giveth His Beloved Sleep

Lyric by
WILLIAM H. GARDNER.

Music by
FRANK E. TOURS.

5 6 2 5

12134-4

THE SONGS OF FRANK E. TOURS

149

ev - er - more. The dark - ness now has flown a - way, They

soon _____ will wake in end - less day. He giv - eth his be -

lov - ed sleep, While an - gels watch o'er them do keep,

He giv - eth His be - lov - ed sleep, While an - gels watch o'er

12134-4

them do keep.

He giv-eth His be - lov - ed sleep, Wher.- e'er they be, on

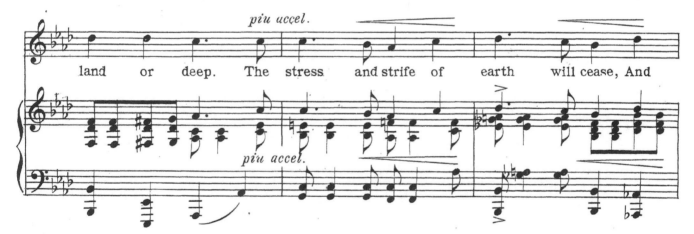

land or deep. The stress and strife of earth will cease, And

they _____ will tread the Paths of Peace. There is _____ no death, the

12134 - 4

soul lives on, To find ___ new joys with each new dawn.

Then, mind not when the shad - ows creep, He giv-eth His be -

lov - ed sleep, Then, mind not when the shad - ows creep,

He giv-eth His be - lov - ed sleep. ___

12134-4

Christmas Songs

SECULAR

Hang Up the Baby's Stocking—Pathetic. Bb, (eb to f)   T
                                                   Wm. Coleman   50

I'm Going to Write to Santa Claus—Juvenile. C, (e to d)
   Lyric by Jessica Moore.   Geo. L. Spaulding   50

I'm Waiting for Santa Claus—Pathetic. D, (c♯ to d)..Dora Burdge   50
   Lyric by Julia Marion Manley.

Night Before Christmas, The—Pathetic. G, (d to e)
   Lyric by Geo. Graff, Jr.   Ernest R. Ball   50

Santie Was Good to Me—Juvenile. G, (d to d)........Alb. H. Fitz   50

Tale of a Turkey, The—Juvenile. G, (d to d)..Geo. L. Spaulding   50
   Lyric by Jessica Moore.

That Christmas Night Just Twenty Years Ago—Pathetic.
   Lyric by O. H. Barr.   Bb (d to f)   Karl Weixelbaum   50

When Christmas Bells Are Ringing—Pathetic. G, (d to e)
                                                C. Paul   50

When Santa Claus Comes Round—Popular. G, (d to c)
   Lyric by Gene Jefferson.   Raymond A. Browne   50

SACRED

Christmas Peace. F, (f to f).............................James L. Gilbert   50
   Lyric by Wm. H. Gardner.

From Manger Unto Throne. Ab (eb to f)......James Lowell Tracy   50
   Lyric by Wm. H. Gardner.

Glory to God in the Highest. G, (e to g)..............Sadie Harrison   50
   Lyric by Wm. H. Gardner.

Hail Thou Blessed Saviour. B, (c to e)..............Henry L. Gideon   50
   Lyric by Wm. H. Gardner.

Prince of Peace, The. Ab, (eb to eb)..................Henry L. Gideon   50
   Lyric by Wm. H. Gardner.

Star of Bethlehem.
   Four Keys: C, (e to g); Bb, (d to f); D, (e to a); Ab, (c to eb)
   Lyric by A. E. Morrow.   Caro Roma   50

Shout the Glad Tidings O'er Vale and Hill.
   Two Keys: C, (d to f); Eb, (e to ab)....................Caro Roma   50
   Lyric by Wm. H. Gardner.

Thou Blessed Man of God. Two Keys: C, (c to e); Eb, (eb to g)
   Lyric by Wm. H. Gardner.   Frank E. Tours

O, Sing Ye Sons of Men. Two Keys: D, (d to d); F, (f to f)
                                        T. Austin-Ball   50

Christmas Bells Ring Sweet and Clear. Eb, (f to f)
   Lyric by Wm. H. Gardner.   Jessie Mae Jewitt   50

JUVENILE BOOKS

Joke On the Toy Maker, A—Operetta.............Geo. L. Spaulding   75
   Book by Jessica Moore.

Up the Chimney—Operetta............................Theo. H. Northrup   75
   Book by S. B. Alexander.

Christmas With the Old Woman Who Lived in a Shoe—Musical Play
   Book by Wm. H. Gardner.   Jessie Mae Jewitt   50

M. WITMARK & SONS   NEW YORK CITY

Thou Blessed Man of God.

(Jesus of Nazareth.)

Christmas Song.

in C

Lyric by
WILLIAM H. GARDNER.

Music by
FRANK E. TOURS.

M.W & SONS. 12136-4

154

DAVIS AND THORSETT

rall.   rall.

rev - 'rent - ly they wor - shipped, Laud - ing His Ho - ly name:_____
an - gels come at mid - night, To praise the Spot - less One._____

rall.   rall.

REFRAIN. Andante.

"All Hail to Thee, Je - sus of Naz - - a - reth, Thou

bring - est good will to men,_____ The seats of the might - y shall

call_____ thee 'Lord,' And right now shall rule a - gain;_____

5590

M.W.& SONS. 12136-4

M.W.& SONS. 12136-4

Davis and Thorsett

THEATRE AND FILM SONGS

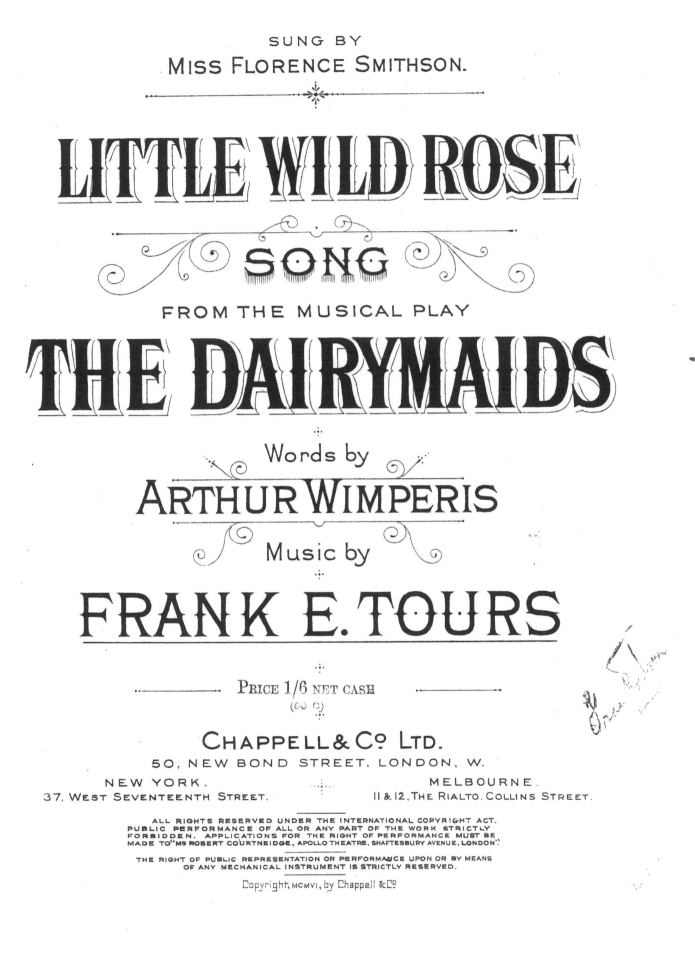

SUNG BY
MISS FLORENCE SMITHSON.

LITTLE WILD ROSE

SONG

FROM THE MUSICAL PLAY

THE DAIRYMAIDS

Words by

ARTHUR WIMPERIS

Music by

FRANK E. TOURS

PRICE 1/6 NET CASH
(60 c)

CHAPPELL & C° LTD.

50, NEW BOND STREET, LONDON, W.

NEW YORK.
37, WEST SEVENTEENTH STREET.

MELBOURNE.
11 & 12, THE RIALTO, COLLINS STREET.

LITTLE WILD ROSE.

SONG.

Words by
ARTHUR WIMPERIS.

Music by
FRANK E. TOURS.

1. On a sea _ girt cliff grew a bud _ ding rose, And oh, she was fair to see,_____ And lov _ ers two came there to woo— The
2. Then the jeal _ ous breeze drew an an _ gry breath, And he cried "You are false to me!"_____ And a blast he blew till her pet _ als flew_____

bum _ ble _ bee, As he sang her his ten _ der song.
cliff a _ gain, Where he sang his song_ of yore.

Wild Rose, lit _ tle wild Rose, You're the world to

me, Tho' you reign se _ rene _ ly, Fair and queen _ ly

I'm but a hum _ ble, bum _ ble _ bee, Wild Rose, lit _ tle

wild Rose, All through my life I shall love you

Dear _ ly, sin _ cere _ ly, my own lit _ tle Rose.

Rose, My own lit _ tle Rose,

My own lit _ tle Rose.

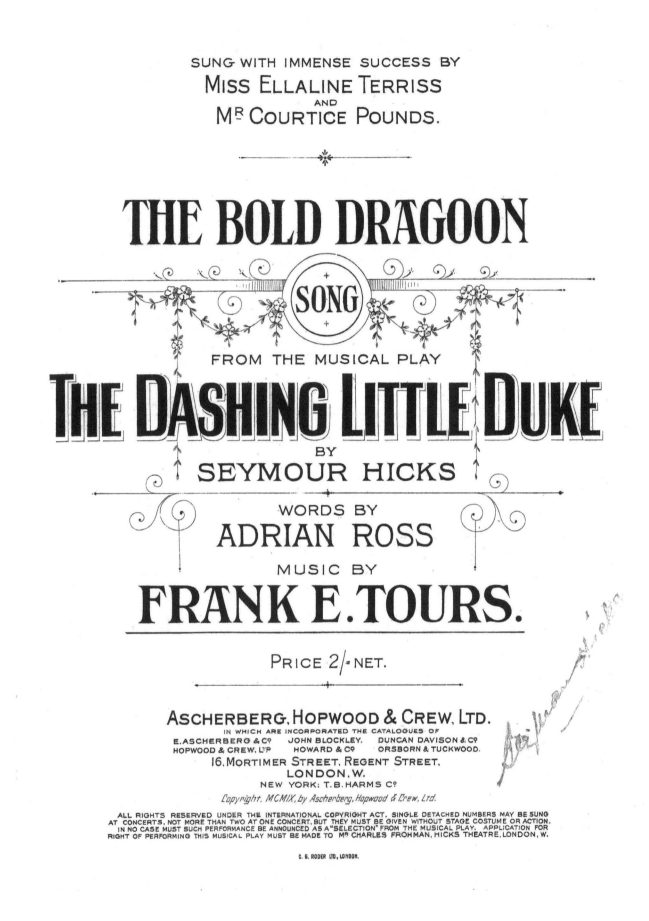

SUNG WITH IMMENSE SUCCESS BY
MISS ELLALINE TERRISS
AND
MR COURTICE POUNDS.

THE BOLD DRAGOON

SONG

FROM THE MUSICAL PLAY

THE DASHING LITTLE DUKE

BY
SEYMOUR HICKS

WORDS BY
ADRIAN ROSS

MUSIC BY
FRANK E. TOURS.

PRICE 2/= NET.

ASCHERBERG, HOPWOOD & CREW, LTD.
IN WHICH ARE INCORPORATED THE CATALOGUES OF
E. ASCHERBERG & Cº   JOHN BLOCKLEY.   DUNCAN DAVISON & Cº
HOPWOOD & CREW, Lº°   HOWARD & Cº   ORSBORN & TUCKWOOD.
16, MORTIMER STREET, REGENT STREET,
LONDON, W.
NEW YORK: T. B. HARMS Cº

Copyright. MCMIX, by Ascherberg, Hopwood & Crew, Ltd.

C. G. RODER LTD, LONDON.

The Bold Dragoon.

Song.

Words by
ADRIAN ROSS.

Music by
FRANK E. TOURS.

1. Oh, the life of a bold dra-goon Is the life for which I hun-ger, For we fight till night and we

THE SONGS OF FRANK E. TOURS

drink till noon, As I did when I was young-er! When the trum-pets blow then we

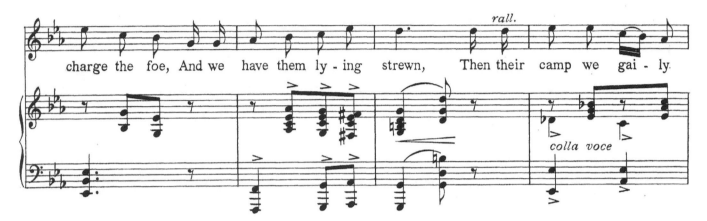

charge the foe, And we have them ly-ing strewn, Then their camp we gai-ly

pil-lage For the maid-ens of the vil-lage Who wel---come a

bold dra-goon, Who wel-come a bold dra-goon!

A. H. & C. Ltd. 4973

DAVIS AND THORSETT

A. H. & C. Ltd. 4973

2. Oh, the life of a bold dra - goon   All with
3. Oh, the life of a bold dra - goon,   It has

glo - ry and gold lace la - den!   We've a   un - i - form that will
joys I'll   soon dis - cov - er,   For his   sword can   slay   and his

take   by storm An - y   wi - dow, wife,   or   maid - en!   For we
coat   is gay.   But he's   fin - est as a   lov - er!   At the

A. H. & C. Ltd. 4973

Davis and Thorsett

sons of Mars are as bright as stars On a night with - out a
look he gives an - y girl that lives Will be fit to sigh and

moon! It's our plea - sure and our du - ty, That in
swoon, But she'll find him read - y for her, For there

bright and man - ly beau - ty, There's none like a
is - n't an a - dor - er That loves like a

bold dra - goon, There's none like a bold dra - goon!
bold dra - goon, That loves like a bold dra - goon!

Ride,   ride,   ride,   In a   cav - al - cade of   war - like splendour!
Ride,   ride,   ride,   O - ver beau - ty that can - not re - sist us,

Ride,   ride,   ride,   With a   cap - tiv - a - ting eas - y stride! Ride,   ride,
Ride,   ride,   ride,   O - ver prud - e - ry and maid - en pride! Ride,   ride,

ride,   And the   wo - men's hearts grow ten - der!   Hear them twit - ter - ing
ride,   Un - til   ev - 'ry girl has kissed us,   Draw your flat - ter - ies,

1.
    2. 𝄋

Round our   glit - ter - ing   Ride,   ride,   ride!   ride!
Charge the   bat - ter - ies,   Ride,   ride,   ride!   ride!

Fine.

A. H. & C. Ltd. 4973

Songs Introduced by

Louise Gunning

IN

"The Balkan Princess"

DIRECTION

SAM S. & LEE SHUBERT Inc.

Theatrical and Music Hall Rights of these Songs are fully protected by
Copyright and MUST NOT be used for public performances
without permission.

M. WITMARK & SONS
NEW YORK · CHICAGO · SAN FRANCISCO · LONDON · PARIS

When I Am All Your Own.

Lyric by
LOUIS WESLYN.

Music by
FRANK E. TOURS.

Some - where with - in the world so wide, dear, You wait for me,
Oft have I won-dered when 'tis fa - ted That we shall meet,

My love to be. Fate can but take me to your side, dear,
With greet-ings sweet. Just as in dreams we have been ma - ted,

5299

M.W.& SONS 11734-3

To make me yours, While life en-dures. 'Tis but in Dream-land that you
In real life, too, I'm meant for you. Tho' I know not where you may

call me, Yet hand in hand, With you I'd stand, Pledg-ing love most true
be, dear, I on-ly know, I love you so, In some sa-cred place,

rallentando.

off-'ring all to you Know-ing harm could ne'er be - fall me.
we'll meet face to face, Your path-way must lead to me, dear.

REFRAIN.
a tempo.

When I am all your own,____ The world will seem____ A joy-ous dream;

a tempo.

The Songs of Frank E. Tours

Held in your arms, dear, Safe from all a-larms, dear, Drift-ing a-down life's

stream. All that I have to give I'll give_ to you a-

lone;_ And just for you I will live, When I_ am_ all your

own. I_ am_ all_ your own._

SWEET NELL

VALSE SONG

WORDS BY

DESMOND CARTER

MUSIC BY

FRANK E. TOURS

[Dedicatory number for the opening of the Plaza Theatre]

PRICE 2/= NET

CHAPPELL & Cº LTD.
50, NEW BOND STREET, LONDON, W.1.
AND SYDNEY.

HARMS INCORPORATED.
62-64, WEST 45TH STREET,
NEW YORK.

7706.

SWEET NELL.

Valse Song.

Words by
DESMOND CARTER.

Music by
FRANK E. TOURS.

1. There is a for-tun-ate lov-er ____ Who
2. Wher-ev-er For-tune may set you ____ Your

some day will come and dis - cov - er_____ This
lov - ers will nev - er for get you._____ The

rose that has bloom'd by the way - side a - lone, And
sound of your laugh - ter will still lin - ger on To

take her and make her his own._____
thrill us long af - ter you're gone._____

rall.

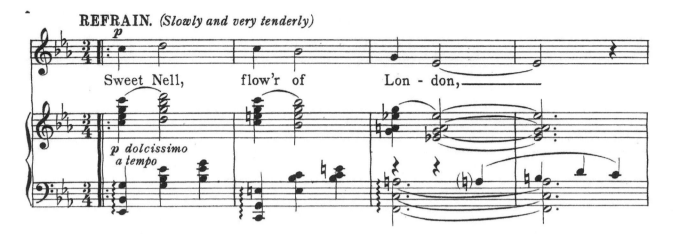

Sweet Nell, flow'r of Lon - don,_____

Some day when for - tune is fair,_____ Smile up - on

those Who have wor-shipp'd the rose On - ly a king can

wear._____ We who have to

28922   Chappell.

178   Davis and Thorsett

lose you_____ Know that all hearts you will

win,_____ Wher - ev - er you reign To us you'll re -

- main Al - ways pret - ty Nell Gwyn._____

Al - ways pret - ty Nell Gwyn._____

28922

CHANSON ALGERIAN

SONG

FEATURED IN

"Beau Geste"

WORDS BY
EDWARD LOCKTON

MUSIC BY
FRANK TOURS
JAMES BRADFORD
AND
HANS SPIALEK

PRICE 2/- NET

Published by

SAM FOX PUBLISHING Co (London) LTD.
SOLE PROPRIETORS
KEITH PROWSE & CO LTD.
42-43, POLAND STREET, LONDON, W I.

Copyright.

DAVIS AND THORSETT

CHANSON ALGERIAN.

Words by
EDWARD LOCKTON.

Music by
FRANK TOURS,
JAMES BRADFORD
and HANS SPIALEK.

Day now is pass - ing in won - der and light,

Hark to the dis - tant call.

Ov - er the world steal the foot - steps of night,

Si - lence reigns ov - er all.

rit.

K.P. & C.º Lt.d. 3149.

Davis and Thorsett

REFRAIN. Tempo commodo.

Sink once more, O ra-diant Sun, in - to thy bed of gold:

Take with thee in-to the night our long - ings man - i - fold.

Low we bow be-fore thy splen-dour Thy pow'r_ un-known,

Bear our spir-its in sur-ren-der To Al - lah's throne.

K.P. & Cº Ltd. 3149.

DAVIS AND THORSETT

"Our Crystal Wedding Day"

Words by
ANNE CALDWELL

Music by
FRANK E. TOURS

7122 - 4

Davis and Thorsett

Lady fas-cin-a-ting, a mirror scin-til-la-ting
Brides-maids in their la-ces, with pret-ty flow-er fa-ces,

Soon will re-flect, you there.____
Wait for the bride's bou-quet.____

Refrain *a tempo*

You will be-long___ to me; I shall be-long___ to you

Old fash-ioned hus____band and wife, dear,

One lit - tle___ ring, won - der - ful - - thing.

Makes you mine for life___ dear,

We'll take our wed - - ding vows un - der the spread - ing boughs

Then as the years___ pass a - way, And

7122-4

DAVIS AND THORSETT

THE SONGS OF FRANK E. TOURS

EDITORS' STATEMENT

PURPOSE

A project to reintroduce to the public a composer whose music has been lost in obscurity for nearly a century raises many questions for those who take it on. As we have considered whether or not the circumstances may be right for Frank Tours' music to be revived, we have also wondered why his music fell into obscurity to begin with. The most obvious cause, generally speaking, is that public affection for most music fades over time; and therefore, when aesthetic fashions change, only the most innovative or idiomatic or universal music survives beyond the lifetime of its composer, when they are alive to promote their work. Another general reason that comes to mind is that the economy of the music industry in any era does not support the perpetuation of all music from the past, and therefore even the most successful music is constantly in competition with new music for its survival in perpetuity. When considering the question of why the music of this particular composer was no longer performed by the end of his lifetime, we also recognize the specific logistical problem that he was never contracted by a single publisher that would have had a vested interest in producing a folio of his best work at any point during the decades that followed the original sheet music going out of print (and, in any case, most of the publishers that issued his music had gone out of business and sold their interests by 1960). The legacy of Frank Tours and his music has been complicated by all of these forces, leaving even the most popular of his songs largely unknown at the end of his life. The primary mission of this project has been to present his most meaningful and well-crafted songs in a volume that also provides the reader with a portrait of the artist and other supplemental materials in the hope that together they will help to create the conditions by which his music may find new champions and audiences in the twenty-first century.

SOURCES AND METHODS

The circumstances that caused Tours' music to become almost completely unknown and unperformed upon his death also left his family as its sole custodial caretakers in the years that followed. While the advent of the internet has made some his sheet music available in a digital form, copies of the majority of his published works were preserved in one place by the composer himself in six large bound volumes that were held for decades by his heirs and their children. Access to these volumes has been the single most important factor in making our project feasible from the outset. From a curatorial standpoint, these books were housed at two residences—one in California and one in Tennessee—and they ultimately needed to be brought together again temporarily for the purpose of making high-resolution digital images that would be suitable for the production of a facsimile edition. The decision to create a facsimile rather than an edition with new engravings was arrived at having considered a variety of factors—some practical, some aesthetic. But being fortunate enough to have a set of clean, well-preserved originals made this decision much easier for us than it would have been otherwise. Weighing the pros and cons of producing a facsimile made us think of the volume in terms of its potential uses for both musicians and non-musicians. Ultimately, it became clear that presenting the original engravings held mostly advantages and only a few disadvantages. Although the original sheet music is far from perfect from an editorial standpoint and, like most popular music from the time, contains many inconsistencies that could be corrected for contemporary musicians, there were only a handful of notational errors among the songs that we wanted to use. Furthermore, the value of providing both the musician and the historically minded aficionado with images of the original sheet music became paramount in our thinking, since these scores could facilitate a greater understanding of the social, cultural, artistic, and economic contexts in which these songs were first presented. Since notational styles in the early twentieth century are no longer in use and are mostly elegant and pleasing to look at, this consideration also outweighed the advantages of using a new standard notation program with its consistency, clarity, and editorial flexibility.

Given the constraints of presenting the music without editorial interventions, we felt that it would be useful to identify errata and inconsistencies that we found in order to show those changes we would have made if we had created new engravings. By indicating markings that we considered to be erroneous, we also hope to encourage a deeper interaction with the scores by performers, particularly students who might be otherwise inclined to accept published music as definitive reflections of the composer's intentions. Our experience with these scores has taught us that the house editors in even the most reputable publishing firms were more concerned with efficiency than clarity, consistency, and accuracy when issuing popular ballads. As a result, inconsistencies in dynamic, tempo, articulation, and pedal markings were ubiquitous in these scores to the extent that we could not find one that would not require at least a few minor changes. But since we did not have access to Tours' manuscripts and therefore do not have definitive evidence of his intentions, we merely offer the observations in our Critical Notes as a point of reference from which the reader may make their own judgements about their usefulness. In particular, we hope that our remarks will promote a more creative response by performers to any questions posed by these issues rather than a more pedantic one. The commentaries at the back of the book, where these issues are discussed, are also a place where we have shared some of our research into a variety of ancillary elements of the songs: biographical information about the lyricists; circumstances of the composer/lyricist collaboration; brief descriptions of outstanding features of the settings (form, harmony, rhythmic scansion, illustration, etc.); technical matters for the vocalist; and core data such as publisher, date of publication, key, and vocal range. The end matter also contains other information about Tours' work and career, including a complete list of published works, a discography, and a reproduction of one of the composer's unpublished songs in manuscript, all of which we are providing to fill in additional details of his life and work.

Since we were only able to include approximately half of the more than seventy of Tours' published songs in this volume, one of the first and most important tasks we had before us as editors was to select the music that would best represent the range and quality of his output. Given our interest in showing his work in several fields of the music industry, we determined that it was important to prioritize some measure of diversity in our selection process rather than using the simple criterion of identifying the best songs or even those that we thought had the best chance of being performed in the future. As a result, there are songs in this collection that may not be as useful or attractive to performers as others that we were not able to include due to limitations of space. In addition to having several subsections for representative examples of his work in theatre, film, and sacred music, we are presenting together songs that were originally published in sets (although they could be purchased individually) to allow the reader to view them as ordered groups and perhaps even encourage singers to perform them that way if they are so inclined. Once we established the general parameters of our selection process,

we searched for every song we could find among Tours' bound personal volumes and in libraries and digital collections. In evaluating his extant songs, we implemented a ranking system that allowed us to identify those that we were certain would make the cut and those that were on the cusp, most of our time necessarily being dedicated to the latter. The criteria that we established while making these choices revolved largely around lyric quality and content, as we came to agree with several contemporary critics who wrote that Tours' musical settings were of a uniformly high quality, whether or not the poetry he chose to set was entirely worthy of his effort. Indeed, some of the texts he set as a young man in England reflect cavalier attitudes toward women that were a product of their time, but are now out of step with twenty-first century social norms. In the interest of providing access to his entire body of work, we will make as many of his published songs as possible available on a dedicated Frank E. Tours website.

With the exception of a few songs chosen for their historical value, our guiding principle in selecting the music for this collection has been to present what we believe to be Tours' best songs in the belief that they are still viable for performance, despite having been forgotten for decades. Indeed, some of the selections we have made will show the extent to which we value them purely for the ease and comfort of their vocal lines. We acknowledge, for instance, that there may be songs that we did not include in this collection that are more compelling from a purely artistic standpoint than "Red Rose." However, this song's elegant vocal line and natural lyric scansion make it very attractive for voice students who are looking for quality song settings of English lyrics, and we believe that voice teachers will welcome many other songs in this collection similarly for their pedagogical value. This collection also offers a balanced selection of repertoire for male and female singers. While Tours set many lyrics that feature a male protagonist, especially among his early songs about romance and courtship, only a handful of songs in this collection—"I Dreamed," "In Flanders' Fields," "Mother o' Mine," "Son of My Heart," and "Sweet Nell" in particular—should only be sung by a man. Moreover, Tours set the words of many female lyricists (e.g. Ellaline Terriss, Elsie Janis, Hilda Hammond Spenser, H. Pearl Humphrey, Irene Castle, and Dorothy K. Thomas), whose poetry can be performed by singers of either gender, and three songs in this volume—"God's Promise," "Jest a-Wearyin' fer You" and "The Long Day"—specifically feature a female protagonist. Though it would be natural for a woman to interpret these songs, men who might consider singing them should take note of the promotional endorsement by John Charles Thomas on the sheet music for "The Long Day."

Most of Tours' songs were composed within a comfortable tessitura that will accommodate amateurs while at the same time presenting significant musical challenges for professionals. In fact, we have estimated that 95% of the songs that are being presented in this volume are set within a medium vocal range of a tenth, which should be suitable for most singers:

Moreover, the tessitura of nearly all the songs lies on the staff in the range of a sixth (f′–d″), which will be satisfying for singers with both medium-low and high voices. The undergraduate singer should be able to quickly take command of the full range of most songs and enjoy being able to execute their expressive choices with relative ease. The more dramatic songs like "Mother o' Mine," "In Flanders' Fields," "Beyond the Sunset," and "No Voice But Yours" could be handled by more advanced students, but these singers would need to possess agility through the *passaggi* and be capable of sustained singing in the higher registers. Although some of Tours' songs were issued in more than one key, these options were not available to us for this book, since we were limited in our choices to the sheet-music originals in the family's bound volumes. These limitations are ameliorated by the fact that most songs were scored in a comfortable range and that the alternate keys were usually within a third. Whenever we have access to other published transpositions, we will make them available on the Frank Tours website (www.franktours.net).

TRADITION, STYLE, AND TERMINOLOGY

Being a traditionalist, Frank Tours employed a musical style that evolved out of his exposure to several accomplished English composers in his youth, most notably his teacher Charles Stanford and his father Berthold Tours. These influences not only formed the bedrock of his compositional style from a technical standpoint, they informed his aesthetic disposition. His teachers at the Royal College of Music surely instilled in him a disciplined conservatism that grounded his musical expression in techniques derived from French and German Romanticism. But while the academic traditionalism that prevailed at the RCM often bred individualism and even defiance among some of its more talented and adventurous students, who embraced modernist agendas that were developing on the continent, in Tours it found a receptive apprentice, a circumstance that could be traced further to his upbringing and his father's guidance. By all accounts a benevolent figure who was serious in his work, Berthold Tours was a composer whose church music was highly regarded, but whose staunch conservatism has relegated his secular music to a depth of obscurity that exceeds even that of Stanford, much of whose music he oversaw the publication of at Novello, Ewer & Co. The elder Tours was a prolific song composer, but one who showed little or no interest

in discovering how the ironic musical language of his distant uncle Robert Schumann might be welcomed by the British public in his own romantic ballads. After all, these were British popular songs often performed in aristocratic salons, and Victorian mores were at stake in these contexts and were not to be threatened as the aesthetic radicalism of Schumann demanded in his battle with the Philistines. In all likelihood, it was the happy and mutually respectful relationship with his father that led Frank Tours to seek to advance the field of the romantic ballad that his father enjoyed success in rather than being an aesthetic agitator seeking to disrupt the continuity of conservative British musical traditions.

Given the middle ground that most of Frank Tours' songs occupy between the Victorian ballad and post-Romantic art song, as well as the instability of the terminology around these musical subgenres, it should not seem out of place or unwelcome to entertain a discussion of song nomenclature in this context. Etymologically speaking, the term "ballad" in referring to songs was already the source of some confusion in the late-nineteenth century. John Ashton wrote with authority in his book *A Century of Ballads* published in 1887 that "in using the word ballad, we must not confound it with the song."[1] While he was referring specifically to the English ballad of the seventeenth century, his explanation is instructive to our consideration of how of it was used in the nineteenth century as well, because it shows how the term had changed from one that referred to topical verse narratives set to pre-existing music to one that referred to romantic or sentimental lyrics set to tuneful music for solo voice and obbligato instrumental accompaniment. The change in connotation likely occurred in the first half of the nineteenth century, when the ballad opera was being transformed by composers such as Michael William Balfe and William Vincent Wallace from a form of musical theatre dominated by the contrafactum, as had been standard since *The Beggar's Opera*, to an English operatic style fashioned after Rossini and Bellini, featuring arias of unadorned melodic elegance. Harold Simpson highlighted this change in his book (also titled) *A Century of Ballads*, when he quoted a writer anonymously as having stated that "[i]n the early part of the nineteenth century ... singers wanted something that would show off their voice more, and composers no longer wanted to be kept to the ballad proper."[2] In this way, the ballad evolved into a song form that emphasized melodic simplicity and lyrical earnestness and became the prevailing form of published English music for voice and piano in the Victorian Era. Frank Tours' father Berthold wrote over one hundred

---

[1] John Aston, *A Century of Ballads* (London: Eliot Stock, 1887), v.

[2] Harold Simpson, *A Century of Ballads* (1810–1910): *Their Composers and Singers, with some Introductory Chapters on "Old Ballads and Ballad Makers"* (London: Mills & Boon, Limited, 1910), 71.

songs for voice and piano in this style that could also be called ballads despite the fact that sheet music covers and catalogues all referred to them simply as songs. And though Frank himself composed music with strong modernist leanings that were unthinkable in the Victorian ballad, he only composed a few works that could comfortably be called art songs. Instead his main contribution to the art of song was in expanding the expressive and technical range of the English ballad and of continuing to work successfully in this tradition well into the twentieth century.

However, as the tradition of English art song began to flourish after 1900, it all but eclipsed the Victorian ballad; and, as a result of the style's perceived aesthetic deficiencies, the term began to acquire a pejorative connotation. Sophie Fuller described the situation candidly in stating that "as the twentieth century progressed, the ballad was increasingly dismissed as sentimental, mawkish rubbish, and the spaces in which it was heard were frequently denigrated."[3] Late in the century, as British art song continued to be celebrated collectively as one of the country's outstanding cultural achievements, the ballads of the previous century were disparaged unmercifully by scholars like Stephan Banfield, whose masterful study *Sensibility and English Song* contains the following condemnation: "by comparison with the *Lieder* of Schumann, Brahms, and Wolf, the *mélodies* of Bizet, Fauré, Duparc, and Debussy, and the songs of Grieg, the overall impression [of Victorian ballads] is one of worthlessness."[4] Since the English ballad of the nineteenth and early twentieth century has been disregarded in academic circles, has been ignored by musicians, and has become virtually unknown to the public, our reluctance to characterize Frank Tours as a composer of ballads should be understandable. However, this project has caused us to reconsider whether these prejudices are still useful today or whether they simply obstruct our view or, at least, cloud our perception of this area of musical history. Again, Fuller has broken the ice on this discussion with her insight that the romantic ballad at its best demanded a charismatic performance practice by singers that is virtually unknown today. Isolated from these complementary interpretive elements, the shortcomings of the ballad as a musical composition are often exposed by music historians and critics who are left to evaluate the works bereft of their most compelling features. Until the advent of the musical recording in the twentieth century, we have had limited information with which to accurately evaluate the music

that composers have made as a springboard for the virtuoso performer's art. Consequently, twentieth century music historians have generally favored the works from previous centuries in which the composer's voice dominates, since it is better documented and therefore more accessible and easily comprehensible through the score.

Insights into defunct musical traditions can elucidate aspects of the working relationship between performer and composer, which can, in turn, shed light on the musical styles of the works that are left behind. Knowing, for instance, that Berthold Tours expected a performance full of personality, warmth, and pathos from a singer like Antoinette Sterling goes a long way to explaining why he composed songs of such earnest simplicity. By contrast, Frank Tours invested more expressive musical content in his song settings than we generally find in the songs of his father. As a result, his scores provide more clues to singers and pianists who are interested in using elements of the original interpretive style in performance. Although expressive markings such as dynamics and tempo modification were often projected carelessly in the published sheet music, the formal and expressive contours of the music itself is usually clear enough in Tours' songs that the very best guide for how to render his scores in performance can be found in the essential musical components of phrase shape, instrumental voicing, and rhythmic texture. From the very first song he published, Frank Tours composed vocal lines that were not merely melodious, but created harmonic interest by frequently using extended chord tones and sonorities that highlighted adventurous and unexpected tonal choices. His tunes were distinctive and refined, but rarely catchy, even though he was constantly surrounded by memorable music as a music director, and many of the productions he led had scores by the best songwriters in show business. It is perhaps telling that, for all of the musical comedy and film songs that he composed, he never had a hit. It was as if he did not conceive of melody as a dominant musical feature of song, but rather as an extension of the harmony, which was equally if not more important to the setting. His harmonic language was sometimes sweet and sometimes bitter, but never bland or acrid. His use of dissonance was always functionally recognizable and sensible, but never routine or derivative. Though he generally preferred order to instability, Tours frequently used modulation and chord progressions that have a distant relationship to the tonal center to illustrate the texts he set in meaningful ways. Since the narrative conventions of the lyrics he chose featured emotional language that often expressed romantic and spiritual yearning, his songs often built to a powerful climax toward the end. His formal sensibility was the area where he was most complacent and reserved, in keeping with his conservative taste for lyrics. Following the regular metric patterns of the verses he favored, binary and A-B-A′ forms and four-measure melodic periods

---

[3] Sophie Fuller "'The Finest Voice of the Century': Clara Butt and Other Concert-Hall and Drawing-Room Singers of Fin-dé-Siècle Britain," in *The Arts of the Prima Donna in the Long Nineteenth Century*, edited by Rachel Cowgill and Hilary Poriss (Oxford: Oxford University Press, 2012), 310–11.

[4] Stephen Banfield, *Sensibility and English Song* (Cambridge: Cambridge University Press, 1985), 3.

were ubiquitous in his music. Even though the lyrics of his songs were not consistently potent as poetic allusion, Tours always set them with an ear for their natural scansion, giving the listener the best possible chance of understanding the words while maintaining a high degree of sophistication and complexity in the musical elements.

PERFORMANCE AND INTERPRETATION

In presenting his songs to the public for the first time, Tours worked with many of the finest singers of his generation. Often the singers who championed his music were veterans of musical theatre and opera, who brought impeccable diction and considerable acting skill to their performances. Maurice Farkoa was a star of British musical comedy, who first drew attention in George Edwardes' *The Artist's Model* in 1895. He became a close associate of Tours when he appeared in *Three Little Maids* as Monsieur de L'Orme and the company subsequently toured the English-speaking world. A noted recitalist, he performed in ballad concerts promoted by Chappell and was associated with Tours' "Through Cupid's Garden," "Wind in the Orchard," and "I Beg Your Pardon." Popular Welsh tenor Ben Davies made his early career in light opera and oratorio, but was best-known later in his career as a recitalist and as a recording artist. The Tours songs he was known to have programmed include "A Meeting," "Mother o' Mine," "The Lilacs," and "Il pleure dans mon coeur." Tours met the English stage actor and baritone Charles Hayden-Coffin when they worked together in Edwardian musical comedy productions, and he became another important early interpreter of "Mother o' Mine." Orville Harrold had been a star of the Manhattan Opera House in New York when he was asked to appear with his colleague Emma Trentini in Naughty Marietta by Victor Herbert in 1910, and the following year Frank Tours dedicated "Oh, Bring Me Love!" to him. Herbert Witherspoon made his debut as a bass with the Metropolitan Opera Company in 1908 where he sang for six seasons. During this time, he sang Tours' dramatic song "Beyond the Sunset" in recital and made the first recording of "Mother o' Mine" for Victor Talking Machine Co. Irish tenor John McCormack was one of the best-known singers of his generation, famous for his work in opera, oratorio, and recital. He performed several Tours songs both in concerts and on records, and his endorsement on sheet music covers brought distinction to several songs, including "Mother o' Mine," "The Littlest of All," and "In Flanders' Fields." Charles Norman Granville, who built his reputation largely as a recitalist and voice teacher (he wrote a treatise on singing called the "Granville Vocal Study Plan"), collaborated with Tours in a "Composition Recital" of M. Witmark & Sons composers presenting their music in 1917, where he sang "Son of My Heart," "No Voice But Yours," and "Norah McCall." John

Charles Thomas made a successful career in opera and light opera in New York and Europe, but he became famous as a recording artist and radio personality beginning in the 1920s and continuing until he retired around 1950. He first worked with Frank Tours in the Broadway revue *Step This Way* in 1916 and then again during the following year in Reginald DeKoven's comic opera *The Highwayman*. Thomas performed "The Long Day" and "Give Me Your Hands" around this time as his career as a recitalist began to grow, and the inscription on the latter claims that the song was composed specifically for his voice. The two men worked together on and off over the next three decades, where they collaborated on radio programs and light opera when they both lived in Los Angeles. John Steel rose to fame as a concert tenor for the *Ziegfeld Follies* and the *Music Box Revue* in the late 1910s and early 1920s. Tours set two of his lyrics ("Hope Dreams" and "You Smile at Dawn") while they worked together on Broadway and Steel surely sang both with the composer at the piano. These and other performers formed a community of artists that composed and performed songs in the ballad tradition that flourished well into the twentieth century, and Frank Tours was at the center of this development.

Once the ballad had gone out of fashion around mid-century, we lost direct contact with its interpretive style and the sensibility that had once been second nature to its practitioners. But since the age of recording began in earnest during the period of the Edwardian ballad, some evidence of this vocal practice was captured in the medium. Though some of the great ballad singers from the period made recordings and these artifacts are undoubtedly useful, there is no better model for a recreation of an original interpretive style for Tours' songs than the many recordings of "Mother o' Mine" that were made by more than a dozen singers over three decades (see Discography of this volume). In addition, we have a transcription of a 1945 radio broadcast by the popular tenor James Melton with Frank Tours conducting a new orchestral arrangement. Not only is this a rare example of Tours conducting his own music, it is an example of how the ballad was still being performed in the 1940s in a way that was fresh and vital rather than nostalgic. Taken together, these performances are the best reflection of the ballad style as it lived on through Tours' masterpiece, even as the broader tradition had all but disappeared from public life. For, just as the ballad repertory was mostly considered paltry and banal in the second half of the twentieth century, the singing style of its most distinguished representatives in the nineteenth and early twentieth centuries was regarded, at least by some, as histrionic and hyper-emotional. J. B. Stean's commentary on the recordings of Clara Butt in his 1974 book *The Grand Tradition* reflects this attitude when he wrote that "[o]n the whole, I think modern taste still pronounces the verdict 'Excessive', but perhaps less emphatically than it might have done, say, twenty years ago."[5] Despite Frank Tours' reliance on compositional elements that leaned toward modernism, his dedication to setting romantic lyrics kept him firmly aligned with the musical aesthetics of the ballad and, likewise, the interpretive tradition found in Butt's recordings, as the many recordings of "Mother o' Mine" affirm. Therefore, if we want to understand these period conventions in order to emulate their style, the value of having access to a broad sample of interpretations over time cannot be overestimated.

There are certain characteristics of musical interpretation that are common to all of the "Mother o' Mine" recordings, from Herbert Witherspoon's stoic rendition in 1907 to the fiery lyricism of Richard Crooks' performance in 1936. But while the sheet music makes it clear that much of the emotionalism of these performances is built into the composition by Tours, close listening with the score reveals how limited Tours' use of expressive markings was. Though "Mother o' Mine" is stylistically different in tone from many of his songs, being more declamatory than lyrical, it can be instructive to isolate and identify some of the interpretive features that are not indicated in the score so that they may be applied to other songs where appropriate. As a practical matter, the dynamics that Tours gives in the score of "Mother o' Mine" are of little use to the singer, partly since they are limited to a few crescendo markings after the opening measures. Despite the absence of any dynamic marking in the vocal part, the singers all take their cue from the *mezzo piano* marking in the introduction, indicating that the *piano* dynamic given below the first entrance of the voice is a suggestion for the accompanist to play in a quiet supportive manner. In fact, some clearly take an even more forceful approach (John Charles Thomas does not sing below *mezzo forte* at any point in the song), perhaps responding to the need to project in the period of acoustic recording. However, most singers do not take the absence of nuanced dynamic markings in the score as an indication that the composer intended a single dynamic to unify the song. Instead they modify their dynamics from phrase to phrase, conforming the expression to the immediate needs of the music and lyrics at any given point. For example, we can clearly hear Richard Crooks sing the antecedent phrases of the melody at the beginning of the song ("If I were hang'd on the highest hill," and "I know whose love would follow me still") with an expansive dynamic of at least *mezzo forte* only to be followed by a relaxation on each of the consequent phrases (addressing his "Mother o' Mine") into a quieter *mezzo piano* or even *piano* to express the comfort and tenderness of feeling it gives him. By the fourth phrase (beginning in the middle of measure 13),

the dynamic naturally expands with the progression to A Minor (vi) and the octave leap in the vocal line. All of the singers respond to this increase of energy in the music and maintain it through two measures despite there being no indication of a *crescendo* in the score. At the downbeat of measure 20, following the second piano interlude and caesura, Tours gives accents but no dynamic marking on the half-diminished "Tristan" chord in the piano. This allows the pianist to determine the right intensity to support the singer's interpretation of this line, which offers a range of options because the vocal line, up to the *crescendo* on the word "soul," is enhanced only by *tenuto* marks and a heavy accent on the word "damn'd." Thus, Tours dispenses with the need for a *forte* marking to make obvious what is clear from the setting. And this remains true through the end of the piece, which every singer properly delivers in impassioned tones, varying in loudness from *forte* to *fortissimo* throughout, even though the biggest dynamic marking the score is *mezzo piano*.

The score for "Mother o' Mine" contains more tempo markings than dynamics, a fact that corresponds to the rhetorical quality of the text and Tours' ear for its declamatory rhythms. Even so, the singers on record enjoyed more freedom to modify the tempo than the score indicates. To begin with, the amount of forward movement throughout the many textures that Tours created to support the vocal line defies the *Adagio* marking that governs the whole song, and most of the singers on record take a tempo that is at least *Andante* (Louis Graveure and Richard Bonelli are notable exceptions). The *ritardando* in measure 8 on the second appearance of the title lyric ("Mother o' Mine") is an expressive gesture that is repeated in measures 12 and 13 and in some performances with an even deeper relaxation of the tempo, despite there being no marking in the score. At the end of measure 8, the *rallentando* in the accompaniment seems to contradict the movement suggested by the melody and the eighth-note texture, and the fact that most accompanists actually accelerate slightly in that spot (including Tours himself) suggests that it may have been an error. Following the instrumental interlude, both the rising melodic line and the tenuto marks over the notes for "If I were drowned" suggest that the singer should bring urgency to this phrase, and the *colla voce* mark does alert the accompanist to this possibility. Not surprisingly, most singers increased the tempo in this section (some more than others), even though the score does not explicitly ask for an *accelerando*. The second instrumental interlude is also generally taken faster than the original tempo despite the absence of any clear indication to increase its movement. Though simply marked *cantabile*, it is natural for the music to drive forward to the caesura once it is released from the *rallentando* and the fermatas at the end of the previous phrase, and the recordings show that there was a clear consensus that the music should

---

[5] J. B. Steane, *The Grand Tradition: Seventy Years of Singing on Record* (Portland, OR: Amadeus Press, 1974), 252–53.

DAVIS AND THORSETT

accelerate in these two measures. Tours gives no indication of any tempo modification from measure 20 through the end of the song, and yet most singers approached this final section with the freedom to push and pull back the tempo to heed the expressive demands of the music and text. The *tenuto* marks and accents in the vocal line along with the whole notes and half notes in the accompaniment suggest that the performer should hold back in the first two measures, which heightens the tension to focus the listener on the existential crisis of physical and spiritual damnation. The flood of energy that is released once the eighth notes return in the accompaniment swells with the dynamic increase that is suggested by the *crescendo* marks from measure 21-26. The singers all drive the tempo forward on the words "I know whose pray'rs would make me whole" and in its emphatic reiteration toward the caesura in measure 27, after which they uniformly slow down as if the score had a *Grave* marking, all the while sustaining the *crescendo* to the final note of the vocal line. The *accelerando* that occurs naturally throughout the final section reminds us of how *crescendo* marks invited performers in the nineteenth century to increase the energy, which included both volume and speed, as an expressive device. Tours knew in 1903 that the urgency of the music and text with expanding dynamics would compel performers to drive the tempo forward as a part of their impassioned delivery, and the song's interpretive tradition (crowned by Tours' own rendering with James Melton in 1945) reflects this.

It was customary for singers of Tours' music to adhere to the rhythm as indicated in the score with a high degree of fidelity. For though it was allied with popular music in its themes and audiences, the ballad in its twentieth-century manifestation was more closely associated with classical styles in its modes and practices. In evaluating the performances of "Mother o' Mine" that we have on record however, we should view the piece as a late- or post-Romantic song, and thus within a tradition that gave performers some latitude in the execution of some idiomatic rhythmic figures. These freedoms are particularly evident in the subtle and specific use of rhythmic variants we find in the recorded performances. For example, the pickup note in the vocal line at the end of measure 13 is modified to an eighth note by at least half of the singers, presumably in order to reduce the dissonance against the grace-note anacrusis figure on the E-dominant sonority (V_7/vi). This modification also reconciles it with the same figure at the end of measure 24. As was previously discussed, the intensity of measure 20 is typically expressed by a broadening of the quarter notes. However, in the recording by Crooks, the same intensification suggested by the score is achieved with what appears at first to be an *accelerando*, but upon closer scrutiny is instead a diminution of the note values to eighths, a change of rhythm that only becomes apparent in the following measure when we hear the dotted quarter.

Lastly, Tours' use of fermatas on both final eighth notes in measure 17 suggests that he wants the tempo to resume on the downbeat. In practice, however, most of the singers ignore this indication in favor of using the final eighth note of the measure as a cue for the instrumental interlude to begin again in time. These rhythmic variants are noteworthy not only as examples of the some of the interpretive freedoms that were acceptable at the time, but also as a reflection of the constraints that governed ballad singing in the twentieth century.

"Mother o' Mine," like the poem upon which it is based, is largely pathetic in tone, even though its theme is ultimately a hopeful one and all its horrors are imagined and not real. Since all of the poetic imagery is forged out of traumatic scenes in the author's imagination, the sound of the voice must bear the weight of these thoughts in order to be credible to the listener and, in turn, to be felt. To express this burden, Tours created a vocal line that is full of falling two-note melismatic figures that require a downward *portamento*, which has a built-in emotional sound, like sighing, on some of the most potent words in the text. The *portamento* phrasing between these intervals—seconds, thirds, and fourths—is a traditional sliding gesture that connects the two notes. By varying degrees, depending upon the singer's skill, taste, and inclination, these gestures also carry emotional content with microtonal *glissandi* that give the downward slide contour and texture that borrows from other vocal expressions of human feeling. Tours wrote these short melismas with the *portamento* in mind, as we can see from the phrase marks connecting the intervals, but even more explicitly from the grace note in measure 14 on the word "would," suggesting that the singer may land on the note of arrival in advance after the slide of a fourth from E to B on the word "tears." The same gesture is indicated in measure 25 on the words "pray'rs would," but using an eighth note instead of a grace note, a variant suggested by the rhythm of the text. The use of an upward *portamento* (rising from B to C using an anticipatory arrival note) by a few of the singers from measure 22 to 23 was suggested by the *crescendo* mark but not specifically indicated in the score. These optional modes of phrasing were an important element of the singer's art in Tours' day, although they have mostly lost their currency among twenty-first century recitalists (they seem to have been retained to a much larger extent in opera). The recordings by Tours' contemporaries show that the *portamento* is not only stylistically congruent with the musical setting but it has an expressive potency that matches the pathos of the text, a fact which argues persuasively for its continued use in this and other Tours songs according to the demands of good taste.

The unprecedented number of recordings of "Mother o' Mine" can be used to inform an interpretive style for all of Tours' songs, according to the basic principles that were operative in the tradition of ballad singing in the first half of the twentieth century. This is particularly useful for a variety of reasons: first, because the interpretive freedoms that were allowed and, in fact, expected are not necessarily a part of our current tradition; and, second, because Tours' published scores were not only lacking in many specific markings that could provide guidance (the few cases of his notating *portamenti* referred to above notwithstanding), but because they were full of inconsistencies that can be confusing, especially to musicians that are inclined to rely heavily upon the score for interpretive directions. For this reason, we have identified as many of these confusing dynamics, tempo indications, articulations, and pedal markings as possible for convenient reference in the critical commentaries that follow, along with relevant information that will make it easy for the performer to access. Again, we hope that these observations will encourage a rational approach to interpreting these scores in a manner that is both stylistically sensitive and creatively individualistic as the composer would have expected from young singers as well as seasoned professionals.

CRITICAL COMMENTARY

The critical commentary for each piece contains as many as five items of information.[1] (1) *Publisher* indicates the company that issued the sheet music used in the facsimile; (2) *Date* provides the year the song was first published; (3) *Key/Range* provides the primary key of the song and the vocal range it requires for performance (in addition to "ossia" or alternate high notes recommended to the singer); (4) *Critical notes* lists errata and inconsistent markings that the editors would have added, removed, or corrected if we had created a new engraving; (5) *Comments* provides information about any or all of the following areas: background information on the lyricist, circumstances of the collaboration, interpretation and critique of the lyric, outstanding features of the musical setting.

The critical notes are given in a telegraphic style similar to that used originally in Charles Hamm's *Irving Berlin: Early Songs*. The measure is identified first, followed by the number of the note or rest within that measure. Notes and rests of any length count as one, regardless of ties. Next, the musical staff is identified, as V, P1, or P2, which indicate the voice part, the upper staff of the piano accompaniment, and the lower staff of the piano accompaniment. The pitches for the vocal ranges are designated by register thus: C-c-c′-c″-c‴, in which c′ is middle C. For example, an entry reading "9.3, P2, no natural before e" reports that, on the third note of measure 9, the lower piano staff of the sheet music lacks a natural for the E below middle C.

The Alternative

Publisher. M. Witmark & Sons
Date. 1904
Key/Range. C Major (c′ – g″)
Critical notes. 1, tempo mark (*Adagio*) is slow for the rhythmic texture; 22.2, P, tempo modification mark (*rallentando*) is contrary to anacrusis leading to *Allegretto*; 31.2, P2, courtesy accidental (c♯) is missing in chord; 35.3, P2, pedal release is missing; 37, P1, courtesy accidental (f♯) is unclear; 43, tempo modification mark (*a tempo*) is missing; 55, tempo modification mark (*poco accelerando*) is missing; 55 dynamic mark (*piano*) is superfluous; pedal marks in the piano part are superfluous.

Comments. Lyricist Arthur Anderson wrote the libretti and/or lyrics for several Edwardian musical comedies (e.g. *The White Chrysanthemum*, *The Girl Behind the Counter*, *Two Merry Monarchs*) then worked on several Broadway shows in the same capacity (e.g. *The Marriage Market*, *The Beauty Spot*, *Chu Chin Chow*). The song's theme of unrequited love becoming a basis for friendship is similar to Wilfred Sanderson's "pal" song "Friend o' Mine" from 1913. One of Tours' most adventurous settings in terms of harmony, it modulates abruptly in the B section to A♭ (♭VI), a distant third-relation key, and then wends its way back to the tonic slowly through D Minor using many chromatic pedal chords.

Beloved

Publisher. M. Witmark & Sons
Date. 1904
Key/Range. D Major (d′ – f♯″)
Critical notes. 2.4, V, dynamic mark (*mezzo piano*) is missing; 6, tempo modification mark (*a tempo*) is missing; 13.6, V, lyric incorrect ("its"); 34, *decrescendo* mark is missing; 34.2, V, lyric incorrect ("gives"); 38.2, V, lyric incorrect ("gives"); 38.4, P, dynamic mark (*mezzo forte*) is missing.

Comments. Lyricist J. Edward Fraser was a performer on the London stage, appearing in *Lady Madcap*, *Mr. Popple*, and as Lord Eynsford with Gertie Millar in *Our Miss Gibbs*. This song was published the year he was a member of the company of *Three Little Maids*, which Frank Tours led as music director on its world tour. In 1920, he wrote the words and music for the British musical comedy *The*

---

[1] The format and text for these Critical Commentaries were suggested by a similar section from *The Music and Scripts of* In Dahomey, edited by Thomas L. Riis (Madison, WI: A-R Editions, 1996) and have been used in this book by permission of the editor.

Widow and the Maid. Fraser's lyric shows the full measure of love and devotion that was possible between young men and women in the Edwardian Era before they had even made their affection known to each other. Since the relationship is aspirational, one could think of the song itself as a serenade or musical love letter to the object of the protagonist's desire. An early example of Tours' gift for long, lyrical melodic lines, each four-measure phrase in the sixteen-measure verse is different in rhythm and shape, while the whole line sounds like one long melodic idea. The coda is a variant on the third phrase and climaxes, appropriately, on the highest note and loudest dynamic in the song. Also appropriate is that fact that the music's expressive high point occurs on the word "worship," since that is, in a secular sense, the song's central theme.

Beyond the Sunset (And God Is Overhead)

Publisher. M. Witmark & Sons
Date. 1911
Key/Range. E Minor (d' – f♯'')
Critical notes. 4.4, V, dynamic mark (*piano*) is missing.
Comments. One of Tours' most dramatic settings, M. Witmark & Sons published it in four keys covering an interval of a fifth. Herbert Witherspoon, an operatic bass, was an early interpreter as indicated on the cover, demonstrating that it is a good song for low voice, despite featuring several sustained notes in the high register. The text by Holman Quinn subtly and convincingly conflates the romantic and religious, and enhances its sacred tone, by borrowing from the "Old Waits Carol" ("The life of man is but a span"). The only Tours song that was published with both English and German lyrics. The melody is constructed in four-measure periods in an overall A-B-A scheme. Modulation to ♭VI begins with a pivot chord in the parallel major of the tonic. The planing chords in the Aeolian mode that color the opening of both A sections have a mystical quality, particularly with the blurring effect caused by the damper pedal being held over the entire measure. The damper pedal should be released with the harmony changes at all other times.

From the Valley

Publisher. Oliver Ditson Company
Date. 1911
Key/Range. D♭ Major (d♭' – f'')
Critical notes. 19–20, P, damper pedal hold over the harmony changes, as at 15–16, should be repeated; pedal marks in the piano part are superfluous.
Comments. The lyric by Elsie Janis, one the finest eccentric comediennes on the Broadway stage during the 1910s, is one of unusual spiritual and poetic depth for a Tours song. The phrase "Valley of Discontent" seems to conflate

two significant literary images: the "valley of the shadow of death" from Psalm 23 and the "winter of our discontent" from Shakespeare's *Richard III*. There is another historical literary allusion in the line "Gather the flowers while you may," which echoes the first line of Robert Herrick's "To the Virgins, To Make Much of Time" ("Gather ye rosebuds while ye may, Old Time is still a-flying"). The form of Tours' setting is A-B-A', but the return of the A material is repeated twice, once at the beginning of A' and once as a bookend codetta. The A section has two six-measure melodic periods, which is uncommon and a welcome change from his standard four-measure phrases. The B section begins with an abrupt modulation to F Major (III) and winds through a more distant C Major (VII), illustrating with its cascades of thirds and blurred harmony the dreamy atmosphere of the poet's memory, when she "lingered at the stream of bliss."

Fury of the Sea

Publisher. The Boston Music Co.
Date. 1924
Key/Range. D♭ Major (c' – f'')
Critical notes. 3-4, P, pedal mark is missing; 5, V, dynamic mark should be *mezzo piano* instead.
Comments. Edmund Goulding's poem, inspired by his own 1922 sailing novel *Fury*, is full of potent language condensed from his descriptive prose about the sea. A British singer who spent his early years in New York working as a performer in vaudeville (he once played the same bill as Nora Bayes at the Palace), Goulding turned his attention to screenwriting during the silent-picture era and is credited with working on dozens of films in the 1920s as both a writer and director. In the sound era, he became an A-list director and worked on several outstanding films over a thirty-year period with Hollywood's leading actors. Tours met Goulding at the Algonquin Round Table, which both men frequented in the early 1920s, and the composer may have suggested that he write the lyric based on imagery from his popular book. Goulding's passionate language inspired Tours' most provocative setting and his most overt attempt at musical illustration. Depicting the motion of a roiling sea, the accompaniment features a relentless series of undulating arpeggios that evoke the ocean's instability and danger, but also the romance it held for the sailor and the poet. Evocative of this instability, the harmony is mostly chromatic and is full of non-functional sonorities and progressions. Moreover, the music only cadences twice, signaling the close of each stanza with unconventional dominant sonorities at 19–20 (♭II₇—I) and 33–34 (i°4₇—I). A radio transcription from 1945 of John Charles Thomas singing the song with an orchestral arrangement (probably by Tours) reveals the full extent of its expressive power. Tours' most ambitious setting, "Fury of the Sea" is

the clearest example of his potential to make a significant contribution to the tradition of American art song in the early twentieth century.

God's Promise

Publisher. Chappell & Co.
Date. 1908
Key/Range. F Major (d′ – f″)
Critical notes. 47, tempo modification mark (*rallentando*) should be *più rall* at 46.3 instead.

Comments. Lyricist Ellaline Terriss was a beloved figure on the London stage, whose story of personal triumph and tragedy in the theatre was well-known in her day. The daughter of actor William Terriss, she rose to fame at the age of sixteen and performed in numerous plays and musical comedies throughout the 1890s and 1900s. She married actor Seymour Hicks in 1895, and the two played together in *The Shop Girl* and *The Circus Girl.* The brutal murder of her father by another actor just before going on stage was the subject of a long court case that made her a sympathetic figure to the British public. Frank Tours first worked with Terriss in 1907, when he was the music director for *The Gay Gordons* starring the Hicks. They became close friends thereafter and were involved in several productions on the London stage, including *The Dashing Little Duke* (with a score by Tours) and *Captain Kidd,* and they were developing another show when Tours immigrated to New York in 1911. The lyric for "God's Promise" was written as a personal expression of maternal affection for Terriss' daughter, Betty, to whom the song was dedicated. It is divided into three sections: the first describes Terriss' married life before her daughter was born and is addressed to Hicks; the second is also directed to her husband and describes (in the most delicate imaginable terms) the couple's connubial bliss in conceiving their child; and the third section is addressed directly to her daughter as the flower they had prayed for—"our Lily"—a gift of divine providence. The poetic meter of the verse is consistently gathered in two groups of four trochees, and Tours' setting varies the rhythm between one type of four-bar musical phrase that emphasizes the quarter-note beats and another that compresses the verse into two measures, using many more eighth notes. He also cleverly brings variety by introducing the eight-note rhythms at the end of the A section and then continuing them into the B section. The image of the lily, representing their child, is given a *leitmotif* by Tours that occurs in all three sections, highlighted by a dominant-seven-flat-nine chord on the first degree ($F_{7(b9)}$) that illustrates the child as an unnamed wish (she makes no explicit mention of the lily flower), as a fetus in the womb, and as their baby after birth. With no explicit religious imagery apart from its references to God, this song has an undeniable spiritual dimension that characterizes the conception and birth of a child as a sacred mystery.

Hope Dreams

Publisher. Unity Music Publishers, Inc.
Date. 1924
Key/Range. D Major (d′ – f♯″)
Critical notes. 4.4, V, dynamic mark (*piano*) is missing; 18.3, P2, dynamic mark (*piano*) should be removed; 50.3, P2, dynamic mark (*piano*) should be removed.

Comments. John Steel's lyric has strong religious overtones without having any explicit sacred or liturgical text or function. Apart from its clear reference to the Christian nativity, the "Star of Hope" was a common literary image of faith and prayer throughout the nineteenth and early twentieth centuries. Steel's arcane language, with its "book of memories," "sacred seal," and "Springtime of roses" is set with a modern tonal language that remarkably does not sound anachronistic. The refrain features one of Tours' most memorable melodies, its long, wavelike phrases reinforced by an octave doubling. This ethereal line, along with the constantly throbbing pedal harmonies in the accompaniment, illustrates the lyric's theme of yearning and supplication.

Hush-a-By, Sweetie

Publisher. Novello & Co.
Date. 1903
Key/Range. A♭ Major (e♭′ – a♭″)
Critical notes. 7, P, tempo modification mark (*colla voce*) should be removed; 11, V, tempo modification (*a tempo*) is missing; 33, P, tempo modification mark (*colla voce*) should be removed; 37, V, tempo modification (*a tempo*) is missing; pedal markings in the piano part are superfluous.

Comments. This was Tours' only song published by Novello, his father's company. The lyricist Edward Oxenford (born in 1848 and not to be confused with Edward deVere, Earl of Oxford) was a prolific poet and librettist who wrote over 2,000 lyrics for songs and contributed the texts for more than fifty operas and cantatas (his best-known lyric in the twentieth century is the English translation of "Funicula, Funiculi"). "Hush-a-By, Sweetie" is a lullaby of both musical and lyrical sweetness with no explicit suggestion of parental anxiety that is common in the genre. Accordingly, the *piano* dynamic throughout is accurate and should be observed. The verses are set with two contrasting sections of eight measures and the refrain is half that length. Tours fashioned a codetta from two measures of the verse, a welcome reprise of the most attractive melodic material in the song.

I Dreamed

Publisher. M. Witmark & Sons
Date. 1911
Key/Range. G Major (d′ – g″)
Critical notes. 4.4, V, dynamic mark (*mezzo piano*) is missing; 16, P, dynamic mark (*piano*) is superfluous; 21, P, dynamic mark (*mezzo forte*) is missing; 29, P, dynamic mark (*mezzo piano*) is missing; 49, P, dynamic mark (*mezzo forte*) is missing; pedal marks in the piano are superfluous.

Comments. The subject of death in the lyric by Holman Quinn is rare among Tours' songs. By concealing the tragedy of a young lover's death within the conceit of the protagonist's dream, Quinn justifies the intensely passionate emotional narrative of the song more than a lyric about love and loss would.

If You Loved Me

Publisher. M. Witmark & Sons
Date. 1914
Key/Range. A Major (e′ – f♯)
Critical notes. Despite being the most detailed score that Tours composed in terms of tempo modification, there is only one dynamic marking in the entire song. Therefore, performers should interpret the song with dynamics that match the energy conveyed by other compositional elements.

Comments. The lyric by Hilda Hammond Spenser has a theme about romantic love that is the inverse of the typical juxtaposition we see in a poem by Petrarch. Instead of the lover experiencing romantic angst while nature is seemingly expressing its joy in springtime, Hammond depicts her lovers (albeit aspirationally) as elated while walking amongst the gloom of winter. Three large sections (A-B-A′) are formally balanced, each with fourteen-measure periods comprised of three phrases in the vocal line (4+4+6). The tonic of the first section (A Major) does not appear until measure 9 and then only briefly, contributing to a sense of movement that is illustrative of the emotional excitement of the protagonist imagining the wonderful possibilities offered by a shared life. The opening F-dominant sonority (♭VI₇) presages the new key the B section (F Major), which modulates through D♭ Major, another descending third-relation key, before returning chromatically to the original key for the recapitulation of the opening material at 37.

In Flanders' Fields

Publisher. M. Witmark & Sons
Date. 1918
Key/Range. D Minor (d′ – f″)
Critical notes. Lyric incorrectly has an apostrophe in the title and throughout the text when it should read "In Flanders Fields" (or "fields" within the lyric); 30, P1, accidental (e♭) is missing; 33.2, P1, left-hand chord accidental (g♯) is missing; 37, P2, courtesy accidental (b♭) missing; 38.4, P2, courtesy accidental (g♮) is missing; 38, P, dynamic mark (*piano*) is missing; 42.2, P2, bass note is incorrect (d not f).

Comments. McCrae's well-known lyric was treated by Tours with careful attention to the sound of the soldier's voice and to the multidimensional message contained within the different sections of the verse. His setting expresses the shifting moods that were contained in McCrae's words as the poet surveyed the death and destruction on the battlefield before him. Tours' use of the version of the poem where the "poppies blow" (instead of "grow") is illustrated by the undulating melodic line through the first six measures, as arpeggiated chords depict the gentle breeze that lift the flower petals from the ground up into the air, the two spaces that the soldiers inhabit in death. Though largely through-composed, the signature melodic phrase that appears first on the words "that mark our place and in the sky" recurs twice, descending through the harmonic minor scale in contrary motion against the haunting opening chord progression. As the voice communicates the soldier's love of life from beyond the grave, the sonorities take on a spectral glow; and when the spirit regains its will to fight, the music matches its power and intensity. Tours alters the poem in only one place by separating the elision on the word "Torch" at 33 and 34, giving the word its place in both phrases for emphasis ("we throw the Torch" and "The Torch be yours") for emphasis. When the opening phrase ("the poppies blow") changes to "Though poppies grow," the melody flattens out on the fifth and becomes chantlike, representing the spirit that remains on the desolate landscape of the quiet, windblown battlefield.

Jest a Wearyin' fer You

Publisher. Joseph Williams, Limited
Date. 1910
Key/Range. A Minor (d′ – f♯″)
Critical notes. 3.3, V, dynamic mark (*piano*) is missing; 7.4, P2, courtesy accidental (a♮) is missing; 15.4, P1, courtesy accidental (c♯) is superfluous; 19, P2, courtesy accidentals (f♮, c♮) are superfluous; 28, P1, left hand indication (*l.h.*) is missing at top of chord; pedal marks in the piano part are superfluous.

Comments. The poem by Frank Lebby Stanton, originally published in *Songs of the Soil* in 1894, was titled "Wearyin' fer You" and consisted of seven stanzas, of which Tours set the first, third, sixth, and seventh. The only specific reference to gender in the poem lies in the fourth stanza: "Comes the wind with sounds that jes'/Like the rustlin' o' your dress." Stanton's poem clearly depicts a domesticated home where, in 1894, it would be nearly impossible to imagine a woman taking a long trip for work, and thus we can only imagine that the woman has left for other reasons that give her absence heartbreaking implications. In her 1901 setting of the poem, Carrie Jacobs-Bond did not use this stanza, being a performer of her own songs whose point of reference in this case was her husband, to whom the song is dedicated. Likewise, rather than identify with Stanton's male protagonist, Tours seems to follow Jacobs-Bonds' model, as if knowing that her popular setting had fixed the idea of a female singer in the public's mind. Though he used different stanzas than Jacobs-Bonds in his setting, he likely also avoided the fourth because it was common in the 1910s for women to be alone at home for long periods while their husbands traveled for work, making for a more plausible and less pathetic scenario. Nonetheless, since there is no clear reference to gender in this version, it can comfortably be sung now by a man or a woman, depending upon the intention of the performer. The bass-chord rhythm in the accompaniment is reminiscent of the plodding footsteps in some of the songs from Schubert's *Winterreise* and could be thought of as the sound of the protagonist pacing through the empty house. The harmony, with distantly related chromatic chords in every measure, is expressive of emotional weariness through its abundance of dissonant sonorities. Few of Tours' song settings have accompaniments that are as free of melody as this one. The prevailing dotted-eighth/sixteenth rhythm in the melody is expressive of the heavy burden of loneliness, and yet Tours gives the listener a welcome relief from the pervasive unequal subdivision (and from the minor mode) in the second part of the A section. Tours' setting of the poem, though it never got the traction that it deserved, having been overshadowed by the success of the version by Carrie Jacobs-Bond, is more effective and nuanced in its treatment of the text than its more famous predecessor, having made the vocal line and harmony an equal partner in the expressiveness of the song.

The Long Day (But I Am Over Here, and He Is Over There!)

Publisher. M. Witmark & Sons
Date. 1918
Key/Range. G Major (b′ – e″)
Critical notes. 3, V, dynamic mark (*piano*) is missing; 3-6, P1, ties are superfluous; 21, P1, fermatas are missing (in both voices); pedal marks in the piano part are superfluous.
Comments. Lyricist George V. Hobart was a humorist and a prolific author of books and libretti for Broadway musicals during the first two decades of the twentieth century. Though they never worked together on a show, Tours and Hobart were both devoted members of the Lambs Club, where they probably met. Hobart's lyric for "The Long Day" is a radical departure from his comedy

work for the *Ziegfeld Follies* and other theatrical productions, as it reveals the author's sensitivity and poetic gift. Particularly appealing is the obvious, but not cloying reference to one of the most famous songs from another well-known member of the Lambs, George M. Cohan. Hobart deftly took Cohan's jingoistic call to arms in "Over There" and used it to remind the audience of the women who were sacrificing on the home front when their loved ones went to war. The elegant simplicity of his lyric is reflected in its traditional elements, such as the trochaic five-syllable lines that are used consistently throughout and the Petrarchian juxtaposition (nature is peaceful, but my heart is not) that comprises the song's primary argument. But while this simplicity is matched by Tours' melodic setting, which is almost completely diatonic, his harmony is highly adventurous, which could be seen as an illustration of the unsettling interior life of the protagonist amidst the external tranquility of the environment and of the outward calm she projects in her community. In the B section of the song's A-B-A′ form, Tours took the verses with the same meter as the outer sections and gave them a different setting that conceals their metric similarity, thus providing the listener a respite from the five-syllable rhythm. One of the few Tours songs explicitly written to be sung by a woman, "The Long Day" was, nonetheless, performed by John Charles Thomas in recital and promoted as such by the publisher.

Mother o' Mine

Publisher. Chappell & Co.
Date. 1903
Key/Range. C Major (d′ – e″)
Critical notes. *Adagio* tempo marking is a slower tempo than the music suggests; 2.3, V, dynamic mark (*piano*) is missing; 8.7, P1, tempo modification mark (*rallentando*) runs contrary to the forward motion of musical line; 12, P, dynamic mark (*ritardando*) is missing; 14, P, dynamic mark (*mezzo forte*) is missing; 16, P1, *decrescendo* and dynamic mark (*piano*) is missing; 25, P, dynamic mark (*forte*) is missing.
Comments. The poem by Rudyard Kipling originally appeared as a preface in an early reprint of his first novel *The Light that Failed*. The setting is through-composed with only two instances of musical repetition of the title phrase ("Mother o' Mine") at 17–18 and 28–31. Tours composed each of the seven iterations of the phrase differently so that the listener does not tire of hearing it over the course of the song. In the middle stanza, he changes meter twice to preserve the natural scansion of the phrase. The music builds throughout the third section and climaxes powerfully at the very end. The setting begins on the tonic, but moves away quickly and does not return until measure 6. Each stanza that depicts the various tribulations that

the protagonist imagines begins on an unstable sonority and does not resolve fully until after the words "Mother o' Mine" are sung. Furthering this sense of instability, the third stanza opens with a succession of unrelated half-diminished chords that only resolve to the tonic eleven bars later at measure 30 for the final time. Though Tours' songs generally have vocal lines that are almost uniformly syllabic, "Mother o' Mine" has no less than eight melismatic two-note downward intervals that emphasize the pathetic tone of the poetry. These traditional sighing figures all highlight key words in the text ("I," "love," "still," "sea," "tears," "me," "prayers," "whole") and call for an emotional tone in the voice to enhance their impact on the listener. Tours' best-known song was commercially recorded by at least sixteen singers between 1907 and 1951. Two other published versions—one by Arthur Classen and another by Leo Ornstein—were published within fifteen years of the Tours setting, but were nonetheless eclipsed by the enduring popularity of the original. A convincing case could be made for this song being considered the high point of the Victorian/Edwardian ballad tradition.

No Voice But Yours (No Hope, No Love, Save That in Your Dear Eyes)

Publisher. M. Witmark & Sons
Date. 1917
Key/Range. D Major (f♯ – a″ [b″ ossia])
Critical notes. 2, P2, fermata in bass is missing; 3.2, V, dynamic mark (*piano*) is missing; 13, V, dynamic mark (*piano*) is missing; 11, P2, fermata is incorrect and belongs at 10, beat 3 instead; 12, P2, fermata in the bass line is missing; 23, P2, fermata is missing; 23.4, P, V, accidentals (b♭) are superfluous; 19.5, V, breath mark interrupts the phrase and should be removed; 22.4, V, breath mark interrupts the phrase and should be removed; 23.4, V, breath mark is superfluous; 23, P, tempo modification mark (*molto rallentando*) should be placed at midpoint of 22 instead; 24.4, V, dotted-eighth/sixteenth figure in vocal part at 24, beat 2 could be sung more comfortably as two eighth notes instead.

Comments. The lyric by Edward Teschemacher was designed to be set to music. The romantic aspiration of the protagonist is made clear in the line "if you are ever mine," despite the poetic language obscuring its specific meaning to some extent. The phrase is elliptical, but its meaning should be understood as "if you are *forever* mine" rather than "if you *ever become* mine." This connotation corresponds to the stage of courtship that precedes engagement during which the lover has experienced the things described in the poem and wishes that they continue for a lifetime. Tours was in the midst of his own courtship of Helen Clarke at the time he set this lyric and so it probably had a greater personal meaning for him than many of the earlier romantic ballads he composed. The two verses are set in binary form with a variation in the second half of the eight-measure period and a climactic five-measure extension at the end. The vocal line is unusually high (including an ossia b″) and sits in the *passaggi* during large portions of the song, presenting technical challenges for the singer, especially in the forte passages.

O, Bring Me Love!

Publisher. M. Witmark & Sons
Date. 1911
Key/Range. F Major (d′ – f″)
Critical notes. 2.2-3, V, the quarter- and eighth-note rests with fermatas should be combined to a dotted quarter with a single fermata; 3.5, P2, bass note should have courtesy accidental (f♮) to clarify the cross-relation (f♯); 11.2, P, tempo modification mark (*rallantando*) is missing; 13, P, tempo modification mark (*a tempo*) is missing; 13, P2, dynamic mark (*sforzando*) is superfluous (similar to 1); 14.2-3, V, the quarter- and eighth-note rests with fermatas should be combined to a dotted quarter with a single fermata; 16.5, P2, bass note should have courtesy accidental (f♮) to clarify the cross-relation (f♯); 23, P, dynamic mark (*fortissimo*) is superfluous; 23, P, tempo modification mark (*a tempo*) is missing; the pedal marks in the piano part are superfluous.

Comments. The lyric by Harold Simpson, who wrote an important history of the ballad in the nineteenth and early twentieth century, is an excellent example of a mediocre text that Tours elevated substantially with his difficult and dramatic musical setting. The message of the protagonist to his lover is set against the backdrop of their parting for some unknown reason. Simpson's elliptical use of the word "love" in the second sentence for both his love and that of his would-be lover ("Oh, bring me [your] love, that [my] love may not be in vain") creates an ambiguity that is not worth the effort it takes to unpack. An even more awkward ambiguity exists in the opening line, which suggests that the lover bring the protagonist tears, when it is in fact the presence of their tears that makes the protagonist cry (this connotation should not be conflated with the phrase "bring me *to* tears"). The lyric's passionate plea mounts throughout the song until it climaxes in dramatic fashion at the end, giving the singer a powerful vehicle to exercise the full extent of their vocal capacity to great effect.

Red Rose

Publisher. Chappell & Co.
Date. 1907
Key/Range. F Major (d′ – f′)
Critical notes. 3, V, dynamic mark (*piano*) is missing; 6, P, dynamic mark (*mezzo forte*) is a mistake; 14.6, P1, tempo

modification mark (*rallentando*) should begin at 13.3, P1 instead; 16.3, P1, tempo modification mark (*tenuto*) is a mistake; 25.2, P2, arpeggio is a mistake; 27.2, P1, courtesy accidental (b♭) is superfluous; 39.1–2, P1, arpeggios should extend through the right-hand chords. Pedal marks in the piano part are superfluous.

Comments. H. Pearl Humphry was a performer in British musical comedies who also was a poet and an essayist. Her lyric was written within a long tradition of poems in English about the rose that includes well-known examples from William Blake, Robert Burns, Christina Rossetti, and Emily Dickenson. While "Red Rose" is not crafted with the same intensity of language as these other poems, Humphry's use of personification to pose questions to the flower is a typical conceit, as is the use of the poetic image to convey the idea of *carpe diem*. Tours uses a modulation from F Major to A Minor (iii) effectively at the recapitulation to illustrate how the "little brown rose" has died. He returns quickly to the tonic and elaborates the melody with a sequence on the line that conveys hope in the moral that facing the end of life with dignity allows you to "glow" even in death. The simplicity and charm of his melody not only matches the delicacy of the poetic imagery, but it makes this song sit quite comfortably in the voice.

Son of My Heart

Publisher. M. Witmark & Sons
Date. 1915
Key/Range. D Major (e′ – g″ [a″ ossia])
Critical notes. 2.4, V, dynamic mark (*mezzo piano*) is missing; 10.3, P1, tempo modification mark (*colla voce*) is missing; 32.3, P1, tempo modification mark (*colla voce*) is missing; 34.2, V, courtesy accidental (f♯) is superfluous; 38.3, V, P1, courtesy accidentals (f♯) are missing; 42.3, V, dynamic mark (*mezzo piano*) is missing; 50.2, P1, caesura mark is missing; 51, V, tempo modification mark (*a little slower*) is missing; 51-53, P2, arpeggios are missing; 55.3, V, P, courtesy accidentals (c♯) are superfluous; 57.5, V, courtesy accidental (c♯) is superfluous; pedal marks in the piano part are superfluous.

Comments. With Edward Teschemacher's sentimental lyric, this song serves as a companion piece to "Mother o' Mine," not only because of its theme of unabashed male familial affection, but because Tours' music is as rich and tuneful a setting as he ever composed. The Irish tone of the music and lyric is more in keeping with the American songs written by and for Chauncey Olcott than any traditional music from Ireland. And yet, the song's fetching theme was created with a palette of harmonic color that was never heard in the music of Ernest Ball. While most composers of sentimental songs in Tin Pan Alley at the time used secondary dominants on at most a few scale degrees, Tours uses some type of non-diatonic seventh chord (dominant,

half-diminished, or diminished) on every step of the chromatic scale except ♭II during the course of the song. Nor was the gracious lilt of the melody constructed with the compositional symmetry of Ball's justifiably famous "When Irish Eyes Are Smiling," with its 32+32-bar binary verse-and-chorus form. Instead, Tours employed a broad A-B-A′ form in which the main section is comprised of four four-measure phrases plus a two-measure tag that are all different, giving the song a constant sense of progression and development. When the melody does recapitulate after forty measures, it returns with new lyrics that warn the boy of the challenges that lie ahead. Although most of the song sits high in the voice, the end brings a powerful climax with five fermatas that call for a sustained fortissimo at the top of the range, conveying the father's heartfelt emotion with an undeniable and touching sincerity.

A Wayside Prayer

Publisher. Boosey & Co.
Date. 1927
Key/Range. A♭ Major (e♭′ – e♭″)
Critical notes. 1.4, P1, fermata should be placed below the chord; 2.6, P1, fermata is missing; 7.2, V caesura is superfluous; 7.2, P2, caesura is missing; 7.2, P2, courtesy accidental (c♮) is missing; 27, V, fermata is missing; pedal marks in the piano part are superfluous (and in several cases have no release marks).

Comments. Tours' penultimate published song (his last song, "West of the Sun," was published twenty years later) is also his most mature musical statement. Not surprisingly, it was the spiritual candor and profundity of the lyric by Elsie Janis, so rare in his body of work, that enabled him to create a song of great expressive depth. The direct appeal to God in the song outside of any formal religious context has a disarming sincerity about it that is likely a reflection of the creators' own non-denominational sacred world view. In fact, the confessional posture of the protagonist is an explicit plea for God to hear the prayer of someone who does not attend church regularly, but who abides by the same ethical values as those who do. Tours sets the verse in three large sections that match the form of the poem. He uses the harmony to illustrate the text at key moments: when the singer is asking for forgiveness, the parallel minor of the tonic darkens the mood; and, when asking for help, having strayed from the path, the protagonist sings a melody that, after modulating to the dominant (E♭), wanders through almost every note of the chromatic scale except f and g (the second and third degrees of the diatonic scale). Beneath this seemingly aimless melodic phrase, the harmony wanders as well, through several tonally unrelated dominant-nine chords (F, E, D♭, E♭, D, B) before arriving home through the dominant sonority (E♭) of the original key of A♭. This circuitous homecoming and recapitulation of the A-theme represents the feeling of security that can come though prayer during times of trial, bewilderment, and doubt.

West of the Sun

Publisher. G. Schirmer, Inc.
Date. 1947
Key/Range. D Major (c♯′ – f″)
Critical notes. 4.2, V, dynamic mark *(mezzo forte)* is missing; 12.2, tempo modification *(ritardando)* is missing; 36, P1, dynamic mark *(mezzo forte)* is superfluous; 46, dynamic mark *(decrescendo)* is missing; 61, dynamic mark *(forte)* is missing; 64.3, P1, tempo modification mark *(rallentando)* is missing.

Comments. Published, remarkably, twenty years after his previous effort, "West of the Sun" is Tours' swan song. The lyric by Dorothy K. Thomas is a dreamscape where lovers return to a tropical paradise where they previously vacationed. The intoxication of romance, of travel, and of the Polynesian islands are intertwined in this lyric, which retains its original appeal due to the fact that Thomas' atmospheric language carefully avoids any reference to the colonialist views that prevailed in the twentieth century among Westerners toward the cultures of the South Pacific. Tours' music, too, is vaguely evocative of the tropics without being derivative of Polynesian music. In fact, he cleverly employed the habañera rhythm to conjure the swaying of the palm trees and a sophisticated harmonic palette to evoke the color and perfume of the landscape. Revealing himself to be still in full possession of his mastery, Tours used the exact same harmonic device—stating the theme in the tonic minor only to be followed two measures later by an abrupt shift to the parallel major—in this song as he did at the beginning of "In Flanders' Fields," illustrating two landscapes that are diametrically opposed in every way with a similar harmonic idea (notably, both songs are also in D Minor). One of Tours' favorite strategies to convey the instability of human emotions, he was successfully able to paint both lyrics with the same brush while depicting, on the one hand, the intoxicating madness of the battlefield during war and, on the other hand, the intoxicating passion of two people being in love in a strange and beautiful land. Formally, this is Tours' most ambitious song, with its seventeen-measure verse and a forty-four-measure chorus. Both sections are binary forms that quickly shift after the return of the beginning material into new ideas that bring a sense of development, climax, and closure. Though presented in $\frac{4}{4}$ (common time), the dance rhythm of the bass, the phrasing of the melody with its heavy emphasis on beats one and three, and, above all, the quarter-note triplet figures that are so abundant in the chorus suggest that this song is actually in $\frac{2}{2}$ (cut time). The interaction of the triplets, which subdivide the half note

beats in three parts, with the habañera bass figure, which subdivide them in two (or four) parts, contribute to a sense of dreamy intoxication in the music. Though the accompaniment is scored in a pianistic manner, its instrumental lines suggest that the song was designed to be orchestrated and that he may have composed it for a film or in hopes of having it recorded by James Melton or Mario Lanza.

I Took a Thought

Publisher. Ascherberg, Hopwood & Crew, Ltd.
Date. 1908
Key/Range. G Minor (d′ – e″)
Critical notes. 3.3. P1, tempo modification mark *(a tempo)* is missing; 20, P1, tempo modification mark *(a tempo)* is missing; 21.8, P1, the final note of the line in the tenor (b′) would have been better placed in the top line so as to make the tie easier to read and since the right hand should play the octave.

Comments. The lyric by Harold Simpson reflects on the power of art, and specifically music, to cheer people when they are feeling down. Tours took the binary form of the poem and set the two stanzas first in G Minor and then G Major, suggesting that he may have wanted to illustrate the poem's narrative as a shift from "grief and pain" to a relief from sorrow at the end.

When We Met

Publisher. Ascherberg, Hopwood & Crew, Ltd.
Date. 1908
Key/Range. D Major (e♯′ – f♯″)
Critical notes. 1, P2, quarter note should be a dotted-half instead; 2, P2, dotted-half rest with fermata is missing; 13, P, tempo modification mark *(a tempo)* is missing; 14.4, P2, alignment of bass note is incorrect; 15, V, courtesy accidental (b♭) is superfluous; 18, P, alignment of beat 1 is incorrect.

Comments. In a similar manner to its companion piece, this song features an illustrative remote modulation at the halfway point. The text painting occurs most strikingly when the music abruptly modulates from D♭ back to D Major at the point in the text where his lover smiled and "the sun shone through" the wintry gloom.

Hidden in Your Heart

Publisher. G. Schirmer
Date. 1917
Key/Range. G Major (d′ – e″)
Critical notes. 24, P2, fermata on bass note is missing; pedal marks in piano part are superfluous.

Comments. Edward Teschemacher's lyric was created to be a courtship serenade. The ultimatum that comes at the end of the first stanza giving the woman a choice between leaving and staying "a while" should be read as a euphemism for a proposal. This reading is corroborated by the fact that he borrows from scripture ("bless you and keep you") to express a verbal commitment reminiscent of the wedding vows. Tours uses some mildly dissonant harmonic colors among his pedal harmonies, but saves his most powerful harmonic borrowing—a dominant sonority on the degree of the minor sixth (♭VI$_7$)—for the words "till Death comes." While Tours composed many love songs, it is notable that he chose these three lyrics about devotion and commitment at a time when he was himself courting Helen Clarke.

Give Me Your Hands

Publisher. G. Schirmer
Date. 1917
Key/Range. B♭ Major (d′ – e♭″)
Critical notes. 1, P2, fermata on bass note is missing; 19.7, P1, fermata on chord is missing; 30, P, tempo modification mark (*a tempo*) is missing; 31, P2, fermata on bass note is missing; pedal marks in piano part are superfluous.

Comments. The second song in this set, also with a lyric by Edward Teschemacher, is similarly built around a request for a sign of mutual devotion. Each successive stanza after the first becomes more euphemistic—first he asks for her hands to hold, then her heart (presumably as one "holds" someone *in* their heart), and lastly her love. Tours' A-B-A′ setting fits the stanzas neatly, and the vocal line is an elegant and natural expression of the text's sentiment without any overt attempts at illustration.

Come Back to Me

Publisher. G. Schirmer
Date. 1917
Key/Range. E♭ Major (d♭′ – d♯″)
Critical notes. 7, P, dynamic mark (*mezzo piano*) is missing; 10.3, P1, P2, enharmonic accidentals (c♯) should be d♭ instead; 28.4, P1, accidental (c♭) is missing; 28.4, P1, courtesy accidental (d♭) is superfluous (likely misplaced); pedal marks in piano part are superfluous.

Comments. Tours set more lyrics by Edward Teschemacher than any other poet during this period. While he could have easily found another text by Teschemacher to go with the first two (and set several other lyrics by him during this period), his choice of this poem by Milton Goldsmith suggests that the songs were gathered after they were composed for this set. Unlike the other two songs in this group, this one is about loss of love through a breakup, as the hope of renewing their "troth" indicates. The uneasiness of sleep is illustrated by the chromatic line and dissonant pedal harmonies in the second half of the first section. Tours manages to match the intensity of the outburst "'Tis misery!" by expanding the same musical materials from measures 7 and 8 dynamically and in the accompaniment to fashion them into a musical climax. The versatility of his musical ideas as well as the naturalness of the musical scansion of the lyrics suggest a high degree of compositional planning in these songs, which is not immediately evident upon first listening.

Before You Came

Publisher. M. Witmark & Sons
Date. 1918
Key/Range. D Major (d′ – f♯″)
Critical notes. 9, V, P, dynamic mark (*mezzo piano*) is missing; 14, P, dynamic mark (*crescendo*) is missing; 30, P, dynamic marks (*mezzo piano*, *piú lento*, and *colla voce*) are missing.

Comments. The lyric for this song, as with all four songs in this set, was written by Irene Castle in homage to her late husband Vernon, who had died in a plane accident that year while training young pilots in Texas during World War I. The Castles had become influential in the early 1910s as a dancing team that drove fashion trends at a time when social dancing was the most popular form of entertainment in the United States. Tours had met the couple during the tour of Irving Berlin's *Watch Your Step* and he maintained a close relationship with Irene during her husband's long absences in Europe and around the United States during the war. When her husband died, Irene's friendship with "Frankie" was surely a source of comfort, not least of which because he gave her a vehicle to express her grief in their collaboration on these songs. "Before You Came" is organized in three long sentences, although the punctuation in the sheet music does not accurately reflect this grammatical structure (for instance, the period at 29 should be a comma, since the next phrase "turning sorrow into song" needs to be in the same sentence as "a little love," both because they are causally connected and because the line with "sorrow" otherwise has no subject or verb). Tours set the first sentence as the first half of the song's binary form using four large musical ideas that give the listener no sense that Castle's poem is in iambic hexameter. The harmonic conceit that illustrates their wandering is the absence of a tonic cadence until the second appearance of the word "came" at the end of the verse. During this harmonic conceit that illustrates the poetic image of life before the lovers met is the fact that Tours never arrives at the tonic until the end of the sentence on the final appearance of the word "came." During this harmonic meandering, Tours illustrated more specifically the line "my lonely soul had wandered far" with parallel dominant sonorities that cause the listener to lose any sense of mooring in D Major. The song climaxes near the end of the second half of the binary form on the words "since you have come to me at last," followed by a series of dominant chords through the circle of fifths on the words "I shall forget the years that passed" that wind inevitably toward a tonal homecoming that is, nonetheless, difficult to see (or hear) in advance. This song is one of Tours' most subtle and sophisticated examples of text painting.

For You and Me

Publisher. M. Witmark & Sons
Date. 1918
Key/Range. F Major (c′ – f″)
Critical notes. 10, P, tempo modification mark (*a tempo*) is missing; 11.3, V, tempo modification mark (Tempo I) is superfluous; 19, P, tempo modification mark (*a tempo*) is missing; 20.2, V, fermata should be placed on the dotted half note; 20.5, P1, P2, all fermatas should be placed on beat 3 quarter notes.

Comments. The lyric in this song concentrates upon the emotions of separation. Castle's imagery of longing—burning lips, throbbing heart—are set by Tours with a series of dominant sonorities that progress gradually around the circle of fifths and back (III_7-VI_7-II_7-V_7-I_7-IV_7-II_7-V_7) toward the goal of the tonic, which arrives at the explanation of why she feels this passion: "Because God made me, dear, for you!" The song climaxes, in typical fashion, toward the end of the second half of the binary with a cadence using a diminished chord built on the first degree ($i°_7$-I) on the word "Eternity." The ♭VI-I figure at the beginning is a bookend gesture that prepares and then reminds the listener of the harmonic adventures within.

So Great Our Love

Publisher. M. Witmark & Sons
Date. 1918
Key/Range. (d′ – f″)
Critical notes. 3, V, dynamic mark (*piano*) is missing; 11, P, tempo modification (*a tempo*) is missing; 24, V, dynamic mark (*piano*) is missing; 26, P, dynamic mark (*crescendo*) is missing; 27, P, dynamic mark (*mezzo forte*) is missing; pedal marks in the piano part are superfluous.

Comments. The three stanzas of this lyric explore three different ways in which their love stood the test of time: through separation, through togetherness, and through eternity. Castle expanded her concept of eternal love in this song to include an explicit description of spirits wandering through the "shadowland," which Tours set on a sharp-eleven-dominant sonority built on the subtonic (♭$VII_{7-\#11}$), a foreign borrowed chord that precedes a cascade of descending sonorities that was unlike anything ever composed for the romantic ballad literature in its harmonic sophistication and daring.

Yesterday, To-day, To-morrow!

Publisher. M. Witmark & Sons
Date. 1918
Key/Range. F Major (c′ – f″)
Critical notes. Pedal marks in the piano part are superfluous.

Comments. As the title suggests, the lyric for this song is built around the poet's description of her various emotional states from before, during, and after her love affair takes place. These three states—the empty feeling of being alone before they met, the joy of finding love and being in love, and the anxiety that an uncertain future brings—were each explored at different points in the previous songs. This song, therefore, provides a summary of the feelings expressed in the entire set. Even so, "Yesterday, To-day, To-morrow!" provides the clearest depiction of Irene Castle's frame of mind when she last saw her husband on a weekend visit just before his tragic death. She describes the events in her book *Castles in the Air*, and though she does her best to conceal her knowledge of the horrible tragedy that was shortly to befall them, the anxiety that accompanied her precarious and temporary happiness with him was palpable, as it is in this song. Tours signals to the listener the destabilizing emotions that animate this song in the opening chords, which introduce shifting foreign parallel sonorities that resolve, but cannot be cleared with the pedal until the next measure, since they occur over a fifth in the deep register of the piano that must be held. In a striking gesture that reveals his mastery of post-Romantic harmony, Tours sets with equal effectiveness the opening stanza about Castle's sadness in the major and the following stanza about her happiness in the minor. His setting of the words "the world seems mad with joy for this/My heart before your feet I lay"—a chromatic rising vocal line, supported by fluctuating consonant and dissonant chords and followed by a swooping melody that descends an octave-and-a-fourth before settling a half note up on D♭—is a stunning example of text painting that rivals anything in the literature of art song. The successive dominant-nine sonorities (VI_9-II_9-V_9) in the retransition to the A′ section are so harmonically disorienting that Tours cleverly cues the singer to the opening note of the melody (A) in the final chord of the interlude. And, the conclusion, which features a climax on the word "sorrow," substitutes a jarring series of descending chromatic dominant chords for a typical cadence, as if to demonstrate the crushing terror of not knowing whether you will ever see the one you love again.

Breaks the Morning

Publisher. M. Witmark & Sons
Date. 1912
Key/Range. A♭ Major (d′ – f″)

Critical notes. 1, P, accents should use the same style for consistency; 25.4, V, lyric should read "brightly gleams *through* dark tomorrows"; 31.6, V, courtesy accidental (f♮) is superfluous; 44.3, P1, accidental (d♭) is missing; 44.4, P1, courtesy accidental (b♭) is missing; 47.3, P1, courtesy accidental (f♮) is missing.

Comments. Lyricist Jessie Villars contributed occasionally to songs for Broadway shows between 1891 and 1908. Tours followed closely the poetic meter of his text in composing the rhythm for his setting, which was created for insertion into a Christian liturgy for Easter morning services. The hymn-like characteristics of the song suggest that a four-part homophonic arrangement of the vocal line would also make an excellent choral anthem.

Thou Blessed Man of God

Publisher. M. Witmark & Sons
Date. 1911
Key/Range. C Major (c′– e″)
Critical notes. 40.4, P2, final two eighth-note rests are missing.

Comments. Lyricist William H. Gardner was a Boston businessman who wrote poetry and lyrics as a "diversion," according to his 1932 obituary in *The New York Times.* Gardner's text, which was intended for Christmas religious services, suggested the verse-and-refrain form of the song. Tours set the two sections in different meters, which enabled him to create a syllabic setting with a natural scansion for each that, nonetheless, are related as compound meters (⁶₄ and ¹²₈). By changing the value of the subdivision from quarter note to eighth note, his setting allows for a seamless change of tempo in the transition from the gracious lullaby rhythm of the verse to the triumphant march of the chorus. The music for this song is reminiscent of the late-romantic liturgical music of Gounod, which Tours' father, Berthold, published at Novello, Ewer & Co. in the 1870s.

He Giveth His Beloved Sleep

Publisher. M. Witmark & Sons
Date. 1911
Key/Range. A♭ Major (e♭′ – f″)
Critical notes. 10, P, dynamic mark (*decrescendo*) is missing; 32, P, dynamic mark (*decrescendo*) is missing.

Comments. This song was created for inclusion in church services and was listed in the Sacred Music category of M. Witmark & Sons' catalogue. Centered on the death and resurrection of Jesus Christ, William H. Gardner's lyric uses the text "His beloved sleep" to invoke the image of the resurrected savior without ever mentioning him by name. In turn, the gift of sleep is given as a reassurance that faith will lead believers to everlasting life. The song's dedication

"by the Author to the beloved memory of his Mother" is by Gardner and not Tours, whose mother died in 1929.

Little Wild Rose

Publisher. Chappell & Co.
Date. 1906
Key/Range. F Major (c′ – f″)
Critical notes. 23, V, tempo modification mark (*a tempo*) is missing.

Comments. This song was introduced in the musical comedy *The Dairymaids*, which opened in 1906 at the Apollo Theatre in London and was imported the following year by Charles Frohman to Broadway with six additional songs by Jerome Kern. Tours shared the responsibility of composing the score for the show with Paul Rubens and lyricist Arthur Wimperis. The number appears in the Addenda of the English vocal score, suggesting that it was composed after the opening for Florence Smithson, who played Hélène in the original production. For some unknown reason, the song was not incorporated into the American production until it went on tour.

The Bold Dragoon

Publisher. Ascherberg, Hopwood & Crew, Ltd.
Date. 1909
Key/Range. E♭ Major (e♭′ – f″)
Comments. *The Dashing Little Duke* was a musical play by Seymour Hicks based upon the 1939 French play *Les Premières Armes de Richelieu.* Hicks had played the role of the young Duc du Richelieu in an 1899 London production of the play, but he handed it over to his wife Ellaline Terriss to turn it into a pants role for the musical version that he wrote and produced. This song was performed by Terriss and Courtice Pounds to emphasize the comedic effect of the gender-crossing character in the title role.

When I Am All Your Own

Publisher. M. Witmark & Sons
Date. 1911
Key/Range. B♭ Major (c♯′ – a♭″ [b♭″ ossia])
Critical notes. 20, P, tempo modification mark (*ritardando*) is missing; 23.5, P1, P2, courtesy accidentals (b♭) are missing; 39, V, P2, fermatas are missing.

Comments. When William Brady and his wife, Grace George, came to London and procured the rights to *The Balkan Princess* for the Shuberts, they also brought Frank Tours with them to be the music director for the Broadway production. When he arrived in New York, he was made to wait for six months by the musicians' union until he could work as a conductor in the theatre and so the producers put him to work as a composer, despite the fact that the purpose of the interpolations was to Americanize the shows. This song, therefore, marks the beginning of Tours' American career and shows signs of his effort to assimilate to the current stylistic trends circa 1911 on Broadway typified by composers such as Karl Hoschna and Jerome Kern.

Sweet Nell

Publisher. Chappell & Co./Harms Incorporated
Date. 1925/1926
Key/Range. E♭ Major (c′ – e♭″ [g″ ossia])
Critical notes. 23–24, P2, pedal mark covering both measures would be clearer than the tied dotted half and would convey the same idea; 24.2, P1, arpeggio is missing; 34.2–3, P1, arpeggios should be removed; 35.1, P1, arpeggio should be removed; 40.2–3, P1, P2, arpeggios are missing; 54.2–3, P1, P2, arpeggios are missing; 58.2–3, P1, P2 (second measure of the second ending) arpeggios are missing; 53–56, typical confusion regarding endings as we see in most popular songs with two verses: the performers are intended to play the second ending during the first and third passes through the music and the first ending the second time through. The better solution would have been to replace the forward-facing repeat sign at 25 with a return sign (§) and then put the second ending given here first with the numbers 1.3. and the first ending given here second with number 2 and a *dal segno* at the end; pedal marks in the piano part are superfluous.

Comments. This song was composed for the 1926 opening of the Plaza Theatre, Paramount Studios' premiere movie palace in London. Frank Tours was hired as the music director for the Plaza, which involved composing music to be performed live for films (which were still silent at that time) in addition to music for the pre-screening entertainment. "Sweet Nell" is an homage to Nell Gwyn, the woman who during the British Restoration (late-17th century) rose from being a poor orange seller to becoming a celebrated actress on the London stage and then the mistress of Charles II and a figure of renown. Her story was the subject of the film *Nell Gwyn* starring Dorothy Gish, and Tours' song was likely also woven into the scoring for the film. The music is a tender and elegant waltz that could have been composed 25 years earlier and thus was likely considered a plausible musical icon for a historical figure in a 1920s costume drama, despite the setting for the movie being from a period more than 200 years earlier.

Chanson Algerian

Publisher. Sam Fox Publishing Co.
Date. 1926
Key/Range. G Minor (d′ – a♭″)
Critical notes. See "Critical notes" for "Sweet Nell" regarding first and second endings.

Comments. Frank Tours began to work for Paramount Pictures as a movie palace music director in 1925. The following year, he was hired as a composer at the studio's Astoria lot. He shared credit for all of his work on the music for *Beau Geste*, a 1926 film starring Ronald Coleman based upon the book by P. C. Wren. This song reunited Tours with one of his most frequent lyric collaborators, Edward Teschemacher, who had changed his name after World War I to Lockton in order to shield him from anti-German sentiment. In retrospect, his lyric for "Chanson Algerian" is more expressive of the orientalism common in American popular arts at the time than the north African culture it attempts to portray. Similarly, the shifting minor modality—between harmonic minor and the Aeolian mode—was a form of musical essentialism that was common in film scores as well as Tin Pan Alley songs with "Arabian" lyrics and themes.

Our Crystal Wedding Day

Publisher. Harms, Inc.
Date. 1924
Key/Range. F Major (c′ – f″)
Critical notes. See "Critical notes" for "Sweet Nell" regarding first and second endings.

Comments. A musical revue featuring no less than nine composers, *Hassard Short's Ritz Revue* was supposed to inaugurate a series, but it never took hold, despite the show's success. Tours contributed at least three songs, including this number from the wedding scene in the Crystal Room at the Ritz.

APPENDICES

APPENDIX 1
Facsimile of Composer's Fair Copy of
"Around the Corner" (unpublished song)

Around the Corner

Poem by
Charles Hanson Towne.

F.E.T.

Charles Hanson Towne
"Around the Corner"
Frank Tours
Moderato
A-round the cor-ner
piu accel
a tempo
I have a friend In this great city that has no end Yet
colla voce
rall
days go by and weeks rush on And be-fore I know it, a year has
gone - And I never see my old friend's face For

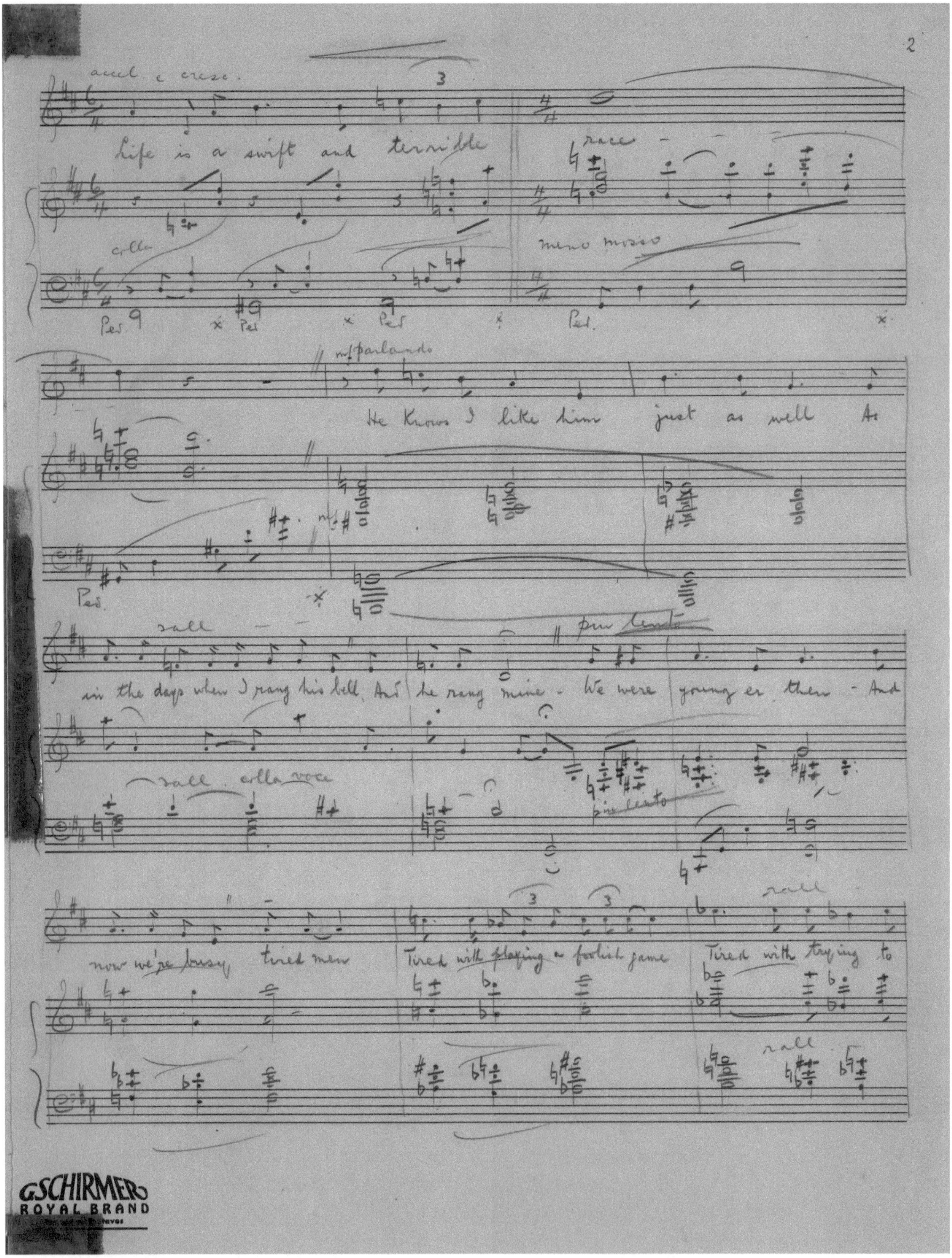
2
accel. e cresc.
Life is a swift and terrible race –
colla
meno mosso
Ped.
mf parlando
He knows I like him just as well As
rall
più lento
in the days when I rang his bell, And he rang mine – We were young er then – And
rall. colla voce
now we're busy tired men
Tired with playing a foolish game
Tired with trying to
G.SCHIRMER
ROYAL BRAND

3.
a tempo
make a name
To-morrow, I say, I will
molto rall
a tempo
call on Jim —
Just to show that I'm thinking of him — But to-
rall
-morrow comes and to-morrow goes, And the distance be-tween us grows and grows
Ped
Tempo primo
Around the corner - yet miles - a-way!
Ped.

DAVIS AND THORSETT

APPENDIX 2
Published Works

Chorus

Short Setting of the Office for the Holy Communion

Orchestra

Coquetry
Girl o' Mine Foxtrot
Girl o' Mine Waltz
The Great Adventure
Hero Land
Midday Dreams
Mother o' Mine
Scene Pastorale
Sun-Land
Tambouretta
Witches' Revel
Sunshine and Shadow Sketches
    Sunset (No. 1)
    The Old Oak Tree (No. 2)
    Snowflakes (No. 3)
    April Showers (No. 4)
    Through the Woods (No. 5)
    Lovers' Lane (No. 6)
The Dashing Little Duke   *Lancers*
The Dashing Little Duke   *Selection*
The Dashing Little Duke   *Waltz*

Violin and Piano

Three Dances
Romance in C
Impromptu Pathetique
Sunshine and Shadow Sketches
    April Showers
    Autumn Leaves
    Jack in the Pulpit
    Lovers' Lane
    Snowflakes
    Sunset
    Through the Woods
    The Dancing Brook
    The Blue Bird
    The Old Oak Tree
    The Harvest Moon
    Wildflowers

Piano solo

Balaria
Cupid—Valse Brilliante
Danse Arabesque
Hero Land
Love's Promise
Romance in C
Tarantelle
Three Dances
Truant Love
Valse Impromptu

Piano Four Hands

Fairyland

Songs for Voice and Piano

The Skelsmerghian Song	(1889)*
O Golden Morn of Love	(1899)
Lover Mine	(1901)
'Tis Passing Strange	
Hush-a-Bye, Sweetie	(1903)
The Matador	
Mother o' Mine	
My Darling	
A Rose Romance	
What the Thrush Said	
The Alternative	(1904)
Beloved	
If You Could Know	
Just You – And I	
Love's Quiet	
Oh! Cupid	
Tatterdemalion	
That Old Sweet Love	
Through Cupid's Garden	
C'est Moi	(1906)
Il pleure dans mon coeur	
The Lilacs	
The Wind in the Orchard	
I Beg Your Pardon	(1907)
The Lovely Fay	
A Meeting	
Red Rose	
Seedtime and Harvest	
Sow If You Will	
Good Horses at the Plow	
Far Away	
The Waggon Groans	
God's Promise	(1908)

*published in 1934

Two Songs
    I Took a Thought
    When We Met
In the Springtime
Just Suppose
Do You?   (1909)
In an Evening Sky
A Surprise
Two Songs   (1910)
I Have a Rose
Love Came to Me
Jest a Wearyin' fer You
Beyond the Sunset   (1911)
From the Valley
He Giveth His Beloved Sleep
I Dreamed
If the Wealth of the World
Were Mine
Just to Forget
Love, Not in Vain
Oh, Bring Me Love!
Parted
A Prayer for You
Thou Blessed Man of God
Waiting for God and Thee
When Summer Days Depart
When You Are Near
A Year Ago
Your Eyes
Breaks the Morning   (1912)
Through All the Years
Apple Time   (1914)
If You Loved Me
Son of My Heart
On the Banks of the Wye   (1915)
My Heart's With You   (1916)
No Voice But Yours
Three Songs of Love   (1917)
    Come Back to Me
    Give Me Your Hands
    Hidden in Your Heart
Four Little Love Songs   (1918)
    Before You Came
    For You and Me
    So Great Our Love
    Yesterday, To-day, To-morrow!
In Flanders' Fields
The Long Day
The Littlest of All
Norah McCall
Love's Coming   (1920)
A Bit of Irish   (1923)
Trees

Hope Dreams	(1924)
Fury of the Sea	
You Smile at Dawn	
Smiling Eyes	(1925)
A Wayside Prayer	(1926)
West of the Sun	(1947)

Music for the Theatre

See-See's So-Hei	(from *See-See*)
Lay Our Heads Together	
Chinese Dolls	
Some People Cannot Take a Hint	
Rather Not	
Who Would Be a Boy	(from *The New Aladdin*)
Opening Chorus—Act II	
The Cadi	
I Want to Be a Mortal	
I'm Lally	
The Gallic Cock	
My Little Girlie	(from *A Country Girl*)
Boy Blue	(from *The Dairymaids*)
Little Wild Rose	
Love Among the Daisies	
The Thrush	
I Must Have a Lot of Little Girls Around Me	
Vocal Score (with Paul Rubens)	
The Dairymaids Selection	
Cupid's Rifle Range	(from *The Little Cherub*)
I Should So Love to Be a Boy	
Opening Chorus—Act II	
*Pierrot and Pierrette**	
Wonderful Night	(from *The Gay Gordons*)
Everybody's Fond of Me	
Gay Lothario Waltz	(from *A Waltz Dream*)
The Kiss Waltz Selection (arr.)	(from *The Kiss Waltz*)
Blue Boy	(from *The Dashing Little Duke*)
The Bold Dragoon	
Lisette	
Love and Pride	
Nobody Cares for Me	
Rose of the World	
Women	
Vocal Score	
The Dashing Little Duke	*Lancers*
The Dashing Little Duke	*Selection*
The Dashing Little Duke	*Waltz*
Love! Love! Love!	(from *The Dollar Princess*)
When I Am All Your Own	(from *The Balkan Princess*)
Oh, You Girls!	(from *La Belle Paree*)
Gay Lothario Waltz	(from *A Waltz Dream*)
They Were Irish	(from *Getting Together*)
Birdies in the Trees	(from *Girl o' Mine*)

DAVIS AND THORSETT

Every Cloud Is Silver Lined
Love Is Just a Fairy Tale
Not So Fast
Omar Khyyam
Telephone Song
To-day Is the Day
Girl o' Mine Fox Trot
Girl o' Mine Waltz
Midsummer Night's Dream   (from *Hassard Short's Ritz Revue*)
Our Crystal Wedding Day
Sun Girl
Mayflowers   (from *Mayflowers*)

Music for film

Sweet Nell   (from *Nell Gwyn*)
Chanson Algerian   (from *Beau Geste*)
The Song of the Legion
Desert Stars   (from *Beau Sabreur*)

APPENDIX 3
Discography

Songs of Frank Tours, recorded between 1907 and 1951

Title	Performer	Label/Issue Number	Recording Date
A Bit of Irish	Theo Karle	Brunswick (rejected)	1924
A Bit of Irish	Theo Karle	Brunswick (rejected)	1924
A Bit of Irish	Colin O'More	Vocalion B9651, B24059	1926
I Beg Your Pardon	Maurice Farkoa	Edison 500	1910
In Flanders' Fields	John McCormack	Victor (rejected)	1918
Mother o' Mine	Herbert Witherspoon	Victor 64071	1907
Mother o' Mine	Emilio de Gogorza	Victor 74188	1908
Mother o' Mine	Vernon Archibald	Columbia A962	1910
Mother o' Mine	John McCormack	Victor 64332	1913
Mother o' Mine	Edward Johnson	Columbia A1673	1914
Mother o' Mine	John McCormack	Victrola 776-B	1915
Mother o' Mine	Imperial Quartet	Victor 18350	1916
Mother o' Mine	Charles Hart	OKeh 1043, Actuelle 020690	1918
Mother o' Mine	Henry Moeller	Gennett 10073-B	1918
Mother o' Mine	Richard Bonelli	Brunswick 5100, 13015	1920
Mother o' Mine	John Charles Thomas	Aeolian Vocalion 30127	1922
Mother o' Mine	Louis Graveure	Columbia A3562	1922
Mother o' Mine	Emilio de Gogorza	Victor 1107	1924
Mother o' Mine	John Charles Thomas	Brunswick 10273	1926
Mother o' Mine	Emilio de Gogorza	Victor 1286	1927
Mother o' Mine	Hugh Donovan	Oriole 873 (b)	1927
Mother o' Mine	Francis Russell	Columbia (Br.) 4501	1927
Mother o' Mine	Conrad Thibault	Victor 24620	1933
Mother o' Mine	Richard Crooks	Victor 1806-B	1936
Mother o' Mine	Leonard Warren	RCA Victor WMD 1630	1951
No Voice But Yours	James Harrod	Columbia (rejected)	1917
No Voice But Yours	John Steel	Victor (rejected)	1920
Smiling Eyes	John Charles Thomas	Brunswick 10274	1927
Sun Girl	Richard Crooks	Victor 45481	1924

Recordings by Frank Tours, music director

Title	Performer	Label/Issue Number	Recording Date
A La Gavotte	Plaza Theatre Orch.	Columbia (Br.) 5193	1926
A Musical Switch (part 1)	Plaza Theatre Orch.	Columbia (Br.) 9196	1926
A Musical Switch (part 2)	Plaza Theatre Orch.	Columbia (Br.) 9196	1926
Alice Blue Gown	Edith Day	Columbia (Br.) F-1044	1920
Bal Masque	Plaza Theatre Orch.	Columbia (Br.) 5403	1926
Castle of Dreams	Edith Day	Columbia (Br.) F-1045	1920

Title	Performer	Label/Issue Number	Recording Date
"Chanson—In Love"/ "Love Everlasting"	Plaza Theatre Orch.	Columbia (Br.) 9157	1926
Dashing Little Duke	The Black Diamonds	Gramophone Monarch 0192	1909
Gipsy Suite (part 1)	Plaza Theatre Orch.	Columbia (Br.) 9241	1926
Gipsy Suite (part 2)	Plaza Theatre Orch.	Columbia (Br.) 9241	1926
Hobbies	Daisy Hancox	Columbia (Br.) F-5	1920
Irene	Edith Day	Columbia (Br.) F-1044	1920
Irene: Medley	Orchestra	Columbia (Br.) 823	1920
Irene: Waltz	Orchestra	Columbia (Br.) 823	1920
Minuet	Plaza Theatre Orch.	Columbia (Br.) 5193	1926
My Hero	John Charles Thomas	Victor 18061	1941
My Lady Dainty	Plaza Theatre Orch.	Columbia (Br.) 5192	1926
Nell Gwyn Overture	Plaza Theatre Orch.	Columbia (Br.) 9167	1926
Pearl o' Mine	Plaza Theatre Orch.	Columbia (Br.) 5403	1926
Pierrette	Plaza Theatre Orch.	Columbia (Br.) 9157	1926
Plymouth-Hoe Overture	Plaza Theatre Orch.	Columbia (Br.) 9167	1926
Sky Rocket	Edith Day	Columbia (Br.) F-1046	1920
Sympathy/That Would Be Lovely/ Forgive	John Charles Thomas Hope Manning	Victor 18061	1941
Tangled Tunes (part 1)	Plaza Theatre Orch.	Columbia (Br.) 2423	1926
Tangled Tunes (part 2)	Plaza Theatre Orch.	Columbia (Br.) 2423	1926
Tangled Tunes (part 3)	Plaza Theatre Orch.	Columbia (Br.) 2424	1926
Tangled Tunes (part 4)	Plaza Theatre Orch.	Columbia (Br.) 2424	1926
The Busy Bee— Morceau Characteristique	Plaza Theatre Orch.	Columbia (Br.) 5192	1926
The Last Part of Every Party	Winnie Collins Margaret Campbell Robert Hale	Columbia (Br.) F-5	1920
The Talk of the Town	Winnie Collins Margaret Campbell Robert Hale	Columbia (Br.) F-1047	1920
To Be Worthy of You	Edith Day	Columbia (Br.) F-1045	1920
To Love You	Edith Day Robert Michaelis	Columbia (Br.) F-1046	1920
Victor Presents a John Charles Thomas Program	John Charles Thomas	RCA Victor M645	1941
We're Getting Away With It	Winnie Collins Margaret Campbell Robert Hale	Columbia (Br.) F-1047	1920